Cover art: Brooklyn Museum of Art, New York, USA/Bridgeman Images

About the Cover Image

Winter Scene in Brooklyn, detail of a street and the Post Office, c. 1817–1820 (oil on canvas), by Francis Guy (born 1760)

Francis Guy was born in London and emigrated to the United States in 1795 at the beginning of the new nation. A self-taught artist, he moved to Brooklyn in 1817, where he painted the quaint village as it then existed. Unlike most landscape paintings of the period, which usually derived from idealized European models, Guy's oil on canvass winter scene depicted ordinary people at work. In Brooklyn, like many places in the young nation, the change from rural to urban occurred gradually. By the 1870s, Guy's painting provided a nostalgic view, especially of the old-fashioned Dutch-style barnyard on the left. Guy painted this scene from the vantage point of his second-story window facing Front Street.

Guide to Analyzing Primary and Secondary Sources

To understand the past, historians look at a variety of evidence — written sources, visual sources, and material artifacts. When they encounter any of these primary sources, historians ask questions. Sometimes historians don't know the answers, but they always ask the questions. As a student, you should ask these questions, too. Asking questions is the first step in writing history. Facts alone do not create history — it is the historian who organizes and interprets the facts in a reasoned and verifiable manner. The books and articles that historians publish after the events or conditions they are studying have occurred are secondary sources. Secondary sources become the basis for teaching and for other historians to use in researching and writing their own studies. Because they are interpretative and open for debate, secondary sources allow historians to move forward by modifying explanations of the past. Historical interpretations are constantly being revised, and *Exploring American Histories*, Fourth Edition, offers you an opportunity to explore this dynamic quality.

Analyzing a Written Primary Source

- What kind of source is this? For example, is it a diary, letter, speech, sermon, court opinion, newspaper article, witness testimony, poem, memoir, or advertisement?
- Who wrote the source? How can you identify the author? Was the source translated by someone other than the author or speaker (for example, Native American speeches translated by whites)?
- When and where was it written?
- Why was the source written? Is there a clear purpose?

- Who was, or who might have been, its intended audience?
- What point of view does it reflect?
- What can the source tell us about the individual(s) who produced it and the society from which he, she, or they came?
- How might individuals' race, ethnicity, class, gender, age, and region have affected the viewpoints in the sources?
- In what ways does the larger historical context help you evaluate individual sources?

Analyzing a Visual or Material Primary Source

- What kind of visual or material source is this? For example, is it a map, drawing, or engraving, a physical object, painting, photograph, census record, or political cartoon?
- Who made the image or artifact, and how was it made?
- When and where was the image or artifact made?
- Can you determine if someone paid for or commissioned it? If so, how can you tell that it was paid for or commissioned?
- Who might have been the intended audience or user? Where might it have originally been displayed or used?

- What message or messages is it trying to convey?
- How might it be interpreted differently depending on who viewed or used it?
- What can the visual or material source tell us about the individual who produced it and the society from which he or she came?
- In what ways does the larger historical context help you evaluate individual sources?

Comparing Multiple Primary Sources

- In what ways are the sources similar in purpose and content? In what ways are they different?
- How much weight should one give to who wrote or produced the source?
- Were the sources written or produced at the same time or at different times? If they were produced at different times, does this account for any of the differences between or among the sources?
- What difference does it make that some sources (such as diaries and letters) were intended to be private and some sources (such

as political cartoons and court opinions) were meant to be public?
- How do you account for different perspectives and conclusions? How might these be affected by the author's relative socioeconomic position or political power in the larger society?
- Is it possible to separate fact from personal opinion in the sources?
- Can the information in the sources under review be corroborated by other evidence? What other sources would you want to consult to confirm your conclusions?

Cautionary Advice for Interpreting Primary Sources

- A single source does not tell the whole story, and even multiple sources may not provide a complete account. Historians realize that not all evidence is recoverable.
- Sources have biases, whether they appear in personal or official accounts. Think of biases as particular points of view, and try to figure out how they influence the historical event and the accounts of that event.
- Sources reflect the period in which they were written or produced and must be evaluated within the historical time frame from which they came. Explain how people understood the world in which they lived, and be careful to avoid imposing contemporary standards on the past. Nevertheless, remember that even in a particular time period people disagreed over significant principles and practices such as slavery, imperialism, and immigration.
- Sources often conflict or contradict each other. Take into account all sides. Do not dismiss an account that does not fit into your interpretation; rather, explain why you are giving it less weight or how you are modifying your interpretation to conform to all the evidence.

Analyzing Secondary Sources

- Secondary sources are written or produced by people who did not participate in or experience first-hand the events that they are analyzing. Secondary sources in history usually appear as scholarly books and articles. Secondary sources underscore that history is an ever-changing enterprise.
- Identify the author's main interpretations.
- Describe the evidence the author uses to make that interpretation.
- Evaluate how well the evidence supports the author's interpretation.
- Describe whether the author considers alternative explanations and points of view.
- Compare the author's account with any other sources you have read.
- Assess whether the author has the credentials for making reliable historical judgments.
- Evaluate whether there is anything in the author's background or experience that might have influenced the author's point of view and interpretation.
- Identify the main audience that the author is addressing.

Comparing Secondary Sources

- Explain how two sources differ in interpretation. To what extent, if any, do they agree?
- Historians are products of their own times. Identify the date of publication for each of the sources and explain how the particular time periods might have shaped the authors' arguments.
- Compare the approaches each author takes to reach an interpretation. Describe whether they are looking at the events mainly from a political, social, cultural, or economic perspective.
- Compare the secondary sources with other secondary sources on the same subject, such as the historical narrative in this textbook.
- Taking these considerations into account, explain which secondary source you find more convincing or how the two interpretations might be combined.

Cautionary Advice for Analyzing Secondary Sources

- The secondary sources in this book are excerpts from longer books or articles. The selections are meant to provide a representative view of the authors' main interpretations and perspectives on the subject. Nevertheless, these excerpts do not show the broad sweep of evidence from which the authors draw their conclusions.
- No excerpt can provide a full appreciation of how historians gather evidence and present and defend their interpretations in a reliable manner. Only a more extensive reading of the secondary source can provide sufficient evidence for judging whether the author has presented a convincing account.
- As with primary sources, secondary sources have biases. Think of biases as particular points of view, and try to figure out how they influence the historical interpretation and the accounts of an event or development.
- Secondary sources often conflict with or contradict each other. Do not dismiss an account that does not fit with your perspective; rather, explain why you are giving it more or less weight or how you are modifying your interpretation to conform to all the arguments made by the authors of the secondary sources.
- Secondary sources reflect the period in which they are written or produced and must be evaluated within the historical time frame from which they originate. This doesn't mean that a newer book or article is more accurate than an older one. Interpretations may differ because new facts have been uncovered, but they are just as likely to change according to the contemporary concerns and perspectives of the authors. Moreover, even when analyzing the same time period, historians often disagree over controversial subjects due to different viewpoints on politics, religion, race, ethnicity, region, class, and gender.

CANADA

Alaska

Greenland
(Den.)

ICELAND

UNITED
KINGDOM

IRELAND

FRANCE

SPAIN

PORTUGAL

Azores
(Port.)

MOROCCO

Canary Is.
(Sp.)

Western Sahara
(Mor.)

CAPE
VERDE

MAURITANIA

SENEGAL

MALI

GAMBIA

GUINEA-BISSAU

GUINEA

SIERRA LEONE

LIBERIA

CÔTE D'IVOIRE

BURKINA FASO

GHANA

UNITED STATES

ATLANTIC
OCEAN

Hawaii

MEXICO

BAHAMAS

DOMINICAN
REPUBLIC

HAITI

CUBA

Puerto Rico (U.S.)

JAMAICA

ST. KITTS AND NEVIS

BELIZE

ANTIGUA AND BARBUDA

GUATEMALA

HONDURAS

Guadeloupe (Fr.)

DOMINICA

EL SALVADOR

Martinique (Fr.)

ST. VINCENT AND THE GRENADINES

NICARAGUA

ST. LUCIA

BARBADOS

GRENADA

COSTA RICA

TRINIDAD AND TOBAGO

GUYANA

PANAMA

VENEZUELA

SURINAME

French Guiana (Fr.)

COLOMBIA

PACIFIC OCEAN

Galápagos Is.
(Ec.)

ECUADOR

PERU

BRAZIL

SAMOA

BOLIVIA

TONGA

PARAGUAY

Easter I.
(Chile)

CHILE

URUGUAY

ARGENTINA

ATLANTIC
OCEAN

0		1,500		3,000 miles

0	1,500	3,000 kilometers

Falkland Is.
(U.K.)

Abbreviations

ALB.	ALBANIA
AUS.	AUSTRIA
BEL.	BELGIUM
B.H.	BOSNIA AND HERZEGOVINA
CR.	CROATIA
CZ. REP.	CZECH REPUBLIC
DEN.	DENMARK
F.Y.R.O.M.	FORMER YUGOSLAV REPUBLIC OF MACEDONIA
HUNG.	HUNGARY
K.	KOSOVO
LUX.	LUXEMBOURG
M.	MONTENEGRO
NETH.	NETHERLANDS
SLK.	SLOVAKIA
SLN.	SLOVENIA
S.M.	SERBIA AND MONTENEGRO
SWITZ.	SWITZERLAND

Exploring American Histories

A SURVEY WITH SOURCES

FOURTH EDITION

VOLUME 1 To 1877

Nancy A. Hewitt

Rutgers University

Steven F. Lawson

Rutgers University

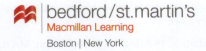

bedford/st.martin's

Macmillan Learning

Boston | New York

To Mary and Charles Takacs, Florence and Hiram Hewitt,
Sarah and Abraham Parker, Lena and Ben Lawson,
Irene and Robert Hewitt, and Ceil and Murray Lawson
who made our American Histories possible.

Vice President: Leasa Burton
Program Director: Erika Gutierrez
Senior Program Manager: William J. Lombardo;
Director of Content Development: Jane Knetzger
Senior Development Editor: Leah R. Strauss
Assistant Editor: Julia Bell
Director of Media Editorial: Adam Whitehurst
Media Editor: Mollie Chandler
Marketing Manager: Melissa Rodriguez
Senior Director, Content Management Enhancement:
   Tracey Kuehn
Senior Managing Editor: Michael Granger
Executive Content Project Manager: Gregory Erb
Workflow Project Manager: Lisa McDowell
Production Supervisors: Robin Besofsky, Robert Cherry
Director of Design, Content Management: Diana Blume
Interior Design: Jerilyn DiCarlo
Cover Design: William Boardman

Cartographer: Mapping Specialists, Ltd.
Text Permissions Editor: Michael McCarty
Text Permissions Researcher: Elaine Kosta, Lumina
   Datamatics
Photo Permissions Editor: Christine Buese
Photo Researcher: Naomi Kornhauser, Cheryl DuBois,
   Lumina Datamatics
Director of Digital Production: Keri deManigold
Media Project Manager: Michelle Camisa
Editorial Services: Lumina Datamatics, Inc.
Copyeditor: Harold Johnson
Indexer: Michael Ferreira
Composition: Lumina Datamatics, Inc.
*Cover Art: Winter Scene in Brooklyn, detail of a street and
   the Post Office,* c. 1817–1820 (oil on canvas), by Francis
   Guy (1760–1820)/Brooklyn Museum of Art, New York,
   USA/Bridgeman Images
Printing and Binding: LSC Communications

Library of Congress Control Number: 2021930838
ISBN: 978-1-319-24449-1 (Combined Edition)
ISBN: 978-1-319-33116-0 (Volume 1)
ISBN: 978-1-319-33126-9 (Volume 2)

Printed in the United States of America.
1 2 3 4 5 6   26 25 24 23 22 21

Acknowledgments

*Text acknowledgments and copyrights appear at the back of the book on page C-1, which
constitutes an extension of the copyright page. Art acknowledgments and copyrights appear on
the same page as the art selections they cover.*

For information, write: Bedford/St. Martin's, 75 Arlington Street, Boston, MA 02116

We are delighted to publish the fourth edition of *Exploring American Histories: A Survey with Sources.* We have sought to provide **a U.S. history survey text that makes a broad and diverse American history accessible** to a new generation of students and instructors. With each edition, our central focus has been to weave written and visual primary sources that represent a rich assortment of American perspectives throughout the book. Users of the previous editions have told us our book gives them and their students opportunities to actively engage with both the narrative of American history and primary sources from that history in a way previously not possible. The new edition's combination of narrative and diverse primary sources is available now for the first time in **Achieve**, Macmillan Learning's innovative new learning platform.

Engage Your Students with Achieve

Exploring American Histories, Fourth Edition, is available in a variety of print and digital formats, with Achieve offering the greatest value. Built with instructors and students in mind, Achieve includes the full-color e-book, gradebook, LearningCurve adaptive quizzing, assessment tools, insights and reporting, and integration options. Whenever an instructor assigns **Achieve** (with the option of bundling the print book at a low cost), students have access to all the resources of *Exploring American Histories*, including its unique collection of source features that appear in every chapter.

The Right Balance between Narrative and Primary Sources. Inspired by our own teaching, we wanted to create a textbook that would provide everything we would want to use in class, in one place. Many texts include some primary sources, but we found the balance between narrative (too much) and primary sources (too few) didn't suit our courses. We crafted the narrative to make room to include more primary sources and integrate them to help

students make the necessary connections that spur them to think critically. *Exploring American Histories* is comprehensive in the essentials of American history, but with a carefully selected amount of detail that is more in tune with what instructors can realistically expect their students to comprehend. *Exploring American Histories* offers a format which provides just the right balance between narrative and primary sources, along with consistent pedagogy that helps students analyze primary-source material.

Building-Blocks Approach to Analyzing Sources. We know that students in the introductory survey course often need help in developing the ability to think critically about primary sources. In the fourth edition, we continue to promote historical thinking skills by providing a consistent pedagogical framework for analyzing sources. In each chapter, our building-blocks approach ensures that students can progress from working with a single source (Guided Primary Source Analysis), to comparing paired sources (Comparative Primary Source Analysis), to tackling a set of sources from varied perspectives (Primary Source Project). In this way, students can increase their confidence and skills in analyzing primary sources. Students also have the chance to evaluate how historians use primary sources to construct their own interpretations (Comparative Secondary Source Analysis). In Achieve, each one of these features includes a short quiz as part of this wrap-around pedagogy.

Progression in Primary Source Work. Each chapter contains seven to eight substantial, featured primary sources — both written and visual — with unique pedagogy aimed at helping students make connections between the sources and the text's major themes. Each source is clearly cross-referenced within the text so that students can connect the source to the narrative text. We also underscore the importance of primary sources by opening each chapter with a **Window to the Past** — a facsimile of some portion of a primary source that appears in the chapter. To help students make connections between the narrative and sources, we embed

Explore prompts at key junctures in the narrative that describe what the sources illuminate. Such integration is designed to help students make a firm connection between the narrative of history and the evidence upon which it is built.

- Each chapter begins with a **Guided Primary Source Analysis** of a textual or visual source, with a headnote offering historical context and questions in the margins to help students consider a specific phrase or feature and analyze the source as a whole. These targeted questions are intended to guide students in reading and understanding a primary source. A **Put It in Context** question prompts students to consider the source in terms of the broad themes of the chapter. A multiple-choice quiz in Achieve for this and the following source features gauges students' understanding of the assignment.

- Next, each chapter contains a **Comparative Primary Source Analysis**, a paired set of primary sources that show contrasting or complementary perspectives on a particular issue. This feature marks a step up in difficulty from the previous Guided Primary Source Analysis by asking students to analyze sources through their similarities and differences. These primary sources are introduced by a single headnote and are followed by **Interpret the Evidence** and **Put It in Context** questions that prompt students to analyze and compare the items and place them in a larger historical framework.

- At the end of every chapter, a **Primary Source Project** provides the capstone of our integrated primary-sources approach. Each Primary Source Project brings together four or five sources focused on a critical issue central to that chapter. It is introduced by a brief overview and ends with **Interpret the Evidence** and **Put It in Context** questions that ask students to draw conclusions based on what they have learned in the chapter and read or seen in the sources.

An Introduction to Secondary Sources. In addition to the primary source features in each chapter, we extend the building-block approach by offering two scholars' perspectives on a significant topic related to the chapter. The **Comparative Secondary Source Analysis** feature includes a brief introduction and **Examine the Sources** and **Put It in Context** questions, which ask students to compare two secondary sources and identify how they reflect the primary sources and narrative of the textbook. For example, for the early republic, chapter 7 provides selections on partisanship in the 1800 election by Eric Burns and John Ferling. Chapter 11, on the expansion of slavery, contrasts a view of enslaved family life offered by Robert Fogelman and Stanley Engerman with one by Deborah Gray White. With respect to the Progressive Era, chapter 19 offers divergent excerpts on reform in the South by C. Vann Woodward and Glenda Elizabeth Gilmore. Chapter 23 on World War II compares a selection on FDR and the Holocaust by David Wyman with that of Richard Breitman and Allan J. Lichtman. These selections demonstrate how historical scholarship, built upon the analysis of primary sources, can generate different interpretations of the same topic. They reinforce the idea that history changes over time, and help students to get a glimpse into the debates among historians.

Variety of Perspectives. We have selected sources that provide multiple perspectives on important issues, including both well-known sources and those that are less familiar. In all time periods, some groups of Americans are far better represented in primary sources than others. Those who were wealthy, well educated, and politically powerful, produced and preserved many primary sources about their lives, and their voices are well represented in this textbook. We have provided sources by Native Americans, enslaved Africans, free blacks, racial and ethnic minorities, immigrants, rural residents, working people, women, and young people. The lives of those who left few primary sources of their own can often be illuminated by carefully reading sources written by elites to see what information they yield about less well-documented groups. The questions that we ask about these sources are intended to help students read between the lines or see beyond the main image to uncover new meanings. Firsthand accounts include paintings, illustrations, sermons, speeches, letters, diaries, newspaper articles, political cartoons, advertisements, and photographs.

We challenge students to consider diverse viewpoints. For example, in chapter 5, students read contradictory testimony and examine an engraving to analyze the events that became known as the Boston Massacre. In chapter 12, they compare the views on the Fugitive Slave Law of a black abolitionist and the president of the United States. In chapter 18, students have to reconcile two very different views by a Chinese immigrant and a Supreme Court justice concerning the status of Chinese Americans in the late nineteenth century. In chapter 28, we ask readers to reconsider the depiction of the 1980s as a conservative decade in light of widespread protests challenging President Reagan's military build-up against the Soviet Union.

Comparing Biographies

We believe that the most appealing entry to the past starts with individuals and how people in their daily lives connect to larger political, economic, cultural, and international developments. Each chapter opens with **Comparing American Histories**, a pair of biographies that showcase individuals who experienced and influenced events in a particular period, and then returns to them throughout the chapter to strengthen the connections and highlight their place in the larger picture. These biographies cover both well-known Americans — such as Daniel Shays, Frederick Douglass, Andrew Carnegie, and Eleanor Roosevelt — and those who never gained fame or fortune — such as the Cherokee chief John Ross, activist Amy Post, labor organizer Luisa Moreno, and World War II internee Fred Korematsu. Introducing such a broad range of biographical subjects illuminates the many ways that individuals shaped and were shaped by historical events. This strategy also makes visible throughout the text the intersections where history from the top down meets history from the bottom up, and the relationships between social and political histories and economic, cultural, and diplomatic developments.

New Content and Updates to the Narrative

We have engaged the most recent scholarship to ensure the most useful and accurate textbook. In addition to more expansive attention to regional, racial, and ethnic diversity, we have updated our approach to a number of other historical developments, such as systemic racism, pandemics, and the development of capitalist systems in various periods. We continue to pay significant attention to African Americans and women and to expand coverage on the histories of Native Americans, Mexican Americans, Latino Americans, and Asian Americans throughout the book in the narrative and sources.

Expanded Coverage of Diversity. We have made updates in each chapter, many of them focused on providing even greater representation of diverse peoples. In chapter 3, for example, the coverage of Native Americans has been amplified and more names of specific tribes are included to highlight the variety and number of Native American nations. Chapter 6 has been reorganized in order to expand coverage of multiethnic, multiracial forces fighting on both sides in the Revolution and to highlight the role and fate of various Native American nations. In chapter 9, there is a fuller discussion of Denmark Vesey and his planned rebellion, and more on anti-black violence in the North. Chapter 10 has been revised to highlight more black people as pioneers of the Antislavery Movement and the section on women's roles has been reorganized to emphasize black women and interracial efforts. Chapter 13 includes new material on Mexican Americans and Tejanos; enslaved blacks as contraband/refugees; and women as nurses, doctors, and soldiers. Chapter 21 includes new coverage of the Tulsa Race Massacre of 1921; the Osage Indians in Oklahoma and the murders to steal their oil rights; and the League of United Latin American Citizens (LULAC), which formed in 1929. Chapter 25 includes coverage of an important case affecting Mexican Americans, *Hernandez v. Texas (1954)*; and also new coverage on systemic racism in the North. Chapter 26 includes coverage of Mexican American activist, Rejes Tijerna, and also the 1968 Bilingual Education Act.

New Biographies. We have continued to diversify the biographies offered in the chapter-opening **Comparing American Histories**. Accordingly, in Volume 1 we introduce 4 new individuals. These include Powhatan, leader of the largest native confederacy in the mid-Atlantic region (chapter 2); Pontiac, head of a pan-tribal alliance to force the British out of their territory (chapter 5); Elizabeth

(Mum Bett) Freeman, whose freedom suit contributed to Massachusetts ending slavery during the American Revolution (chapter 6); and José Antonio Menchaca, a Tejano military leader who fought for Texas independence (chapter 11). In Volume 2 we now include Pauli Murray, the African American civil rights activist and feminist (chapter 27); Demetria Martinez, the Mexican American writer and immigrant advocate (chapter 28); and Alicia Garza, the African American community organizer and co-founder of Black Lives Matter (chapter 29).

New Primary Source Projects. Volume 1 and Volume 2 each contain two new primary source projects. Chapter 9 offers a project on Cherokee engagement with white society and the chapter 12 project now focuses on the debates over secession. Chapter 19 provides a project on women's suffrage and the ratification of the nineteenth amendment, and chapter 20 includes a project on the 1918 influenza pandemic

Adjustments to Chapter Organization. The major organizational change in Volume 1 is the movement of the secession debates and the beginning of the Civil War from chapter 13 to chapter 12. This allows for extended discussions in chapter 13 of American Indians, Mexican Americans, African Americans, and women during the Civil War, and of black refugees who used the chaos of war to claim their independence.

In Volume 2, we have added material on the extremely divisive 2020 presidential election and Joseph Biden's victory over Donald Trump in the final chapter. Chapter 29 covers the COVID-19 pandemic; the police killings of George Floyd and Breonna Taylor and the nationwide protests they inspired; the collapse of the U.S. economy caused by the pandemic; the January 6, 2021 insurrection at the Capitol; and the subsequent second impeachment of Trump. These events are still unfolding and we intend to provide a framework to help students understand these controversial issues as they evolve.

New Maps and Figures. In Volume 1, we added maps on tribal locations of native peoples at the time of European contact (chapter 1) and revised maps to clarify the role of Native Americans in the American Revolution (chapter 6). We also added a table on migration to the Americas that illustrates the movement of Europeans as well as the forced migration of Africans (chapter 4). In Volume 2, we have added a table on World War I casualties by country (chapter 20); a table on nuclear warheads in the United States, Soviet Union, and United Kingdom, 1945–1960 (chapter 24); a revised table on immigrant growth by home region, 1981–2010 (chapter 28); and a new map on U.S. intervention in Central America and the Caribbean, 1954–1989 (chapter 28). In Achieve, every chapter includes a Map Quiz related to one of the chapter maps that helps students build their geographic literacy skills. We have also changed about one-quarter of the illustrations from the previous edition.

Achieve: Helping Instructors Teach with Digital Resources

Exploring American Histories is now available for the first time in **Achieve**, Macmillan Learning's new complete course platform, which provides access to the narrative as well as a wealth of primary sources and other features, along with assessments and robust insights and reports at the ready, all in one accessible and affordably priced product. Achieve also includes a downloadable e-book for reading offline. Whenever an instructor assigns **Achieve**, students have access to all the resources of the print text (*Exploring American Histories: A Survey with Sources*), including its special features and its primary and secondary sources.

Helping Students Understand the Narrative. Like the print book, each chapter in the **Achieve e-book** includes the following elements to help students make sense of their reading: **Learning Objectives** in the chapter openers prepare students to read the chapter with clear goals in mind; **chapter conclusions** summarize the chapters to help students identify main developments; **Review & Relate** questions help students focus on main themes and concepts presented in each major section of the chapter; **key terms** in boldface highlight important content. All terms are explained in the narrative as well as defined in a glossary at the end of the book; and the **Chapter Review** lets students review key terms, important concepts, and notable events.

Adaptive Learning with LearningCurve. Achieve offers access to **LearningCurve**, an online adaptive learning tool that helps students actively rehearse what they have read and foster a deeper understanding and retention of the material. With this adaptive quizzing, students accumulate points toward a target score as they go, giving the interaction a game-like feel. Feedback for incorrect responses explains why the answer is incorrect and directs students back to the text to review before they attempt to answer the question again. The end result is a better understanding of the key elements of the text. Instructors who actively assign LearningCurve report that their students come to class prepared for discussion and their students enjoy using it. In addition, LearningCurve's reporting feature allows instructors to quickly diagnose which concepts students are struggling with so they can adjust lectures and activities accordingly.

Nurturing Skill Development. Further opportunities for skill development are available through the special activities provided in **Achieve**, many of which are available for the first time with the fourth edition of *Exploring American Histories*. These easy-to-use assignments include new **chronology exercises**, new **reflection activities** that invite students to reflect on what they have read in each chapter, **instructor activity guides** that instructors can use for either remote or in-person collaborative learning, **source and feature quizzes**, **research and writing tutorials with quizzes**, and more. Achieve is a rich asset for instructors who want to support students however they encounter them, whether teaching in a face-to-face, hybrid, or fully remote setting. *Exploring American Histories* combines an engaging narrative with a rich set of digital and print features that promote the comprehension of content, active learning, and skill development. (To learn more about the benefits of LearningCurve, Achieve, and the different versions to package with these digital tools, see the Versions and Supplements section on page xxi.)

Companion Primary Source Reader. For instructors who value even more options, a **companion primary source reader** is available in Achieve and as a printed text. *Thinking through Sources for Exploring American Histories* in **Achieve** provides an additional primary source project for each chapter along with activities. These activities supply self-graded exercises that help students not only understand the sources but also think critically about them. First, a short **quiz after each source** offers students the opportunity to check their understanding of materials that often derive from quite distant times and places. Some questions focus on audience, purpose, point of view, limitations, or context, while others challenge students to draw conclusions about the source or to compare one source with another. And a **Draw Conclusions from the Evidence activity** challenges students to assess whether a specific piece of evidence drawn from the sources supports or challenges a stated conclusion. Collectively these assignments create an active learning environment where reading with a purpose is reinforced by immediate feedback and support. This feedback for each rejoinder creates an active learning environment where students are rewarded for reaching the correct answer through their own process of investigation. **Achieve** is thus a rich asset for instructors who want to support students in all settings, from traditional lectures to "flipped" classrooms. *Exploring American Histories* seeks to promote active learning in various ways.

Teaching with Primary Sources. We understand that the instructor's role is crucial in teaching students how to analyze primary-source materials and develop interpretations. Instructors can use the primary sources in many different ways — as in-class discussion prompts, for take-home writing assignments, and as the basis for exam questions — and also in different combinations with primary sources throughout or across chapters being compared and contrasted with one another.

- **The Instructor's Manual.** The Instructor's Manual for *Exploring American Histories* (available in Achieve) provides a wealth of creative suggestions for using the primary source program effectively. We have written a section, entitled **"Teaching American Histories with Primary Sources,"** which provides ideas and resources for both new and experienced faculty. It offers basic guidelines for teaching students how to analyze sources critically and suggests ways to integrate selected primary sources into lectures, discussions, small group projects, and writing assignments. We also suggest ideas for linking in-text primary sources with the opening biographies, maps, and illustrations in a particular chapter and for using the **Primary Source Projects** to help students understand the entangled histories of the diverse groups that comprise North America and the United States. (See the Versions and Supplements section on page xxi for more information on all the available instructor resources.)

- **Guide to Analyzing Primary and Secondary Sources.** This checklist at the start of the Achieve e-book gives students a quick and efficient lesson on how to read and analyze sources and what kinds of questions to ask in understanding them. We know that many students find primary sources intimidating. Eighteenth and nineteenth century sources contain spellings and language often difficult for modern students to comprehend. Yet, students also have difficulty with contemporary primary sources because in the digital age of Facebook and Twitter they are exposed to information in tiny fragments and without proper verification. Thus, the checklist will guide students in how to approach sources from any era and what to look for in exploring them.

Acknowledgments

We wish to thank the talented scholars and teachers who were kind enough to give their time and knowledge to help us with our revision, as well as those who provided advice in preparation for previous editions. Historians who provided special insight for the fourth edition include the following:

Jonathan Atkins, *Berry College;*
Joseph Cullon, *Worcester State University;*
Nancy Duke, *Daytona State College;*
Jared Eberle, *Oklahoma State University-Stillwater;*
Gary Edwards, *Arkansas State University-Main Campus;*
Keona Ervin, *University of Missouri-Columbia;*
Gabrielle Everett, *Jefferson College;*
Roger Flynn, *Anderson University;*
Melissa Franson, *SUNY College at New Paltz;*
Portia Hopkins, *Lee College;*

Richard Hughes, *Illinois State University;*
Tracy K'Meyer, *University of Louisville;*
Daniel Kotzin, *Medaille College;*
Stephanie Laffer, *University of West Georgia;*
Florence Lemoine, *Cosumnes River College;*
Alexander Marriott, *Alvin Community College;*
Jim McIntyre, *Moraine Valley Community College;*
Robert Parkinson, *Binghamton University-SUNY;*
Donald Seals, *Kilgore College;*
Sean Trundle, *University of Nebraska-Lincoln;*
Trey Welborn, *Georgia College & State University; and*
Adrienne Winans, *Utah Valley University.*

We are also grateful to those who provided ideas and suggestions for previous editions:

Rob Alderson, *Perimeter College at Georgia State University;*
Benjamin Allen, *South Texas College;*
Daniel Allen, *Trinity Valley Community College;*
Leann Almquist, *Middle Georgia State University;*
Christine Anderson, *Xavier University;*
Uzoamaka Melissa C. Anyiwo, *Curry College;*
Rebecca Arnfeld, *California State University, Sacramento;*
David Arnold, *Columbia Basin College;*
Brian Alnutt, *Northampton Community College;*
Anthony A. Ball, *Housatonic Community College;*
Terry A. Barnhart, *Eastern Illinois University;*
John Belohlavek, *University of South Florida;*
Edwin Benson, *North Harford High School;*
Paul Berk, *Christian Brothers University;*
Deborah L. Blackwell, *Texas A&M International University;*
Jeff Bloodworth, *Gannon University;*
Carl Bon Tempo, *University at Albany–SUNY;*
Thomas Born, *Blinn College;*
Margaret Bramlett, *St. Andrews Episcopal High School;*
Martha Jane Brazy, *University of South Alabama;*
Lauren K. Bristow, *Collin College;*
Tsekani Browne, *Duquesne University;*
Jon L. Brudvig, *Dickinson State University;*
Richard Buckelew, *Bethune-Cookman University;*
Timothy Buckner, *Troy University;*
Dave Bush, *Shasta College;*
Monica Butler, *Seminole State College of Florida;*

Barbara Calluori, *Montclair State University;*

Julia Schiavone Camacho, *The University of Texas at El Paso;*

Jacqueline Campbell, *Francis Marion University;*

Amy Canfield, *Lewis-Clark State College;*

Michael Cangemi, *Binghamton University;*

Roger Carpenter, *University of Louisiana, Monroe;*

Dominic Carrillo, *Grossmont College;*

Mark R. Cheathem, *Cumberland University;*

Keith Chu, *Bergen Community College;*

Laurel A. Clark, *University of Hartford;*

Myles L. Clowers, *San Diego City College;*

Remalian Cocar, *Georgia Gwinnett College;*

Lori Coleman, *Tunxis Community College;*

Wilbert E. Corprew, *SUNY Broome;*

Hamilton Cravens, *Iowa State University;*

Audrey Crawford, *Houston Community College;*

Vanessa Crispin-Peralta, *Moorpark College;*

John Crum, *University of Delaware;*

David Cullen, *Collin College;*

Gregory K. Culver, *Austin Peay State University;*

Alex G. Cummins, *St. Johns River State College;*

Robert Chris Davis, *Lone Star College–Kingwood;*

Susanne Deberry-Cole, *Morgan State University;*

Julian J. DelGaudio, *Long Beach City College;*

Patricia Norred Derr, *Kutztown University;*

Thomas Devine, *California State University, Northridge;*

Tom Dicke, *Missouri State University;*

Andy Digh, *Mercer University;*

Gary Donato, *Massachusetts Bay Community College;*

John Donoghue, *Loyola University Chicago;*

Timothy Draper, *Waubonsee Community College;*

David Dzurec, *University of Scranton;*

Susan Eckelmann, *University of Tennessee, Chattanooga;*

George Edgar, *Modesto Junior College;*

Keith Edgerton, *Montana State University Billings;*

Taulby Edmondson, *Virginia Tech;*

Ashton Ellett, *University of Georgia;*

Blake Ellis, *Lone Star College;*

Christine Erickson, *Indiana University–Purdue University Fort Wayne;*

Keona K. Ervin, *University of Missouri;*

Todd Estes, *Oakland University;*

Gabrielle Everett, *Jefferson College;*

Julie Fairchild, *Sinclair Community College;*

Robert Glen Findley, *Odessa College;*

Randy Finley, *Georgia Perimeter College;*

Tiffany Fink, *Hardin-Simmons University;*

Kirsten Fischer, *University of Minnesota;*

Michelle Fishman-Cross, *College of Staten Island;*

Roger Flynn, *TriCounty Technical College;*

Jeffrey Forret, *Lamar University;*

Jonathan Foster, *Great Basin College;*

Kristen Foster, *Marquette University;*

Sarah Franklin, *University of North Alabama;*

Michael Frawley, *University of Texas of the Permian Basin;*

Susan Freeman, *Western Michigan University;*

Nancy Gabin, *Purdue University;*

Kevin Gannon, *Grand View University;*

Benton Gates, *Indiana University–Purdue University Fort Wayne;*

Bruce Geelhoed, *Ball State University;*

Mark Gelfand, *Boston College;*

Robert Genter, *Nassau Community College;*

Jason George, *The Bryn Mawr School;*

Judith A. Giesberg, *Villanova University;*

Dana Goodrich, *Northwest Vista College;*

Sherry Ann Gray, *Mid-South Community College;*

Chad Gregory, *Tri-County Technical College;*

Patrick Griffin, *University of Notre Dame;*

Audrey Grounds, *University of South Florida;*

Abbie Grubb, *San Jacinto College–South;*

Kenneth Grubb, *Wharton County Junior College;*

Larry Grubbs, *Georgia State University;*

Aaron Gulyas, *Mott Community College;*

Scott Gurman, *Northern Illinois University;*

Melanie Gustafson, *University of Vermont;*

Ashley Haines, *Mt. San Antonio College;*

Dennis Halpin, *Virginia Tech;*

Hunter Hampton, *University of Missouri;*

Tona Hangen, *Worcester State University;*

Brian Hart, *Del Mar College;*

Paul Hart, *Texas State University;*

Paul Harvey, *University of Colorado Colorado Springs;*

Stephen Henderson, *William Penn University;*

Kimberly Hernandez, *University of Wisconsin-Milwaukee;*

Lacey A. Holley-McCann, *Columbia State Community College;*

Woody Holton, *University of Richmond;*

Vilja Hulden, *University of Arizona;*

Creed Hyatt, *Lehigh Carbon Community College;*

Colette A. Hyman, *Winona State University;*

Brenda Jackson-Abernathy, *Belmont University;*

Joe Jaynes, *Collin College;*

Troy R. Johnson, *California State University, Long Beach;*

Shelli Jordan-Zirkle, *Shoreline Community College;*

Stephen Katz, *Community College of Philadelphia;*

Lesley Kauffman, *San Jacinto College-Central;*

Jennifer Kelly, *The University of Texas at Austin;*

Kelly Kennington, *Auburn University;*

Andrew E. Kersten, *University of Wisconsin–Green Bay;*

Tina M. Kibbe, *Lamar University;*

Melanie Kiechle, *Virginia Tech;*

Janilyn M. Kocher, *Richland Community College;*

Don Knox, *Wayland Baptist University;*

Max Krochmal, *Duke University;*

Peggy Lambert, *Lone Star College;*

Stephanie Lamphere, *Sierra College;*

Jennifer R. Lang, *Delgado Community College;*

Todd Laugen, *Metropolitan State University of Denver;*

Carolyn J. Lawes, *Old Dominion University;*

John Leazer, *Carthage College;*

Marianne Leeper, *Trinity Valley Community College;*

Alan Lehmann, *Blinn College–Brenham;*

John S. Leiby, *Paradise Valley Community College;*

Leslie Leighton, *Georgia State University;*

Mitchell Lerner, *The Ohio State University;*

Carole N. Lester, *University of Texas at Dallas;*

Amanda Littauer, *Northern Illinois University;*

Matthew Loayza, *Minnesota State University, Mankato;*

Gabriel J. Loiacono, *University of Wisconsin Oshkosh;*

Carmen Lopez, *Miami Dade College;*

Robert Lyle, *University of North Georgia;*

John F. Lyons, *Joliet Junior College;*

Lorie Maltby, *Henderson Community College;*

Christopher Manning, *Loyola University Chicago;*

Amani Marshall, *Georgia State University;*

Phil Martin, *San Jacinto College–South;*

David Mason, *Georgia Gwinnett College;*

Marty D. Matthews, *North Carolina State University;*

Eric Mayer, *Victor Valley College;*

Suzanne K. McCormack, *Community College of Rhode Island;*

David McDaniel, *Marquette University;*

J. Kent McGaughy, *Houston Community College, Northwest;*

Alan McPherson, *Howard University;*

Sarah Hand Meacham, *Virginia Commonwealth University;*

Jason Mead, *Johnson University;*

Brian Craig Miller, *Emporia State University;*

Robert Miller, *California State University, San Marcos;*

Brett Mizelle, *California State University, Long Beach;*

Mark Moser, *The University of North Carolina at Greensboro;*

Ricky Moser, *Kilgore College;*

Jennifer Murray, *Coastal Carolina University;*

Peter C. Murray, *Methodist University;*

Steven E. Nash, *East Tennessee State University;*

Chris Newman, *Elgin Community College;*

David Noon, *University of Alaska Southeast;*

Richard H. Owens, *West Liberty University;*

Alison Parker, *College at Brockport, SUNY;*

Craig Pascoe, *Georgia College;*

David J. Peavler, *Towson University;*

Linda Pelon, *McLennan Community College;*

Laura A. Perry, *University of Memphis;*

Wesley Phelps, *University of St. Thomas;*

Jamie Pietruska, *Rutgers University;*

Sandra Piseno, *Clayton State University;*

Merline Pitre, *Texas Southern University;*

Eunice G. Pollack, *University of North Texas;*

Kimberly Porter, *University of North Dakota;*

Cynthia Prescott, *University of North Dakota;*

Gene Preuss, *University of Houston;*

Sandra Pryor, *Old Dominion University;*

Rhonda Ragsdale, *Lone Star College;*

Ray Rast, *Gonzaga University;*

Michaela Reaves, *California Lutheran University;*

Peggy Renner, *Glendale Community College;*

Steven D. Reschly, *Truman State University;*

Barney J. Rickman, *Valdosta State University;*

Pamela Riney-Kehrberg, *Iowa State University;*

Paul Ringel, *High Point University;*

Jason Ripper, *Everett Community College;*

Timothy Roberts, *Western Illinois University;*

Glenn Robins, *Georgia Southwestern State University;*

Alicia E. Rodriquez, *California State University, Bakersfield;*

Mark Roehrs, *Lincoln Land Community College;*

Patricia Roessner, *Marple Newtown High School;*
John G. Roush, *St. Petersburg College;*
James Russell, *St. Thomas Aquinas College;*
Eric Schlereth, *The University of Texas at Dallas;*
Gregory L. Schneider, *Emporia State University;*
Debra Schultz, *Kingsborough Community College, CUNY;*
Ronald Schultz, *University of Wyoming;*
Stanley K. Schultz, *University of Wisconsin–Madison;*
Scott Seagle, *University of Tennessee at Chattanooga;*
Donald Seals, *Kilgore College;*
Sharon Shackelford, *Erie Community College;*
Donald R. Shaffer, *American Public University System;*
Gregory Shealy, *Saint John's River State College;*
Cathy Hoult Shewring, *Montgomery County Community College;*
Jill Silos-Rooney, *Massachusetts Bay Community College;*
David J. Silverman, *The George Washington University;*
Beth Slutsky, *California State University, Sacramento;*
Andrea Smalley, *Northern Illinois University;*
Karen Smith, *Emporia State University;*
Molly Smith, *Friends School of Baltimore;*
Suzie Smith, *Trinity Valley Community College;*
Troy Smith, *Tennessee Tech University;*
David L. Snead, *Liberty University;*
David Snyder, *Delaware Valley College;*
David Soll, *University of Wisconsin-Eau Claire;*
Gary Sprayberry, *Columbus State University;*
Jodie Steeley, *Merced College;*
Bethany Stollar, *Tennessee State University;*
Bryan E. Stone, *Del Mar College;*
Jason Stratton, *Bakersfield College;*
Emily Straus, *SUNY Fredonia;*
Kristen Streater, *Collin College;*
Joseph Stromberg, *San Jacinto College–Central;*
Jean Stuntz, *West Texas A&M University;*
Sarah Swedberg, *Colorado Mesa University;*
Nikki M. Taylor, *University of Cincinnati;*
Heather Ann Thompson, *Temple University;*
Timothy Thurber, *Virginia Commonwealth University;*
Christopher Thrasher, *Calhoun Community College;*
T. J. Tomlin, *University of Northern Colorado;*
Jeffrey Trask, *Georgia State University;*
Laura Trauth, *Community College of Baltimore County–Essex;*
Russell M. Tremayne, *College of Southern Idaho;*

Laura Tuennerman-Kaplan, *California University of Pennsylvania;*
Linda Upham-Bornstein, *Plymouth State University;*
Mark VanDriel, *University of South Carolina;*
Kevin Vanzant, *Tennessee State University;*
Ramon C. Veloso, *Palomar College;*
Morgan Veraluz, *Tennessee State University;*
Vincent Vinikas, *The University of Arkansas at Little Rock;*
David Voelker, *University of Wisconsin–Green Bay;*
Melissa Walker, *Converse College;*
William Wantland, *Mount Vernon Nazarene University;*
Ed Wehrle, *Eastern Illinois University;*
David Weiland, *Collin College;*
Eddie Weller, *San Jacinto College-South;*
Shane West, *Lone Star College-Greenspoint Center;*
Geoffrey West, *San Diego Mesa College;*
Kenneth B. White, *Modesto Junior College;*
Matt White, *Paris Junior College;*
Anne Will, *Skagit Valley College;*
John P. Williams, *Collin College;*
Zachery R. Williams, *University of Akron;*
Gregory Wilson, *University of Akron;*
Kurt Windisch, *University of Georgia;*
Jonathan Wlasiuk, *The Ohio State University;*
Timothy Wright *Shoreline Community College;*
Timothy L. Wood, *Southwest Baptist University;*
Nancy Beck Young, *University of Houston;*
Maria Cristina Zaccarini, *Adelphi University;*
Nancy Zens, *Central Oregon Community College; and*
Jean Hansen Zuckweiler, *University of Northern Colorado*

We want to thank Bob and Sharon Constantine and Richard and Bobbie Sirmons for their good company and sustenance during the pandemic and other critical events of 2020. In addition a number of scholars generously answered our questions for this fourth edition and provided research critical to our latest revisions: Catherine Brekus, Lisa Brooks, Ellen Hartigan-O'Connor, April Haynes, Maeve Kane, William Link, Tiya Miles, Theda Perdue, Manisha Sinha, Amy Murrell Taylor, Kevin Vrevich, and Brenda Withington. We also appreciate the help the following scholars, archivists, and students gave us in providing the information we needed at critical points in the writing of earlier editions of this text: Lori Birrell, Julia Bowes, Leslie Brown, Andrew Buchanan, Gillian Carroll, Susan J. Carroll, Jacqueline Castledine, Derek Chang, Paul Clemens, Dorothy Sue Cobble, Jane Coleman-Harbison, Alison Cronk, Kayo Denda, Elisabeth Eittreim, David Foglesong, Phyllis Hunter, Tera Hunter, Molly Inabinett, Kenneth Kvamme, William Link, James Livingston, Julia Livingston, Justin Lorts, Melissa Mead, Gilda Morales, Andrew Preston, Vicki L. Ruiz, Julia Sandy-Bailey, Susan Schrepfer, Bonnie Smith, Melissa Stein, Margaret Sumner, Camilla Townsend, Jessica Unger, Anne Valk, and Melinda Wallington. We also want to thank Rob Heinrich and Julia Sandy for their work in compiling the primary source projects for the first edition of the companion source reader, *Thinking through Sources: Exploring American Histories.*

We would particularly like to applaud the many hardworking and creative people at Bedford/St. Martin's (Macmillan Learning) who guided us through the labyrinthine process of writing this fourth edition. No one was more important to us than Leah Strauss, our editor with a keen eye and a light touch, and William Lombardo, senior executive program manager, who has seen us through all four editions. They were joined by an excellent team at Macmillan, including Erika Gutierrez, senior program director; Gregory Erb, executive content project manager; Julia Bell, assistant editor; Mollie Chandler, media editor; Stephanie Sosa, associate editor; and Melissa Rodriguez, senior marketing manager. We thank cover designer, William Boardman, and Naomi Kornhauser for image research for which we are grateful. We will always remain thankful to Sara Wise and Patricia Rossi for their advice about and enthusiasm for a primary source-based American History textbook and to Joan Feinberg, who had the vision that guided us through every page of this book. Thanks as well to Michael Rosenberg whose enthusiasm inspired us to keep thinking anew about the past. Finally, we would like to express our gratitude to our friends and family who have encouraged us through every edition and have even read the book without it being assigned.

Nancy A. Hewitt and Steven F. Lawson

Adopters of *Exploring American Histories* and their students have access to abundant digital and print resources and tools, including documents, assessment and presentation materials, the acclaimed *Bedford Series in History and Culture* volumes, and much more. *Exploring American Histories* is now available for the first time in Achieve, Macmillan Learning's new complete course platform, which provides access to the narrative as well as a wealth of primary sources and other features, along with assessments and robust insights and reports at the ready, all in one affordably priced product. Achieve also includes a downloadable e-book for reading offline. See the following text for more information, visit the book's catalog site at macmillanlearning.com, or contact your local Macmillan Learning sales representative.

Get the Right Version and Volume for Your Class — Digital, Print, and Value Options.

Whether it's a digital course platform, e-book, print book, a value option, or a package combining digital and print products, *Exploring American Histories* is available in a variety of volumes and formats so you can choose what works best for your course. The comprehensive *Exploring American Histories* includes a full-color art and map program and a rich set of features and primary and secondary sources. Digital options for the comprehensive version include the full course platform of Achieve for *Exploring American Histories* (see below for the description of Achieve's benefits), as well as e-books. The comprehensive version is also available in print in three volume options. For great value in a streamlined product, *Exploring American Histories*, **Value Edition**, offers the unabridged narrative and selected two-color art and maps — without special features or primary or secondary sources — at a steep discount. The Value Edition is available in e-book format, as

well as print, in three volume options, with loose-leaf format available for the least expensive price option. For the best value, purchase Achieve on its own or package it with the print version of your choice for a small add-on cost. *Exploring American Histories* is available in the following volume configurations:

- **Combined Volume** (Chapters 1–29). Available in Achieve (1- and 2-term subscriptions), e-books, and print volumes for the comprehensive and Value editions.
- **Volume 1: To 1877** (Chapters 1–14). Available in Achieve (1- and 2-term subscriptions), e-books, and print volumes for the comprehensive and Value editions, including loose-leaf format for the Value editions.
- **Volume 2: Since 1865** (Chapters 14–29). Available in Achieve (1- and 2-term subscriptions), e-books, and print volumes for the comprehensive and Value editions, including loose-leaf format for the Value editions.

As noted below, any of these volumes can be packaged with additional titles for a discount. To get ISBNs for discount packages, visit **macmillanlearning.com** or contact your Macmillan Learning sales representative.

Achieve READ & PRACTICE Assign Achieve — A Comprehensive Course Platform with E-book, Skill-Building Assessments, and Analytics for Instructors

Affordably priced, intuitive and easy to use, Achieve is a breakthrough solution for building students' skills and confidence in history courses. Achieve for *Exploring American Histories* includes the rich resources and skill-building content of the e-books for the complete comprehensive text and companion reader, *Thinking through Sources for Exploring American Histories* alongside a robust set of summative and formative assessments — many autograded — that help students build confidence in their mastery of the material, reflect on their learning, and build critical, higher-level thinking skills. Achieve for *Exploring American Histories* includes LearningCurve adaptive quizzing that — when assigned — helps ensure students do the reading before class; autograded exercises that teach students how to build a thesis and support an argument; quizzes that check student comprehension of primary sources and boxed features; chapter summative quizzes that test student knowledge after they've completed the reading; tutorials with quizzing that build skills such as working with primary sources and avoiding plagiarism; assignable chapter reflection questions that encourage students to engage with their learning; active reading activities that help students read actively for key concepts; class activity guides that can be used in synchronous and asynchronous courses; and iClicker polling questions that engage students during class. These features, plus additional primary source documents, map quizzes, customizable test banks, and detailed reports on student progress make Achieve an invaluable asset for any instructor.

Achieve easily integrates with course management systems, and with fast ways to build assignments and organize content, it lets teachers build the courses they want to teach while holding students accountable. For more information, or to arrange a demo or class test, contact us at **historymktg@macmillan.com**.

LearningCurve Assign LearningCurve So Your Students Come to Class Prepared

Students using Achieve receive access to LearningCurve for *Exploring American Histories*. Assigning LearningCurve in place of reading quizzes is easy for instructors, and the reporting features help instructors track overall class trends and spot topics that are giving students trouble so they can adjust their lectures and class activities. This online learning tool is popular with students because it was designed to help them rehearse content at their own pace in a nonthreatening, game-like environment. The feedback for wrong answers provides instructional coaching and sends students back to the book for review. Students answer as many questions as necessary to reach a target score, with repeated chances to revisit material they haven't mastered. When LearningCurve is assigned, students come to class better prepared.

iClicker iClicker Student App, Active Learning Simplified

The iClicker student app offers simple, flexible tools to help you give students a voice and facilitate active learning in the classroom. Students can participate with the devices they already bring to class using our iClicker student mobile app (which works with smart phones, tablets, or laptops). We've now integrated iClicker with Macmillan's Achieve to make it easier than ever to synchronize grades and promote engagement — both in and out of class. iClicker can be used synchronously through its polling feature, or asynchronously for assignments. To learn more, talk to your Macmillan Learning sales representative or visit us at **www.iclicker.com**.

Take Advantage of Instructor Resources

Bedford/St. Martin's has developed a rich array of teaching resources for this book and for this course. They range from lecture and presentation materials and assessment tools to course management options. Most can be found in Achieve or can be downloaded or ordered at **macmillanlearning.com**.

Instructor's Resource Manual. The Instructor's Resource Manual offers both experienced and first-time instructors tools for presenting textbook material in engaging ways. It includes content learning objectives, annotated chapter outlines, and strategies for teaching with the textbook, plus suggestions on how to get the most out of LearningCurve, and a survival guide for first-time teaching assistants.

Guide to Changing Editions. Designed to facilitate an instructor's transition from the previous edition of *Exploring American Histories* to the new edition, this guide presents an overview of major changes as well as of changes in each chapter.

Online Test Bank. The test bank includes a mix of fresh, carefully crafted multiple-choice, short-answer, and essay questions for each chapter. Some of the multiple-choice questions feature a map as the prompt. All questions appear in easy-to-use test bank software that allows instructors to add, edit, re-sequence, filter by question type, and print questions and answers. Instructors can also export questions into a variety of course management systems.

The Bedford Lecture Kit: *Lecture Outlines, Maps, and Images.* Look good and save time with *The Bedford Lecture Kit*. This resource includes fully customizable multimedia presentations built around chapter outlines that are embedded with maps, figures, and images from the textbook and are supplemented by more detailed instructor notes on key points and concepts.

Print, Digital, and Custom Options for More Choice and Value

For information on packages and discounts up to 50%, visit **macmillanlearning.com**, or contact your local Macmillan Learning sales representative.

Thinking through Sources for Exploring American Histories, **Third Edition.** This companion reader provides an additional primary source project with four to five written and visual sources focused on a central topic to accompany each chapter of *Exploring American Histories*. To aid students in approaching and interpreting the sources, the project for each chapter contains an introduction, document headnotes, and questions for discussion. This companion reader is an exceptional value for students and offers plenty of assignment options for instructors, and is included in Achieve with autograded quizzes for each source. *Thinking through Sources for Exploring American*

Histories is also available on its own as a downloadable e-book.

Bedford Document Collections. These affordable, brief document projects provide five to seven primary sources, an introduction, historical background, and other pedagogical features. Each curated project — designed for use in a single class period and written by a historian about a favorite topic — poses a historical question and guides students through analysis of the sources. Examples include "What Caused the Civil War?"; "The California Gold Rush: A Trans-Pacific Phenomenon"; and "War Stories: Black Soldiers and the Long Civil Rights Movement." These primary source projects are available in a low-cost, easy-to-use digital format or can be combined with other course materials in Bedford Select to create an affordable, personalized print product. For more information on using Bedford Select to customize your course materials with these and other resources, visit **macmillanlearning.com/bedfordselect**.

Bedford Tutorials for History. Designed to provide resources relevant to individual courses, this collection of over a dozen brief units, each 16 pages long and loaded with examples, guides students through basic skills such as using historical evidence effectively, working with primary sources, taking effective notes, avoiding plagiarism and citing sources, and more. For more information, visit **macmillanlearning .com/historytutorials**.

The Bedford Series in History and Culture. Now available in low-cost e-books as well as print volumes, the more than 100 titles in this highly praised series combine first-rate scholarship, historical narrative, and important primary documents for undergraduate courses. Each title is brief, inexpensive, and focused on a specific topic or period. Recent titles in the series include: *The Chinese Exclusion Act and Angel Island: A Brief History with Documents*, by Judy Yung; *The Life of P.T. Barnum, Written by Himself, with Related Documents*, edited with an introduction by Stephen Mihm; and *The California Gold Rush: A Brief History with Documents*, by Andrew C. Isenberg. For a complete list of titles, visit **macmillanlearning.com**. Package discounts are available.

Trade Books. History titles published by sister companies Hill and Wang; Farrar, Straus and Giroux; Henry Holt and Company; St. Martin's Press; Picador; and Palgrave Macmillan are available at a 50% discount when packaged with Bedford/St. Martin's textbooks. For more information, visit **macmillanlearning.com/tradeup**.

A Pocket Guide to Writing in History. Available in a low-cost e-book as well as in print and updated to reflect changes made in the 2017 Chicago Manual of Style revision, this portable and affordable reference tool by Mary Lynn Rampolla provides reading, writing, and research advice useful to students in all history courses. Concise yet comprehensive advice on approaching typical history assignments, developing critical reading skills, writing effective history papers, conducting research, using and documenting sources, and avoiding plagiarism — enhanced with practical tips and examples throughout — has made this slim reference a best-seller. Deep discounts are available when bundled with a survey textbook.

A Student's Guide to History. Available in a low-cost e-book as well as in print and updated to reflect changes made in the 2017 Chicago Manual of Style revision, this complete guide to success in any history course provides the practical help students need to be successful. In addition to introducing students to the nature of the discipline, author Jules Benjamin teaches a wide range of skills from preparing for exams to approaching common writing assignments, and explains the research and documentation process with plentiful examples. Deep discounts are available when bundled with a survey textbook.

Brief Contents

Contents

---

chapter 4

Religious Strife and Social Upheavals 1680–1754 *107*

chapter 5

War and Empire 1754–1774   143

chapter 6

The American Revolution 1775–1783   177

---

chapter 7

Forging a New Nation 1783–1800   *211*

---

chapter 10

Social and Cultural Ferment in the North 1820–1850   319

chapter 13

Civil War 1861–1865   *427*

Maps, Figures, and Tables

Maps

Figures and Tables

How to Use This Book

Use the chapter tools to focus on what's important as you read.

Learning Objectives preview what you will learn in the chapter.

Comparing American Histories biographies at the start of each chapter personalize the history of the period by describing the life of two individuals.

Review & Relate questions review key concepts at the end of each major section and repeat in the chapter review.

Learning Objectives

After reading this chapter you will be able to:

- Explain the relationship between the beginning of armed conflict and patriots' decision to declare independence.

- Understand the choices of colonists, American Indians, and African Americans to support or oppose independence.

- Analyze the military strategies of the British and the Americans in 1776–1777, the roles that various allies played, the importance of women and other groups on the home front, and the significance of smallpox among colonial soldiers.

- Explain the major accomplishments of and conflicts within the new state and federal governments during the Revolution.

- Analyze the shift of warfare to the South and West from 1778 to 1781; the importance of American Indians, foreign allies, and colonial soldiers in patriot victories there; and the challenges Americans faced once they defeated the British.

Comparing American Histories

One of the foremost pamphleteers of the patriot cause, **Thomas Paine** was born in 1737 in England, where his parents trained him as a corset maker. Eventually he left home and found work as a seaman, a teacher, and a tax collector. He drank heavily and beat both his wives. Yet he also taught working-class children to read and pushed the British government to improve the working conditions and pay of tax collectors. In 1772 Paine was fired from his government job, but a pamphlet he wrote had caught the eye of Benjamin Franklin, who persuaded him to try his luck in the colonies.

Arriving in Philadelphia in November 1774 at age thirty-seven, Paine secured a job on the *Pennsylvania Magazine*. The newcomer quickly gained in-depth political knowledge of the intensifying conflicts between the colonies and Great Britain. He also gained patrons for his political tracts among Philadelphia's economic and political elite. When armed conflict with British troops erupted in April 1775, colonial debates over whether to declare independence intensified. Pamphlets were a popular means of influencing these debates, and Paine wrote one entitled *Common Sense* to tip the balance in favor of independence.

Published in January 1776, *Common Sense* proved an instant success. It provided a rationale for independence and an emotional plea for creating a new democratic republic. Paine urged colonists to separate from England and establish a political structure that would ensure liberty and equality for all Americans. "A government of our own is our natural right," he concluded. "'Tis time to part."

When *Common Sense* was published, an enslaved woman known as Bett was working for the Ashleys in Sheffield, Massachusetts. She was born to enslaved parents around 1742 in Claverack, New York, on the estate of Peiter Hogeboom. When Hogeboom's daughter Hannah married John Ashley, around 1750, the young Bett was given to them as a wedding present. Bett worked for the Ashleys for the next thirty years. Sometime in the late 1760s or early 1770s, the Ashleys allowed Bett to marry, and she gave birth to a daughter, Little Bett. By the 1770s, "Mum" Bett had gained skills as a nurse and midwife.

John Ashley, a wealthy lawyer and landowner, had fought in the French and Indian War. As conflicts between Britain and the colonies escalated, he joined the patriot cause. In January 1773, eleven patriots, including lawyer Theodore Sedgwick, met at his home. They drew up a series of resolutions known as the Sheffield Resolves that decried British tyranny and demanded individual rights. They were printed in the

(left) **Thomas Paine** Library of Congress, Prints and Photographs Division, Washington, D.C. [LC-DIG-pga-12728]
(right) **Elizabeth Freeman (Mum Bett)** Bridgeman Images

178

---

delegates from twelve colonies approved the Declaration, with only New York abstaining. Independence was publicly proclaimed on July 4 when the Declaration was published as a broadside to be circulated throughout the colonies.

Review & Relate

| What challenges did Washington face after accepting command of the Continental Army? | How and why did proponents of independence prevail in the debates that led to the Declaration of Independence? |

Use the building blocks approach to primary sources to strengthen your interpretive skills.

STEP 1 Guided Primary Source Analysis

Near the start of each chapter, a **Guided Analysis** of a textual or visual source with annotated questions in the margins models how to analyze a specific phrase or detail of the source as well as the source as a whole.

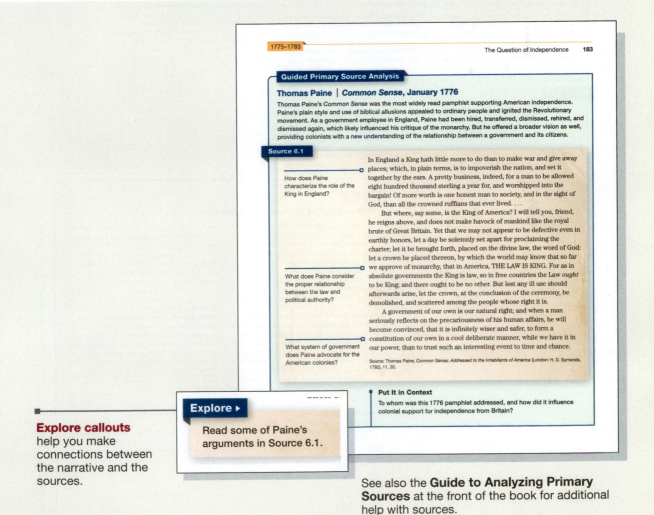

Guided Primary Source Analysis

Thomas Paine | *Common Sense*, January 1776

Thomas Paine's *Common Sense* was the most widely read pamphlet supporting American independence. Paine's plain style and use of biblical allusions appealed to ordinary people and ignited the Revolutionary movement. As a government employee in England, Paine had been hired, transferred, dismissed, rehired, and dismissed again, which likely influenced his critique of the monarchy. But he offered a broader vision as well, providing colonists with a new understanding of the relationship between a government and its citizens.

Source 6.1

How does Paine characterize the role of the King in England?

In England a King hath little more to do than to make war and give away places; which, in plain terms, is to impoverish the nation, and set it together by the ears. A pretty business, indeed, for a man to be allowed eight hundred thousand sterling a year for, and worshipped into the bargain! Of more worth is one honest man to society, and in the sight of God, than all the crowned ruffians that ever lived. . . .

But where, say some, is the King of America? I will tell you, friend, he reigns above, and does not make havock of mankind like the royal brute of Great Britain. Yet that we may not appear to be defective even in earthly honors, let a day be solemnly set apart for proclaiming the charter; let it be brought forth, placed on the divine law, the word of God: let a crown be placed thereon, by which the world may know that so far we approve of monarchy, that in America, THE LAW IS KING. For as in

What does Paine consider the proper relationship between the law and political authority?

absolute governments the King is law, so in free countries the Law *ought* to be King; and there ought to be no other. But lest any ill use should afterwards arise, let the crown, at the conclusion of the ceremony, be demolished, and scattered among the people whose right it is.

A government of our own is our natural right; and when a man seriously reflects on the precariousness of his human affairs, he will become convinced, that it is infinitely wiser and safer, to form a constitution of our own in a cool deliberate manner, while we have it in

What system of government does Paine advocate for the American colonies?

our power, than to trust such an interesting event to time and chance.

Source: Thomas Paine, *Common Sense; Addressed to the Inhabitants of America* (London: H. D. Symonds, 1792), 11, 20.

Put It in Context

To whom was this 1776 pamphlet addressed, and how did it influence colonial support for independence from Britain?

Explore ▶

Read some of Paine's arguments in Source 6.1.

Explore callouts help you make connections between the narrative and the sources.

See also the **Guide to Analyzing Primary Sources** at the front of the book for additional help with sources.

Next, each chapter progresses to the **Comparative Primary Source Analysis**, a paired set of documents that reveal contrasting or complementary perspectives on a particular issue or event.

Comparative Primary Source Analysis

Women and Free Blacks Claim Rights in the Nation

Limited in their civil and political rights and educational and economic opportunities, some women and African Americans demanded change. Many white women focused on gaining greater access to education. In the first selection, Judith Sargent Murray, a well-educated Massachusetts writer, insists that women are rational creatures who can make important contributions to society. Blacks had far fewer opportunities since the vast majority were enslaved, and even free blacks faced numerous restrictions. In the second selection, three free black men in Charleston, South Carolina petition the state legislature for increased judicial rights.

Source 7.2

Judith Sargent Murray | On the Equality of the Sexes, 1790

Are we [women] deficient in reason? . . . [I]f an opportunity of acquiring knowledge hath been denied us, the inferiority of our sex cannot fairly be deduced from thence. . . . May we not trace its source in the difference of education, and continued advantages? Will it be said that the judgment of a male of two years old, is more sage than that of a female's of the same age? . . . But from that period what partiality! . . . As their years increase, the sister must be wholly domesticated, while the brother is led by the hand through all the flowery paths of science. . . . Now, was she permitted the same instructors as her brother, . . . for the employment of a rational mind an ample field would be opened. In astronomy she might catch a glimpse of the immensity of the Deity, and thence she would form amazing conceptions of the august and supreme Intelligence. In geography she would admire Jehovah in the midst of his benevolence; thus adapting this globe to the various wants and amusements of its inhabitants. In natural philosophy she would adore the infinite majesty of heaven, clothed in condescension; and as she traversed the reptile world, she would hail the goodness of a creating God. . . . Will it be urged that those acquirements

Source 7.3

Petition from Free Blacks of Charleston, 1791

That in the enumeration of free citizens by the Constitution of the United States for the purpose of representation of the Southern states in Congress your memorialists [petitioners] have been considered under that description as part of the citizens of this state.

Although by the fourteenth and twenty-ninth clauses in an Act of Assembly made in the year 1740 . . . commonly called the Negro Act, now in force, your memorialists are deprived of the rights and privileges of citizens by not having it in their power to give testimony on oath in prosecutions on behalf of the state; from which cause many culprits have escaped the punishment due to their atrocious crimes, nor can they give their testimony in recovering debts due to them, or in establishing agreements made by them within the meaning of the Statutes of Frauds and Perjuries in force in this state except in cases where persons of color are concerned, whereby they are subject to great losses and repeated injuries without any means of redress.

That by the said clauses in the said Act, they are debarred of the rights of free citizens by being subject to a trial without the benefit of a jury and subject to prosecution by testimony of slaves without oath by which they are placed on the same footing.

Your memorialists show that they have at all times since the independence of the United States contributed and do now contribute to the support of the government by cheerfully paying their taxes proportionable to their property with others who have been during such period, and now are, in full enjoyment of the rights and immunities of citizens, inhabitants of a free independent state.

Source: Petition of Thomas Cole, Peter Bassnett Matthewes, and Matthew Webb to the South Carolina Senate, January 1, 1791, Records of the General Assembly, no. 181.

Interpret the Evidence

1. What kind of rights do Judith Sargent Murray and the free blacks in Charleston claim for women and free African Americans, respectively?
2. What explains the differences in the rights demanded by Murray and the black petitioners and the ways they justify those claims?

Put It in Context

What do these documents reveal about the positions of white women and free black men during the formation of the United States?

STEP 3 Comparative Secondary Source Analysis

Next, the **Comparative Secondary Source Analysis**, presents two secondary sources by historians that offer differing perspectives on an important historical issue or event.

Partisan Campaigning in the Election of 1800

While the election of 1796 was the first to involve candidates chosen by opposing parties, it was decidedly civil compared to that of 1800. Partisan differences intensified as divisions over domestic and foreign policies led each side to view the other as a threat to fundamental American values. Historians agree that the election of 1800 — between Federalist John Adams and Democratic-Republican Thomas Jefferson — marks a critical moment in U.S. history because it necessitated the peaceful transfer of power from one political party to another. Yet it was also marked by vitriol spewed by partisan newspapers. Eric Burns suggests that Federalists attacked Jefferson because they could not imagine a peaceful transfer of power to their opponents, while John Ferling focuses on the growing strength and reach of Democratic-Republican newspapers.

Source 7.4

Eric Burns | Federalists Attack Thomas Jefferson, 2006

[W]ould Federalists willingly and peacefully hand power over to their political enemies . . . , men whom they not only loathed but also considered dangerous to the rep[. . .] economic growth an[. . .] to everything they ch[. . .]

The answer, at l[. . .] newspapers were co[. . .] to make sure that the[. . .] on the transfer of po[. . .] despised, they began[. . .] most dire of predicti[. . .] Jefferson be elected [. . .] *Hudson Bee* . . . , "the[. . .] set on our holy religi[. . .] prostrated, and some[. . .]

the title the Goddess of Reason, will preside in the Sanctuaries now devoted to the Most High." . . .

The [Democratic-]Republican counterattack

Source 7.5

John Ferling | Democratic-Republicans Attack John Adams, 2013

While most of the candidates avoided the hustings [public platforms], party activists were busy. For the most part, both sides spread their messages through pamphlets, broadsides, and newspapers. The Federalists had a decided edge in the press, but [Democratic-]Republican newspapers had climbed up from 15 percent of the total in 1796 to nearly one-third by 1800. The [Democratic-] Republicans were better organized for disseminating information, as they established committees of correspondence to funnel publications to the hinterland. . . .

Some [Democratic-]Republican penmen limned [depicted] Adams as a monarchist . . . , but their essayists focused mostly on the Federalist program. One writer after another attacked the

Alien and Sedition Acts, the taxes levied to pay for the debt . . . , and the very existence of a standing army. Much of their ink was [also] spilled on Hamilton's economic program. . . .

The abuse . . . directed against Hamilton paled in comparison to the calumny heaped on Jefferson. . . . Federalists charged that Jefferson's residence in France had transformed him into a dangerous radical. . . . A Federalist newspaper in Virginia alleged that Jefferson had a slave mistress. . . . [And] Federalists twisted Jefferson's advocacy of religious freedom in *Notes on the State of Virginia* to brand him an atheist.

Source: John Ferling, *Jefferson and Hamilton: The Rivalry That Forged a Nation* (New York: Bloomsbury Press, 2014), 320–321.

Examine the Sources

1. How do Ferling and Burns differ in their assessments of Federalist and Democratic-Republican attacks on each other's presidential candidates?
2. How effective are Ferling and Burns in using primary sources to make their argument? Do you find one argument more compelling than the other, and if so, why?

Put It in Context

Given the fierce attacks on Jefferson, what explains his victory in the 1800 election?

Examine the Sources questions help you evaluate and compare the historians' interpretations.

Finally, the **Primary Source Project** includes four or five sources that focus on a central topic and provide the opportunity to draw deeper conclusions.

Primary Source Project 7

Debating the Constitution in New York State

▶ As Americans considered the proposed Constitution, which groups sought to increase and which groups sought to restrict federal power and why?

Although the Constitution was eventually approved by all thirteen states, the battle over its ratification revealed a deeply divided nation. Antifederalist delegates dominated conventions in Massachusetts, Virginia, and New York; and when Massachusetts and Virginia finally ratified the Constitution by close votes, the New York convention was still in session.

As elsewhere, New York delegates debated questions of representation, the increased powers of the federal government, and a bill of rights. Before the convention opened, James Madison, Alexander Hamilton, and John Jay offered fellow New Yorkers pro-Constitution arguments in *The Federalist Papers* (Source 7.6). At the convention, Hamilton emphasized the need for a strong central government in which checks and balances limited the power of any single branch and insisted on accommodating the views of diverse groups, including southern slaveowners (Source 7.8).

A secretary recorded the speeches of Hamilton and other delegates. Melancton Smith was a large landowner and a New York City merchant, but he led the state's Antifederalists and questioned the expansion of federal power and the limits on representation (Source 7.7). John Williams, a farmer from rural Washington County and thus a more typical Antifederalist, criticized the Constitution more adamantly. He distrusted federal power, disliked the system of representation, and worried about America's moral decline (Source 7.9). However, the

Federalists eventually prevailed, w Smith, and twenty-eight other delega and Williams one of the twenty-seven slim victory elated the Federalist ne *Massachusetts Centinel*, which tracke that ratified the Constitution (Source 7.

The intensity of these debates competing ideas and interests among also shows the willingness of Federalis mise on issues like a bill of rights whi creating a new political structure.

Source 7.6

James Madison │ *Federalist* The Union as a Safeguard A Domestic Faction and Insur November 1787

James Madison wrote the most signific pro-Constitution essays known collect *Federalist Papers*. In this essay, Madis the widely held belief that republican g were most likely to succeed when they and compact. He argued instead that a diverse population in which various factions competed for support would keep any one faction from subverting the freedom of other groups.

To the People of the State of New York:

AMONG the numerous advantages promised by a well-constructed Union, none deserves to be more accurately developed than its tendency to break and control the violence of faction. The friend of popular

Source 7.7

Melancton Smith │ Antifederalist Argument at the New York State Convention, June 1788

Melancton Smith was unusually wealthy for an Antifederalist delegate. Smith worked alongside Alexander Hamilton in the New York Manumission Society, which encouraged the gradual abolition of slavery. But while Hamilton accepted the three-fifths compromise as necessary, Smith found it odious. He also embraced the traditional view that republics were best governed by smaller governmental bodies.

In the discussion of this question, he [Smith] was disposed to make every reasonable concession, and, indeed, to sacrifice every thing for a union, except the liberties of his country. . . .

The defects of the Old Confederation needed as little proof as the necessity of an Union. But there was no proof in all this that the proposed Constitution was a good one. Defective as the Old Confederation is, . . . no one could deny but it was possible we might have a worse government. . . .

Use the Chapter Review to identify significant historical events and how they fit together over time.

Review the **Timeline of Events**, which shows the relationship among chapter events.

Timeline of Events

1783	Continental Army officers threaten to mutiny
1784	Treaty of Fort Stanwix
1785	Northwest Ordinance passed
	Annapolis Convention
1786–1787	Shays's Rebellion
1787	Constitutional Convention in Philadelphia
	Northwest Ordinance revised
1788	U.S. Constitution ratified
1789	Alexander Hamilton named secretary of the treasury
	Judiciary Act of 1789 passed
1789–1799	French Revolution
1790–1794	Little Turtle leads pan-Indian alliance in the Ohio valley
1791	Bill of Rights ratified
1793	Neutrality Proclamation
	Yellow fever epidemic paralyzes Philadelphia
1794	Whiskey Rebellion
	African Methodist Episcopal Church founded
1796	Jay Treaty and Pinckney Treaty ratified
	Democratic-Republican Party established
1798	Alien and Sedition Acts passed
1800	Election of Thomas Jefferson as president

Key Terms

Treaty of Fort Stanwix, *214*
Northwest Ordinance, *217*
republican motherhood, *220*
Shays's Rebellion, *222*
Virginia Plan, *225*
New Jersey Plan, *225*
three-fifths compromise, *225*
Federalists, *226*
Antifederalists, *227*

Bill of Rights, *228*
Jay Treaty, *232*
Whiskey Rebellion, *233*
Treaty of Greenville, *234*
Pinckney Treaty, *234*
Democratic-Republicans, *236*
XYZ affair, *236*
Alien and Sedition Acts, *237*
Virginia and Kentucky Resolutions, *237*

Study the **Key Terms** list to see if you can define each term and describe its significance.

Review & Relate

1. What challenges did the new nation face in the immediate aftermath of the Revolutionary War?
2. How did farmers, financial leaders, foreign nations, and Indians react to government efforts to address challenges after the Revolution?
3. How did America's experience of the Revolutionary War change the lives of African Americans and women?
4. What do uprisings by farmers and debtors tell us about social and economic divisions in the early Republic?
5. What issues attracted the most intense debate during the drafting and ratification of the Constitution? Why?
6. How did Hamilton's policies stabilize the national economy, and why did they nonetheless arouse opposition?
7. How did events overseas shape domestic American politics and frontier policy in the 1790s?
8. What common concerns underlay the Whiskey Rebellion and Shays's Rebellion? How did the U.S. government deal differently with each?
9. What were the main issues dividing the Federalists and the Democratic-Republicans?
10. What do the Alien and Sedition Acts and the election of 1800 tell us about political partisanship in late-eighteenth-century America?

Answer the **Review & Relate questions**, which prompt you to recall major concepts in each section.

241

Mapping Global Frontiers

to 1590

Window to the Past

Universalis Cosmographia, 1507

This image of the Americas was engraved on one of the first world maps of the sixteenth century. The elongated shape was based on information supplied by early European explorers. ▸ **To learn more about this primary source, see Source 1.1 on page 11.**

After reading this chapter you will be able to:

- Describe the diverse societies that populated the Americas prior to European exploration.

- Explain the reasons for European exploration and expansion, and compare the impact of this expansion on Europe and Africa.

- Evaluate the reasons for Europeans' success in reaching the Americas, and compare the impact of the Columbian exchange on American Indians, Africans, and Europeans.

- Analyze how the Spanish created an empire in the Americas, and describe the impact of Spain's empire building on Indian empires and European nations.

Comparing American Histories

In 1519 a young Indian woman named **Malintzin** was thrust into the center of dramatic events that transformed not only her world but also the world at large. As a young girl, Malintzin, whose birth name is lost to history, lived in the rural area of Coatzacoalcos on the frontier between the expanding kingdom of the Mexica and the declining Mayan states of the Yucatán peninsula. Raised in a noble household, Malintzin was fluent in Nahuatl, the language of the Mexica.

(*left*) **Portrait of Malintzin (detail)** Gianni Dagli Orti/Shutterstock
(*right*) ***Universalis Cosmographia*, 1507 (detail)** Library of Congress, Geography and Map Division

In 1515 or 1516, when she was between the ages of eight and twelve, Malintzin was taken by or given to Mexica merchants, perhaps as a peace offering to stave off military attacks. She then entered a well-established trade in slaves, consisting mostly of women and girls, who were sent eastward to work in the expanding cotton fields or the households of their owners. She may also have been forced into a sexual relationship with a landowner. Whatever her situation, Malintzin learned the Mayan language during her captivity.

In 1517 Mayan villagers sighted Spanish adventurers along local rivers and drove them off. But in 1519 the Spaniards returned. The Maya's lightweight armor made of dense layers of cotton, cloth, and leather and their wooden arrows were no match for the invaders' steel swords, guns, and horses. Forced to surrender, the Maya offered the Spaniards food, gold, and twenty enslaved women, including Malintzin. The Spanish leader, Hernán Cortés, baptized the enslaved women and assigned each of them Christian names, although the women did not consent to this ritual. Cortés then divided the women among his senior officers, giving Malintzin to the highest-ranking noble.

Already fluent in Nahuatl and Mayan, Malintzin soon learned Spanish. Within a matter of months, she became the Spaniards' chief translator. As Cortés moved into territories ruled by the Mexica (whom the Spaniards called Aztecs), his success depended on his ability to understand Aztec ways of thinking and to convince subjugated groups to fight against their despotic rulers. Malintzin thus accompanied Cortés at every step, including his triumphant conquest of the Aztec capital in the fall of 1521.

At the same time that Malintzin played a key role in the conquest of the Aztecs, **Martin Waldseemüller** sought to map the frontiers along which these conflicts erupted. Born in present-day Germany in the early 1470s, Waldseemüller enrolled at the University of Fribourg in 1490, where he probably studied theology. He would gain fame, however, as a cartographer, or mapmaker.

In 1507 Waldseemüller and Mathias Ringmann, working at a scholarly religious institute in St. Dié in northern France, produced a map of the world, a small globe, and a Latin translation of the four voyages of the Italian explorer Amerigo Vespucci. The map and the globe, entitled *Universalis Cosmographia*, depict the "known" world as well as the "new" worlds recently discovered by European explorers. The latter include an elongated territory labeled *America*, set between the continents of Africa and Asia. It was named in honor of Amerigo Vespucci, who first recognized that the lands Columbus reached were part of a separate continent. The map, covering some 36 square feet, offered a view of the world never before attempted.

In 1516 Waldseemüller produced an updated map of the world, the *Carta Marina*. Apparently in response to challenges regarding Vespucci's role in discovering new territories, he substituted the term *Terra Incognita* ("unknown land") for the region he had earlier labeled America. But the 1507 map had already circulated widely, and *America* became part of the European lexicon. ■

A comparison of the personal histories of Malintzin and Martin Waldseemüller highlights the profound consequences of contact between the peoples of Europe and those of the Americas. The Mexica, or Aztec, and the Spanish were most affected during this period, but France and England would soon also seek footholds in the Americas. For millennia, travel and communication between the two sides of the Atlantic had been extremely limited. Then, in the sixteenth century — and despite significant obstacles — animals, plants, goods, ideas, and people began circulating between Europe and what became known as America. Malintzin and Waldseemüller, in their very different ways, helped map the frontiers of this global society and contributed to the dramatic transformations that followed.

Native Peoples in the **Americas**

The first people in the Americas almost certainly arrived as migrants from northeast Asia, but the timing of such migrations remains in doubt. They likely began at least 25,000 years ago. It is also difficult to estimate the population of the Americas before contact with Europeans. Estimates range from 37 million to 100 million. It is clear, however, that the vast majority of people lived within a few hundred miles of the equator, and the smallest number — perhaps 4 to 7 million — lived in present-day North America. By the fifteenth century, like other regions of the world, the Americas were home to diverse societies, ranging from coastal fishing villages to nomadic hunter-gatherers to settled horticulturalists to city-centered empires.

Native Peoples Develop Diverse Cultures.

The settlement of the Americas was encouraged by the growth of glaciers on the North American continent between about 38,000 and 14,000 B.C.E. This development led to a dramatic drop in sea levels and created a land bridge in the Bering Strait, between present-day Siberia and Alaska, called **Beringia**. The first migrations may have occurred about 20,000 to 25,000 years ago, during a warming trend when melting glaciers retreated from large areas of land. During the warming trend, some settlers probably traveled from the northeastern region of the Asian Steppe (southern Siberia) to Beringia, following herds of mammoths, musk oxen, and woolly rhinoceroses. Then, 15,000 to 20,000 years ago, descendants of some of these settlers followed coastal pathways and the Pacific shore line, taking advantage of the rich maritime resources. These coastal journeys may help explain how Asiatic migrants peopled vast areas of South America in just a few thousand years. As immense expanses of ice returned to many regions some 13,000 years ago, the routes that migrants could follow shifted and forced many groups to push inland or further south.

Whether over land or sea, those moving inland had to skirt melting glaciers to find better hunting grounds and more abundant plant life. When the mammoths and other large game disappeared from large areas about 10,000 years ago, people became more dependent on smaller game, fish, roots, berries, and other plant foods to survive. At the same time, new groups of migrants headed east from Beringia. These included Inuit and Aleut peoples who arrived in present-day Alaska thousands of years after more southern areas had been settled (Map 1.1).

Between 8000 and 2000 B.C.E., some communities in the Americas began establishing agricultural systems that encouraged more stable settlements and population growth. **Horticulture** — a form of agriculture in which people work small plots of land with simple tools — became highly developed in the area of present-day Mexico. There men and women developed improved strains of maize (or Indian corn). They also cultivated protein-rich beans, squash, tomatoes, potatoes, and manioc (a root vegetable, also known as cassava or yucca root). The combination of beans, squash, and corn offered an especially nutritious diet while maintaining the fertility of the soil. Moreover, high yields produced surplus food that could be stored or traded to neighboring communities.

By 500 C.E., complex societies, rooted in intensive agriculture, began to thrive in the equatorial region. Between 500 and 1500 C.E., the spread of maize cultivation northward into the present-day American Southwest and beyond fostered economic developments that necessitated irrigation and led to the diversification of native societies. Small bands of hunters and gatherers continued to thrive in deserts and forests while impressive civilizations arose on swamplands and grasslands, and in the mountains.

The Aztecs, the Maya, and the Incas.

Three significant civilizations emerged by the early sixteenth century: Aztec and Mayan societies in the equatorial region and Inca society along the Pacific coast in present-day Peru. Technologically advanced and with knowledge of mathematics and astronomy, these societies were characterized by vast mineral wealth, large urban centers, highly ritualized religions, and complex political systems. Unlike their counterparts in Europe, Asia, and Africa, they did not develop the wheel to aid in transportation, nor did they have steel tools and weapons. Since most of their commerce was carried out over land or along rivers and coastlines, they did not build large boats. They also lacked horses, which had disappeared from the region thousands of years earlier. Still, the Aztecs, Maya, and Incas established grand cities and civilizations.

Around 1325 C.E., the **Aztecs**, who called themselves Mexica, built their capital, Tenochtitlán, on the site of present-day Mexico City. Seminomadic warriors who invaded and then settled the region, the Aztecs drew on local residents' knowledge of irrigation and cultivation and adopted their written language. Aztec commoners, who tilled communally owned lands, were ruled over by priests and nobles. The nobles formed a warrior class and owned vast estates on which they employed both serfs and slaves captured from non-Aztec communities in the region. Priests promised fertility — for the land and its people — but demanded human sacrifices, including thousands of men and women from captured tribes. To sustain their society, Aztecs extended their trade networks, offering pottery, cloth, and leather goods in exchange for textiles and obsidian to make sharp-edged tools and weapons. As Malintzin's story illustrates, enslaved women were an important component of this trade.

MAP 1.1   The Settling of the Americas

Beginning about 25,000 B.C.E., Asian peoples likely migrated to America across a land bridge after expanding glaciers lowered sea levels. Others probably followed the coastline in boats. As glaciers retreated over several centuries, they opened corridors along which people migrated, leaving traces in archaeological sites in present-day Wisconsin, New Mexico, Florida, Central America, and Chile.

When Malintzin was sold to a Mayan village by Aztec merchants, she was being traded from one grand civilization to another. The **Maya** slowly settled the Yucatán peninsula and the rain forests of present-day Guatemala between roughly 900 B.C.E. and 300 C.E. They established large cities that were home to skilled artisans and developed elaborate systems for irrigation and water storage. Farmers worked the fields and labored to build huge stone temples and palaces for rulers who claimed to be descended from the gods. Learned men developed mathematical calculations, astronomical systems, hieroglyphic writing, and a calendar.

Yet the Mayan civilization began to decline around 800 C.E. An economic crisis, likely the result of drought and exacerbated by heavy taxation, probably drove peasant families into the interior. While many towns and religious sites were abandoned, some communities survived the crisis and reemerged as thriving city-states. By the early sixteenth century, they were trading with the Aztecs.

The **Incas** developed an equally impressive civilization in the Andes Mountains along the Pacific coast. The Inca empire, like the Aztec empire, was built on the accomplishments of earlier societies. At the height of their power, in the fifteenth century, the Incas controlled some 16 million people spread over 350,000 square miles. They constructed an expansive system of roads and garrisons to ensure the flow of food, trade goods, and soldiers from their capital at Cuzco through the surrounding mountains and valleys.

The key to Inca success was the cultivation of fertile mountain valleys. Cuzco, some eleven thousand feet above sea level, lay in the center of the Inca empire, with the Huaylas and Titicaca valleys on either side. Here residents cultivated potatoes and other crops on terraces watered by an elaborate irrigation system. Miners dug gold and silver from the mountains, and artisans crafted the metals into jewelry and decorative items. Thousands of laborers constructed elaborate palaces and temples. And like the Aztec priests, Inca priests sacrificed humans to the gods to stave off natural disasters and military defeat.

Native Cultures to the North.

To the north of these grand civilizations, smaller societies with less elaborate cultures thrived. In present-day Arizona and New Mexico, the Mogollon and Hohokam established communities around 500 C.E. The Mogollon were expert potters, while the Hohokam, migrating north from Mexico, developed extensive irrigation systems. Farther north, in present-day Utah and Colorado, the ancient Pueblo people built adobe and masonry homes

Female Figurine, Peru, c. 1430–1532 This figurine made of gold depicts a Mamacona, who was similar to a nun in Incan society. Daughters of the nobility or young women of exceptional beauty lived in temple sanctuaries and dedicated themselves to the sun god, Inti. They served the Inca people and priests. The multicolored woolen robe and gold pin indicate this woman's special status. Werner Forman/Universal Images Group/Getty Images cut into cliffs around 750 C.E. After migrating south and constructing large buildings that included administrative offices, religious centers, and craft shops, the Pueblo returned to their cliff dwellings in the 1100s for protection from invaders. There, drought eventually caused them to disperse into smaller groups.

Farther north on the plains that stretched from present-day Colorado into Canada, hunting societies developed around herds of bison. A weighted spear-throwing device, called an *atlatl*, allowed hunters to capture smaller game, while nets, hooks, and snares allowed them to catch birds, fish, and small animals. Societies in the Great Plains as well as the Great Basin (between the Rockies and the Sierra Nevada) generally remained small and widely scattered. Given the arid conditions in these regions, communities needed a large expanse of territory as they followed migrating animals or seasonal plant sources. Here the adoption of the bow and arrow, in about 500 C.E., proved the most significant technological development.

Other native societies, like the Mandan, settled along rivers in the heart of the continent (present-day North and South Dakota). The rich soil along the banks fostered farming, while forests and plains attracted diverse animals for hunting. Around 1250 C.E., however, an extended drought forced these settlements to contract, and competition for resources increased among Mandan villages and with other native groups in the region.

Hunting-gathering societies also emerged along the Pacific coast, where the abundance of fish, small game, and plant life provided the resources to develop permanent settlements. The Chumash Indians, near present-day Santa Barbara, California, harvested resources from the land and the ocean. Women gathered acorns and pine nuts, while men fished and hunted. The Chumash, whose villages sometimes held a thousand inhabitants, participated in regional exchange networks up and down the coast.

Even larger societies with more elaborate social, religious, and political systems developed near the Mississippi River. A group that came to be called the **Hopewell people** established a thriving culture there in the early centuries C.E. The river and its surrounding lands provided fertile fields and easy access to distant communities. Centered in present-day southern Ohio and western Illinois, the Hopewell constructed towns of four to six thousand people. Artifacts from their burial sites reflect extensive trading networks that stretched from the Missouri River to Lake Superior, and from the Rocky Mountains to the Appalachian region and Florida.

Beginning around 500 C.E., the Hopewell culture gave birth to larger and more complex societies that flourished in

Cliff Palace at Mesa Verde   This cliff dwelling of some 150 rooms is the largest remaining in North America. It was built by the Anasazi (later known as Pueblo) people around 1200 C.E. and inhabited for about a century. Located in Mesa Verde National Park in southwestern Colorado, it was part of the Anasazi ancestral homeland shown in Map 1.2. David Watkins/Shutterstock the Mississippi River valley and to the south and east. As bows and arrows spread into the region, people hunted more game in the thick forests. But Mississippian groups also learned to cultivate corn. By providing a staple crop, corn allowed the population to expand dramatically. More complex political and religious systems developed in which elite rulers gained greater control over the labor of farmers and hunters. Mississippian peoples created massive earthworks sculpted in the shape of serpents, birds, and other creatures. Some earthen sculptures stood higher than 70 feet and stretched longer than 1,300 feet. Mississippians also constructed huge temple mounds that could cover nearly 16 acres.

By about 1100 C.E., the Cahokia people established the largest Mississippian settlement, near present-day St. Louis, which may have housed ten to thirty thousand inhabitants (Map 1.2). Powerful chieftains extended trade networks from the Great Lakes to the

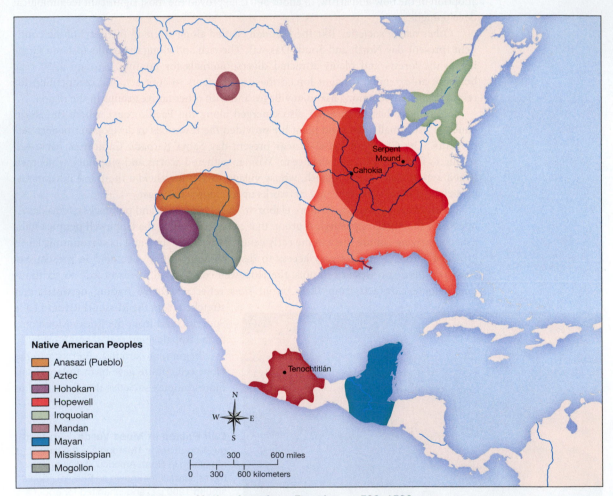

Native American Peoples

- Anasazi (Pueblo)
- Aztec
- Hohokam
- Hopewell
- Iroquoian
- Mandan
- Mayan
- Mississippian
- Mogollon

Serpent Mound

Cahokia

Tenochtitlán

MAP 1.2   Native American Peoples, c. 500–1500 C.E.

Many distinct cultures developed in the Americas in the ten centuries before 1500. Some societies, like the Mississippians, developed extensive trade networks over land or along rivers and coastlines. Societies in the same region often learned from those who preceded them, such as the Aztec from the Maya, but other groups battled over scarce resources.

Gulf of Mexico, conquered smaller villages, and created a centralized government. Shells from the Atlantic coast, copper from the Great Lakes, buffalo hides from the Great Plains, and other items found at Cahokian sites provide evidence of a trade network that extended across large parts of North America. By the 1200s, however, deforestation, drought, and perhaps disease, affected the Cahokian people, as did overhunting. Many settlements dispersed. After 1400, political turmoil and increased warfare among native peoples joined with environmental changes to ensure the decline of Mississippian culture.

Review & Relate

▪ Compare and contrast the Aztecs, Incas, and Maya. What similarities and differences do you note?

▪ How did the societies of North America differ from those of the equatorial zone and the Andes?

Europe Expands Its Reach

The complex societies that emerged in the Americas were made possible by an agricultural revolution that included the establishment of crop systems, the domestication of animals, and the development of tools. This agricultural revolution, spurred by the end of the Wisconsin glaciation, transformed eastern North America in the 1100s and 1200s C.E. Even more dramatic developments had occurred centuries earlier — between 4000 and 3000 B.C.E — in the Fertile Crescent of the Middle East and in China. Increased productivity there ensured population growth and allowed attention to science, trade, politics, religion, and the arts. Over millennia, knowledge from these civilizations made its way into Europe. At the height of the Roman Empire in the early centuries C.E., dense global trade networks connected the peoples of Europe, Africa, and Asia. With the decline of Roman power in western Europe, those connections broke down, but commercial ties continued to thrive among diverse peoples surrounding the Mediterranean Sea. Portuguese explorers, denied access to that rich Mediterranean world by the politics of the period, instead sought trade routes along the coast of Africa. Increased trade with African kingdoms by Portugal and other European societies included the purchase of slaves. This lucrative and devastating commerce would expand dramatically as European nations colonized the Americas.

The Mediterranean World. Beginning in the seventh century Islam proved one of the most dynamic cultural, political, and military forces in the world. By the ninth century, Islamic (also known as Muslim) regimes created an Arab empire that controlled most of southwest Asia and North Africa and conquered parts of the Iberian peninsula in Europe. In the eleventh and twelfth centuries, Catholic leaders launched several military and religious campaigns to reclaim Jerusalem and other sites associated with Jesus for the Church. Later known as the **Crusades**, these campaigns largely failed, but they enhanced the roles of Italian merchants, who profited from both outfitting Crusaders and opening new trade routes to the East. Moreover, these campaigns inspired explorers and adventurers throughout Europe.

In the Middle East, inhabitants had managed to survive droughts and other ecological crises and sustain productive economic systems. In the Mediterranean world, this productivity depended on technological advances in irrigation and navigation and a vast network of slave-trading centers and enslaved laborers. It was the productivity of agriculture — developed centuries earlier than in Europe or America—that allowed societies along the southern Mediterranean, in northern Africa, and in southwest Asia to excel in astronomy, mathematics, architecture, and the arts.

Medieval European states proved far less adept at staving off human and environmental disasters. Besieged by drought and disease as well as wars and peasant rebellions, rulers across the continent expended most of their resources on trying to sustain their population and protect their borders. In the 1340s, as Europeans began to trade with various regions of Asia, flea-infested rats carried the bubonic plague and other epidemic diseases on board ships and into European seaports. From the 1340s to the early fifteenth century, the bubonic plague—later called the **Black Death**—periodically ravaged European cities and towns. The initial **pandemic**—a deadly disease that covers a wide geographic area—spread across Europe between 1346 and 1350, killing about 36 million people, half of Europe's population. A century-long war between France and England added to the death and destruction.

By the early fifteenth century, the plague had retreated from much of Europe, and the climate had improved. Only then were European peoples able to benefit significantly from the riches of the East. Smaller populations led to an improved standard of living. Then rising birthrates and increased productivity, beginning in Italian city-states, fueled a resurgence of trade with other parts of the world. The profits from agriculture and commerce allowed the wealthy and powerful to begin investing in the arts and luxury goods. Indeed, a cultural **Renaissance** (from the French word for "rebirth") flourished in the Italian city-states and then spread to France, Spain, the Low Countries, and central Europe.

This cultural rebirth went hand in hand with political unification as more powerful rulers extended their control over smaller city-states and principalities. A vibrant and religiously tolerant culture had existed in Muslim Spain from the eighth to the tenth century, but that was followed by a long period of persecution of Christians. When Christians began reconquering Spain after 1200, Muslims and Jews alike became targets. Then in 1469, the marriage of Isabella of Castile and Ferdinand II of Aragon sealed the unification of Christian Spain. By 1492 their combined forces expelled the last Muslim conquerors from the Iberian peninsula. Promoting Catholicism to create a more unified national identity, Isabella and Ferdinand launched an Inquisition against supposed heretics and executed or expelled some 200,000 Jews as well. Despite the brutality of the reconquest and the Inquisition, Catholic Spain had the wealth and military power to forge its own trade networks with North Africa, India, and other Asian lands.

Explore ▶

For two cartographers' vision of the world during this period, see Source 1.1.

Yet Italy controlled the most important routes through the Mediterranean, so leaders in Spain and neighboring Portugal sought alternate paths to riches. Their efforts were aided by explorers, missionaries, and merchants who traveled to Morocco, Turkey, India, and other distant lands. They brought back trade goods and knowledge of astronomy, shipbuilding, mapmaking, and navigation that allowed Iberians to venture farther south along the Atlantic coast of Africa and, eventually, west into the uncharted Atlantic Ocean.

Portugal Pursues Long-Distance Trade. Cut off from the Mediterranean by Italian city-states and Muslim rulers in North Africa, Portugal looked toward the Atlantic. Although a tiny nation, Portugal benefited from the leadership of its young prince, Henry,

Guided Primary Source Analysis

Martin Waldseemüller and Mathias Ringmann | *Universalis Cosmographia*, 1507

In 1507 German cartographers Waldseemüller and Ringmann produced a map of the "known" world, which included those areas in the Western Hemisphere recently discovered by European explorers. They were the first to use the term *America*, and their *Universalis Cosmographia* was also the first map to show the Americas as separate from Asia. The map was printed from wood engravings and produced in twelve sections covering 36 square feet.

Source 1.1

Library of Congress, Geography and Map Division

What does the shape of the Americas suggest about European understandings of these two continents?

Why do the cartographers place Africa and Europe at the center of this map?

What does the size and shape of the Indian Ocean indicate about European knowledge of and interest in the surrounding countries?

Put It in Context

How did this new map of the world both reflect and reinforce European nations' growing interest in trade with Africa and Asia?

who launched explorations of the African coast in the 1420s, hoping to find a passage to India via the Atlantic Ocean. Prince Henry — known as Henry the Navigator — gathered information from astronomers, geographers, mapmakers, and craftsmen in the Arab world and recruited Italian cartographers and navigators along with Portuguese scholars, sailors, and captains. He then launched a systematic campaign of exploration, observation, shipbuilding, and long-distance trade that revolutionized Europe and shaped developments in Africa and the Americas.

Prince Henry and his colleagues developed ships known as caravels — vessels with narrow hulls and triangular sails that were especially effective for navigating the coast of West Africa. His staff also created state-of-the-art maritime charts, maps, and astronomical tables; perfected navigational instruments; and mastered the complex wind and sea currents along the African coast. Soon Portugal was trading in gold, ivory, and slaves from West Africa.

In 1482 Portugal built Elmina Castle, a trading post and fort on the Gold Coast (present-day Ghana). Further expeditions were launched from the castle; five years later, a fleet led by Bartolomeu Dias rounded the Cape of Good Hope, on the southernmost tip of Africa. This feat demonstrated the possibility of sailing directly from the Atlantic to the Indian Ocean. Vasco da Gama followed this route to India in 1497, returning to Portugal in 1499, his ships laden with valuable cinnamon and pepper.

By the early sixteenth century, Portuguese traders had wrested control of the India trade from Arab fleets. They established fortified trading posts at key locations on the Indian Ocean and extended their expeditions to Indonesia, China, and Japan. Within a decade, the Portuguese had become the leaders in international trade. Spain, England, France, and the Netherlands competed for a share of this newfound wealth by developing long-distance markets that brought spices, ivory, silks, cotton cloth, and other luxury goods to Europe.

With expanding populations and greater agricultural productivity, European nations developed more efficient systems of taxation, built larger military forces, and adapted gunpowder to new kinds of weapons. The surge in population provided the men to labor on merchant vessels, staff forts, and protect trade routes. More people began to settle in cities, which grew into important commercial centers. Slowly, a form of capitalism based on market exchange, private ownership, and capital accumulation and reinvestment developed across much of Europe.

European Encounters with West Africa.
Enslaved Africans were among the most lucrative commodity traded by European merchants. Slavery had been practiced in Europe, America, Africa, and other parts of the world for centuries. The enslaved were often captives of war or individuals sold in payment for deaths or injuries to conquering enemies. In some places, including Roman society, slavery was inheritable. In others, such as Anglo-Saxon England, slaves were sometimes sold along with the land they had worked. In other areas, enslaved men and women retained some legal rights and bondage was not passed on to their children. With the advent of European participation in the African slave trade and increased African demand for European goods, the system of bondage changed. The scale of the trade expanded significantly, transforming Europe and Africa and eventually the Americas.

In the fifteenth century, Europeans were most familiar with North Africa, a region deeply influenced by Islam and characterized by large kingdoms, well-developed cities, and an extensive network of trading centers. In northeast Africa, including Egypt, city-states flourished, with ties to India, the Middle East, and China. In northwest Africa, Timbuktu linked North Africa to empires south of the Great Desert as well as to Europe. Here African slaves labored for wealthier Africans in a system of bound labor long familiar to Europeans.

As trade with western Africa increased, however, Europeans came into contact with communities that lived by hunting and subsistence agriculture. This unleashed conflict among Africans even within the same kingdom. In 1526, Mvemba A Nzinga, king of the Kongo, wrote to the king of Portugal, John III, complaining "that many of our people, keenly desirous as they are of the wares and things of your Kingdoms, . . . seize many of our people," including freedmen and noblemen, "and take them to be sold to the white men." To stop this illegal commerce, Nzinga asked that Portuguese men entering the Kongo immediately inform noblemen and court officials and comply with existing rules of trade. Nzinga's request was ignored.

By the mid-sixteenth century, European nations established competing forts along the African coast from the Gold Coast and Senegambia in the north to the Bight of Biafra and West Central Africa in the south. Increasingly, the enslaved Africans shipped from these forts came from communities that had been raided or conquered by more powerful groups. They arrived at the coast exhausted, hungry, dirty, and with few clothes. They worshipped gods unfamiliar to Europeans, and their cultural customs and social practices seemed strange and primitive. Over time, the image of the West African slave came to dominate European visions of the entire continent.

As traders from Portugal, Spain, Holland, and England brought back more enslaved Africans, negative depictions took deeper hold. Woodcuts and prints circulated in Europe in which half-naked Africans appeared more like apes than humans while biblical stories reinforced notions of Africans as inherently inferior. In the Bible, Ham had sinned against his father, Noah. Noah then cursed Ham's son Canaan to a life of slavery. Increasingly, European Christians considered Africans the "sons of Ham," infidels assigned

African Salt Cellar This ivory salt cellar was carved in the fifteenth or sixteenth century in Sierra Leone, on the West African coast and was made for sale to Portuguese traders. The artisan depicted traditional geometric designs and African reptiles but clothed the four male and four female African figures in items of European dress. Werner Forman Archive/Bridgeman Images by God to a life of bondage. This self-serving idea was used to justify the enslavement of black men, women, and children.

Of course, these distorted images of West Africans did not reflect the diverse peoples and societies that made their home in the area's tropical rain forests, plains, and savannas. Still, as the slave trade expanded in the sixteenth and seventeenth centuries, it destabilized large areas of western and central Africa, with smaller societies decimated by raids and even larger kingdoms damaged by the extensive commerce in human beings.

Some Africans, particularly rulers of the most powerful African kingdoms, were active participants in the slave trade. For instance, because women were more highly valued by Muslim traders in North Africa and Asia, African traders steered women to these profitable markets. At the same time, African societies organized along matrilineal lines — where goods and political power passed through the mother's line — tried to protect women against enslavement. Other groups sought to limit the sale of men.

Ultimately, men, women, and children were captured by African as well as Portuguese, Spanish, Dutch, and English traders. Europeans did not institute a system of perpetual slavery, in which enslavement was inherited from one generation to the next. Instead, Africans formed another class of bound labor, alongside peasants, indentured servants, criminals, and apprentices. Few distinctions among bound laborers were based on race. Wealthy Englishmen, for instance, viewed both African and Irish laborers as ignorant and unruly heathens. However, as Europeans began to conquer and colonize the Americas and demands for labor increased dramatically, ideas about race and slavery would change significantly.

Review & Relate

- How and why did Europeans expand their connections with Africa and the Middle East in the fifteenth century?

- How did early European encounters with West Africans influence Europeans' ideas about African peoples and reshape existing systems of slavery?

Worlds Collide

In the 1520s and 1530s, Spain and Portugal chartered traders to ship enslaved Africans to the Caribbean, Brazil, Mexico, and Peru. The success of this trade relied heavily on the efforts of European cartographers, who used information from explorers and adventurers to map these areas. The maps illustrate the growing connections among Europe, Africa, and the Americas even as they also reflect the continued dominance of the Mediterranean region, the Middle East, India, and China in European visions of the world. Yet that world was changing rapidly as Europeans introduced guns, horses, and new diseases to the Americas and came in contact with previously unknown flora and fauna. The resulting exchange of plants, animals, and germs transformed the two continents as well as the wider world.

Europeans Cross the Atlantic.

The first Europeans to discover lands in the western Atlantic were Norsemen. In the late tenth century, Scandinavian seafarers led by Erik the Red reached Greenland. Sailing still farther west, Erik's son Leif led a party that discovered an area in North America that they called Vinland, near the Gulf of St. Lawrence. The Norse established a small settlement there around 1000 C.E., and people from Greenland continued to visit Vinland for centuries. By 1450, however, the Greenland settlements had disappeared.

Nearly a half century after Norse settlers abandoned Greenland, a Genoese navigator named Christopher Columbus visited the Spanish court of Ferdinand and Isabella and proposed an **Enterprise of the Indies**. Portuguese explorers used this name for the region that included present-day South Asia and Southeast Asia and surrounding islands. Because Italian city-states controlled the Mediterranean and Portugal dominated the routes around Africa, Spain sought a third path to the rich Eastern trade. Columbus claimed he could find it by sailing west across the Atlantic to Japan, China, or the Indies themselves.

Columbus's 1492 proposal was timely. Having just expelled the last Muslims and Jews from Granada and imposed Catholic orthodoxy on a now-unified nation, the Spanish monarchs sought to expand their empire. After winning Queen Isabella's support, the Genoese captain headed off in three small ships with ninety men. They stopped briefly at the Canary Islands and then headed due west on September 6, 1492.

Columbus had calculated the distance to Japan, which he judged the nearest island, based on Ptolemy's division of the world into 360 degrees of north-south lines of longitude. But in making his calculations, Columbus made a number of errors that led him to believe that it was possible to sail from Spain to Asia in about a month. The miscalculations nearly led to mutiny, but disaster was averted when a lookout finally spotted a small island on October 12. Columbus named the island San Salvador and made contact with local residents, whom he named Indians in the belief that he had found East Indies islands near Japan or China. Columbus was impressed with their warm welcome and considered the gold jewelry Indians wore as a sign of great riches in the region.

Explore ▶

Read two accounts by early explorers of their encounters with native peoples in Sources 1.2 and 1.3.

Columbus and his crew were welcomed as heroes when they returned to Spain in March 1493. Their discovery of islands seemingly unclaimed by any known power led the pope to confer Spanish sovereignty over all lands already claimed or to be claimed 100 leagues west of the Cape Verde Islands. A protest by Portugal soon led to a treaty that moved the line 270 leagues farther west, granting Portugal control of territory that became Brazil and Spain control of the rest of what became known as South America.

Europeans Explore the Americas. Columbus made three more voyages to the Caribbean to claim land for Spain and sought to convince those who accompanied him to build houses, plant crops, and cut logs for forts. But the men had come for gold, and when the Indians stopped trading willingly, the Spaniards used force to claim their riches. Columbus sought to impose a more rigid discipline but failed. On his final voyage, he introduced a system of *encomienda*, by which leading men received land and the labor of all Indians residing on it. By the time of Columbus's death in 1506, the islands he had discovered were dissolving into chaos as traders and adventurers fought with Indians and one another over the spoils of conquest. By then, no one believed that Columbus had discovered a route to China, but few people understood the revolutionary importance of the lands he had found.

Nonetheless, Columbus's voyages inspired others to head across the Atlantic (Map 1.3). In 1497 another Genoese navigator, John Cabot (or Caboto), sailing under the English flag, reached an island off Cape Breton in the North Atlantic, where he discovered good cod

Comparative Primary Source Analysis

Who Are These Native People?

European explorers portrayed native peoples in disparate ways, shaped by individual experiences and the larger context in which they wrote. When Christopher Columbus landed in the West Indies in October 1492, he kept a journal that highlighted the value of his discoveries to his Spanish sponsors, including friendly and submissive natives. Nearly thirty years later, when Ferdinand Magellan landed in the present-day Philippines, his crew had already suffered disease, starvation, and desertion. It soon became embroiled in a deadly conflict between native groups. Antonio Pigafetta, a paying passenger on that voyage, described this more brutal encounter in his journal for April 1521.

Source 1.2

Christopher Columbus | Description of His First Encounter with Indians, 1492

I [believed] . . . that we might form great friendship, for I knew that they were a people who could be more easily freed and converted to our holy faith by love than by force, gave to some of them red caps, and glass beads to put round their necks, and many other things of little value, which gave them great pleasure, and made them so much our friends that it was a marvel to see. They afterwards came to the ship's boats where we were, swimming and bringing us parrots, cotton threads in skeins, darts, and many other things; and we exchanged them for other things that we gave them, such as glass beads and small bells. In fine [In short], they took all, and gave what they had with good will. It appeared to me to be a race of people very poor in everything.

They go as naked as when their mothers bore them, and so do the women, although I did not see more than one young girl. . . . They have no iron, their darts being wands without iron, some of them having a fish's tooth at the end. . . . They should be good servants and intelligent, for I observed that they quickly took in what was said to them, and I believe that they would easily be made Christians, as it appeared to me that they had no religion. I, our Lord being pleased, will take hence, at the time of my departure, six natives for your Highnesses, that they may learn to speak.

Source: *The Journal of Christopher Columbus (during His First Voyage, 1492–93) and Documents Relating to the Voyages of John Cabot and Gaspar Corte Real* (London: Hakluyt Society, 1893), 37–38.

fishing but met no local inhabitants. He continued down the Atlantic coast, at one point being able to see Cuba to the east according to Cabot's son Sebastian. Over the next several years, John and Sebastian made more trips to North America. Although England failed to follow up on their discoveries, in 1500, a Spanish mapmaker showed British flags planted along the Atlantic coast as far south as present-day Florida.

More important at the time, Portuguese and Spanish mariners continued to explore the western edges of the Caribbean. Amerigo Vespucci, a Florentine merchant, joined one such voyage in 1499. It was Vespucci's account of his journey that led Martin Waldseemüller

Source 1.3

Antonio Pigafetta | Journal, 1521

When day came, our men leaped into the water up to our thighs, forty-nine of them. . . . The boats could not come in closer because of certain rocks in the water. . . . [When the natives saw that we were firing muskets without any result] . . . they cried out determined to stand firm . . . shooting so many arrows and hurling bamboo lances, charred pointed stakes, stones and mud at the Captain [Magellan] that he could scarce defend himself. When the Captain saw this he sent some men to burn their houses to frighten them. And when they saw their houses burning they were all the more fierce. . . . And so great a number came upon us that they pierced the right leg of the Captain with a poisoned arrow, wherefore he ordered that they gradually retreat. . . . [But] they had so many spears, darts and stones that they [the soldiers] could not withstand them, and the artillery of the fleet was so far away that it could not help them.

And our men withdrew to the shore, fighting all the while. . . . They [the natives] recognized the Captain and so many assailed him that twice they knocked his sallet [helmet] from his head. And he, like a good knight, continued to stand firm with a few others, and they fought thus for more than an hour. . . . An Indian threw his bamboo spear into his [the Captain's] face and he immediately killed him [the native] with his own spear. . . . And the Captain tried to draw his sword and was able to draw it only half way, because he had been wounded in the arm with a spear. . . . The Christian king [a rival chief who converted to Christianity] would have helped us but . . . the Captain bade him not to leave the ship. . . . When the king learned that the Captain was dead he grieved much, and not without cause.

Source: *The Voyage of Magellan, the Journal of Antonio Pigafetta*, trans. Paula Spurlin Paige (Englewood Cliffs, NJ: Prentice-Hall, 1969), 76–78.

Interpret the Evidence

1. How might Columbus's journal entry, which was circulated among clerics and officials in Spain, have shaped Spanish views about native peoples in the 1490s?
2. What does Pigafetta's description of the battle between Magellan's forces and native warriors suggest about how Spanish explorers viewed the native peoples they encountered in the Philippines? How does the response of the Christianized chief complicate our understanding of Spanish-native encounters?

Put It in Context

How might changing expectations and perceptions of native peoples between the 1490s and the 1520s have affected the actions of explorers as they encountered groups in newly discovered locations?

to identify the new continent he charted on his 1507 *Universalis Cosmographia* as "America." Meanwhile, Spanish explorers subdued tribes like the Arawak and Taino in the Caribbean and headed toward the mainland. In 1513 Vasco Nuñez de Balboa traveled across the Isthmus of Darien (now Panama) and became the first known European to see the Pacific Ocean. That same year, the Spanish explorer Juan Ponce de León explored a peninsula that he named Florida and claimed it for Spain. Although British explorers had earlier claimed the territory, it was Spain that erected the first forts there, and they maintained control for 250 years.

MAP 1.3   European Explorations in the Americas, 1492–1536
Early explorers, funded by Spain, sought trade routes to Asia or gold, silver, and other riches in the Americas. The success of these voyages encouraged adventurous Spaniards to travel throughout the West Indies, South America, and regions immediately to the north. It also inspired the first expeditions by the French and the English in North America.

Ferdinand Magellan launched an even more impressive expedition in August 1519 when he, with the support of Charles V of Spain, sought a passageway through South America to Asia. In October 1520, after fifteen months of struggle and travail, his crew discovered a strait at the southernmost tip of South America that connected the Atlantic and Pacific Oceans. Ill with scurvy and near starvation, the crew reached Guam and then the Philippines in March 1521. Magellan died there a month later, but one of his five ships and eighteen of the original crew finally made it back to Seville in September 1522, having successfully circumnavigated the globe. Despite the enormous loss of life and equipment, Magellan's lone ship was loaded with valuable spices and detailed information for cartographers, and his venture allowed Spain to claim the Philippine Islands.

Mapmaking and Printing. Waldseemüller's 1507 map reflected the expanding contacts among Europe, Africa, and the Americas. Over the following decades, cartographers charted newly discovered islands, traced coastlines and bays, and situated each new piece of data in relation to lands already known.

The dissemination of geographical knowledge was greatly facilitated by advances in information technology. The Chinese had developed a form of printing with wood blocks in the tenth century, and woodcut pictures appeared in Europe in the fifteenth century. In the 1440s, German craftsmen invented a form of movable metal type in which each letter was created in a separate mold. This allowed printers to rearrange the type for each page and create multiple copies of a single manuscript more quickly and more cheaply than ever before. Between 1452 and 1455, Johannes Gutenberg, a German goldsmith, printed some 180 copies of the Bible with movable type. Although this was not the first book printed using the new system, Gutenberg's Bible marked a revolutionary change in the production and circulation of written texts.

Innovations in printing helped publicize Portuguese and Spanish explorations, the travels of European adventurers, and the atlases created by Waldseemüller and other cartographers. Italian craftsmen contributed by manufacturing paper that was thinner and cheaper than traditional vellum and parchment. Books were still expensive, and they could be read only by the small minority of Europeans who were literate. Still, mechanical printing rapidly increased the speed with which knowledge was circulated. The enhanced ability to exchange ideas encouraged their expression and ensured the flow of information among scholars and rulers across Europe.

Codex Mendoza, c. 1540   The Codex Mendoza depicted histories of indigenous communities. This image shows a list of taxes paid by conquered peoples to the Aztec king and, after 1519, the Spanish crown. They included beads, feathers, and jaguar skins. DEA PICTURE LIBRARY/Getty Images

The peoples of the Americas had their own ways of charting land, waterways, and boundary lines and of circulating information. The Maya, for instance, developed a system of glyphs—images that represented prefixes, suffixes, numbers, people, or words. Scribes carved glyphs into large flat stones, or *stela*, providing local residents with histories of important events. In settled farming villages, this system communicated information to a large portion of the population. But it could not serve, as printed pages did, to disseminate ideas more widely. Similarly, the extant maps created by the Maya, Aztecs, and other native groups tended to focus on specific locales. Still, we know that these groups traded across long distances, so they must have had some means of tracing rivers, mountains, and villages beyond their own communities.

The Columbian Exchange. The Spaniards were aided in their conquest of the Americas by germs as well as maps, guns, and horses. Because native peoples in the Western Hemisphere had had almost no contact with the rest of the world for millennia, they lacked immunity to most germs carried by Europeans. A series of pandemics caused by measles, typhus, smallpox, and other diseases decimated communities throughout the hemisphere. Disease and warfare first eradicated the Arawak and Taino on Hispaniola, wiping out some 300,000 people. In the Inca empire, the population plummeted from about 9 million in 1530 to less than half a million by 1630. Among the Aztecs, the Maya, and their neighbors, the population collapsed from some 40 million people around 1500 to about 3 million a century and a half later. The germs spread northward as well, leading to pandemics among the Pueblo peoples of the Southwest and the Mississippian cultures of the Southeast.

These demographic disasters—far more devastating than the bubonic plague in Europe—were part of what historians call the **Columbian exchange**. This exchange also involved animals, plants, and seeds and affected Africa and Asia as well as Europe and the Americas. The transfer of flora and fauna and the spread of diseases transformed the economies and environments of all four continents. Initially, the catastrophic decline in Indian populations ensured the victory of Spain and other European powers over American populations. Africans' partial immunity to malaria and yellow fever then made them attractive to Europeans seeking laborers for Caribbean islands after the native population was decimated. At the same time, African coconuts and bananas were traded to Europe, while European traders provided their African counterparts with iron and pigs. Asia also participated in the exchange, introducing both Europe and Africa to sugar, rice, tea, and highly coveted spices.

America, in turn, provided Europeans with high-yielding, nutrient-rich foods like maize and potatoes, as well as new indulgences like tobacco and cacao. The East Indies had the perfect climate for producing sugar, an enormously profitable trade item. After discovering that sugar could be produced on Caribbean islands, the region became known as the West Indies. When mixed with cacao, sugar created an addictive drink known as chocolate.

In exchange for products that America offered to Europe and Africa, these continents sent rice, wheat, rye, lemons, and oranges as well as horses, cattle, pigs, chickens, and honeybees to the Western Hemisphere (Map 1.4). The grain crops transformed the American landscape, particularly in North America, where wheat became a major food source. Cattle

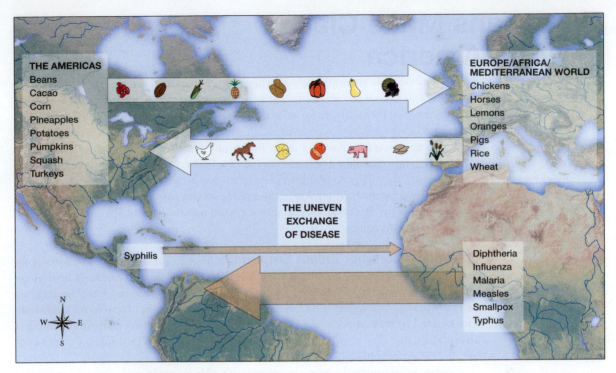

THE AMERICAS
Beans
Cacao
Corn
Pineapples
Potatoes
Pumpkins
Squash
Turkeys

**EUROPE/AFRICA/
MEDITERRANEAN WORLD**
Chickens
Horses
Lemons
Oranges
Pigs
Rice
Wheat

**THE UNEVEN
EXCHANGE
OF DISEASE**

Syphilis

Diphtheria
Influenza
Malaria
Measles
Smallpox
Typhus

MAP 1.4   The Columbian Exchange, Sixteenth Century

When Europeans made contact with Africa and the Americas, they initiated an exchange of plants, animals, and germs that transformed all three continents. The contact among these previously isolated ecosystems caused dramatic transformations in food, labor, and mortality. American crops changed eating habits across Europe, while diseases devastated native populations even as foreign grains and domesticated animals thrived in the Americas.

and pigs, meanwhile, changed native diets, while horses inspired new methods of farming, transportation, and warfare throughout the Americas.

The Columbian exchange benefited Europe far more than the Americas. Initially, it also benefited Africa, providing new crops with high yields and rich nutrients. Ultimately, however, the spread of sugar and rice to the West Indies and European cravings for tobacco and cacao increased the demand for labor, which could not be met by the declining population of Indians. This situation ensured the expansion of the African slave trade to the Americas. The consequences of the Columbian exchange were thus monumental for the peoples of all three continents.

Review & Relate

■ What were the short-term consequences in both Europe and the Americas of Columbus's voyages?

■ How did the Columbian exchange transform both the Americas and Europe?

Europeans Make Claims to **North America**

With the help of native translators, warriors, and laborers, Spanish soldiers called **conquistadors** conquered some of the richest and most populous lands in South America in the early sixteenth century. The conquered Inca and Aztec empires produced vast quantities of gold and silver, making Spain the treasure-house of Europe and ensuring its dominance on the continent for several decades. Some Spaniards headed north, hoping to find gold in the southern regions of North America or develop new routes to Asia. Following Spain's successes, rulers of other European nations began to fund expeditions to North America. France and England both launched efforts to claim colonies in the Americas. However, they failed to find the riches Spain had acquired. By the late sixteenth century, Spanish supremacy in the Americas and the wealth acquired there transformed the European economy. But conquest also raised critical questions about Spanish responsibilities to God and humanity.

Spaniards Conquer Indian Empires. Although rulers in Spain supposedly set the agenda for American ventures, it was difficult to control the campaigns of their emissaries at such a distance. The Spanish crown held the power to grant successful leaders vast amounts of land and Indian labor via the encomienda system. But the leaders themselves then divided up their prizes to reward those who served under them, giving them in effect an authority that they sometimes lacked in law. This dynamic helped make Cortés's conquest of the Aztecs possible.

Diego de Velásquez, the Spanish governor of Cuba, granted Cortés the right to explore and trade along the coast of South America. He gave him no authority, however, to attack native peoples in the region or claim land for himself. But seeing the possibility for gaining great riches, Cortés forged alliances with local rulers willing to join the attack against the Aztec chief, Montezuma. From the perspective of local Indian communities, Cortés's presence offered an opportunity to strike back against the brutal Aztec regime.

Despite their assumption of cultural superiority, many Spaniards who accompanied Cortés were astonished by Aztec cities, canals, and temples, which rivaled those in Europe. Seeing these architectural wonders may have given some soldiers pause about trying to conquer the Indian kingdom. But when Montezuma presented Cortés with large quantities of precious objects, including gold-encrusted jewelry, as a peace offering, he alerted Spaniards to the vast wealth awaiting them in the Aztec capital.

An Inca with Smallpox   Baltasar Jaime Martínez Compañón served as the bishop of Trujillo, Peru in the 1780s. He created a nine-volume codex for King Charles IV of Spain, which included 1,411 watercolor paintings tracing the history of native communities. This picture from Volume II shows an indigenous woman with smallpox isolated in a small hut.   Album/Art Resource, NY

When Cortés and his men marched to Tenochtitlán in 1519, Montezuma was indecisive in his response. After an early effort to ambush the Spaniards failed, the Aztec leader allowed Cortés to march his men into the capital city, where they took Montezuma hostage. In response, Aztec warriors attacked the Spaniards, but Cortés and his men managed to fight their way out of Tenochtitlán. They suffered heavy losses and might have been crushed by their Aztec foes but for the alliances forged with native groups in the surrounding area. Given time to regroup, the remaining Spanish soldiers and their allies attacked the Aztecs with superior steel weapons, horses, and trained dogs and gained a final victory.

The Spanish victory was also aided by the germs that soldiers carried with them. Smallpox swept through Tenochtitlán in 1521, killing thousands and leaving Montezuma's army severely weakened. This human catastrophe as much as military resources and strategies allowed Cortés to conquer the capital that year. He then claimed the entire region as New Spain, assigned soldiers to construct the new capital of Mexico City, and asserted Spanish authority over the native groups that had allied with him.

As news of Cortés's victory spread, other Spanish conquistadors sought gold and glory in the Americas. Most important, in 1524 Francisco Pizarro conquered the vast Inca empire in present-day Peru. Once again, the Spaniards were aided by the spread of European diseases and smaller tribes' hatred of Inca rule. This victory ensured Spanish access to vast supplies of silver in Potosí (in present-day Bolivia) and the surrounding mountains. It also ensured the spread of enslaved African labor from plantation agriculture to mining. Spain was now in control of the most densely populated regions of South America, which also contained the greatest mineral wealth. Still, the diversity of populations in these regions — wealthy Spanish *encomenderos*, much poorer Spanish soldiers, Indians, and Africans — concerned authorities. In response, the Spanish developed a caste system that defined the status of these diverse populations and ensured that Spaniards remained at the top of the hierarchy even as wealthy landowners distinguished themselves from their poorer countrymen. In one decade, life for Aztecs and other Indians as well as the Spanish changed dramatically. **See Primary Source Project 1: Indian and Spanish Encounters in the Americas, 1519–1530, page 32.**

Spanish Adventurers Head North.
In 1526, a company of Spanish women and men traveled from the West Indies as far north as the Santee River in present-day South Carolina. They planned to settle in the region and then search for gold and other valuables. The effort failed, but two years later Pánfilo de Narváez — one of the survivors — led four hundred soldiers from Cuba to Florida's Tampa Bay. Seeking precious metals, the party instead confronted hunger, disease, and hostile Indians. The ragtag group continued to journey along the Gulf coast, until only four men, led by Álvar Núñez Cabeza de Vaca, made their way from Galveston Bay back to Mexico City. In both cases, native peoples effectively defended their political sovereignty, economic prosperity, and religious beliefs.

A decade later, in 1539, a survivor of Narváez's ill-fated venture — a North African named Esteban — led a party of Spaniards from Mexico back north. Lured by tales of Seven Golden Cities, the party instead encountered Zuñi Indians, who attacked the Spaniards and killed Esteban. Still, the men who returned to Mexico passed on stories of large and wealthy cities. Hoping to find fame and fortune, Francisco Vásquez de Coronado launched a grand expedition northward in 1540. Angered when they failed to discover fabulous wealth, Coronado and his men terrorized the region, burning towns, killing residents, and stealing goods before returning to Mexico.

Hernando de Soto headed another effort to find wealth in North America. An experienced conquistador, de Soto received royal authority in 1539 to explore Florida. That spring he established a village near Tampa Bay with more than six hundred Spanish, Indian, and African men, and a few women. A few months later, de Soto and the bulk of his company traveled up the west Florida coast with Juan Ortiz, a member of the Narváez expedition and an especially useful guide and interpreter. That winter, the expedition traveled into present-day Georgia and the Carolinas in an unsuccessful search for riches (Map 1.5).

On their return trip, de Soto's men engaged in a brutal battle with local Indians led by Chief Tuskaloosa. Although the Spaniards claimed victory, they lost a significant number of men and horses and most of their equipment. Fearing that word of the disaster would reach

MAP 1.5   Spanish Explorations in North America, 1528–1542

Spanish explorers in North America hoped to find gold and other treasures. Instead, they encountered difficult terrain and native peoples hostile to Spanish intruders. Many Spaniards died on these expeditions, and they failed to discover new sources of wealth. But they laid the foundations for Spanish settlements in Florida, northern Mexico, and California while devastating local Indian populations.

Spain, de Soto steered his men away from supply ships in the Gulf of Mexico and headed back north. The group traveled into present-day Tennessee, then turned west, and in May 1541 became the first Europeans to report seeing the vast Mississippi River. Crossing it, they journeyed on into Arkansas, Oklahoma, and Texas. By the winter of 1542, the expedition had lost more men and supplies to Indians, and de Soto had died. The remaining members finally returned to Spanish territory the next summer.

The lengthy journey of de Soto and his men brought European diseases into new areas, leading to epidemics and the depopulation of once-substantial native communities. At the same time, the Spaniards left horses and pigs behind, creating new sources of transportation and food for native peoples. Although most Spaniards considered de Soto's journey a failure, the Spanish crown claimed vast new territories. Two decades later, in 1565, Pedro Menéndez de Avilés established a mission settlement on the northeast coast of Florida, named St. Augustine. It became the first permanent European settlement in North America. Still, unlike the conquest of central and South America, the colonization of North America forced Spaniards to accept some of the native people's political and economic systems, religious beliefs, and even gender roles. When they refused to do so, open rebellions often resulted.

Europeans Compete in North America.

Spain's early ventures in North America helped inspire French and English explorers to establish their own footholds on the continent. The French entered the race for empire in 1524, when an Italian navigator named Giovanni da Verrazano led a French company along the coast of North America. Landing initially near Cape Fear on the Carolina coast, the expedition headed north, sailing into what would become New York harbor. Verrazano then continued north, claiming lands all along the coast for France.

A decade later, in 1534, the Frenchman Jacques Cartier sailed to the Gulf of St. Lawrence. In two subsequent expeditions, Cartier pushed deeper into the territory known as Canada. Although he failed to discover precious metals or the elusive passage to the Pacific Ocean, he did trade for furs with local Indians. Cartier also inspired a French nobleman, the Sieur de Roberval, and several hundred followers to attempt a permanent settlement at Quebec in 1542. But the project was abandoned within a year because of harsh weather, disease, and high mortality.

English interest in North America was ignited by Spanish and French challenges to claims John Cabot had made along the Atlantic coast in the 1490s. To secure these rights, the English needed to colonize the disputed lands. Since the English crown did not have funds to support settlement, the earliest ventures were financed by minor noblemen who hoped to gain both wealth and the crown's favor. The earliest of these, in Newfoundland and Maine, failed.

The most promising effort to secure an English foothold was organized by Sir Walter Raleigh. Claiming all the land north of Florida for England, Raleigh called the vast territory Virginia (after Elizabeth I, "the Virgin Queen"). In 1585 Raleigh sent a group of soldiers to found a colony on Roanoke Island, off the coast of present-day North Carolina. The colony would establish England's claims and allow English sailors stationed there to seize Spanish ships laden with valuables. This venture lasted less than a year. In 1587 Raleigh tried again, sending a group of 117 men, women, and children to Roanoke. However, when supply ships came to fortify the settlement in 1590, the settlers had all disappeared, their fate unknown.

By 1590, then, nearly a century after Columbus's initial voyage, only Spain had established permanent colonies in the Americas, mostly in the West Indies, Mexico, and South America. The French and the English, despite numerous efforts, had not sustained a single ongoing settlement by the end of the sixteenth century. Yet neither nation gave up hope of benefiting from the wealth of the Americas.

Spain Seeks Dominion in Europe and the Americas.

The continued desire of European nations to gain colonies in the Americas resulted from the enormous wealth garnered by Spanish conquests. That wealth transformed economies throughout Europe. Between 1500 and 1650, Spanish ships carried home more than 180 tons of gold and 16,000 tons of silver from Mexico and Potosí. About one-fifth of this amount was taken by the Spanish crown for taxes; the rest was dispersed among supporters of the expeditions; family and friends of those who conquered lands, gained *encomiendas*, or participated in trade; and soldiers and sailors who returned from America. The money was spent mainly on luxury goods imported from the Americas, Asia, or other European nations. Very little of this wealth was invested in improving conditions at home. Indeed, the rapid infusion of gold and silver fueled inflation, making it harder for ordinary people to afford the necessities of life.

In one area, however, employment for the poor expanded rapidly. Spain's King Philip II (r. 1556–1598) used American gold and silver to fund a variety of military campaigns, ensuring an endless demand for soldiers and sailors. The king, a devout Catholic, claimed to be doing God's work as Spain conquered Italy and Portugal, including the latter's colonies in Africa, and tightened its grip on the Netherlands, which had been acquired by Spain through marriage in the early sixteenth century.

Despite the obvious material benefits, the Spaniards were not blind to the enormous human costs of colonization, and the conquest of the Americas inspired heated debates within Spain. Catholic leaders believed that the conversion of native peoples to Christianity was critical to Spanish success in the Americas. However, most royal officials and colonial agents viewed the extraction of precious metals as far more important. They argued that cheap labor was essential to creating wealth. Yet brutal conditions led to the death of huge numbers of Indians, which made it nearly impossible to convert others to Catholicism.

By 1550, tales of the widespread torture and enslavement of Indians convinced the Spanish king Carlos V (r. 1519–1556) to gather a group of theologians, jurists, and philosophers at Valladolid to discuss the moral and legal implications of conquest. Bartolomé de Las Casas took a leading role in defending the rights of Indians. A former conquistador and Dominican friar, Las Casas had spent many years preaching to Indians in America. "And so what man of sound mind," he asked, "will approve a war against men who are harmless, ignorant, gentle, temperate, unarmed, and destitute of every human defense?" Las Casas argued that even if Spain defeated the Indians, the souls of those killed would be lost to God, while among the survivors "hatred and loathing of the Christian religion" would prevail. He even suggested replacing Indian labor with African labor, apparently less concerned with the souls of black people.

Juan Ginés de Sepúlveda, the royal historian, attacked Las Casas's arguments. Although he had never set foot in America, he read reports of cannibalism and other violations of "natural law" among native peoples. Since the Indians were savages, the

Spanish Torturing Indians　In the late 1500s, Theodor de Bry and his sons created a series of detailed and graphic engravings of interactions between Spanish soldiers and American Indians based on reports from explorers and missionaries. Some portrayed Spaniards torturing Indians. These popular illustrations led critics to protest the Spanish conquest of the Americas, which they labeled the "Black Legend." Beinecke Rare Book and Manuscript Library, Yale University

Explore ▶

Read two historians' interpretations of Indian responses to Spanish rule in Secondary Sources 1.4 and 1.5.

civilized Spaniards were obligated to "destroy barbarism and educate these people to a more humane and virtuous life." If they refused such help, Spanish rule "can be imposed upon them by force of arms." Although Ginés de Sepúlveda spoke for the majority at Valladolid, Las Casas and his supporters continued to press their case as Spain expanded its reach into North America.

At the same time, American riches increasingly flowed beyond Spain's borders. The Netherlands was a key beneficiary of this wealth, becoming a center for Spanish shipbuilding and trade. Still, the Dutch were never completely under Spanish control, and they traded gold, silver, and other items to France, England, and other European nations. Goods also followed older routes across the Mediterranean to the Ottoman empire, where traders could make huge profits on exotic items from the Americas. Thus, while some Europeans suffered under Spanish power, others benefited from the riches brought to the continent.

Indians in the New Spanish Empire

While Theodor De Bry depicted and Bartolomé de Las Casas denounced the cruelty Spanish conquistadores visited on Indians in the Americas, most Indians who survived the conquest were forced to accommodate to their new rulers. Many had already been conquered and even enslaved by more powerful Indian societies like the Aztec or Maya. Finding a way to survive did not mean that Indians wholly accepted Spanish authority, but it did require wielding more subtle forms of resistance or finding ways to benefit from the new imperial system. Camilla Townsend and Jane Mangan wrote their books about the Spanish conquest at nearly the same time. However, Townsend focuses on an individual woman translator during the Spanish conquest of Mexico while Mangan highlights the economic strategies of women and men who survived Spain's conquest of the Inca Empire.

Source 1.4

Camilla Townsend | An Indian Woman Aids in the Conquest of Mexico, 2006

It was not simply that the Spanish needed their translators in order to find their way and obtain requisite food and water. They needed them for far more than this — for the conquest itself. . . .

[Malintzin] knew that her survival was dependent on the Spaniards' survival, so she was motivated to observe them carefully; undoubtedly her years as a slave had honed her skills in that regard. . . . [B]y all accounts she learned Spanish and Spanish ways quickly. . . . By 1524 . . . Malintzin did all his [Cortés'] translation between Spanish, Nahuatl, and Maya.

For Malintzin could do more than repeat what others said in a foreign vocabulary. . . . [S]he could speak in different registers and thus make a necessary point more effectively. . . . [The] Spaniards who depended on her competence seemed to like and admire her. Bernal Diaz [a Spanish conquistador who wrote a history of the conquest] . . . conveys that she spoke to them archly or coquettishly if need be — in other words, that she knew how to handle her Spanish male audience. Such an approach, however, would never have worked with her Nahua audiences, who were also largely male. With them, . . . she spoke like . . . "a lady of power," not . . . like a playful girl. A playful girl should respect her elders, not tell them what to do. She knew this and adjusted her tone accordingly.

She was to need all her skills, linguistic and otherwise, as they [the Spanish army] marched from the sea to Tenochtitlan.

Source: Camilla Townsend, *Malintzin's Choices: An Indian Woman in the Conquest of Mexico* (Albuquerque: University of New Mexico Press, 2006), 58–59.

By the late sixteenth century, the desire for a greater share of those riches revitalized imperial dreams among the French and English as well as the Dutch.

Review & Relate

- What motivated the Spanish to conquer and colonize the Americas?

- What were the consequences in Europe of Spain's acquisition of an American empire?

Source 1.5

Jane E. Mangan | Indians Seek to Benefit from Spanish Conquest, 2005

History has made Potosí as infamous for its forced labor draft, known as the *mita*, as it was famous for its silver. . . . [T]he Spanish victimization of native Andeans through the mita is indisputable. . . .

The early modern Dutch engraver Theodor de Bry provided one of the most enduring visual images of the mine labor. . . . because it portrayed the Indians' victimization by the Spanish. . . . [But] had de Bry's European contemporaries been able to turn their view 180 degrees from the mines and face the town center of Potosí, an equally compelling . . . scene would have appeared. Sixteenth-century Potosí resident Luis Capoche['s] . . . view of the bustling marketplace highlights . . . areas where Andean historians have modified a De Bry-like image of Indians as victims of Spanish colonization. . . . Economic historians have revealed that highland native Andean groups, like the Lupaqas and the Carangas, made a business trading coca, foodstuffs, and llamas. . . . [H]istorians of mining and labor have shown how Indians stole silver to sell for profit (and thus boosted the brisk exchange in the marketplace). . . .

In the same era that Capoche observed the market plaza, Cuzco native Catalina Palla marketed bread and coca on credit to indigenous residents of Potosí. The mother of several children with Spanish men, Palla dressed in finely woven native textiles known as *cumbi*. Engaged in urban and economic and social exchanges that included both native Andeans and Spaniards, Palla was representative of an urban marketeer. . . .

[Yet others], like Bartolina, brewed *chicha* [corn beer] for the Spaniard Francisca Nieto for pitiful wages. . . ."

Source: Jane E. Mangan, *Trading Roles: Gender, Ethnicity, and the Urban Economy in Colonial Potosí* (Durham, N.C.: Duke University Press, 2005), 4–5 and 7.

Examine the Sources

1. Identify the main points of Townsend's and Mangan's interpretations of Indian responses to the Spanish conquest, evaluating differences and similarities in their arguments.
2. Many of the sources on native peoples come from European observers. What are the challenges in using these sources to understand native experiences in Mexico and Potosí?

Put It in Context

How does recognizing the ways that indigenous people accommodated to Spanish authority shape your overall evaluation of the Spanish conquest and of the individual Indians and Indian communities that survived that conquest?

Conclusion: A Transformed America

For centuries, Asian peoples migrated to the Americas by land and sea. They developed an astonishing array of cultures and societies, from small hunting-and-gathering bands to complex empires. In the fourteenth and fifteenth centuries, extensive commercial and political networks existed among the Mississippians, the Aztecs, and the Incas, although only the latter two continued to thrive by the late 1400s. In southern Europe, too, during the fifteenth century, economic, cultural, and political advances fueled interest in long-distance trade and exploration. Italy and Portugal led these efforts, but their monopoly of trade routes across the Mediterranean and around Africa to Asia forced Spain to look west in hopes of gaining access to China and the Indies. In doing so, the Spanish unexpectedly came into contact with the Americas.

When Spanish explorers happened upon Caribbean islands and the nearby mainland, they created contacts between populations that would be dramatically transformed in a matter of decades. While native residents of the Americas were sometimes eager to trade with the newcomers and to form alliances against their traditional enemies, they fought against those they considered invaders. Yet some of the most significant invaders — plants, pigs, and especially germs — were impossible to defend against. Even Europeans seeking peaceful relations with native inhabitants or bent on conversion rather than conquest brought diseases that devastated local populations, and plants and animals that transformed their landscape, diet, and traditional ways of life.

Waldseemüller died in 1521 or 1522, so he did not see the most dramatic changes that his remarkably accurate maps inspired. Malintzin, however, experienced those changes firsthand. She watched as disease ravaged rural villages and the capital city of Tenochtitlán. She encountered horses, pigs, attack dogs, and other European animals. She ate the foods and wore the clothes that her Spanish captors provided. In 1522, Malintzin gave birth to Cortés's son; two years later, she served as interpreter when he ventured north to conquer more territory. In 1526 or 1527, however, she married a Spanish soldier, Juan Jaramillo, settled in Mexico City, and bore two more children. As more and more Spaniards, including the first women, settled in New Spain, Malintzin realized that her children would grow up in a world very different from the one in which she was raised.

From 1490 to 1590, the most dramatic and devastating changes for native peoples occurred in Mexico, the West Indies, Central America, and South America. Events there presaged what would happen throughout the Americas. As Spanish conquistadors ventured into Florida and the Gulf Coast and French and English explorers sought to gain footholds along the Atlantic seaboard, they carried sufficient germs, seeds, and animals to transform native societies even before Europeans established permanent settlements in North America.

In the century to come, contacts and conflicts between native peoples and Europeans would escalate as France, England, and the Netherlands joined Spain in colonizing North America. Conflicts among European nations and among Indian nations also multiplied as they struggled to control land, labor, and trade. Moreover, as Indian populations died out in some regions and fended off conquest in others, Europeans turned increasingly to the trade in Africans to provide the labor to produce enormously profitable items like sugar, coffee, and tobacco.

Timeline of Events

25,000–13,000 B.C.E.	First northeast Asians migrate to the Americas
900 B.C.E.–300 C.E.	Maya settle Yucatán peninsula
500 C.E.	Mogollon and Hohokam settle in southwestern North America; spread of maize cultivation northward begins
500–1400	Mississippian peoples establish complex cultures
800	Mayan civilization begins to decline
1000	Norse settle in North America
1325	Aztecs build Tenochtitlán
1340s	Black Death (bubonic plague) in Europe
1400–1500	Inca empire reaches its height
1440s	Portuguese begin to trade along the coast of West Africa
1452–1455	Johannes Gutenberg prints Bibles using movable type
1469	Unification of Spain
1487	Bartolomeu Dias rounds the Cape of Good Hope
1492	Spain expels Muslim conquerors and Jews
	Christopher Columbus's first voyage to the Americas
1497	Vasco da Gama sails to India
1507	Martin Waldseemüller and Mathias Ringmann publish *Universalis Cosmographia*
1519	Malintzin captured by Spaniards
1519–1521	Hernán Cortés conquers the Aztecs
1519–1522	Ferdinand Magellan's fleet circumnavigates the globe
1524	Francisco Pizarro conquers the Incas
1587	English settle Roanoke Island

Key Terms

Beringia, *3*

horticulture, *4*

Aztecs, *4*

Maya, *6*

Incas, *6*

Hopewell people, *7*

Crusades, *9*

Black Death, *10*

pandemic, *10*

Renaissance, *10*

Enterprise of the Indies, *15*

encomienda, *15*

Columbian exchange, *20*

conquistadors, *22*

Review & Relate

1. Compare and contrast the Aztecs, Incas, and Maya. What similarities and differences do you note?

2. How did the societies of North America differ from those of the equatorial zone and the Andes?

3. How and why did Europeans expand their connections with Africa and the Middle East in the fifteenth century?

4. How did early European encounters with West Africans influence Europeans' ideas about African peoples and reshape existing systems of slavery?

5. What were the short-term consequences in both Europe and the Americas of Columbus's voyages?

6. How did the Columbian exchange transform both the Americas and Europe?

7. What motivated the Spanish to conquer and colonize the Americas?

8. What were the consequences in Europe of Spain's acquisition of an American empire?

Indian and Spanish Encounters in the Americas, 1519–1530

▶ Evaluate the significance of the cultural misunderstandings between Indians and the Spanish in shaping political, social, and economic relations in the early sixteenth century.

The arrival of Europeans in the Americas in the fifteenth century reshaped the society, culture, and economy of the entire world. For the Indians who had inhabited the region for thousands of years, these encounters began a story of devastation. Europeans came in search of wealth and glory (see Source 1.8). They brought with them superior firepower and, more significantly, deadly diseases that led to the dramatic decline of the Indian population. After the Spanish explorer Hernán Cortés conquered the Aztec city of Tenochtitlán in 1521, Spain emerged as the world's preeminent empire.

On the local level, the Columbian exchange of plants, animals, diseases, and ideas between Europe, Africa, and the Americas meant a clash of distinct cultures (see Sources 1.7 and 1.9). The Spanish questioned the Indians' religions, social norms, and work habits. They sought to impose Catholicism and control the Indians' labor, and they used extreme means to reach these ends (Source 1.6). The Indians tried to resist the imposition of Spanish culture, but a variety of factors related to differences in power, cultural views, and economic systems among the many Indian societies that occupied present-day Mexico and the Gulf Coast undermined their efforts.

The following documents explore early contact between Europeans, specifically the Spanish, and Indians, primarily the Aztecs. As you read, consider the many levels of cultural misunderstanding and misinterpretation that occurred when these worlds collided.

Source 1.6

Hernán Cortés | Letter to King Charles I, 1520

Hernán Cortés wrote a series of letters to the Spanish king Charles I detailing his experiences and progress in Mexico. In the following excerpt from his second letter, Cortés explains how the Indians refused to accept Catholicism and the rule of the Spanish king. He then describes military actions that he carried out against the Indians.

When I undertook to [read] my requirements in due form, through the interpreters whom I had brought with me, and . . . the more diligent I was to admonish and require them to keep the peace, just so much the more diligent were they in committing hostilities upon us, and, seeing that neither requirements nor protests were of any avail, we began to defend ourselves as best we could, and thus they kept us fighting, until we found ourselves in the midst of an hundred thousand warriors, who surrounded us on all sides. This went on all day long, until about an hour before sunset, when they retired. In this fight I did them a good deal of harm with about half a dozen cannon, and five or six muskets, forty archers, and thirteen horsemen . . . without our receiving any hurt from them. . . . And it truly appeared that it was God who battled for us, because amongst such a multitude of people, so courageous and skilled in fighting, and with so many kinds of offensive arms, we came out unhurt.

That night I fortified myself in a small tower of their idols, which stood on a small hill, and afterwards, at daybreak, I left two hundred men and all the artillery in the camp. As I was the attacking party I went out towards evening with the horsemen, and a hundred foot soldiers, and four hundred Indians whom I had brought from Cempoal, and three hundred from Yztacmastitan. Before the enemy had time to assemble, I set fire to five or six small places of about a hundred houses each, and brought away about four hundred prisoners, both men and women, fighting my way back to my camp without their doing me any harm. At daybreak the following morning, more than a hundred and forty-nine thousand men, covering all the country, attacked our camp so determinedly that some of them penetrated into it, rushing about, and thrusting with their swords at the Spaniards. We mustered against them, and Our Lord was pleased so to aid us, that, in about four hours, we managed that they should no more molest us in our camp. . . .

The next day I again went out before daybreak, in another direction, without having been observed by the enemy, taking with me the horsemen, a hundred foot-soldiers, and the friendly Indians. I burned more than a hundred villages, one of which had more than three thousand houses, where the villagers fought with me, though there were no other people there. As we carried the banner of the Holy Cross, and were fighting for our Faith, and in the service of Your Sacred Majesty, to Your Royal good fortune God gave us such a victory that we slew many people without our own sustaining any injury. . . .

Messengers came from the chiefs the next day, saying that they wished to become vassals of Your Highness and my friends, beseeching me to pardon their past fault; and they brought me provisions, and certain feather-work which they use, and esteem and prize. I answered that they had behaved badly, but that I was satisfied to be their friend, and pardon them for all they had done. . . .

When we had somewhat rested, I made a sally [foray] one night . . . taking a hundred foot[men], the friendly Indians, and the horsemen; and about a league from our camp five horses and mares fell, unable to go on, so I sent them back. Although those who accompanied me, said that I ought to return, as this was an evil omen, I still pushed ahead, confiding in God's supremacy above everything. Before

daybreak I fell upon two towns, in which I slaughtered many people, but I did not want to burn the houses, so as to avoid attracting the attention of other people who were very near. When day dawned I fell upon another large town, . . . and, as I had surprised them, I found them unarmed, and the women and children, running naked through the streets; and we did them some harm. Seeing they could offer no resistance, a certain number of the inhabitants came to beseech me not to do them further injury, for they desired to become vassals of Your Highness, and my friends.

Source: Francis Augustus MacNutt, ed. and trans., *Fernando Cortés: His Five Letters of Relation to the Emperor Charles V* (Cleveland: Arthur H. Clark, 1908), 201–3, 205–6.

Source 1.7

Aztec Priests | Respond to the Spanish, 1524

As Indian resistance to the *requerimiento* — the requirement for obedience to the Catholic Church — indicated, most Aztecs did not want to renounce their own religion in favor of Catholicism. In 1524 twelve Franciscan friars organized a series of meetings with Aztec political and religious leaders, who defended the legitimacy of their own customs. In the 1560s another friar published the notes from these meetings, providing insight into how Aztec leaders viewed the differences between their own beliefs and those of the Spanish.

You say that we [the Aztecs] do not recognize the being that is everywhere, lord of heaven and earth. You say our gods are not true gods. The new words that you utter are what confuse us; due to them we feel foreboding. Our makers [our ancestors] who came to live on earth never uttered such words. They gave us their *laws*, their ways of doing things. They believed in the gods, served them and honored them. They are the ones who taught us everything, the gods' being served and respected. Before them we eat earth [kiss the ground]; we bleed; we pay our debts to the gods, offer incense, make sacrifice. . . . Indeed, we live by the grace of those gods. They rightly made us out of the time, the place where it was still dark. . . . They give us what we go to sleep with, what we get up with [our daily sustenance], all that is drunk, all that is eaten, the produce, corn, beans, green maize, chia. We beg from them the water, the rain, so that things grow upon the earth.

The gods are happy in their prosperity, in what they have, always and forever. Everything sprouts and turns green in their home. What kind of place is the land of Tlaloc [the god of rain]? Never is there any famine there, nor any illness, nor suffering. And they [the gods] give people virility, bravery, success in the hunt, [bejeweled] lip rings, blankets, breeches, cloaks, flowers, tobacco, jade, feathers and gold.

Since time immemorial they have been addressed, prayed to, taken as gods. It has been a very long time that they have been revered. . . . These gods are the ones who established the mats and thrones [that is, the inherited chieftainships], who gave people nobility, and kingship, renown and respect.

Will we be the ones to destroy the ancient traditions of the Chichimeca, the Tolteca, the Colhuaca? [No!] It is our opinion that there is life, that people are born, people are nurtured, people grow up, [only] by the gods' being called upon, prayed to. Alas, o our lords, beware lest you make the common people do something bad. How will the poor old men, the poor old women, forget or erase their upbringing, their education? May the gods not be angry with us. Let us not move towards their anger. And let us not agitate the commoners, raise a riot, lest they rebel for this reason, because of our saying to them: address the gods no longer, pray to them no longer.

Source: Camilla Townsend, ed. and trans., *American Indian History: A Documentary Reader* (Malden, MA: Wiley-Blackwell, 2009), 29–30.

Source 1.8

Hernán Cortés and Malintzin Meet Montezuma at Tenochtitlán, 1519

This image, depicting Cortés and Malintzin meeting Montezuma in November 1519, is one of eighty illustrations from a sixteenth-century mural cycle detailing the conquest of Mexico and its aftermath. The originals were painted by Tlaxcalan artists and represent an Indian perspective on these events. Malintzin is standing between Cortés (seated) and Montezuma (in gold robe). The Spanish and Aztec leaders are accompanied by leading warriors.

Gianni Dagli Orti/Shutterstock

Source 1.9

Álvar Núñez Cabeza de Vaca | *La Relación*, c. 1528

In 1528 a group of Spaniards sailed from Cuba to Tampa Bay in present-day Florida. After failing to find great riches, the survivors tried to return to Cuba but were washed ashore at Galveston Bay. Álvar Núñez Cabeza de Vaca and three other men survived the expedition, but only after enduring a nine-year, six-hundred-mile trek across Texas and Mexico and enslavement by Indians. In an account of his journey, Cabeza de Vaca described his experiences on the Isla de Malhado (Island of Misfortune) off the coast of Texas.

All the people of this country go naked; only the women cover part of their bodies with a kind of wool that grows on trees. The girls go about in deer skins. They are very liberal towards each other with what they have. There is no ruler among them. All who are of the same descendancy [ancestry] cluster together. There are two distinct languages spoken on the island; those of one language are called Capoques, those of the other Han. They have the custom, when they know each other and meet from time to time, before they speak, to weep for half an hour. After they have wept the one who receives the visit rises and gives the other all he has. The other takes it, and in a little while goes away with everything. Even sometimes, after having given and obtained all, they part without having uttered a word. There are other very queer customs, but having told the principal ones and the most striking, I must now proceed to relate what further happened to us. . . .

I had to remain with those same Indians of the island for more than one year, and as they made me work so much and treated me so badly I determined to flee and go to those who live in the woods on the mainland, and who are called those from Charruco. . . .

Among many other troubles I had to pull the eatable roots out of the water and from among the canes where they were buried in the ground, and from this my fingers had become so tender that the mere touch of a straw caused them to bleed. . . . This is why I went to work and joined the other Indians. Among these I improved my condition a little by becoming a trader, doing the best in it I could, and they gave me food and treated me well.

They entreated me to go about from one part to another to get the things they needed, as on account of constant warfare there is neither travel nor barter in the land.

So, trading along with my wares I penetrated inland as far as I cared to go and along the coast as much as forty or fifty leagues. My stock consisted mainly of pieces of seashells and cockles, and shells with which they cut a fruit which is like a bean, used by them for healing and in their dances and feasts. This is of greatest value among them, besides shell-beads and other objects. These things I carried inland, and in exchange brought back hides and red ochre with which they rub and dye their faces and hair; flint for arrow points, glue and hard canes wherewith to make them, and tassels made of the hair of deer, which they dye red. This trade suited me well because it gave me liberty to go wherever I pleased; I was not bound to do anything and no longer a slave. Wherever I went they treated me well, and gave me to eat for the sake of my wares. My principal object in doing it, however, was to find out in what manner I might get further away. . . .

My sufferings, while trading thus, it would take long to tell; danger, hunger, storms and frost overtaking me often in the open field and alone, and from which through the mercy of God, Our Lord, I escaped. For this reason I did not go out trading in winter, it being the time when the Indians themselves remain in their huts and abodes, unable to go out or assist each other.

Nearly six years I spent thus in the country, alone among them and naked, as they all were themselves.

Source: Adolph F. Bandelier, ed., *The Journey of Álvar Núñez Cabeza de Vaca and His Companions from Florida to the Pacific, 1528–1536* (New York: A. S. Barnes, 1905), 71–76.

Interpret the Evidence

1. How does Hernán Cortés treat his Indian adversaries (Source 1.6) and how does he justify this treatment and to whom? What conflicts among the Indians themselves are revealed in Cortés's letter?

2. How do the Aztec priests respond to Spanish criticisms of their religion? Why do they refuse to abandon their gods (Source 1.7)?

3. What does the mural image, created by Tlaxcalan Indians, suggest about the relative power of Montezuma and Cortés at this meeting and the possibilities for conflict or cooperation between them (Source 1.8)? Given the information in Sources 1.6 and 1.7, what concerns might Malintzin, as the translator, have about conveying information to each leader?

4. What does Álvar Núñez Cabeza de Vaca find surprising about Indian culture, and how might that reflect differences between the Spanish and Indians (Source 1.9)? How does his story differ from the information provided in Sources 1.6, 1.7, and 1.8?

Put It in Context

What do these sources reveal about Spanish-Indian relations throughout the conquest period?

How did news of these encounters shape debates among Spanish religious leaders over the conquest in the 1550s?

What roles did religion, military power, and economic interests play in the differing perspectives among the Indians, among Spaniards, and between the Indians and the Spanish?

Colonization and Conflicts

1580–1680

Window to the Past

William Nahaton, Petition to Free an Indian Slave, 1675

William Nahaton, a Christianized Indian in Massachusetts Bay, sent this petition to gain the release of a relative whom he feared would be sold into slavery by the English. While hundreds of native people were sold into slavery, petitions for their release were rare. This petition offers important insights into the views of an Indian who had chosen to adopt many English ways. ▶ **To learn more about this primary source, see Source 2.6 on page 66.**

After reading this chapter you will be able to:

■ Discuss the impact of the Reformation and Counter-Reformation and the emerging Atlantic economy on European nations and their goals in the American colonies.

■ Evaluate the ways that European demands for land and trade, upheavals among indentured servants, and the emergence of slavery transformed the lives of Indians and colonists in diverse regions of North America.

■ Analyze the influence of Puritanism on New England's development and how religious and political upheavals in England fueled Puritan expansion and conflicts with Indians in that region.

Comparing American Histories

A boy named Wahunsenacawh was born in the 1540s to a powerful family of Algonquian-speaking Indians in the Middle Atlantic region west of Chesepiooc (Chesapeake) Bay. As an adult, he inherited leadership of a group of four to six Algonquian-speaking tribes. By the early 1600s, through diplomacy and force, Wahunsenacawh expanded this confederacy to about thirty tribes comprising some 12,000–15,000 inhabitants. Now called **Powhatan**, meaning the chief of chiefs, he lived at Werowocomoco, an ancient Indian site along the York River.

(*left*) **Powhatan, from John Smith, General Historie of Virginia** Library of Congress, 3b20538
(*right*) **Anne Hutchinson** Portrait of Anne Hutchinson (1591–1643) Bridgeman Images

In April 1607, a boatload of 104 Englishmen led by Captain John Smith arrived in Chesapeake Bay and founded a settlement south of the York River. They named it Jamestown in honor of King James I and claimed the land for England. When news of their arrival reached Powhatan, the powerful chief likely hoped that this small community of light-skinned men might bring goods to trade.

When Powhatan's younger brother discovered Smith and two of his Jamestown comrades in the chief's territory that December, he brought them to Powhatan. While Smith was eventually released, his two comrades were executed. Powhatan likely performed an adoption ceremony for Smith to bring him and the English settlement under Powhatan's authority. In a typical ceremony, Powhatan would send one of his daughters — in this case, twelve-year-old Pocahontas — to indicate that the captive was spared. Captain Smith, who had just seen two comrades slain, did not understand the meaning of the ceremony or why he was spared. Anticipating further violence, he returned to Jamestown and urged residents to build fortifications for security.

The following fall, colonists elected Smith president of the Jamestown council. He insisted that colonists must intimidate the Indians and labor on farms and fortifications daily. Many colonists were opposed or ill-prepared to undertake such labors. Instead, hungry colonists demanded or seized corn from Indian villages. This mystified Powhatan: "What will it availe you to take that by force [which] you might quickly have by love, or destroy them that provide you food?"

Dissatisfied with Smith, the Virginia Company imposed a new set of leaders in 1609. When the situation deteriorated further, Powhatan again had to consider how to deal with what he likely viewed as ungrateful newcomers.

While the Virginia Company contemplated its economic interests, other Englishmen and women contemplated their souls. Critics of the Church of England formed a number of dissenting congregations in the early seventeenth century, part of a Protestant Reformation that swept across Europe. The Virginia Company benefited from this upheaval by offering legal charters to private investors, including dissenting Pilgrims in 1620. Other dissenters, including Puritans in 1630, gained royal charters from the English government.

Anne Hutchinson, a forty-five-year-old wife and mother, joined the Puritan migration. Born in Lincolnshire, England, in 1591, Anne was well educated when she married William Hutchinson, a merchant, in 1612. The Hutchinsons and their children began attending Puritan sermons, and in 1634 they followed the Reverend John Cotton to Massachusetts Bay.

Anne Hutchinson was well-versed in the Bible, and Reverend Cotton urged her to hold prayer meetings in her home for pregnant and nursing women who did not attend regular services. Hutchinson, like Cotton, preached that individuals must rely solely on God's grace rather than a saintly life or good works to ensure salvation. Many Puritan

ministers had come to oppose this position, but Hutchinson did not retreat.

Her intransigence shocked Puritan leaders, who were embroiled in a deadly war with the powerful Pequot nation. In August 1637, with Hutchinson's following expanding, Puritan leaders condemned her meetings. Refusing to recant her views, Hutchinson was put on trial that November. She mounted a vigorous defense, but the Puritan judges convicted her of heresy and banished her from Massachusetts Bay. Hutchinson's family, and dozens of followers moved to the recently established colony of Rhode Island. Although safe from her critics, she would eventually succumb to an Indian attack. ■

C omparing the American histories of Powhatan and Anne Hutchinson illustrates the complex relationships between Indians and English settlers as well as among colonists themselves. Because silver and gold were not found north of Mexico, English, French, and Dutch colonists depended on farming, fishing, and trade as their entrée to the growing Atlantic economy. These efforts required either negotiating with Indians or taking their lands. Although Indian confederacies and communities in northern regions were smaller than the Maya and Inca Empires, they resisted European dominion for much longer. This necessitated ever-shifting alliances between European colonizers and Indian nations. The resulting conflicts dramatically transformed the lives of American Indians and European colonists between 1580 and 1680.

Religious, Economic, and Imperial Transformations

The Puritans were part of a relatively new religious movement known as **Protestantism** that had emerged around 1520. Protestants challenged Catholic policies and practices but did not form a single church of their own. Instead, they formed distinct denominations in various regions of Europe. Catholics sought to counter their claims by revitalizing their faith, reasserting control, and converting Indians in lands they claimed in North America. These religious conflicts shaped developments across North America. So, too, did the search for commercial success as France, the Netherlands, and England sought a foothold in North America. Whether seeking conversions, land, trading partners, or military allies, Europeans were forced to negotiate with or conquer diverse Indian nations and confederacies, each of which had its own economic and military interests to consider.

The Protestant Reformation. Critiques of the Catholic Church multiplied in the early sixteenth century, driven by papal involvement in conflicts among monarchs and corruption among church officials. But the most vocal critics focused on immorality, ignorance, and absenteeism among clergy. These anticlerical views appeared in popular songs and printed images as well as in learned texts by theologians such as Martin Luther.

Luther, a professor of theology in Germany, believed that faith alone led to salvation, which could be granted only by God. He challenged the Catholic Church's claim that individuals could achieve salvation by buying indulgences, which were documents that absolved the buyer of sin. The church profited enormously from these sales, but they suggested that God's grace could be purchased. In 1517 Luther wrote an extended argument against indulgences and sent it to the local bishop. His writings soon gained a wider audience.

Luther's followers, who protested Catholic practices, became known as Protestants. His teachings circulated widely through sermons and printed texts, and his claim that ordinary people should read and reflect on the Scriptures appealed to the literate middle classes. Meanwhile his attacks on indulgences and corruption attracted those who resented the church's wealth and priests' indifference to their flocks. In Switzerland, John Calvin developed a version of Protestantism in which civil magistrates and reformed ministers ruled over a Christian society. Calvin argued that God had decided at the beginning of time who was saved and who was damned. Calvin's idea, known as predestination, energized Protestants who understood salvation as a gift from an all-knowing God in which the "works" of sinful humans played no part.

The Protestant Reformation quickly spread through central and northern Europe. English rulers too, came under the influence of Protestantism in the 1530s, although for different reasons. When the pope refused to annul the marriage of King Henry VIII (r. 1509–1547) and Catherine of Aragon, Henry denounced papal authority and established the **Church of England**, or Anglicanism, with himself as "defender of the faith." Despite the king's conversion to Protestantism, the Church of England retained many Catholic practices.

In countries like Spain and France with strong central governments and powerful ties to the Catholic Church, a strong Catholic Counter-Reformation largely quashed Protestantism. Yet, Catholic leaders also initiated reforms to counter their critics. In 1545 Pope Paul II called together a commission of cardinals, known as the Council of Trent (1545–1563), which founded new seminaries to train priests and returned monastic orders to their spiritual foundations. Both Protestant and Catholic leaders urged followers to spread their faith across the Atlantic, and religious minorities sought a safe haven there.

Just as important, political struggles erupted between Catholic and Protestant rulers in Europe, inspiring more people to migrate to North America. Many were attracted by economic opportunities while others were forced to labor on their behalf. Together, these migrants fueled an expanding Atlantic economy built on fish, furs, sugar, and increasingly slavery.

Spain's Global Empire Declines.
As religious conflicts escalated in Europe, Spaniards in America continued to push north in hopes of expanding their empire. The nature of Spanish expansion, however, changed. As a result of the Council of Trent and the Catholic Counter-Reformation, Spain increasingly emphasized its religious mission. Thus Spanish authorities decided in 1573 that missionaries rather than soldiers should direct new settlements. Franciscan priests began founding missions on the margins of Pueblo villages north of Mexico. They named the area Nuevo México (New Mexico), and many learned Indian languages. In the following decades, some twenty thousand Pueblo women and men converted to Catholicism. However, many still retained traditional beliefs and practices, which missionaries tried, unsuccessfully, to eradicate through flogging and other punishments.

San Esteban del Rey Mission
Opened in 1644 after fourteen years of construction, this Spanish mission in present-day New Mexico provided instruction in Christianity and Hispanic customs for the Acoma (Pueblo) people. To this end, Spanish missionaries prohibited traditional Pueblo practices such as performing dances and wearing masks. The mission was one of the few to survive Pueblo revolts in the late seventeenth century. age fotostock/Superstock

At the same time, Franciscans tried to force the Pueblo people to adopt European ways. They insisted that men rather than women farm the land and that Indians speak, cook, and dress like Spaniards. Missionaries also largely ignored Spanish laws intended to protect Indians from coerced labor, demanding that Pueblos build churches, provide the missions with food, and carry their goods to market. Wealthy landowners who followed the missionaries into New Mexico also demanded tribute in the form of goods and labor.

In 1598 Juan de Oñate, from a wealthy mining family, established a trading post and fort in the upper Rio Grande valley. The 500 soldiers who accompanied him seized corn and clothing from Pueblo villages and murdered or raped those who resisted. Indians at the Acoma pueblo confronted these soldiers, and eleven Spaniards were killed. The Spanish retaliated, slaughtering 500 men and 300 women and children. Fearing reprisals, most Spaniards withdrew from the region.

In 1610 Spaniards returned, founded Santa Fe, and established a network of missions and estates owned by *encomenderos*, Spanish elites granted land and the right to exploit Indian labor. This time the Pueblo people largely accepted the new situation. While they feared military reprisals if they challenged Spanish authorities, they also sought Spanish protection following a period of drought, disease, and raids by Apache and Navajo tribes. Yet their faith in the Franciscans' spiritual power faded when conditions did not improve. Although Spain maintained a firm hold on Florida and its colonies in the West Indies, it focused most of its efforts in the West, allowing other European powers to expand into eastern North America.

France Enters the Race for Empire. In the late sixteenth century, French, Dutch, and English investors became increasingly interested in gaining a foothold in North America. First, however, they had to break Catholic Spain's grip on the Atlantic world. The Protestant Reformation helped shape the alliances that shattered Spain's American monopoly. As head of the Church of England, Queen Elizabeth I (King Henry VIII's daughter, r. 1558–1603) sought closer political and commercial ties with Protestant nations like the Netherlands. The queen also assented to, and benefited from, raids on Spanish ships by Francis Drake and other privateers. In 1588 King Philip II of Spain (r. 1556–1598) decided to punish England for these attacks and its intervention in the Netherlands. He sent a massive armada to spearhead the invasion of England. However, the English, aided by Dutch ships and lucky weather conditions, defeated the armada and ensured that the two nations could compete for riches and colonies in North America.

Although French rulers shared Spain's Catholic faith, they, too, were rivals and sought greater access to North American colonies. Once in North America, the French adopted attitudes and policies that differed significantly from those of Spain. This was due in part to their interest in trade rather than conquest. The French had profited from fishing the North Atlantic since the mid-sixteenth century, but their efforts to establish settlements in Newfoundland and Nova Scotia met with fierce Indian resistance. Gradually French traders established relations with local Indians, exchanging iron kettles and other European goods for valuable beaver skins.

By the early seventeenth century, France's King Henry IV (r. 1589–1610) sought to profit more directly from the North American trade. With the Edict of Nantes (1598), the king ended decades of religious wars by granting political rights and limited toleration to French Protestants, known as Huguenots, many of whom had sought refuge in North America. He then focused on developing the lucrative Atlantic trade in fish and furs. Samuel de Champlain, sponsored by a French fur-trading company, founded that nation's first permanent settlement in North America in 1608 at Quebec. Accompanied by several dozen men, Champlain joined a Huron raid on the Iroquois, who resided south of the Great Lakes. By using guns, the French helped ensure a Huron victory and a powerful ally for the French. But the battle also fueled lasting bitterness among the Iroquois.

Trade relations flourished between the French and their Indian allies. Both became part of the flourishing **Atlantic economy**, in which traders and colonists in the Americas exchanged European goods with Indian nations, which in turn provided those European countries with fish, furs, and other increasingly valuable items. The commercial character of the French venture was made clear by the relatively few French men and even fewer women who settled in North America. Government policies discouraged mass migration as did reports of short growing seasons and severe winters. Cardinal Richelieu, the king's chief minister, urged priests and nuns to migrate to New France but barred further emigration by Protestant Huguenots. Thus into the 1630s, French settlements in North America consisted largely of fishermen, fur traders, and Catholic missionaries. Fur traders were critical to sustaining French land claims and warding off encroachment by the English, whose villages radiated out from Massachusetts Bay. The French journeyed throughout eastern Canada, aided by the Huron tribe, and established a fortified trading post at Montreal in 1643. Over the next three decades, the French pushed farther west, feeding Europe's growing market for beaver skins. However, as they extended the fur trade beyond the St. Lawrence River valley, they left their Huron allies behind.

As the Dutch entered the fur trade via forts along the Hudson River, Iroquois in that region sought to keep the Huron from trading their high-quality furs to the Dutch (Map 2.1). With guns supplied by Dutch merchants, the Iroquois led a series of assaults on Huron villages. In this way, they also secured captives to restore their population, which was decimated by disease.

As they ventured west, some Frenchmen took Indian wives, who were skilled at tanning and drying animal pelts and provided companionship and kinship ties to powerful native leaders. Despite Catholic criticism of these marriages, they strengthened commercial

MAP 2.1   Approximate Tribal Locations at First Contact with Europeans

Maps of early European colonies in North America often highlight the locations of Spanish, French, Dutch, and English settlements. However, it was the complex network of native communities, with their pre-existing patterns of settlement, migration, trade, and conflict, which profoundly shaped how these European colonies developed.

Explore ▶

In Source 2.1, read a Catholic nun's report of a Huron woman's complaints about the Jesuits.

relations and fostered French alliances with the Ojibwe and Dakota nations in the Great Lakes region. These alliances, in turn, created a middle ground in which economic and cultural exchanges led to a remarkable degree of mutual adaptation. The mixed-race children of French men and Indian women, known as **metis**, became translators, guides, and traders themselves. French traders also benefited from Indian technology, especially canoes, while natives adopted iron cooking pots and European cloth.

Still, France could only capitalize on its North American colonies by maintaining profits from the fur trade. In moving ever westward, French traders carried European diseases into

Guided Primary Source Analysis

A French Nun Reports a Huron Woman's View of the Jesuits, 1640

Jesuit missionaries and Ursuline nuns brought the Catholic faith to Indians in New France along with germs and guns. In this letter, the nun Marie de L'Incarnation writes to her superiors about the views expressed by an elderly and respected Huron woman. She conveys a report she heard about this woman, who told her village that the Jesuits, known as Black Robes, were destroying their communities. L'Incarnation summarizes and then analyzes the Huron woman's speech.

Source 2.1

What is the Huron woman's evidence of the Jesuits' danger to her people?

What are the sources, in her experience, of the Jesuits' power to do harm?

How does Marie de L'Incarnation interpret the message of this Huron woman?

It's the Black Robes who are making us die by their spells. Listen to me, I will prove it by reasons that you will recognize as true. They set themselves up in a village where everyone is feeling fine; no sooner are they there, but everyone dies except for three or four people. They move to another place, and the same thing happens. They visit cabins in other villages, and only those where they have not entered are exempt from death and illness. Don't you see that when they move their lips in what they call prayer, spells are coming out of their mouths? It's the same when they read their books. They have big pieces of wood [guns] in their cabins by which they make noise and send their magic everywhere. If they are not promptly put to death, they will end up ruining the country, and no one will be left, young or old. . . .

When she stopped speaking, everyone agreed that this was true, . . . [and] it seemed true . . . , for wherever the [Jesuit] Fathers went, God permitted death to accompany them so as to render more pure the faith of those who converted.

Source: Marie de L'Incarnation, *Correspondance*, ed. Dom Guy Oury (Abbaye de Saint-Pierre, 1971), trans. Natalie Zemon Davis, *Women on the Margins: Three Seventeenth-Century Lives* (Cambridge, MA: Harvard University Press, 1995), 111–12.

▌ Put It in Context

How might this account of a Huron woman's perspective have been transformed in its retelling and translation? Despite these changes, what can it tell us about Huron interactions with Catholic priests and nuns in the early 1600s?

new areas, intensified warfare among native groups, and stretched their small population of settlers ever thinner. However fragile their empire, French explorers, traders, and priests extended their reach beyond the Great Lakes and by 1681 moved southward along the Mississippi to a territory they named Louisiana in honor of King Louis XIV (r. 1643–1715).

The conflicts between commerce and conversion in Spanish America were far less severe in New France. French traders relied on Indian allies, and some French Jesuit priests also sought to build on native beliefs and learn Indians' languages and customs. Although Catholics assumed that their own religious beliefs and cultural values were superior to those of the Indians, many sought to engage native inhabitants on their own terms. Thus one French Jesuit employed the Huron belief that "our souls have desires which are inborn and concealed" to explain Christian doctrines of sin and salvation to potential converts. Still, missionaries — like traders — carried deadly germs, and Catholics sought conversion, not mutual adaptation. While many Indian nations benefited from their alliances with the French in the short term, the long-term costs proved devastating.

The Dutch Expand into North America.

The Protestant Dutch had no interest in bringing religion to Indians in America. From the beginning, their goals were almost purely economic. As Spain's shipbuilding center, the Netherlands had benefited from the wealth pouring in from South America, and an affluent merchant class emerged. However, the Dutch also embraced Calvinism and sought to separate themselves from Catholic Spain. In 1581 the Netherlands declared independence from King Philip II (r. 1556–1598). Although Spain refused to recognize the new status for several decades, by 1600 the Netherlands was both a Protestant haven and the trading hub of Europe. Indeed, the Dutch East India Company controlled trade routes to much of Asia and parts of Africa.

With technology and skills developed under Spanish control, the Dutch became central to the Atlantic economy as well. In 1609 they established a fur-trading center on the Hudson River in present-day New York, which was part of what became known as the middle colonies. The small number of Dutch traders developed friendly relations with important Mohawk and Munsee communities, which were linked respectively to Iroquois and Algonquian allies. Dutch authorities recognized Indian sovereignty and insisted land be purchased rather than taken from local Indians. In 1614, the trading post was moved south to Fort Orange, near present-day Albany. The Dutch fur trade also benefitted England and Russia, where artisans created beaver hats from the raw skins shipped to Amsterdam.

In 1624, to fend off French and English raids on ships sent downriver from Fort Orange, the Dutch established New Amsterdam on Manhattan Island, which they purchased from the Lenape Indians. The new settlement was organized by the Dutch West India Company, which was chartered three years earlier. New Amsterdam attracted a diverse community of traders, fishermen, artisans, and farmers. It was noted for its religious toleration as well as the independence of its female colonists. Dutch wives, unlike other European women, retained their separate legal status after marriage. Husbands and wives shared property, and widows often inherited businesses as well as domestic goods. Indeed, Dutch trading networks were rooted in networks of kin and community that stretched east, south, and west from Amsterdam to Cape Town, Java, Guyana, New Amsterdam, and beyond. By the 1630s, the Dutch would play a major role in the Atlantic slave trade, eventually transporting more than half a million enslaved Africans to the Americas.

Early Dutch settlers in New Netherland developed peaceful relations with the Mohawk and Munsee, who also rooted their trade networks in kin and community relations. However, by the 1630s, as colonists established farms along the Hudson River and Long Island, amid large communities of Algonquian Indians, tensions escalated. Then, in 1639, Governor Willem Kieft demanded an annual tribute in wampum or grain. Local Algonquians resisted, raiding Dutch farms on the frontier and killing at least two colonists. Raids and killings continued on both sides. In 1643, Kieft launched a surprise attack on an Indian encampment on Manhattan Island, murdering eighty people, mostly women and children. Outraged Algonquians burned and looted homes north of the city, killed livestock, and murdered settlers. For two decades, sporadic warfare continued. The Algonquians suffered some 1,000 deaths compared to 200 settlers.

New Amsterdam   This engraving on copper offers one of the oldest extant images of New Amsterdam. It captures the thriving commercial center of New Netherland at the tip of Manhattan. It also illustrates the importance of enslaved Africans to the colony's success and the significant role played by Dutch women as well as men in its economic development. New York Public Library/Bridgeman Images

Amid these devastating conflicts, the Dutch continued to trade for furs with Mohawks along the upper Hudson River. This powerful tribe had the backing of the even more powerful Iroquois Confederacy. The confederacy's ties to Indians farther west allowed the Mohawk to provide beaver skins to Dutch traders long after beavers died out in the Hudson valley. Still, the Mohawk people did not deceive themselves. As one chief proclaimed in 1659, "The Dutch say we are brothers and that we are joined together with chains, but that lasts only so long as we have beavers."

Meanwhile reports of atrocities by Indians and the Dutch circulated in the Netherlands, damaging New Amsterdam's reputation and slowing migration. A series of wars with their former ally England further weakened Dutch power in America. In 1664, England sent a naval convoy to take New Amsterdam. Exhausted by decades of unrelenting conflict, the Dutch surrendered to the English without a fight.

Review & Relate

◾ How did the Protestant Reformation and Catholic Counter-Reformation shape the course of European expansion in the Americas?

◾ How did the French and Dutch colonies in North America differ from the Spanish empire to the south, and how were these differences shaped by Indian nations?

The English Seek an Empire

The English, like the French and the Dutch, entered the race for an American empire well after the Spanish. England did not have a permanent settlement in the Americas until the founding of **Jamestown** at the mouth of Chesapeake Bay in 1607. In the 1620s, the English established settlements in the West Indies, which quickly became the economic engine of English colonization. Expansion into these areas demanded new modes of labor to ensure a return on investment. Large numbers of indentured servants crossed the Atlantic and enslaved Indians labored throughout the English colonies, while growing numbers of Africans were forced onto ships for sale in the Americas. Meanwhile, the rapid expansion of English settlement increased military conflicts with Indian nations and fueled tensions among settlers.

The English Establish Jamestown. England's success in colonizing North America depended in part on a new economic model in which investors purchased shares in joint-stock companies that could raise large amounts of money quickly. If the venture succeeded, investors shared the profits. If they failed, no investor suffered the whole loss. In 1606 a group of London merchants formed the Virginia Company, and King James I granted them the right to settle a vast area of North America, from present-day New York to North Carolina.

Some of the men that the Virginia Company recruited as colonists were gentlemen who hoped to get rich through the discovery of precious metals. They also recruited skilled artisans and laborers to launch the settlement, many of whom hoped to gain wealth and status. A few men who planned to stay for an extended period brought their wives, which was almost unheard of among the Spanish and French. Arriving on the coast of North America in April 1607, the colonists established Jamestown along a river, a site they chose mainly for its easy defense knowing that it lay within territory controlled by a large confederation of Indians. Although bothered by the settlement's mosquito-infested environment, the colonists focused their energies on constructing buildings, producing food, and searching for gold and silver.

The Englishmen quickly made contact with the Indian chief Powhatan, who presided over a confederation of some thirty tribes, which surrounded the small Jamestown settlement. The **Powhatan Confederacy** was powerful, and for the first two years English settlers depended on its generosity to survive. While a severe drought between 1606 and 1612 caused a shortage of food among both Indians and the English, the problem was exacerbated in Jamestown by some colonists' refusal to engage in manual labor. Moreover, the nearby water was tainted by salt from the ocean and diseases festered in the low-lying area, killing more than half of the original settlers.

Powhatan assisted the settlers in hopes they would provide him with English cloth, iron hatchets, and even guns. His capture and subsequent release of John Smith in 1607 suggests his interest in trading with the newcomers even as he sought to subordinate them. But leaders like Captain Smith considered Powhatan and his warriors a threat rather than an asset. When unable to feed themselves that first year, Jamestown residents raided Indian villages for corn and other food, making Powhatan increasingly wary. The settlers' decision to construct a fort only bolstered the Indians' concern.

Meanwhile the Virginia Company devised a plan to stave off the collapse of its colony. It started selling seven-year joint-stock options to raise funds and recruited new settlers to produce staple crops, glassware, or other items for export. Interested individuals who could not afford to invest cash could sign an indenture for service in Virginia. After seven years, these indentured servants would gain their freedom and receive a hundred acres of land. In

June 1609, a new contingent of colonists attracted by this plan — five hundred men and a hundred women — sailed for Jamestown.

The new arrivals, however, had not brought enough supplies to sustain the colony through the winter. Powhatan did offer some aid, but Indians, too, suffered shortages that winter. A "starving time" settled on Jamestown. By the spring of 1610, seven of every eight settlers who had arrived in Jamestown since 1607 were dead.

That June, the sixty survivors decided to abandon the colony and sail for home. They were surprised to meet three English ships in the harbor loaded with supplies and three hundred more settlers. Emboldened by fresh supplies and an enlarged population, Jamestown's new leaders adopted an aggressive military posture, attacking native villages, burning crops, killing many Indians, and taking others captive. They believed that such brutality would convince neighboring tribes to obey English demands for food and labor.

Tobacco Fuels Growth in Virginia.   It was not military aggression, however, but the discovery of a viable cash crop that saved the English colony. Orinoco tobacco, grown in the West Indies and South America, sold well in England and Europe. Virginia colonist John Rolfe began to experiment with its growth in 1612, just as the drought lifted. Production of the leaf soared as eager English investors poured seeds, supplies, and labor into Jamestown. Exports multiplied rapidly, from 2,000 pounds in 1615 to 40,000 pounds five years later and an incredible 1.5 million pounds by 1629.

However, tobacco cultivation exacerbated tensions between colonists and Indians. As production increased, prices declined. Farmers could increase their profits only by obtaining

Scene on an American Tobacco Plantation   Pomet, physician to the French King Louis XIV included this engraving in his *A Compleat History of Drugs*, published in London in 1725. It shows a tobacco plant on the right as enslaved men, women, and children process the leaves on the left. Photo12/Universal Images Group via Getty Images more land and more laborers. In response, the Virginia Company offered land to indentured laborers who spent seven years clearing new fields and creating more plantations. Yet in most cases, the Powhatan Confederacy already claimed the land granted to these would-be colonists.

Despite growing conflicts over land, Powhatan tried one last time to create an alliance between his confederacy and the English settlers. Perhaps he was encouraged by the return of rain and hoped that increased productivity would ease relations with the English. In 1614, he allowed his daughter Pocahontas, who had spent considerable time in Jamestown, to marry John Rolfe, forging the kind of familial bond that created alliances between Indian tribes. Pocahontas converted to Christianity and two years later traveled to England with Rolfe and their infant son. While there, however, she fell ill and died in 1617. The next year, Powhatan died, and his younger brother Opechancanough took over as chief. Rolfe and his son returned to Virginia, but relations between colonists and the confederacy once again deteriorated.

The English crown made clear its intentions in 1619 by granting Virginia colonists the right to establish a local governing body, the **House of Burgesses**. Its members could make laws and levy taxes, although the English governor or the company council in London held veto power. The Virginia Company also resolved to recruit more female settlers as a way to increase the colony's population. More young women and men arrived as **indentured servants**, working in the fields and homes of more affluent Englishmen for a set period of time in exchange for passage to America. Also in 1619, an English ship carried the first boatload of twenty Africans to Jamestown. They were bound as indentured servants to farmers desperate for labor.

Although the English colony still hugged the Atlantic coast, its geographical expansion and enhanced political authority increased conflict with native inhabitants. In March 1622, after repeated English incursions on land cleared and farmed by Indians, Chief Opechancanough launched a surprise attack that killed nearly a third of the colonists. In retaliation, Englishmen assaulted native villages, killed inhabitants, burned cornfields, and sold Indian captives into slavery.

The English proclaimed victory in 1623, but hostilities continued for nearly a decade. The very next year, King James asserted his authority over the colony by annulling the Virginia Company charter. He appointed the governor and a small advisory council, required that legislation passed by the House of Burgesses be ratified by the Privy Council, and demanded that property owners pay taxes to support the Church of England. These regulations became the model for royal colonies throughout North America.

Matoaks als Rebecka daughter to the mighty Prince Powhatan Emperour of Attanoughkomouck als virginia converted and baptized in the Christian faith, and wife to the wor.ll Mr Joh Rolff.

Engraving of Pocahontas, 1616 Simon van de Passe created this portrait of Pocahontas during her visit to England in 1616. The engraving was commissioned by the Virginia Company to promote settlement in Jamestown. It was the only portrait of Pocahontas made before her death in London. While van de Passe clothes her in English aristocratic style, he retains her dark complexion and direct gaze. Library of Congress, Rare Book Division [LC-USZ62-8104]

Still, royal proclamations could not halt Indian opposition. In 1644, the Powhatan Confederacy launched a second uprising against the English, killing hundreds of colonists. After two years of bitter warfare, Chief Opechancanough was finally captured and then killed. With the English population now too large to eradicate, the remaining members of the Confederacy either moved to new areas or submitted to English authority.

Expansion, Rebellion, and the Emergence of Slavery.

By the 1630s, despite continued conflicts with Indians, Virginia was well on its way to commercial success. The most successful tobacco planters acquired growing numbers of indentured servants, including some Africans as well as thousands of English and Irish immigrants. Between 1640 and 1670, some 40,000 to 50,000 of these servants and immigrants settled in Virginia and neighboring Maryland (Map 2.2). Maryland was founded in 1632 when King Charles I, the successor to James I, granted most of the territory north of Chesapeake Bay to Cecilius Calvert and appointed him Lord Baltimore. Calvert was among the minority of English who remained a Catholic, and he planned to create Maryland as a refuge for his persecuted co-worshippers. Appointing his brother Leonard Calvert as governor, he carefully recruited the first colonists, including artisans and farmers (mainly Protestant) as well as wealthy merchants and aristocrats (mostly Catholic). When conflict festered between the Catholic elite and the Protestant majority, Governor Calvert convinced the Maryland assembly to pass an Act of Religious Toleration in 1649, granting religious freedom to all Christians.

Taken together, Maryland and Virginia formed the Chesapeake region of the English empire — a crucial engine of the Atlantic economy. Both colonies relied on tobacco to produce the wealth that fueled their growth, and both introduced African labor to complement the supply of white indentured servants. Still, neither colony initially developed a legal code of slavery. From 1650 on, however, improved economic conditions in England meant fewer

MAP 2.2   The Growth of English Settlement in the Chesapeake, c. 1650

With the success of tobacco, English plantations and forts spread along the James River and north to St. Mary's. By 1650 most Chesapeake Indian tribes had been vanquished or forced to move north and west. The fall line, which marked the limit of navigable waterways, kept English settlements close to the Atlantic coast but also ensured easy shipment of goods.

A Susquehannock Warrior John Smith published a remarkably accurate map of Virginia in 1612. It included major geographical features and the names of some 200 Indian towns. Smith placed a sketch of a Susquehannock warrior in the upper right-hand corner; at his feet, Smith noted that the Susquehannock were "a Gyant-like people." This map was widely used for seven decades. Beinecke Rare Book and Manuscript Library, Yale University

English men and women were willing to gamble on a better life in North America. Even though the number of African laborers remained small until late in the century, colonial leaders increased their control over that population. Most importantly, in 1660 the House of Burgesses passed an act that allowed black laborers to be enslaved and in 1662 defined slavery as an inherited status passed on from mothers to children. Maryland followed suit two years later.

The march toward full-blown racial slavery had begun in Barbados, which established the model that Chesapeake authorities followed. The booming sugar industry on the island spurred the development of plantation slavery, and both proved critical to the Atlantic economy. In 1660 blacks in Barbados formed a majority of the population. Twenty years later, there were seventeen enslaved Africans for every white indentured servant on Barbados. The growth of slavery on the island depended almost wholly on imports from Africa since enslaved persons there died faster than they could reproduce themselves. In the context of high death rates, brutal working conditions, and massive imports, Barbados systematized its slave code, defining enslaved Africans as chattel—that is, as mere property more akin to livestock than to human beings.

While enslaved Africans would become, in time, a crucial component of the Chesapeake labor force, indentured servants made up the majority of bound workers in Virginia and Maryland for most of the seventeenth century. They, too, labored under harsh conditions and severe punishments, including beating, whipping, and branding, for a variety of infractions. Some white servants made common cause with black laborers who worked side by side with them on tobacco plantations. They ran away together, stole goods from their masters, and planned uprisings and rebellions.

By the 1660s and 1670s, the population of indentured servants who had become free formed a growing and increasingly unhappy class. Most were struggling economically, working as common laborers or tenants on large estates. Meanwhile, those who claimed land on the frontier were confronted by hostile Indians like the Susquehannock. Virginia governor Sir William Berkeley, who levied taxes to support nine forts along the frontier, had little patience with the complaints of these colonists. His priorities were securing sufficient labor for wealthy tobacco

Explore ▶

In Sources 2.2 and 2.3, analyze the experiences of indentured servants in Maryland.

Comparative Primary Source Analysis

Indentured Servants in the Chesapeake

Indentured servants, who generally worked for tobacco farmers in seventeenth-century Maryland and Virginia, had little control over their lives. They could ask local courts or county councils, however, to intervene if they were severely abused. In Source 2.2 Sarah Tailer accuses her master and mistress of physical abuse. Although she did not win this case, evidence of repeated abuse led the court to free her two years later. In Source 2.3, the Virginia General Assembly (also known as the House of Burgesses) granted freedom to Elizabeth Key, the daughter of a white father and an enslaved mother. An Assembly Committee accepted Key's claim that she had been an indentured servant, not a slave.

Source 2.2

Sarah Tailer Charges Captain and Mrs. Thomas Bradnox with Abuse, 1659

A Court holden on Kent the first day of October 1659

Sarah Tailer Complaineth to the Majestrate mr Joseph [W]ickes of divers wronges & abuses given her by her Master and Mrs, Capt Thomas Bradnox & Mary his wife. . . .

John Jenkins sworne in Court Examined saith That he never saw Capt Bradnox or his wife strike his Servant Sarah Tailer with either Bulls pisle [whip] or Rope but he saw the said Sarah have a blacke place crosse one of her shoulders & this Deponent heard her Mrs give her som bad words. . . .

Tobias [W]ells on oath saith that he saw Sarah Tailer Stript & on her backe he saw severall blacke spotts and on her Arme a great black spott about as broad as his hand. . . .

Mr Joseph [W]ickes doth Informe the Court that Mrs Mary Bradnox broake the peace in strikeinge her Sarvant before him beinge a Majestrate, And on the time when the said Sarvant was there to make her Complaint which the said [M]r [W]ickes could not in Justice passe by or suffer, which was one blow or stroke with a Ropes ende.

Source: J. Hall Pleasants, ed., *Archives of Maryland*, vol. 54, *Proceedings of the County Courts of Kent, 1648–1676* (Baltimore: Maryland Historical Society, 1937), 167–69.

planters and maintaining the profitable deerskin trade with the Algonquian Indians. Frontier settlers' call for an aggressive Indian policy would hurt both.

Impatient frontiersmen refused to accept Berkeley's stance, and in late 1675, attacked Indians in the region. Unlike colonial leaders back east, frontier settlers generally considered all Indians hostile. Thus, rather than attacking only the Susquehannock, they also assaulted Indians allied with the English. Moreover, when local Virginia militiamen surrounded a Susquehannock village, they ignored pleas for peace and murdered five chiefs. Susquehannock warriors retaliated with raids on frontier farms. Amid this open warfare, Governor Berkeley still refused to send troops, and disgruntled farmers sought the leadership of Nathaniel Bacon. Bacon came from a wealthy family and was related to Berkeley by marriage. Yet he defied the governor's authority and called up an army to attack Indians across the colony. **Bacon's Rebellion** had begun. Frontier farmers formed an important part of Bacon's coalition; but affluent planters who had been left out of Berkeley's inner circle also joined Bacon in hopes of gaining access to power and profits. Even many bound laborers, black and white, assumed that anyone who opposed the governor was on their side.

Report of a Committee of the Assembly Concerning the Freedom of Elizabeth Key, 1656

It appeareth to us that shee is the daughter of Thomas Key [a white planter] . . . by a fine imposed upon the said Thomas for getting her mother with Child. . . . That she hath bin by verdict of a Jury . . . in the County of Northumberland found to be free by several oaths. . . . That by the Comon Law the Child of a Woman slave begot by a freeman ought to bee free. That she hath bin long since Christened. . . . That Thomas Key sould her only for nine years to Col Higginson with several conditions to use her more Respectfully than a Comon servant or a slave. . . . For theise reasons, wee conceive the said Elizabeth ought to bee free and that her last Master should give her Corn and Cloathes and give her satisfaction for the time shee hath served longer then Shee ought to have done.

Source: "A Report of a Committee from the Assembly Concerning the Freedome of Elizabeth Key," in Warren M. Billings, ed., *The Old Dominion in the Seventeenth Century: A Documentary History of Virginia, 1609–1689* (Chapel Hill: University of North Carolina Press, 1975), 167.

Interpret the Evidence

1. What does the case of Sarah Tailer suggest about the ability of white indentured servants to use the courts to address their grievances?
2. How did the Northumberland County Court and the Assembly Committee justify granting freedom to Elizabeth Key?

Put It in Context

How do these court cases help us understand legal efforts in the 1660s to redefine the status of blacks and the gradual replacement of indentured servants with enslaved laborers thereafter?

In the summer of 1676, Governor Berkeley declared Bacon guilty of treason. Rather than waiting to be captured, Bacon led his army toward Jamestown. Berkeley then arranged a hastily called election to undercut the rebellion. Even though Berkeley rescinded the right of men without property to vote, Bacon's supporters won control of the House of Burgesses, and Bacon won new adherents. These included "news wives," lower-class women who spread information about oppressive conditions to aid the rebels. As Bacon's army marched across Virginia, his men plundered the plantations of Berkeley and his supporters. In September they reached Jamestown after the governor and his administration fled across Chesapeake Bay. The rebels burned the capital to the ground, victory seemingly theirs.

Only a month later, however, Bacon died of dysentery, and the movement he formed unraveled. Governor Berkeley quickly reclaimed power. He hanged twenty-three rebel leaders and incited his followers to plunder the estates of planters who had supported Bacon. But he could not undo the damage to Indian relations on the Virginia frontier. Bacon's army had killed or enslaved hundreds of once-friendly Indians and left behind a tragic and bitter legacy.

Another important consequence of the rebellion was that wealthy planters and investors realized the depth of frustration among poor whites willing to make common cause with their black counterparts. Having regained power, white planters worked to crush any such interracial alliance. Virginia legislators began to improve the conditions and rights of poor white settlers while imposing new restrictions on blacks. In 1672, in an effort to meet the growing demand for labor in the West Indies and the Chesapeake, King Charles II chartered the Royal African Company to carry enslaved Africans to North America.

Enslaved Indians from Virginia were also being shipped to the West Indies. That trade, which began in the mid-1600s, resulted from tribes like the Westos raiding other Indian communities and exchanging captives to the English for guns. By the 1660s, the Westos used their guns to prey on Indians further south who were still using bows and arrows. They sold these enslaved Indians to English traders in Charles Town, a thriving port in South Carolina. In 1682, Westos themselves were sold into slavery after being defeated by Shawnee Indians working for other Carolina traders.

The English Compete for West Indies Possessions.
While tobacco held great promise in Virginia, investors were eager to find other lucrative exports to increase profits via the Atlantic economy. Some turned their sights on the West Indies. In the 1620s, the English developed permanent settlements on St. Christopher, Barbados, and Nevis (Map 2.3). English migrants settled in especially large numbers in Barbados and brought in white indentured servants, many Irish and Scotch, to cultivate tobacco and cotton and raise livestock.

In the 1630s, falling tobacco prices resulted in economic stagnation on Barbados. By that time, however, a few planters were considering another avenue to wealth: sugarcane. English and European consumers absorbed as much sugar as the market could provide, but

Sugar Manufacturing in the West Indies   This seventeenth-century engraving, which was later colorized, depicts the use of enslaved labor in the production of sugar in the West Indies. The Dutch, English, and French used slaves to plant sugarcane and then cut, press, and boil it to produce molasses. The molasses was turned into rum and refined sugar, both highly profitable exports. Sarin Images/ Granger

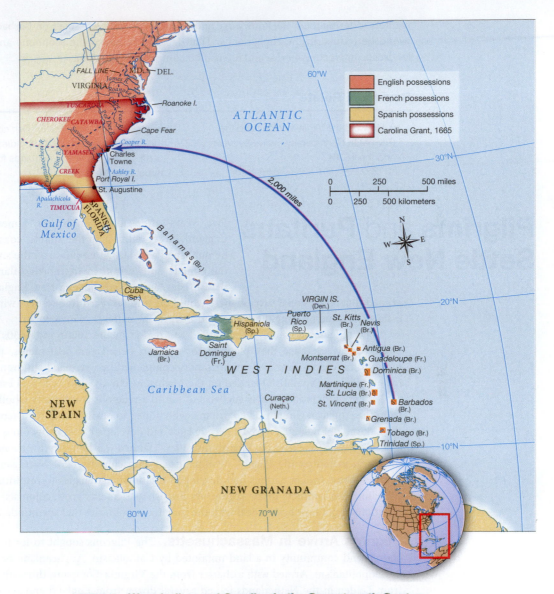

MAP 2.3 West Indies and Carolina in the Seventeenth Century

Beginning in the 1630s, sugar cultivation transformed West Indies colonies. The British consumed sugar in large quantities, ensuring the economic success of Barbados and its neighbors and a vast increase in the enslaved population. In the 1660s, Barbados planters obtained a charter for Carolina and sent many early settlers — white planters and merchants as well as enslaved laborers — to this mainland colony.

producing sugar was difficult, expensive, and labor-intensive. In addition, the sugar that was sent from America needed further refinement in Europe before being sold to consumers. The Dutch had built the best refineries in Europe, but their small West Indies colonies could not supply sufficient raw material. By 1640 they formed a partnership with English planters, offering them the knowledge and financing to cultivate sugar on Barbados, which would be refined in the Netherlands. That decision reshaped the economic and political landscape of North America and intensified competition for labor.

Review & Relate

■ How did the Virginia colony and the Powhatan Confederacy evolve between 1607 and the 1670s?

■ How did the growth of English colonies on the mainland and in the West Indies shape conflicts in Virginia and demands for labor throughout North America?

Pilgrims and Puritans Settle New England

Five years after John Smith left Jamestown for England, he set out to map the Atlantic coast. In 1616, he published a tract that emphasized the similarity of the climate and terrain in the north Atlantic to the British Isles, and called the area New England. Smith argued that commercial success there would depend on recruiting settlers with the necessary skills and offering them land and a say in the colony's management.

The religious dissenters who settled the region in the 1620s and 1630s embraced Smith's ideas. Because they planned to establish permanent settlements, their ships brought merchants, farmers, and artisans accompanied by wives and children. **Pilgrims** (also known as Separatists) landed on the Massachusetts coast in 1620 and established a settlement at Plymouth. Their goal was to found a religious community wholly separate from the Anglican Church. The Puritans, who hoped to purify rather than separate from the Church of England, arrived a decade later and developed their own colony in Massachusetts Bay. Yet the land the English dissenters claimed was home to diverse native communities, including the Pequot, Wampanoag, Massachusetts, and Narragansett. Over decades, these Indian nations had developed diplomatic strategies to minimize, though not eliminate, conflicts in the region. As English settlements grew, colonists, too, faced questions about how best to deal with the Indian communities that surrounded them.

Pilgrims Arrive in Massachusetts. The Pilgrims sought to form a separate church and community in a land untainted by Catholicism, Anglicanism, or European cosmopolitanism. Armed with a charter from the Virginia Company, thirty-five Pilgrims from Leiden in the Netherlands joined several dozen from England and set sail on the *Mayflower* in September 1620.

Battered by storms, the ship veered off course, landing at Cape Cod in present-day Massachusetts in early December. Before leaving the ship, the settlers, led by William Bradford, signed a pact to form a "civill body politick." This **Mayflower Compact**, which was the first written constitution adopted in North America, followed the Separatist model of a self-governing religious congregation.

After several forays along the coast, the Pilgrims located an uninhabited village surrounded by cornfields where they established their new home, Plymouth. Uncertain of native intentions, the Pilgrims were unsettled by sightings of Indians. They did not realize that a smallpox epidemic brought by English fishermen or European sailors had ravaged the area between 1616 and 1619, killing a large percentage of the local Indian population. Initially, fevers and other diseases proved deadly to the settlers as well. By the spring of 1621, only half of the original Pilgrims remained alive.

Desperate to find food, the survivors were stunned when two English-speaking Indians — Samoset (Abenaki) and Squanto (Patuxet) — appeared at Plymouth that March. Both had been captured as young boys by European explorers. Squanto showed them how to plant corn and where to fish. He also served as an interpreter and intermediary for Pilgrims, who negotiated a fragile peace with Massasoit, chief of the Wampanoag tribe. Although concerned by the power of English guns, Massasoit hoped to create an alliance that would assist him against his traditional native enemies. With Wampanoag assistance, the surviving Pilgrims soon regained their health.

In summer 1621, reinforcements arrived from England, and the next year the Pilgrims received a charter granting them rights to Plymouth Plantation and a degree of self-government. Although some Pilgrims hoped to convert the Indians, other leaders favored a more aggressive stance. One Indian nation, the Massachusetts, posed an especially serious threat. In 1623 Captain Miles Standish led an attack on its main village after kidnapping and killing the chief and his younger brother. Standish's strategy, though controversial, ensured that Massasoit, the colonists' Wampanoag ally, was now the most powerful chief in the region.

The Puritan Migration.

A new group of dissenters, the **Puritans**, was also making plans to develop an American settlement. Puritans believed that their country's church and government had grown corrupt and was being chastened by an all-powerful God. During the early seventeenth century, the English population boomed but harvests failed, leading to famine, crime, unemployment, and inflation. The enclosure movement, in which land-lords fenced in fields and hired a few laborers and tenants to replace a large number of peasant farmers, increased the number of landless vagrants. At the same time, the English cloth industry nearly collapsed under the weight of competition from abroad. In the Puritans' view, these problems were divine punishments for the nation's sins.

The Puritans envisioned New England as a safe haven from God's wrath. In 1623, affluent Puritans had received a royal charter for the Massachusetts Bay Company. Under Puritan lawyer John Winthrop's leadership, they made plans for their own North American colony. Unlike Pilgrims, Puritans believed that England and the Anglican Church could be redeemed. By prospering spiritually and materially in America, they could establish a model "City upon a Hill" that would inspire reform among residents of the mother country.

The Puritans who arrived in North America in 1630 were better supplied, more prosperous, and more numerous than both the Plymouth and Jamestown pioneers. The Puritans, who sailed on seventeen ships, included ministers, merchants, craftsmen, and farmers. Many arrived with their entire families. The community benefited from being well supplied and including substantial numbers of women who provided critical domestic and farm labor and ensured a high birthrate.

The first Puritan settlers arrived north of Plymouth in 1630 and named their community Boston, after the port city in England from which they had departed. Once established, they relocated the Massachusetts Bay Company's capital and records to New England, thereby converting their commercial charter into the founding document of a self-governing colony. They instituted a new kind of polity in which adult male church members participated in the election of a governor, deputy governor, and legislature.

Although the Puritans suffered a difficult first winter, they quickly recovered and soon cultivated sufficient crops to feed themselves and a steady stream of new migrants. During the 1630s, some eighteen thousand Puritans migrated to New England. Even without a cash crop like tobacco or sugar, their colony flourished.

Eager to take advantage of abundant land in the area, the close-knit community spread quickly beyond its original boundaries. Most Puritans sought friendly relations with local Indians, especially the Massachusetts, but this did not stop their expansion into native lands. As new settlements ringed the original at Boston, the legislature established townships with governing bodies that supported a local church and school. By the time the migration of Puritans slowed around 1640, Massachusetts Bay had become a thriving commercial center. They shipped codfish, lumber, grain, pork, and cheese to England in exchange for manufactured goods and to the West Indies for rum and molasses. This trade, along with a relatively healthy climate, and a fairly equal ratio of women to men, ensured a stable and prosperous colony.

The Puritans and Pilgrims also benefited from the smallpox epidemic of 1633–1634. Plymouth Governor William Bradford reported a mortality rate of 95 percent in some native villages, including the Pequot. This powerful tribe, located at the mouth of the Connecticut River, controlled the regional trade in wampum — strings of shells used in intertribal trade and diplomacy. Bradford considered the fact that the English were spared when the Pequot were not as the "marvelous goodnes and providens of God."

While Puritans were pleased that more land was now available for settlement, some sought to convert their Indian neighbors to Christianity. Puritan missionaries taught Indian pupils how to read the Bible, and a few exceptional students attended Harvard College, founded in 1636. Wawaus, a Nipmuck convert, was apprenticed to a printer and given the name James Printer. He eventually worked the first printing press in America, which was installed at the Harvard Indian College. In an effort to wean converts from their traditional customs and beliefs, missionary John Eliot created "praying towns," where Christian Indians could live among others who shared their faith. They were also protected from English settlers seeking to exploit them. As with other native converts, most "praying Indians" continued to embrace traditional rituals and beliefs alongside Christian practices.

The Puritan Worldview. Opposed to the lavish rituals and rigid hierarchy of the Church of England and believing that few Anglicans truly felt the grace of God, Puritans set out to establish a simpler form of worship. They focused on their inner lives and on the purity of their church and community. Puritans followed Calvin, believing in an all-knowing God whose true Word was presented in the Bible. The biblically sanctioned church was a congregation formed by a group of believers who made a covenant with God. Only a small minority of people, known as Saints, were granted God's grace.

Whether one was a Saint and thereby saved was predetermined by and known only to God. Still, some Puritans believed that the chosen were likely to lead a saintly life. Visible signs included a passionate response to the preaching of God's Word, a sense of doubt and despair over one's soul, and that wonderful sense of reassurance that came with God's "saving grace." God's hand in the world appeared in nature as well. Comets and eclipses, as well as epidemics, were considered "remarkable providences."

Shared religious beliefs helped forge a unified community where faith guided civil as well as spiritual decisions. While ministers were discouraged from holding political office, political leaders were devout Puritans who were expected to promote a godly society.

Mrs. Elizabeth Freake and Baby Mary This anonymous 1674 portrait shows Elizabeth Freake, the wife of merchant John Freake, and their eighth child. Large families helped ensure Puritan expansion and financial success. Here Elizabeth and her daughter capture Puritan simplicity in their white head coverings and aprons. But they display their family's wealth and John Freake's commercial ties through their silk gowns and embroidered cloth. Bridgeman Images

Leaders and most followers believed in a hierarchical society. In determining who got land and how much, Puritan leaders assured that wealthier families would continue to thrive. These men also served as judge and jury for those accused of crimes or sins. Their leadership was largely successful, yet almost from the beginning, some Puritans challenged fundamental aspects of religious teachings and, in the process, the community itself.

Dissenters Challenge Puritan Authority. In the early 1630s, Roger Williams, a Salem minister, criticized Puritan leaders for not being sufficiently pure in their rejection of the Church of England and the English monarchy. Embracing separatist views, he moved to Plymouth, but soon criticized their relation to the Church of England as well. He also attacked the king and the royal charter, convinced that colonists should only gain land in New England through legitimate purchase from the various Indian tribes. Returning to Salem in 1633, Williams soon set off a conflict between Salem and the General Court over whether he should be allowed to preach given his claims about the church, the king, and the

Explore ▸

Explore two perspectives on North American colonies as models of Britain and models for America in Secondary Sources 2.4 and 2.5.

charter. In October 1635, the General Court finally banished Williams from Massachusetts Bay because of his "diverse, new and dangerous ideas." He moved south with a dozen followers, eventually buying land from the Narragansetts and establishing the community of Providence in an area beyond the bounds of the royal charter. He forged an alliance with the Narragansett, the most powerful nation in the region, that lasted forty years. Williams and his followers insisted on "liberty of conscience" and a clear separation of church and state. Thus, unlike Massachusetts Bay, Providence welcomed Quakers and Jews to the community and also became home to the first Baptist church in America.

A year after Williams's departure, Anne Hutchinson was accused of sedition, or trying to overthrow the government by challenging colonial leaders. She was put on trial in November 1637. An eloquent orator, Hutchinson ultimately claimed that her authority to

Colonial Models of and for English Society

From the late nineteenth century to the 1970s, most historians of colonial North America argued that New England offered a closer model *of* the home country, England, than did other colonies and that it served as an important model *for* American society generally. In the 1980s and 1990s, scholars such as Jack Greene claimed instead that the colonial Chesapeake more closely mirrored not only seventeenth-century English society but also England's other colonies in Ireland and the West Indies. They noted that the focus on New England, where the number of enslaved persons was far smaller than elsewhere in the British colonies, allowed colonial historians to marginalize the role of slavery in American society. Alan Taylor is among a younger generation of scholars who acknowledge the distinctiveness of New England's colonial development but highlight the importance of Puritan ideals and prosperity to Euro-American society. However, these historians also acknowledge the darker sides of Puritan life.

Source 2.4

Jack P. Greene | The Chesapeake as Model of and for English Society, 1988

As long as they could continue to believe that New England, the region of colonial British America in which black slavery was least well entrenched, was indeed the most direct and important source of later American sociocultural patterns, historians could continue to perpetuate the comforting illusion that slavery . . . had never been central to American culture but had always only been a marginal institution confined to the cultural peripheries of the colonial British American world. . . .

[Yet] between 1630 and 1660, the Chesapeake colonies represented a much closer approximation of old England than did the puritan colonies of Connecticut and Massachusetts Bay. . . .

In its permissiveness, lack of social cohesion, . . . slowly developing community spirit, religious pluralism, secular orientation, competitiveness,

acquisitiveness, high levels of property concentration, . . . reliance upon dependent servant labor, treatment of labor as a disposable commodity, mobility, strong orientation for large-scale production for the market . . . , Chesapeake society reflected, and in only a few instances to an exaggerated degree, characteristics that were deeply and undeniably English. . . .

Chesapeake society before 1660 exhibited impulses and social and cultural configurations that were broadly representative of those in the first generations of settlement all over the early modern English world — with the notable exception of the orthodox New England colonies.

Source: Jack P. Greene, *Pursuits of Happiness: The Social Development of Early Modern British Colonies and the Formation of American Culture.* (Chapel Hill: University of North Carolina Press, 1988), 35–36, 53.

challenge Puritan leaders came from "an immediate revelation" from God, "the voice of his own spirit to my soul." Since Puritans believed that God spoke only through the intermediary of properly appointed male ministers, her claim was condemned as heretical.

Hutchinson was seen as a threat not only because of her religious beliefs but also because she was a woman. The Reverend Hugh Peter, for example, reprimanded her at trial: "You have stept out of your place, you have rather bine a Husband than a Wife and a preacher than a Hearer; and a Magistrate than a Subject." Many considered her challenge to

Source 2.5

Alan Taylor | New England Puritans Develop Anglo-American Ideals, 2001

The Puritans understood in spiritual terms many causes that we might define as "economic." They interpreted the wandering beggars, increased crime, cloth trade depression, and famine [in England] as divine afflictions meant to punish a guilty land that wallowed in sin. . . .

To redeem their hope for a brighter future, many Puritans sought a distant refuge. . . .

By colonial standards, New England attracted an unusual set of emigrants. . . . Most seventeenth-century English emigrants were poor young single men who lacked prospects in the mother country. Seeking regular meals in the short term and a farm in the long, they gambled their lives as indentured servants in the Chesapeake or the West Indies. In contrast, most of the New England colonists could pay their own way and emigrated as family groups. . . .

Compared with other colonial regions, New England was a land of relative equality, broad (albeit moderate) opportunity, and thrifty, industrious, and entrepreneurial habits that sustained an especially diverse and complex economy. . . . And nowhere else in colonial America did colonists enjoy readier access to public worship and nearly universal education. That those ideals remain powerful in our own culture attests to the enduring importance of the Puritan legacy. But those accomplishments also had a dark side, especially the intolerance of dissenters. . . . And, . . . the pursuit of Puritan ideals and Puritan prosperity depended upon dispossessing the Indians and transforming their land.

Source: Alan Taylor, *American Colonies: The Settling of North America*. (New York: Penguin Books, 2001), 167, 169, and 186.

Examine the Secondary Sources

1. How do Green and Taylor understand the relationship of the Chesapeake and New England colonies, respectively, to England? To British North America?
2. Based on the descriptions offered by Green and Taylor, which elements of Chesapeake and New England society are most similar to Great Britain and which are most characteristic of British North America?

Put It in Context

Were differences between English colonies greater than differences among English, French, and Dutch colonies? How did European colonies, taken together, differ from the Indian tribes and confederacies among whom they settled?

Puritan authority more serious because she also challenged traditional gender hierarchies. Once banished, Hutchinson and her followers joined Williams's Rhode Island colony.

Wars in Old and New England. Alongside confrontations with Anne Hutchinson and Roger Williams, Puritans faced threats from their Indian neighbors. The Pequot nation had been allies of the English for several years but increasingly protested colonists' continued expansion into their territory. Some Puritans feared they "would cause all the

Indians in the country to join to root out all the English." With the Pequot weakened by smallpox, English leaders used the death of two Englishmen in 1636 to justify a military expedition against them. The Narragansett, who were rivals of the Pequot, allied with the English in the **Pequot War**. After months of bloody conflict, the English and their Indian allies launched a brutal attack on a palisaded Pequot village in May 1637 that left some four hundred men, women, and children dead. At the Treaty of Hartford in 1638, the English stripped the decimated tribe of their sovereignty and their name.

Puritans in England were soon engaged in armed conflict as well, against other Englishmen. Differences over religion, taxation, and royal authority had strained relations between Protestants in Parliament and the crown for decades, as James I (r. 1603–1625) and his son Charles I (r. 1625–1649) sought to consolidate their own power at Parliament's expense. In 1642 the relationship between Parliament and King Charles I broke down completely, and the country descended into civil war. Puritan Oliver Cromwell emerged as the leader of the Protestant parliamentary forces, and after several years of fighting, he claimed victory. Charles I was executed, Parliament established a republican commonwealth, and bishops and elaborate rituals were banished from the Church of England. Cromwell ruled England as a military dictator until his death in 1658. By then, much of England had tired of religious conflict and Puritan rule, so Charles I's son, Charles II (r. 1660–1685), was invited to return from exile on the continent and restore the monarchy and the Church of England. In 1660, when Charles II acceded to the throne, the Puritans recognized that their only hope for building a godly republic lay in North America.

During the civil war of the 1640s, English settlements had grown rapidly as a result of both natural increase and migration. Taking control of more and more native lands, English communities stretched from Connecticut through Massachusetts and Rhode Island and north to Maine. Colonial governments began establishing fortified towns along their northern frontier to serve as a buffer between the French and Indians, on one side, and southern English towns, including Boston, on the other. Despite their military purpose, the towns were settled by families. Male inhabitants worked on the town's defenses and served in local militias. However, when fighting erupted, women also took up arms, and all residents were at risk of being wounded, killed, or captured.

The English king and Parliament, embroiled in war at home, paid little attention to events in North America, allowing these New England colonies to develop with little oversight. In 1664, after the restoration of the monarchy, the English wrested control of New Amsterdam from the Dutch and renamed it New York. A decade later, the English could claim dominance—in population, trade, and politics—over other European powers vying for empires along the northern Atlantic coast.

The spread of English control was still contested, however, by diverse Indian groups. In 1651, Plymouth leaders tried to force the elderly Wampanoag chief Massasoit, their longtime ally, to grant them lands along the Ktetit (later Taunton) River. He refused, declaring that only Weetamoo, his kinswoman and the "Squa Sachem" of that region, could authorize such a grant. Weetamoo, like Anne Hutchison, challenged English assumptions about gender roles and refused to bow to the will of English authorities. She married Massasoit's son, Wamsutta, and became sister-in-law to Metacom, another Wampanoag leader. But she still retained power over the territory she brought to this family alliance.

Numbers, however, were on the side of the English. Only 15,000 to 16,000 native people remained in New England by 1670, a loss of some 80 percent over fifty years. Meanwhile the English population reached more than 50,000. In 1671 the English at Plymouth demanded that the Wampanoag, who had been their allies since the 1620s, surrender their guns and be ruled by English law. Instead, many Indians hid their weapons and, over the next several years, raided frontier farms and killed some settlers. English authorities responded by hanging three Wampanoag men, and tightening their frontier defenses.

In 1662, Metacom, called King Philip by the English, became chief of the Wampanoag. Initially, he continued friendly relations with Puritans. But their efforts to continually expand into Wampanoag and other Indian territories angered him. By 1675, he argued that Europeans must be forced out of the region if Indians were to survive. As conflicts erupted between Indians and colonists that fall, Metacom and his party took refuge with the widowed Weetamoo. The English insisted that Metacom/King Philip had initiated the war but were convinced they could win an easy victory. Nonetheless, the General Court declared that residents of fortified towns—women and men—must not flee but remain "for the defence of such places." Metacom's forces allied with Nipmucks and smaller groups of other Algonquian-speaking communities, attacking fortified towns and outlying villages. They also launched assaults on Plymouth and Providence and marched within twenty miles of Boston. While the Narragansett had declared their neutrality early in the war, they offered sanctuary to noncombatants from warring tribes. As a result, their long-time English allies declared war on them in November 1675.

As the conflict continued into 1676, it became increasingly brutal. That February, Wampanoag attacked the town of Lancaster and took captives, including Mary Rowlandson and her children. They then marched into the Great Swamp, where Indians fled to regroup, and Rowlandson was assigned to work for Weetamoo. The English meanwhile allied with remnants of the Pequot along with Mohawks and Mohegans. Metacom and the Wampanoag pushed west, hoping to ally with more powerful tribes like the Mohawk. Instead the Mohawk attacked the Wampanoag while English, Pequot, and Mohegan forces ambushed the Narragansett and attacked enemy villages, killing hundreds of Indians and selling hundreds more into slavery in the West Indies. **See Primary Source Project 2: King Philip's War, page 66.**

Attacks on colonial towns and Indian villages continued into 1676. That August, English troops finally killed Metacom, but the war continued. The remaining Wampanoag, Narragansett, and Nipmuck moved north and west, seeking aid from other Indians as they ran short of men, guns, and food. Finally, the Treaty of Casco Bay ended the war in April 1678.

While some 1,000 English settlers were killed and dozens were taken captive during the war, Indian losses were even more catastrophic. Food shortages and disease combined with military deaths to kill at least 4,000 men, women, and children, about a quarter of the remaining Indian population of New England. Indian power in southern New England collapsed as survivors moved north and gradually intermarried with tribes allied with the French. After the carnage spilled into New York, Iroquois leaders and colonists met at Albany in 1677 to salvage their lucrative fur trade. Forming an alliance to forestall future conflicts, they ensured that furs and land would continue to define the complex relations between Indians and Europeans across the northern colonies.

Review & Relate

■ How did Puritan religious views shape New England's development?

■ Why did conflict between New England settlers and the region's Indians escalate over the course of the seventeenth century and with what consequences?

Conclusion: European Empires in **North America**

When Powhatan died in 1618, English, French and Dutch efforts to colonize North America had barely begun. Over the next seventy years, those efforts would look very different from the Spanish conquest they initially hoped to replicate. Powhatan's efforts to bring Jamestown under his control or into a productive alliance collapsed because English success required permanent settlement, abundant land, and sufficient laborers. Alliances with Indians were important for French, Dutch, and English colonists along the Atlantic coast. But they were constantly undermined by European expansion and the need for cheap labor. Success in the burgeoning Atlantic economy—whether through tobacco, sugar, or furs and whether led by commercial interests or religious dissenters—depended as importantly on economic ties and political alliances (or conflicts) back home. Success also often required that European women and men rethink their economic and social roles, adapting to conditions in North America.

European colonists found different ways to prosper in Virginia, Canada, New England, and New Amsterdam, but they still faced daunting choices. Most important, should they create alliances with local Indians for sustenance and trade, or should they seek to dominate them and take what they needed? John Smith, Miles Standish, and many other colonial leaders supported an aggressive policy, much like that of Spain. However, some Europeans in New England, New Amsterdam, and Canada advocated a less violent approach. Many French Jesuit priests and Puritans like Roger Williams focused on the spiritual and material benefits of conversion. Far more argued that building alliances was the most effective means of advancing trade and gaining land, furs, and other goods valued by Europeans. Conflicts over religious beliefs and government support for frontier settlers also created divisions among European settlers. The banishment of Anne Hutchinson from Massachusetts Bay in 1636 and the response to Bacon's Rebellion in Virginia in 1676 revealed the lengths to which colonial leaders would go to protect their power and authority.

Such internal divisions were often intertwined with or overwhelmed by conflicts with Indians. Although English, Dutch, and French colonists profited from trade relations and military alliances with Indian nations, conflicts and wars repeatedly erupted along the Atlantic Coast. European settlers fought the Powhatan Confederacy in the 1620s and 1640s, the Pequot in the 1630s, Algonquian-speaking tribes in New Netherland in the 1640s, and the Susquehannock in Virginia and the Wampanoag and Narragansett in New England in the 1670s. While the French did not go to war with their Huron allies, they left them to fight alone against the Iroquois when the fur trade moved west. The exhaustion of furs along the Atlantic coast increased the vulnerability of other Indian communities as well. Devastated by European-borne diseases and without valuable items to trade, their very survival was at stake. Indians in New Amsterdam as well as New England resisted the many losses they suffered, often with violence. Anne Hutchinson and her six youngest children had moved to the outer reaches of New Netherland in 1642 after the death of her husband. A year later, she and five of her children were killed by Indians in response to Governor William Kieft's slaughter of peaceful Indians in the region.

As European settlements expanded beyond the Atlantic coast in the late seventeenth century, their prosperity continued to depend on trade goods and land that were often in Indian hands. At the same time, a growing demand for labor led wealthier settlers to seek an increased supply of indentured servants from Europe and enslaved workers from Africa. Over the next half century, relations between settlers and Indians, between wealthy and poor settlers, between whites and blacks, and among European nations vying for empires would grow even more complicated and conflicted.

Timeline of Events

1517	Protestant Reformation begins
1530s	England breaks with the Roman Catholic Church
1545–1563	Council of Trent
1598	Acoma pueblo uprising, Edict of Nantes
1607	Jamestown founded
1608	French settle in Quebec
1609	Dutch settle on the Hudson River
1612–1614	Tobacco cultivation begins in Virginia
1619	First Africans arrive in Virginia
1620	Pilgrims found Plymouth settlement
1622	Powhatan Confederacy attack Virginia colonists
1624	Dutch establish New Amsterdam
1630	Puritans found Massachusetts Bay colony
1632	Maryland founded
1635	Roger Williams moves to Rhode Island
1636–1637	Pequot War
1637	Anne Hutchinson banished from Massachusetts Bay colony
1642–1649	English civil war
1643-1645	Governor Kieft's war against Indians in New Netherland
1644	War between Powhatan Confederacy and Virginia colonists
1660	Monarchy restored in England
1660–1664	Virginia and Maryland establish lifelong, inherited slavery
1664	Dutch surrender New Amsterdam to the English
1675–1676	King Philip's War
1676	Bacon's Rebellion

Key Terms

Protestantism, *39*

Church of England, *40*

Atlantic economy, *42*

metis, *43*

Jamestown, *47*

Powhatan Confederacy, *47*

House of Burgesses, *49*

indentured servants, *49*

Bacon's Rebellion, *52*

Pilgrims, *56*

Mayflower Compact, *56*

Puritans, *57*

Pequot War, *62*

King Philip's War, *63*

Review & Relate

1. How did the Protestant Reformation and Catholic Counter-Reformation shape the course of European expansion in the Americas?

2. How did the French and Dutch colonies in North America differ from the Spanish empire to the south, and how were these differences shaped by Indian nations?

3. How did the Virginia colony and the Powhatan Confederacy evolve between 1607 and the 1670s?

4. How did the growth of the English colonies on the mainland and in the West Indies shape conflicts in Virginia and demands for labor throughout North America?

5. How did Puritan religious views shape New England's development?

6. Why did conflict between New England settlers and the region's Indians escalate over the course of the seventeenth century and with what consequences?

King Philip's War

▶ How does King Philip's War illuminate differences among Indians and among the English as well as those between the Indians and the English?

Tensions between Indians and colonists in New England periodically flared into open warfare. In the 1660s those tensions escalated once again. Metacom, also known as King Philip, became grand sachem of the Wampanoag in 1662. Especially troubled by English encroachments on native lands, he forged an alliance that brought together two-thirds of the region's Indian population. While the Narragansett sought to remain neutral, Metacom's New England Confederation coordinated attacks on outlying settlements, burning fields, taking captives, and killing colonists.

In 1675 Indian attacks on New England towns escalated, and the English then captured Indians and sold them into slavery (Source 2.6). As the situation deteriorated, the Rhode Island colony sent representatives to meet with King Philip in June. Some colonists and Indian leaders also met independently (Sources 2.7 and 2.8). However, these diplomatic efforts failed as Indians sought preservation and English sought domination. In September, the New England Confederation, which included English colonies in Massachusetts and Connecticut, declared war. Fighting continued for more than a year, leading to the deaths of 1,000 colonists and more than 4,000 Indians. Edward Randolph, a customs agent, criticized both colonists and Indians for their parts in the conflict (Source 2.9). The English finally gained the upper hand in August 1676 with the help of Indian allies. Soldiers led by Captain Benjamin Church ambushed Metacom/King Philip near Bristol, Rhode Island, and killed him. To the English, the death of King Philip signaled the end of the war, but conflicts between colonists and native communities continued for years. In 1682 Mary Rowlandson published an account of her captivity, which was widely read by New Englanders (Source 2.10).

Because there are fewer Indian sources, historians have struggled to develop a balanced picture of the war. William Nahaton (Source 2.6) provides the view of a Christianized Indian, and other documents offer information about Indian perceptions of the war even though written by the English.

Source 2.6

William Nahaton | Petition to Free an Indian Slave, 1675

The English sold a number of Indians into slavery before and during King Philip's War. Many English colonists petitioned the government of Massachusetts Bay to stop this practice as did Indians. William Nahaton, an Indian who had embraced Christianity, sent this petition to convince colonial leaders to release a relative who was about to be sold into slavery in the West Indies.

To the honored counsel now siting at boston to the humble petition of william [n]ahaton hee humbly sheweth.

I have seing a woman taken by the mohegins and now brought to boston which woman although she did belong to [King] phillip his Company yet shee is a kinn to me and all so to john hunter as severall of the indians of punkapoag do know[.] my humble and right request there fore to the Renowned Counsel is that if it may stand with there pleasure and with out furtur inconvenience her Life may be spared and her Liberty granted under such conditions as the honored Counsel see most fit: shee being a woman whatever her mind hath been it is very probable she hath not dun much mischefe and if the honored counsel shall plese so grant me that favor I shall understand to leve her at punkapoag[.] . . . I shall obtaine so much favor from the honored counsel which will further oblige him who is your honored to command william [n]ahaton.

Source: Massachusetts State Archives, Massachusetts Archives, Series 45X, Vol. 176.

Benjamin Church | A Visit with Awashonks, Sachem of the Sakonnet, 1716

Benjamin Church was an aide to Plymouth governor Josiah Winslow and a captain in the militia. In 1674 he built on land claimed by sachems Weetamoo and Awashonks. English leaders tried, but failed, to acquire clear title to these lands. In June 1675 Church and Awashonks met in her Sakonnet community. While Church insisted King Philip was preparing for war, he did not mention the English were doing the same. He urged Awashonks to put her people under English protection. Once war erupted, Awashonks sought protection with the Narragansett, who sought to remain neutral. Captain Church's company led many raids and eventually killed Metacom. In 1716 Church's son, Thomas, published his father's memoir, *Entertaining Account of King Philip's War.*

The next Spring advancing, while Mr. Church was diligently settling his new Farm, stocking, leasing, and disposing of his Affairs, and had a fine prospect of doing no small things; and hoping that his good success would be inviting unto other good Men to become his Neighbours; Behold! The rumor of a War between the English and the Natives gave check to his projects. People began to be very jealous of the Indians, and indeed they had no small reason to suspect that they had form'd a design of War upon the English. Mr. Church had it daily suggested to him that the Indians were plotting a bloody design. That Philip the great Mount-hope Sachem was leader therein: and so it prov'd, he was sending his Messengers to all the Neighbouring Sachems, to ingage them in a Confederacy with him in the War.

Among the rest he sent Six Men to Awashonks Squaw-Sachem of the Sogkonate [Sakonnet] Indians, to engage her in his Interests: Awashonks so far listened unto them as to call her Subjects together, to make a great Dance, which is the custom of that Nation when they advise about Momentous Affairs. But what does Awashonks do, but sends away two of her Men that well understood the English Language . . . to invite Mr. Church to the Dance. Mr. Church upon the Invitation, immediately takes with him Charles Hazelton his Tennants Son, who well understood the Indian Language, and rid [rode] down to the Place appointed: Where they found hundreds of Indians gathered together from all Parts of her Dominion. Awashonks her self in a foaming Sweat was leading the Dance. But she was no sooner sensible of Mr. Churches arrival, but she broke off, sat down, calls her Nobles round her, orders Mr. Church to be invited into her presence. Complements being past, and each one taking Seats. She told him, King Philip had sent Six Men of his with two of her People that had been over at Mount-hope, to draw her into a confederacy with him in a War with the English. . . .

Then Mr. Church turn'd to Awashonks, and told her, if Philip were resolv'd to make War, her best way would be to knock those Six Mount-hopes on the head, and shelter her self under the Protection of the English: upon which the Mount-hopes were for the present Dumb. . . .

Then he told Awashonks he thought it might be most advisable for her to send to the Governour of Plymouth, and shelter her self, and People under his Protection. She lik'd his advice, and desired him to go on her behalf to the Plymouth Government, which he consented to: And at parting advised her what ever she did, not to desert the English Interest, to joyn with her Neighbours in a Rebellion which would certainly prove fatal to her. He mov'd none of his Goods from his House that there might not be the least umbrage from such an Action. She thank'd him for his advice, and sent two of her Men to guard him to his House; which when they came there, urged him to take care to secure his Goods, which he refused for the reasons before mentioned. But desired the Indians that if what they feared should happen, they would take care of what he left, and directed them to a Place in the woods where they should dispose them; which they faithfully observed.

Source: Benjamin Church, *The History of King Philip's War* (Boston: John Kimball Wiggin, 1865), 5–11.

Source: John Easton, "A Relation of the Indian War," in *A Narrative of the Causes Which Led to Philip's Indian War, of 1675 and 1676* (Albany: J. Munsell, 1858), 13–15.

Source 2.8

John Easton | A Relation of the Indian War, 1675

As conflicts between English settlers and Indians intensified, a meeting was arranged for June 1675 between Metacom and John Easton, attorney general of the Rhode Island colony. At this meeting, Metacom related the Indians' many complaints, which included the sale of liquor to Indians, the destruction of their crops, and their mistreatment under the colonial justice system. The meeting was unsuccessful in preventing further violence, and by the end of the month King Philip's War erupted.

Another Grievance was, when their King sold Land, the English would say, it was more than they agreed to, and a Writing must be prove against all them, and some of their Kings had dun Rong [done wrong] to sell so much. He left his Peopell [people] none, and some being given to Drunknes the English made them drunk and then cheated them in Bargains, but now their Kings were forewarned not for to part with Land, for nothing in Comparison to the Value thereof. Now home [some] the English had owned for King or Queen, they would disinherit, and make another King that would give or sell them these Lands; that now they had no Hopes left to keep any Land. Another Grievance, the English Catell [cattle] and Horses still increased; that when they removed 30 Miles from where English had any thing to do, they could not keep their Corn from being spoiled, they never being used to fence, and thought when the English bought Land of them they would have kept their Catell upon their owne Land. Another Grievance, the English were so eager to sell the Indians Lickers [liquor], that most of the Indians spent all in Drunknes, and then ravened upon the sober Indians, and they did believe often did hurt the English Cattel, and their King could not prevent it.

Source 2.9

Edward Randolph | Report on the War, 1676

Edward Randolph was an English customs official sent to the colonies to investigate colonial compliance with English laws. He criticized the Puritan colonies for pursuing political autonomy, like coining money and administering their own oath of allegiance, and called for greater control by Parliament. Randolph's reports to his superiors in London also described the outbreak of violence in 1676. He reported what he saw as the causes of the war, criticizing the actions of both colonists and Indians.

Various are the reports and conjectures of the causes of the late Indian wars. Some impute it to an imprudent zeal in the magistrates of Boston to Christianize those heathens, before they were civilized, and enjoining them to the strict observation of their laws, which, to people so rude and licentious hath proved even intolerable; and that the more, for while the magistrates, for their profit, severely put the laws in execution against the Indians, the people on the other side, for lucre [money] and gain, intice and provoke the Indians to the breach thereof, especially to drunkenness, to which these people are so generally addicted, that they will strip themselves to the skin to have their fill of rum and brandy.

The Massachusetts government having made a law that every Indian being drunk should pay ten shillings or be whipped, according to the discretion of the magistrate, many of these poor people willingly offered their backs to the lash, to save their money. Upon the magistrate finding much trouble and no profit to arise to the government by whipping, did change that punishment of the whip into ten days' work, for such as would not or could not pay the fine of ten shillings; which did highly incense the Indians. . . .

Others impute the cause to arise from some injuries offered to the Sachem Philip; for he being possessed of a tract of land called Mount Hope, a very fertile, pleasant and rich soil, some English had a mind to dispossess him thereof, who, never wanting some pretence or other to attain their ends, complained of injuries done by Philip and his Indians to their stock and cattle. Whereupon the Sachem [King] Philip was often summoned to appear before the magistrates, sometimes imprisoned, and never released but upon parting with a considerable part of his lands.

But the government of the Massachusetts . . . do declare [the following acts] are the great and provoking evils which God hath given the barbarous heathen commission to rise against them: . . .

For men wearing long hair and perriwigs made of women's hair.

For women wearing borders of hair and cutting, curling and laying out their hair and disguising themselves by following strange fashions in their apparel.

For profaneness of the people in not frequenting their [church] meetings, and others going away before the blessing is pronounced.

For suffering the Quakers to dwell among them, and to set up their thresholds by God's thresholds, contrary to their old laws and resolutions, with many such reasons.

But whatever was the cause, the English have contributed very much to their misfortunes, for they first taught the Indians the use of arms and admitted them to be present at all their musters and trainings, and showed them how to handle, mend and fix their muskets, and have been constantly furnished with all sorts of arms by permission of the government, so that the Indians are become excellent fire-men.

Source: John Norris McClintock, *History of New Hampshire* (Boston: B. B. Russell, 1888), 79–80.

Source 2.10

Mary Rowlandson | Narrative of Captivity, 1682

In February 1675, the Wampanoag and their allies attacked Lancaster, Massachusetts, set fire to the town and killed many residents. Mary Rowlandson and her three children were captured and forced to flee with the Wampanoag. During her captivity, Rowlandson labored as a servant for Weetamoo, the "Squa Sachem." Six-year-old Sarah Rowlandson died, but Mary and two other children survived. They were ransomed after eleven weeks and reunited with their family. After the war, Rowlandson published an account of her captivity that highlighted the ways her Puritan faith helped her survive the ordeal. The Nipmuck convert James Printer set the type for the book, which became one of the most popular publications of its era.

Upon a *Friday*, a little after noon we came to this River. When all the company was come up, and were gathered together, I thought to count the number of them, but they were so many, and being somewhat in motion, it was beyond my skil. In this travel, because of my wound, I was somewhat favored in my load; I carried only my knitting work and two quarts of parched meal: Being very faint I asked my mistress to give me one spoonfull of the meal, but she would not give me a taste. They quickly fell to cutting dry trees, to make Rafts to carry them over the river: and soon my turn came to go over: By the advantage of some brush which they had laid upon the Raft to sit upon, I did not wet my foot (which many of themselves at the other end were mid-leg deep) which cannot but be acknowledged as a favour of God to my weakened body, it being a very cold time. I was not before acquainted with such kind of doings or dangers. *When thou passeth through the waters I will be with thee, and through the rivers they shall not overflow thee*, Isai. 43.2. A certain number of us got over the River that night, but it was the night after the Sabbath before all the company was got over. On the *Saturday* they boyled [boiled] an old Horses leg which they had got, and so we drank of the broth, as soon as they thought it was ready, and when it was almost all gone, they filled it up again.

The first week of my being among them, I hardly ate any thing; the second week, I found my stomach grow very faint for want of something; and yet it was very hard to get down their filthy trash: but the third week, though I could think how formerly my stomach would turn against this or that, and I could starve or die before I could eat such things, yet they were sweet and savory to my taste. I was at this time knitting a pair of white cotton stockins for my mistriss [Weetamoo] and had not yet wrought upon a Sabbath day; when the Sabbath came they bade me go to work; I told them it was the Sabbath-day, and desired them to let me rest, and told them I would do as much more tomorrow; to which they answered me, they would break my face. And here I cannot but take notice of the strange providence of God in preserving the heathen: They were many hundreds, old and young, some sick, and some lame, many had *Papooses* [infants] at their backs, the greatest number at this time with us, were *Squaws*, and they travelled with all they had, bag and baggage, and yet they got over this River aforesaid; and on *Munday* they set their *Wigwams* on fire, and away they went: On that very day came the English Army after them to this River, and saw the smoak of their *Wigwams*, and yet this River put a stop to them. God did not give them courage or activity to go over after us; we were not ready for so great a mercy as victory and deliverance; if we had been, God would have found out a way for the *English* to have passed this River, as well as for the *Indians* with their *Squaws* and *Children*, and all their Luggage. . . .

On Munday *(as I said) they set their* Wigwams *on fire, and went away.* It was a cold morning, and before us there was a great Brook with ice on it; some waded through it, up to the knees & higher, but others went till they came to a Beaver dam, and I amongst them, where through the good providence of God, I did not wet my foot. I went along that day mourning and lamenting, leaving farther my own Country, and travelling into the vast and howling *Wilderness*, and I understood something of *Lot's* Wife's Temptation, *when she looked back.* We came that day to a great Swamp, by the side of which we took up our lodging that night. When I came to the brow of the hill, that looked toward the Swamp, I thought we had been come to a great *Indian* Town (though there were none but our own Company). The *Indians* were as thick as the trees: it seemed as if there had been a thousand Hatchets going at once: if one looked before one, there was nothing but *Indians*, and behind one, nothing but *Indians*, and so on either hand, I my self in the midst, and no Christian soul near me, *and yet how hath the Lord preserved me in safety! Oh the experience that I have had of the goodness of God, to me and mine!*

Source: Henry S. Nourse, ed., *The Narrative of the Captivity and the Restoration of Mrs. Mary Rowlandson* (Lancaster, MA, 1903), 17–20.

Interpret the Evidence

1. What does William Nahaton's petition (Source 2.6) reveal about English leaders' main goal when dealing with the Indians, Christian and non-Christian?

2. What types of complaints did the Wampanoag have against the English, and which seem the most grievous (Sources 2.7, 2.8, and 2.9)? What do these complaints reveal about how colonists viewed the Wampanoag?

3. What motivated Benjamin Church to meet with Awashonks (Source 2.7)? What does his account suggest about the difficult choices faced by Indians and colonists as conflicts escalated?

4. What does Edward Randolph's description of the causes of the war (Source 2.9) reveal about how the conflict was viewed by Englishmen who were not colonists? How do his perceptions compare with those of Benjamin Church and John Easton (Sources 2.7 and 2.8)?

5. How does Mary Rowlandson employ religion to explain the events that happen to her during her captivity (Source 2.10)? What does the enormous popularity of her book indicate about the place of religion and of Indians in New England in the 1680s?

Put It in Context

King Philip's War was one of the bloodiest in American history. From these documents, how do you explain its ferocity?

What does the war and its outcome suggest about the trajectory of Indian-English relations from 1620 to 1680?

Colonial America amid Global Change

1680–1754

Enslaved Blacks Working on a Tobacco Plantation, c. 1750

In the mid-eighteenth century, an unknown artist drew this picture of tobacco farmers and enslaved laborers. The London printers Bowles and Carver sold it as a cheap penny print. A valuable colonial export, tobacco was embedded in the popular imagination and the Atlantic economy. Farmers took out loans to ship tobacco via wholesalers in Charleston or New Orleans and to pay merchants in London for its sale. The resulting loans were repaid with profits from those sales, profits that also underwrote the purchase of enslaved laborers from the West Indies. ▶ **To learn more about this primary source, see Source 3.8 on page 104.**

Peter Newark American Pictures/Bridgeman Images

After reading this chapter you will be able to:

- Compare the development of Spanish, French, and English colonies from the late sixteenth to the mid-seventeenth century.

- Analyze the effects of European wars on relations among different groups of European colonists and among diverse Indian nations.

- Examine how the American colonies became part of a global trading network.

- Describe the changing character of labor in the English colonies, including the expansion of African and Indian slavery.

Comparing American Histories

In 1729, at age thirty, **William Moraley Jr.** signed an indenture to serve a five-year term as a "bound servant" in the "American Plantations." This was not what his parents had imagined for him. The son of a journeyman watchmaker, Moraley received a good education and was offered a clerkship with a London lawyer. But Moraley preferred London's pleasures to legal training. At age nineteen, out of money, he was forced to return home and become an apprentice watchmaker for his father. Moraley made a poor apprentice, and in 1725, his father rewrote his will, leaving him just 20 shillings. When Moraley's father died unexpectedly, his more generous widow gave her son 20 pounds. Moraley headed back to London in 1728.

(*left*) **Indentured Servant** (No image of William Moraley exists) Granger

(*right*) **Fabric dyed with indigo** (No image of Eliza Lucas Pinckney exists) Cooper Hewitt, Smithsonian Design Museum/Art Resource, NY

Times were hard in London, and Moraley failed to find work. After being imprisoned for debt, he sold his labor for five years in return for passage to America. Arriving in the colonies in December 1729, William was indentured to Isaac Pearson, a Quaker clockmaker and goldsmith in Burlington, New Jersey. Preferring to live in a large city like Philadelphia, he ran away but was soon captured. Most runaway servants had their contracts extended, but Moraley did not. For the next three years, he worked for Pearson alongside another indentured servant and an enslaved boy. Pearson allowed William to travel the countryside fixing clocks and watches, and the servant observed the far worse conditions of enslaved workers. Perhaps having recouped his investment, Pearson released Moraley from his contract two years early.

Moraley spent the next twenty months traveling the northern colonies, but found no steady employment. Hounded by creditors, he returned to England, penniless and unemployed. In 1743, hoping to cash in on popular interest in adventure tales, he published an account of his travels. In the book, entitled *The Infortunate, the Voyage and Adventures of William Moraley, an Indentured Servant*, he offered a poor man's view of eighteenth-century North America. Like so much else in Moraley's life, the book was not a success.

In 1738, while Moraley was trying to carve out a career as a writer, sixteen-year-old **Eliza Lucas**, the eldest daughter of Colonel George Lucas, arrived at Wappoo, her father's estate near Charleston, South Carolina. Eliza was born on Antigua, in the West Indies, where her father served with the British army and owned a sugar plantation worked by enslaved laborers. The move to the Carolinas was necessitated by her mother's ill health, but it created an unusual opportunity for Eliza. When Colonel Lucas was called back to Antigua in May 1739, he left Eliza in charge of his estate.

For the next five years, Eliza Lucas managed Wappoo and two other Carolina plantations owned by her father. Rising each day at 5 a.m., she checked on the fields and the enslaved laborers who worked them, balanced the books, nursed her mother, taught her younger sister to read, and wrote to her younger brothers at school in England. Eliza improved the value of her family's estates by experimenting with new crops. With her father's enthusiastic support, she cultivated indigo, a plant used for making textile dyes. Her success, however, ensured the expansion of the estate's enslaved labor force.

Eliza Lucas was soon encouraging neighboring planters to follow her lead. With financial aid from the colonial legislature and Parliament, indigo became a profitable export from South Carolina, second only to rice. One of the neighbors she befriended was Charles Pinckney, whom she would later marry, adding her enslaved laborers and landholdings to his. ∎

Comparing the American histories of William Moraley and Eliza Lucas illuminates profound shifts in the global economy. Labor and goods from the Atlantic economy now became fully integrated into trade networks from Europe to Asia and Africa. Between 1680 and 1750, indentured servants, enslaved Africans and Indians, planters, soldiers, merchants, and artisans traveled along these new trade networks. So, too, did sugar, rum, tobacco, indigo, cloth, and a host of other items. As England, France, and Spain expanded their empires, colonists developed new crops for export and increased the demand for manufactured goods from elsewhere. Yet the vibrant, increasingly global economy was fraught with peril. Economic crises, the uncertainties of maritime navigation, and outbreaks of war caused constant disruptions. For some Europeans, the opportunities offered by colonization outweighed the dangers; for others, fortune was less kind, and the results were disappointing, even disastrous. Enslaved Africans faced even more devastating circumstances as slavery and the slave trade expanded exponentially. So, too, did many Indians caught between expanding European settlements and powerful native adversaries.

Europeans Expand Their Claims

Beginning with the restoration of the monarchy in 1660, English kings began granting North American land and commercial rights to men who were loyal to the crown. France and Spain also expanded their empires in North America, and all three frequently came into conflict with each other in the late seventeenth and early eighteenth centuries. At the same time, American Indians challenged European efforts to displace them from their homelands while also attempting to establish new communities beyond colonists' reach.

English Colonies Grow and Multiply. Shortly after Charles II (r. 1660–1685) was restored to the English throne, Connecticut and Rhode Island requested and received royal charters that granted them some local authority. These charters could be changed only with the agreement of both parties, and Connecticut and Rhode Island maintained this local autonomy throughout the colonial period. In other colonies, however, Charles II asserted his authority by rewarding loyal supporters with land grants and commercial rights, which could more easily be changed or revoked than royal charters could. He also appointed his supporters to the newly formed Lords of Trade and Plantations, which advised the English Privy Council on policies in the far-flung English empire. He was even more generous with his brother James, the Duke of York. Charles II granted him control over all the lands between the Delaware and Connecticut Rivers, once known as New Netherland, but now known as New York. He then conveyed the adjacent lands to investors who established the colonies of East and West Jersey. Finally, Charles II repaid debts to Admiral Sir William Penn by granting his son huge tracts of land in the Middle Atlantic region. Six years later, William Penn Jr. left the Church of England and joined the Society of Friends, or Quakers. This radical Protestant sect was severely persecuted in England, so the twenty-two-year-old Penn turned his holdings into a Quaker refuge named Pennsylvania.

Between 1660 and 1685, York, Penn, and other English gentlemen were established as the overseers of a string of **proprietary colonies** from Carolina to New York. Although Charles II could have intruded into the government of these colonies, he rarely did. Instead, local conditions and the proprietor's vision largely dictated what was possible. Most proprietors envisioned the creation of a manorial system in their colony, one in which they and other gentry presided over workers producing goods for export. In practice, however, a range of relationships emerged between property owners and workers. For instance, small farmers and laborers in northern Carolina rose up and forced proprietors there to offer land at reasonable prices and a semblance of self-government. In the southern part of Carolina, however, English planters with West Indies connections dominated. They created a mainland version of Barbados by introducing enslaved Africans as laborers, carving out plantations, and trading with the West Indies.

William Penn provided a more progressive model of colonial rule. He established friendly relations with the local Lenni-Lenape Indians and drew up a Frame of Government in 1681 that recognized religious freedom for all Christians. It also allowed all property-owning men to vote and hold office. Under Penn's leadership, Pennsylvania attracted thousands of middling farm families, most of them Quakers, as well as artisans and merchants.

Charles II's death in 1685 marked an abrupt shift in crown-colony relations. His successor, James II (r. 1685–1688), instituted a more authoritarian regime both at home and abroad. He consolidated the colonies in the Northeast and established tighter controls. His royal officials banned town meetings, challenged land titles granted under the original colonial charters, and imposed new taxes. Fortunately for the colonists, the Catholic James II alienated his subjects in England as well as in the colonies, inspiring a bloodless coup in 1688, the so-called **Glorious Revolution**. His Protestant daughter Mary (r. 1689–1694) and her husband, William of Orange (r. 1689–1702), then ascended the throne, introducing more democratic systems of governance in England and the colonies. Two years later, John Locke, a physician and philosopher, wrote a widely circulated treatise supporting the initiatives of William and Mary by insisting that government depended on the consent of the governed.

Eager to restore political order and create a commercially profitable empire, William and Mary established the new colony of Massachusetts (which included Plymouth, Massachusetts Bay, and Maine) and restored town meetings and an elected assembly. But the 1692 charter also granted the English crown the right to appoint a royal governor and officials to enforce customs regulations. It ensured religious freedom to members of the Church of England and allowed all male property owners (not just Puritans) to be elected to the assembly. In Maryland, too, the crown imposed a royal governor and replaced the Catholic Church with the Church of England as the established religion. And in New York, wealthy English merchants won the backing of the newly appointed royal governor, who instituted a representative assembly and supported a merchant-dominated Board of Aldermen. In 1696, William consolidated various bodies related to policies in England's far-flung plantations into the Lord Commissioners for Trade and Plantations, known as the Board of Trade. Taken as a whole, William and Mary's policies instituted a partnership between England and colonial elites by allowing colonists to retain long-standing local governmental institutions while also asserting royal authority to appoint governors and ensure the influence of the Church of England (Table 3.1).

TABLE 3.1   English Colonies Established in North America, 1607–1750

Colony	Date	Original Colony Type	Religion	Status in 1750
Virginia	1624	Royal	Church of England	Royal
Massachusetts	1630	Charter	Congregationalist	Royal with charter
Maryland	1632	Proprietary	Catholic	Royal
Connecticut	1662	Charter	Congregationalist	Charter
Rhode Island	1663	Charter	No established church	Charter
Carolina	1663	Proprietary	Church of England	
North	1691	Proprietary		Royal
South	1691	Proprietary		Royal
New Jersey	1664	Proprietary	Church of England	Royal
New York	1664	Proprietary	Church of England	Royal
Pennsylvania	1681	Proprietary	Quaker	Proprietary
Delaware	1704	Proprietary	Lutheran/Quaker	Proprietary
Georgia	1732	Charter	Church of England	(Royal 1752)
New Hampshire (separated from Massachusetts)	1691	Royal	Congregationalist	Royal

In the early eighteenth century, England's North American colonies took the form that they would retain until the revolution in 1776. In 1702 East and West Jersey united into the colony of New Jersey. Delaware separated from Pennsylvania in 1704. By 1710 North Carolina became fully independent of South Carolina. Finally, in 1732, the colony of Georgia was chartered as a buffer between Spanish Florida and the plantations of South Carolina. At the same time, settlers pushed back the frontier in all directions.

The Pueblo Revolt and Spain's Fragile Empire.
Meanwhile Spain's forces in North America were spread dangerously thin. In Florida, Indians resisted the spread of Spanish cattle ranching in the 1670s. Some moved their settlements north to the Carolina border, wooed by the English who eagerly exchanged European goods for deerskins. The efforts of the English to interfere with Spanish-Indian trade networks fueled growing tensions along this Anglo-Spanish frontier. To the west, in New Mexico, open conflict erupted between Spanish and Pueblo peoples when war broke out in Europe in 1702. Tensions between Spanish missionaries and *encomenderos* and the Pueblo nation had simmered for decades (see "Spain's Global Empire Declines" in chapter 2). Relations worsened in the 1670s when a drought led to famine in the area and brought a revival of Indian rituals that the Spaniards considered heretical and threatening. Meanwhile, Spanish forces were failing to protect the Pueblos against devastating raids by Apache and Navajo warriors, while Catholic prayers failed to stop Pueblo deaths in a 1671 epidemic.

When some Pueblos returned to their traditional priests, Spanish officials hanged three Indian leaders for idolatry and whipped and incarcerated forty-three others. Among those punished was Popé, a militant Pueblo. Upon his release, Popé began planning a broad-based revolt. On August 10, 1680, seventeen thousand Pueblo Indians initiated a coordinated assault on numerous Spanish missions and forts. They destroyed buildings and farms, burned crops and houses, and smeared excrement on Christian altars. The Spaniards retreated to Mexico without launching any significant counterattack.

Still, the Spaniards reconquered parts of New Mexico in the 1690s, aided by growing internal conflict among the Pueblos and raids by the Apache. The governor general of New Spain worked hard to subdue the province and in 1696 crushed the rebels and opened new lands for settlement. Meanwhile Franciscan missionaries improved relations with the Pueblos by allowing them to retain more indigenous practices.

Yet despite the Spanish reconquest, in the long run the **Pueblo revolt** limited Spanish expansion by strengthening other indigenous peoples in the region. In the aftermath of the revolt, some Pueblo refugees moved north and taught the Navajo how to grow corn, raise sheep, and ride horses. Through the Navajo, the Ute, Shoshone, and Comanche peoples also gained access to horses. By the 1730s, the Comanches launched mounted bison hunts as well as raids on other Indian nations. At Taos, they traded Indian captives into slavery for more horses and guns. Thus the Pueblo provided other Indian nations with the means to support larger populations, wider commercial networks, and more warriors. These nations continued to contest Spanish rule.

At the same time, Spain sought to reinforce its claims to Texas (named after the Tejas Indians) in response to French settlements in the lower Mississippi valley. In the early eighteenth century, Spanish missions and forts appeared along the route from San Juan Batista to the border of present-day Louisiana. Although small and scattered, these outposts were meant to ensure Spain's claim to Texas. But the presence of large and powerful Indian nations, including the Caddo and the Apache, forced Spanish residents to accept many native customs in order to maintain their presence in the region.

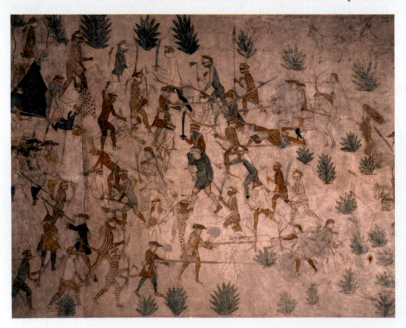

Ambush of the Villasur Expedition, c. 1720   An unknown artist painted this battle scene on buffalo hide. In 1720, Spanish soldiers and Pueblo warriors tried to expel the French from the lower Mississippi River valley. Instead, French soldiers and their Indian allies ambushed the expedition and killed forty-five men. Two of the dead, Spanish Father Juan Minguez and Pueblo leader Joseph Naranjo, are shown here in the center. MPI/Archive Photos/Getty Images

France Seeks Land and Control. Louis XIV of France (r. 1643–1715) claimed absolute power derived from what he believed was his divine right to rule. One of his missions was to extend the boundaries of France's North American colonies. Still, French efforts were focused more on exploration and trade than on settlement. In 1682 French adventurers and their Indian allies journeyed from the *Pays d'en Haut*, the Upper Country surrounding the Great Lakes, down the Mississippi River. Led by the French explorer René-Robert Cavelier, Sieur de La Salle, the party traveled to the Gulf of Mexico and claimed all the land drained by the river's tributaries for France. The new territory of Louisiana promised great wealth, but its development stalled when La Salle failed in his attempt to establish a colony.

Still eager for a southern outlet for furs, the French did not give up. After several more attempts at colonization in the early eighteenth century, French settlers maintained a toehold along Louisiana's Gulf coast. Most important, Pierre LeMoyne d'Iberville and his brother established forts at Biloxi and Mobile bays, where they traded with local Choctaw Indians. They recruited settlers from Canada and France, and these two small outposts survived despite conflicts among settlers, pressure from the English and the Spanish, a wave of epidemics, and a lack of supplies from France. Nevertheless, Louisiana counted only three hundred French settlers by 1715.

Continuing to promote commercial relations with diverse Indian nations, the French built a string of missions and forts along the upper Mississippi and Illinois Rivers. The most important of these, Kaskaskia (just south of Cahokia), developed into a multicultural community of Indian farmers and artisans, French fur traders, and Jesuit missionaries. These outposts in the continent's interior allowed France to challenge both English and Spanish claims to North America. In addition, extensive trade with a range of Indian nations ensured that French power was far greater than the small number of French settlers suggests.

Review & Relate

- What role did the crown play in the expansion of the English North American colonies in the second half of the seventeenth century?

- How did the development of the Spanish and French colonies in the late seventeenth century differ from that of the English colonies?

European Wars and American Consequences

The importance of the Atlantic economy in the late seventeenth and early eighteenth centuries ensured that developments in Europe would reshape American colonies. From 1689 until 1713, Europe was in an almost constant state of war, with continental conflicts spilling over into colonial possessions in North America. The result was increased tensions between colonists of different nationalities and diverse Indian nations as well as between Indians and colonists and between colonists and their home countries.

Colonial Conflicts and Indian Alliances. France was at the center of much of the European warfare of the period. Louis XIV hoped to expand France's borders and gain supremacy in Europe. To this end, he built a powerful professional army under state authority. Having gained victories in the Spanish Netherlands, Flanders, Strasbourg, and Lorraine, the French army seemed invincible.

Between 1689 and 1697, France and England fought their first sustained war in North America, **King William's War**. The war began over conflicting French and English interests on the European continent, but it soon spread to the American frontier when English and Iroquois forces attacked French and Huron settlements around Montreal and northern New York.

Although neither side had gained significant territory when peace was declared in 1697, the war had important consequences. Many colonists serving in the English army died of battle wounds, smallpox, and inadequate rations. Those who survived resented their treatment and the unnecessary deaths of so many comrades. The Iroquois fared even worse. Their fur trade was devastated, and hundreds of Mohawks and Oneidas were forced to flee from France's Huron, Ottawa, Ojibwe, and Potawatomi allies along the eastern Great Lakes. Moreover, "French Indians" and Iroquois continued to attack each other for years after the peace settlement. Finally, in 1701, the Iroquois agreed to end their raids and remain neutral in all future European conflicts. Wary of further European entanglements, Iroquois leaders focused on rebuilding their tattered confederacy.

Taking advantage of French military success, Antoine Laumet de La Mothe, Sieur de Cadillac, founded Fort Pontchartrain du Detroit in 1701 on a strategic strait on the Detroit River that joined the Great Lakes and linked the St. Lawrence and Mississippi Rivers. Established at what was then the western point of European settlement, Cadillac envisioned a post that would consolidate French control of the fur trade by forestalling England's advance into the region and reinforcing France's trade relations with Indian nations to the East and the West. Detroit consolidated France's eastern and western fur-trading networks and provided a longer growing season for settlers than Montreal or Quebec.

Still, neither the peace treaty of 1701 nor the establishment of Fort Detroit could end European battles over North America's lands and resources. Indeed, as Indian agents and traders from the various colonial powers learned Indian languages, negotiated with diverse tribes, intermarried with or converted Indian families, and joined in Indian rituals, it became impossible to disentangle European conflicts from North American economic and political networks.

A second protracted conflict, known as the **War of the Spanish Succession** (1702–1713) or Queen Anne's War, had even more devastating effects on North America. The conflict erupted in Europe when Charles II of Spain (r. 1665–1700) died without an heir, launching a contest for the Spanish kingdom and its colonies. France and Spain squared off against England, the Netherlands, Austria, and Prussia. In North America, however, it was England and her Indian allies that faced France, Spain, and their Indian allies. Each European nation sought to gain additional territory, while Indians hoped to increase the value of their alliances.

After more than a decade of savage fighting, Queen Anne's War ended in 1713 with the Treaty of Utrecht, which sought to secure a prolonged peace by balancing the interests of the great powers in Europe and their colonial possessions. By then, England had consolidated power at home by incorporating Scotland into Great Britain through the 1707 Act of Union. In 1713, a weakened France surrendered Newfoundland, Nova Scotia, and the Hudson Bay Territory to England, while Spain granted England control of St. Kitts in the West Indies, Gibraltar, and Minorca as well as the right to sell African slaves in its American colonies. Europeans' Indian allies did not participate in these negotiations, though those who fought with the English benefitted from that nation's expansion into new North American markets. Still, neither the treaty nor Britain's consolidation forestalled further conflict. Indeed, Spain, France, and Britain all strengthened fortifications along their North American borders (Map 3.1).

MAP 3.1 European Empires and Indian Nations in North America, 1715–1750
European nations competed with one another and with numerous Indian nations for control of vast areas of North America. Although wars continually reshaped areas under European and Indian control, this map shows the general outlines of the empires claimed by each European nation, the key forts established to maintain those claims, and the major Indian nations in each area.

Indians Resist European Encroachment. The seemingly ceaseless European conflicts in North America put incredible pressure on Indian peoples to choose sides. It was increasingly difficult for native peoples in colonized areas to remain autonomous, yet Indian nations were not simply pawns of European powers. Some actively sought European allies against their native enemies, and nearly all desired European trade goods like cloth, guns, and horses. The most powerful confederacies, like the Iroquois in New York and the Choctaw in the lower Mississippi River valley, played one European power off another. This became more difficult as the French and Spanish lost ground to the English in North America.

Moreover, as colonial expansion and trade led to war, the power of young male warriors increased in many tribes. In societies like the Cherokee and Iroquois, in which older women had long held significant economic and political authority, this change threatened traditional gender and generational relations. In addition, struggles among English, French, and Spanish forces both reinforced conflicts among Indian peoples that existed before European settlement and created new ones.

The trade in guns was especially significant in escalating conflicts among tribes in the Southeast during the late seventeenth century. By that period, the most precious commodity Indians in the region had to trade were Indian captives sold as slaves. Indians had always taken captives in war, but some of those captives had been adopted into the victorious nation. Now, however, war was almost constant in many areas, and captives were more valuable when sold as slaves to Europeans. The English in Carolina encouraged the Westo and later the Savannah nation to raid tribes in Spanish Florida, exchanging their captives for guns. The Chickasaws ranged further west, raiding tribes across the Mississippi River and then force-marching their captives to Charleston for sale. As slave raiding spread across the Anglo-Spanish borders, more peaceful tribes were forced to acquire guns for self-protection. In addition, many Indian nations were forced off traditional lands by slave-raiding Indian foes. Some of these displaced groups merged to form new tribes, like the Yamasee in the Southeast.

Indian slave traders both intensified the violence among native peoples and spread European diseases further west. The Great Southeastern Smallpox epidemic that raged from 1696 to 1700 erupted first among European colonists and enslaved Africans but then swept through Indian communities across the Southeast and west to the Mississippi valley. It devastated Indian societies that had been displaced and weakened by warfare and slave raiding and created crises even for those, like the Yamasee, who had sustained their alliance with the English by enslaving other Indians.

The vicious cycle of guns and enslavement convinced some southern Indians to develop a pan-Indian alliance in the 1710s similar to that forged by New England Indians in the 1670s (see "Wars in Old and New England" in chapter 2). First, a group of Tuscarora warriors, hoping to gain support from other tribes, launched an attack on North Carolina settlements in September 1711. In the **Tuscarora War** that followed, South Carolina colonists came to the aid of their North Carolina countrymen and persuaded the Yamasee, Catawba, and Cherokee nations to join forces against the Tuscarora. Meanwhile political leaders in North Carolina convinced a competing group of Tuscarora to ally with the colonists. By 1713 the war was largely over, and in 1715 the Tuscarora signed a peace treaty and forfeited their lands. Many then migrated north and were accepted as the sixth nation of the Iroquois Confederacy.

The end of the Tuscarora War did not mean peace, however. The Yamasee people remained deeply in debt to British merchants as the trade in deerskins and slaves moved west. Yet they were no longer able to secure sufficient captives to meet colonists' demands. The Yamasee also needed to adopt more captives as their own population shrank from disease and war. In turn, British colonists in South Carolina imported more African slaves to meet their need for labor. As the situation deteriorated, the Yamasee secured allies among the Creek and Cherokee and in 1715 launched an all-out effort to force the British out. For the next two years, this Yamasee-led coalition warred against the South Carolina militia. The British gained victory in the **Yamasee War** only after the Cherokee switched their allegiance to the colonists in early 1716. The final Indian nations withdrew from the conflict in 1717, and a fragile peace followed.

Explore ▶

For a Tuscarora appeal to avoid war, see Source 3.1.

While the Yamasee War did not oust the British, it transformed the political landscape of native North America. In its aftermath, the Creek and Catawba tribes emerged as powerful new confederations, the Cherokee became the major trading partner of the British, and the Yamasee nation was seriously weakened. Moreover, as the Cherokee allied with the British, the Creek and the Caddo tribes strengthened their alliance with the French.

Despite the British victory, colonists on the Carolina frontier faced raids on their settlements for decades to come. In the 1720s and 1730s, settlers in the Middle Atlantic colonies also experienced fierce resistance to their westward expansion. And attacks on New Englanders along the Canadian frontier periodically disrupted settlement there. Still, many Indian tribes were pushed out of their homelands. As they resettled in new regions, they alternately allied and fought with native peoples already living there. At the same time, the trade in Indian slaves expanded in the west as the French and the Spanish competed for economic partners and military allies.

Conflicts on the Southern Frontier.

Indians were not the only people to have their world shaken by war. By 1720 years of warfare and upheaval had transformed the mind-set of many colonists. Although most considered themselves loyal British subjects, many believed that British proprietors remained largely unconcerned with the colonies' welfare. Others resented the British army's treatment of colonial militia and Parliament's unwillingness to aid settlers against Indian attacks. Moreover, the growing numbers of settlers who arrived from other parts of Europe had little investment in British authority.

The impact of Britain's ongoing conflicts with Spain during the 1730s and 1740s illustrates this development. Following the Yamasee War, South Carolina became a royal colony, and its profitable rice and indigo plantations spread southward. Then, in 1732, Parliament established Georgia (named after King George II, r. 1727–1760) on lands north of Florida as a buffer between Carolina colonists and their longtime Spanish foes.

Spanish authorities were furious at this expansion of British territorial claims. Thus in August 1739, a Spanish naval ship captured an English ship captain who was trading illegally in the Spanish West Indies and severed his ear. In response, Great Britain attacked St. Augustine and Cartagena (in present-day Colombia), but its troops were repulsed. In 1742 Spain sent troops into Georgia, but the colonial militia pushed back the attack. By then, the American war had become part of a more general European conflict. Once again France and Spain joined forces while Great Britain supported Germany in Europe. When the war ended in 1748, Britain had ensured the future of Georgia and reaffirmed its military superiority. Once again, however, victory cost the lives of many colonial settlers and soldiers, and some colonists began to wonder whether their interests and those of the British government were truly the same.

Guided Primary Source Analysis

The Tuscarora Appeal to the Pennsylvania Government, 1710

Shortly before the outbreak of a pan-Indian war led by the Tuscarora, a delegation from that nation traveled to Pennsylvania to negotiate with British colonial officials and representatives of the Iroquois Confederacy. The views of Tuscarora representatives Iwaagenst Terrutawanaren and Teonnottein are summarized below by two white officials, John French and Henry Worley, who sought to present the arguments of the Indians. The Pennsylvania government subsequently denied their requests. The Iroquois were apparently more sympathetic since, when the war ended in 1715, the Tuscarora became the sixth nation of the Iroquois Confederacy.

Source 3.1

At Conestogo, June 8th, 1710.

The Indians were told that according to their request we were come from the Govr. and Govmt. to hear what proposals they had to make anent [about] a peace, according to the purport of their Embassy from their own People.

What groups did the Tuscarora representatives speak for, and what does this suggest about political dynamics within the Tuscarora nation?

They signified to us by a Belt of Wampum, which was sent from their old Women, that those Implored their friendship of the Christians & Indians of this Govmt., that without danger or trouble they might fetch wood & Water.

The second Belt was sent from their Children born, & those yet in the womb, Requesting that Room to sport & Play without danger of Slavery, might be allowed them.

The third Belt was sent from their young men fitt to Hunt, that privilege to leave their Towns, & seek provision for their aged, might be granted to them without fear of Death or Slavery.

What are the most important demands of the Tuscarora?

The fourth was sent from the men of age, Requesting that the Wood, by a happy peace, might be as safe for them as their forts.

The fifth was sent from the whole nation, requesting peace, that thereby they might have Liberty to visit their Neighbours.

The sixth was sent from their Kings and Chiefs, Desiring a lasting peace with the Christians & Indians of this Govmt., that thereby they might be secured against those fearful apprehensions they have for these several years felt. . . .

What is the most immediate concern of the Tuscarora?

These Belts (they say) are only sent as an Introduction, & in order to break off hostilities till next Spring, for then their Kings will come and sue for the peace they so much Desire.

Source: Sherman Day, *Historical Collections of the State of Pennsylvania* (Philadelphia: George W. Gorton, 1853), 391–92.

Put It in Context

To what extent does the Tuscarora appeal illuminate important concerns of other Indian tribes in the early 1700s?

Once again, Indians were caught up in these ongoing disputes among Europeans. While both French and Spanish forces attacked the British along the Atlantic coast, they sought to outflank each other in the lower Mississippi River valley and Texas. With the French relying on Caddo, Choctaw, and other Indian allies for trade goods and defense, the Spaniards needed to expand their alliances beyond those with the Tejas. In 1749, Spaniards agreed to stop kidnapping and enslaving Apache women and children and, instead, negotiated peace with that powerful Indian nation.

The British meanwhile became increasingly dependent on a variety of European immigrants to defend colonial frontiers against the French, Spaniards, and Indians. Certainly many Anglo-Americans moved westward as coastal areas became overcrowded, but frontier regions also attracted immigrants from Scotland and Germany who sought refuge and economic opportunity in the colonies. Many headed to the western regions of Virginia and Carolina and to Georgia in the 1730s and 1740s. Meanwhile, South Carolina officials recruited Swiss, German, and French Huguenot as well as Scots-Irish immigrants in the 1740s. Small communities of Jews settled in Charleston as well. Gradually many of these immigrants moved south into Georgia, seeking more and cheaper land. Thus when Spanish, French, or Indian forces attacked the British colonial frontier, they were as likely to face Scots-Irish and German immigrants as Englishmen.

Review & Relate

◾ How did the European wars of the late seventeenth and early eighteenth centuries impact relations between colonists and England?

◾ How were Indian alliances and conflicts, with other Indians and with European nations, shaped by the trade in slaves and guns and by wars between European powers?

The **Benefits** and Costs of **Empire**

The combined forces of global trade and international warfare altered the political and economic calculations of imperial powers. This was especially true for British North America, where colonists settled as families and created towns that provided key markets for Britain's commercial expansion. Over the course of the eighteenth century, British colonists became increasingly avid consumers of products from North America and around the world. Meanwhile the king and Parliament sought greater control over these far-flung commercial networks.

Colonial Traders Join Global Networks.

In the late seventeenth and early eighteenth centuries, trade became truly global. Not only did goods from China, India, the Middle East, Africa, and North America gain currency in England and the rest of Europe, but the tastes of European consumers also helped shape which goods were produced in other parts of the world. For instance, by the early eighteenth century the Chinese were making porcelain teapots and bowls specifically for the English market. The trade in cloth, tea, tobacco, and sugar was similarly influenced by European tastes. The exploitation of enslaved African laborers contributed significantly to this global commerce. They were a crucial item of trade in their own right, and their labor in the Americas ensured steady supplies of sugar, rice, tobacco, and indigo for the world market.

MAP 3.2   North Atlantic Trade in the Eighteenth Century

North Atlantic trade provided various parts of the British empire with raw materials, manufactured goods, and labor. Many ships traveled between only two regions because they were equipped to carry particular kinds of goods — slaves, grains, or manufactured goods. Ultimately, however, people and goods were exchanged among four key points: the West Indies, mainland North America, West Africa, and Great Britain.

By the early eighteenth century, both the volume and the diversity of goods multiplied. Silk, calico, porcelain, olive oil, wine, and other items were carried from Asia to Europe and the American colonies, while cod, mackerel, shingles, pine boards, barrel staves, rum, sugar, rice, indigo, and tobacco filled ships from America. A healthy trade also grew up within North America as New England fishermen, New York and Charleston merchants, and Caribbean planters met one another's needs. Salted cod and mackerel flowed to the Caribbean, and rum, molasses, and enslaved laborers flowed back to the mainland. This commerce required ships, barrels, docks, warehouses, and wharves, all of which ensured a lively trade in lumber, tar, pitch, and rosin (Map 3.2).

The flow of information was critical to the flow of goods and credit. By the early eighteenth century, coffeehouses flourished in port cities around the Atlantic, providing access to the latest news. Merchants, ship captains, and traders met in person to discuss new ventures and to keep apprised of recent developments. British and American periodicals reported on parliamentary legislation, commodity prices in India and Great Britain, the state of trading houses in China, the outbreak of disease in foreign ports, and stock ventures in London. Still, these markets were volatile. In 1720 shares in the British South Seas Company, which had risen to astronomical heights, collapsed. Thousands of investors, including William Moraley's father, lost a great deal of money.

Imperial Policies Focus on Profits.

European sovereigns worked to ensure that this international trade and their colonial possessions benefited their own European treasuries. In the late seventeenth century, both Louis XIV and his English rivals embraced a system known as **mercantilism**, which centered on the maintenance of a favorable balance of trade, with more gold and silver flowing into the home country than flowed out. In France, finance minister Jean-Baptiste Colbert honed the system. Beginning in the 1660s, he taxed foreign imports while removing all barriers to trade within French territories. Colonies provided valuable raw materials that could be used to produce manufactured items for sale to foreign nations and to colonists.

While France's mercantile system was limited by the size of its empire, England benefited more fully from such policies. The English crown had access to a far wider array of natural resources from which to manufacture goods and a larger market for these products. Beginning in 1660, Parliament passed a series of **Navigation Acts** that required merchants to conduct trade with the colonies only in English-owned ships. In addition, certain items imported from foreign ports had to be carried in English ships or in ships with predominantly English crews. Finally, a list of "enumerated articles"—including tobacco, cotton, sugar, and indigo—had to be shipped from the colonies to England before being reexported to foreign ports. Thus the crown benefited directly or indirectly from nearly all commerce conducted by its colonies. But colonies, too, often benefited as when Parliament subsidized the development of indigo in South Carolina.

East Prospect of the City of Philadelphia c. 1778

This view of Philadelphia from New Jersey was originally published as a sepia-toned engraving in *London Magazine* in 1761. The colored engraving was published in 1778 to highlight the bustling commercial activity in the city, which became the seat of the federal government that July. From The New York Public Library, https://digitalcollections.nypl.org/items/510d47d9-7ac4-a3d9-e040-e00a18064a99

In 1663 Parliament expanded its imperial reach through additional Navigation Acts, which required that goods sent from Europe to English colonies also pass through British ports. And a decade later, ship captains had to pay a duty or post bond before carrying enumerated articles between colonial ports. These acts ensured not only greater British control over shipping but also additional revenue for the crown as captains paid duties in the West Indies, mainland North American, and British ports. Beginning in 1673, England sent customs officials to the colonies to enforce the various parliamentary acts. By 1680, with a consolidated Board of Trade coordinating business with the colonies, London, Bristol, and Liverpool all thrived as barrels of sugar and tobacco and stacks of deer and beaver skins were unloaded at their docks and bolts of dyed cloth and cases of metal tools and guns were put on board for the return voyage. As mechanization and manufacturing expanded in England, Parliament sought to keep the profits at home by quashing nascent industries in the colonies. It thus prohibited the sale of products such as American-made textiles (1699), hats (1732), and iron goods (1750). In addition, Parliament worked to restrict trade among the North American colonies, especially between those on the mainland and in the West Indies.

Despite the increasing regulation, American colonists could own British ships and transport goods produced in the colonies. Indeed, by the mid-eighteenth century, North American merchants oversaw 75 percent of the trade in manufactures sent from Bristol and London to the colonies and 95 percent of the trade with the West Indies. Ironically, then, a system established to benefit Great Britain ended up creating a mercantile elite in British North America. Most of those merchants traded in goods, but some traded in human cargo.

The Atlantic Slave Trade.

Parliament chartered the Royal African Company in 1672 as Britain expanded its role in the Atlantic slave trade. Between 1700 and 1808, some 3 million captive Africans were carried on British and Anglo-American ships, about 40 percent of the total of those sold in the Americas in this period (Figure 3.1). Probably half a million Africans died on the voyage across the Atlantic. Huge numbers also died in Africa, while being marched to the coast or held in forts waiting to be forced aboard ships. Yet despite this astounding death rate, the slave trade yielded enormous profits and had far-reaching consequences: The Africans whom British traders bought and sold transformed labor systems in the colonies, fueled international trade, and enriched merchants, planters, and their families and communities.

European traders worked closely with African merchants to gain their human cargo, trading muskets, metalware, and linen for men, women, and children. Originally many of those sold into slavery were captives of war. But by the time British and Anglo-American merchants became central to this notorious trade, their contacts in Africa were procuring labor in any way they could. Over time, African traders moved farther inland to fill the demand, devastating large areas of West Africa, particularly the Congo-Angola region, which supplied some 40 percent of all Atlantic slaves.

The trip across the Atlantic, known as the **Middle Passage**, was a brutal and often deadly experience for Africans. Exhausted and undernourished by the time they boarded the large oceangoing vessels, the captives were placed in dark and crowded holds. Most had been poked and prodded by slave traders, and some had been branded to ensure that a trader received the exact individuals he had purchased. Once in the hold, they might wait for weeks before the ship finally set sail. By that time, the foul-smelling and crowded hold

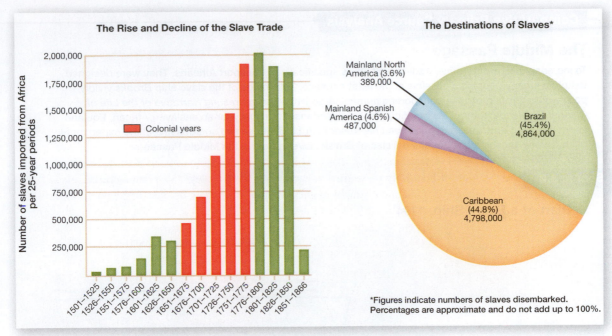

FIGURE 3.1   The Slave Trade in Numbers, 1501–1866

Extraordinary numbers of Africans were shipped as slaves to other parts of the world from the sixteenth to the nineteenth century. The slave trade transformed mainland North America, Brazil, and the West Indies. What broad patterns about the African slave trade can you infer from this data?

Source: Estimates Database. 2009. Voyages: Trans-Atlantic Slave Trade Database, http://www.slavevoyages.org/tast/assessment/estimates.faces. Accessed June 15, 2010.

Explore ▸

Examine two sources that reveal the horrors of the Middle Passage in Sources 3.2 and 3.3.

became a nightmare of disease and despair. There was never sufficient food or fresh water for the captives, and women especially were subject to sexual abuse by crew members. Many captives could not communicate with each other since they spoke different languages, and none of them knew exactly where they were going or what would happen when they arrived.

Those who survived the voyage were likely to find themselves in the slave markets of Barbados or Jamaica, where they were put on display for potential buyers. Once purchased, the enslaved workers went through a period of seasoning as they regained their strength, became accustomed to their new environment, and learned commands in a new language. Some did not survive seasoning, falling prey to malnutrition and disease or committing suicide. Others adapted to the new circumstances and adopted enough European or British ways to carry on even as they sought means to resist the shocking and oppressive conditions.

Seaport Cities and Consumer Cultures.   The same trade in human cargo that brought misery to millions of Africans provided traders, investors, and plantation owners with huge profits that helped turn America's Atlantic seaport cities into centers of culture and consumption. Charleston was one of the main ports receiving African slaves in the early 1700s, and Eliza Lucas was impressed with its prosperous character. Arriving in 1738,

Comparative Primary Source Analysis

The Middle Passage

To increase their profits, slave traders built ships specifically to transport Africans. They were designed to hold as many people as possible at the least expense. This image of the slave ship *Brooks* vividly portrays the profit motive in transporting human cargo while *The Interesting Narrative of the Life of Olaudah Equiano* captures the horrific personal experience. Unusually for an enslaved African, Equiano learned to read and write and purchased his freedom in 1766. These two sources reveal the experiences of enslaved Africans as well as the policies of British slave traders in the Middle Passage.

Source 3.2

Plan of a Slave Ship, 1794

Universal History Archive/UIG/Getty Images

Source 3.3

The Interesting Narrative of the Life of Olaudah Equiano, 1789

At last, when the ship we were in had got in all her cargo, they made ready with many fearful noises, and we were all put under deck, so that we could not see how they managed the vessel. . . . [N]ow that the whole ship's cargo were confined together, it became absolutely pestilential. The closeness of the place, and the heat of the climate, added to the number in the ship, which was so crowded that each had scarcely room to turn himself, almost suffocated us. This produced copious perspirations, so that the air soon became unfit for respiration, from a variety of loathsome smells, and brought on a sickness among the slaves, of which many died, thus falling victims to the improvident avarice, as I may call it, of their purchasers. This wretched situation was again aggravated by the galling of the chains, now become insupportable; and the filth of the necessary tubs, into which the children often fell, and were almost suffocated. The shrieks of the women, and the groans of the dying, rendered the whole a scene of horror almost inconceivable.

Happily perhaps for myself I was soon reduced so low here that it was thought necessary to keep me almost always on deck; and from my extreme youth I was not put in fetters. . . . One day, when we had a smooth sea and moderate wind, two of my wearied countrymen who were chained together (I was near them at the time), preferring death to such a life of misery, somehow made through the nettings and jumped into the sea: immediately another quite dejected fellow, who, on account of his illness, was suffered to be out of irons, also followed their example. . . . Those of us that were the most active were in a moment put down under the deck, and there was such a noise and confusion amongst the people of the ship as I never heard before, to stop her, and get the boat out to go after the slaves. However two of the wretches were drowned, but they got the other, and afterwards flogged him unmercifully for thus attempting to prefer death to slavery.

Source: *The Interesting Narrative of the Life of Olaudah Equiano, or Gustavus Vassa, The African, Written by Himself* (London, 1789), 78–82.

Interpret the Evidence

1. What aspects and challenges of the slave trade does the plan of a slave ship emphasize?
2. How does the narrative of Olaudah Equiano complement and deepen our understanding of the image of the ship?

Put It in Context

What do these sources reveal about the role of the Middle Passage in transforming African captives into slaves?

she noted that "the Metropolis is a neat pretty place. The inhabitants [are] polite and live in a very gentile [genteel] manner." North American seaports, with their elegant homes, fine shops, and lively social seasons, did capture the most dynamic aspects of colonial life. Although cities like New York, Boston, Philadelphia, Baltimore, and Charleston contained less than 10 percent of the colonial population, they served as focal points of economic, political, social, and cultural activity.

Affluent urban families created a consumer revolution in North America. Changing patterns of consumption challenged traditional definitions of status. Less tied to birth and family pedigree, status in the colonies became more closely linked to financial success and a genteel lifestyle. Successful men of humble origin, even those of Dutch, Scottish, French, and Jewish heritage, might join the British-dominated colonial gentry.

Of those who made this leap in the early eighteenth century, Benjamin Franklin was the most notable. Franklin was apprenticed to his brother, a printer, an occupation that matched his interest in books, reading, and politics. At age sixteen, Benjamin published (anonymously) his first essays in his brother's paper, the *New England Courant*. Two years later, a family dispute led Benjamin to try his luck in New York and then Philadelphia. His fortunes were fragile, but unlike William Moraley Jr., he combined hard work with a quick wit, good luck, and political connections, which together led to success. In 1729 Franklin purchased the *Pennsylvania Gazette* and became the colony's official printer.

While Franklin worried about the concentration of wealth in too few hands, most colonial elites in the early eighteenth century happily displayed their profits. Leading merchants in Boston, Salem, New York, and Philadelphia emulated British styles and built fine homes that had separate rooms for sleeping, eating, and entertaining guests. Mercantile elites also redesigned the urban landscape, donating money for brick churches and stately town halls. They constructed new roads, wharves, and warehouses to facilitate trade, and they invested in bowling greens and public gardens.

The Potter Family of Rhode Island, c. 1740   The portrait (artist unknown) shows John Potter, a wealthy landowner and slave trader, his wife, two other women, and an enslaved boy. The family's wealth is evident in their clothing, fine tea service, and enslaved servant. Potter's large farm in South Kingston sat on land taken from the Narragansett tribe. Potter later became a Quaker and freed his enslaved workers. The Newport Historical Society (53.3). Estate of E. L. Winters.

The spread of international commerce created a lively cultural life in thriving colonial cities. The colonial elite replicated British fashions, including elaborate tea rituals. In Boston, the wives of merchants served fine teas imported from East Asia in cups and saucers from China while decorated bowls held sugar from the West Indies. However, the emergence of a colonial aristocracy also revealed growing inequality. Wealthy urban merchants and professionals lived alongside a middling group of artisans and shopkeepers and a growing class of unskilled laborers, widows, orphans, the elderly, the disabled, and the unemployed. In seaport cities, enslaved laborers might live in their owners' homes or be relegated to separate and impoverished communities. In New York City, which boasted the second largest slave market in the mainland colonies in the 1710s, blacks were regularly buried outside the city limits. The frequent wars of the late seventeenth and early eighteenth centuries contributed to these economic and social divisions by boosting the profits of merchants, shipbuilders, and artisans. They temporarily improved the wages of seamen as well. But in their aftermath, rising prices, falling wages, and a lack of jobs led to the concentration of wealth in fewer hands.

Review & Relate

■ What place did North American colonists occupy in the eighteenth-century global trade network?

■ How and with what success did the British government maintain control over the colonial economy and ensure that it served Britain's economic and political interests?

Labor in North America

What brought the poor and the wealthy together was the demand for labor. Labor was sorely needed in the colonies, but this did not make it easy to find steady, high-paying employment. Many would-be laborers had few skills and faced fierce competition from other workers for limited, seasonal labor. Moreover, a majority of European immigrants and nearly all Africans arrived in America with significant limits on their freedom.

Finding Work in the Colonies.   The lack of demand for free laborers was rooted in many employers' preference for indentured servants, apprentices, or others who came cheap and were bound by contract. Some employed criminals or purchased enslaved workers, who would provide years of service for a set price. Free laborers who sought a decent wage and steady employment needed to match their desire to work with skills that were in demand.

When William Moraley ended his indenture and sought work, he discovered that far fewer colonists than Englishmen owned timepieces, leaving him without a useful trade. So he tramped the countryside, selling his labor when he could, but found no consistent employment. Thousands of other men and women, most without Moraley's education or skills, also found themselves at the mercy of unrelenting economic forces.

Many poor men and women found jobs building homes, loading ships, or spinning yarn. But they were usually employed for only a few months a year. The rest of the time they scrounged for bread and beer, begged in the streets, or stole what they needed. Most lived in ramshackle buildings filled with cramped and unsanitary rooms. Children born into such squalid circumstances were lucky to survive their first year. Those raised in seaport cities might earn a few pence running errands for captains or sailors, but they would never have access to the bounteous goods unloaded at the docks.

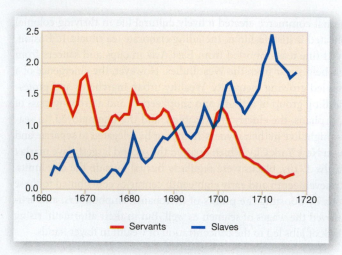

FIGURE 3.2   Indentured Servants and Slaves in Six Maryland Counties, 1662–1717

This chart illustrates a dramatic shift in the Chesapeake labor force between 1662 and 1717. Although based on a study of estate inventories from six Maryland counties, what does the trend shown here suggest about the larger transition in the use of white indentured servants and black slaves on Chesapeake farms? Based on Gloria L. Main, *Tobacco Colony: Life in Early Maryland, 1650–1720* (Princeton: Princeton University Press, 1982), 26.

By the mid-eighteenth century, older systems of labor, like indentured servitude, began to decline in many areas. In some parts of the North and across the South, white servants were gradually replaced by enslaved Africans (Figure 3.2). At the same time, farm families who could not usefully employ all their children bound out sons and daughters to more prosperous neighbors. Apprentices, too, competed for positions. Unlike most servants, apprentices contracted to learn a trade. They trained under the supervision of a craftsman, who gained cheap labor by promising to teach a young man (and most apprentices were men) his trade. But master craftsmen limited the number of apprentices they accepted to maintain the value of their skills.

Another category of laborers emerged in the 1720s. A population explosion in Europe and the rising price of wheat and other items convinced many people to seek passage to America. Shipping agents offered them loans for their passage that were repaid when the immigrants found a colonial employer who would redeem (that is, repay) the agents. In turn, these **redemptioners**, who often traveled with families, labored for the employer for a set number of years. The redemption system was popular in the Middle Atlantic colonies, especially among German immigrants who hoped to establish farms on the Pennsylvania frontier. While many succeeded, their circumstances could be extremely difficult.

Large numbers of convicts, too, entered the British colonies in the eighteenth century. Jailers in charge of Britain's overcrowded prisons offered inmates the option of transportation to the colonies. Hundreds were thus bound out each year to American employers. The combination of indentured servants, redemptioners, apprentices, and convicts ensured that as late as 1750 the majority of white workers — men and women — in the British colonies were bound to some sort of contract.

Some white workers also competed with slaves, especially in the northern colonies. Africans and African Americans formed only a small percentage of the northern population, just 5 percent from Pennsylvania to New Hampshire in 1750. In the colony of New York, however, blacks formed about 14 percent of inhabitants. While some enslaved blacks worked on agricultural estates in the Hudson River valley and New Jersey, even more labored as household servants, dockworkers, seamen, and blacksmiths in New York City alongside British colonists and European immigrants. In addition, some British **enslavers** in the West Indies moved to the mainland and brought their African workers with them. Isaac Royall, for example, traded enslaved Africans as well as sugar and rum from his plantation in Antigua. After surviving a hurricane, smallpox epidemic, and slave revolt on the island, he moved to an estate on the Mystic River in Massachusetts in 1737 with his family and 27 enslaved laborers.

Coping with Economic Distress.
Some white workers who were bound by contracts felt common cause with their black counterparts. But whites had a far greater chance of gaining their freedom even before slavery was fully entrenched in colonial law. Still, several challenges confronted white servants, apprentices, redemptioners, and convicts looking to purchase land, open a shop, or earn a decent wage. First, white women and men who gained their freedom from indentures or other contracts had to compete for jobs with a steady supply of redemptioners, convicts, and apprentices as well as other free laborers. Second, by the early eighteenth century, many areas along the Atlantic coast faced a land shortage that threatened the fortunes even of long-settled families. Finally, a population boom in Britain's North American colonies produced growing numbers of young people seeking land and employment. Thus many free laborers migrated from town to town and from country to city seeking work. They hoped to find farmers who needed extra hands for planting and harvesting, ship captains and contractors who would hire them to load or unload cargo or assist in the construction of homes and churches, or wealthy families who needed cooks, laundresses, or nursemaids.

Seasonal and temporary demands for labor created a corps of transient workers. Many New England towns developed systems to "warn out" those who were not official residents. Modeled after the British system, warning-out was meant to ensure that strangers did not become public dependents. Still, being warned did not mean immediate removal. Sometimes transients were simply warned that they were not eligible for poor relief. At other times, constables returned them to an earlier place of residence. In many ways, warning-out served as an early registration system, allowing authorities to encourage the flow of labor, keep residents under surveillance, and protect the town's coffers. But it rarely aided those in need of work.

Residents who were eligible for public assistance might be given food and clothing or boarded with a local family. Many towns began appointing Overseers of the Poor to deal with the growing problem of poverty. By 1750 every seaport city had constructed an almshouse that sheltered white residents without other means of support. In 1723 the Bridewell prison was added to Boston Almshouse, built in 1696. A workhouse was opened on the same site in 1739 to employ the "able-bodied" poor in hopes that profits from it would help fund the almshouse and prison. Still, these efforts at relief fell far short of the need, especially in hard economic times.

Rural Americans Face Changing Conditions.
While seaport cities and larger towns fostered a growing cohort of individuals who lived outside traditional households, families remained the central unit of economic organization in rural areas, where the vast majority of Americans lived. Yet farm households, too, had been drawn into the Atlantic economy and the increasingly global circulation of goods and people.

In areas along the Atlantic coast, rural families became part of commercial networks in a variety of ways. Towns and cities needed large supplies of vegetables, meat, butter, barley, wheat, and yarn. Farm families sold these goods and bought sugar, tea, and other imported items that diversified their diet. Few rural families purchased ornamental or luxury items, but cloth or cheese bought in town saved hours of labor at home. Just as important, coastal communities like Salem, Massachusetts and Wilmington, Delaware that were once largely rural became thriving commercial centers in the late seventeenth century.

In New England, the land available for farming shrank as the population soared. In the original Puritan colonies, the population rose from 100,000 in 1700 to 400,000 in 1750. Many parents were no longer able to provide their children with sufficient land for profitable farms. The result was increased migration to the frontier, where families were more dependent on their own labor and a small circle of neighbors. And even this option was not accessible to all. Before 1700, servants who survived their indenture had a good chance of securing land, but by the mid-eighteenth century only two of every ten were likely to become landowners.

In the Middle Atlantic region, the population surged from 50,000 in 1700 to 250,000 in 1750. The increase was due in part to the rapid rise in wheat prices, which leaped by more than 50 percent in Europe. Hoping to take advantage of this boon, Anglo-Americans, Germans, Scots-Irish, and other immigrants flooded into the region in the early eighteenth century. By the 1740s, German families had created self-contained communities in western Pennsylvania, New York's Mohawk River valley, and the Shenandoah Valley of Virginia. They worshipped in German churches, read German newspapers, and preserved German traditions. Meanwhile Scots-Irish immigrants established churches and communities in New Jersey, central Pennsylvania, and western Maryland and Virginia (Map 3.3).

Further south, immigrants could acquire land more easily, but their chances for economic autonomy were increasingly influenced by the spread of slavery. As hundreds and then thousands of Africans were imported into the Carolinas in the 1720s and 1730s, economic and political power became more entrenched in the hands of planters and merchants. Increasingly, they controlled the markets, wrote the laws, and set the terms by which white as well as black families lived. Farms along inland waterways and on the frontier were crucial in providing food and other items for urban residents and for planters with large labor forces. But farm families increasingly depended on commercial and planter elites to set the prices and market their goods. Those outside this market economy subsisted largely on what they could grow or exchange with neighbors. In addition, as slave raiding increased among Indians, now equipped with guns, many frontier settlements were caught in the crosshairs of wars among native peoples and with English and Spanish communities.

Slavery Takes Hold in the South. The rise of African slavery reshaped the South in numerous ways. A major shift from white indentured servants to black slaves began in Virginia after 1676 and soon spread across the Chesapeake (see Figure 3.2). The Carolinas, meanwhile, developed as a slave society from the start. That is, the Carolinas were not just a society that included enslaved labor, but one in which slavery shaped the political and social as well as the economic structure of the colony. Enslaved workers

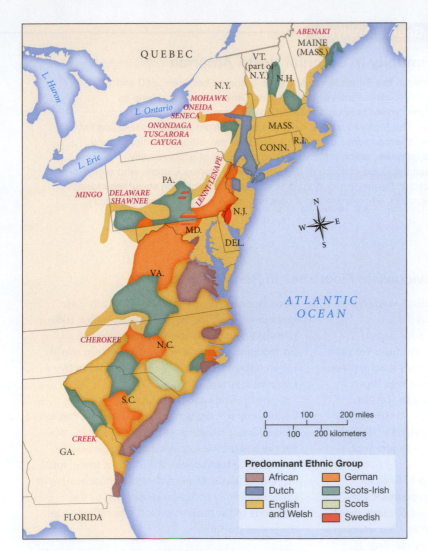

MAP 3.3   Ethnic and Racial Diversity in British North America, 1750

By 1750 British North America was a far more diverse region than it had been fifty years earlier. In 1700 the English dominated most regions, while the Dutch controlled towns and estates in the Hudson River valley. By 1750, however, growing numbers of African Americans, German and Scots-Irish immigrants, and smaller communities of other ethnic groups predominated in various regions.

Predominant Ethnic Group

- African
- Dutch
- English and Welsh
- German
- Scots-Irish
- Scots
- Swedish

allowed for the expanded cultivation of cash crops like tobacco, rice, and indigo, which promised high profits for planters as well as merchants. But these developments also made southern enslavers more dependent on the global market and limited opportunities for poorer whites and all blacks. Enslavers' need for more and more land also ensured that Indians and many whites were pushed farther west, sparking more conflicts along the frontier.

In the 1660s, as tobacco cultivation spread across the Chesapeake, the Virginia Assembly had passed a series of laws that defined slavery as a distinct status based on racial identity and passed to future generations. The enactment of these **slave laws** was driven largely by the growing need for labor, which neither enslaved Indians nor indentured servants could fill. Modeling

Explore ▶

Read two historical interpretations of white settlers in colonial Pennsylvania in Secondary Sources 3.4 and 3.5.

Comparative Secondary Source Analysis

Individualism and Community in Colonial North America

The majority of Europeans who entered the British North American colonies between 1680 and 1750 came as indentured servants, slaves, or other forms of bound labor. Others, however, came as independent farmers, artisans, or merchants seeking economic advancement, religious liberty, or political sanctuary. This latter group has received a great deal of attention from scholars searching for the historical roots of a distinctive American sense of individualism or of the nation's ethnic, cultural, and religious diversity. The middle colonies, which attracted a large number of economically independent immigrants, have been the focus of much of this scholarship. James Lemon, who analyzes a broad swath of European colonists in Pennsylvania, comes to a different conclusion about their ideas and identities than does James Henretta, who focuses on a specific group in a particular community.

Source 3.4

James T. Lemon | Individualism Flourishes in Pennsylvania, 1972

[The] supporters of individualism were not only the more affluent citizens [of Pennsylvania] but also those who moved elsewhere to seek better opportunities for their families. Undoubtedly their views were fostered by a sense that the environment was "open." As individuals, they were ready in spirit to conquer the limitless continent, to subdue the land. . . . We can see the early signs of liberal North America in Pennsylvania as much as anywhere. . . .

The migrants were . . . largely from the middle stratum of western European society. Because they came from the middle class, these settlers brought with them certain characteristics that came to mark Pennsylvania's society. . . . These migrants sought a better life, possessed certain skills, and were neither wealthy nor poverty stricken, at least when they left their homeland. . . . [F]or nearly a century after 1680 [Pennsylvania] possessed a reputation for providing the best chance in the western world for an improved standard of living and life free of external restraint.

The balance was shifting away from the community toward the individual . . . and this led to significant results in early Pennsylvania. Most people sought sites on good land or as near as possible to Philadelphia, the focus of trade; most organized family farms rather than cooperative or manorial farms; and most responded to the demands of the market, which was reflected in the use of the land.

Source: James T. Lemon, *The Best Poor Man's Country: A Geographical Study of Early Southeastern Pennsylvania.* (Baltimore, Md.: John Hopkins University Press, 1972), xv–xvi, 5–7.

their laws on statutes passed earlier in Barbados, political leaders ensured that Africans and their descendants would spend their entire lives laboring for white owners. Slavery became a status inherited through the mother, which could not be changed by converting to Christianity. And enslavers were granted the right to kill enslaved workers who resisted their authority. In 1680 the Virginia Assembly made it illegal for "any negro or other slave to carry or arme himself with any club, staffe, gunn, sword, or any other weapon of

Source 3.5

James A. Henretta | Ethnic and Religious Bonds Foster Community, 1978

[V]oluntary concentrations of like-minded settlers indicate the importance of communal values, of people who preferred to share a religious or ethnic identity. . . .

Most of the German immigrants who arrived in Lancaster, Pennsylvania, in 1744 settled on the lots laid out by Dr. Adam Simon Kuhn, the leading German resident, rather than on land offered by the English proprietor, Alexander Hamilton. These linguistic and religious ties extended beyond settlement patterns to encompass economic relationships. . . . [T]he main business connections of the merchants of Lancaster, whether they were Jewish or Quaker or German, were with their co-religionists in Philadelphia. . . .

[T]he weight of the evidence indicates that these decisions were not made for narrowly economic or utilitarian reasons: the felt need to maintain a religious or ethnic identity was as important a consideration as the fertility of the soil or the price of the land in determining where a family would settle. . . . These ethnic, linguistic, or religious ties did not reflect a coherent ideological system, a planned communitarian culture similar to the highly organized Moravian settlement at Bethlehem, Pennsylvania. These bonds among families, neighbors, and fellow church members were informal; nonetheless, they circumscribed the range of individual action among the inhabitants of Pennsylvania and laid the foundations for a rich and diverse cultural existence.

Source: James A. Henretta, "Families and Farms: Mentalité in Pre-Industrial America," *William and Mary Quarterly* 35:1 (1978), 4–5.

Examine the Sources

1. How do Lemon and Henretta differ in their historical interpretations of white settlers in colonial Pennsylvania?
2. Explain how the experiences of New England and Chesapeake colonists might be used to support and/or complicate Lemon's and Henretta's interpretations.

Put It in Context

Analyze how the experiences of slaves and indentured servants challenge the interpretation of Lemon or Henretta. How might the Tuscarora Indians in Source 3.1 have responded to the visions of colonial Pennsylvania offered by Lemon and Henretta?

defence or offence." Nor could the enslaved leave their enslaver's premises without a certificate of permission. Increasingly harsh laws in Virginia and Maryland coincided with a rise in the number of Africans imported to the colonies. The rate of importation also ensured the decline of the free black population in the Chesapeake. In 1668 one-third of all Africans and African Americans in Virginia and Maryland were still free, but the numbers dwindled year by year. Once the Royal African Company started supplying the

Chesapeake with slaves directly from Africa in the 1680s, the pace of change quickened. By 1750, 150,000 blacks resided in the Chesapeake, and only about 5 percent remained free. **See Primary Source Project 3: Tobacco and Slavery, page 103.**

Direct importation from Africa had other negative consequences on the lives of the enslaved. Far more men than women were imported, skewing the sex ratio in a population that was just beginning to form families and communities. Enslaved women, like men, performed heavy field work, and few bore more than one or two children. When these conditions, along with brutal work regimens, sparked resistance by the enslaved, fearful whites imposed even stricter regulations, further distinguishing between white indentured servants and enslaved blacks.

While slavery in the Carolinas was influenced by developments in the Chesapeake, it was shaped even more directly by practices in the British West Indies. Many wealthy families from Barbados, Antigua, and other sugar islands — including that of Colonel Lucas — established plantations in the Carolinas. At first, they brought enslaved laborers from the West Indies to oversee cattle and pigs and assist in the slaughter of livestock and curing of meat for shipment back to the West Indies. Some of the enslaved grew rice, using techniques learned in West Africa, to supplement their diet. Their owners soon realized that rice might prove very profitable. Although not widely eaten in Europe, rice could provide cheap and nutritious food for sailors, orphans, convicts, and peasants. Relying initially on Africans' knowledge, enslavers began cultivating rice for export. (See Map 2.2 in chapter 2.)

The need for African rice-growing skills and the fear of attacks by Spaniards and Indians led Carolina owners to grant the enslaved rights unheard of in the Chesapeake or the West Indies. Initially enslaved laborers were allowed to carry guns and serve in the militia. For those who nonetheless ran for freedom, Spanish and Indian territories offered refuge. Still, most stayed, depending for support on bonds they had developed in the West Indies. The frequent absence of owners also offered enslaved Carolinians greater autonomy.

Yet as rice cultivation expanded from the 1690s through the early 1700s, slavery in the Carolinas turned more brutal. The Assembly, which included large numbers of enslavers, enacted harsher and harsher slave codes to ensure control of the growing labor force. No longer could the enslaved carry guns, join militias, meet in groups, or travel without a pass. At the same time, the increase in the direct importation of enslaved

TO BE SOLD, on board the Ship *Bance-Island*, on tuesday the 6th of *May* next, at *Ashley-Ferry*; a choice cargo of about 250 fine healthy **NEGROES**, just arrived from the Windward & Rice Coast. —The utmost care has already been taken, and shall be continued, to keep them free from the least danger of being infected with the SMALL-POX, no boat having been on board, and all other communication with people from *Charles-Town* prevented.

Austin, Laurens, & Appleby.

N. B. Full one Half of the above Negroes have had the SMALL-POX in their own Country.

Sale of Slaves in Charleston, South Carolina   Henry Laurens, one of the major slave traders in Charleston, formed a partnership with two other men to import enslaved Africans to North America. This ad focuses on the health of the 250 Africans they are offering for sale, half of whom have developed immunity to smallpox. Being from the Rice Coast, they were also likely skilled in cultivating rice. Library of Congress, Prints and Photographs Division [LC-USZ62-10293]

Africans skewed gender balances and disrupted older community networks. New military patrols by whites enforced laws and labor practices. Some plantations along the Carolina coast turned into virtual labor camps, where thousands of mostly enslaved men worked under harsh conditions with no hope of improvement.

By 1720 blacks outnumbered whites in the Carolinas, and fears of slave rebellions inspired South Carolina officials to impose even harsher laws and more brutal enforcement measures. When Eliza Lucas developed indigo as a cash crop alongside rice in the 1740s, the demand for slave labor increased further. Although far fewer enslaved laborers — about 40,000 by 1750 — resided in South Carolina than in the Chesapeake, they constituted more than 60 percent of the colony's total population.

Africans Resist Their Enslavement.

Enslaved laborers in British North America resisted their subjugation in a variety of ways. Similar to Indians, they sought to retain customs, foods, belief systems, and languages from their homelands. They tried to incorporate work patterns passed down from one generation to the next into new environments. They challenged masters and overseers by refusing to work, breaking tools, feigning illness, and other means of disputing whites' authority. Some ran for freedom, others fought back in the face of punishment, and still others used arson, poison, or other means to defy owners. A few planned revolts.

However, the consequences for resisting were severe, from whipping, mutilation, and branding to summary execution. Fearful of rebellion, whites often punished people falsely accused of planning revolts. Yet some enslaved workers did plot insurrections against their owners or whites in general. Indeed, northern as well as southern colonies lived with the threat of slave rebellion. In New York City in 1712, several dozen enslaved Africans and Indians set fire to a building. When whites rushed to the scene, the insurgents attacked them with clubs, pistols, axes, and staves, killing eight and injuring many more. The rebels were soon defeated by the militia, however. Authorities executed eighteen insurgents, burning several at the stake as a warning to others. Six of those imprisoned committed suicide. In 1741 a series of suspicious fires in the city led to accusations against a white couple who owned an alehouse where free and enslaved blacks gathered to drink. To protect herself from prosecution, an Irish indentured servant testified that she had overheard discussions of an elaborate plot involving black and white conspirators. Frightened of any hint that poor whites and blacks might make common cause, authorities immediately arrested suspects and eventually executed 34 people, including 4 whites. They also banished 72 blacks from the city. Among those executed was Cuffee, an enslaved laborer who claimed that "a great many people have too much, and others too little."

The most serious slave revolt, however, erupted in South Carolina, just a few miles from Wappoo, the Lucas plantation. A group of recently imported Africans led the **Stono rebellion** in 1739. On Sunday, September 9, a group of enslaved men stole weapons from a country store and killed the owners. They then marched south, along the Stono River, beating drums and recruiting others to join them. Torching plantations and killing whites along the route, they had gathered more than fifty insurgents when armed whites overtook them. In the ensuing battle, dozens of rebels died. The militia, along with Indians hired to assist them, killed another twenty over the next two days and then captured a group of forty, who were executed without trial.

This revolt reverberated widely in a colony where enslaved blacks outnumbered whites nearly two to one, direct importation from Africa was at an all-time high, and Spanish authorities in Florida promised freedom to enslaved runaways. In 1738 the Spanish governor formed a black militia company, and he allowed thirty-eight fugitive families to settle north of St. Augustine and build Fort Mose for their protection. When warfare erupted between Spain and Britain over commercial rivalries in 1739, enslaved Carolinians may have seen their chance to gain freedom en masse. But as with other rebellions, this one failed, and the price of failure was death.

Review & Relate

- What were the sources of economic and social inequality in North America in the early eighteenth century?

- How did the laws and conditions under which poor black and white workers lived during the late seventeenth and early eighteenth centuries differ?

Conclusion: Changing Fortunes in British North America

Global commerce, international wars, and immigration reshaped the economy and geography of North America between 1680 and 1750. Many colonists and some Indians thrived as international trade boomed. In seaport cites, a consumer revolution transformed daily life, fueling the emergence of a colonial elite and the demand for skilled artisans. Others found greater opportunities by pushing inland and establishing farms and communities along new frontiers. But many people failed to benefit from these changes. Indians continued to be dispossessed of their land as white settlers pushed west. As European populations increased, the spread of lethal diseases and nearly constant warfare dealt heavy blows to native communities. To survive, more powerful Indian tribes enslaved more captives from weaker ones to exchange for guns from colonists. At the same time, many indentured servants found it impossible to obtain land or decent wages after they gained their independence. Moving to the frontier in hopes of finding unsettled land, they too became caught up in cycles of war and disease. Still, even if white servants and unskilled workers struggled, they had the benefit of freedom. Black workers were increasingly forced into slavery, with the shrinking percentage of free blacks suffering from intensifying discrimination against the race as a whole. The consequences of international trade and imperial conflicts only widened the gap between economically successful whites, poor whites, weakened Indians, and enslaved blacks.

Increased mechanization and the growth of manufacturing in England contributed to the differences among these Americans. After failing to find an economic foothold in the colonies, indentured servant William Moraley Jr. returned to England where he made and repaired cheap watches, which were now being turned out in large numbers. Other indentured servants remained in the colonies once free but found it increasingly difficult to obtain land or a living wage. In northern cities and across the South, they increasingly competed with enslaved blacks. These same changes had far more positive effects for some colonists. The mechanization of cloth production in England demanded vast amounts of raw material from the English countryside and the colonies. It ensured, for example, the profitability of indigo. This crop benefited South Carolina planters like Eliza Lucas and — after her marriage in 1744 — her husband, Charles Pinckney, a successful planter himself. Still, profits from indigo and other crops could be gained only through enslaving hundreds of laborers and expanding further into Indian territories.

Eliza Pinckney's sons became important leaders in South Carolina, and despite their English education and the benefits they gained through British trade, both developed a strong belief in the rights of the colonies to control their own destinies. Like many American colonists, they were spurred by the consumer revolution, geographical expansion, growing ethnic diversity, and conflicts with Indian and European enemies to develop a mind-set that differed significantly from their counterparts in England. Yet this turn away from the religious and political beliefs that had sustained colonists for generations soon spurred a series of revivals that initially reinforced the importance of faith but ultimately challenged the authority of traditional institutions.

chapter **3** review

Timeline of Events

Key Terms

Review & Relate

1. What role did the crown play in the expansion of the English North American colonies in the second half of the seventeenth century?

2. How did the development of the Spanish and French colonies in the late seventeenth century differ from that of the English colonies?

3. How did the European wars of the late seventeenth and early eighteenth centuries impact relations between colonists and England?

4. How were Indian alliances and conflicts, with other Indians and with European nations, shaped by the trade in slaves and guns and by wars between European powers?

5. What place did North American colonists occupy in the eighteenth-century global trade network?

6. How and with what success did the British government maintain control over the colonial economy and ensure that it served Britain's economic and political interests?

7. What were the sources of economic and social inequality in North America in the early eighteenth century?

8. How did the laws and conditions under which poor black and white workers lived during the late seventeenth and early eighteenth centuries differ?

Tobacco and Slavery

▶ **Explain the roles that legislators, planters, and enslaved workers played in the production of tobacco and describe the challenges they faced.**

Tobacco was a popular commodity among Europeans, and they relied on colonies like Virginia and Maryland to provide it. Consumption and production expanded dramatically between the 1670s and the 1750s. The 17.5 million pounds of tobacco exported from the Chesapeake in 1672 leapt to nearly 51 million pounds by 1750. While many small farmers cultivated tobacco with only the aid of family members or indentured servants, increased demand drove others to seek new sources of labor. Laws that codified the status of the enslaved encouraged more planters to invest in Africans (Source 3.6).

Many tobacco planters worried about how to balance proper care of enslaved laborers, in whom they had invested significant capital, with their willingness to use brutal forms of discipline (Sources 3.7 and 3.9). At the same time, these enslavers sought to promote a positive image that would appeal to consumers and English authorities (Source 3.8). While large slave owners could find themselves deeply in debt when prices fell, they were still likely to gain the greatest profits from the tobacco trade.

As tobacco production increased in Virginia, so did the importation of enslaved Africans. While 4,000 Africans were imported in the 1690s, more than 15,000 arrived in the 1730s. By 1740, natural reproduction added to the steady rise in Virginia's African American population. The vast majority of black Virginians were enslaved, and the greatest number worked in tobacco. While much of the work of clearing fields, weeding, and hoeing was considered unskilled, the cutting, stemming, and packing of tobacco leaf required considerable skill (Sources 3.8 and 3.9). In response to the arduous labor and harsh discipline, some enslaved laborers ran away and others organized collective escapes (Source 3.10). However, most of Virginia's enslaved workers remained locked into the tobacco cycle, along with their children and grandchildren.

Source 3.6

Virginia Slave Laws, 1662 and 1667

As the demand for labor on tobacco farms increased in the mid-seventeenth century and the flow of white indentured servants to Virginia slowed, tobacco planters imported more Africans to fill their labor needs. In the 1660s Virginia legislators passed a series of laws to clarify the status of this new category of worker. Several were based on laws in effect in the West Indies, including the 1662 law that defined slavery as an inherited position.

[1662]
WHEREAS some doubts have arisen whether children got by any Englishman upon a negro woman should be slave or free, *Be it therefore enacted and declared by this present grand assembly,* that all children borne in this country shall be held bond or free only according to the condition of the mother, *And* that if any christian shall commit fornication with a negro man or woman, he or she so offending shall pay double the fines imposed by the former act.

[1667]

WHEREAS some doubts have risen whether children that are slaves by birth, and by the charity and piety of their owners made pertakers of the blessed sacrament of baptisme, should by vertue of their baptisme be made free; *It is enacted and declared by this grand assembly, and the authority thereof*, that the conferring of baptisme doth not alter the condition of the person as to his bondage or freedome; that diverse masters, freed from this doubt, may more carefully endeavour the propagation of christianity by permitting children, though slaves, or those of greater growth if capable to be admitted to that sacrament.

Source: William W. Hening, ed., *The Statutes at Large; Being a Collection of All Laws of Virginia, from the First Session of the Legislature in the Year 1619* (Samuel Pleasants, 1810), 2:170, 260.

Source: William W. Hening, ed., *The Statutes at Large; Being a Collection of All Laws of Virginia, from the First Session of the Legislature in the Year 1619* (Samuel Pleasants, 1810), 2:170, 260.

Source 3.7

Joseph Ball Instructs His Nephew on Managing Enslaved Workers, 1743

Joseph Ball of Stratford, England, owned a tobacco plantation named Morattico in Lancaster County, Virginia. He lived in England, where he practiced law, so he employed his nephew Joseph Chinn to manage his estate. Ball sent Chinn detailed instructions about handling crops, livestock, the overseer, and the enslaved workers. He also visited Morattico regularly. This letter from February 1743 focuses on Chinn's care of the enslaved.

I will have what Goods I send to Virginia to the use of my Plantation there, kept in my House at Morattico.

If I should not send Goods enough, you must Supply the rest out of the stores there with my Tobacco.

The Coarse Cotton . . . was assign'd for blankets for my Negroes: there must be four yards a half to each Blanket. They that have [now] two blankets already; that is one tolerable one, and one pretty good one, must have what is wanting to make it up, 4½ yards in a blanket. And Everyone of the workers must have a Good Suite of the Welsh Plain [wool] made as it should be. Not to[o] Scanty, nor bobtail'd. And Each of the Children must have a Coat of Worser Cotton . . . and two shirts or shifts of ozenbrig [coarse linen] and the Workers must Each of them have Summer Shirtfs of the brown Rolls. And All the workers must have Good strong Shoes, & stockings; and they that go after the Creatures [livestock], or Much in the Wet, must have two pair of Shoes . . . and all must be done in Good time; and not for Winter to be half over before they get their summer Clothes; as the Common Virginia fashion is.

If any of the Negroes should be sick, let them ly by a Good fire; and have fresh Meat & brot[h]; and blood, and vomit [purge] them, as you shall think proper. . . . I would have no Doctor unless in very violent Cases: they Generally do more harm than Good. . . .

Let not the overseers abuse my People. Nor let them abuse their overseer.

Let the Breeding Wenches have Baby Clothes, for wh[ic]h you may tear up old sheets, or any other old Linen . . . (I shall Send things proper hereafter) and let them have Good Midwives; and what is necessary. Register all the Negro Children that shall be born and after keep an account of their ages among my Papers.

Source: Joseph Ball Letterbook, 1743–1759, in *Correspondence of Joseph Ball, 1743–1780*, Library of Congress.

Source: Joseph Ball Letterbook, 1743–1759, in *Correspondence of Joseph Ball, 1743–1780*, Library of Congress.

Source 3.8

Penny Print of Enslaved Blacks and Plantation Owner, c. 1750

This wood engraving was published by English author and engraver Frederick W. Fairholt in his 1859 book, *Tobacco, Its History and Associations*. The engraving was based on a cheap mid-eighteenth-century print sold by London printers Bowles and Carver. It depicts a prosperous colonial plantation owner and manager with bare-chested slaves packing and rolling hogsheads of tobacco. Well-dressed whites oversee the work while ships wait to transport the tobacco to England. The overhead banner honors Indians who introduced tobacco to the English.

A TOBACCO PLANTATION

Source 3.9

Richard Corbin Describes How to Become a Successful Planter, 1759

Richard Corbin (c. 1708–1790) owned tobacco plantations in King and Queen County, Virginia, and served as a burgess and receiver general of Virginia. Here he writes to his new manager, James Semple, describing his duties as well as the work of overseers and enslaved laborers. Corbin describes the crucial processes in preparing cut leaves for market — "striking" them down from the rafters where they are hung to cure; "stripping" the leaves from the stalk; and "stemming," or rolling, individual leaves, which are then "prized" or packed in a hogshead.

As it will be Necessary to . . . Suggest to you my Thoughts upon the business you have undertaken, I shall endeavor to be particular and Circumstanial. . . .

Observe a prudent and a Watchful Conduct over the Overseers that they attend their business with diligence; keep the Negroes in good order and enforce obedience by the Example of their own Industry, wch [which] is a more effectual method in every respect . . . than Hurry and Severity; the ways of Industry are constant and regular, not to be in a hurry at one time and do nothing at another, but to be always Usefully and Steadily employed. . . .

Take an Exact account of all the Negroes & Stocks [animals] at each Plantation and send to me; & tho[ugh] once a year may be sufficient to take this acct, yet it will be advisable to see them once a Month at least, as such an Inspection will fix more closely the overseers attention to these points.

As complaints have been made by the Negroes in respect to their provision of corn, I must desire you to put that matter under such a Regulation, as your own Prudence will dictate. . . . The allowance to be sure is Plentiful and they ought to have their Belly full but care must be taken with this Plenty that no Waiste [waste] is Committed. . . .

Tob[acc]o h[ogs]h[ea]ds [large casks] should always be provided the 1st Week in Sept; every morning of that month is fit for Striking & Stripping; every morning therefore of this month, they should Strike as much Tob[acc]o as they can strip whilst the Dew is upon the Ground and what they Strip in the morning must be Stem'd in the Evening; this method constantly practiced, the Tobacco will be prised before Christmas, Weigh well, and at least one hhd in Ten gained by finishing the Tob[acc]o thus early.

Source: Richard Corbin to Mr. James Semple, January 1, 1759, Richard Corbin Letterbook, Manuscript DMS 1971.5, John D. Rockefeller, Jr. Library, Colonial Williamsburg Foundation.

Source 3.10

Lieutenant Governor William Gooch to the Board of Trade, London, 1729

William Gooch served as lieutenant governor and governor of the Virginia colony from 1727 to 1749. His success depended in large part on his support for Virginia's tobacco planters, who comprised the colony's ruling elite. His frequent letters to the Board of Trade in London addressed planters' and the board's concerns regarding trade relations, debt collection, the quality of tobacco, and, in the letter below, resistance among some enslaved workers.

Some time after my last [letter] a number of negroes, about fifteen, belonging to a new plantation, . . . formed a design to withdraw from their master and to fix themselves in the fastnesses of the neighbouring mountains: they had found means to get into their possession some arms and ammunition, and they took along with them some provisions, their cloaths, bedding and working tools; but the Gentleman to whom they belonged with a party of men made such diligent pursuit after them, that he soon found them out in their settlement, a very obscure place among the mountains, where they had already begun to clear the ground, and obliged them after exchanging a shot or two by which one of the slaves was wounded, to surrender and return back, and so prevented for this time a design which might have proved as dangerous to this country, as is that of the negroes in the mountains of Jamaica to the inhabitants of that island. Tho' this attempt has happily been defeated, it ought nevertheless to awaken us into some effectual measures for preventing the like hereafter, it being certain that a very small number of negroes once settled in those parts, would very soon be encreas'd by the accession of other runaways and prove dangerous neighbours to our frontier inhabitants.

Source: Lt. Gov. William Gooch to Board of Trade, June 29, 1729, *Calendar of State Papers, Colonial Series, America and the West Indies, 1728–1729* (London, 1937), 414–15, in Paul G. E. Clemens, ed., *The Colonial Era: A Documentary Reader* (Malden, MA: Blackwell, 2008), 135–36.

Interpret the Evidence

1. Why did Virginia lawmakers decide that the status of the enslaved should pass through the mother's (rather than father's) line and would be unaffected by baptism (Source 3.6)?

2. What do the descriptions of "Negro" life and labor by Joseph Ball and Richard Corbin reveal about the attitudes of Virginia planters toward enslaved workers (Sources 3.7 and 3.9)? Because no slaves in the region and time period left us direct descriptions of their lives, what limitations do these sources present for historians?

3. How does the engraving (Source 3.8) distinguish between the roles of white planters and managers and black enslaved workers? As a penny print, how would this image shape ideas about slavery among the English?

4. What issues about slave life on a tobacco plantation are raised by Lieutenant Governor William Gooch (Source 3.10), and how do they compare with the image presented in the engraving (Source 3.8) and the writings by enslavers (Sources 3.7 and 3.9)?

Put It in Context

What were the relationships among the growing demand for tobacco, the actions of Virginia politicians and planters, and the lives of enslaved laborers?

What were the greatest challenges faced by white colonists (including those who owned slaves and those who did not) and by black laborers as the Atlantic slave trade expanded between 1680 and 1750?

Religious Strife and Social Upheavals

1680–1754

Window to the Past

Isaac Royall Jr and His Family, 1741

In 1737, Isaac Royall Sr. moved his family and 27 enslaved workers from his Antigua plantation to Massachusetts after facing drought, storms, and a slave rebellion. Two years later, Royall Sr. died and left his estate to his son, Isaac Royall Jr., aged twenty. A year earlier, Royall Jr. had married Elizabeth McIntosh, the daughter of a wealthy neighbor, ensuring his place among colonial elites. He joined the Governor's Council in 1752 and in 1779 left a bequest to Harvard College to establish the first professorship of law. ▶ To learn more about this primary source, see Source 4.2 on page 114.

Historical & Special Collections, Harvard Law School Library

After reading this chapter you will be able to:

- Explain the relationships among religious, economic, and political tensions and accusations of witchcraft.

- Describe family dynamics, particularly between husbands and wives, and how they changed over time and differed by class and region.

- Understand the ways that economic development, increasing diversity, and continued expansion fueled conflicts among various groups in the early eighteenth century.

- Explain the emergence of the Great Awakening and identify its critics and legacies.

- Describe how the Great Awakening shaped political developments in the 1730s and 1740s.

Comparing American Histories

The son of a Scots-Irish clergyman, **Gilbert Tennent** was born in Vinecash, Ireland, in 1703 and at age fifteen moved with his family to Philadelphia. After receiving an M.A. from Yale College in 1725, Gilbert was ordained a Presbyterian minister in New Brunswick, New Jersey, with little indication of the significant role he would play in a denominational schism.

Tennent entered the ministry at a critical moment, when leaders of a number of denominations had become convinced that the colonies were descending into spiritual apathy. Tennent dedicated himself to sparking a rebirth of Christian commitment, and by the mid-1730s he had gained

(*left*) **Gilbert Tennent** Granger
(*right*) **Gravestone of Sarah Grosvenor** Jessica C. Linker

fame as a revival preacher. At the end of the decade, Tennent journeyed through the middle colonies with Englishman George Whitefield, an Anglican preacher known for igniting powerful revivals. In the fall of 1740, following the death of his wife, Tennent launched his own evangelical "awakenings."

Revivals inspired thousands of religious conversions across denominations, but they also fueled conflicts within established churches. Presbyterians in Britain and America disagreed about whether only those who had had a powerful, personal conversion experience were qualified to be ministers. Tennent made his opinion clear by denouncing unconverted ministers in his sermons, a position that led to his expulsion from the Presbyterian Church in 1741. But many local churches sought converted preachers, and four years later a group of ejected pastors formed a rival synod that trained its own evangelical ministers.

While ministers debated the proper means of saving sinners, ordinary women and men searched their souls. In Pomfret, Connecticut, **Sarah Grosvenor** certainly feared for hers in the summer of 1742 when the unmarried nineteen-year-old realized she was pregnant. Her situation was complicated by her status in the community. She was the daughter of Leicester Grosvenor, an important landowner, town official, and member of the Congregational Church.

The pew next to Sarah and her family was occupied by Nathaniel Sessions and his sons, including the twenty-six-year-old Amasa, who had impregnated Sarah. Many other young women became pregnant out of wedlock in the 1740s, but families accepted the fact as long as the couple married before the child was born. However, Amasa refused to marry Sarah and suggested instead that she have an abortion.

Although Sarah was reluctant to follow this path, Amasa insisted. When herbs traditionally used to induce a miscarriage failed, Amasa introduced Sarah to John Hallowell, a doctor who claimed he could remove the fetus with forceps. After admitting her agonizing situation to her older sister Zerviah and her cousin Hannah, Sarah allowed Hallowell to proceed. He finally induced a miscarriage, but Sarah soon grew feverish, suffered convulsions, and died ten days later.

Apparently Sarah's and Amasa's parents were unaware of the events leading to her demise. Then in 1745, a powerful religious revival swept through the region, and Zerviah and Hannah suffered great spiritual anguish. It is likely they confessed their part in the affair since that year officials brought charges against Amasa Sessions and John Hallowell for Sarah's death. At the men's trial, Zerviah and Hannah testified about their roles and those of Sessions and Hallowell. There was to be no earthly justice, however. Hallowell was found guilty but escaped punishment by fleeing to Rhode Island. Sessions was acquitted and remained in Pomfret, where he married and became a prosperous farmer. ■

Comparing the American histories of Gilbert Tennent and Sarah Grosvenor reveals the power of the religious forces — later called the Great Awakening — that swept through the colonies in the early eighteenth century. Those forces are best understood in the context of larger social, economic, and political changes. By the early eighteenth century, many young people became more independent of their parents and developed tighter bonds with siblings, cousins, and neighbors their own age. Towns and cities developed clearer hierarchies by class and status, which could protect wealthier individuals from being punished for their misdeeds. A double standard of sexual behavior became more entrenched as well, with women subject to greater scrutiny than men for their sexual behavior. These changes occurred as more German and Scots-Irish immigrants brought their own familial ideals and religious beliefs to the colonies. As they pushed settlement westward, they confronted Indians and former servants who were also hoping to find peace and economic opportunity in those areas. Amid these transformations, most young women managed to avoid the fate of Sarah Grosvenor. Still, pastors like Gilbert Tennent feared precisely such consequences if the colonies — growing ever larger and more diverse — did not reclaim their religious foundations.

An **Ungodly Society?**

As American colonists became more engaged in international and domestic commerce, spiritual commitments appeared to wane. In New England, Congregational ministers condemned the apparent triumph of worldly ambition over religiosity. Nonetheless, some ministers saw economic success as a reward for godly behavior even as they worried that wealth and power opened the door to sin. In the late seventeenth century, these anxieties deepened when accusations of witchcraft erupted across southern New England.

The Rise of Religious Anxieties. In 1686 the Puritan minister Samuel Sewell railed against the behavior of Boston mercantile elites. Citing examples of their depravity in his diary, including drunkenness and cursing, he claimed that such "high-handed wickedness has hardly been heard of before." Sewell was outraged as well by popular practices such as donning powdered wigs in place of God-given hair, wearing scarlet and gold jackets rather than simple black cloth, and offering toasts rather than prayers.

While Sewell spoke for many Puritans concerned with the consequences of commercial success, other religious leaders tried to meld old and new. The Reverend Cotton Mather complained that many colonists showed greater interest in the latest fashions than in the state of their souls. Yet he was attracted by the luxuries available to colonists and hoped to make his own son "a more finished Gentleman." Mather was also fascinated by new scientific endeavors and supported inoculations for smallpox, which others viewed as challenging God's power.

Certainly news of the Glorious Revolution in England (1688) offered Puritans hope of regaining their customary authority (see "English Colonies Grow and Multiply" in chapter 3). But the outbreak of King William's War in 1689 quickly ended any notion of an easy return to peace and prosperity. Instead, continued conflicts at home and abroad and renewed fears of Indian attacks on rural settlements heightened colonists' sense that Satan was at work in the region. Soon, accusations of witchcraft joined outcries against other forms of ungodly behavior.

Cries of Witchcraft. Belief in witchcraft had been widespread in Europe and England for centuries. It was part of a general belief in supernatural causes for events that could not otherwise be explained — severe storms, an eclipse, a rash of deaths among livestock. When a community began to suspect witchcraft, they often pointed to individuals who challenged cultural norms. Women who were quarrelsome, eccentric, poor, or simply too independent were easy to imagine as cavorting with evil spirits and invisible demons.

Witchcraft accusations tended to be most common in times of change and uncertainty. Over the course of the seventeenth century, colonists had begun to spread into new areas seeking more land and greater economic opportunities. But expansion brought with it confrontations with Indians, exposure to new dangers, and greater vulnerability to a harsh environment. As the stress of expansion mounted, witchcraft accusations emerged. Some 160 individuals, mostly women, were accused of witchcraft in Massachusetts and Connecticut and 15 were put to death between 1647 and 1691. Many of the accused were poor, childless, or disgruntled women, but widows who inherited property also came under suspicion, especially if they fought for control against male relatives and neighbors.

The social and economic complexities of witchcraft accusations are well illustrated by the most famous American witch-hunt, the Salem witch trials of the early 1690s. In 1692 residents of Salem, Massachusetts confronted conflicts between long-settled farmers and newer mercantile families, political uncertainties following the Glorious Revolution in England, ongoing threats from Indians, and quarrels over the choice of a new minister. These tensions were brought to a head when the Reverend Samuel Parris's daughter and niece learned voodoo lore and exotic dances from the household's West Indian slave, Tituba. The daughters and servants of neighboring families also became entranced by Tituba's tales and began to tell fortunes, speak in gibberish, and contort their bodies into painful positions. When the girls were questioned about their strange behavior, they pointed not only to Tituba but also to other people in the community. They first accused an elderly female pauper and a homeless widow of bewitching them, but later singled out respectable churchwomen as well as a minister, a wealthy merchant, and a four-year-old child.

Within weeks, more than one hundred individuals, 80 percent of them women, stood accused of witchcraft. Governor William Phips established a special court to handle the cases, over which the Reverend Samuel Sewell presided. Twenty-seven of the accused came to trial, and twenty were found guilty based on testimony from the girls and on spectral evidence, that is, evidence that came to the girls in dreams or visions. In court, the young accusers writhed, shook, and cried out in pain as spirits of the accused, invisible to everyone else, pinched, choked, and bit them. Based on such evidence, nineteen people were hanged, and one was pressed to death with stones.

Explore ▶

Read the appeal of a woman accused of witchcraft in Source 4.1.

But when accusations reached into prominent Salem and Boston families, Governor Phips ended the proceedings and released the remaining suspects. In the following months, leading ministers and colonial officials condemned the use of spectral evidence, and some young accusers recanted their testimony.

The Salem trials illuminate far more than beliefs in witchcraft. The trials pitted the daughters and servants of prosperous farmers against the wives and widows of recently arrived merchants. The accusers included young women like nineteen-year-old Mercy Lewis, who was bound out as a servant when her parents were killed by Indians. Fear of attack from hostile Indians, hostile officials in England, or hostile neighbors fostered anxieties in Salem, as it did in many colonial communities. Other anxieties also haunted the accusers. A shortage of land led many New England men to seek their fortune farther west, leaving young women with fewer opportunities to marry. Battles over inheritance forestalled marriages as well. Thomas Putnam Jr., who housed three of the accusers, was in the midst of such a battle. It left his three sisters—the accusers' aunts—in limbo as they awaited legacies that could enhance their marriage prospects. As young women in Salem forged tight bonds in the face of such uncertainties, they turned their anger not against men, but instead against older women, including respectable "goodwives" like Abigail Faulkner.

Review & Relate

- What factors led to rising tensions within colonial communities in the early 1700s?

- How did social, economic, and political tensions contribute to an increase in accusations of witchcraft?

Family and Household Dynamics

Concerns about marriage, property, and inheritance were not limited to Salem or to New England. As the American colonies became more populous and the numbers of women and men more balanced, husbands sought greater control over the behavior of household members while the legal and economic rewards available to most women declined. Yet some women improved their situation by wielding their skills as midwives, brewers, or even plantation managers to benefit themselves and their families.

Women's Changing Status. In most early American colonies, the scarcity of women and workers ensured that many white women gained economic and legal leverage. In the first decades of settlement in the Chesapeake, where women were in especially short supply and mortality was high, young women who arrived as indentured servants and completed their term might marry older men of property. If the husbands died first, widows often took control of the estate and passed on the property to their children. Even in New England, where the numbers of men and women were more balanced from the beginning, the crucial labor of wives in the early decades of settlement was sometimes recognized by their control of family property after a husband's death.

Guided Primary Source Analysis

Abigail Faulkner Appeals Her Conviction for Witchcraft, 1692

While most women accused of witchcraft in Salem were marginal to society, Abigail Faulkner was the daughter of a minister and the wife of a large landowner. Nonetheless, she was declared guilty on the basis of spectral evidence and the charges made by "bewitched" girls. When Faulkner's execution was postponed, she petitioned Governor Phips to release her. Faulkner was released, but only after Massachusetts officials stepped in and ended the trials.

Source 4.1

The humblee Petition of Abigall: Falkner unto his Excellencye S'r W'm Phipps knight and Govern'r of their Majestyes Dominions in America: humbly sheweth

That your poor and humble Petitioner having been this four monthes in Salem Prison and condemned to die having had no other evidences against me but the Spectre Evidences and the Confessors w'ch Confessors have lately since I was condemned owned to my selfe and others and doe still own that they wronged me and what they had said against me was false: and that they would not that I should have been put to death for a thousand worldes for they never should have enjoyed themselves againe in this world; w'ch undoubtedly I shouled have been put to death had it not pleased the Lord I had been with child. Thankes be to the Lord I know my selfe altogether Innocent & Ignorant of the crime of witchcraft w'ch is layd to my charge: as will appeare at the great day of Judgment (May it please yo'r Excellencye) my husband about five yeares a goe was taken w'th fitts w'ch did very much impaire his memory and understanding but w'th the blessing of the Lord upon my Endeavors did recover of them againe but now through greife and sorrow they are returned to him againe as bad as Ever they were: I having six children and having little or nothing to subsist on being in a manner without a head [husband] to doe any thinge for my selfe or them and being closely confined can see no otherwayes but we shall all perish Therfore may it please your Excellencye your poor and humble petition'r doe humbly begge and Implore of yo'r Excellencye to take it into yo'r pious and Judicious consideration that some speedy Course may be taken w'th me for my releasement.

Source: Paul Boyer and Stephen Nissenbaum, eds., *The Salem Witchcraft Papers, Verbatim Transcripts of the Legal Documents of the Salem Witchcraft Outbreak of 1692* (New York: Da Capo Press, 1977), 1:333–34.

What evidence does Faulkner provide of her innocence?

What saved Faulkner from being executed initially?

How does Faulkner try to persuade Governor Phips of the need for immediate action?

Put It in Context

How might the conviction of a woman like Abigail Faulkner have helped bring an end to the Salem witch trials?

TABLE 4.1   Sex Ratios in the White Population for Selected Colonies, 1624–1755

Date	Colony	White Male Population	White Female Population	Females per 100 Males
1624–1625	Virginia	873	222	25
1660	Maryland	c. 600	c. 190	32
1704	Maryland	11,026	7,136	65
1698	New York	5,066	4,677	92
1726	New Jersey	15,737	14,124	90
1755	Rhode Island	17,860	17,979	101

By the late seventeenth century, however, as the sex ratio in the Chesapeake evened out, white women lost the opportunity to marry "above their class" (see Table 4.1). And across the colonies, more widows lost control of family estates. Even though women still performed vital labor, the spread of indentured servitude and slavery lessened the recognition of wives' contributions, while in urban areas the rise of commerce highlighted their role as consumers rather than producers. As a result, most wives and daughters of English colonists were assigned primarily domestic roles. They also found their legal and economic rights restricted to those accorded their female counterparts in Great Britain.

According to English common law, a wife's status was defined as *feme covert*, which meant that she was legally covered over by (or hidden behind) her husband. The husband controlled his wife's labor, the house in which she lived, the property she brought into the marriage, and any wages she earned. He was also the legal guardian of their children, and through the instrument of his will could continue to control the household after his death.

With the growth and diversity of colonial towns and cities, the **patriarchal family** — a model in which fathers held absolute authority over wives, children, and servants — came to be seen as a crucial bulwark against disorder. Families with wealth were especially eager to control the behavior of their sons and daughters as the parents sought to build social, commercial, and political alliances. The refusal of Amasa Sessions to marry Sarah Grosvenor, for instance, may have resulted from his father's expectation of a better match.

Explore ▶

Compare the images of elite women conveyed in a family portrait and a personal letter in Source 4.2 and 4.3.

Working Families.   Still, for most colonial women and men, daily rounds of labor shaped their lives more powerfully than legal statutes or inheritance rights. Husbands and wives depended on each other to support the family. By the early eighteenth century, many colonial writers promoted the idea of marriage as a partnership, even if the wife remained the junior partner.

This concept of marriage as a partnership took practical form in communities across the colonies. In towns, the wives of artisans often learned aspects of their husband's craft and assisted their husbands in a variety of ways. Given the overlap between homes and workplaces in the eighteenth century, women often cared for apprentices, journeymen, and laborers as well as their own children. Husbands meanwhile labored alongside their subordinates and represented their families' interests to the larger community. Both spouses were expected to provide models of godliness and to encourage prayer and regular church attendance among household members.

Comparative Primary Source Analysis

Elite Women's Lives in the North American Colonies

By the 1740s, elite women were viewed as paragons of piety and domesticity. Many also contributed wealth and management skills to family enterprises. The painting by Robert Feke (Source 4.2) portrays Elizabeth and Isaac Royall of Medford, Massachusetts, with their daughter and a sister of each. Isaac's estate was built on his deceased father's trade in rum, sugar, and slaves from Antigua while his place in the colonial elite was ensured by his marriage to Elizabeth McIntosh. Elizabeth cared for the family and managed a staff that included a dozen slaves. In Source 4.3, twenty-year-old Eliza Lucas, born on Antigua, describes her typical routine. Although young and single, she managed her father's South Carolina plantations, adding substantially to the family's wealth and to the enslaved population that worked the estate.

Source 4.2

Isaac Royall and His Family, 1741

Historical & Special Collections, Harvard Law School Library

Source 4.3

Eliza Lucas | Letter to Miss Bartlett, London, c. 1742

Why, my dear Miss B, will you so often repeat your desire to know how I triffle away my time. . . . [H]ere it is.

In general then I rise at five o'Clock in the morning, read till Seven, then take a walk in the garden or field, see that the Servants [slaves] are at their respective business, then to breakfast. The first hour after breakfast is spent at my musick, the next is constantly employed in recolecting something I have learned least . . . , such as French and short hand. . . . I devote the rest of the time till I dress for dinner to our little Polly and two black girls who I teach to read, and if I have my papa's approbation (my Mamas I have got) I intend [them] for school mistres's for the rest of the Negroe children. . . . [After dinner, musick and then] the rest of the afternoon in Needle work till candle light, and from that time to bed read or

write. . . . I have particular matter for particular days. . . . Mondays my musick Master is here. Tuesday my friend Mrs. Chardon (about 3 miles distant) and I are constantly engaged to each other, she at our house one Tuesday—I at hers the next, and this is one of the happiest days I spend at Woppoe. Thursday the whole day . . . is spent in writing, either on the business of the plantation, or letters to my friends. Every other Fryday . . . we go a vizeting so that I go abroad once a week and no oftener. . . .

O! I had like to forgot the last thing I have done a great while. I have planted a large figg orchard with design to dry and export them. . . . [W]as I to tell you how great an Estate I am to make this way . . . you would think me far gone in romance.

Source: Eliza Lucas Pinckney Letterbook, 1739–1762, South Carolina Historical Society.

Interpret the Evidence

1. What do the positions of the Royall family members, their clothing, and the furnishings indicate about the family's and the women's status?
2. How does Eliza Lucas's description of her activities compare with those you imagine the Royall women perform? In what ways do these sources reflect or challenge patriarchal ideals?

Put It in Context

How did the profits of slavery and the slave trade shape the lives of elite women in northern and southern colonies?

On farms, where the vast majority of colonists lived, women and men played crucial if distinct roles. In general, wives and daughters labored inside the home as well as in the surrounding yard with its kitchen garden, milk house, chicken coop, dairy, or washhouse. Husbands and sons worked the fields, kept the livestock, and managed the orchards. Many families supplemented their own labor with that of servants, slaves, or hired field hands. And surplus crops and manufactured goods such as cloth or sausage were exchanged with neighbors or sold at market, creating an economic network of small producers.

Indeed, by the late seventeenth and early eighteenth centuries, many farm families in long-settled areas participated in a household mode of production. Men lent each other tools and draft animals and shared grazing land, while women gathered to spin, sew, and quilt. Individuals with special skills like midwifery or blacksmithing assisted neighbors, adding farm produce or credit to the family ledger. One woman's cheese might be bartered for another woman's jam. A family that owned the necessary equipment might brew neighbors' barley and malt into beer, while a family with a loom would turn yarn into cloth. The system of exchange, managed largely through barter, allowed individual households to function even as they became more specialized in what they produced. Whatever cash was obtained could be used to buy sugar, tea, and other imported goods.

Harvest Scene   Mary Woodhull was born on Long Island in 1743 and created this colorful needlepoint sampler sometime before her marriage to Amos Underhill. Such decorative samplers were often hung in the family parlor to illustrate the young woman's ideals and skills to prospective husbands. Interestingly here, both the woman and the man are holding scythes used to cut the grain. Granger

Reproduction and Women's Roles. Maintaining a farm required the work of both women and men, which made marriage an economic as well as a social and religious institution. In the early eighteenth century, more than 90 percent of white women married. By 1700 a New England wife who married at age twenty and survived to forty-five bore an average of eight children, most of whom lived to adulthood. In the Chesapeake, mortality rates remained higher and the sex ratio still favored men. It thus took another generation for white women in that region to come close to the reproductive rates of their northern counterparts.

Harsh conditions of labor and poor nutrition and health care ensured that fertility rates among enslaved Africans and African Americans remained much lower than those among whites in the early eighteenth century. And fewer infants survived to adulthood. It was not until the 1740s that the majority of enslaved laborers were born in the colonies rather than imported. By then, some southern enslavers, especially those owning larger estates, began to realize that encouraging reproduction made good economic sense. Still, enslaved women, most of whom worked in the fields, gained only minimal relief from their labors during pregnancy.

Colonial mothers who were free combined childbearing and child rearing with a great deal of other work. While some affluent families could afford wet nurses and nannies, most women fended for themselves or hired temporary help for particular tasks. In rural areas, mothers with babies on hip and children under foot hauled water, fed chickens, collected eggs, picked vegetables, prepared meals, spun thread, and manufactured soap and candles. Children were at constant risk of disease and injury, but were spared the overcrowding, the raw sewage, and the foul water that marked ever-growing cities.

Infants were the most vulnerable to disease, and parents were relieved when their children passed their first birthdays. Colonists feared the deaths of mothers as well. In 1700 roughly one out of thirty births ended in the mother's death. Women who bore six to eight children thus faced death on a regular basis. One minister urged pregnant women to prepare their souls, "For ought you know your Death has entered into you."

When a mother died while her children were still young, her husband was likely to remarry soon afterward in order to maintain the family and his farm or business. Even though fathers held legal guardianship over their children, there was little doubt that child rearing, especially for young children, was women's work. Many husbands acknowledged this role, prayed for their wives while in labor, and sought to ease their domestic burdens near the end of a pregnancy. But some women gained little help or protection from their husbands.

The Limits of Patriarchal Order. While most white families accepted the idea of female subordination in return for patriarchal protection, there were signs of change in the early eighteenth century. Sermons against fornication; ads for runaway spouses, servants, and slaves; reports of domestic violence; poems about domineering wives; petitions for divorce; and legal suits charging rape, seduction, or breach of contract make clear that ideals of patriarchal authority did not always match the reality. It is impossible to quantify the frequency with which women contested their subordination, but a variety of evidence points to increasing tensions around issues of control — by husbands over wives, fathers over children, and men over women.

Women's claims about men's misbehavior were often demeaned as gossip, but gossip could be an important weapon for those who had little chance of legal redress. In colonial communities, credit and trust were central to networks of exchange, so damaging a man's reputation could be a serious matter. Still, gossip was not as powerful as legal sanctions.

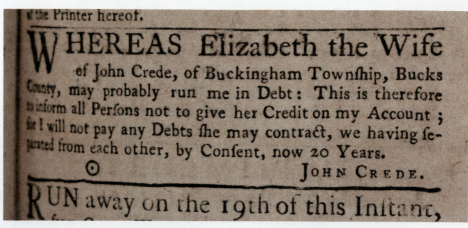

WHEREAS Elizabeth the Wife of John Crede, of Buckingham Township, Bucks County, may probably run me in Debt: This is therefore to inform all Persons not to give her Credit on my Account; for I will not pay any Debts she may contract, we having separated from each other, by Consent, now 20 Years.

                                   JOHN CREDE.

RUN away on the 19th of this Instant,

Advertising a Married Couple's Separation Although it was difficult to obtain a legal divorce, husbands and wives sometimes abandoned each other or agreed to separate. In this June 1743 notice in the *Pennsylvania Gazette*, John Crede notified merchants and other creditors that he would not pay debts contracted by his wife, Elizabeth, from whom he claimed to have been separated for twenty years. Library of Congress

Thus some women who bore illegitimate children, suffered physical and sexual abuse, or were left penniless by a husband who drank might seek assistance from the courts.

Divorce was as rare in the colonies as it was in England. In New England, colonial law allowed for divorce, but few were granted and almost none to women before 1750. In other colonies, divorce could be obtained only by an act of the colonial assembly and was therefore confined to the wealthy and powerful. If a divorce was granted, the wife usually received an allowance for food and clothing. Yet without independent financial resources, she nearly always had to live with relatives. Custody of any children was awarded to fathers who had the economic means to support them, although infants or young girls might be assigned to live with the mother. A quicker and cheaper means of ending an unsatisfactory marriage was to abandon one's spouse. Again wives were at a disadvantage since they had few means to support themselves or their children. Colonial divorce petitions citing desertion and newspaper ads for runaway spouses suggest that it was husbands who fled in at least two-thirds of such cases.

In the rare instances when women did obtain a divorce, they had to bring multiple charges against their husbands. Domestic violence, adultery, or abandonment alone was insufficient to gain redress. Indeed, ministers and relatives were likely to counsel abused wives to change their behavior or suffer in silence. Even evidence of brutal assaults on a wife rarely led to legal redress because physical punishment was widely accepted and husbands had the legal right to "correct" their wives and children.

Single women also faced barriers in seeking legal redress. By the late seventeenth century, church and civil courts in New England gave up on coercing sexually active couples to marry. Judges, however, continued to hear complaints of seduction or breach of contract brought by the fathers of single women who were pregnant but unmarried. Had Sarah Grosvenor survived the abortion, her family could have sued Amasa Sessions on the grounds that he gained "carnal knowledge" of her through "promises of marriage." If the

TABLE 4.2   Sexual Coercion Cases Downgraded in Chester County, Pennsylvania, 1731–1739

Date	Defendant/Victim	Charge on Indictment in Testimony	Charge in Docket
1731	Lawrence MacGinnis/Alice Yarnal	Assault with attempt to rape	None
1731	Thomas Culling/Martha Claypool	Assault with attempt to rape	Assault
1734	Abraham Richardson/Mary Smith	Attempted rape	Assault
1734	Thomas Beckett/Mindwell Fulfourd	Theft (testimony of attempted rape)	Theft
1734	Unknown/Christeen Pauper	(Fornication charge against Christeen)	None
1735	Daniel Patterson/Hannah Tanner	Violent assault to ravish	Assault
1736	James White/Hannah McCradle	Attempted rape/adultery	Assault
1737	Robert Mills/Catherine Parry	Rape	None
1738	John West/Isabella Gibson	Attempt to ravish/assault	Fornication
1739	Thomas Halladay/Mary Mouks	Assault with intent to ravish	None

Source: Sharon Block, *Rape and Sexual Power in Early America* (Chapel Hill: University of North Carolina Press). Data from Chester County Quarter Sessions Docket Books and File Papers, 1730–1739.

plaintiffs won, the result was no longer marriage, however, but financial support for the child. In 1730 in Concord, Massachusetts, Susanna Holding sued a farmer, Joseph Bright, whom she accused of fathering her illegitimate child. When Bright protested his innocence, Holding found townsmen to testify that the farmer, "in his courting of her . . . had designed to make her his Wife." In this case, the abandoned mother mobilized members of the community, including men, to uphold popular understandings of patriarchal responsibilities. Without such support, women were less likely to win their cases.

Women who were raped faced even greater legal obstacles than those who were seduced and abandoned. In most colonies, rape was a capital crime, punishable by death, and all-male juries were reluctant to find men guilty. Unlikely to win and fearing humiliation in court, few women charged men with rape. Yet more did so than the records might show since judges and justices of the peace sometimes downgraded rape charges to simple assault or fornication, that is, sex outside of marriage (Table 4.2).

Young white women had the best chance of gaining support and redress for seduction or rape if they confided in their parents or other elders. But by the mid-eighteenth century, young people were seeking more control over their sexual behavior and marriage prospects. Certain behaviors — sons settling in towns distant from their parents, younger daughters marrying before their older sisters, and single women finding themselves pregnant — increased noticeably. In part, these trends were natural consequences of colonial growth and mobility. The bonds that once held families and communities together began to loosen. But in the process, young women's chances of protecting themselves against errant and abusive men diminished. Just as important, even when they faced desperate situations, young women like Sarah Grosvenor increasingly turned to sisters and friends for help rather than fathers or ministers.

Poor women, especially those who labored as servants, had even fewer options. Servants faced tremendous obstacles in obtaining legal independence from masters or mistresses who beat or sexually assaulted them. Colonial judges and juries generally refused to declare a man who was wealthy enough to support servants guilty of criminal acts against them. Moreover, poor women generally and servants in particular were regularly depicted as lusty and immoral, making it unlikely that they would gain the sympathy of white judges or juries. Enslaved workers faced many of the same obstacles and had even less hope of prevailing against brutal owners. Thus for most servants and slaves, running away was their sole hope for escaping abuse. However, if they were caught, their situation would likely worsen. Even poor whites who lived independently had little chance of addressing issues of domestic violence, seduction, or rape through the courts.

Review & Relate

▪ Why and how did the legal and economic circumstances of colonial women decline between 1650 and 1750? How did the circumstances of black and white women compare?

▪ How did patriarchal ideals of family and community shape life and work in colonial America? What happened when men failed to live up to those ideals?

Diversity and Competition in Colonial Society

As the English colonies in North America expanded, divisions increased between established families living in long-settled regions—whether on rural farmsteads or in urban homesteads—and the growing population of women and men with few resources. Although most white colonists still hoped to own their own land and establish themselves as farmers, artisans, or shopkeepers, fewer were likely to succeed than in the past. By 1760 half of all white men in North America owned no property. This growing class cleavage was accompanied by increasing racial, national, and religious diversity, which fostered greater economic competition and social conflict.

Population Growth and Economic Competition.
After 1700, the population grew rapidly across the colonies. In 1700 about 250,000 people lived in England's North American colonies. By 1725 that number had doubled, and fifty years later it reached 2.5 million. Much of the increase was due to natural reproduction, but in addition nearly 250,000 immigrants and enslaved Africans arrived in the colonies between 1700 and 1750.

Because more women and children arrived than in earlier decades, higher birthrates and a more youthful population resulted. At the same time, most white colonists in North America enjoyed a better diet than their counterparts in Europe and had access to more abundant natural resources. In the eighteenth century, these colonists began living longer, with more adults surviving to watch their children and grandchildren grow up.

However, as the population soared, the chance for individuals to obtain land or start a business of their own diminished. Those white men and women who had established businesses early generally expanded to meet new needs, making it more difficult for others to compete. The vast majority who planned to make their living from the land found the soil exhausted in long-settled regions. As white colonists sought to carve out farms on the frontier, they found themselves facing forests and swamps or areas already claimed by Indian, French, or Spanish residents. While owning land did not automatically lead to prosperity, most individuals who were landless could only find work as tenant farmers, laborers, or in

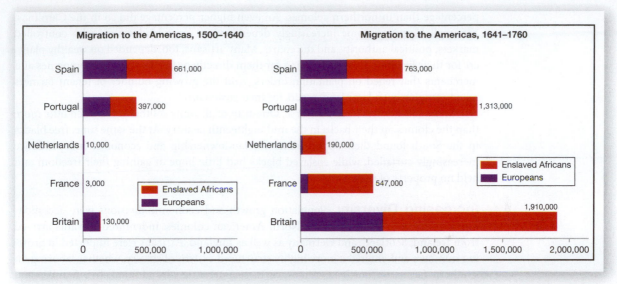

FIGURE 4.1   Transatlantic Migrations, 1500–1640 & 1641–1750

This figure charts the changing population of the Americas from 1500 to 1760. By recording the changing population of various European migrants as well as that of enslaved Africans, the figure reveals the centrality of slavery to the development of the Americas. Which European nation imported the largest number of enslaved Africans in each period, and which European nation held the greatest percentage of enslaved Africans relative to their population?

Source of Data: Stanley L. Engerman and Kenneth L. Sokoloff, "Factor Endowments, Institutions, and Differential Paths of Growth Among New World Economies: A View from Economic Historians of the United States," in *How Latin America Fell Behind: Economic Histories of Brazil and Mexico, 1800–1914*, ed. Stephen Haber (Stanford University Press, 1997), 264.

other unskilled occupations. In the South Carolina backcountry, a visitor in the mid-eighteenth century noted that many white residents "have nought but a Gourd to drink out of, nor a Plate, Knive or Spoon, a Glass, Cup, or anything."

In prosperous parts of the Middle Atlantic colonies like Pennsylvania, many white landless laborers abandoned rural life and searched for urban opportunities. They moved to Philadelphia or other towns and cities in the region, seeking jobs as dockworkers, street vendors, or servants, or as apprentices in one of the skilled trades. But newcomers found the job market flooded with poor whites and free and enslaved blacks. The chances for significant advancement over their lifetime were growing slim (Figure 4.1).

In the South, too, divisions between rich and poor became more pronounced in the early decades of the eighteenth century. Tobacco was the most valuable product in the Chesapeake, and the largest tobacco planters, who owned the most enslaved workers, lived in relative luxury. Although they did not build the kind of fancy plantation homesteads that would appear in the mid-nineteenth century, they benefitted enormously from the thriving Atlantic economy. Planters developed mercantile contacts — including among slave traders — in seaport cities on the Atlantic coast and in the Caribbean. They also imported luxury goods from Europe and began deploying some of their enslaved women as domestic workers to relieve wives and daughters of the strain of household labor.

Even small farmers could purchase and maintain a farm and profit from the tobacco trade. In 1750 two-thirds of white families farmed their own land in Virginia, a larger percentage than in northern colonies. An even higher percentage did so in the Carolinas. Yet small farmers became increasingly dependent on large landowners, who controlled markets, political authority, and the courts. Many artisans, too, depended on wealthy planters for their livelihood, either working for them directly or for the shipping companies and merchants that relied on plantation orders. And the growing number of tenant farmers relied completely on large landowners for their sustenance.

Some southerners fared far worse. One-fifth of all white southerners owned little more than the clothes on their backs in the mid-eighteenth century. At the same time, free blacks in the South found their opportunities for landownership and economic independence increasingly curtailed, while enslaved blacks had little hope of gaining their freedom and held no property of their own.

Increasing Diversity. Population growth and economic divisions were accompanied by increased diversity in the North American colonies. Indentured servants arrived from Ireland, Scotland, and Germany as well as England. Africans were imported in growing numbers and entered a more highly structured system of slavery, whether laboring on southern farms, on northern estates, or in seaport cities. In addition, free families and redemptioners from Ireland, Scotland, the German states, and Sweden came in ever-larger numbers and developed their own communities and cultural institutions. More colonists had also spent time in the Caribbean before settling on the mainland. And the frontiers of British North America were filled with American Indians and French and Spanish settlers.

As the booming population demanded more land, colonists pushed westward to find territory that either was not claimed by others or could be purchased. At the beginning of the eighteenth century, German and Scots-Irish immigrants joined Anglo-American settlers in rural areas of New Jersey, Pennsylvania, and Delaware. In Pennsylvania, many immigrants settled along the Schuylkill and Susquehanna Rivers amid Iroquois, Algonquian, and Siouan towns and negotiated with Indians to obtain farmland. At the same time, Delaware and Shawnee groups, who were pushed out of New Jersey and the Ohio valley by pressure from settlers there, also moved into this region. They negotiated with colonists, the colonial government, and other Indian groups to establish their own towns. All along the Pennsylvania frontier, the lines between Indian and immigrant settlements blurred. Still, many communities prospered in the region, with white settlers exchanging European and colonial trade goods with Indians to gain access to their orchards, waterways, and lands (Map 4.1).

In the 1720s and 1730s, however, Scots-Irish settlers flooded into Pennsylvania when bad harvests and high rents caused them to flee oppressive conditions back home. The new immigrants overwhelmed native communities that had welcomed earlier settlers. The death of William Penn in 1718 exacerbated the situation as his sons and closest advisers struggled to gain control over the colony. Indians were increasingly pushed to the margins as growing numbers of European settlers crowded the frontier.

Expansion and Conflict. As more and more colonists sought economic opportunities on the frontier, conflicts erupted between earlier British and newer immigrant settlers as well as among immigrant groups. In Pennsylvania, Dutch, Scots-Irish, and German colonists took each other to court, sued land surveyors, and even burned down cabins built by their immigrant foes. For longtime British settlers, such acts only reinforced their sense that

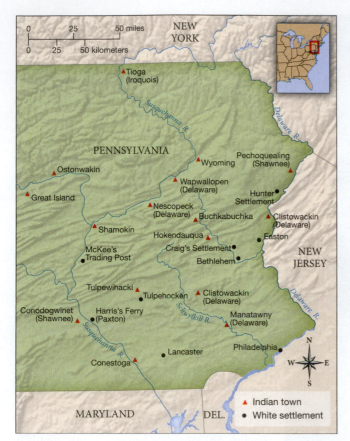

MAP 4.1   Frontier Settlements and Indian Towns in Pennsylvania, 1700–1740

German and Scots-Irish immigrants to Pennsylvania mingled with Indian settlements in the early eighteenth century as Delaware and Shawnee groups were pushed west from New Jersey. In the 1720s and 1730s, however, European migration escalated dramatically in the fertile river valleys. In response, once-independent Indian tribes joined the Delaware and Shawnee nations to strengthen their position against the influx of colonists.

From *At the Crossroads: Indians & Empires on a Mid-Atlantic Frontier, 1700–1763* by Jane T. Merritt, Published for the Omohundro Institute of Early American History and Culture. Copyright © 2003 by the University of North Carolina Press. Used by permission of the publisher. www.uncpress.unc.edu.

recent immigrants were a threat to their society. In 1728 James Logan, William Penn's long-time secretary, complained that the "Palatines [Germans] crowd in upon us and the Irish yet faster." For Logan, these difficulties were exacerbated by what he considered the "idle," "worthless," and "indigent" habits of Scots-Irish and other recent arrivals.

Anglo-Americans hardly set high standards themselves, especially when negotiating with Indians. Even in Pennsylvania, where William Penn had established a reputation for relatively fair dealing, the desire for Indian land led to dishonesty and trickery. Conflicts among Indian nations aided colonial leaders in prying territory from them. Hoping to assert their authority over the independent-minded Delaware Indians, Iroquois chiefs insisted that they held rights to much of the Pennsylvania territory and therefore must be the ones to negotiate with colonial officials. Those colonial authorities, however, produced a questionable treaty supposedly drafted by Penn in 1686 that allowed them to claim large portions of the contested territory. James Logan "discovered" a copy of this treaty, which allowed the English to control an area that could be walked off in a day and a half. Seeking to maintain control of at least some territory, the Iroquois finally agreed to this **Walking Purchase**. The sachems of the far smaller Delaware tribe were then pressured into letting Pennsylvania officials walk off the boundaries. By the time the Delaware acquiesced in the fall of 1737, Pennsylvania surveyors had already marked off the "shortest and best course," which allowed

Lappawinsa 1757   Lappawinsa was a Delaware chief who signed the Walking Purchase Treaty in 1737. The signers did not know that colonial surveyors had marked the best route and hired runners to "walk off" the territory. Gustavus Hesselius, who migrated from Sweden to Philadelphia in 1711, painted six portraits of native chiefs. They were considered among the most realistic for this period. DEA Picture Library/Getty Images

them to extend the boundaries by at least thirty miles beyond those set in the original, and questionable, treaty.

The rapid expansion of the colonial population ensured that conflicts between Indian and colonial leaders over land rights would continue. Meanwhile migrants and immigrants on the frontier increasingly claimed land simply by taking control of it, building houses, and planting crops regardless of Indian claims. This led to conflicts with diverse Indian communities, with English officials who demanded legal contracts and deeds, and among immigrants who settled in the same area.

These conflicts contrasted with developments around the Great Lakes where French traders and Algonquian inhabitants forged military and economic alliances. In this region, which the French called *Pays d'en Haut* (upper country), French colonists and Indians sought diplomatic solutions to problems to protect mutually beneficial trade relations. These relationships also helped fend off challenges from other European and indigenous groups.

Some religiously minded immigrants also worked to improve relations with Indians in Pennsylvania, at least temporarily. The tone had been set by William Penn's Quakers, who generally accepted Indian land claims and tried to pursue honest and fair negotiations. German Moravians who settled in eastern Pennsylvania in the 1740s also developed good relations with area tribes. On Pennsylvania's western frontier, Scots-Irish Presbyterians established alliances with Delaware and Shawnee groups. These alliances, however, were rooted less in religious principles than in the hope of profiting from the fur trade as Indians sought new commercial partners when their French allies became too demanding.

Explore ▶

Compare two perspectives on French Indian relations in New France in Sources 4.4 and 4.5.

Bethlehem, Pennsylvania, 1757   This painting by Nicholas Garrison shows Bethlehem sixteen years after its settlement by German Moravians. The Moravians fled religious persecution in Germany in the early 1700s and established communal societies in Pennsylvania and New Jersey. Moravians pooled their labor and resources so they could sustain farms and shops, establish separate schools for their children, and missionize among local Indians. Art Resource, NY

Still, by the mid-eighteenth century, tensions escalated between English and French officials in the region and intensified among various immigrant and religious communities and with Indian communities. The distinct religious traditions and the dramatically different visions of Indian-settler relations drawn from these traditions also sharpened boundaries within and between colonial communities. German Moravians and Scots-Irish Presbyterians in Pennsylvania established churches and schools separate from their Quaker neighbors, while Puritan New Englanders remained suspicious of Quakers as well as other Protestant sects. Moravians and other German sects also flourished in Georgia and the Carolinas, and nearly all sought to isolate themselves from the influences of other groups.

Some religious groups were isolated as much by force as by choice. While most early Irish immigrants were Protestant, by the early eighteenth century more Irish Catholics began to arrive. Then in 1745 some forty thousand Scots who had supported the Catholic monarchs in England prior to the Glorious Revolution were shipped to the Carolinas after a failed rebellion. Even long-settled Catholics, like those in Maryland, were looked on with suspicion by many Protestants. Although only a few hundred Jewish families resided in the

Comparative Secondary Source Analysis

Finding a Middle Ground in New France

Scholars have generally emphasized conflict, including open warfare, between American Indians and European colonists. More recently, historians of the early colonial period have explored the effects of the Columbian Exchange, especially of germs and epidemics, on Indian-European relations. A third framework for analyzing these relations developed in the early 1990s when historians explored areas of North America where native peoples, traders, and settlers sought accommodations that would allow the development of economic and military alliances. Such accommodations in the *Pays d'en Haut*, the Upper Country of New France, allowed some Indian nations to thrive while others fell victim to these new alliances.

Source 4.4

Richard White │ Cultural Accommodation on the Middle Ground, 1991

The process of accommodation described [here] certainly involves cultural change, but it takes place on what I call the middle ground. The middle ground is the place in between: in between cultures, peoples, and in between empires and the nonstate world of villages. It is a place where many of the North American subjects and allies of empire lived. It is the area between the historical foreground of European invasion and occupation and the background of Indian defeat and retreat. On the middle ground diverse peoples adjust their differences through what amounts to a process of creative, and often expedient, misunderstandings. People try to persuade others who are different from themselves by appealing to what they perceive to be the values and practices of those others. They often misinterpret and distort both the values and the practices of those they deal with, but from these misunderstandings arise new meanings and through them new practices—the shared meanings and practices of the middle ground. This accommodation took place for long periods of time in large parts of the colonial world where whites could neither dictate to Indians nor ignore them. Whites needed Indians as allies, as partners in exchange, as sexual partners, as friendly neighbors. . . .

The world of the *pays d'en haut* . . . is a joint Indian-white creation. Within it well-known European and Anglo-American names appear: . . . Sir Jeffrey Amherst, William Johnson, Daniel Boone, George Washington, . . . and Thomas Jefferson, So, too, do well-known Indian names such as Pontiac and Tecumseh.

Source: Richard White, *The Middle Ground* (Cambridge, UK: Cambridge University Press, 1991), ix and xiii.

colonies by 1750, they too were seen as outsiders. Still, they formed small but enduring communities in a number of seaport cities, where they established synagogues and developed a variety of mercantile ventures.

Africans brought new ideas and practices to North America as well. Transported by force to an unknown land, they may have found religious faith particularly important. Enslaved blacks included some Catholics from regions long held by the Portuguese and a

Brett Rushforth | Indian Slavery and Cultural Accommodation, 2014

This study explores the relationship between indigenous and Atlantic slaveries in New France, a colony centered on the Saint Lawrence River and stretching westward to a region the French called the **Pays d'en Haut,** or Upper Country. . . . Between about 1660 and 1760, French colonists and their Native allies enslaved thousands of Indians, keeping them in the towns and villages of New France, or shipping them to the French Caribbean. . . . Unlike many American colonies, where Indian slaves were replaced by Africans in the early stages of settlement, Native slavery predominated in New France throughout the colony's final century. . . .

The slave trade grew from, and indeed offers a strong example of, these intercultural negotiations in the *Pays d'en Haut.* As the region's Natives encountered French traders and eventually settlers

in the second half of the seventeenth century, they greeted them with rituals and gifts to signal their friendship and to invite the newcomers into an alliance. Among the most significant of these gifts were enslaved enemies, offered as a sign of trust and evidence of Native power. From these beginnings, Natives and the French developed a sustained slave trade built upon decades of small-scale exchanges of bodies, goods, and ideas. Slavery reveals a somber dimension to cultural accommodation in the *Pays d'en Haut,* showing that its success was often founded on a shared commitment to violence. Yet even this violence was a product of mutual adaptation and produced new cultural forms that persisted for generations.

Source: Brett Rushforth, *Bonds of Alliance: Indigenous and Atlantic Slaveries in New France* (Chapel Hill: University of North Carolina Press, 2014), 10–11.

Examine the Sources

1. To what degree does Rushforth's interpretation of Indian cultural accommodation support White's thesis about the middle ground?
2. Explain how one specific event or development from this chapter not explicitly mentioned in the excerpts above could be used to support White's or Rushforth's interpretation.

Put It in Context

Compare relations between Indians and colonists in British North America with those in New France as analyzed by White and Rushforth.

few thousand Muslims, but many Africans initially embraced religious beliefs that were largely unknown to their Anglo-American masters.

As religious affiliations in the colonies multiplied, they reinforced existing concerns about spiritual decline and exacerbated cleavages rooted in nationality, class, and race. These developments heightened concerns among many well-established families over the future of British culture and institutions in North America.

Review & Relate

- How and why did economic inequality in the colonies increase in the first half of the eighteenth century?

- How did population growth and increasing diversity contribute to conflict among and anxieties about the various groups inhabiting British North America?

Religious Awakenings

Whether rooted in fears that worldly concerns were overshadowing spiritual devotion or that growing religious diversity was undermining the power of the church, many Protestant ministers lamented the state of faith in eighteenth-century America. Church leaders in Britain and the rest of Europe shared their fears. Ministers eager to address this crisis of faith — identified in the colonies as **New Light clergy** — worked together to reenergize the faithful and were initially welcomed, or at least tolerated, by more traditional **Old Light clergy**. But by the 1740s, fears that the passionate New Light clergy had gone too far led to a backlash.

The Roots of the Great Awakening.   By the eighteenth century, the **Enlightenment**, a European cultural movement that emphasized rational and scientific thinking over traditional religion and superstition, had taken root in the colonies, particularly among elites. The development of a lively print culture spread the ideas of Enlightenment thinkers like the English philosopher John Locke, the German intellectual Immanuel Kant, and the French writer Voltaire across the Atlantic. These thinkers argued that through reason humans could discover the laws that governed the universe and thereby improve society. Benjamin Franklin, a leading printer in Philadelphia, was one of the foremost advocates of Enlightenment ideas in the colonies. His experiments with electricity reflected his faith in rational thought, and his publication of the *Pennsylvania Gazette* and *Poor Richard's Almanac* spread such ideas throughout the colonies in the 1720s and 1730s.

As more colonists were influenced by Enlightenment thought, they became more accepting of religious diversity, which had spread as settlers from diverse countries and denominations arrived in the English colonies. At the same time, Enlightenment ideas could undermine the religious vitality of the colonies. Many Enlightenment thinkers believed in a Christian God but rejected the revelations and rituals that defined traditional church practices and challenged ministerial claims that God was directly engaged in the daily workings of the world.

There were, however, countervailing forces. The German **Pietists** in particular challenged Enlightenment ideas that had influenced many Congregational and Anglican leaders in Europe. Pietists decried the power of established churches and urged individuals to follow their hearts rather than their heads in spiritual matters. Persecuted in Germany, Pietists migrated to Great Britain and North America, where their ideas influenced Scots-Irish Presbyterians and members of the Church of England. John Wesley, the founder of Methodism and a professor of theology at Oxford University, taught Pietist ideas to his students, including George Whitefield. Like the German Pietists, Whitefield considered the North American colonies a perfect venue for restoring intensity and emotion to religious worship.

Some colonists had begun rethinking their religious commitments before Whitefield or the Pietists arrived. By 1700 both laymen and ministers voiced growing concern with the state of colonial religion. Preachers educated in England or at colonial colleges like Harvard and William and Mary often emphasized learned discourse over passion. At the same time, there were too few clergy to meet the demands of the rapidly growing population in North America. In many rural areas, residents grew discouraged at the lack of ministerial attention. Meanwhile urban churches increasingly reflected the class divisions of the larger society, with wealthier members paying substantial rents to seat their families in the front pews. Farmers and shopkeepers rented the cheaper pews in the middle of the church, while the poorest congregants sat on free benches at the very back or in the gallery. Educated clergy might impress the richest parishioners with their learned sermons, but they did little to move the spirits of the congregation at large.

Still, this fear of religious declension was rooted almost solely in the behaviors of white men. While some colonial ministers sought to Christianize Indians, they never considered Indians' own forms of spiritual worship as an indication of religiosity. Nor did they include African Americans in their estimates of colonial piety. Perhaps more surprisingly, white women's religious devotion was considered problematic. In 1692, the Boston minister Cotton Mather declared, "there are fare more godly women in the world than godly men." As the witchcraft trials unfolded, he estimated that women comprised 75 to 80 percent of many Boston area congregations. He saw this as cause for concern, not rejoicing.

Concerns about the declining importance of religion, at least among men, continued into the eighteenth century even as denominations and churches multiplied. In 1719 the Reverend Theodorus Frelinghuysen, a Dutch Reformed minister in New Jersey, sought to reclaim religious enthusiasm by emphasizing parishioners' emotional investment in Christ. The Reverend William Tennent, the father of Gilbert Tennent, arrived in neighboring Pennsylvania with his family about the same time. He despaired that Presbyterian ministers were too few in number to reach the growing population and, like Frelinghuysen, feared that their approach was too didactic. Tennent soon established his own one-room academy to train his sons and other young men for the ministry. Though disparaged by Presbyterian authorities, the school attracted devout students.

Jonathan Edwards, a Congregational minister in Northampton, Massachusetts, joined Enlightenment ideas with religious fervor. A brilliant scholar who studied natural philosophy and science as well as theology, Edwards viewed the natural world as powerful evidence of God's design. He came to view the idea that God elected some individuals for salvation and others for damnation as a source of mystical joy. Although Edwards wrote erudite books and essays, he proclaimed that "our people do not so much need to have their heads stored [with knowledge] as to have their hearts touched." From 1733 to 1735, his sermons on God's absolute sovereignty over man initiated a revival in Northampton that reached hundreds of parishioners.

A few years earlier, Gilbert Tennent had begun urging his flock in New Brunswick, New Jersey to embrace "a true living faith in Jesus Christ." He took his lead from Frelinghuysen, who viewed conversion as a three-step process: Individuals must be convinced of their sinful nature, experience a spiritual rebirth, and then behave piously as evidence of their conversion. Tennent embraced these measures, believing they could lance the "boil" of an unsaved heart and apply the "balsam" of grace and righteousness. Then in 1739 Tennent met Whitefield, who launched a wave of revivals that revitalized and transformed religion across the colonies.

MAP 4.2   Religious Diversity in 1750

Despite the universal appeal of Whitefield and other New Light ministers, religious diversity had increased by 1750. Baptist churches multiplied in New England, where Congregationalists long held sway, while Presbyterian and Lutheran churches spread across the South where Anglicanism was the established church. Non-evangelical houses of worship, such as Quaker meeting houses and Jewish synagogues, also gradually increased in number.

An Outburst of Revivals.

Whitefield was perfectly situated to extend the series of revivals that scholars later called the **Great Awakening**. Gifted with a powerful voice, he understood that the expanding networks of communication and travel—developed to promote commerce—could also be used to promote religion. Advertising in newspapers and broadsides and traveling by ship, coach, and horseback, Whitefield made seven trips to the North American colonies beginning in 1738. He reached audiences from Georgia to New England to the Pennsylvania backcountry and inspired ministers in the colonies to expand upon his efforts.

In 1739 Whitefield launched a fifteen-month preaching tour that reached tens of thousands of colonists. Like Edwards, Frelinghuysen, and Tennent, he asked individuals to invest less in material goods and more in spiritual devotion. If they admitted their depraved and sinful state and truly repented, God would hear their prayers. Whitefield danced across the platform, shouted and raged, and gestured dramatically, drawing huge crowds everywhere he went. He attracted 20,000 women and men to individual events, at a time when the entire city of Boston counted just 17,000 residents.

New Light ministers carried on Whitefield's work throughout the 1740s, honing their methods and appeal. Less concerned with denominational affiliation than with core beliefs, they denounced urbane and educated clergy, used extemporaneous oratorical styles and outdoor venues to attract crowds, and invited colonists from all walks of life to build a common Christian community. Some became itinerant preachers, preferring to carry their message throughout the colonies than be constrained by a single church (Map 4.2).

New Light clergy appealed to large numbers of women and also brought young people to religion by the thousands. In addition, thousands of colonists, especially men who were already church members were "born again," recommitting themselves to their faith. Poor women and men who felt little connection to preaching when they sat on the back benches eagerly joined the crowds at outdoor revivals, where they could stand as close to the pulpit as a rich merchant.

Religious Dissension.

Initially, the Great Awakening drew support from large numbers of ministers because it increased religious enthusiasm and church attendance throughout the colonies. After decades of competition from secular concerns, religion once again took center stage. But the early embrace by Old Light clergy diminished as revivals spread farther afield, as critiques of educated clergy became more pointed, and as worshippers left established congregations for new churches. A growing number of ministers and other colonial leaders began to fear that revivalists were providing poor whites, free blacks, women, and even the enslaved with compelling critiques of those in power. By 1742, some Old Light ministers and colonial officials began openly critiquing evangelical revivalists. **See Primary Source Project 4: Awakening Religious Tensions, page 138.**

Itinerant preachers in the South seemed especially threatening as they invited blacks and whites to attend revivals together and proclaimed their equality before God. Although New Light clergy rarely attacked slavery directly, they implicitly challenged racial hierarchies. In the North, too, revivalists attracted African Americans and Indians by emphasizing communal singing and emotional expressions of the spirit, which echoed traditional African and indigenous practices.

Increasingly, Old Light ministers and local officials questioned New Light techniques and influences. One of the most radical New Light preachers, James Davenport, attracted huge crowds when he preached in Boston in the early 1740s. Drawing thousands of colonists to Boston Common day after day, Davenport declared that the people "should drink rat poison rather than listen to corrupt, unconverted clergy." Boston officials finally called a grand jury into session to silence him "on the charge of having said that Boston's ministers were leading the people blindfold to hell."

Even some New Light ministers, including Tennent, considered Davenport extreme. Yet revivals continued throughout the 1740s and beyond. Although they lessened in intensity in many areas, local revivals continued through the 1760s. In Newport, Rhode Island, for instance, Sarah Osborn led a series of revivals in 1766–1767. Osborn was a poor woman with little formal education who had experienced early widowhood, the death of her only son, a second marriage to a widower with three sons, and chronic struggles with depression and disease. She underwent a dramatic conversion in 1742, but her second husband soon suffered a breakdown and the family declared bankruptcy a year later. Osborn then took up teaching while writing a memoir focused on her struggles to follow God's path. In the 1760s, when no evangelical preacher could be found to minister to local residents, Osborn opened her home for prayer and contemplation. Although the central tenets of revivalist preaching — criticisms of educated clergy, itinerancy, and extemporaneous preaching — worked against the movement's institutionalization, it provided space for individual converts to take up the work in their own way. The Great Awakening thus echoed across the colonies into the 1770s, its influence felt in attitudes and practices as well as in churches and meetings.

For example, when, in 1750, King George II (r. 1727–1760) threatened to appoint an Anglican bishop for the North American colonies, many North American ministers, both Old Light and New, resisted the appointment. Most colonists had become used to religious diversity and toleration, at least for Protestants, and had little desire to add church officials to the existing hierarchies of colonial authorities. In various ways, revivalists also highlighted the democratic tendencies in the Bible, particularly in the New Testament. Even as they proclaimed God's wrath against sinners, they also preached that a lack of wealth and power did not diminish a person in God's eyes. And revivalists honed a style of passionate and popular preaching that would shape American religion as well as politics for centuries to come. This mode of communication had immediate application as colonists mobilized to resist what they saw as tyrannical actions by colonial officials and others in authority.

Review & Relate

- What was the relationship between the Enlightenment and the religious revivals of the early eighteenth century?

- What was the immediate impact of the Great Awakening, and what were its legacies for American religious and social life?

Political Awakenings

The effects of eighteenth-century religious awakenings rippled out from churches and revivals to influence social and political relations. New Light clergy allowed colonists to view their resistance to traditional authorities as part of their effort to create a better and more just world. Experiences of self-government, Enlightenment ideas, and protests against perceived corruption in the imperial system also led some colonists to question the right of those in power to impose their will on the community as a whole.

Changing Political Relations. The settlements of the seventeenth century could be regulated with a small number of officials, and in most colonies male settlers agreed on who should rule. However, with geographical expansion, population growth, and commercial development, colonial officials—whether appointed by the crown or selected by local residents—found themselves confronted with a more complex, and more contentious, situation. In New England, most colonies developed participatory town meetings that elected members to their colonial legislatures. In the South, wealthy planters exercised greater authority locally and colony-wide, but they still embraced ideals of self-governance and political liberty.

Throughout the British American colonies, officials were usually educated men who held property and had family ties to other colonial elites. Although ultimate political authority—or sovereignty—rested with the king and Parliament, local officials made many decisions because the king and Parliament were too distant to regulate daily life. Another factor that weakened the power of royal officials was the tradition of town meetings and representative bodies, like the Virginia House of Burgesses, that gave colonists a stake in their own governance. Officials in England and the colonies assumed that most people would defer to those in authority, and they minimized resistance by holding public elections in which freemen cast ballots by voice vote. Not surprisingly, those with wealth and power continued to win office.

Still, evidence from throughout the colonial period indicates that deference to authority was not always sufficient to maintain order. Roger Williams and Anne Hutchinson, Bacon's Rebellion, King Philip's War, the Stono rebellion, the Salem witchcraft trials, and the radical preaching of James Davenport make clear that not everyone willingly supported their supposed superiors. These episodes of dissent and protest were widely scattered across time and place. But as the ideas disseminated by New Light clergy and Enlightenment thinkers converged with changing political relations, resistance to established authority became more frequent and more collective.

Dissent and Protest. Local protests against colonial authorities had a long history. Some settlers challenged colonial leaders' repeated demands for more men and higher taxes to support New England's almost continuous wars against Indians. From the 1670s on, women petitioned authorities for tax relief as well as their men folks' "relief from service." In 1706, five wives of poor fisherman in Marblehead, Massachusetts opposed "with force and arms" colonial officials who sought to confiscate their property for non-payment of taxes. As war raged on, refugees flooded eastern towns and colonists faced injury, capture, or death. By the 1730s, many families insisted they had paid enough when officials repeated their calls for men and money, which led to new rounds of protests.

The issues and methods of protest varied, but collectively they indicate a growing sense of political and economic autonomy among North American colonists. Some protests focused on royal officials like governors and Royal Navy captains; others focused on local authorities, merchants, or large landowners. Whatever the target of resistance, colonists demonstrated their belief that they had rights worth protecting, even against those who held legitimate authority.

Access to reasonably priced food, especially bread, inspired numerous riots. During the 1730s, the price of bread—a critical staple in colonial diets—rose despite falling wheat prices and a recession in seaport cities. Bread rioters attacked grain warehouses, bakeries, and shops, demanding more bread at lower prices. In New England, such uprisings were often led by women, who were responsible for putting bread on the table. When grievances involved domestic or consumer issues, women insisted they had the right to be heard. That idea was reinforced by evangelical clergy's insistence on one's moral obligations to society.

View of Main Street, Boston   Boston's broad Main Street, which ran from the Town Hall to the South Church, was used by laborers, merchants, political leaders, and soldiers. This scene was engraved by the German artist Franz Xavier Habermann, who specialized in scenes of North American cities. The buildings and clothing reflect a European view of Boston's commerce and affluence in the mid-eighteenth century. © RMN-Grand Palais/Art Resource, NY

Public markets also sparked collective protests. In 1737, for instance, Boston officials decided to construct a public market and charge fees to farmers who sold their goods there. Small farmers, who were used to selling produce from the roadside for free, clashed with officials and with larger merchants over the venture. Many Boston residents supported the protesters because the market fees would lessen competition and raise prices. Initially, residents petitioned city officials. When they received no response, opponents demolished the market building and stalls in the middle of the night. Local authorities could find no witnesses to the crime.

Access to land was also a critical issue for colonists. Beginning in the 1740s, protests erupted on estates in New Jersey and along the Hudson River in New York over the leasing policies of landlords as well as the amount of land controlled by speculators. Here, again, tenants and squatters petitioned colonial officials, received no response, and then took collective action. They formed associations, targeted specific landlords, and then burned barns, attacked livestock, and emptied houses and farm buildings of furniture and tools. Embracing Enlightenment ideas of "natural law," they also established regional committees to hear grievances and formed "popular" militia companies and courts to mete out justice to recalcitrant land owners. When landlords and colonial officials called out local militia to arrest the perpetrators, they failed to consider that militia members were often the same poor men whose protests they ignored.

In seaport cities, a frequent source of conflict was the **impressment** of colonial men who were forcibly drafted into service in the Royal Navy. Viewed as a sign of the corrupt practices of imperial authorities, the challenge to impressment energized diverse groups of colonists. Sailors, dockworkers, and men drinking at taverns along the shore, black and white, feared being pressed into military service. Colonial officials, worried about labor shortages, petitioned the British government to stop impressment. Still, it was working men who faced the navy's high mortality rates, bad food, rampant disease, and harsh discipline who fought back against both British and colonial authorities. In 1747 in Boston, a general impressment effort led to three days of rioting. An observer noted that "Negros, servants, and hundreds of seamen seized a naval lieutenant, assaulted a sheriff, and put his deputy in stocks, surrounded the governor's house, and stormed the Town House (city hall)." Such riots did not end the system of impressment, but they showed that many colonists now refused to be deprived of what they considered their natural rights.

The religious upheavals and economic uncertainties of the 1730s and 1740s led colonists to challenge officials with greater frequency than in earlier decades. They justified their actions in evangelical or Enlightenment terms. Most protests also accentuated class lines as small farmers and craftsmen, their wives, and poor whites and free blacks fought against merchants, landowners, and local officials. However, the resistance to impressment proved that colonists could mobilize across economic differences when British policies affected diverse groups.

Transforming Urban Politics. The development of cross-class alliances in the 1730s and 1740s was also visible in the more formal arena of colonial politics. Beginning in the 1730s, some affluent political leaders in cities like New York and Philadelphia began to seek support from a wider constituency. In most cases, conflicts among elites led to these appeals to the "popular" will. In 1731, for instance, a new royal charter confirmed New York City's existence as a "corporation" and stipulated the rights of freemen (residents who could vote in local elections after paying a small fee) and freeholders (individuals, whether residents or not, who held property worth £40 and could vote on that basis). A large number of artisans, shopkeepers, and laborers acquired the necessary means to vote, and shopkeepers and master craftsmen now sat alongside wealthier men on the Common Council. Yet most laboring men did not participate actively in elections until 1733, when local elites led by Lewis Morris sought to mobilize the mass of voters against royal officials, like Governor William Cosby, appointed in London.

Morris, a wealthy man and a judge, joined other colonial elites in believing that the royal officials recently appointed to govern New York were tied to ministerial corruption in England. As chief justice of the provincial court, Morris ruled against Governor Cosby in a suit the new governor brought against his predecessor. Cosby then suspended Morris from office. In the aftermath, Morris and his supporters took his case to the people, who were suffering from a serious economic depression. The Morrisites launched an opposition newspaper, published by apprentice printer John Peter Zenger, to mobilize artisans, shopkeepers, and laborers around an agenda to stimulate the economy and elect men supportive of workers to the city's common council.

In his *New-York Weekly Journal*, Zenger leaped into the political fray, accusing Governor Cosby and his cronies of corruption, incompetence, election fraud, and tyranny. The vitriolic attacks led to Zenger's indictment for seditious libel and his imprisonment in November 1734. At the time, libel related only to whether published material undermined government authority, not whether it was true or false. But Zenger's lead attorney, Andrew Hamilton of Philadelphia, argued that truth must be recognized as a defense against charges of libel. Appealing to a jury of Zenger's peers, Hamilton proclaimed, "It is not the cause of a poor printer, nor of New York alone, which you are now trying. . . . It is the best cause. It is the cause of liberty." In response, jurors ignored the law as written and acquitted Zenger.

Although the decision in the Zenger case did not lead to a change in British libel laws, it did signal the willingness of colonial juries to side with fellow colonists against king and Parliament in at least some situations. Building on their success, Morris and his followers continued to gain popular support. In 1737 his son, Lewis Morris Jr., was appointed speaker of the new Assembly, and the Assembly appointed Zenger as its official printer. But soon the group fell into disarray when royal officials offered political prizes to a few of their leaders. Indeed, the elder Morris accepted appointment as royal governor of New Jersey, after which he switched allegiances and became an advocate of executive authority. Nonetheless, the political movement he led had aroused ordinary freemen to participate in elections, and newspapers and pamphlets increasingly attacked corrupt officials and threats to the rightful liberties of British colonists.

Even as freemen gained a greater voice in urban politics, they could challenge the power of colonial leaders only when the elite were divided. Moreover, the rewards they gained sometimes served to reinforce class divisions. Thus many city workers benefited when the elder Morris used his influence to ensure the building of the city's first permanent almshouse in 1736. The two-year project employed large numbers of artisans and laborers in a period of economic contraction. Once built, however, the almshouse became a symbol of the growing gap between rich and poor. Its existence was also used by future city councils as a justification to eliminate other forms of relief, leaving the poor in worse shape than before.

The rising inequality of wealth was especially apparent in the largest cities of British North America — New York, Philadelphia, Boston, and Charleston — but economic distinctions were also growing in smaller cities and towns. As the price of some goods, such as sugar and tobacco, fell in the 1750s, more colonists were able to afford them. At the same time, however, the expansion of transatlantic trade ensured that wealthier colonists had growing access to silver plates, clocks, tea services, bed and table linens, and other luxury goods. With British exporters extending more credit to colonial merchants and affluent white consumers, the division between rich and poor became increasingly visible to colonists of all backgrounds.

Review & Relate

- How did ordinary colonists, both men and women, black and white, express their political opinions and preferences in the first half of the eighteenth century?

- How did politics bring colonists together across economic lines in the first half of the eighteenth century? When did politics highlight and reinforce class divisions?

Conclusion: A Divided Society

By 1754 religious and political awakenings had transformed colonists' sense of their relation to spiritual and secular authorities. Both Gilbert Tennent and Sarah Grosvenor were caught up in these transitions. As a man and a minister, however, Tennent had far more power to control his destiny than did Grosvenor. While wives and daughters in elite families benefited from their wealth and position, they were also constrained by the strictures of the patriarchal family. Women who were poor, indentured, or enslaved were forced into the greatest dependency on male employers and civic officials. Even women in farm and artisanal families depended on loving husbands and fathers to offset the strictures of patriarchal authority. While few colonists conceived of themselves as part of a united body politic, women probably identified most deeply with their family, town, or church. Still, in certain circumstances, such as ongoing colonial wars, women insisted on their right to protect their households by resisting colonial authorities. Nonetheless, women and men thought of themselves as English, or Scots-Irish, or German, rather than more broadly American. At best, they claimed identity as residents of Massachusetts, New Jersey, or South Carolina rather than British North America.

Between the 1680s and the 1750s, the diversity and divisions among colonists increased as class, racial, religious, and regional differences multiplied across the colonies. Immigrants from Germany, Ireland, and Scotland created their own communities; religious awakenings led to cleavages among Protestants and between them and other religious groups; and economic inequality deepened in seacoast cities. At the same time, conflicts between Indians and settlers intensified along the frontier as growing numbers of enslaved Africans reshaped economic and social relations in the urban North and the rural South.

By midcentury, the colonies as a whole had been transformed in significant ways. Religious leaders gained renewed respect, colonial assemblies wrested more autonomy from royal hands, freemen participated more avidly in political contests, printers and lawyers insisted on the rights and liberties of colonists, and local communities defended those rights in a variety of ways. When military conflicts brought British officials into more direct contact with their colonial subjects in the following decade, they sought to check these trends, with dramatic consequences.

Timeline of Events

Key Terms

patriarchal family, *113*

Walking Purchase, *123*

New Light clergy, *128*

Old Light clergy, *128*

Enlightenment, *128*

Pietists, *128*

Great Awakening, *130*

impressment, *134*

Review & Relate

1. What factors led to rising tensions within colonial communities in the early 1700s?

2. How did social, economic, and political tensions contribute to an increase in accusations of witchcraft?

3. Why and how did the legal and economic circumstances of colonial women decline between 1650 and 1750?

4. How did patriarchal ideals of family and community shape life and work in colonial America? What happened when men failed to live up to those ideals?

5. How and why did economic inequality in the colonies increase in the first half of the eighteenth century?

6. How did population growth and increasing diversity contribute to conflict among and anxieties about the various groups inhabiting British North America?

7. What was the relationship between the Enlightenment and the religious revivals of the early eighteenth century?

8. What was the immediate impact of the Great Awakening, and what were its legacies for American religious and social life?

9. How did ordinary colonists, both men and women, black and white, express their political opinions and preferences in the first half of the eighteenth century?

10. How did politics bring colonists together across economic lines in the first half of the eighteenth century? When did politics highlight and reinforce class divisions?

Awakening Religious Tensions

▶ **Evaluate the relationship between the Great Awakening and the Enlightenment in the British American colonies.**

The Great Awakening and the Enlightenment were two of the most influential developments in the early eighteenth-century colonies. Although often considered as oppositional, some advocates of the Enlightenment, including Benjamin Franklin, respected New Light preachers, and some New Light preachers, such as Sarah Osborne, embraced Enlightenment ideas (Sources 4.6 and 4.10). Ultimately, conflicts over the Great Awakening came mainly from Old Light preachers who feared the disruption of traditional church structures and discipline and from civic leaders who feared the social disruption fostered by New Light revivals.

Certainly there were significant differences between the rational approach of scientific observers and the passionate preaching of Jonathan Edwards and George Whitefield (Sources 4.7 and 4.9). Still, many revivalist preachers and reborn converts used natural metaphors to express spiritual ideas, asked for tangible evidence of salvation, elevated the individual above religious authorities, and embraced the idea of progress (Sources 4.7 and 4.10). Differences were at least as great between New Light and Old Light ministers. Old Light ministers initially embraced the Awakening as a way to revive religiosity in the colonies. But as revivalist preachers grew more popular and outspoken, Old Lights became increasingly uneasy. By 1742 the controversial actions of itinerant preachers like James Davenport led Old Light ministers, newspaper editors, and civic leaders to critique the movement as a whole (Source 4.8). One concern of many critics was the challenge the Awakening posed to established relations of class and status. At mass revivals, women and men, old and young, upper and lower classes, and even blacks and whites mingled. And sermons often included pointed critiques of colonial elites (Sources 4.8 and 4.10). Still, the Great Awakening continued in British North America into the 1760s, revitalizing as well as challenging the established order.

Source 4.6

Benjamin Franklin | On George Whitefield, The Great Revivalist, 1739

Benjamin Franklin, the Philadelphia printer, inventor, and politician, was an ardent advocate of the Enlightenment. But he was also interested in popular causes and thus attended one of Whitefield's sermons in Philadelphia in 1739, and several thereafter. While Franklin remained a religious skeptic, he and Whitefield became friends. In his *Autobiography* Franklin printed several of Whitefield's sermons and described the preacher's power.

In 1739 arriv'd among us from England the Rev. Mr. Whitefield, who had made himself remarkable there as an itinerant Preacher. . . . The Multitudes of all Sects and Denominations that attended his Sermons were enormous and it was [a] matter of Speculation to me who was one of the Number, to observe the extraordinary

Influence of his Oratory on his Hearers, and how much they admir'd and respected him, notwithstanding his common Abuse of them, by assuring them they were naturally *half Beasts and half Devils*. It was wonderful to see the Change soon made in the Manners of our Inhabitants; from being thoughtless or indifferent about Religion, it seem'd as if all the World were growing Religious. . . .

He us'd indeed sometimes to pray for my Conversion, but never had the Satisfaction of believing that his Prayers were heard. . . .

He had a loud and clear Voice, and articulated his Words and Sentences so perfectly that he might be heard and understood at a great Distance, especially as his Auditors [audience], however numerous, observ'd the most exact Silence. He preach'd one Evening from the Top of the Court House Steps, which are in the middle of Market Street, and on the West Side of Second Street which crosses it at right angles. Both Streets were fill'd with his Hearers to a considerable distance. Being among the hindmost in Market Street, I had the Curiosity to learn how far he could be heard, by retiring backwards down the Street towards the River; and I found his Voice distinct till I came near Front Street. . . . Imagining then a Semicircle, of which my Distance should be the Radius, and that it were fill'd with Auditors, . . . I computed that he might well be heard by more than Thirty Thousand. . . .

His delivery . . . was so improv'd by frequent Repetitions that every Accent, every Emphasis, every Modulation of Voice, was so perfectly well turn'd and well plac'd, that without being interested in the Subject, one could not help being pleas'd with the Discourse, a Pleasure of much the same kind with that receiv'd from an excellent Piece of Music. This is an Advantage itinerant Preachers have over those who are stationary: as the latter cannot well improve their Delivery of a Sermon by so many Rehearsals.

Source: *The Autobiography of Benjamin Franklin, The Unmutilated and Correct Version*, comp. and ed. John Bigelow (New York: G. P. Putnam's Sons, 1912), 220–25.

Jonathan Edwards | Sinners in the Hands of an Angry God, 1741

Before enrolling at Yale College at age twelve, Jonathan Edwards studied natural history and wrote an essay titled "The Flying Spider." However, his adult fame came from his theological works; his ministry at Christ Church in Northampton, Massachusetts; and his sermons, which he delivered in a quiet yet emotive voice. He first delivered "Sinners in the Hands of an Angry God" at a revival in Enfield, Connecticut, in 1741. Religious opposition to the revivals eventually forced Edwards from his Northampton pulpit, but he continued to publish and to preach, including to New England Indians.

There is nothing that keeps wicked Men at any one Moment, out of Hell, but the meer Pleasure of GOD.

By the meer Pleasure of God, I mean his sovereign Pleasure, his arbitrary Will, restrained by no Obligation, hinder'd by no manner of Difficulty, any more than if nothing else but God's meer Will had in the least Degree, or in any Respect whatsoever, any Hand in the Preservation of wicked Men. . . .

He is not only able to cast wicked Men into Hell, but he can most easily do it. . . .

We find it easy to tread on and crush a Worm that we see crawling on the Earth; so 'tis easy for us to cut or singe a slender Thread that any Thing hangs by; thus easy is it for God when he pleases to cast his Enemies down to Hell. . . .

[What] Use may be of [an] *Awakening* to unconverted Persons in this Congregation[?] . . . That World of Misery, that Lake of burning Brimstone is extended abroad under you. . . .

You probably are not sensible of this. . . . [But] if God should let you go, you would immediately sink and swiftly descend & plunge into the bottomless Gulf, and your healthy Constitution, and your own Care and Prudence, and best Contrivance, and all your Righteousness, would have no more Influence to uphold you and keep you out of Hell, than a Spider's Web would have to stop a falling Rock. . . .

The God that holds you over the Pit of Hell, much as one holds a Spider, or some loathsome Insect, over the Fire, abhors you, and is dreadfully provoked. . . .

[But] now you have an extraordinary Opportunity, a Day wherein CHRIST has flung the Door of Mercy wide open, and stands in the Door calling and crying with a loud Voice to poor Sinners. . . .

And you that are *young* Men, and *young* Women, will you neglect this precious Season that you now enjoy, when so many others of your Age are renouncing all youthful Vanities, and flocking to CHRIST? You especially have now an extraordinary Opportunity; but if you neglect it, it will soon be with you as it is with those Persons that spent away all the precious Days of Youth in Sin, and are now come to such a dreadful pass in blindness and hardness. . . .

Therefore let every one that is out of CHRIST, now awake and fly from the Wrath to come. The Wrath of almighty GOD is now undoubtedly hanging over great Part of this Congregation: Let every one fly out of *Sodom: Haste and escape for your Lives, look not behind you, escape to the Mountain, least you be consumed.*

Source: Jonathan Edwards, *"Sinners in the Hands of an Angry God," A Sermon Preached at Enfield, July 8, 1741* (Boston: S. Kneeland and T. Grant, 1741), 5, 12–13, 15, 23–24, 25.

Source 4.8

Newspaper Report on James Davenport, 1743

James Davenport, whose popular sermons denounced Old Light clergy as corrupt and worldly, was a controversial New Light minister. During the early 1740s, his behavior became increasingly erratic, culminating in a public burning of "immoral" books in New London, Connecticut, in 1743. Davenport also urged his audience to throw luxury items and clothing into the fire. Davenport even took off his own pants and threw them into the fire. His actions, and the ensuing controversy, caused some New Light ministers to turn against Davenport, and by 1744 he issued a public apology for his behavior. The following selection from a Boston newspaper describes the incident in New London.

Multitudes hasten'd toward the Place of Rendezvous, directing themselves by the Clamor and Shouting, which together, with the ascending Smoak [smoke] bro't them to one of the most public Places in the Town, and there found these good People encompassing a Fire which they had built up in the Street, into which they were casting Numbers of Books, principally on Divinity, and those that were well-approved by Protestant Divines, viz. . . . Mr. Russel's Seven Sermons, one of Dr. Colman's, and one of Dr. Chauncy's Books, and many others. Nothing can be more astonishing than their insolent Behaviour was during the Time of their Sacrifice, as 'tis said they call'd it; whilst the Books were in the Flames they cry'd out, *Thus the Souls of the Authors of those Books, those of them that are dad [dead], are roasting in the Flames of Hell; and that the Fate of those surviving, would be the same, unless speedy Repentance prevented:* On the next Day they had at the same Place a second Bonfire of the like Materials, and manag'd in the same manner. Having given this fatal Stroke to Heresy, they made ready to attack Idolatry, and sought for Direction, as in the Case before; and then Mr. [Davenport] told them to look at Home first, and that they themselves were guilty of idolizing their Apparel, and should therefore divest themselves of those Things especially which were for Ornament, and let them be burnt: Some of them in the heighth of their Zeal, conferred not with Flesh and Blood, but fell to stripping and cast their Cloaths [clothes] down at their Apostle's Feet; one or two hesitated about the Matter, and were so bold as to tell him they had nothing on which they idoliz'd: He reply'd, that such and such a Thing was an Offence to him; and they must down with them. . . . Next Mr. [Davenport] pray'd himself; and now the Oracle spake clear to the Point, without Ambiguity, and utter'd that *the Things must be burnt*; and to confirm the Truth of the Revelation, took his wearing Breeches, and hove them with Violence into the Pile, saying, *Go you with the Rest.*

Source: "Religious Excess at New London," *Boston Weekly Post-Boy*, March 28, 1743, in *The Great Awakening: Documents on the Revival of Religion, 1740–1745*, ed. Richard L. Bushman (New York: Institute of Early American History and Culture, 1970), 51–52.

George Whitefield Preaching, c. 1760

Paintings and engravings of the Great Awakening highlighted the most famous preachers and the diverse women and men who attended revivals. This painting by English artist John Collet captures an outdoor revival and shows Whitefield's appeal to a mixed audience of women and men. Collet was known for his satirical images of English life, so it is not clear whether the inclusion of working people and dogs is meant to illustrate or demean Whitefield's broad appeal.

Bridgeman Images

Sarah Osborn | Letter to Reverend Joseph Fish, February 28, 1767

Sarah Osborn began holding meetings in her home in 1766, but her spiritual views were shaped in the 1740s. She heard Whitfield preach in Newport, Rhode Island in 1740 and experienced her own spiritual rebirth in 1742. The next year, she completed a spiritual memoir, and in the following decades wrote hundreds of letters, including to ministers such as Gilbert Tennant, and diary entries. In the 1760s, she began holding religious meetings in her home. By 1767, the numbers of people that gathered to hear her reached hundreds each week. Here she writes Reverend Joseph Fish, a Newport preacher and spiritual guide since the 1740s.

And now, believing Zion's cause is as dear as ever to my venerable friend, permit me to set myself as a child in the presence of her father to give you the most satisfactory account of my conduct as to religious affairs. . . . I will begin with the great one respecting the poor blacks on Lord's Day evening, . . . And first let me assure you,

Sir, it would be the joy of my heart to commit it to superior hands did any arise for their help. . . .

I only read to them, talk to them, and sing a psalm or hymn with them. . . . They call it school, and I would rather it be called almost anything that is good than meeting, I [am] reluct[ant] so much at being thought head of anything that bears that name. . . .

[M]inisters and magistrates send their [black and white] servants and approve, and masters and mistresses frequently send me presents, . . . speaking of the good effects that, through the blessing of the Lord, it has had upon their servants. . . .

In December [1766] I was affrighted at the throng [of black worshippers] and greatly feared that it would indeed be as the river Jordan overflowing all the banks. . . . I told Deacon Coggeshall so. . . . He [finally] said I might send him some white boys too, for they pressed in likewise. . . .

There is usually thirty-odd young girls every Monday evening, . . . The children for catechizing on Thursday afternoon hold on with surprising cheerfulness and steadiness, . . . The room is usually full, consisting of all denominations. . . .

Oh, I trust our God is in the midst of us, does pour out on us a spirit of prayer and supplications. . . .

Source: Catherine A. Brekus, ed., *Sarah Osborne's Collected Writings* (New Haven: Yale University Press, 2017), 264–69.

Interpret the Evidence

1. How does Benjamin Franklin's description of George Whitefield compare to the painting of the English evangelist, and how might the Enlightenment have influenced Franklin's views of Whitefield (Sources 4.6 and 4.9)?

2. What aspects of God's will and human sin does Jonathan Edwards emphasize in his sermon? How is Edwards's interest in science revealed in Source 4.7?

3. Why does James Davenport (Source 4.8) encourage his followers to burn religious books by Old Light ministers as well as items considered idolatrous? How does the Boston newspaper respond to the resulting bonfires?

4. How does the image in Source 4.9 compare to Sarah Osborn's description of the meetings she holds at her home (Sources 4.9 and 4.10)? What aspects of these sources and of Edwards's sermon (Source 4.7) do Old Light ministers and civic leaders find threatening?

Put It in Context

How do these documents help explain the appeal of the Great Awakening, particularly to women, workers, African Americans, and other non-elites?

What ideas or practices from the revivals and the Enlightenment influenced colonists' responses to imperial and colonial authorities in the 1740s and beyond?

chapter 5

War and Empire

1754–1774

Window to the Past

Paul Revere, Etching of the Boston Massacre, 1770

Print culture, including etchings, became increasingly important in the late eighteenth century as a way to publicize events across the American colonies and in Britain. Paul Revere printed and sold this etching, entitled "The Bloody Massacre," from an engraving by the young artist Henry Pelham. Below the image, Revere adds a poem he wrote and the names of the men killed. ▶ **To learn more about this primary source, see Source 5.8 on page 173.**

Library of Congress, Prints and Photographs Division [LC-DIG-ppmsca-01657]

After reading this chapter you will be able to:

- Describe the causes and consequences of the French and Indian War from the perspective of Great Britain, the colonists, and warring Indian communities.

- Explain how British policies following the French and Indian War fostered colonial and Indian grievances.

- Analyze the major British policy changes that affected the colonies between 1764 and 1774 and how colonial responses to them became more unified.

Comparing American Histories

Praised as the father of the United States, **George Washington** remained a loyal British subject for forty-three years. He was born in 1732 to a prosperous farm family in eastern Virginia. When his father died in 1743, George became the ward of his half-brother Lawrence, who took control of the family's Mount Vernon estate. Lawrence's father-in-law, William Fairfax, was an agent for one of the chief proprietors of the colony. When George was sixteen, William hired him to help survey land on Virginia's western frontier.

(*left*) **George Washington** Granger
(*right*) **Pontiac (Ottawa war chief)** Peter Newark American
Pictures/Bridgeman Images

As a surveyor, George journeyed west and came into contact with Indians, friendly and hostile, as well as colonists seeking land. He began investing in western properties, but when Lawrence Washington died in 1752, George suddenly became head of a large estate. He gradually expanded Mount Vernon's boundaries and its enslaved workforce, increasing its profitability.

At the same time, Washington was appointed Lieutenant Colonel in the Virginia militia. In Fall 1753 Virginia's governor sent him to warn the French against encroaching on British territory in the Ohio River valley. The French commander rebuffed Washington and, within six months, gained control of a British post in western Pennsylvania and named it Fort Duquesne. With help from Indians hostile to the French, Washington led a surprise attack on Fort Duquesne in May 1754. The governors of Virginia and North Carolina responded by providing more troops to the newly promoted Colonel Washington. However, the French responded with a much larger force and compelled Washington to surrender.

Washington's fortunes improved when he married the wealthy widow Martha Dandridge Custis in 1759. Now with even more land to defend, Washington supported efforts to extend Britain's North American empire westward to create a buffer against European and Indian foes.

Like Washington, **Pontiac** gained fame as a warrior. However, he fought on the side of the French. He was born between 1712 and 1725 near Lake Erie to parents of mixed native lineage. Around 1723, his family settled in an Ottawa village near the French Fort Detroit. By 1747, Pontiac had become an Ottawa war chief and fought alongside other Indians and the French to defeat British-backed Hurons in the Ohio valley. Then in 1760, British troops defeated French forces at Quebec, essentially ending French control in the region, leaving their native allies without European support.

The next year, General Jeffrey Amherst assumed control of colonial Indian policy as British troops took over French forts and built new ones on native lands. When British colonists pushed further into the Great Lakes/Ohio valley region, Delaware prophet Neolin urged native people to reject European goods and return to traditional ways. His support grew when

France ignored the rights of its Indian allies by ceding its North American lands to Britain in the Peace of Paris in February 1763. That spring, Pontiac held war councils, urging participants from neighboring tribes to join the Ottawa in an attack on Fort Detroit.

Nine hundred warriors from six tribes laid siege to the fort, and Pontiac quickly rose from a local war chief to a regional spokesman for native rights. Indigenous leaders throughout the region organized attacks on other British forts between 1763 and 1766. Initially this decentralized alliance was powerful enough to keep the British from gaining control over the lands France granted them in the Peace of Paris. ◼

Comparing the American histories of Washington and Pontiac reveals the challenges faced by colonists and native peoples in the mid-eighteenth century. North America offered many white colonists greater opportunities for advancement than they could achieve back home, but as the colonial population swelled, discord intensified. Conflicts between white settlers and Indian communities, especially in frontier regions, were nearly continuous through the 1760s. As European wars spilled across the Atlantic and colonial wars entangled European rivals, religious, economic, and political strife intensified with momentous consequences. Still, at least through 1774, as colonists in British North America sought to defeat or pacify Indian nations, they negotiated with colonial and parliamentary authorities over policies they viewed as unfair or abusive.

Imperial Conflicts and Indian Wars, 1754–1763

The war that erupted in the Ohio valley in 1754 sparked an enormous shift in political and economic relations in colonial North America. What began as a small-scale, regional conflict expanded into a brutal and lengthy global war. Known as the French and Indian War in North America and as the Seven Years' War in Great Britain and Europe, the extended conflict led to a dramatic expansion of British territory in North America and to increasing demands from American colonists for more control over their own lives.

The Opening Battles. July 1754 marked a critical point in colonial and Indian relations in British North America. Even before the British learned of Washington's defeat in the Ohio valley, they sought to protect the colonies against further threats from the French and their Indian allies. The British were especially interested in cementing an alliance with the powerful Iroquois Confederacy, composed of six northeastern tribes. In June, officials had invited a delegation from the confederacy to a July meeting with colonial representatives at Albany, New York. Benjamin Franklin had a different view of the meeting. He drew up a Plan of Union that would establish a council of representatives from the various colonial assemblies to debate issues of frontier defense, trade, and territorial expansion. Their deliberations would be overseen by a president-general appointed by the British crown. Despite the proposed council's involvement in Indian affairs, Franklin excluded Iroquois or other Indian representatives from his plan.

Although the **Albany Congress** created stronger bonds among a small circle of colonial leaders, it failed to establish a firmer alliance with the Iroquois or resolve problems of colonial governance. The Mohawk warrior and sachem Hendrick Peters Theyanoguin,

Join or Die   Benjamin Franklin created the first political cartoon in American history to accompany an editorial he wrote in the *Pennsylvania Gazette* in 1754. Franklin's cartoon urged the mainland British colonies to unite politically during the French and Indian War. Legend had it that a snake could come back to life if its severed sections were attached before dusk. Library of Congress, LC-USZC4-5315

a member of the Iroquois Confederacy, urged British representatives at the Congress to take forceful action against their common enemies. However, by the time his views were reported in the British press, Iroquois representatives angered by their exclusion from Franklin's plan broke off talks with the British. The Plan of Union was also rejected by colonial delegates, who were unwilling to give up any of their autonomy in military, trade, and political matters to some centralized assembly. Meanwhile royal officials worried that the debates in Albany might force the crown's hand in dealing with the French and their Indian allies.

If war was going to erupt between the British and the French, the Iroquois could not afford to have the outcome decided by imperial powers alone. Indeed, for most Indians, contests among European nations for land and power offered them the best chance of survival in the eighteenth century. They gained leverage as long as opposing imperial powers needed their trade goods and their military and political support. Their leverage would be far more limited if one European nation controlled most of North America.

Still, Indian tribes adopted different strategies. The Delaware, Miami, Ottawa, and Shawnee nations, for example, allied themselves with the French, hoping that a French victory would stop British colonists from invading their settlements in the Ohio River valley. Members of the Iroquois Confederacy, on the other hand, tried to play one power against the other, hoping to win concessions from the British in return for their military support. The Creek, Choctaw, and Cherokee nations also sought to perpetuate the existing stalemate among European powers by bargaining alternately with the British in Georgia and the Carolinas, the French in Louisiana, and the Spaniards in Florida. Faced with incursions into their lands, some Indian tribes, like the Abenaki in northern New England, launched preemptive attacks on colonial settlements.

The British government soon decided to send additional troops to defend its American colonies against attacks from Indians and intrusions from the French. General Edward Braddock arrived with two regiments in 1755, seeking to expel the French from Fort Duquesne. At the same time, colonial militia units were sent to battle the French and their Indian allies along the New York and New England frontiers. Colonel Washington joined Braddock as his

Colonel George Washington   This 1772 oil painting by Charles Willson Peale portrays George Washington as a colonel in the Virginia militia. Washington commanded this militia during the French and Indian War following the death of General Braddock. After the war, Washington prospered as a planter and land speculator. Granger

personal aide-de-camp. Within months, however, Braddock's forces were ambushed, bludgeoned by French and Indian forces, and Braddock was killed.

Other British forces fared little better during the next three years. Despite having far fewer colonists in North America than the British, the French had established extensive trade networks that helped them gain support from numerous Indian nations in a protracted war. Alternating guerrilla tactics with conventional warfare, the French captured several important forts, built a new one on Lake Champlain, and moved troops deep into British territory. The ineffectiveness of the British and colonial armies also encouraged Indian tribes along the New England and Appalachian frontiers to reclaim land from colonists. Bloody raids devastated many outlying settlements, leading to the death and capture of hundreds of Britain's colonial subjects.

A Shift to Global War. Whereas earlier wars had originated in Europe and spread to American colonies, French victories in North America inspired their European foes to contest British imperial claims elsewhere in the world. In 1756 France and Great Britain officially declared war against each other. Eventually Austria, Russia, Sweden, most of the German states, and Spain allied with France, while Portugal and Prussia sided with Great Britain. Naval warfare erupted in the Mediterranean Sea and the Atlantic and Indian Oceans. Battles were also fought in Europe, the West Indies, India, and the Philippines. By the end of 1757, Britain and its allies had been defeated in nearly every part of the globe. The war appeared to be nearing its end, with France in control.

However, in summer 1757, William Pitt took charge of the British war effort. He poured soldiers and arms into North America along with young and ambitious officers like Henry Bouquet. His strategy energized colonial and British forces, while Prussian forces held the line in Europe. By the summer of 1758, the tide began to turn. In July, British generals recaptured the fort at Louisburg on Cape Breton Island, a key to France's defense of Canada. Then British troops with Bouquet and Washington's aid seized Fort Duquesne, which was renamed Fort Pitt. Other British forces captured Fort Frontenac along the St. Lawrence River, while Prussia defeated France and its allies in Europe and Britain gained key victories in India (Map 5.1). In 1759 General Jeffrey Amherst recaptured Forts Ticonderoga and Crown Point on Lake Champlain while General James Wolfe attacked a much larger French force in Quebec. Despite heavy casualties, including Wolfe himself, the British won Quebec and control of Canada.

MAP 5.1   The French and Indian War, 1754–1763

Clashes between colonial militia units and French and Indian forces erupted in North America in 1754. The conflict helped launch a wider war that engulfed Europe as well as the West Indies and India. In the aftermath of this first global war, Britain gained control of present-day Canada and India, but France retained its West Indies colonies.

Cherokee warriors had allied with British forces to defeat France at Pennsylvania's Fort Duquesne in 1758. The alliance was sealed in part by Britain building Fort Loudon, its first fort west of the Appalachian Mountains, as a base for trade and military protection for native allies. Initially, relations were cordial, and some soldiers stationed there married Cherokee women. However, after Virginia settlers attacked Cherokee warriors returning south from Pennsylvania, some Cherokee retaliated. The situation escalated with the Cherokee hoping to drive colonists out of their hunting grounds. Attacks continued on both sides, and open warfare erupted in 1759. During this Anglo-Cherokee War, Cherokee warriors laid siege to Fort Loudon. However, the Cherokee wives of British soldiers smuggled in food, and their authority over households and agriculture made it impossible to stop the effort. Fort Loudon finally did fall, but by then a smallpox epidemic weakened

Cherokee forces. General Jeffrey Amherst then sent 2,800 troops to invade Cherokee territory and end the conflict. British and Scottish soldiers along with colonial militias and their Indian allies sacked fifteen Cherokee villages; killed men, women, and children; and burned acres of fields. A peace agreement was finally signed in fall 1761.

The Costs of Victory.

Despite Wolfe's victory in 1760 and the end of the Cherokee threat the following year, the war dragged on in North America, Europe, India, and the West Indies until 1763. By then, however, King George III had tired of Pitt's grand strategy and dismissed him. He then opened peace negotiations with France and agreed to give up a number of conquered territories in order to finalize the **Peace of Paris** in 1763. Other countries were ready to negotiate as well. To regain control of Cuba and the Philippines, Spain ceded Florida to Great Britain. While France was expelled from North America, it rewarded Spanish support by granting Spain Louisiana and all French lands west of the Mississippi River. Despite these concessions, the British empire reigned supreme, regaining control of India as well as North America east of the Mississippi, all of Canada, and a number of Caribbean islands.

The wars that erupted between 1754 and 1763 reshaped European empires, transformed patterns of global trade, and initially seemed to tighten bonds between North American residents and the mother country. Yet the Peace of Paris did not resolve many of the problems that had plagued the colonies before the war, and it created new ones as well.

The incredible cost of the war raised particularly difficult problems. Over the course of the war, the national debt of Great Britain had more than doubled. At the same time, as the North American colonies grew and conflicts erupted along their frontiers, the costs of administering them increased fivefold. With an empire that stretched around the globe, the British crown and Parliament were forced to consider how to pay off war debts, raise funds to administer their far-flung territories, and keep sufficient currency in circulation for expanding international trade. Just as important, the Peace of Paris ignored the claims of Indian tribes to the territories that France and Spain turned over to Great Britain. Nor did the treaty settle contested claims among the colonies themselves over lands in the Ohio River valley and elsewhere along British North America's new frontiers.

Battles and Boundaries on the Frontier.

The sweeping character of the British victory encouraged thousands of colonists to move farther west, into lands once controlled by France. This exacerbated tensions that were already rising on the southern and western frontiers of British North America. Sporadic assaults on native communities and frontier settlements continued for years. For backcountry settlers, these conflicts fueled resentments not only against Indians but also against eastern political leaders who rarely provided sufficient resources for frontier defense.

The most serious conflict erupted in the Ohio River valley when Indians there realized the consequences of British victories. When the British captured French forts along the Great Lakes and in the Ohio valley in 1760, they immediately antagonized local Indian groups by hunting and fishing on tribal lands and depriving villages of much-needed food. British traders also defrauded Indians on numerous occasions and General Amherst stopped traditional obligations of gift giving, reduced the value of beaver skins, and refused to provide native traders with guns or ammunition.

The harsh realities of the British regime led some Indians to seek a return to ways of life that preceded the arrival of white men. A Delaware visionary named Neolin preached that Indians had been corrupted by contact with Europeans and urged them to purify themselves by returning to their ancient traditions, abandoning white ways, and reclaiming their lands. Neolin was a prophet, not a warrior, but his message inspired others, including the Ottawa leader Pontiac.

In early 1763, news arrived that France was about to cede all of its North American lands to Britain and Spain without any effort to protect the territory of its former Indian allies. Pontiac then convened a council of more than four hundred Ottawa, Ojibwe, and Huron leaders near Fort Detroit. Drawing on Neolin's vision, he proclaimed, "It is important my brothers, that we should exterminate from our land this nation [Britain], whose only object is our death. . . . we can no longer supply our wants the way we were accustomed to do with our Fathers the French." Having mobilized a half dozen tribes, Pontiac laid siege to Fort Detroit in May 1763. Soon some eighteen Indian nations, including the Chippewa, were attacking British frontier outposts and white settlements along the Great Lakes, Virginia, and Pennsylvania frontier (Map 5.2).

Accounts of Pontiac's rebellion sparked outrage among settlers and British troops. Many colonists did not distinguish between friendly and hostile Indians. In December 1763, a group of men from Paxton Creek, Pennsylvania raided families of peaceful, Christian Conestoga Indians near Lancaster, killing thirty. Protests from eastern colonists infuriated the Paxton Boys, who then marched on Philadelphia demanding protection from "savages" on the frontier. Benjamin Franklin negotiated a truce between the Paxton Boys and the Pennsylvania authorities, though it did not settle the fundamental issues over protection of western settlers.

Convinced that it could not endure these costly frontier clashes, the British crown issued a proclamation in October 1763 forbidding colonial settlement west of a line running down the Appalachian Mountains to create a buffer between Indians and colonists. Nonetheless, Parliament ordered Colonel Bouquet to subdue hostile Indians in the Ohio region the next year, and battles between British troops and tribes allied with Pontiac continued across the Great Lakes region. While diverse native leaders, such as the Chippewa chief Minavavana, initiated attacks on scattered British forts, British emissaries focused their diplomatic efforts solely on Pontiac. In October 1763, having failed to capture Fort Detroit, Pontiac moved further west but continued to encourage militant resistance to the British occupation. In July 1766, Sir William Johnson, the British Superintendent of Indian Affairs, finally met Pontiac at Fort Ontario in upstate New York, and formally ended hostilities. Pontiac had sought to end European encroachment in his region, but the widespread Indian attacks he inspired instead led the British to increase their military presence in order to quell native uprisings.

Still, Parliament's establishment of the **Proclamation Line of 1763** did temporarily slow colonists' westward movement. However, it heightened tensions over land and wealth. Small farmers, backcountry settlers, and squatters had hoped to improve their lot by acquiring rich farmlands won in the long and bloody French and Indian War. Instead, they watched wealthy speculators claim these western lands, certain that the Proclamation was merely "a temporary expedient to quiet the Minds of the Indians." George Washington alone acquired tens of thousands of acres west of the Proclamation Line, land that was once home to native tribes.

Conflicts over Land and Labor Escalate.
Conflicts among colonists and with Britain were not confined to frontier regions. Land riots directed against the leasing policies of landlords and the greed of speculators had plagued New York's Hudson valley

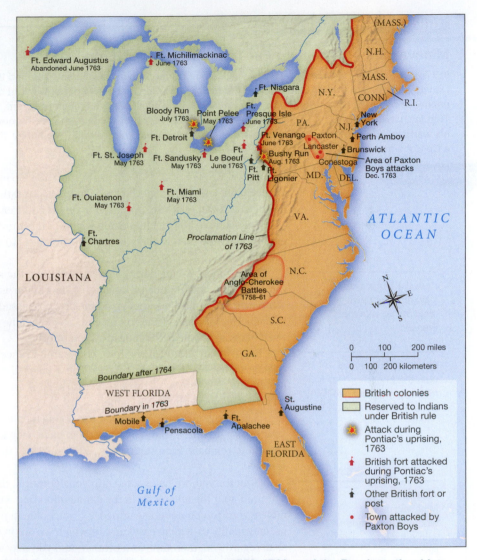

MAP 5.2   British Conflicts with Indians, 1758–1763, and the Proclamation Line

The entrance of British troops into former French territory in the Ohio River valley following the French and Indian War fueled conflicts with Indian nations. Colonists in Pennsylvania and the Carolinas also battled with Indians, including tribes who were allies or remained neutral during the war. Parliament established the Proclamation Line to limit westward expansion and thereby diminish such hostilities.

Explore ▶

Read part of Minavavana Speech to Fur Trader Alexander Henry, in Source 5.1.

and New Jersey before the war, and these struggles continued into the 1760s. New clashes also occurred in the Carolinas as settlers stood up to landlords and government officials.

While the French and Indian War raged, the owners of large estates along the Hudson River raised rents and reduced the rights of tenants. In the early eighteenth century, the titles to some of these estates were challenged by small

Guided Primary Source Analysis

Minavavana | Speech to Fur Trader Alexander Henry, 1761

In 1761, Alexander Henry, a twenty-two-year-old fur trader born in New Jersey, traveled through central Canada in hopes of trading with tribes in the region. Knowing that native peoples might consider him an enemy since his parents were English, he traveled with a small party, a French assistant, and few weapons. That fall, while visiting Fort Michilimackinac, Henry was visited by Minavavana, a Chippewa chief, and sixty of his warriors. Henry recorded Minavavana's speech, which was translated by Mr. Farley, the French husband of a Chippewa woman.

Source 5.1

Englishman, you know that the French king is our father. He promised to be such; and we, in return, promised to be his children. . . .

Englishman, it is you that made war with this our father. You are his enemy; and how then, could you have the boldness to venture among us, his children? . . . .

How did Minavavana view the Chippewa relationship with the French?

Englishman, we are informed that our father, the king of France, is old and infirm; and that being fatigued . . . has fallen asleep. During his sleep, you have taken advantage of him, and possessed yourselves of Canada. But his nap is almost at an end. . . . [W]hen he does awake, what must become of you? He will destroy you utterly!

How did Minavavana view the English following their defeat of the French?

Englishman, although you have conquered France, you have not conquered us! We are not your slaves. These lakes, these woods and mountains, were left to us by our ancestors. They are our inheritance; and we will part with them to none. . . .

[T]he king of France, employed our young men to make war upon your nation. In this warfare, many of them have been killed; and it is our custom to retaliate, until such times as the spirits of the slain are satisfied. . . .

What explains Minavavana's willingness to trade with Alexander Henry?

[B]ut for you, we have taken into consideration, that you have ventured your life among us, in the expectation that we should not molest you. You do not come armed. . . ; you come in peace, to trade with us, and supply us with necessaries, of which we are in much want. We shall regard you, therefore, as a brother; and you may sleep tranquilly, without fear of the Chipewas.

Source: Alexander Henry, *Travels and Adventures in Canada and Indian Territories between 1760 and 1766* [1809] (Boston: Little and Brown, 1901).

Put It in Context

What does Minavavana's speech reveal about the position of France's Indian allies after England's conquest of Canada?

The Indians Delivering Up English Captives, 1766   This hand-colored engraving was based on a Benjamin West sketch made in 1764 when Colonel Henry Bouquet led an army of 1,500 men into the Ohio territory. His mission was to force the Shawnee and Delaware to accept the Peace of Paris and release all English captives. The image suggests that not all captives wanted to leave their Indian families. Library of Congress, Prints and Photographs Division [LC-USZC2-1595]

landowners and tenants, but even where legitimate titles existed, tenants declared a moral right to own the land they had long farmed. The manors and estates of the Hudson valley, they claimed, were more appropriate to a feudal government than to an enlightened empire.

Farmers in neighboring New Hampshire were drawn into battles over land when the king's Privy Council in London decided in 1764 that the Green Mountains belonged to New York rather than New Hampshire. Landlords along the Hudson River hoped to expand eastward into this region, but the farmers already living there claimed they had bought the land in good faith and deserved to keep it. The farmers launched guerrilla warfare against New York authorities and large landowners as well as against New York farmers who claimed land that New Hampshire families had cleared and settled. These Green Mountain Boys, led by Ethan Allen, refused to recognize New York authorities as legitimate and established their own local governments and popular courts.

Inspired by the Green Mountain Boys as well as uprisings in New Jersey, tenants in the Hudson valley banded together in 1765 and 1766. Under the leadership of Irish immigrant William Prendergast, a group of tenants calling themselves Levellers refused to pay rent and instead claimed freehold title to the land they farmed. New York tenants petitioned the colonial assembly and sought redress in a variety of ways. But landowners refused to negotiate, and Prendergast concluded that "there was no law for poor men." All of these groups developed visible, well-organized networks of supporters, targeted specific landlords, sought redress first through colonial courts and assemblies, and then established popular militias and other institutions to govern themselves and to challenge those in authority. Although led by men, such community protests required the support of women as well, who took on extra household and agricultural duties while their husbands and sons built resistance movements.

Review & Relate

▪ How did the French and Indian War and the subsequent peace treaty affect relations among Britain, American Indian nations, and American colonies?

▪ How did the French and Indian War and the increasing power of large landowners contribute to conflict between average colonists and colonial elites?

Postwar British Policies and Colonial Unity

Even as ordinary colonists challenged the authority of economic and political elites, colonial leaders tried to persuade the disaffected to turn their anger against royal authorities in Britain. By highlighting colonists' rights as British subjects, local traditions of self-rule, and Enlightenment ideas, these leaders slowly gained support. Some of them even joined earlier opponents in arguing for the rights of the individual. The imposition of new British policies in the decade following the French and Indian War, from 1764 to 1774, was equally important in nurturing common grievances and uniting colonists across regional and economic differences. For instance, the Proclamation Line of 1763 eventually inspired widespread dissent as poor farmers, large landowners, and speculators sought to expand westward. A second policy, impressment, by which the Royal Navy forced young colonial men into military service, also aroused anger across regions and classes. At the same time, the Great Awakening provided colonists with shared ideas about moral principles and new techniques for mass communication. Finally, Britain's efforts to repay its war debts by taxing colonists and its plan to continue quartering troops in North America led colonists to forge intercolonial protest movements.

Common Grievances. Like the Proclamation Line, which denied all colonists the right to settle beyond the Appalachian Mountains, the policy of impressment affected port city residents of all classes. Impressment had been employed by the British during the extended wars of the eighteenth century to procure seamen. While plucking poor men from ports throughout the British Empire, the Royal Navy faced growing resistance to this practice in the American colonies from merchants and common folk alike. Because many free black men worked in jobs tied to the sea, they, too, joined impressment protests.

Impressment by the British   This eighteenth-century engraving depicts the harsh impressment of men into the British navy. Set in England, this illustration shows that impressment was widely practiced at home. Thus the British government did not single out colonists for special mistreatment. Chronicle/Alamy

Seamen and dockworkers had good reason to fight off impressment agents. Men in the Royal Navy faced low wages, bad food, harsh punishment, rampant disease, and high mortality. As the practice escalated with each new war, the efforts of British naval officers and impressment agents to capture new "recruits" met violent resistance, especially in the North American colonies where several hundred men might be impressed at one time. In such circumstances, whole communities joined in the battle.

In the aftermath of the French and Indian War, serious impressment riots erupted in Boston, New York City, and Newport, Rhode Island. Increasingly, poor colonial seamen and dockworkers — white and black — made common cause with the owners of merchant ships and mercantile houses who depended on their labor. Colonial officials — mayors, governors, and customs agents — were caught in the middle. Some upheld the Royal Navy's right of impressment; others tried to placate both naval officers and local residents; and still others resisted what they saw as an oppressive imposition on the rights of colonists. Both those who resisted British authority and those who sought a compromise had to gain the support of the lower and middling classes to succeed.

Employers and politicians who opposed impressment gained an important advantage if they could direct the anger of colonists away from themselves and toward British policies. The decision of British officials to continue quartering troops in the colonies gave local leaders another opportunity to join forces with ordinary colonists. Colonial towns and cities were required to quarter (that is, house and support) British troops even after the Peace of Paris was signed. Some were housed in individual homes, adding to the burdens of housewives who were forced to provide soldiers' food, laundry, and other necessities. While the troops were intended to protect the colonies, they also provided reinforcements for impressment agents and surveillance over other illegal activities like smuggling and domestic manufacturing. Thus a range of issues and policies began to bind colonists together through common grievances against the British Parliament.

Forging Ties across the Colonies.

The ties forged between poorer and wealthier colonists over issues of westward expansion, impressment, and quartering grew stronger in the 1760s, but they tended to be localized in seaport cities or in specific areas of the frontier. Creating bonds across the colonies required considerably more effort in a period when communication and transportation beyond local areas were limited. Means had to be found to disseminate information and create a sense of common purpose if the colonists were going to persuade Parliament to take their complaints seriously. One important model for such intercolonial communication was the Great Awakening.

By the 1750s, the Great Awakening was marked more by dissension than by unity as new denominations continued to split off from traditional churches. For example, in the Sandy Creek region of North Carolina, radical Protestants formed the Separate Baptists, who proclaimed a message of absolute spiritual equality. From the late 1750s through the 1770s, Separate Baptists converted thousands of small farmers and farmwives, poor whites, and enslaved women and men and established churches throughout Virginia, Georgia, and the Carolinas.

Like Separate Baptists, Methodists, Dunkards, Moravians, and Quakers also offered southern residents religious experiences that highlighted spiritual equality. Some dissenting preachers invited slaves and free blacks to attend their services alongside white farm families and laborers. Slaveholders and other elite southerners considered such practices outrageous and a challenge to the political as well as the social order.

Most women and men who converted to Separate Baptism, Methodism, or other forms of radical Protestantism did not link their religious conversion directly to politics. But as more and more ordinary colonists and colonial leaders voiced their anger at offensive British policies, evangelical techniques used to rouse the masses to salvation became important for mobilizing colonists to protest. Still, colonial leaders, especially in areas with large enslaved populations, did not imagine Africans and African Americans as part of their audience.

Even though the Great Awakening had spent its religious passion in most parts of North America by the 1760s, the techniques of mass communication and critiques of opulence and corruption it initiated provided emotional and practical ways of forging ties among widely dispersed colonists. Many evangelical preachers had condemned the lavish lifestyles of colonial elites and the spiritual corruption of local officials. Now in the context of conflicts with Great Britain, colonial leaders used such rhetoric to paint Parliament and British officials as aristocrats with little faith and less compassion.

The public sermons and mass gatherings used during the Great Awakening to inspire loyalty to a greater moral cause could now be translated into forms applicable to political protest. The efforts of Great Britain to assert greater control over its North American colonies provided colonial dissidents an opportunity to test out these new ways to forge inter-colonial ties.

Great Britain Seeks Greater Control.
Until the French and Indian War, British officials and their colonial subjects coexisted in relative harmony. Economic growth led Britain to ignore much of the smuggling and domestic manufacturing that took place in the colonies, since such activities did not significantly disrupt Britain's mercantile policies (see "Imperial Policies Focus on Profits" in chapter 3). Similarly, although the king and Parliament held ultimate political sovereignty, or final authority, over the American colonies, it was easier to allow some local control over political decisions, given the communication challenges created by distance.

This pattern of **benign** (or "salutary") **neglect** led some American colonists to view themselves as more independent of British control than they really were. Many colonists came to see smuggling, domestic manufacturing, and local self-governance as rights rather than privileges. Thus when British officials decided to assert greater control, many colonists protested.

To King George III and to Parliament, asserting control over the colonies was both right and necessary. In 1763 King George appointed George Grenville to lead the British government. As Prime Minister and Chancellor of the Exchequer, Grenville faced an economic depression in England, rebellious farmers opposed to a new tax on domestic cider, and growing numbers of unemployed soldiers returning from the war. He believed that regaining political and economic control in the American colonies could help resolve these crises at home.

Eighteenth-century wars, especially the French and Indian War, cost a fortune. British subjects in England paid taxes to help offset the nation's debts, even though few of them benefited as directly from the British victory as did their counterparts in the American colonies. The colonies would cost the British treasury more if the crown could not control colonists' movement into Indian territories, limit smuggling and domestic manufacturing, and house British troops in the colonies cheaply.

To reassert control, Parliament launched a three-pronged program. First, it sought stricter enforcement of existing laws and reorganized the Board of Trade to centralize policies and ensure their implementation. The **Navigation Acts**, which prohibited smuggling, established guidelines for legal commerce, and set duties on trade items, were the most important laws to be enforced. Second, Parliament extended wartime policies into peacetime. For example, the Quartering Act of 1765 ensured that British troops would remain in the colonies to enforce imperial policies. Colonial governments were expected to support them by allowing them to use vacant buildings or extra rooms in colonial homes and providing them with food and supplies.

The third part of Grenville's colonial program was the most important. It called for the passage of new laws to raise funds and reestablish the sovereignty of British rule. The first revenue act passed by Parliament was the American Duties Act of 1764, known as the **Sugar Act**. It imposed an **import duty**, or tax, on sugar, coffee, wines, and other luxury items. The act actually reduced the import tax on foreign molasses, which was regularly smuggled into the colonies from the West Indies, but insisted that the duty be collected. The crackdown on smuggling increased the power of customs officers and Britain established the first vice-admiralty courts in North America to ensure that the Sugar Act raised money for the crown. That same year, Parliament passed the Currency Act, which prohibited colonial assemblies from printing paper money or bills of credit. Taken together, these provisions meant that colonists would pay more money into the British treasury even as the supply of money (and illegal goods) diminished in North America.

Some colonial leaders protested the Sugar Act through speeches, pamphlets, and petitions, and Massachusetts established a **committee of correspondence** to circulate concerns to leaders in other colonies. However, dissent remained disorganized and ineffective. Nonetheless, the passage of the Sugar and Currency Acts caused anxiety among many colonists, which was heightened by passage of the Quartering Act the next year. Colonial responses to these developments marked the first steps in an escalating conflict between British officials and their colonial subjects.

Review & Relate

■ Why did British policymakers believe they were justified in seeking to gain greater control over Britain's North American colonies?

■ How did Britain's postwar policies help to expand and unify protests across the colonies?

Resistance to Britain Intensifies

Over the next decade, between 1764 and 1774, the British Parliament sought to extend its political and economic control over the American colonies, and colonists periodically resisted. With each instance of resistance, Parliament demanded further submission to royal authority. With each demand for submission, colonists responded with greater assertions of their rights and autonomy. Still, no one imagined that a revolution was in the making.

The Stamp Act Inspires Coordinated Resistance. Grenville decided next to impose a stamp tax on the colonies similar to that long used in England. The stamp tax required that a revenue stamp be affixed to all transactions involving paper items, from

No Stamp Act Teapot   This creamware teapot was made in Staffordshire, England for the colonial market. It was likely produced after March 1766 to commemorate the repeal of the Stamp Act. English manufacturers were worried about losing the American market and were thus pleased when colonial protests led to the law's repeal. Courtesy the Colonial Williamsburg Foundation

newspapers and contracts to playing cards and diplomas. Grenville announced his plans in 1764, a full year before Parliament enacted the **Stamp Act** in the spring of 1765. The tax was to be collected by colonists appointed for the purpose, and the money was to be spent at the direction of Parliament for "defending, protecting and securing the colonies." To the British government, the Stamp Act seemed completely fair. After all, Englishmen paid on average 26 shillings in tax annually, while Bostonians averaged just 1 shilling. Moreover, the act was purposely written to benefit the American colonies.

The colonists viewed it in a more threatening light. The Stamp Act differed from earlier parliamentary laws in three important ways. First, by the time of its passage, the colonies were experiencing rising unemployment, falling wages, and a downturn in trade. All of these developments were exacerbated by the Sugar, Currency, and Quartering Acts passed by Parliament the previous year. Second, critics viewed the Stamp Act as an attempt to control the *internal* affairs of the colonies. It was not an indirect tax on trade, paid by importers and exporters, but a direct tax on daily business. Third, such a direct intervention in the economic affairs of the colonies unleashed the concerns of both local officials and ordinary residents that Parliament was taxing colonists who had no representation in its debates and decisions.

By announcing the Stamp Act a year before its passage, Grenville allowed colonists plenty of time to organize their opposition. In New York City, Boston, and other cities, merchants, traders, artisans, and their wives and daughters formed groups dedicated to the repeal of the Stamp Act. Soon Sons of Liberty, Daughters of Liberty, Sons of Neptune, Vox Populi, and similar organizations emerged to challenge the imposition of the Stamp Act. Even before the act was implemented, angry mobs throughout the colonies attacked stamp distributors. Some were beaten, others tarred and feathered, and all were forced to take an oath never to sell British stamps.

Colonists lodged more formal protests with the British government as well. The Virginia House of Burgesses, led by Patrick Henry, acted first. It passed five resolutions, which it sent to Parliament, denouncing taxation without representation. The Virginia Resolves were reprinted in many colonial newspapers and repeated by orators to eager audiences in Massachusetts and elsewhere. At the same time, the Massachusetts House adopted a circular letter — a written protest circulated to the other colonial assemblies — calling for a congress to be held in New York City in October 1765 to consider the threat posed by the Stamp Act.

In the meantime, popular protests multiplied. The protests turned violent in Boston, where **Sons of Liberty** leaders like Samuel Adams, a Harvard graduate and town official, organized mass demonstrations. Adams modeled his oratory on that of itinerant preachers, but with a political twist. Other activists used more visual means of inspiring their audiences. At dawn on August 14, 1765, the Boston Sons of Liberty hung an effigy of stamp distributor Andrew Oliver on a tree and called for his resignation. A mock funeral procession, joined by farmers, artisans, apprentices, and the poor, marched to Boston Common. The crowd, led by shoemaker and French and Indian War veteran Ebenezer Mackintosh, carried the fake corpse to the Boston stamp office and destroyed the building. Demonstrators saved pieces of lumber, "stamped" them, and set them on fire outside Oliver's house. Oliver, wisely, had already left town.

Oliver's brother-in-law, Lieutenant Governor Thomas Hutchinson, arrived at the scene and tried to quiet the crowd, but he only angered them further. They soon destroyed Oliver's stable house, coach, and carriage, which the crowd saw as signs of aristocratic opulence.

The battle against the Stamp Act unfolded across the colonies with riots, beatings, and resignations reported from Newport, Rhode Island, to New Brunswick, New Jersey, to Charles Town (later Charleston), South Carolina. On November 1, 1765, when the Stamp Act officially took effect, not a single stamp agent remained in his post in the colonies.

Protesters carefully chose their targets: stamp agents, sheriffs, judges, and colonial officials. Even when violence erupted, it remained focused, with most crowds destroying stamps and stamp offices first and then turning to the private property of Stamp Act supporters. These protests made a mockery of notions of deference toward British rule. But they also revealed growing autonomy on the part of middling- and working-class colonists who attacked men of wealth and power, sometimes choosing artisans rather than wealthier men as their leaders. However, this was not primarily a class conflict because many wealthier colonists made common cause with artisans, small farmers, and the poor. Indeed, colonial elites considered themselves the leaders, inspiring popular uprisings through the power of their political arguments and oratorical skills. Still, they refused to support actions they considered too radical.

It was these more affluent protesters who dominated the Stamp Act Congress that met in New York City in October 1765. It brought together twenty-seven delegates from nine colonies. The delegates petitioned Parliament to repeal the Stamp Act, arguing that taxation without representation was tyranny. Delegates then urged colonists to boycott British goods and refuse to pay the stamp tax. Yet they also proclaimed their loyalty to king and country.

The question of representation became a mainstay of colonial protests. Whereas the British accepted the notion of "virtual representation," by which members of Parliament gave voice to the views of particular classes and interests, the North American colonies had developed a system of representation based on locality. According to colonial leaders, only members of Parliament elected by colonists could represent their interests.

Even as delegates at the Stamp Act Congress declared themselves loyal, if disaffected, British subjects, they participated in the process of developing a common identity in the American colonies. Christopher Gadsden of South Carolina expressed the feeling most directly. "We should stand upon the broad common ground of natural rights," he argued. "There should be no New England man, no New-Yorker, known on the continent, but all of us Americans."

Eventually the British Parliament was forced to respond to colonial protests and even more to rising complaints from English merchants and traders whose business had been damaged by colonists' boycott. Parliament repealed the Stamp Act in March 1766, and King George III granted his approval a month later. Victorious colonists looked forward to a new and better relationship between themselves and the British government.

From the colonists' perspective, the crisis triggered by the Stamp Act demonstrated the limits of parliamentary control. Colonists had organized effectively and forced Parliament to repeal the hated legislation. Protests had erupted across the colonies and attracted support from a wide range of colonists. Individual leaders, like Patrick Henry of Virginia and Samuel Adams of Massachusetts, became more widely known through their fiery oratory and their success in appealing to the masses. The Stamp Act agitation also demonstrated the growing influence of ordinary citizens who led parades and demonstrations and joined in attacks on stamp agents and the homes of British officials. The protests also revealed the growing power of the written word and printed images in disseminating ideas among colonists. Broadsides, political cartoons, handbills, newspapers, and pamphlets circulated widely, reinforcing discussions and proclamations at taverns, rallies, demonstrations, and more formal political assemblies.

For all the success of the Stamp Act protests, American colonists still could not imagine in 1765 that protest would ever lead to open revolt against British sovereignty. More well-to-do colonists were concerned that a revolution against British authority might fuel a dual revolution in which small farmers, tenants, servants, white and enslaved, laborers, and even women would rise up against their political and economic superiors in the colonies. Even most middling- and working-class protesters believed that the best solution to the colonies' problems was to gain greater economic and political rights within the British Empire, not to break from it.

The Townshend Act.

The repeal of the Stamp Act in March 1766 led directly to Parliament's passage of the Declaratory Act. That act declared that Parliament had the authority to pass any law "to bind the colonies and peoples of North America" closer to Britain. No new tax or policy was established; Parliament simply wanted to proclaim Great Britain's political supremacy in the aftermath of the successful stamp tax protests.

Following this direct assertion of British sovereignty, relative harmony prevailed in the colonies for more than a year. Then in June 1767, Charles Townshend, the new chancellor of the Exchequer, rose to power in England. He persuaded Parliament to return to the model offered by the earlier Sugar Act. The **Townshend Act**, like the Sugar Act, instituted an import tax on a range of items sent to the colonies, including glass, lead, paint, paper, and tea.

Now, however, even an indirect tax led to immediate protests and calls for a boycott of taxed items. In February 1768, Samuel Adams wrote a circular letter reminding colonists of the importance of the boycott, and the Massachusetts Assembly disseminated it to other colonial assemblies. In response, Parliament posted two more British army regiments in Boston and New York City to enforce the law. Angry colonists did not retreat when confronted by this show of military force. Instead, a group of outspoken colonial leaders demanded that colonists refuse to import goods of any kind from Britain.

John Dickinson, a prominent Pennsylvania attorney and Quaker, had published a critique of the Stamp Act, which was sent to Britain as the first protest against Parliament's efforts to tax the colonists. In 1767 and 1768, he wrote a series of letters attacking the

A Patriot Merchant's Mansion   Jeremiah Lee, the wealthiest merchant in Massachusetts, moved his family into a newly built Marblehead mansion in 1768. It was decorated with hand-carved moldings, furniture made by colonial craftsmen, and hand-painted wallpaper from England. Despite his strong ties to British commercial circles, he was an ardent patriot and friend of Samuel Adams and used his wealth to promote the colonists' cause.
© Lucinda Lambton/Bridgeman Images

Townshend Act, presenting himself as an ordinary colonist by using the pen name "A Farmer." Dickinson argued that any duty on goods was a tax and insisted, "Those who are taxed without their own consent, given by themselves, or their representatives, are slaves. We are taxed without our own consent given by ourselves, or our representatives. We are therefore—I speak it with grief—I speak it with indignation—we are slaves." Only a boycott could demonstrate colonists' insistence on their rights as British subjects.

More than previous efforts to resist British authority, this boycott depended on the support of women, who were generally in charge of the day-to-day purchase of household items. Wives and mothers were expected to boycott a wide array of British goods, while single women and widows who supported themselves as shopkeepers were expected to refrain from selling British goods. Women were also called upon to provide substitutes for boycotted items. Thus mothers and daughters produced homespun clothing, brewed herbal teas, and expanded their gardens.

Despite the hardships, many colonial women embraced the boycott. As twenty-two-year-old Charity Clarke wrote to a friend in England, "If you English folks won't give us the liberty we ask . . . I will try to gather a number of ladies armed with spinning wheels [along with men] who shall learn to weave & keep sheep, and will retire beyond the reach of arbitrary power." Other women also organized spinning bees in which dozens of participants produced yards of homespun cloth, the wearing of which symbolized female commitment to the cause.

Refusing to drink tea offered women another way to protest parliamentary taxation. In February 1770, more than "300 Mistresses of Families, in which number the Ladies of the Highest Rank and Influence," signed a petition in Boston and pledged to abstain from drinking tea. Dozens of women from less prosperous families signed their own boycott agreement.

Explore ▶

See Sources 5.2 and 5.3 for two different types of dissent.

The Boston Massacre.   Boston women's refusal to drink tea and their participation in spinning bees were part of a highly publicized effort to make their city the center of opposition to the Townshend Act. Printed propaganda, broadsides, demonstrations, and rallies announced to the world that Bostonians rejected Parliament's right to impose its will, or at least its taxes, on the American colonies. Angry over Parliament's policies, Boston men also considered the soldiers, who moonlighted for extra pay, as economic competitors. Throughout the winter of 1769–1770, boys and young men reacted by harassing the growing number of British soldiers stationed in the city.

Comparative Primary Source Analysis

Protesting the Stamp Act

The announcement of the Stamp Act in 1764 ignited widespread protests throughout the colonies. Colonial governments petitioned Parliament for its repeal, crowds attacked stamp agents and distributors, broadsides and newspapers denounced "taxation without representation," and boycotts and mass demonstrations were organized in major cities. As Source 5.2 shows, London merchants also protested, arguing that they were losing revenue because of colonial boycotts of British goods. Source 5.3 celebrates the repeal of the Stamp Act by depicting a funeral for the act led by its supporters. Dr. William Scott, who published letters supporting the Stamp Act in a London newspaper, leads the procession.

Source 5.2

London Merchants Petition to Repeal the Stamp Act, 1766

And that, in consequence of the trade between the colonies and the mother country, as established and permitted for many years, and of the experience which the petitioners have had of the readiness of the Americans to make their just remittances to the utmost of their real ability, they have been induced to make and venture such large exportations of British manufactures, as to leave the colonies indebted to the merchants of Great Britain in the sum of several millions sterling; at that at this time the colonists, when pressed for payment, appeal to past experience, in proof of their willingness; but declare it is not in their power, at present, to make good their engagements, alleging, that the taxes and restrictions laid upon them, and the extension of the jurisdiction of vice admiralty courts established by some late acts of parliament, particularly . . . by an act passed in the fifth year of his present Majesty, for granting and applying certain stamp duties, and other duties, in the British colonies and plantations in America, with

several regulations and restraints, which, if founded in acts of parliament for defined purposes, are represented to have been extended in such a manner as to disturb legal commerce and harass the fair trader, have so far interrupted the usual and former most fruitful branches of their commerce, restrained the sale of their produce, thrown the state of the several provinces into confusion, and brought on so great a number of actual bankruptcies, that the former opportunities and means of remittances and payments are utterly lost and taken from them; and that the petitioners are, by these unhappy events, reduced to the necessity of applying to the House, in order to secure themselves and their families from impending ruin; to prevent a multitude of manufacturers from becoming a burthen to the community, or else seeking their bread in other countries, to the irretrievable loss of this kingdom; and to preserve the strength of this nation entire.

Source: Guy Steven Callender, *Selections from the Economic History of the United States, 1765–1860* (Boston: Ginn, 1909), 146–147.

On the evening of March 5, 1770, young men began throwing snowballs at the lone soldier guarding the Boston Customs House. An angry crowd began milling about was joined by a group of sailors led by Crispus Attucks, an ex-slave of mixed African and Indian ancestry. The guard called for help, and Captain Thomas Preston arrived at the scene with

Source 5.3

The Repeal, 1766

Library of Congress, Prints and Photographs Division [LC-USZ62-21264]

Interpret the Evidence

1. How do the petition and the cartoon emphasize the economic arguments against the Stamp Act? What role, if any, do arguments about political representation play in these documents?

2. Who do you think was the intended audience for each of these documents? What evidence can you find in each document to support your answer?

Put It in Context

What do these documents suggest about relations among the colonies, British merchants, and Parliament more generally in 1766?

seven British soldiers. He appealed to the "gentlemen" present to disperse the crowd. Instead, the harangues of the crowd continued, and snowballs, stones, and other projectiles flew in greater numbers. Then a gun fired, and soon more shooting erupted. Eleven men in the crowd were hit, and four were "killed on the Spot," including Attucks.

Despite confusion about who, if anyone, gave the order to fire, colonists expressed outrage at the shooting of men on the streets of Boston. Samuel Adams and other Sons of Liberty recognized the incredible potential for anti-British propaganda. Adams organized a mass funeral for those killed, and thousands watched the caskets being paraded through the city. Newspaper editors and broadsides printed by the Sons of Liberty labeled the shooting a "massacre." But when the accused soldiers were tried in Boston for the so-called **Boston Massacre**, the jury acquitted six of the eight of any crime. Still, ordinary colonists as well as colonial leaders were growing more convinced that British rule had become tyrannical and that such tyranny must be opposed. **See Primary Source Project 5: The Boston Massacre, page 171.**

To ensure that colonists throughout North America learned about the Boston Massacre, committees of correspondence formed once again to spread the news. These committees became important pipelines for sending information about plans and protests across the colonies. They also circulated an engraving by Bostonian Paul Revere that suggested the soldiers purposely shot at a peaceful crowd.

Parliament was already considering the repeal of the Townshend duties, and in the aftermath of the shootings, public pressure increased to do so. Merchants in England and North America insisted that parliamentary policies had resulted in economic losses on both sides of the Atlantic. In response, Parliament repealed all of the Townshend duties except the one on tea, which it retained to demonstrate its political authority to tax the colonies.

Continuing Conflicts at Home.

As colonists in Boston and other seaport cities rallied to protest British taxation, other residents of the thirteen colonies continued to challenge authorities closer to home. In the same years as the Stamp Act and Townshend Act protests, tenants in New Jersey and the Hudson valley continued their campaign for economic justice. So, too, did a group called the **Regulators** in central North Carolina. Its leaders included Hermon Husband, a Separatist Baptist, who wrote pamphlets and helped organize the Sandy Creek Association in 1766 to assist poorer farmers and squatters in the region. Conflicts escalated when the North Carolina Assembly, dominated by the eastern slaveholding elite, approved a measure in 1768 to build a stately mansion for Governor Tryon with public funds. Outraged frontier farmers withheld their taxes, took over courthouses, and harassed corrupt local officials. While Governor Tryon claimed that Parliament abused its power in taxing the colonies, he did not recognize such abuses in his own colony. Instead, he increasingly viewed the Regulators as traitors. In spring 1771, he recruited a thousand militiamen to quell what he considered open rebellion on the Carolina frontier. The Regulators amassed two thousand farmers to defend themselves, although Husband, a pacifist, was not among them. But when twenty Regulators were killed and more than a hundred wounded at the Battle of Alamance Creek in May 1771, he surely knew many of the fallen. Six of the defeated Regulators were hanged a month later. Many local residents harbored deep resentments against colonial officials for what they viewed as the slaughter of honest, hardworking men.

Resentments against colonial leaders were not confined to North Carolina. An independent Regulator movement emerged in South Carolina in 1767. Far more effective than their North Carolina counterparts, South Carolina Regulators seized control of the western regions of the colony, took up arms, and established their own system of frontier justice. In 1769 the South Carolina Assembly negotiated a settlement with the Regulators, establishing new parishes in the colony's interior that ensured greater representation for frontier areas and extending colonial political institutions, such as courts and sheriffs, to the region.

Tea and Widening Resistance.

Tea and Widening Resistance. For a brief period after the Boston Massacre, conflicts within the colonies generally overshadowed protests against British policies. During this period, the tea tax was collected, the increased funds ensured that British officials in the colonies were less dependent on local assemblies to carry out their duties, and general prosperity seemed to lessen the antagonism between colonists and royal authorities. In May 1773, however, all that changed. That month Parliament passed a new act that granted the revered but financially struggling East India Company a monopoly on shipping and selling tea in the colonies. Although this did not add any new tax or raise the price of tea, it did fuel a new round of protests.

Samuel Adams, Patrick Henry, Christopher Gadsden, and other radicals had continued to view the tea tax as an illegal imposition on colonists and refused to pay it as a matter of principle. They had established committees of correspondence to keep up the pressure for a colony-wide boycott, and Adams published and circulated "Rights of the Colonies," a pamphlet that listed a range of grievances against British policies. Their concerns became the basis for a new round of protests when Parliament, many of whose members invested in the East India Company, granted its monopoly. By eliminating colonial merchants from the profits to be made on tea and implementing a monopoly for a single favored company, Parliament pushed merchants into joining with radicals to demand redress.

Explore ▶

See Sources 5.4 and 5.5 for different perspectives on how colonists' identities changed in the 1760s and 1770s.

Committees of correspondence quickly organized another colony-wide boycott. In some cities, like Charleston, South Carolina, tea was unloaded from East India Company ships but never sold. In others, like New York, the ships were turned back at the port. Only in Boston, however, did violence erupt as ships loaded with tea sat anchored in the harbor. On the night of December 16, 1773, the Sons of Liberty organized a "tea party." After a massive rally against British policy, a group of about fifty men disguised as Indians boarded the British ships and dumped forty-five tons of tea into the sea.

Although hundreds of spectators knew who had boarded the ship, witnesses refused to provide names or other information to British investigators. The Boston Tea Party was a direct challenge to British authority and resulted in large-scale destruction of valuable property.

Parliament responded immediately with a show of force. The **Coercive Acts**, passed in 1774, closed the port of Boston until residents paid for the tea, moved Massachusetts court cases against royal officials back to England, and revoked the colony's charter in order to strengthen the authority of royal officials and weaken that of the colonial assembly. The British government also approved a new Quartering Act, which forced Boston residents to accommodate more soldiers in their homes or build more barracks.

The royal government passed the Coercive Acts to punish Massachusetts and to discourage similar protests in other colonies. Instead, the legislation, which colonists called the **Intolerable Acts**, spurred a militant reaction. Committees of correspondence spread news of the fate of Boston and of Massachusetts. Colonial leaders, who increasingly identified themselves as patriots, soon formed committees of safety — armed groups of colonists who gathered weapons and munitions and vowed to protect themselves against British encroachments on their rights and institutions. Other colonies sent support, both political and material, to Massachusetts and instituted a wider boycott of British goods. In Edenton, North Carolina, a group of women published a proclamation stating their allegiance to the cause of liberty by refusing to serve or drink British tea. The statement received widespread attention in the American and British press, some laudatory and some satirical.

Comparative Secondary Source Analysis

Colonial Identities in Eighteenth Century British North America

In the 1760s and early 1770s, colonists on mainland North America increasingly resisted Parliament's imposition of policies they considered burdensome and unfair. The great distance between England and mainland North America had allowed colonists to develop relatively autonomous institutions and ideas over the previous century. In addition, a growing proportion of colonists emigrated from places other than the British Isles. Still, many colonists were closely bound to Britain and British culture by familial and religious ties, commercial exchanges, and books and newspapers. As political relations between Britain and its mainland colonies frayed in the 1760s and 1770s, did the balance between colonists' British and American identities shift? Gordon Wood focuses on leaders and the literate population in arguing that colonists remained far more similar to than different from Britons. Jon Butler explores the racial and ethnic diversity of American colonists, which, he argues, led them toward distinctive American ideas and institutions.

Source 5.4

Gordon Wood | Britain's Influence on Colonial Identities, 1993

In our enthusiasm to contrast the "traditional" society of the mother country with the "modernity" of the colonies, we have often overlooked how dominantly British and traditional the colonists' culture was; indeed, in some respects colonial society was more traditional than that of the mother country. Most colonial leaders in the mid-eighteenth century thought of themselves not as Americans but as Britons. They read much the same literature, the same law books, the same history, as their brethren at home, and they drew most of their conceptions of society and their values from their reading. Whatever sense of unity the disparate colonies of North America had came from their common tie to the British crown and from their membership in the British Empire. Most colonists knew more about events in London than they did about occurrences in neighboring colonies. They were provincials living on the edges of a pan-British world, and all the more British for that.

Source: Gordon Wood, *The Radicalism of the American Revolution.* Vintage Books, 1993, p. 12.

At the same time, a group of patriots meeting in Williamsburg, Virginia in the spring of 1774 called for colonies to send representatives to a **Continental Congress** to meet in Philadelphia the following September. Delegates planned to discuss how to recalibrate relations between the North American colonies and Great Britain.

By passing the Coercive Acts, Parliament had hoped to dampen long-smoldering conflicts with the colonies. Instead, they flared even brighter, with radical leaders committing themselves to the use of violence, moderate merchants and shopkeepers making common cause with radicals, and ordinary women and men embracing a boycott of all British goods.

The Continental Congress and Colonial Unity. When the Continental Congress convened in Philadelphia in September 1774, fifty-six delegates represented every colony but Georgia. Many of these men—and they were all men—had met before. Some had worked

Source 5.5

Jon Butler | American Influences on Colonial Identities, 2000

The transformation of the [British mainland] colonies between 1680 and 1770 exhibited the settlers' increasing fascination with power and authority, a determination to make the world anew in yet untested images. Men and women of all kinds pressed on to control their own destiny, sometimes collectively, sometimes individually as America's population, economy, secular life, and religion became more complex and variegated. Colonists created a far more independent economy than their "colonial" status might have suggested was desirable or possible. Most European settlers extended and enlivened traditional religious expression in the New World. Africans and American Indians shaped new cultures and modes of living under extraordinarily difficult conditions. Provincial politics gave European settlers persuasive control over colonial affairs. A vigorous secular life emulated European models but moved to New World rhythms and concerns.

Modernity could also support and even create new problems that would afflict America and much of the modern world for decades, even centuries. Most spectacularly, the slaveholding that overwhelmed Spanish America and the British Caribbean by the 1650s, was perfected in the British mainland colonies after 1680. . . .

The result was America in its aspirations, its character, its flaws, and its achievements—a surprising America that seventeenth-century immigrants never imagined. The transformations occurring between 1680 and 1770 made the term "America" increasingly indelible. They made the direction of American history unmistakable, even if they did not make it inevitable.

Source: Jon Butler, *Becoming America: The Revolution Before 1776.* Harvard University Press, 2000, pp. 3 and 4.

Examine the Sources

1. How do Wood and Butler differ in their historical interpretation of colonial identity in the eighteenth century?
2. Which individuals discussed in this chapter support the main arguments of Wood? Which support the main arguments of Butler?

▌ Put It in Context

How might Wood's and Butler's views of colonial identities have changed if they focused more attention on frontier settlers, women, Indians, and/or poor colonists?

together in the Stamp Act Congress in 1765; others had joined forces in the intervening years on committees of correspondence or in petitions to Parliament. Still, the representatives disagreed on many issues. Some were radicals like Samuel Adams, Patrick Henry, and Christopher Gadsden. Others held moderate views, including George Washington and John Dickinson of Pennsylvania. And a few, like John Jay of New York, voiced more conservative positions.

Despite their differences, all the delegates agreed that the colonies must resist further parliamentary encroachments on their liberties. They talked not of independence but rather of reestablishing the freedoms that colonists had enjoyed in an earlier period. Washington voiced the sentiments of many. Although opposed to the idea of independence, he echoed John Locke by refusing to submit "to the loss of those valuable rights and privileges, which are essential to the happiness of every free State, and without which life, liberty, and property are rendered totally insecure."

Virtual Representation, 1775 This print shows an English lord threatening to shoot a colonist while a Parliament member declares, "I give you that man's money for my use." The American responds, "I will not be robbed." Meanwhile, Britannia heads into "The pit prepared for others"; Boston burns in the background; and a French monk prays with Quebec behind him. Such cartoons were widely used to arouse anti-British sentiments. Library of Congress, 3a053113

To demonstrate their unified resistance to the Coercive Acts, delegates called on colonists to continue the boycott of British goods and to end all colonial exports to Great Britain. Committees were established in all of the colonies to coordinate and enforce these actions. Delegates also insisted that Americans were "entitled to a free and exclusive power of legislation in their several provincial legislatures." By 1774 a growing number of colonists supported these measures and the ideas on which they were based.

The delegates at the Continental Congress could not address all the colonists' grievances, and most had no interest in challenging race, class, or gender relations within the colonies themselves. Nonetheless, it was a significant event because the congress drew power away from individual colonies and local organizations and placed the emphasis instead on colony-wide plans and actions. To some extent, the delegates also shifted leadership of the protests away from militant artisans, like Ebenezer Mackintosh, and put planning back in the hands of men of wealth and standing, including radicals like Samuel Adams. Moreover, even as they denounced Parliament, many representatives felt a special loyalty to the king and sought his intervention to rectify relations between the mother country and the colonies.

Review & Relate

∎ How and why did colonial resistance to British policies escalate in the decade following the conclusion of the French and Indian War?

∎ How did internal social and economic divisions shape the colonial response to British policies?

Conclusion: Liberty within Empire

From the Sugar Act in 1764 to the Continental Congress in 1774, colonists reacted strongly to parliamentary efforts to impose greater control over the colonies. Their protests grew increasingly effective as colonists developed organizations, systems of communication, and arguments to buttress their position. Residents of seacoast cities like Boston and New York City developed especially visible and effective challenges, in large part because they generally had the most to lose if Britain implemented new economic, military, and legislative policies.

In frontier areas, such as the Hudson valley, the southern backcountry, and the Great Lakes region, complaints against British tyranny vied with those against colonial land speculators and officials throughout the 1760s and 1770s. Still, few of the white agitators questioned the right of white colonists to claim Indian lands or enslave African labor. While frontier settlers railed against British and colonial officials who limited their access to land and failed to protect them from Indians, most would rather make common cause with wealthy critics of Great Britain than with neighboring native tribes.

One other tie bound the colonists together in 1774. No matter how radical the rhetoric, the aim continued to be resistance to particular policies and greater liberty within the British Empire, not independence from it. Moreover, despite some colonists' opposition to certain parliamentary acts, many others supported British policies. Indeed, the majority of colonists did not participate in protest activities. Most small farmers and backcountry settlers were far removed from urban centers of protest, while poor families in seaport cities who purchased few items to begin with had little interest in boycotts of British goods. Finally, some colonists hesitated to consider open revolt against British rule for fear of a revolution from below. The activities of land rioters, Regulators, evangelical preachers, female petitioners, African American converts to Christianity, and native communities on the frontier reminded well-established settlers that the colonies harbored their own tensions and conflicts.

The fates of Pontiac and George Washington suggest the uncertainties that plagued the British colonies and individuals residing there. It is not clear whether Indians in the Great Lakes region heard about colonists' rejection of the Stamp Act or their growing resistance to British policies. If Pontiac had, he may have supported the British. By 1766, Pontiac was accused of becoming arrogant, believing the power he gained with British authorities gave him greater importance among his own people. Former Ottawa supporters forced him to flee their village in 1768. He resettled further west and told British officials that he was no longer recognized as a chief. The following year, a Peoria warrior killed Pontiac to avenge Pontiac's earlier assault on his uncle. The Peoria band council had approved the assassination. However, Pontiac still loomed large among white settlers, and in the early nineteenth century, officials in Michigan and Illinois named cities in his honor.

Even before Pontiac's death, George Washington had shifted his focus from the frontier conflicts against the French to colonial resistance to British authority. In 1774, he attended the Continental Congress. He then took command of the volunteer militia companies in the colonies and chaired the committee on safety in his home county. Although still opposed to rebellion, he was nonetheless preparing for it. Washington likely agreed with the great British parliamentarian Edmund Burke who, on hearing of events in the American colonies, lamented, "Clouds, indeed, and darkness, rest upon the future." Despite Washington's early failures against French forces in Pennsylvania, he would lead colonists through the darkness and ensure his place in the history of a burgeoning nation.

chapter 5 review

Timeline of Events

Key Terms

Review & Relate

1. How did the French and Indian War and the subsequent peace treaty affect relations among Britain, American Indian nations, and American colonies?

2. How did the French and Indian War and the increasing power of large landowners contribute to conflict between average colonists and colonial elites?

3. Why did British policymakers believe they were justified in seeking to gain greater control over Britain's North American colonies?

4. How did Britain's postwar policies help to expand and unify protests among colonists?

5. How and why did colonial resistance to British policies escalate in the decade following the conclusion of the French and Indian War?

6. How did internal social and economic divisions shape the colonial response to British policies?

The Boston Massacre

▶ **Why did these individuals portray the events of March 5, 1770 so differently, and what do these differences suggest about how the Boston Massacre escalated tensions between British officials and colonists?**

The Boston Massacre was a critical episode in the American independence movement. The origins of this skirmish between Bostonians and British troops lay in the passage of the Townshend Act in 1767, three years before the so-called massacre. The following documents reveal the chaos of that night from the differing perspectives of Bostonians and British soldiers.

There was widespread resistance to the Townshend duties, including public demonstrations, petitions, and boycotts against British goods. The situation in Boston became so tense that four thousand British troops were brought in to enforce the Townshend Act. In late February 1770, a British sympathizer tore down an anti-British poster, and an angry mob then threw stones at his house and hit his wife. The homeowner fired into the crowd and killed an eleven-year-old boy. A mass funeral for the boy set the stage for the events of March 5.

On that chilly evening, an exchange between young men and a British officer outside the Customs House escalated with supporters joining both sides. Church bells were rung, bringing more colonial sailors and soldiers to the scene (Source 5.7). Captain Thomas Preston, the officer in charge, called in reinforcements to regain control (Source 5.9). As Bostonians overwhelmed the British regulars, someone fired his gun. A number of British soldiers then followed suit, killing four men immediately, including Crispus Attucks, and seriously injuring two others (Sources 5.6 and 5.9). Some colonial leaders used the event to promote the patriot cause (Sources 5.7 and 5.8).

Within the month, as contradictory accounts circulated, Preston and eight British soldiers were indicted for murder. They were tried in October 1770. Unable to find attorneys, Preston appealed directly to patriot John Adams, who agreed to take the case to ensure a fair trial. Adams provided a strong defense (Source 5.10), resulting in the acquittal of Preston, who was tried separately, and of six of the other eight soldiers. Two soldiers were found guilty of murder, a charge later reduced to manslaughter.

Source 5.6

Deposition of William Wyatt, March 7, 1770

Just two days after the Boston Massacre, city officials began deposing dozens of witnesses to the event. They later published their descriptions as part of a pamphlet that criticized the event as a "Horrid Massacre." The following selection is from the testimony of William Wyatt and describes his version of the scene just as British soldiers were loading their weapons.

That last Monday evening, being the fifth day of March current, I was in Boston, down on Treat's wharf, where my vessel was lying, and hearing the bells ring, supposed there was a fire in the town, whereupon I hastened up to the

Town-house, on the south side of it, where I saw an officer of the army lead out of the guard-house there seven or eight soldiers of the army, and lead them down in seeming haste, to the Custom-house on the north side of King street, where I followed them, and when the officer had got there with the men, he bid them face about. I stood just below them on the left wing, and the said officer ordered his men to load, which they did accordingly, with the utmost dispatch, then they remained about six minutes, with their firelocks rested and bayonets fixed, but not standing in exact order. I observed a considerable number of young lads, and here and there a man amongst them, about the middle of the street, facing the soldiers, but not within ten or twelve feet distance from them; I observed some of them, viz., the lads, etc., had sticks in their hands, laughing, shouting, huzzaing, and crying fire; but could not observe that any of them threw anything at the soldiers, or threatened any of them. Then the said officer retired from before the soldiers and stepping behind them, towards the right wing, bid the soldiers fire; they not firing, he presently again bid 'em fire, they not yet firing, he stamped and said, "Damn your bloods, fire, be the consequence what it will"; then the second man on the left wing fired off his gun, then, after a very short pause, they fired one after another as quick as possible, beginning on the right wing; the last man's gun on the left wing flashed in the pan, then he primed again, and the people being withdrawn from before the soldiers, most of them further down the street, he turned his gun toward them and fired upon them. Immediately after the principal firing, I saw three of the people fall down in the street; presently after the last gun was fired off, the said officer, who had commanded the soldiers (as above) to fire, sprung before them, waving his sword or stick, said, "Damn ye, rascals, what did ye fire for?" and struck up the gun of one of the soldiers who was loading again, whereupon they seemed confounded and fired no more.

Source: *A Short Narrative of the Horrid Massacre in Boston Perpetrated in the Evening of the Fifth Day of March, 1770, by the Soldiers of the 29th Regiment* (Boston, 1770), republished with additional material by John Doggett Jr. (New York, 1849), 72.

Source 5.7

Account of Boston Massacre Funeral Procession, March 12, 1770

One week after the Boston Massacre, a massive public funeral was held for the four victims who had already died: Samuel Gray, Samuel Maverick, James Caldwell, and Crispus Attucks. Shops were closed, church bells marked the event in Boston and nearby Charlestown and Roxbury, and Bostonians of all ranks attended the funeral.

Last Thursday, agreeable to a general request of the inhabitants, and by the consent of parents and friends, were carried to their grave in succession, the bodies of Samuel Gray, Samuel Maverick, James Caldwell, and Crispus Attucks, the unhappy victims who fell in the bloody massacre of the Monday evening preceding!

On this occasion most of the shops in town were shut, all the bells were ordered to toll a solemn peal, as were also those in the neighboring towns of Charlestown, Roxbury, etc. The procession began to move between the hours of 4 and 5 in the afternoon; two of the unfortunate sufferers, Messrs. James Caldwell and Crispus Attucks, who were strangers [not residents of Boston], borne from Faneuil Hall, attended by a numerous train of persons of all ranks; and the other two, Mr. Samuel Gray, from the house of Mr. Benjamin Gray (his brother), on the north side of the Exchange, and Mr. Maverick, from the house of his distressed mother, Mrs. Mary Maverick, in Union Street, each followed by their respective relations and friends: The several hearses forming a junction in King Street, the theatre of the inhuman tragedy! proceeded from thence through the Main Street, lengthened by an immense concourse of people, so numerous as to be obliged to follow in ranks of six, and brought up by a long train of carriages belonging to the principal gentry of the town. The bodies were deposited in one vault in the middle burying ground. The aggravated circumstances of their death, the distress and sorrow visible in every countenance, together with the peculiar solemnity with which the whole funeral was conducted, surpass description.

Source: *Boston Gazette and Country Journal*, March 12, 1770.

Paul Revere | Etching of the Boston Massacre, 1770

Published three weeks after the Boston Massacre, Paul Revere's famous etching of the event stirred anti-British sentiment among the colonists. Revere had produced an earlier sketch that showed the position of Attucks, Caldwell, and the other men killed near the Customs House. The etching that circulated widely, however, was based on an engraving by another artist, Henry Pelham, which depicted an organized line of British soldiers firing into a crowd of unarmed colonists. At the time of the Boston Massacre, Revere was a prominent silversmith and a member of the Sons of Liberty.

Library of Congress, Prints and Photographs Division [LC-DIG-ppmsca-01657]

Account of Captain Thomas Preston, June 25, 1770

Captain Thomas Preston, the officer in charge on March 5, was tried separately from the other soldiers. His trial centered on whether he had ordered his men to fire on the crowd. Assuming that defendants in criminal trials would perjure themselves to gain an acquittal, English legal custom prohibited them from testifying. But Preston presented his version of events to British authorities just a week after the event, strenuously denying the charges against him. That account was published in the *Boston Gazette* on March 12, 1770; later appeared in London papers; and was republished in the *Boston Evening-Post* on June 25, 1770.

On Monday night about Eight o' Clock two Soldiers were attacked and beat. But the Party of the Towns-People, in order to carry Matters to the utmost Length, broke into two Meeting-Houses, and rang the Alarm Bells, which I supposed was for Fire as usual, but was soon undeceived. About Nine some of the Guard came to and informed me, the Town-Inhabitants were assembling to attack the Troops, and that the Bells were ringing as the Signal for that Purpose, and not for Fire, and the Beacon intended to be fired to bring in the distant People of the Country. This, as I was Captain of the Day, occasioned my repairing immediately to the Main-Guard. In my Way there I saw the People in great Commotion, and heard them use the most cruel and horrid Threats against the Troops. In a few Minutes after I reached the Guard, about an hundred People passed it, and went towards the Custom-House, where the King's Money is lodged. They immediately surrounded the Sentinel posted there, and with Clubs and other Weapons threatened to execute their Vengeance on him. I was soon informed by a Townsman, their Intention was to carry off the Soldier from his Post, and probably murder him. On which I desired him to return for further Intelligence; and he soon came back and assured me he heard the Mob declare they would murder him. This I feared might be a Prelude to their plundering the King's Chest. I immediately sent a non-commissioned Officer and twelve Men to protect both the Sentinel and the King's-Money, and very soon followed myself, to prevent (if possible) all Disorder; fearing lest the Officer and Soldiery by the Insults and Provocations of the Rioters, should be thrown off their Guard and commit some rash Act. They soon rushed through the People, and, by charging their Bayonets in half Circle, kept them at a little Distance. Nay, so far was I from intending the Death of any Person, that I suffered the Troops to go to the Spot where the unhappy Affair took Place, without any Loading in their Pieces, nor did I ever give Orders for loading them. This remiss Conduct in me perhaps merits Censure; yet it is Evidence, resulting from the Nature of Things, which is the best and surest that can be offered, that my Intention was not to act offensively, but the contrary Part, and that not without Compulsion. The mob still increased, and were more outrageous, striking their clubs or bludgeons one against another, and calling out, "Come on you rascals, you bloody backs, you lobster scoundrels, fire if you dare, G–d damn you, fire and be damned; we know you dare not"; and much more such language was used. At this time I was between the soldiers and the mob, parleying with and endeavouring all in my power to persuade them to retire peaceably; but to no purpose. They advanced to the points of the bayonets, struck some of them, and even the muzzles of the pieces, and seemed to be endeavouring to close with the soldiers. On which some well-behaved persons asked me if the guns were charged. I replied, yes. They then asked me if I intended to order the men to fire. I answered no, by no means; observing to them that I was advanced before the muzzles of the men's pieces, and must fall a sacrifice if they fired; that the soldiers were upon the half-cock and charged bayonets, and my giving the word fire under those circumstances would prove me no officer. While I was thus speaking, one of the soldiers, having received a severe blow with a stick, stepped a little on one side and instantly fired, on which turning to and asking him why he fired without orders, I was struck with a club on my arm, which for some time deprived me of the use of it, which blow, had it been placed on my head, most probably would have destroyed me. On this a general attack was made on the men by a great number of heavy clubs, and snowballs being thrown at them, by which all our lives were in imminent danger; some persons at the same time from behind calling out, "Damn your bloods, why don't you fire?" Instantly three or four of the soldiers fired, one after another, and directly after three more in the same confusion and hurry.

The mob then ran away, except three unhappy men who instantly expired, in which number was Mr. Gray, at whose rope-walk the prior quarrel took place; one more is since dead, three others are dangerously, and four slightly wounded. The whole of this melancholy affair was transacted in almost 20 minutes. On my asking the soldiers why they fired without orders, they said they heard the word "Fire" and supposed it came from me. This might be the case, as many of the mob called out "Fire, fire," but I assured the men that I gave no such order, that my words were, "Don't fire, stop your firing."

Source: *Supplement to the Boston Evening-Post*, June 25, 1770.

Source 5.10

John Adams | Defense of the British Soldiers at Trial, October 1770

A descendant of Puritans, John Adams was a Harvard graduate, Enlightenment thinker, and lawyer. He wrote some of the most important legal defenses of colonial rights in response to Parliament's passage of the Stamp Act. A staunch patriot, Adams agreed to defend the British soldiers because he believed that everyone deserved a fair trial. This decision did not injure Adams's reputation. Indeed, he was elected to the Massachusetts General Court (legislature) while preparing for the trial.

shall endeavour to make some few observations on the testimonies of the witnesses, such as will place the facts in a true point of light. . . .

The next witness is Dodge, he says, there were fifty people near the soldiers pushing at them; now the witness before says, there were twelve sailors with clubs, but now here are fifty more aiding and abetting of them, ready to relieve them in case of

need; now what could the people expect? It was their business to have taken themselves out of the way; some prudent people by the Town-house told them not to meddle with the guard, but you hear nothing of this from these fifty people; no, instead of that, they were huzzaing and whistling, crying damn you, fire! why don't you fire? So that they were actually assisting these twelve sailors that made the attack; he says the soldiers were pushing at the people to keep them off, ice and snow balls were thrown, and I heard ice rattle on their guns, there were some clubs thrown from a considerable distance across the street. . . .

. . . When the multitude was shouting and huzzaing, and threatening life, the bells ringing, the mob whistling, screaming, and rending like an Indian yell, the people from all quarters throwing every species of rubbish they could pick up in the street, and some who were quite on the other side of the street throwing clubs at the whole party, Montgomery in particular smote with a club and knocked down, and as soon as he could rise and take up his firelock, another club from afar struck his breast or shoulder, what could he do? Do you expect he should behave like a stoic philosopher lost in apathy? . . . It is impossible you should find him guilty of murder. You must suppose him divested of all human passions, if you don't think him at the least provoked, thrown off his guard, and into the furor brevis [brief madness], by such treatment as this. . . .

. . . Facts are stubborn things; and whatever may be our wishes, our inclinations, or the dictates of our passions, they cannot alter the state of facts and evidence: nor is the law less stable than the fact; if an assault was made to endanger their lives, the law is clear, they had a right to kill in their own defence; if it was not so severe as to endanger their lives, yet if they were assaulted at all, struck and abused by blows of any sort, . . . this was a provocation, for which the law reduces the offence of killing, down to manslaughter, in consideration of those passions in our nature, which cannot be eradicated. To your candor and justice I submit the prisoners and their cause.

Source: Frederick Kidder, *History of the Boston Massacre, March 5, 1770* (Albany, NY: J. Munsell, 1870), 249, 252, 257–58.

Interpret the Evidence

1. What are the major similarities and differences between the testimonies of William Wyatt and Captain Preston (Sources 5.6 and 5.9)?

2. How does Revere's portrayal (Source 5.8) compare with the testimonies of Wyatt (Source 5.6) and Preston (Source 5.9)? Who was the primary audience for Revere's engraving?

3. How might the funeral procession (described in Source 5.7) have incited popular sentiment against the British before March 5?

4. Why does John Adams challenge the eyewitness accounts of the event (Source 5.10) and how is he able to convince a Boston jury to acquit most of the British soldiers?

Put It in Context

What events occurred between March 1770 and March 1774 that heightened the meaning of the Boston Massacre for colonial patriots?

Evaluate how the deaths of the five colonists and the outcome of the trial changed the way patriots and ordinary colonists viewed the British authorities.

The American Revolution
1775–1783

Window to the Past

A Fire Burns British-Occupied New York City

New York City was home to avid patriots and devoted loyalists. The city of 25,000 was a center of trade with an excellent harbor. Patriots initially occupied the city. But in summer 1776, British General William Howe launched an assault; and by September, patriots retreated to Harlem. Within days of British troops entering Manhattan, a raging fire destroyed homes, churches, and businesses. ▶ **To learn more about this primary source, see Source 6.3 on page 187.**

Library of Congress, Prints and Photographs Division [LC-USZC2-402]

After reading this chapter you will be able to:

- Explain the relationship between the beginning of armed conflict and patriots' decision to declare independence.

- Understand the choices of colonists, American Indians, and African Americans to support or oppose independence.

- Analyze the military strategies of the British and the Americans in 1776–1777, the roles that various allies played, the importance of women and other groups on the home front, and the significance of smallpox among colonial soldiers

- Explain the major accomplishments of and conflicts within the new state and federal governments during the Revolution.

- Analyze the shift of warfare to the South and West from 1778 to 1781; the importance of American Indians, foreign allies, and colonial soldiers in patriot victories there; and the challenges Americans faced once they defeated the British.

Comparing American Histories

One of the foremost pamphleteers of the patriot cause, **Thomas Paine** was born in 1737 in England, where his parents trained him as a corset maker. Eventually he left home and found work as a seaman, a teacher, and a tax collector. He drank heavily and beat both his wives. Yet he also taught working-class

(*left*) **Thomas Paine** Library of Congress, Prints and Photographs Division, Washington, D.C. [LC-DIG-pga-12728]
(*right*) **Elizabeth Freeman (Mum Bett)** Bridgeman Images

children to read and pushed the British government to improve the working conditions and pay of tax collectors. In 1772 Paine was fired from his government job, but a pamphlet he wrote had caught the eye of Benjamin Franklin, who persuaded him to try his luck in the colonies.

Arriving in Philadelphia in November 1774 at age thirty-seven, Paine secured a job on the *Pennsylvania Magazine*. The newcomer quickly gained in-depth political knowledge of the intensifying conflicts between the colonies and Great Britain. He also gained patrons for his political tracts among Philadelphia's economic and political elite. When armed conflict with British troops erupted in April 1775, colonial debates over whether to declare independence intensified. Pamphlets were a popular means of influencing these debates, and Paine wrote one entitled *Common Sense* to tip the balance in favor of independence.

Published in January 1776, *Common Sense* proved an instant success. It provided a rationale for independence and an emotional plea for creating a new democratic republic. Paine urged colonists to separate from England and establish a political structure that would ensure liberty and equality for all Americans. "A government of our own is our natural right," he concluded. "'Tis time to part."

When *Common Sense* was published, an enslaved woman known as Bett was working for the Ashleys in Sheffield, Massachusetts. She was born to enslaved parents around 1742 in Claverack, New York, on the estate of Peiter Hogeboom. When Hogeboom's daughter Hannah married John Ashley, around 1750, the young Bett was given to them as a wedding present. Bett worked for the Ashleys for the next thirty years. Sometime in the late 1760s or early 1770s, the Ashleys allowed Bett to marry, and she gave birth to a daughter, Little Bett. By the 1770s, "Mum" Bett had gained skills as a nurse and midwife.

John Ashley, a wealthy lawyer and landowner, had fought in the French and Indian War. As conflicts between Britain and the colonies escalated, he joined the patriot cause. In January 1773, eleven patriots, including lawyer Theodore Sedgwick, met at his home. They drew up a series of resolutions known as the Sheffield Resolves that decried British tyranny and demanded individual rights. They were printed in the colonies and sent to Parliament. When war erupted in spring 1775, Colonel Ashley was too old to serve, but Bett's husband, whose name is unknown, joined the local militia. He was apparently killed in the war.

In 1780, Hannah Ashley tried to hit one of the enslaved workers, perhaps Little Bett, and Mum Bett intervened. She received a severe blow from a heated shovel and readily showed the scar as evidence of Ashley's brutal treatment. That same year, Mum Bett heard the newly ratified Massachusetts Constitution read aloud. It included the proposition that "All men

are born free and equal, and have certain natural, essential, and unalienable rights." Soon after, Mum Bett contacted Theodore Sedgwick, whose antislavery sentiments were well-known, and asked his help in suing for her freedom. Her case and that of another Ashley slave named Brom led the county court to rule that "there can be no such thing as perpetual servitude of a rational creature." Mum Bett took the name **Elizabeth Freeman** and moved to the home of Theodore Sedgwick, where she was respected and paid for her work. ■

Comparing the American histories of Thomas Paine and Elizabeth Freeman demonstrates how the American Revolution transformed individual lives as well as the life of the nation. Paine had failed financially and personally in England but gained fame in the colonies through his skills as a patriot pamphleteer. Freeman was born into slavery, taken from her parents, and forced to watch as her daughter was abused. Then the claims of patriots led to her freedom. While the American Revolution offered opportunities for both Paine and Freeman, most Americans had to choose sides long before it was clear whether the colonists could defeat Great Britain. Moreover, the lengthy war (1775–1783) took a toll on families and communities across the thirteen colonies. Moreover, even with English converts like Paine and homegrown supporters like Freeman, the patriots would need foreign allies to achieve victory. And battlefield victory could not ensure political stability in the new nation.

The **Question** of **Independence**

The Continental Congress that met to protest the Coercive Acts adjourned in October 1774, but delegates reconvened in May 1775. During the intervening months, patriot leaders honed their arguments for resisting British tyranny, and committees of correspondence circulated the latest news. While some patriots began advocating resistance in the strongest terms, the eruption of armed clashes between British soldiers and local farmers created the greatest push for independence. It also led the Continental Congress to establish the Continental Army in June 1775. A year later, in July 1776, the congress declared independence.

Armed Conflict Erupts. As debates over independence intensified, patriots along the Atlantic coast expanded their efforts. The Sons of Liberty and other patriot groups spread propaganda against the British, gathered and stored weapons, and organized and trained local militia companies. In addition to boycotting British goods, female patriots manufactured bandages and bullets. Some northern colonists freed enslaved African Americans who agreed to enlist in the militia. Others kept close watch on the movements of British troops.

On April 18, 1775, Boston patriots observed British movement in the harbor. British soldiers were headed to Lexington, intending to confiscate guns and ammunition hidden there and in neighboring Concord and perhaps arrest patriot leaders. To warn his fellow patriots, Paul Revere raced to Lexington on horseback but was stopped on the road to Concord by the British. By that time, however, a network of riders was spreading the alarm and alerted Concord residents of the impending danger.

Early in the morning of April 19, the first shots rang out on the village green of Lexington. After a brief exchange between British soldiers and local militiamen — known as minutemen for the speed with which they assembled — eight colonists lay dead. The British troops then marched on Concord, where they burned colonial supplies. By then, patriots in nearby towns had been alerted. Borrowing guerrilla tactics from native peoples, colonists hid behind trees, walls, and barns and battered the British soldiers as they marched back to Boston, killing 73 and wounding 200.

Word of the conflict traveled quickly. Outraged Bostonians attacked British troops and forced them to retreat to ships in the harbor. The victory was short-lived, however, and the British soon regained control of Boston. But colonial forces entrenched themselves on hills just north of the city. Then in May, Ethan Allen and his Green Mountain Boys joined militias from Connecticut and Massachusetts to capture the British garrison at Fort Ticonderoga, New York. The battle for North America had begun.

The Battle of Bunker Hill   On June 16, 1775, 2,500 British infantry sought to dislodge 1,500 patriot volunteers from Breeds Hill, 600 yards below Charlestown's strategic Bunker Hill. Although the British managed to root out the patriots during a third assault, more than a thousand British soldiers were wounded or killed. British General Thomas Gage lost his command, and the Royal Army no longer seemed invincible. akg-images

When the **Second Continental Congress** convened in Philadelphia on May 10, 1775, the most critical question for delegates like Pennsylvania patriot John Dickinson was how to ensure time for discussion and negotiation. Armed conflict had erupted, but should, or must, revolution follow? Other delegates, including Patrick Henry, insisted that independence was the only appropriate response to armed attacks on colonial residents.

Just over a month later, on June 16, British forces under General Sir William Howe attacked patriot fortifications on Breed's Hill and Bunker Hill, north of Boston. The British won the **Battle of Bunker Hill** when patriots ran out of ammunition. But the redcoats—so called because of their bright red uniforms—suffered twice as many casualties as the patriots. The victory allowed the British to maintain control of Boston for nine more months, but the heavy losses emboldened patriot militiamen. Both armies were also fighting smallpox. Howe used the time in Boston to inoculate British troops against the disease, an effective but dangerous cure since some percentage of those inoculated were likely to die.

Building a Continental Army.

The Battle of Bunker Hill convinced the Continental Congress to establish an army for the defense of the colonies. They appointed forty-three-year-old George Washington as commander in chief, and he headed to Massachusetts to take command of militia companies already engaged in battle. Since the congress had not yet proclaimed itself a national government, Washington depended largely on the willingness of local militias to accept his command and of individual colonies to supply soldiers, arms, and ammunition. Throughout the summer of 1775, Washington wrote numerous letters to patriot political leaders detailing the army's urgent need for men and supplies. He also sought to remove incompetent officers and improve order among the troops.

As he worked to forge a disciplined army, Washington and his officers developed a twofold military strategy. They sought to drive the British out of Boston and to secure the colonies from attack by British forces and their Indian allies in New York and Canada. In November 1775, American troops under General Richard Montgomery captured Montreal. However, the difficult trek in cold weather and the spread of smallpox decimated the patriot reinforcements led by General Benedict Arnold, and American troops failed to dislodge the British from Quebec.

Smallpox continued to threaten the patriot cause. The Continental Congress refused to let troops be inoculated, fearing the loss of too many men. Still, huge numbers were dying across the north, including Major General John Thomas, Commander of the Continental Army in Quebec. John Adams claimed, "The smallpox is ten times more terrible than Britons, Canadians and Indians, together." In fact, native people died at a higher rate than any other group. By mid-July 1776, an estimated three thousand men of the Northern Army were sick, most with smallpox. Eventually the epidemic eased, but it returned in different regions throughout the revolution.

Despite the disastrous outcome of the Canadian invasion, the Continental Army secured important victories in the winter of 1775–1776. On May 10, 1775, a small force of Green Mountain Boys from Vermont, led by Ethan Allen and Benedict Arnold, captured the small British garrison at Fort Ticonderoga. General Henry Knox later retrieved forty-three cannons captured at the fort to improve Washington's position outside Boston. In March 1776, with the cannons positioned on Dorchester Heights, Washington bombarded the British and drove them from Boston. Eventually the British retreated to Nova Scotia.

Reasons for Caution and for Action.

When the British retreated from Boston, the war had already spread into Virginia. In spring 1775, local militias forced Lord Dunmore, Virginia's royal governor, to take refuge on British ships in Norfolk harbor. Dunmore encouraged white servants and enslaved blacks to join him there. Hundreds of black men fought with British troops when the governor led his army back into Virginia in November 1775. After the Battle of Great Bridge, Dunmore reclaimed the governor's mansion and issued an official proclamation that declared "all indent[ur]ed Servants, Negroes or others (appertaining to Rebels)" to be free if they were "able and willing to bear Arms" for the British.

Dunmore's Proclamation, offering freedom to enslaved men who fought for the crown, reinforced earlier challenges to social hierarchies. During the 1760s, Baptist preachers repudiated class and racial distinctions and, even in the South, invited poor whites and enslaved blacks to their services. By 1775, 15 percent of whites in Virginia and hundreds of African Americans had joined Baptist churches. In England itself, a group of radicals drew on anti-authoritarian ideas developed during the English Civil War (1642–1651) to criticize British rule over its expanding empire. Through pamphlets and newspapers, their ideas circulated widely in the colonies. In addition, Enlightenment thinkers generally emphasized individual talent over inherited privilege, a view reinforced by the success of a man like Thomas Paine.

Still, many delegates at the Continental Congress, which included large planters, successful merchants, and professional men, hesitated to act. They held out hope for a negotiated settlement that would increase the colonies' political liberty without disrupting social and economic hierarchies. However, the king and Parliament refused to compromise in any way with the rebellious colonies. Instead, in December 1775, the king prohibited any negotiation or trade with the colonies, increasing the leverage of radicals who argued independence was a necessity. The January 1776 publication of Thomas Paine's *Common Sense* bolstered their case. Paine wielded both biblical references and Enlightenment ideas in his best-selling pamphlet. It impressed patriot leaders as well as ordinary farmers and artisans, who debated his ideas at taverns and coffeehouses.

Explore ▶

Read some of Paine's arguments in Source 6.1.

By the spring of 1776, a growing number of patriots believed that independence was necessary. Colonies began to take control of their legislatures and instruct their delegates to the Continental Congress to support independence. Meanwhile, the congress requested economic and military assistance from France. And in May, the congress advised colonies that had not yet done so to establish independent governments.

Still, many colonists opposed the idea of breaking free from Britain. Charles Inglis, the rector at Trinity Church in New York City, insisted that "limited monarchy is the form of government which is most favorable to liberty."

Declaring Independence.

As colonists argued back and forth, Richard Henry Lee of Virginia introduced a motion to the Continental Congress in early June 1776 declaring that "these United Colonies are, and of right ought to be, Free and Independent States." A heated debate followed with Lee and John Adams arguing passionately for independence. Eventually, even more cautious delegates, like Robert Livingston of New York, were convinced. Livingston concluded that "they should yield to the torrent if they hoped to direct it." He then joined Adams, Thomas Jefferson, Benjamin Franklin, and Roger Sherman on a committee to draft a formal statement justifying independence.

Guided Primary Source Analysis

Thomas Paine | *Common Sense*, January 1776

Thomas Paine's *Common Sense* was the most widely read pamphlet supporting American independence. Paine's plain style and use of biblical allusions appealed to ordinary people and ignited the Revolutionary movement. As a government employee in England, Paine had been hired, transferred, dismissed, rehired, and dismissed again, which likely influenced his critique of the monarchy. But he offered a broader vision as well, providing colonists with a new understanding of the relationship between a government and its citizens.

Source 6.1

How does Paine characterize the role of the King in England?

What does Paine consider the proper relationship between the law and political authority?

What system of government does Paine advocate for the American colonies?

In England a King hath little more to do than to make war and give away places; which, in plain terms, is to impoverish the nation, and set it together by the ears. A pretty business, indeed, for a man to be allowed eight hundred thousand sterling a year for, and worshipped into the bargain! Of more worth is one honest man to society, and in the sight of God, than all the crowned ruffians that ever lived. . . .

But where, say some, is the King of America? I will tell you, friend, he reigns above, and does not make havock of mankind like the royal brute of Great Britain. Yet that we may not appear to be defective even in earthly honors, let a day be solemnly set apart for proclaiming the charter; let it be brought forth, placed on the divine law, the word of God: let a crown be placed thereon, by which the world may know that so far we approve of monarchy, that in America, THE LAW IS KING. For as in absolute governments the King is law, so in free countries the Law *ought* to be King; and there ought to be no other. But lest any ill use should afterwards arise, let the crown, at the conclusion of the ceremony, be demolished, and scattered among the people whose right it is.

A government of our own is our natural right; and when a man seriously reflects on the precariousness of his human affairs, he will become convinced, that it is infinitely wiser and safer, to form a constitution of our own in a cool deliberate manner, while we have it in our power, than to trust such an interesting event to time and chance.

Source: Thomas Paine, *Common Sense; Addressed to the Inhabitants of America* (London: H. D. Symonds, 1792), 11, 20.

Put It in Context

To whom was this 1776 pamphlet addressed, and how did it influence colonial support for independence from Britain?

Thirty-three-year-old Jefferson took the lead in preparing the declaration, building on ideas expressed by Paine, Adams, and Lee. He also drew on language used in dozens of "declarations" written by town meetings, county officials, and colonial assemblies. The earliest, the 1773 Sheffield Resolves, proclaimed that "Mankind in a state of nature are equal, free, and independent of each other, and have a right to the undisturbed enjoyment of their lives, their liberty and property." These words are echoed in the most famous line of the Declaration of Independence: "We hold these truths to be self-evident, that all men are created equal, that they are endowed by their Creator with certain unalienable Rights, that among these are Life, Liberty and the pursuit of Happiness." Jefferson was also inspired by the Virginia Declaration of Rights drafted by George Mason in May 1776. This and several similar documents insisted on religious freedom, a right that many colonists viewed as evidence of their being uniquely blessed with liberty. Another central principle was the contract theory of government, proposed by the seventeenth-century British philosopher John Locke. Locke argued that sovereignty resided in the people, who submitted voluntarily to laws and authorities in exchange for protection of their life, liberty, and property. The people could reconstitute or overthrow a government that abused its powers. Jefferson summarized this argument and then listed the abuses and crimes perpetrated by King George III against the colonies, which justified the patriots' decision to break their contract with British authorities.

Once prepared, the **Declaration of Independence** was debated and revised. In the final version, all references to slavery were removed. But delegates agreed to list among the abuses suffered by the colonies the fact that the king "excited domestic insurrections amongst us," referring to the threat posed by Dunmore's Proclamation. On July 2, 1776, delegates from twelve colonies approved the Declaration, with only New York abstaining. Independence was publicly proclaimed on July 4 when the Declaration was published as a broadside to be circulated throughout the colonies.

Review & Relate

- What challenges did Washington face after accepting command of the Continental Army?

- How and why did proponents of independence prevail in the debates that led to the Declaration of Independence?

Choosing Sides

Perhaps half of American colonists actively supported the patriots, and a fifth actively supported the British. The rest tried to stay neutral or were largely indifferent unless the war came to their doorstep. Both patriots and loyalists included men and women from all classes and regions. African Americans and Indians also provided critical support to both sides, hoping to improve their status in the revolution's aftermath.

Recruiting Supporters. Men who took up arms against the British before independence was declared and the women who supported them clearly demonstrated their commitment to the patriot cause. In some colonies, patriots organized local committees, courts, and assemblies to assume governance should British officials lose their authority. White servants and enslaved blacks in Virginia who fled to British ships or marched with Lord Dunmore made their loyalties known as well. Some native tribes, too, declared their allegiance early in the conflict. In May 1775, Colonel Guy Johnson, the new

Joseph Brant/Thayendanegea   The Mohawk chief Joseph Brant was born into a family with close ties to the British Superintendent of Indian Affairs, William Johnson. Brant attended Eleazar Wheelock's Indian school and helped translate the Bible into Mohawk. One of the most famous Indians of his day, Brant visited England twice, seeking assurances of land for the Mohawk. The famed portraitist Gilbert Stuart captured Brant after his 1786 visit to London. VCG Wilson/Corbis via Getty Images

British superintendent for Indian affairs, sought refuge in Canada. He was accompanied by 120 British loyalists and 90 Mohawk warriors led by their mission-educated chief, Joseph Brant (Thayendanegea), and his sister Mary (Konwatsi'tsiaienni), a Mohawk diplomat.

The Continental Congress recognized the importance of native allies to the outcome of any colonial war. It appointed commissioners from the "United Colonies" to meet with representatives of the Iroquois Confederacy in August 1775. While Brant's Mohawk warriors were already committed to the British, some Oneida Indians, influenced by missionaries and patriot sympathizers, wanted to support the colonies. Others, however, urged neutrality, at least for the moment.

Once independence was declared, there was far more pressure to choose sides. The stance of political and military leaders and soldiers was clear. But to win against Great Britain required the support of a large portion of the civilian population as well. As battle lines shifted back and forth across New England, the Middle Atlantic region, and the South, civilians caught up in the fighting were faced with difficult decisions.

Many colonists who remained loyal to the king found safe haven in cities like New York, Newport, and Charleston, which remained under British control throughout much of the war. **Loyalist** men were welcomed by the British army. Still, colonists who made their loyalist sympathies clear risked a good deal. When British troops were forced out of cities or towns they had temporarily occupied, loyalist women and men faced harsh reprisals. Patriots had no qualms about invading the homes and businesses of loyalists and destroying or confiscating property.

Many loyalists were members of the economic and political elite. Others came from ordinary backgrounds. Many tenants, small farmers, and enslaved workers joined the loyalist cause in defiance of landlords, speculators, and wealthy planters. Many poorer loyalists lived in the Hudson valley, their sympathy for the British heightened by the patriot commitments of the powerful men who controlled the region. When the fighting moved into the Carolinas, members of a group called the Regulators—poor frontier farmers who challenged the domination of patriot leaders among the eastern elite—also supported the British.

Explore ▶

For images of African Americans' varied responses to the war, see Sources 6.2 and 6.3.

Perhaps most important, the majority of Indian nations ultimately sided with the British. The Mohawk, Seneca, and Cayuga nations in the North and the Cherokee and Creek nations in the South were among Great Britain's leading allies. Although British efforts to limit colonial migration, such as the Proclamation Line of 1763, had failed, most native leaders still believed that a British victory offered the only hope of ending further encroachments on their territory.

African Americans in New York City Amid the Upheavals of 1776

On July 9, the day New York's Provincial Congress approved the Declaration of Independence, a rowdy crowd of soldiers and civilians toppled a statue of King George III. However, an etching of the event presents it as the work of African Americans, with most whites simply observing (Source 6.2). In a second etching, by François Xavier Haberman (Source 6.3), Manhattan burns only days after British troops occupied the city in September. The fire burnt a mile-long swath through the area as redcoats beat suspected patriots and white and black residents carried items from burning buildings.

Source 6.2

Slaves Destroy Statue of King George III in New York City, July 1776

Library of Congress, Prints and Photographs Division [LC-USZ62-2202]

Choosing Neutrality. Early in the war, many tribes followed the Iroquois in proclaiming their neutrality. This included the Delaware and Shawnee in the Ohio River valley and the Oneida in Connecticut. The Oneida's chief warriors declared that the English and patriots were "*two brothers of one blood. We are unwilling to join on either side in such a contest.*" But patriots often refused to accept Indian neutrality. Indeed, colonial troops killed the Shawnee chief Cornstalk under a flag of truce in 1777, leading that nation to ally, finally, with the British.

Source 6.3

A Fire Burns British-Occupied New York City, September 1776

Library of Congress, Prints and Photographs Division [LC-USZC2-402]

Interpret the Evidence

1. Why might an American artist depict the destruction of the statue of King George III as the work mainly of blacks? What roles are whites playing in this portrayal?

2. What meanings might be attached to black and white residents carrying items out of burning buildings after the British occupation of Manhattan? Why are the blacks here and in Source 6.2 shown as barely clothed?

Put It in Context

Given the limited choices available to most African Americans during the American Revolution, what advantages or disadvantages were created when the patriots or the British gained control of areas where they lived?

Colonists who sought to remain neutral during the war also faced hostility. Some 80,000 Quakers, Mennonites, Amish, Shakers, and Moravians considered war immoral and embraced neutrality. These men refused to bear arms, hire substitutes, or pay taxes to new state governments. The largest number of religious pacifists lived in Pennsylvania. Despite Quakerism's deep roots there, pacifists were treated as suspect by both patriots and loyalists.

Explore ▶

For two historians' perspectives on what led colonists to revolt against British rule, see Sources 6.4 and 6.5.

In June 1778, Pennsylvania authorities jailed nine Mennonite farmers who refused to take an oath of allegiance to the revolutionary government. Their worldly goods were sold by the state, leaving their wives and children destitute. Quakers were routinely fined and imprisoned for refusing to support the patriot cause and harassed by British authorities in the areas they controlled. At the same time, Quaker meetings regularly disciplined members who offered aid to either side. Philadelphia Quakers disowned Betsy Ross after she married a non-Quaker who fought with the patriots and then sewed flags herself for the Continental Army and Navy.

Committing to Independence.   After July 4, 1776, the decision to support independence took on new meaning. If the United States failed to win the war, all those who actively supported the cause could be considered traitors. The families of Continental soldiers faced especially difficult decisions as the conflict spread and soldiers moved farther and farther from home. Men too old or too young to fight proved their patriotism by gathering arms and ammunition and patrolling local communities.

Some female patriots accompanied their husbands, fiancés, or brothers as camp followers, cooking, washing clothes, nursing, and providing other services for soldiers. Most patriot women remained at home, however, and demonstrated their commitment by raising funds, gathering information, and, perhaps most importantly, sending clothes, bedding, and medicine to soldiers at the front. The Continental Army was desperately short of supplies from the beginning of the war. Northern women were urged to increase cloth production, while southern women were asked to harvest crops for hungry troops. The response was overwhelming. Women in Hartford, Connecticut produced 1,000 coats and vests and 1,600 shirts in 1776 alone. Across the colonies, women collected clothing door-to-door and opened their homes to sick and wounded soldiers.

Phillis Wheatley   This portrait of Phillis Wheatley appears facing the title page of her book of poems, printed in London in 1773. It was painted by another Boston slave, Scipio Moorhead. Phillis Wheatley converted to Christianity and sided with the patriots in the Revolution. She won her freedom but never gained sufficient support to publish another book of poems. Library of Congress, Prints and Photographs Division [LC-USZ62-56850]

Some African American women also became ardent patriots. Phillis Wheatley of Boston, whose owners taught her to read and write, published a collection of poems in 1776 and sent a copy to General Washington. She urged readers to recognize Africans as children of God. Rewarded with freedom by her master, Wheatley was among a small number of blacks who actively supported the patriot cause. Still, the vast majority of blacks were enslaved. While some escaped and joined the British in hopes of gaining their freedom, most were not free to choose sides.

Review & Relate

▪ How did colonists choose sides during the Revolutionary War? What factors influenced their decisions?

▪ Why would some Indian tribes try to stay neutral during the conflict? Why did most of those who chose sides support the British?

Fighting for Independence, 1776–1777

After July 4, 1776, battles between British and colonial troops intensified, but it was not until December that the patriots celebrated a major military victory. The rebellion faced a formidable set of challenges. Over the course of the eighteenth century, Great Britain had developed the world's most powerful military force, including a huge navy. Moreover, once independence was declared, the colonists lost their main trading partner and had to find ways to sustain their economy while funding a war. To succeed, the patriots needed support from men and women on the home front as well as the battlefront and assistance from Europeans experienced in fighting the British. It took two years for the patriots and the Continental Army to gain traction against British forces.

British Troops Gain Early Victories. In the summer of 1776, when General Washington tried to lead his army out of Boston to confront British troops set to invade New York City, many soldiers deserted and returned home. They believed that New York men should defend New York. Among the soldiers who remained with Washington, many were landless laborers whose wives and sisters followed the troops as their only means of support. Although Washington tried to rid the army of these camp followers, a few hundred women continued to travel with the troops, providing critical services to ordinary soldiers. Ultimately, Washington arrived in New York with 19,000 men, many of whom were poorly armed and poorly trained, and some of whom were coerced into service by local committees of safety. Camp followers nursed, washed, and cooked for these men.

Throughout the summer, British ships sailed into New York harbor or anchored off the coast of Long Island. General Howe, hoping to overwhelm the colonists, ordered 10,000 troops to march into the city in the weeks immediately after the Declaration of Independence was signed. Still, the Continental Congress rejected Howe's offer of peace and a royal pardon.

So Howe prepared to take control of New York City by force and then march up the Hudson valley, isolating New York and New England from the rest of the rebellious colonies. He was aided by some 8,000 Hessian mercenaries (Germans being paid to fight for the British). On August 27, 1776, British forces clashed with a far smaller contingent of Continentals on Long Island. More than 1,500 patriots were killed, wounded, or taken prisoner in the fierce fighting.

In September, British troops occupied Manhattan. A raging fire, thought but never proved to be arson, destroyed or damaged nearly a quarter of Manhattan's 4,000 buildings, briefly halting their advance. Meanwhile, Washington and his men continued to retreat.

Comparative Secondary Source Analysis

Americans Decide to Revolt against British Rule

Historians have long debated why, between the years 1774 and 1776, a large number of American colonists decided to revolt against British rule. Until 1774, colonists protested British policies, such as taxes or impressment, but hoped to reform, not overthrow, the imperial system. By 1776, however, a significant proportion of American colonists changed course and demanded independence from the British Crown. As historians assess the most important factors that account for this change, some, including Bernard Bailyn, highlight the role of ideas and their circulation among colonial leaders. Others, represented by Timothy Breen, focus on the anger against Britain and passion for a distinctly American notion of liberty among patriot insurgents.

Source 6.4

Bernard Bailyn | The Importance of Ideas, 1967

[T]he American Revolution was above all else an ideological, constitutional, political struggle. . . . [The pamphlets read for this study] confirmed . . . my belief that the intellectual developments in the decade before Independence led to a radical idealization and conceptualization of the previous century and half of American experience, and that it was this intimate relationship between Revolutionary thought and the circumstances in eighteenth-century America that endowed the Revolution with its peculiar force and made it so profoundly a transforming event. . . .

The pamphlets . . . reveal the influence of Enlightenment thought, and . . . show the effective force of certain religious ideas, of the common law, and also of classical literature; but they reveal most significantly the close integration of these elements . . . [with] still another tradition. . . . This distinctive influence had been transmitted most directly to the colonists by a group of early eighteenth-century radical publicists and opposition politicians in England who carried forward into the eighteenth century . . . the peculiar strain of anti-authoritarianism bred in the upheaval of the English Civil War. . . .

[T]he fear of a comprehensive conspiracy against liberty throughout the English-speaking world—a conspiracy believed to have been nourished in corruption, and of which, it was felt oppression in America was only the most immediately visible part—lay at the heart of the Revolutionary movement. . . .

For the primary goal of the American Revolution . . . was not the overthrow or even the alteration of the existing social order but the preservation of political liberty. . . .

Source: Bernard Bailyn, *The Ideological Origins of the American Revolution* (Cambridge: Belknap Press of Harvard University Press, 1967), pp. vi–ix and 19.

By November, the British had captured Fort Lee in New Jersey and attacked the Continental Army at Fort Washington, north of New York City. Washington then led his weary troops and camp followers into Pennsylvania, while the Continental Congress, fearing a British attack on Philadelphia, fled to Baltimore.

Although General Howe might have ended the patriot threat right then by an aggressive campaign, he wanted to wear down the Continental Army and force the colonies to sue

Source 6.5

Timothy H. Breen | Insurgents Mobilize, 2010

The [essence] of our Revolution—indeed, of any successful revolution—was the willingness of a sufficient number of people to take up arms against an unelected imperial government that no longer served the common good. This moment occurred in America sometime in mid-1774. . . .

Insurgencies are not movements for the faint of heart. They certainly involve a lot more than a commitment to a set of intellectual principles. What is demanded of us, therefore, is a greater appreciation of the kinds of passions that have energized insurgencies throughout world history. Our revolutionary lexicon will include popular anger and rage, and a feeling of betrayal—harsh concepts perhaps, but ones that better reflect the actual revolutionary process than do those encountered in abstract histories of political thought.

The argument is not that insurgents did not have ideas about politics. They did. But these were ideas driven by immediate passions; they were amplified through fear, fury and resentment.

Moreover, evangelical religion played a much larger role in motivating revolutionary resistance than most historians have recognized. . . .

To be sure, the insurgents did not fight for democracy, but by inviting so many new participants into the political process on the local level and by rejecting a monarchical system of government, with its attendant aristocratic privilege, they transformed the colonial political culture. Thousands of Americans . . . invented new, highly effective forms of popular resistance. . . .

Revolutions do not sustain themselves through ideas alone. . . . [T]he evidence of ordinary Americans mobilizing in response to parliamentary insults and an army of occupation, forging common bonds of sympathy throughout all thirteen colonies, and creating an infrastructure to support and drive forward revolution in the years ahead of the Declaration of Independence is overwhelming.

Source: Timothy H. Breen, *American Insurgents, American Patriots: The Revolution of the People* (New York: Hill & Wang, 2010), pp. 10–12 and 16.

Examine the Sources

1. How do Bailyn and Breen differ in their interpretation of why Americans chose to revolt against British rule in the mid-1770s?
2. What evidence from this chapter supports the view of Bailyn or Breen as to why so many Americans embraced the idea of revolution from 1774 to 1776?

Put It in Context

How would you weigh the importance of the ideas promoted by patriot leaders and the anger and resentment that fueled popular support in 1774–1776 over the entire course of the Revolutionary War?

for peace. Washington did not have the troops or arms to launch a major assault, and he hoped that the British would accept American independence once they saw the enormous effort it would take to defeat the colonies. So the war continued.

Patriots Prevail in New Jersey. The Continental Army did not gain a single military victory between July and December 1776. Fortunately for Washington, Howe followed the European tradition of waiting out the winter months and returning to combat after the spring thaw. This gave the patriots the opportunity to regroup, repair weapons and wagons, and recruit soldiers. Yet Washington was reluctant to face the cold and discomfort of winter with troops discouraged by repeated defeats and retreats.

Camped in eastern Pennsylvania, Washington learned that Hessian troops had been sent to occupy the city of Trenton, New Jersey, just across the Delaware River. On Christmas Eve, Washington attacked Trenton in an icy rain, and the Continentals quickly routed the surprised Hessians. They then marched on Princeton and defeated regular British troops on January 3, 1777. The British army soon retreated from New Jersey, settling back into New York City, and the Continental Congress returned to Philadelphia. By mid-January 1777, it seemed clear to both sides that the conflict would be harder, more costly, and more deadly than anyone had imagined.

Then smallpox once again spread through the Continental Army. When quarantining troops proved insufficient, Washington insisted on inoculating his men. He did so with speed and secrecy while the winter provided a break from fighting. Fortunately, only one percent of his troops died as a result of inoculation.

A Critical Year of Warfare.
The British army emerged from winter camp in spring 1777. Its regular army units, American loyalists, Indian allies, Hessians, and naval men-of-war were concentrated largely in New York City and Canada. The Continental forces, numbering fewer than 5,000 men, were then entrenched near Morristown, New Jersey, and Washington feared that an aggressive British assault might succeed.

Meanwhile, the Continental Congress in Philadelphia feared that the British would seek to capture the city and split the United States in two. General Howe did indeed plan on capturing Philadelphia, hoping to force a patriot surrender. Although Washington's force was too small to defeat Howe's army, it delayed his advance by guerrilla attacks and skirmishes. En route, Howe learned that he was expected to reinforce General John Burgoyne's soldiers, who were advancing south from Canada. Instead he continued to Philadelphia and captured it in September 1777 after Burgoyne and his 7,200 troops had regained control of Fort Ticonderoga in July. Burgoyne continued south, but by late July his forces had to stop until supplies from Canada and reinforcements from Howe and General Barry St. Leger reached them.

St. Leger was marching his British troops east through New York State, and Joseph Brant and his sister Molly Brant were gathering a force of Mohawk, Seneca, and Cayuga warriors to support them. But on August 6, they suffered a stunning defeat. In the **Battle of Oriskany** in New York, a band of German American farmers led by General Nicholas Herkimer held off the British advance, allowing Continental General Arnold to reach nearby Fort Stanwix with reinforcements. On August 23, the British troops and their native allies retreated to Canada (Map 6.1).

When General Howe's reinforcements also did not materialize, Burgoyne faced a brutal onslaught in northern New York. In September patriot forces defeated the British at Freeman's Farm, with the British suffering twice the casualties of the Continentals. Fighting intensified in early October, when Burgoyne lost a second battle at Freeman's Farm. Ten days later, he surrendered his remaining army of 5,800 men to General Gates at nearby Saratoga, New York.

The Continental Army's victory in the **Battle of Saratoga** stunned the British. It undercut the significance of Howe's victory at Philadelphia and indicated the general's

MAP 6.1 The War in the North, 1775–1778

After early battles in Massachusetts, patriots invaded Canada but failed to capture Quebec. The British captured New York City in 1776 and Philadelphia in 1777. New Jersey remained a battle zone. As British forces headed into New York State, they were joined by Iroquois. Although patriots defeated the combined force at Saratoga, battles continued throughout central New York and Pennsylvania.

misunderstanding of the nature of the war he was fighting. Meanwhile, the patriot victory energized Washington and his troops as they dug in at Valley Forge for another long winter. It also gave Benjamin Franklin, the Continental Congress envoy to Paris, greater leverage for convincing French officials to support American independence.

Patriots Gain Critical Assistance.

Despite significant Continental victories in the fall of 1777, the following winter proved especially difficult. The quarters at **Valley Forge** were again marked by bitter cold, poor food, inadequate clothing, and scarce supplies. A French volunteer arrived to see "a few militia men, poorly clad, and for the most part without shoes; many of them badly armed." Many recent recruits were also poorly trained. Critical assistance arrived with Baron Friedrich von Steuben, a Prussian officer recruited by Benjamin Franklin, who took charge of drilling soldiers. Other officers experienced in European warfare also joined the patriot cause that winter: the Marquis de Lafayette of France, Johann Baron de Kalb of Bavaria, and Thaddeus Kosciusko and Casimir Count Pulaski, both of Poland. The Continental Army continued to be plagued by problems of recruitment, discipline, wages, and supplies. But the contributions of foreign volunteers, along with the leadership of Washington and his officers, sustained the military effort.

Patriots on the home front were also plagued by problems in 1777–1778. Families living in battlefield areas were especially vulnerable to the shifting fortunes of war. When British troops captured Philadelphia in fall 1777, a British officer commandeered the home of Elizabeth Drinker, a Quaker matron. An angry Drinker reported that the officer moved in with "3 Horses 2 Cows 2 Sheep and 3 Turkeys." Women who lived far from the conflict were isolated from such intrusions but were forced to fend for themselves with husbands at the front. Meanwhile, wives of patriot leaders, anxious to end the conflict, formed voluntary societies, like the Ladies Association of Philadelphia led by Esther De Berdt Reed, to provide critical resources for the army. **See Primary Source Project 6: Women in the Revolution, page 207.**

While most women worked tirelessly on the home front, some continued to cast their fate with the army. Camp followers provided critical services to the military throughout the revolution and suffered, as the troops did, from scarce supplies and harsh weather. Some women also served as spies and couriers for British or Continental forces. Lydia Darragh, a wealthy Philadelphian, eavesdropped on conversations among the British officers who occupied her home and carried detailed reports to Washington hidden in the folds of her dress. Deborah Champion, the daughter of a high-ranking officer in the Continental Army, traveled from Connecticut to Boston to deliver secret messages from her father to George Washington. Accompanied by Aristarchus, an enslaved household laborer, Champion was stopped by British soldiers on several occasions but her mission was never discovered. Others, like Nancy Hart Morgan of Georgia, took more direct action. She lulled half a dozen British soldiers into a sense of security at dinner, hid their guns, and shot two before neighbors came to hang the rest.

Some patriot women took up arms on the battlefield. Margaret Corbin accompanied her husband to the front lines. When her husband was killed at Fort Washington in November 1776, Corbin took his place loading and firing cannons. In addition, a small number of women disguised themselves as men and enlisted as soldiers. Deborah Sampson, an indentured servant in Massachusetts, knew male servants who were recruited into the Continental Army. Late in the war, she disguised herself as a man and enlisted as Robert Shurtliff in a

Massachusetts regiment. Sampson served for more than a year, benefitting from lax standards of hygiene and her muscular frame. When a doctor discovered that "Robert" was a woman, Sampson was honorably discharged.

Surviving on the Home Front. Whether black or white, enslaved or free, women and children faced hardship, uncertainty, loneliness, and fear as a result of the war. Even those who did not directly engage enemy troops took on enormous burdens during the conflict. Farm wives plowed and planted and carried on their domestic duties as well. In cities, women worked ceaselessly to find sufficient food, wood, candles, and cloth to maintain themselves and their children.

As the war intensified, Continental and British forces slaughtered cattle and hogs for food, stole corn and other crops or burned them to keep the enemy from obtaining supplies, looted houses and shops, and kidnapped or liberated enslaved laborers and free servants. Some home invasions turned savage. Both patriot and loyalist papers in New York, Philadelphia, and Charleston reported cases of rape.

In these desperate circumstances, many women asserted themselves in order to survive. When merchants hoarded goods in order to make greater profits from rising prices, housewives raided stores and warehouses and took the supplies they needed. Others learned as much as they could about family finances and submitted claims to local officials when their houses, farms, or businesses were damaged or looted. Growing numbers of women banded together to assist one another, help more impoverished families, and supply troops with badly needed clothes, food, bandages, and bullets.

Review & Relate

- How did the patriot forces fare in 1776? How and why did the tide of war turn in 1777?
- What role did colonial women and foreign men play in the conflict in the early years of the war?

Governing in Revolutionary Times

Amid the constant upheavals of war, patriot leaders established new governments. At the national level, responsibilities ranged from coordinating and funding military operations to developing diplomatic relations with foreign countries and Indian nations. At the state level, constitutions had to be drafted and approved, laws enforced, and military needs assessed and met. Whether state or national, new governments had to assure their followers that they were not simply replacing old forms of oppression with new ones. Yet few states moved to eliminate the most oppressive institution in the nation, slavery.

Colonies Become States. For most of the war, the Continental Congress acted in lieu of a national government while the delegates worked to devise a more permanent structure. The congress depended mainly on states for funds and manpower. In 1777, delegates drafted the **Articles of Confederation**, creating a central government with limited powers. They submitted the Articles to the states for approval, and eight of the thirteen states had ratified the plan by mid-1778. Still, nearly three more years passed before the last state, Maryland, approved the Articles.

Without a formal central government, state governments played crucial roles throughout the war. Even before the Continental Congress declared American independence, some colonies had forced royal officials to flee and established new state governments. Some states abided by the regulations in their colonial charters or by English common law. Others created new governments based on a written constitution.

These constitutions reflected the opposition to centralized power fueled by the struggle against British tyranny. In Pennsylvania, patriots developed one of the most democratic constitutions. The governor was replaced by an executive council. The legislature consisted of a single house elected by popular vote. Legislators could only serve for four in any seven years to discourage the formation of a political aristocracy. Although Pennsylvania's constitution was among the most radical, all states limited centralized power in some way.

Most states adopted Virginia's model and included in their constitutions a bill of rights that ensured citizens freedom of the press, freedom of elections, speedy trials by one's peers, humane punishments, and the right to form militias. Some states also insisted on people's freedom of speech and assembly, the right to petition and to bear arms, and equal protection of the laws. The New Jersey constitution of 1776 enfranchised all free inhabitants who met the property qualifications, thereby allowing some single and widowed women and free blacks to vote. However, most new state constitutions allowed only white men with property to vote, and nearly all granted significant power to the legislative branch, where white men of property dominated.

Patriots Divide over Slavery. Although state constitutions were revolutionary in many respects, few of them addressed the issue of slavery. Only Vermont abolished slavery in its 1777 constitution. Legislators in Pennsylvania approved a gradual abolition law by which slaves born after 1780 could claim their freedom at age twenty-eight. In Massachusetts, Mum Bett and Brom successfully sued for their freedom in county court in 1781. Another enslaved laborer sued for his freedom shortly afterward. Quock Walker was promised his freedom at age 21. However, his master died and his widow's second husband, Nathaniel Jennison, refused to release Walker, who fled to a nearby farm. Jennison retrieved Walker and beat him severely. After a series of court cases, the Massachusetts Supreme Court, citing Bett and Brom's case, ruled in 1783 that slavery conflicted with the state constitution. Although the state legislature never abolished slavery in Massachusetts, the institution had died out in the state by 1790.

In southern states like Virginia, the Carolinas, and Georgia, life for enslaved people grew increasingly harsh during the war. Because British forces promised freedom to blacks who fought with them, slave owners and patriot armies in the South did everything possible to ensure that African Americans did not make it behind British lines. When the British retreated, some generals, like Lord Dunmore and Sir Henry Clinton, took black volunteers with them. But thousands more were left behind to fend for themselves.

Nonetheless, the American Revolution dealt a blow to human bondage. For many blacks, Revolutionary ideals required the end of slavery. Northern free black communities grew rapidly during the war, especially in seaport cities. In the South, too, thousands of the formerly enslaved gained freedom, either by joining the British army or by fleeing in the midst of battlefield chaos. As many as one-quarter of South Carolina's enslaved women and men had emancipated themselves by the end of the Revolution. Yet as the Continental

Congress worked toward developing a framework for a national government, few delegates considered abolishing slavery immediately throughout the country. Instead, some hoped to limit enslavement and slave trading in ways that would lead to its ultimate demise.

France Allies with the Patriots.

In the midst of war, the Continental Congress considered an alliance with France far more critical to success than abolishing slavery. France's long rivalry with Britain made it a likely ally, and the French government had secretly provided funds to the patriots early in the war. In December 1776, the Continental Congress sent Benjamin Franklin to Paris to serve as its unofficial liaison. Franklin was enormously successful, securing supplies and becoming a favorite among the French aristocracy and ordinary citizens alike. Individual French officers, such as Marquis de Lafayette, arrived in North America, helped train Continental troops, and led them into battle.

The French were initially unwilling to forge a formal compact with the upstart patriots. Only after their victory at Saratoga in October 1777 did King Louis XVI agree to an alliance. The following February, the French approved trading rights between the United States and all French possessions. France then recognized the United States as an independent nation, relinquished French territorial claims on mainland North America, and sent troops to reinforce the Continental Army. In return, the United States promised to defend French holdings in the Caribbean. A year later, Spain allied itself with France to protect its own North American holdings.

British leaders responded by declaring war on France. Yet doing so ensured that military conflicts would spread well beyond North America and military expenditures would skyrocket. French forces attacked British outposts in Gibraltar, the Bay of Bengal, Senegal in West Africa, and Grenada in the West Indies. At the same time, the French supplied the United States with military officers, weapons, funds, and critical naval support.

Faced with this new alliance, Britain's prime minister, Lord North (1771–1782), decided to concentrate British forces in New York City. This tactic forced the British army to abandon Philadelphia in summer 1778. For the remainder of the war, New York City provided the sole British stronghold in the North, serving as a supply center and prisoner-of-war camp.

The Marquis de La Fayette with an Aide-de-Camp
This eighteenth-century portrait of the Marquis de Lafayette was painted by a Frenchman during the Revolution. It shows him with his aide-de-camp, probably from the French West Indies. Lafayette joined the Continental Army in September 1777, led patriot forces in numerous battles, camped at Valley Forge, and trapped British forces under General Cornwallis at the decisive Siege of Yorktown. Archives Charmet/Bridgeman Images

Raising Armies and Funds.

The French alliance did create one unintended problem for the Continental Army. When Americans heard that France was sending troops, fewer men volunteered for military service. Local officials had the authority to draft men into the army or to accept substitutes for draftees. In the late 1770s, some draftees forced enslaved men to take their place; others hired landless laborers, the handicapped, or the mentally unfit as substitutes.

As the war spread south and west in 1778–1779, Continental forces were stretched thin, and enlistments faltered further. Soldiers faced injury, disease, and shortages of food and ammunition. They also risked capture by the British, one of the worst fates to befall a Continental. Considered traitors by the British, most captives were held on ships in New York harbor. They faced filthy accommodations, a horrid stench, inadequate water, and widespread disease and abuse. Altogether, between 8,000 and 11,000 patriots died in British prisons in New York — more than died in battle.

Even if the British had allowed the Continental Congress to aid prisoners, it could do little, given the financial problems it faced. With no authority to impose taxes on American citizens, the congress had to borrow money from wealthy patriots, accept loans from France and the Netherlands, and print money of its own — some $200 million by 1780. However, money printed by the states was used far more widely than were Continental dollars. "Continentals" depreciated so quickly that by late 1780 it took one hundred continentals to buy one silver dollar's worth of goods. In 1779, with the cost of goods skyrocketing, housewives, sailors, and artisans in Philadelphia and other cities attacked merchants who were hoarding goods, forcing officials to distribute food to the poor.

The congress finally improved its financial standing slightly by using a $6 million loan from France to back certificates issued to wealthy patriots. Meanwhile states raised money through taxes to provide funds for government operations, backing for its paper money, and other expenses. Most residents found such taxes particularly burdensome given wartime inflation, and even the most patriotic began to protest their inevitable increase. Thus the financial status of the new nation remained precarious.

Indians and Patriots Battle for Land.

Although the congress sought alliances with additional Indian nations, colonists' desire to control native lands counteracted such efforts. Most Indian nations had long-standing complaints against colonists who intruded on their lands, and many patriot leaders made it clear that victory would mean further expansion into Indian territories. Indeed some native peoples viewed the patriots' war more as an imperial conquest than a political revolution. In addition, both the British and patriots recruited increasingly diverse fighting forces as the war continued.

In the late 1770s, British forces and their Indian allies fought bitter battles against patriot militias and Continental forces all along the New York and Pennsylvania frontier. The August 1777 battle of Oriskany, which led to the surrender of British General Burgoyne to Continental forces in October, revealed the increasingly multiethnic and multiracial character of the war. German-American farmers fought for the patriots alongside Oneida Indians and Anglo-American soldiers against British soldiers aided by Hessian (that is, German) mercenaries and Mohawk Indians. With members of the Iroquois Confederacy — Oneida and Mohawk — fighting against each other, the confederacy itself became a victim of the revolution.

For nearly three years, patriots and their Indian allies battled British and tribal forces throughout the Mohawk River valley. The British side destroyed patriot settlements, ruined crops, killed civilians, and took women and children captive. Patriots retaliated against the village of Mohawk chief Joseph Brant, killing men, women, and children. In turn, Brant called on his warriors "to defend their Lands and Liberty against the Rebels," who sought to become "sole Masters of this Continent." When Mohawk warriors attacked the village of Cherry Valley, they killed twice as many civilians as soldiers. In May 1779, as retaliatory attacks continued throughout the region, Washington ordered General John Sullivan to undertake the "total destruction and devastation" of Iroquois villages. Mary Jemison, an Irish immigrant captured by Indians in 1755, recalled, "they destroyed every article of the food kind that they could lay their hands on. A part of our corn they burnt, and threw the remainder into the river. They burnt our houses, killed what few cattle and horses they could find, destroyed our fruit trees, and left nothing but the bare soil and timber." The assaults eventually forced thousands of Indians, sick and starving, to flee to British-controlled Fort Niagara.

Patriots and native tribes also battled along the Pennsylvania frontier, where militia leaders' refusal to differentiate between allies and enemies escalated conflicts. Delaware and Shawnee chiefs had pledged support to the patriots, but in fall 1778, patriot forces killed two Shawnee chiefs. Despite apologies from the Continental Congress, another Delaware chief died two months later, also likely killed by militia. Indians allied with patriots viewed such acts as a war of extermination and some changed sides.

By March 1782, the escalating violence bled into the Ohio River valley when one hundred sixty Pennsylvania militiamen attacked a Moravian Mission at Gnadenhutten. Claiming they were seeking revenge for attacks on their frontier settlements, the patriots killed and scalped ninety-six Delaware Indians as they kneeled in prayer. The patriots then piled the victims' bodies in mission buildings before burning the entire community to the ground. Both the Moravians and their Indian converts were pacifists, but they had aided the patriots as guides and spies. Although some patriot leaders condemned the attack, the soldiers were never punished. The massacre caused outrage among their Indian allies.

Conflicts Escalate on the Frontier.

In present-day Tennessee, Cherokee who sided with the British became targets of patriot troops. Six thousand patriot soldiers laid waste to thirty-six native villages in 1778. They claimed it was in retaliation for the killing of white intruders along the Watauga River by a renegade Cherokee warrior. Cherokee and Shawnee warriors then attacked Fort Boonesborough, which Daniel Boone had established in 1775 in present-day Kentucky. In July 1778, patriot leader George Rogers Clark led Kentucky militiamen and Canadian volunteers sympathetic to the patriots in attacks on the British fort at Kaskaskia on the Mississippi River. Meanwhile the British, hoping to extend their frontier, established Fort Vincennes on the Ohio River. In a surprise February attack, Clark's troops — strengthened by French soldiers — sought to capture the fort. To convince the British commander to surrender, Clark's men tomahawked four Indian captives to death in view of British forces. Once Fort Vincennes surrendered, colonists from Virginia began pouring into the region.

Intent on keeping their control of the northern frontier, the British commander at Fort Michilimackinac on Lake Huron recruited Sioux, Chippewa, and Sauk warriors to attack Spanish forces along the Mississippi, while soldiers at Fort Detroit armed Ottawa, Fox, and

Miami warriors to assault American settlers flooding into the Ohio River valley. Clark tried to capture Fort Detroit, but failed. However, Spanish troops defeated British-allied Indian forces at St. Louis, increasing patriot control in the region (Map 6.2).

As British soldiers, patriots, and native tribes engaged in increasingly brutal battles on the western frontier, Connecticut, Georgia, New York, Massachusetts, and Virginia claimed

MAP 6.2   The War in the West and the South, 1777–1782

Between 1780 and 1781, major battles between Continental and British troops took place in Virginia and the Carolinas, and the British general Cornwallis finally surrendered at Yorktown, Virginia in October 1781. But patriot forces also battled British troops and their Indian allies from 1777 to 1782 in the Ohio River valley, the lower Mississippi River, and the Gulf coast.

they already controlled large portions of the region. The states hoped to use these lands to reward soldiers and expand their settlements. However, those claims were challenged by other states, like Maryland, whose boundaries were fixed. They argued that if such lands were "wrested from the common enemy by the blood and treasure of the thirteen States," they should be considered "common property," to be parcelled out by Congress. After lengthy debate, New York State finally ceded its western claims to the Continental Congress in 1780, and federal officials assumed that the remaining states would follow suit.

Even this achievement was dampened by an outbreak of "break-bone fever" in August 1780 in Philadelphia, home to the Continental Congress. It affected young and old, women and men, blacks and whites. Severe pains in the head, back, and limbs accompanied a high fever. The famed physician Benjamin Rush, who treated a thousand Philadelphians between August and October, noted that in some cases the disease produced hemorrhagic symptoms, leading occasionally to death. Many who recovered suffered physical and mental weakness for an extended period. When the fever abated in October, the outcome of the revolution was still uncertain.

By March 1781, with land disputes settled among the rebellious states, the outcome looked more hopeful. When Maryland ratified the Articles of Confederation, a new national government was finally formed, unifying the rebellious states just as it appeared they would gain their independence. Still, the congress's guarantee that western lands would be "disposed of for the common benefit of the United States" made clear the imperial intentions of the Confederation government and ensured continued conflicts with native peoples.

Review & Relate

- What values and concerns shaped state governments during the Revolutionary War?

- What issues and challenges did American Indian tribes face as the Continental Army and Continental Congress fought for independence from the British?

Winning the War and the Peace, 1778–1783

From 1778 to 1781, the revolutionary battlefront moved south as well as west. The king, who believed that southern colonists' sympathies were more loyalist than patriot, insisted on pursuing a southern strategy. The patriots' eventual victory rested on a combination of superb strategy, their French and Spanish allies, and the continued support of affluent men and women. Still, even after the surrender of Britain's army in October 1781, the war dragged on while peace terms were negotiated. The celebrations following the signing of a peace treaty were themselves tempered by protests among Continental soldiers demanding back pay and by the realization of the new nation's looming challenges.

War Rages in the South. While war raged along the frontier, British troops sought to regain control of southern states from Georgia to Virginia. They captured Savannah, Georgia in 1778 and soon extended their control over the entire state. When General Clinton was called north later that year, he left the southern campaign in the hands of Lord Charles Cornwallis.

In May 1780, General Cornwallis reclaimed Charleston, South Carolina. He then evicted patriots from the city, purged them from the state government, gained military control of the state, and imposed loyalty oaths on all Carolinians able to fight. To aid his efforts, local loyalists organized militias to battle patriots in the interior. Banastre Tarleton led one especially vicious company of loyalists who slaughtered civilians and murdered many who surrendered. In retaliation, patriot planter Thomas Sumter organized 800 men who showed a similar disregard for regular army procedures, raiding largely defenseless loyalist settlements near Hanging Rock, South Carolina in August 1780.

As retaliatory violence erupted in the interior of South Carolina, General Gates marched his Continental troops south to join 2,000 militiamen from Virginia and North Carolina. But his troops were exhausted and short of food, and on August 16 Cornwallis won a smashing victory against the combined patriot forces at Camden, South Carolina (see Map 6.2). Soon after news of Gates's defeat reached General Washington, he heard that Benedict Arnold, commander at West Point, had defected to the British.

Suddenly, British chances for victory seemed more hopeful. Cornwallis was in control of Georgia and South Carolina, and local loyalists were eager to gain control of the southern countryside. Meanwhile Continental soldiers in the North mutinied in early 1780 over enlistment terms and pay. Despite patriot victories along the Ohio and Mississippi rivers, patriot morale back east was low, funds were scarce, and civilians were growing weary of the war.

Yet somehow the patriots prevailed. A combination of luck, strong leadership, frontier militia, and French support turned the tide. In October 1780, when Continental hopes looked especially bleak, a group of 800 frontier sharpshooters routed loyalist troops at King's Mountain in South Carolina. The victory kept Cornwallis from advancing into North Carolina and gave the Continentals a chance to regroup.

Shortly after the battle at King's Mountain, Washington sent General Nathanael Greene to replace Gates as head of southern operations. Taking advice from local militia leaders like Daniel Morgan and Francis Marion, Greene divided his limited force into even smaller units. Marion and Morgan each led 300 Continental soldiers into the South Carolina back-country, picking up hundreds of local militiamen along the way. At the village of Cowpens, Morgan inflicted a devastating defeat on Tarleton's much larger force.

Despite their victory, Continental forces were spread thin and retreated in order to regroup. Cornwallis, enraged at the patriot victory, pursued these Continental forces, but his troops had outrun their cannons, and Greene circled back and attacked them at Guilford Court House. Although Cornwallis eventually forced the far smaller Continental company to withdraw from the battlefield, British troops suffered enormous losses. In August 1781, frustrated at the ease with which patriot forces still found local support in the South, he hunkered down in Yorktown on the Virginia coast and waited for reinforcements from New York.

Washington now coordinated strategy with his French allies. Comte de Rochambeau marched 5,000 troops south from Rhode Island to Virginia as General Lafayette led his troops south along Virginia's eastern shore. At the same time, French naval ships headed north from the West Indies. One unit cut off a British fleet trying to resupply Cornwallis by sea. Another joined up with American privateers to bombard Cornwallis's forces. By mid-October, British supplies had run out, and it was clear that reinforcements would not be forthcoming. On October 19, 1781, the British army admitted defeat.

An Uncertain Peace. The Continental Army had managed the impossible. It had defeated the British army and won the colonies' independence. Yet even with the surrender after the **Battle of Yorktown**, the war continued in fits and starts. Peace negotiations in Paris dragged on as French, Spanish, British, and American representatives sought to settle a host of issues. Meanwhile, British forces challenged Continental troops in and around New York City.

Some Continental soldiers continued to fight, but others focused on the long-festering issue of overdue wages. When the congress decided in June 1783 to discharge the remaining troops without providing back pay, a near mutiny erupted in Pennsylvania. Nearly three hundred soldiers marched on the congress in Philadelphia, and Washington sent troops to put down the mutiny. Bloodshed was avoided when the Pennsylvania soldiers agreed to accept half pay and certificates for the remainder. Still, the issue of back pay would continue to plague the nation.

Meanwhile patriot representatives in Paris—Benjamin Franklin, John Adams, and John Jay—continued to negotiate peace terms. Rising antiwar sentiment on the British home front forced the government's hand. But the Comte de Vergennes, the French foreign minister, opposed the Americans' republican principles and refused to consider the American delegates as his political equals. Given the importance of the French to the American victory, the congress had instructed its delegates to defer to French wishes. This blocked the American representatives from signing a separate peace with the British.

Eventually, however, U.S. delegates finalized a treaty that secured substantial benefits for the young nation. The United States gained control of all lands south of Canada and north of Louisiana and Florida stretching to the Mississippi River. In addition, the treaty recognized the United States to be "free Sovereign and independent states." Spain signed a separate treaty with Great Britain in which it regained control of Florida. Once again, despite their role in the war, none of the Indian nations that occupied the lands under negotiation were consulted.

When the **Treaty (Peace) of Paris** was finally signed on September 2, 1783, thousands of British troops and their supporters left the colonies for Canada, the West Indies, or England. British soldiers on the western frontier were supposed to be withdrawn at the same time, but they remained for many years and continued to foment hostilities between Indians in the region and U.S. settlers along the frontier.

The evacuation of the British also entailed the exodus of thousands of African Americans who had fought against the patriots. At the end of the war, British officials granted certificates of manumission (freedom) to more than 1,300 men, 900 women, and 700 children. Most of these freed blacks settled in Nova Scotia, where they received small allotments of land from the British. Still, they generally lacked the resources to make such homesteads profitable in the cold climate. Despite these obstacles, some created a small Afro-Canadian community in Nova Scotia, while others migrated to areas considered more hospitable to black residents, such as Sierra Leone.

A Surprising Victory. Americans had managed to defeat one of the most powerful military forces in the world. That victory resulted from the convergence of many circumstances. Certainly Americans benefited from fighting on their own soil. Their knowledge of the land and its resources as well as earlier experiences fighting against Indians and the French helped prepare them for battles against the British.

Just as important, British troops and officers were far removed from centers of decision making and supplies. Even supplies housed in Canada could not be easily transported the

"Evacuation Day" and Washington's Triumphal Entry into New York City, November 25, 1783 Masses of Americans turned out to cheer General Washington and his officers as they retook control of New York City following the Peace of Paris. This 1879 print was likely made from an earlier painting. It highlights the joy felt by men, women, and children whose hopes for the new United States replaced their dismay at the long years of war and British occupation. Library of Congress, LC-DIG-pga-02468

relatively short distance into New York. British commanders were often hesitant to make decisions independently, but awaiting instructions from England proved costly on several occasions, especially since strategists in London often had little sense of conditions in America.

Both sides depended on outsiders for assistance, but here, too, Americans gained the advantage. The British army relied heavily on German mercenaries, Indian allies, and freed blacks to bolster its regular troops. In victory, such "foreign" forces were relatively reliable, but in defeat, many of them chose to look out for their own interests. The patriots failed to secure permanent alliances with the largest indigenous tribes and in the late 1770s lost native support. Instead, the patriots fought alongside French and Spanish armies well prepared to challenge British troops and motivated to gain advantages for France and Spain if Britain was defeated.

Perhaps most important, a British victory was nearly impossible without conquering the American colonies one by one. Because a large percentage of colonists supported the patriot cause, British troops had to contend not only with Continental soldiers but also with an aroused citizenry fighting for its independence.

Review & Relate

▪ How and why did the Americans win the Revolutionary War?

▪ What uncertainties and challenges did the new nation face in the immediate aftermath of victory?

Conclusion: Legacies of the Revolution

After the approval of the Declaration of Independence, Thomas Hutchinson, the British official who had gained fame during the Stamp Act upheavals in Boston, charged that patriot leaders had "sought independence from the beginning." But the gradual and almost reluctant move from resistance to revolution in the American colonies suggests otherwise. When faced with threats from British troops, a sufficient number of colonists took up arms to create the reality of war, and this surge of hostilities finally gave the advantage to those urging independence.

The victory over Great Britain won that independence but left the United States confronting difficult problems. Most soldiers simply wanted to return home and reestablish their former lives. But the government's inability to pay back wages and the huge debt the nation owed to private citizens and state and foreign governments ensured difficult economic times ahead. These problems affected American Indians and African Americans as well as whites. Using western lands to reward officers and soldiers who had not received full pay intensified conflicts along the new nation's western frontier. Warfare between settlers and Indians west of the Appalachian Mountains continued for decades. At the same time, slave owners seeking more fertile fields also expanded into the trans-Appalachian region. By 1800 they had carried tens of thousands of enslaved blacks into Kentucky, Tennessee, and the Mississippi Territory. Separated from families back east, enslaved men and women on the frontier engaged in backbreaking labor without the support or camaraderie of the communities left behind.

Although faced with far better opportunities than enslaved laborers, many white soldiers still found the adjustment to postwar life difficult. As former soldiers struggled to reestablish farms and businesses and pay off debts accrued while fighting for independence, many received no compensation for their wartime service until the early 1800s.

Political leaders tried to address the concerns of former soldiers and ordinary citizens while they developed a new government. Within a few years of achieving independence, financial distress among small farmers and tensions with Indians on the western frontier intensified concerns about the ability of the confederation government to secure order and prosperity. While some patriots demanded a new political compact to strengthen the national government, others feared replicating British tyranny.

In the decade following the Revolution, leading patriots engaged in heated disagreements over the best means to unify and stabilize the United States. However, key leaders like Thomas Jefferson, Benjamin Franklin, and John Adams were living abroad as ambassadors, strengthening U.S. ties to Britain and France. In 1787 Thomas Paine, too, left for England, where he wrote pamphlets supporting the French Revolution. He eventually moved to France, but his radical political ideas led to his imprisonment there, and he returned to the United States upon his release. Even here, however, Paine was maligned for his attacks on organized religion and private property. Thus he played no part in the intense debates about how to secure the political future of the United States. Elizabeth Freeman followed political debates among patriots in the Sedgwick home, where she continued her work as a housekeeper and caretaker for the children. In 1808, she retired to a house near her daughter's home in Stockbridge and spent time with her grandchildren. When she died in 1829, her contribution to the end of slavery in Massachusetts was clear, but so too was its expansion across much of the nation.

Timeline of Events

Key Terms

Second Continental Congress, *181*

Battle of Bunker Hill, *181*

Dunmore's Proclamation, *182*

Common Sense, *182*

Declaration of Independence, *184*

loyalist, *185*

Battle of Oriskany, *192*

Battle of Saratoga, *192*

Valley Forge, *194*

Articles of Confederation, *195*

Battle of Yorktown, *203*

Treaty (Peace) of Paris, *203*

Review & Relate

1. What challenges did Washington face after accepting the command of the Continental Army?

2. How and why did proponents of independence prevail in the debates that led to the Declaration of Independence?

3. How did colonists choose sides during the Revolutionary War? What factors influenced their decisions?

4. Why would some Indian tribes try to stay neutral during the conflict? Why did most of those who chose sides support the British?

5. How did the patriot forces fare in 1776? How and why did the tide of war turn in 1777?

6. What role did colonial women and foreign men play in the conflict in the early years of the war?

7. What values and concerns shaped state governments during the Revolutionary War?

8. What issues and challenges did American Indian tribes face as the Continental Army and Continental Congress fought for independence from the British?

9. How and why did the Americans win the Revolutionary War?

10. What uncertainties and challenges did the new nation face in the immediate aftermath of victory?

Women in the Revolution

▶ **What did women gain from the opportunities created by the American Revolution, and which women gained, or lost, the most?**

The Revolutionary War had a tremendous impact on the lives of women, and many helped shape the course of that conflict. Women faced fears and hardships brought on by absent men, inadequate supplies, enemy soldiers, and nearby battles. But the war also expanded opportunities for them in the public sphere. They ran family farms and shops, raised money, and produced homespun goods while defending themselves and their homes. Some women also spied on enemy officers, provided medical care for soldiers, engaged in diplomatic efforts, and took up arms on the battlefield. Many women gained new skills and felt pride in their contributions to the cause in which they believed. Although many women cast their efforts in a political light, patriot and British leaders rarely treated them as equal partners in the revolution.

The following documents reflect a wide variety of women's Revolutionary-era experiences. Some Anglo-American women, like Christian Barnes (Source 6.6), remained loyal to Great Britain and suffered attacks by patriot neighbors and soldiers. Mohawk leader Mary Brant was also a loyalist. Although widely recognized for her diplomatic skills, she still suffered at the hands of some British officers (Source 6.8). Patriot Abigail Adams, wife of political leader John Adams, sought greater rights for women in the new nation, though she could only plead with her husband to take action (Source 6.7). Other women with connections to patriot political and military leaders, such as Esther De Berdt Reed, raised funds for Continental troops (Source 6.9), contributing significantly to the patriot victory. At the same time, Mum Bett, an enslaved African American, turned revolutionary rhetoric to her advantage and successfully sued for her freedom (Source 6.10).

Source 6.6

Christian Barnes | Letter to Elizabeth Inman, April 29, 1775

As the conflict intensified between Great Britain and America, colonists were forced to choose sides. Whether patriots or loyalists, women were often terrorized by enemy soldiers. One such woman was Christian Barnes, the wife of a well-known loyalist who fled to Marlborough, Massachusetts to avoid capture by the colonial government. The following selection is from a letter written by Barnes in the spring of 1775, in which she describes a frightening visit by a colonial soldier.

It is now a week since I had a line from my dear Mrs. Inman, in which time I have had some severe trials, but the greatest terror I was ever thrown into was on Sunday last. A man came up to the gate and loaded his musket, and before I could determine which way to run he entered the house and demanded a dinner. I set him the best I had upon the table. He was not contented, but insisted upon bringing in his gun and dining with me; this terrified the young folks, and they ran out of the house. I went in and endeavored to pacify him by every method in my power, but I found it was to no purpose. He still continued to abuse me, and said that when he had eat his dinner he should want a horse and if I did not let him have one he would blow my brains out. He pretended to have an order from the General for one of my horses, but did not produce it.

His language was so dreadful and his looks so frightful that I could not remain in the house, but fled to the store and locked myself in. He followed me and declared he would break the door open. Some people very luckily passing to meeting prevented his doing any mischief and staid by me until he was out of sight, but I did not recover from my fright for several days. The sound of drum or the sight of a gun put me into such a tremor that I could not command myself. I have met with but little molestation since this affair, which I attribute to the protection sent me by Col. Putnam and Col. Whitcomb. I returned them a card of thanks for their goodness tho' I knew it was thro' your interest I obtained this favor. . . . The people here are weary at his [Mr. Barnes's] absence, but at the same time give it as their opinion that he could not pass the guards. . . . I do not doubt but upon a proper remonstrance I might procure a pass for him through the Camp from our two good Colonels. . . . I know he must be very unhappy in Boston. It was never his intention to quit the family.

Source: Nina M. Tiffany, ed., *Letters of James Murray, Loyalist* (Boston, 1901), 187–88.

Source 6.7

Abigail Adams | Letter to John Adams, March 31, 1776

Abigail Adams wrote detailed letters to John Adams while he was serving as a delegate to the Continental Congress in Philadelphia. She moved to Braintree, Massachusetts during the British occupation of Boston but described conditions in the city and surrounding area. She often highlighted the difficulties faced by the civilian population and their responses to them. But Abigail Adams also discussed specifically political matters, as here where she calls on her husband to grant women more legal rights under the new government.

Do not you want to see Boston; I am fearfull of the small pox, or I should have been in before this time. I got Mr. Crane to go to our House and see what state it was in. I find it has been occupied by one of the Doctors of a Regiment, very dirty, but no other damage has been done to it . . . am determined to get it cleand as soon as possible. . . .

I feel very differently at the approach of spring to what I did a month ago. We knew not then whether we could plant or sow with safety, . . . but now we feel as if we might sit under our own vine and eat the good of the land. . . .

I long to hear that you have declared an independency—and by the way in the new Code of Laws which I suppose it will be necessary for you to make I desire you would Remember the Ladies, and be more generous and favourable to them than your ancestors. Do not put such unlimited power into the hands of the Husbands. Remember all Men would be tyrants if they could. If perticuliar care and attention is not paid to the Laidies we are determined to foment a Rebelion, and will not hold ourselves bound by any Laws in which we have no voice, or Representation.

That your Sex are Naturally Tyrannical is a Truth so thoroughly established as to admit of no dispute, but such of you as wish to be happy willingly give up the harsh title of Master for the more tender and endearing one of Friend. Why then, not put it out of the power of the vicious and the Lawless to use us with cruelty and indignity with impunity.

Source: Abigail Adams to John Adams, March 31–April 5, 1776, Adams Family Papers, Massachusetts Historical Society, Digital Adams Project, http://www.masshist.org/digitaladams/archive/doc?id=L17760331aa&bc=%2Fdigitaladams%2Farchive%2Fbrowse%2Fletters_1774_1777.php.

Source 6.8

Mary Brant | Letter to Capt. Daniel Claus, Montreal, 5 October 1779

Mohawk leader Mary (Molly) Brant (Konwatsi'tsiaienni) supported Britain during the American Revolution. She had befriended Colonel John Butler during the French and Indian War and also worked closely with Captain Clause. In the late 1750s, Brant lived with Sir William Johnson, the British Superintendent of Indian Affairs, as his wife and bore him eight children. Brant entertained many distinguished indigenous and colonial guests, including her brother Joseph Brant, at Fort Johnson. She also advised William on diplomatic issues. In 1774, when Johnson died, his nephew Guy Johnson inherited his position and estate and dismissed Brant and her children from their home. He also slashed support for Indian loyalists and took charge of Fort Niagara.

I have written to Col. [John] Butler and my brother [Joseph Brant] acquainting them with my situation, desiring their advice, as I was left no directions concerning myself and family. Only when a vessel arrived, I could get a passage to Niagara. I have been promised by Col. [Guy] Johnson at Montreal, that I should hear from the Gen'l [Haldmiand] and have his direction in order to be provided at whatever place my little service should be wanted which you know I am always ready to do. Should you think [it] proper to speak to the General [Haldmiand] on that [head I] will be much obliged to you. The Indians are a good deal dissatisfied on acct of the Col. [Johnson]'s hasty temper, which I hope he will soon drop. Otherwise it may be disadvantageous. I need not tell you that whatever is promised or told them it ought to be performed.

Those from Canada are most dissatisfied on account of his [Col. Johnson's] taking more note of those that are suspected of being [disloyal] than them that are known to be Loyal. I tell this only to you that you advise him on that head.

Meantime beg leave to be remembered to all your family from sir your well wisher.

Source: Mary Brant, Carleton Island, to Captain Daniel Claus, Montreal, October 5, 1779, Public Archives Canada Publique, MG19 Folio 1, vol.2:135–136, http://heritage.canadiana.ca/view/oocihm.lac_reel_c1478/442?r=0&s=4

Source 6.9

Esther De Berdt Reed | The Sentiments of an American Woman, 1780

Esther De Berdt Reed lived in England until her marriage to merchant Joseph Reed in 1770. Joseph was a leading Philadelphia patriot and was elected president (governor) of Pennsylvania during the war. In June 1780, Esther Reed, the mother of five young children and recently recovered from smallpox, called on women to aid the Continental Army. Her broadside "The Sentiments of an American Woman" was the foundation of the Ladies Association of Philadelphia, whose members raised large sums by soliciting contributions from women door-to-door.

Who knows if persons disposed to censure, and sometimes too severely with regard to us, may not disapprove our appearing acquainted even with the actions of which our sex boasts? We are at least certain, that he cannot be a good citizen who will not applaud our efforts for the relief of the armies which defend our lives, our possessions, our liberty? . . .

We know that at a distance from the theatre of war, if we enjoy any tranquility, it is the fruit of your watchings, your labours, your dangers. If I live happy in the midst of my family; if my husband cultivates his field, and reaps his harvest in peace; if, surrounded with my children, I myself nourish the youngest, and press it to my bosom, without being affraid of seeing myself separated from it, by a ferocious enemy; if the house in which we dwell; if our barns, our orchards are safe at the present time from the hands of those incendiaries, it is to you that we owe it. And shall we hesitate to evidence to you our gratitude? Shall we hesitate to wear a cloathing more simple; hair dressed less elegant, while at the price of this small privation, we shall deserve your benedictions. Who, amongst us, will not renounce with the highest pleasure, those vain ornaments, when she shall consider that the valiant defenders of America will be able to draw some advantage from the money which she may have laid out in these; that they will be better defended from the rigours of the seasons, that after their painful toils, they will receive some extraordinary and unexpected relief; that these presents will perhaps be valued by them at a greater price, when they will have it in their power to say: *This is the offering of the Ladies*. The time is arrived to display the same sentiments which animated us at the beginning of the Revolution, when we renounced the use of teas, however agreeable to our taste, rather than receive them from our persecutors; when we made it appear to them that we placed former necessaries in the rank of superfluities, when our liberty was interested; when our republican and laborious hands spun the flax, prepared the linen intended for the use of our soldiers; when exiles and fugitives we supported with courage all the evils which are the concomitants of war. Let us not lose a moment; let us be engaged to offer the homage of our gratitude at the altar of military valour, and you, our brave deliverers, while mercenary slaves combat to cause you to share with them, the irons with which they are loaded, receive with a free hand our offering, the purest which can be presented to your virtue,

BY AN AMERICAN WOMAN

Source: Esther De Berdt Reed, "The Sentiments of an American Woman" (Philadelphia: John Dunlop, 1780).

Bridgeman Images

Source 6.10

Elizabeth "Mum Bett" Freeman, 1811

Mum Bett, an enslaved domestic worker, sued her owner John Ashley, Esq., for her freedom with the aid of lawyer Theodore Sedgwick. She was inspired to act by her mistress's beating of her daughter and by overhearing conversations about the new Massachusetts state constitution, which declared "all men . . . free and equal." A jury at the Berkshire County Court of Common Pleas set her free in 1781, after which she worked for the Sedgwick family for three decades. This portrait was painted by Susan Anne Ridley Sedgwick, Theodore's daughter-in-law, when Freeman was sixty-nine years old.

Interpret the Evidence

1. What types of activities did female patriots undertake in the service of American independence (Sources 6.7, 6.9, and 6.10)? What challenges did female loyalists face (Sources 6.6 and 6.8)?

2. How did assumptions about the proper roles of elite white women prior to the war shape their experiences during the Revolution and affect the ways they described those experiences (Sources 6.6, 6.7, and 6.9)?

3. How did Mary Brant and Mum Bett (Elizabeth Freeman) seek to improve their lives and those of other Indians and African Americans during the Revolution (Sources 6.8 and 6.10)? How did their positions as loyalist and partriot, respectively, shape their efforts?

4. What dangers or constraints did women face during the war, and how did they justify the public actions they took?

Put It in Context

How would you compare white women's experiences of the American Revolution to those of African American and American Indian women and to the experiences of white men?

How did the efforts of patriot women shape the outcome of the war?

Forging a New Nation

1783–1800

Window to the Past

Eleventh Pillar of the Great National Dome

During 1788, the thirteen states held conventions to decide whether to ratify the plan for the federal government laid out under the new Constitution. Newspapers followed the proceedings closely, and many created visual images to track the progress of ratification. The *Massachusetts Centinel*, shown here, used Greek pillars to represent each state. ▶ **To learn more about this primary source, see Source 7.10 on page 246.**

After reading this chapter you will be able to:

- Analyze the major threats to the new nation after the Revolution.

- Explain which groups of Americans were marginalized in this period and how they responded to the changes that occurred.

- Describe the chief debates over the Constitution and its ratification.

- Evaluate the ways that the young nation's economic policies affected its relations with European nations abroad and on the U.S. frontier and fostered partisanship in politics.

- Describe how the presidency of John Adams exacerbated differences between Federalists and Democratic-Republicans and led to Thomas Jefferson's election in 1800.

Comparing American Histories

One of six children born to Irish parents in Hopkinton, Massachusetts, **Daniel Shays** received little formal education. In 1772, age twenty-five, he married, had a child, and settled into farming. But in April 1775, he, his father, and his brother raced toward Concord to meet the British forces. By June, he was among the patriots defending Bunker Hill.

After distinguished service in the Continental Army, Shays purchased a farm in Pelham, Massachusetts in 1780 and hoped to return to a

(*left*) **Daniel Shays** Granger
(*right*) **Alexander Hamilton** Library of Congress, Prints and Photographs Division [LC-DIG-pga-03160]

normal life. Instead, economic turmoil roiled the region and the nation. Many farmers had fallen into debt while fighting for independence. They returned to an economic recession and increased taxes as state governments labored to repay wealthy creditors and fund their portion of the federal budget. In western Massachusetts, many farmers faced eviction. Shays kept his farm and represented his town at county conventions that petitioned the state government for economic relief. However, the legislature largely ignored the farmers' concerns.

In 1786, angered by the state's failure to act, armed groups of farmers attacked courthouses throughout western Massachusetts. Although a reluctant leader, Shays headed the largest band of more than a thousand farmer-soldiers.

The uprising, known as Shays's Rebellion, alarmed many state and national leaders who feared such insurgencies might emerge elsewhere. Among those outraged by the rebels was **Alexander Hamilton**, a young New York politician. Hamilton was born illegitimate and impoverished in the British West Indies. Orphaned at eleven, he was apprenticed to a firm of merchants that sent him to the American colonies. There Hamilton was drawn into the activities of radical patriots and joined the Continental Army as a colonel in 1776. He had some success as captain of an artillery company before General George Washington invited him to serve as one of his aides.

During the war, Hamilton fell in love with Elizabeth Schuyler, who came from a wealthy New York family. They married in December 1780. After the war, Hamilton used military and marital contacts to establish himself as a lawyer and financier in New York City. In 1786, Hamilton was elected to the New York State legislature, where he focused on improving the state's finances, and served as a delegate to a convention on interstate commerce held in Annapolis, Maryland. Hamilton and several other delegates advocated a stronger central government. They pushed through a resolution calling for a second convention "to render the constitution of the Federal Government adequate to the exigencies of the Union."

Although the initial response to the call was lukewarm, the eruption of Shays's Rebellion and the government's financial problems soon convinced many political leaders that change was necessary. Although Hamilton played only a small role in the 1787 convention in Philadelphia, he worked tirelessly for ratification of the Constitution drafted there.

When the new federal government was established in 1789, Hamilton became the nation's first secretary of the treasury. ■

C omparing the histories of Daniel Shays and Alexander Hamilton demonstrates that while patriots came together to win the Revolutionary War, they did not share a common vision of the new nation. Despite the suppression of Shays's Rebellion, the grievances that fueled the uprising persisted. Americans differed significantly over how best to resolve them. By 1787, demand for a stronger central government led to the ratification of a new U.S. Constitution. Hamilton played a leading role in advocating and establishing the new government, particularly by seeking to stabilize and strengthen the national economy. While many political and economic elites applauded his efforts, other national leaders and many ordinary citizens opposed them. These differences, exacerbated by foreign and frontier crises, eventually led to the development of competing political parties and the first contested presidential election in American history.

Financial, Frontier, and Foreign Problems

The United States faced serious financial instability in its formative years. The situation was so desperate that Continental Army officers threatened to march on the confederation congress if they did not receive their pay. Other issues also threatened the emerging nation. Conflicts between settlers and Indian tribes in western areas forced the confederation government to attend more closely to its frontier territories. Meanwhile, Spain closed the port of New Orleans to U.S. trade as individual states struggled to regulate domestic and foreign commerce. Off the coast of North Africa, Barbary pirates attacked U.S. merchant ships. Diplomatic relations with European powers were crucial, but they were hampered by America's outstanding war debts and the relative weakness of the confederation government.

Continental Officers Threaten Confederation. As the American Revolution ground to an end, issues of military pay sparked conflict. Uprisings by ordinary soldiers were common but successfully put down. Complaints from Continental officers, however, posed a greater problem. In 1780 they had extracted a promise from the Continental Congress for half pay for life but had received no compensation since. In December 1782, officers encamped at Newburgh, New York, awaiting a peace treaty, petitioned the confederation government for back pay for themselves and their soldiers, again with no success. By March 1783, most soldiers had returned home without pay, but some five hundred officers remained at Newburgh. Many confederation leaders were sympathetic to the officers' plight and hoped to use pressure from this formidable group to enhance the powers of the congress.

Alexander Hamilton had been pressing state governments to grant the confederation congress a new duty of 5 percent on imported goods, thereby providing the federal government with an independent source of revenue. Perhaps threats of an uprising by officers could convince states like New York to agree to the collection of this import duty. Quietly encouraged by political supporters, dissident officers circulated veiled threats of a military takeover. However, on March 15 the officers were confronted by General George Washington. In an emotional speech, he urged them to respect civilian control of the government. Most officers quickly retreated from their "infamous propositions." At the same time, congressional leaders promised the officers full pay for five years. However, lacking sufficient funds, they could provide only "commutation certificates," promising future payment.

Indians, Land, and the Northwest Ordinance.

One anonymous petitioner at Newburgh suggested that the officers move as a group to "some unsettled country" and let the confederation fend for itself. In reality, no such unsettled country existed beyond the thirteen states. Numerous indigenous nations and growing numbers of American settlers claimed control of western lands. In 1784 some two hundred leaders from the Iroquois, Shawnee, Creek, Cherokee, and other nations gathered in St. Louis, where they complained to the Spanish governor that the Americans were "extending themselves like a plague of locusts."

Despite the continued presence of British and Spanish troops in the Ohio River valley, the United States hoped to convince Indian nations that it controlled the territory. In October 1784, U.S. commissioners met with Iroquois delegates at Fort Stanwix, New York and demanded land cessions in western New York and the Ohio valley. When the Seneca chief Cornplanter and other leaders refused, the commissioners insisted that "you are a subdued people" and must submit. An exchange of gifts and captives taken during the Revolution finally ensured the deal. Iroquois leaders not at the meeting disavowed the **Treaty of Fort Stanwix**. But the confederation government insisted it was legal, and New York State began surveying and selling the land. With a similar mix of negotiation and coercion, U.S. commissioners signed treaties at Fort McIntosh, Pennsylvania (1785), and Fort Finney, Ohio (1786), claiming lands held by the Wyandots, Delawares, Shawnees, and others.

As eastern Indians were increasingly pushed into the Ohio River valley, they crowded onto lands already claimed by other native peoples. Initially, these migrations increased conflict among Indians, but eventually some leaders used this forced intimacy to launch pan-Indian movements against further American encroachment on their land.

Indians and U.S. political leaders did share one concern: the vast numbers of squatters, mainly white men and women, living on land to which they had no legal claim. In fall 1784 George Washington traveled west to survey nearly thirty thousand acres of territory he had been granted as a reward for military service. He found much of it occupied by squatters who refused to acknowledge his ownership. Such flaunting of property rights deepened his concerns about the fragility of the confederation government.

The confederation congress was less concerned about individual property rights and more with the refusal of Virginia and Massachusetts to cede the western lands they claimed to federal control. Mistakenly believing that the issue was largely settled once New York ceded her lands, the congress spent another five years—until 1785—negotiating with Virginia and Massachusetts officials before the two states finally relinquished their claims north of the Ohio River (Map 7.1).

Explore ▶

See Source 7.1 for a pan-Indian perspective on relations with the U.S. government.

Guided Primary Source Analysis

United Indian Nations Council | Message to Congress, 1786

Following the Revolutionary War, one of the most pressing issues that the confederation government faced was the disposition of western lands. Although the U.S. government negotiated with a number of Indian tribes to gain clear title to western lands, it often negotiated in secret with only a few leaders and backed negotiations with the threat of force. A pan-Indian council meeting was called in 1786 at which various leaders protested the confederation government's actions. The speech was addressed to the confederation congress and expressed the Indians' united stance and their hopes for fair and open dealings with the United States.

Source 7.1

How would you characterize the tone of this speech? What might this suggest about native peoples' purpose and audience?

What kinds of "mischief" do you think the Indians are referring to here?

What does this Council consider the most important ways to ensure fair treaty negotiations?

To the Congress of the United States of America:

Brethren of the United States of America: It is now more than three years since peace was made between the King of Great Britain and you, but we, the Indians, were disappointed, finding ourselves not included in that peace, according to our expectations: for we thought that its conclusion would have promoted a friendship between the United States and Indians, and that we might enjoy that happiness that formerly subsisted between us and our elder brethren. . . . In the course of our councils, we imagined we hit upon an expedient that would promote a lasting peace between us.

Brothers: We are still of the same opinion as to the means which may tend to reconcile us to each other; and we are sorry to find, although we had the best thoughts in our minds, during the beforementioned period, mischief has, nevertheless, happened between you and us. We are still anxious of putting our plan of accommodation into execution, and we shall briefly inform you of the means that seem most probable to us of effecting a firm and lasting peace and reconciliation: the first step towards which should, in our opinion, be, that all treaties carried on with the United States, on our parts, should be with the general voice of the whole confederacy, and carried on in the most open manner, without any restraint on either side; and especially as landed matters are often the subject of our councils with you, a matter of the greatest importance and of general concern to us, in this case we hold it indispensably necessary that any cession of our lands should be made in the most public manner, and by the united voice of the confederacy; holding all partial treaties as void and of no effect.

Source: *American State Papers, Class II: Indian Affairs* (Washington, 1832), 1:8.

Put It in Context

Why have Indians chosen to send this message to the congress from the United Indian Nations Council rather than from their individual nations?

MAP 7.1 Cessions of Western Land, 1782–1802

Beginning under the Articles of Confederation, political leaders sought to resolve competing state claims to western territory based on colonial charters. The confederation congress and then the U.S. Congress gradually persuaded states to cede their lands and create a "national domain," though without taking into account native land claims. Part of this domain was organized as the Northwest Territory.

To regulate this vast territory, Thomas Jefferson drafted the **Northwest Ordinance** in 1785. It provided that the territory be surveyed and divided into adjoining townships. He hoped to carve nine small states out of the region to enhance the representation of western farmers and to ensure the continued dominance of agrarian views in the national government. The congress revised his proposal, however, stipulating that only three to five states be created from the vast territory and thereby limiting the future clout of western settlers in the federal government.

The population of the territory grew rapidly, with speculators buying up huge tracts of land and selling smaller parcels to eager settlers. In response, congressional leaders modified the Northwest Ordinance in 1787, clarifying the process by which territories could become states. The congress appointed territorial officials and guaranteed residents the basic rights of U.S. citizens. After a territory's population reached 5,000, residents could choose an assembly, but the territorial governor retained the power to veto legislation. When a prospective state reached a population of 60,000, it could apply for admission to the United States. Thus the congress established an orderly system by which territories became states in the Union.

In a very limited way, the 1787 ordinance also addressed racial concerns in the region. It encouraged fair treatment of Indian nations but did not include any means of enforcing

Thomas Jefferson's Map of Western Territories   Jefferson drew this 1784 map of the western territories, showing nine states in the region north of the Ohio River. He proposed giving land to settlers to encourage rapid settlement and discourage speculation and suggested prohibiting slavery in the region. Land taxes would provide funds to the federal government. Congress revised his plan significantly before adopting the Northwest Ordinance in 1785. Clements Library, University of Michigan such treatment and failed to resolve tribal land claims. It also abolished slavery throughout the Northwest Territory but mandated the return of any enslaved workers fleeing their owners in other states to forestall a flood of fugitives.

The 1787 legislation did not address territory south of the Ohio River. As American settlers streamed into areas that became Kentucky and Tennessee, they confronted Creek, Choctaw, and Chickasaw tribes, well supplied with weapons by Spanish traders, as well as Cherokee who had sided with the British during the Revolution. The resulting conflicts in the region were largely ignored by the national government for the next quarter century.

Depression and Debt. Disputes over western lands were deeply intertwined with the economic difficulties that plagued the new nation. Victory in the Revolution was followed by years of economic depression and mushrooming debt. While the war fueled the demand for domestic goods and ensured high employment, both the demand and the jobs declined in peacetime. International trade was also slow to recover from a decade of disruption. Meanwhile the nation was saddled with a huge war debt. Individuals, the states, and the federal government all viewed western lands as a solution to their problems despite the fact that no government held secure title to these territories. Farm families could start over on "unclaimed" land; states could distribute land in lieu of cash to veterans or creditors; and congress could sell land to fund its debts. Even if authorities had gained clear titles, there was never enough land to meet these competing needs.

Some national leaders, including Hamilton, focused on other ways of repaying the war debt. Fearing that wealthy creditors would lose faith in a nation that could not repay its debts, they urged states to grant the federal government a percentage of import duties as a way to increase its revenue. But states had their own problems. Legislators in Massachusetts and other states passed hard-money laws that required debts to be repaid in gold or silver rather than in paper currency. Affluent creditors favored these measures to ensure repayment in full. But small farmers, including veterans, who had borrowed paper money during the war, now had to repay those loans in hard currency as the money supply shrank. Taxes, too, were rising as states sought to cover the interest on wartime bonds held by wealthy investors.

Failures of American diplomacy weakened the nation's economy further. In 1783 the British Parliament denied the United States the right to trade with the British West Indies. The following year, Spain, seeking leverage over disputed western territories, prohibited U.S. ships from accessing the port of New Orleans. Spain and Great Britain also threatened U.S. sovereignty by conspiring with American citizens on the frontier and promising them protection from Indians. At the same time, British troops remained in forts on America's western frontier and urged native allies to harass settlers there.

Review & Relate

▪ What challenges did the new nation face in the immediate aftermath of the Revolutionary War?

▪ How did farmers, financial leaders, foreign nations, and Indians react to government efforts to address challenges after the Revolution?

On the Political Margins

A young nation, the United States was forced to the political margins in international affairs. At the same time, some groups within the nation were marginalized as well. Small farmers suffered in the postwar period, but they were not alone. Church leaders who had enjoyed government support in the colonial period now had to compete for members and funds. African Americans, whose hopes for freedom had been raised by the Revolution, continued to fight for an end to enslavement and full-fledged citizenship. Many women also faced challenges as they sought to enhance their role in the nation.

Separating Church and State. Government support of churches ended in most states with the establishment of the United States. Anglican churches had long benefited from British support and taxed residents to support their ministry during the Revolution. But in 1786, the Virginia Assembly approved the Statute of Religious Freedom, which made church attendance and support voluntary. Many other states followed Virginia's lead and removed government support for established churches.

Churches that had dominated the various colonies now faced greater competition. Especially in frontier areas, Baptists and Methodists, the latter of which broke off from the Anglican Church in 1784, gained thousands of converts. The Society of Friends, or Quakers, and the Presbyterians also gained new adherents, while Catholics and Jews experienced greater tolerance than in the colonial era. This diversity ensured that no single religious voice or perspective dominated the new nation. Instead, denominations competed for members, money, and political influence.

Some Protestant churches were also challenged from within by free blacks who sought a greater role in church governance. In 1794 Richard Allen, who had been born enslaved, led a small group of Philadelphia blacks in founding the first African American church in the United States. Initially, this African Methodist Episcopal Church remained within the larger Methodist fold. By the early 1800s, however, Allen's church served as the basis for the first independent black denomination.

African Americans Struggle for Rights. It was no accident that the first independent black church was founded in Philadelphia, which attracted large numbers of free blacks after Pennsylvania adopted a gradual emancipation law in 1780. Although the northern states with the largest enslaved populations — New York and New Jersey — did not pass such laws until 1799 and 1804, respectively, the free black population increased throughout the region.

Many free blacks were migrants from the South, where tens of thousands of enslaved women and men gained their freedom during or immediately following the Revolution. Only a few slave owners took Revolutionary ideals to heart and emancipated their slaves following the war. Others emancipated slaves in their wills, but family members did not always carry out those wishes. In addition, a few states prohibited the importation of slaves from Africa immediately following the Revolution. Still, the enslaved population continued to grow rapidly, and southern legislators made it increasingly difficult for owners to free their slaves and for free blacks to remain in the region.

The limits on emancipation in the South nurtured the growth of free black communities in the North, especially in seaport cities like Philadelphia, New York, and New Bedford. Most African Americans focused on finding jobs, supporting families, and securing the

Richard Allen   Born enslaved in Delaware in 1760, Richard Allen purchased his freedom from his master and moved to Philadelphia. This pastel and chalk drawing by an unknown artist shows Allen, a gifted preacher and community leader, in 1784. A decade later, when the white-led Methodist Church began segregating its congregation, Allen founded the African Methodist Episcopal Church, the first independent black church in the United States. The Granger Collection, New York

freedom of enslaved relatives. Others, like Richard Allen, sought to establish churches, schools, and voluntary societies and to claim a political voice. Black women and men also established fraternal, literary, and educational societies, calling for the abolition of slavery and civil and political rights for free blacks.

Some northern states, such as New Jersey, granted property-owning blacks the right to vote. Others, such as Pennsylvania, did not specifically exclude them. Yet this was largely because the number of African Americans enfranchised remained small. Small numbers of white women and men aided blacks in their struggles. The Society of Friends, the only religious denomination to oppose slavery in the colonial period, became more outspoken in the 1780s and 1790s. Many Friends, also known as Quakers, withdrew from the slave trade and freed their enslaved workers. Quaker Anthony Benezet, a writer and educator, advocated tirelessly for the abolition of slavery and directed a school for blacks founded by the Society of Friends. Patriot leader and Quaker John Dickinson conditionally manumitted (that is, freed) several dozen enslaved workers on his Delaware farm in 1777. Still, because of a state law that required a bond be paid for each individual freed, Dickinson did not free the last of his enslaved laborers until 1786. A year earlier, a group of wealthy white men organized the New York Manumission Society, which promoted the gradual abolition of slavery in the state. However half of the thirty members held slaves or were involved in the slave trade, including Alexander Hamilton who bought and sold enslaved blacks for his father-in-law. Although these men were more outspoken on the issue of slavery than most whites, their gradualist approach failed to slow the growth of slavery in the wider nation.

Women Seek Wider Roles.
Quaker women as well as men testified against slavery in the 1780s, writing statements on the topic in the Society's separate women's meetings. Although few other women experienced such spiritual autonomy, many gained a greater sense of economic and political independence during the Revolution.

Abigail Adams had written her husband John in 1776, "[I]f perticuliar care and attention is not paid to the Laidies we are determined to foment a Rebellion" (see Source 6.7 in chapter 6). While she and other elite women sought a more public voice, only New Jersey granted women — property-owning single women or widows — the right to vote. The vast majority of women could only shape political decisions by influencing their male relatives and friends. Fortunately, many leaders of the early Republic viewed wives and mothers as necessary to the development of a strong nation. In 1787 Dr. Benjamin Rush, in his *Essay on Female Education*, developed a concept that historians later labeled **republican motherhood**. He claimed that women could best shape political ideas and relations by "instructing their sons in principles of liberty and

Explore ▶

Compare the claims for rights made by a northern woman and southern free blacks in Sources 7.2 and 7.3.

government." To prepare young women for this role, Rush suggested educating them in literature, music, composition, geography, history, and bookkeeping.

Judith Sargent Murray offered a more radical approach, arguing that "girls should be enabled to procure for themselves the necessaries of life; independence should be placed within their grasp" (see Source 7.2). A few American women in the late eighteenth century did receive broad educations. Some ran successful businesses; wrote plays, poems, and histories; and established urban salons where women and men discussed the issues of the day. In 1789 Massachusetts became the first state to institute free elementary education for all children, and female academies also multiplied in this period. While schooling for affluent girls was often focused on preparing them for domesticity, the daughters of artisans and farmers learned practical skills, including writing and basic math, to assist in the family enterprise.

While women's influence was praised in the post-Revolutionary era, states rarely expanded women's rights. All states limited women's economic autonomy, although a few allowed married women to enter into business. Divorce was also legalized in many states but was still available only to the wealthy and well connected. Meanwhile women were excluded from juries, legal training, and, with rare exceptions, voting rights.

African American and Indian women lived under much more severe constraints. Most black women were enslaved, and those who were free could usually find jobs only as domestic servants or agricultural workers. Among indigenous nations, years of warfare enhanced men's role as warriors and diplomats while limiting women's political influence. U.S. government officials and Protestant missionaries encouraged native peoples to embrace gender roles that mirrored those of Anglo-American culture, further diminishing women's authority. Moreover, women forced to move west with their tribes lost traditional authority tied to their control of land.

Indebted Farmers Fuel Political Crises.
Unlike blacks, Indians, and women, white farmers and workingmen actively sought to expand their political role in the new nation. Under constitutions written during the Revolution, most state governments broadened the electorate, allowing men with less property (or in rare cases no property) to vote and hold office. They also increased representation from western areas of the state.

Still, the economic interests of small farmers and workers diverged sharply from those of wealthy merchants and large landowners. As conflicts between debtors and creditors escalated between 1783 and 1787, state governments came down firmly on the side of the wealthy. But indebted farmers did not give up. They voted, petitioned, and protested to gain more favorable policies. When that failed, debt-ridden farmers in New Hampshire marched on the state capital in September 1786, demanding reform. Cavalry units confronted them and quickly seized and imprisoned the leaders.

Assaults on national authority worried many political leaders far more than farmers' uprisings. The continued efforts of Great Britain and Spain to undercut U.S. sovereignty and ongoing struggles with Indian nations posed especially serious threats. When James Madison and Alexander Hamilton attended the 1785 convention in Annapolis to address problems related to interstate commerce, they discovered that their concerns about the weakness of the confederation were shared by many large landowners, planters, and merchants. Despite these concerns, state legislatures were reluctant to give up the powers conferred on them under the Articles of Confederation.

Comparative Primary Source Analysis

Women and Free Blacks Claim Rights in the Nation

Limited in their civil and political rights and educational and economic opportunities, some women and African Americans demanded change. Many white women focused on gaining greater access to education. In the first selection, Judith Sargent Murray, a well-educated Massachusetts writer, insists that women are rational creatures who can make important contributions to society. Blacks had far fewer opportunities since the vast majority were enslaved, and even free blacks faced numerous restrictions. In the second selection, three free black men in Charleston, South Carolina petition the state legislature for increased judicial rights.

Source 7.2

Judith Sargent Murray │ On the Equality of the Sexes, 1790

Are we [women] deficient in reason? . . . [I]f an opportunity of acquiring knowledge hath been denied us, the inferiority of our sex cannot fairly be deduced from thence. . . . May we not trace its source in the difference of education, and continued advantages? Will it be said that the judgment of a male of two years old, is more sage than that of a female's of the same age? . . . But from that period what partiality! . . . As their years increase, the sister must be wholly domesticated, while the brother is led by the hand through all the flowery paths of science. . . . Now, was she permitted the same instructors as her brother, . . . for the employment of a rational mind an ample field would be opened. In astronomy she might catch a glimpse of the immensity of the Deity, and thence she would form amazing conceptions of the august and supreme Intelligence. In geography she would admire Jehovah in the midst of his benevolence; thus adapting this globe to the various wants and amusements of its inhabitants. In natural philosophy she would adore the infinite majesty of heaven, clothed in condescension; and as she traversed the reptile world, she would hail the goodness of a creating God. . . . Will it be urged that those acquirements would supersede our domestick duties. I answer that every requisite in female economy is easily attained; and, with truth I can add, that when once attained, they require no further mental attention. Nay, while we are pursuing the needle, or the superintendency of the family, I repeat, that our minds are at full liberty for reflection; that imagination may exert itself in full vigor; and that if a just foundation is early laid, our ideas will then be worthy of rational beings. . . . [I]s it reasonable, that a candidate for immortality . . . be allowed no other ideas, than those which are suggested by the mechanism of a pudding, or the sewing the seams of a garment?

Source: *Massachusetts Magazine*, March 1790, 132–35.

Still, it was **Shays's Rebellion**, an armed uprising of indebted farmers in western Massachusetts in 1786–1787, that crystallized patriot fears about the limits of the confederation model. In January 1787, a thousand farmer-soldiers led by Daniel Shays headed to the federal arsenal at Springfield, Massachusetts to seize guns and ammunition. While the farmers fought hard, they were routed by state militia and pursued by governor

Petition from Free Blacks of Charleston, 1791

That in the enumeration of free citizens by the Constitution of the United States for the purpose of representation of the Southern states in Congress your memorialists [petitioners] have been considered under that description as part of the citizens of this state.

Although by the fourteenth and twenty-ninth clauses in an Act of Assembly made in the year 1740 . . . commonly called the Negro Act, now in force, your memorialists are deprived of the rights and privileges of citizens by not having it in their power to give testimony on oath in prosecutions on behalf of the state; from which cause many culprits have escaped the punishment due to their atrocious crimes, nor can they give their testimony in recovering debts due to them, or in establishing agreements made by them within the meaning of the Statutes of Frauds and Perjuries in force in this state except in cases where persons of color

are concerned, whereby they are subject to great losses and repeated injuries without any means of redress.

That by the said clauses in the said Act, they are debarred of the rights of free citizens by being subject to a trial without the benefit of a jury and subject to prosecution by testimony of slaves without oath by which they are placed on the same footing.

Your memorialists show that they have at all times since the independence of the United States contributed and do now contribute to the support of the government by cheerfully paying their taxes proportionable to their property with others who have been during such period, and now are, in full enjoyment of the rights and immunities of citizens, inhabitants of a free independent state.

Source: Petition of Thomas Cole, Peter Bassnett Matthewes, and Matthew Webb to the South Carolina Senate, January 1, 1791, Records of the General Assembly, no. 181.

Interpret the Evidence

1. What kind of rights do Judith Sargent Murray and the free blacks in Charleston claim for women and free African Americans, respectively?
2. What explains the differences in the rights demanded by Murray and the black petitioners and the ways they justify those claims?

Put It in Context

What do these documents reveal about the positions of white women and free black men during the formation of the United States?

James Bowdoin's army. Many rebel leaders were captured; others, including Shays, escaped to Vermont and New York. Four were convicted and two were hanged before Bowdoin granted amnesty to the others in hopes of avoiding further conflict.

Still the message was clear to many political leaders. On December 26, 1786, Washington had written Henry Knox to express his concerns about the rebellion and upheavals

Daniel Shays   This sketch is the only eighteenth-century illustration in existence of Daniel Shays (on the left in this detail). He stands with Jacob Shattuck, another antigovernment leader. The picture appeared in a pro-Constitution Boston almanac, which ridiculed the two rebels by showing them in fancy uniforms and holding swords, in contrast to what would have been their usual homespun appearance. National Portrait Gallery, Smithsonian Institution

along the frontier: "If the powers [of the central government] are inadequate, amend or alter them; but do not let us sink into the lowest states of humiliation and contempt." Hamilton agreed, claiming that Shays's Rebellion "marked almost the last stage of national humiliation."

Review & Relate

- How did America's experience of the Revolutionary War change the lives of African Americans and women?

- What do uprisings by farmers and debtors tell us about social and economic divisions in the early Republic?

Reframing the American Government

The delegates who met in Philadelphia in May 1787 did not agree on the best way to reform the government. Some delegates, like James Monroe of Virginia, hoped to strengthen the existing government by amending the Articles of Confederation. Others joined with Madison and Hamilton, who argued for a new governmental structure. Once representatives agreed to draft a new constitution, they still disagreed over questions of representation, the powers of state and national governments, and the limits of popular democracy. Significant compromises had to be reached on these issues to frame a new Constitution.

Other issues arose once the Constitution was ratified and George Washington was inaugurated as president. The government needed to be organized and staffed. A system for levying, collecting, and distributing funds had to be put in place. Diplomatic relations with foreign powers and indigenous nations needed to be reestablished. A bill of rights, demanded by many state ratifying conventions, had to be drafted and approved. Finally, both proponents and opponents of the Constitution had to be convinced that this new government could respond to the varied needs of its citizens.

The Constitutional Convention of 1787.   The fifty-five delegates who attended the Philadelphia convention were composed of white, educated men of property. Two-thirds were lawyers, and half had been Continental Army officers. While only eight had signed the Declaration of Independence eleven years earlier, a majority had served in the confederation congress and seven as governors during the confederation period. The elite status of the delegates and the absence of many leading patriots raised concern among those who saw the convention as a threat to the rights of states and of citizens. Indeed, Patrick Henry refused to serve as a delegate, Rhode Island sent no representatives, and some delegates left the meeting in frustration or refused to sign the Constitution that the convention finally proposed. The leaders who hammered out the compromises and wrote and revised the Constitution were those who feared the fragility of the existing confederation. Not wanting to alarm the public, delegates agreed to meet in secret until they had hammered out a new framework of government.

On May 25, the convention opened, and delegates quickly turned to the key question: Revise the Articles of Confederation or draft an entirely new document? The majority of men came to Philadelphia with the intention of amending the Articles. However, a core group who sought a more powerful central government had met before the convention and drafted a plan to replace the Articles. This **Virginia Plan** proposed a strong centralized state, including a bicameral (two-house) legislature in which representation was to be based on population. Members of the two houses would select the national executive and the national judiciary, and would settle disputes between states. Although most delegates opposed the Virginia Plan, it launched discussions in which strengthening the central government was assumed to be the goal.

Discussions of the Virginia Plan raised another issue that nearly paralyzed the convention: the question of representation. Heated debates pitted large states against small states, even though political interests were not necessarily determined by size. Yet delegates held on to size as the critical issue in determining representation. In mid-June, William Patterson introduced the **New Jersey Plan**, which highlighted the needs of smaller states. In this plan, Congress would consist of only one house, with each state having equal representation.

With few signs of compromise, the convention finally appointed a special committee to hammer out the problem of representation. Their report broke the logjam. Members of the House of Representatives were to be elected by voters in each state; members of the Senate would be appointed by state legislatures. Representation in the House would be determined by population — counted every ten years in a national census — while in the Senate, each state, regardless of size, would have equal representation. While the Senate had more authority than the House in many areas, only the House could introduce funding bills.

Included within this compromise was one of the few direct considerations of slavery at the Philadelphia convention. With little apparent debate, the committee decided that representation in the House of Representatives was to be based on an enumeration of the entire free population and three-fifths of "all other persons," that is, enslaved persons. If delegates had moral scruples about this **three-fifths compromise**, most found them outweighed by the urgency of settling the troublesome question of representation.

Still, slavery was on the minds of delegates. In the same week that the Philadelphia convention tacitly accepted the institution of slavery, the confederation congress in New York City outlawed slavery in the Northwest Territory. News of that decision likely inspired representatives from Georgia and South Carolina to insist that the Constitution protect the slave trade, at least for the immediate future. Delegates in Philadelphia agreed that the importation of slaves would not be interfered with for twenty years. Another provision guaranteed the return of enslaved fugitives to their owners. At the same time, northern delegates insisted that the three-fifths formula be used in assessing taxation as well as representation, ensuring that the South paid for the increased size of its congressional delegation with increased taxes.

Two other issues provoked considerable debate in the following weeks. All delegates supported federalism, a system in which states and the central government shared power, but they disagreed over the balance of power between them. They also disagreed over the degree of popular participation in selecting national leaders. The new Constitution increased the powers of the central government significantly. For instance, Congress would now have the right to raise revenue by levying and collecting taxes and tariffs and coining money; raise armies; regulate interstate commerce; settle disputes between the states; establish uniform rules for the naturalization of immigrants; and make treaties with foreign nations and Indian tribes. But Congress could veto state laws only when those laws challenged "the supreme law of the land," and states retained all rights that were not specifically granted to the federal government.

One of the important powers retained by the states was the right to determine who was eligible to vote even as the Constitution regulated the influence eligible voters would have in national elections. Members of the House of Representatives were to be elected directly by popular vote for two-year terms. Senators — two from each state — were to be selected by state legislatures for a term of six years. Selection of the president was even further removed from voters. The president would be selected by an Electoral College, and state legislatures would decide how to choose its members. Finally, the federal judicial system was to be wholly removed from popular influence. Justices on the Supreme Court were to be appointed by the president and approved by the Senate. Once approved, they served for life to protect their judgments from the pressure of popular opinion. In addition, the Constitution created a separation of powers between these three branches — legislative, executive, and judicial — that limited the authority of each.

When the final debates concluded, only thirty-nine of the original delegates agreed to sign the document. They also agreed that approval by nine states, rather than all thirteen, would make the Constitution the law of the land. Some delegates sought formal reassurance that the powers granted the federal government would not be abused and urged inclusion of a bill of rights, like the Virginia Declaration of Rights. But weary men eager to finish their business voted down the proposal. On September 17, 1787, the Constitution was approved and sent to the states for ratification.

Americans Battle over Ratification.

The confederation congress sent the document to state legislatures and asked them to call conventions to consider ratification. These conventions could not modify the document, but only accept or reject it. Thousands of copies of the Constitution also circulated in newspapers and as broadsides. Pamphleteers, civic leaders, and ministers proclaimed their opinions publicly while ordinary citizens in homes, shops, and taverns debated the wisdom of establishing a stronger central government.

Fairly quickly, two sides emerged. The **Federalists**, who supported ratification, came mainly from urban and commercial backgrounds and lived in towns and cities along the Atlantic coast. They considered a stronger central government essential to the economic and political stability of the nation. Their opponents were generally more rural, less wealthy, and more likely to live in interior or frontier regions. Labeled **Antifederalists**, they opposed increasing the powers of the central government.

The pro-Constitution position was presented in a series of editorials that appeared in New York newspapers in 1787 to 1788 and published collectively as *The Federalist Papers*. The authors James Madison, John Jay, and Alexander Hamilton articulated broad principles embraced by supporters of the Constitution. Alexander Hamilton wrote two essays on impeachment, a system devised in medieval England that allowed Parliament to remove a King's ministers, judges, or other officials for "high Crimes and Misdemeanors." The most important essay, however, was *Federalist* No. 10 in which Madison countered the common wisdom that small units of government were most effective in representing the interests of their citizens and avoiding factionalism. He argued that in large units, groups with competing interests had to collaborate and compromise, providing the surest check on the "tyranny of the majority." **See Primary Source Project 7: Debating the Constitution in New York State, page 242.**

Still, Antifederalists worried that a large and powerful central government could lead to tyranny. Small farmers claimed that a strong congress filled with merchants, lawyers, and planters was likely to place the interests of creditors above those of ordinary (and indebted) Americans. Even some wealthy patriots, like Mercy Otis Warren of Boston, feared that the Constitution would empower a few individuals who cared little for the "true interests of the people." And the absence of a bill of rights concerned many Americans.

Federalists worked in each state to soften their critics by persuasive arguments, flattering hospitality, and the promise of a bill of rights once the Constitution was ratified. The quick ratification of the Constitution by Delaware, Pennsylvania, New Jersey, Georgia, and Connecticut by January 1788 strengthened the Federalist position. Federalists also gained the support of influential newspapers based in eastern cities and tied to commercial interests.

Still, the contest in many states was heated. In Massachusetts, Antifederalists, including leaders of Shays's Rebellion, gained the majority among convention delegates. Federalists worked hard to overcome the objections of their opponents, even drafting a preliminary bill of rights. On February 6, Massachusetts delegates voted 187 to 168 in favor of ratification. Maryland and South Carolina followed in April and May. A month later, New Hampshire Federalists won a close vote, making it the ninth state to ratify the Constitution.

However, two of the most populous and powerful states — New York and Virginia — had not yet ratified. Passionate debates erupted in both ratifying conventions, and Federalists decided it was prudent to wait until these states acted before declaring victory. After promising that a bill of rights would be added quickly, Virginia Federalists finally won the day by a few votes. A month later, New York, too, approved the Constitution by a narrow margin. The divided nature of the votes, and the fact that two states (North Carolina and Rhode Island) had still not ratified, meant that the new government would have to prove itself quickly (Table 7.1).

Organizing the Federal Government.

Most political leaders hoped that the partisanship of the ratification battle would fade away with the Constitution approved. The Electoral College's unanimous decision to name George Washington the first president and John Adams as vice president helped calm the political turmoil. The two took office in April 1789, launching the new government.

TABLE 7.1 Votes of State-Ratifying Conventions

State	Date	For	Against
Delaware	December 1787	30	0
Pennsylvania	December 1787	46	23
New Jersey	December 1787	38	0
Georgia	January 1788	26	0
Connecticut	January 1788	128	40
Massachusetts	February 1788	187	168
Maryland	April 1788	63	11
South Carolina	May 1788	149	73
New Hampshire	June 1788	57	47
Virginia	June 1788	89	79
New York	July 1788	30	27
North Carolina	November 1788	194	77
Rhode Island	May 1790	34	32

To bring order to his administration, Washington appointed well-known leaders to head three departments — State, War, and Treasury. Thomas Jefferson was named secretary of state; Henry Knox, secretary of war; and Alexander Hamilton, secretary of the treasury. He also appointed Samuel Osgood, a New York merchant and politician whose home became Washington's residence in the city, as Postmaster General. The president then selected Edmund Randolph to serve as his attorney general, the first step toward establishing a Department of Justice.

Congress, meanwhile, worked to establish a judicial system. The Constitution called for a Supreme Court but provided no specific guidelines. The Judiciary Act of 1789 established a Supreme Court composed of six justices along with thirteen district courts and three circuit courts to hear cases appealed from the states. Congress also quickly produced a bill of rights. Representative James Madison gathered more than two hundred resolutions passed by state ratifying conventions and honed them down to twelve amendments, which Congress approved and submitted to the states for ratification. In 1791 ten of the amendments were ratified, and these became the **Bill of Rights**. It guaranteed the rights of individuals and states in the face of a powerful central government, including freedom of speech, the press, and religion as well as the right to bear arms, petition the government, and be tried by a jury.

Hamilton Forges an Economic Agenda.
The new government's leaders recognized that without a stable economy, the best political structure could falter. Thus Hamilton's appointment as secretary of the treasury was especially significant. In formulating his economic policy, Hamilton's main goal was to establish the nation's credit. Paying down the debt and establishing a national bank would strengthen the United States in the eyes of the world and tie wealthy Americans more firmly to the federal government.

Hamilton advocated funding the national debt at face value and assuming the remaining state debts as part of the national debt. To pay for this policy, he planned to raise revenue through government bonds and new taxes. Hamilton also called for the establishment of a central bank to carry out the financial operations of the United States. In three major reports to Congress — on public credit and a national bank in 1790 and on manufactures in 1791 — he laid out a system of state-assisted economic development.

Hamilton's proposal to repay at face value the millions of dollars in securities issued by the confederation was particularly controversial. Thousands of soldiers, farmers, and shopkeepers had been paid with these securities during the war; but needing money in its aftermath, most sold them to speculators for a fraction of their value. These speculators would make enormous profits if the securities were paid off at face value. One of the policy's most ardent critics, Patrick Henry, claimed that Hamilton's policy was intended "to erect, and concentrate, and perpetuate a large monied interest" that would prove "fatal to the existence of American liberty." Despite such passionate opponents, Hamilton gained the support of Washington and other key Federalists.

The federal government's assumption of the remaining state war debts also faced fierce opposition, especially from southern states like Virginia that had already paid off their debt. Hamilton again won his case, though this time only by agreeing to "redeem" (that is, reimburse) states that had repaid their debts. In addition, Hamilton and his supporters had to agree to move the nation's capital from Philadelphia to a more central location along the Potomac River.

Funding the national debt, assuming the remaining state debts, and redeeming state debts already paid would cost $75.6 million (about $1.5 billion today). But Hamilton believed maintaining some debt was useful. He thus proposed establishing a Bank of the

United States, funded by $10 million in stock to be sold to private stockholders and the national government. The bank would serve as a repository for federal revenues and grant loans and sell bills of credit to merchants and investors, thereby creating a permanent national debt. This, he argued, would bind investors to the United States, turning the national debt into a "national blessing."

Not everyone agreed. Jefferson and Madison argued vehemently against the Bank of the United States, noting that there was no constitutional sanction for a federal bank. Hamilton fought back, arguing that Congress had the right to make "all Laws which shall be necessary and proper" for carrying out the provisions of the Constitution. Once again, he prevailed. Congress chartered the bank for a period of twenty years, and Washington signed the legislation into law.

The final piece of Hamilton's plan focused on raising revenue. Congress quickly agreed to pass tariffs on a range of imported goods, which generated some $4 million to $5 million annually. Some congressmen viewed these tariffs as a way to protect new industries in the United States, from furniture to shoes. An excise tax, paid by the producer or seller rather than the consumer, was placed on a variety of goods, notably whiskey. It generated another $1 million each year.

Hamilton's financial policies proved enormously successful in stabilizing the American economy, repaying outstanding debts, and tying men of wealth to the new government. The federal bank effectively collected and distributed the nation's resources. Commerce flourished, revenues rose, and confidence revived among foreign and domestic investors. And while the United States remained an agricultural nation, Hamilton's 1791 "Report on the Subject of Manufactures" foreshadowed the growing significance of industry, which gradually lessened U.S. dependence on European nations.

Review & Relate

▪ What issues attracted the most intense debate during the drafting and ratification of the Constitution? Why?

▪ How did Hamilton's policies stabilize the national economy, and why did they nonetheless arouse opposition?

Years of Crisis, 1792–1796

By 1792 Hamilton had succeeded in implementing his plan for U.S. economic development. Yet as Washington began his second term in the spring of 1793, signs of strain appeared throughout the nation. The French Revolution posed challenges to foreign trade and diplomacy. Migration to the frontier increased, which intensified conflicts between Indians and white settlers and increased hostilities between the United States and Great Britain. Yellow fever swept through Philadelphia and other cities, causing fear and disrupting political and economic life. Finally, the excise tax on whiskey fueled armed protests among frontier farmers. This cluster of crises split the Federalists into warring factions during Washington's second term.

Foreign Trade and Foreign Wars.
Jefferson and Madison led the opposition to Hamilton's policies. Their supporters were mainly southern Federalists who envisioned the country's future rooted in agriculture, not the commerce and industry supported by Hamilton and his allies. Jefferson agreed with the Scottish economist Adam Smith that an

international division of labor could best provide for the world's people. Americans could supply Europe with food and raw materials in exchange for manufactured goods. When wars in Europe, including a revolution in France, disrupted European agriculture in the 1790s, Jefferson's views were reinforced.

Although trade with Europe remained the most important source of goods and wealth for the United States, some merchants expanded into other parts of the globe. In the mid-1780s, the first American ships reached China, where they traded ginseng root and sea otter pelts for silk, tea, and chinaware. Still, events in Europe had a far greater impact on the United States at the time than those in the Pacific world.

The French Revolution (1789–1799) was especially significant for U.S. politics. The ideals of freedom of speech, assembly, and religion declared in America's Declaration of Independence resonated with French men and women who opposed the tyrannical rule of their King, Louis XVI. The resulting uprising disrupted French agriculture, increasing demand for American wheat, while the efforts of French revolutionaries to institute an egalitarian republic gained support from many Americans. The followers of Jefferson and Madison formed Republican societies, and members adopted the French term *citizen* when addressing each other. At the same time, the importance of workers and farmers among France's revolutionary forces reinforced critiques of the "monied power" that drove Federalist policies.

Americans Trade with China   This painting by a Chinese artist c. 1800 shows the Hongs at Canton, where ships from foreign countries arrived to unload and load goods. The foreign ships were limited to this small area outside Canton's city walls. There each nation established a trading post identified by its national flag and overseen by a Chinese merchant. © Sotheby's/ akg-images

In late 1792, as French revolutionary leaders began executing thousands of their opponents in the Reign of Terror, wealthy Federalists grew more anxious. The beheading of King Louis XVI horrified them, as did the revolution's condemnation of Christianity. Some members of Republican societies also criticized the brutal turn of the revolution. When France declared war against Prussia, Austria, and finally Great Britain, U.S. merchants worried about the impact on trade. In response, President Washington proclaimed U.S. neutrality in April 1793, prohibiting Americans from providing support or war materials to any belligerent nations—including France or Great Britain.

While the Neutrality Proclamation limited the shipment of certain items to Europe, Americans simultaneously increased trade with colonies in the British and French West Indies. Indeed, U.S. ships captured much of the lucrative sugar trade. At the same time, farmers in the Chesapeake and Middle Atlantic regions filled the growing demand for wheat in Europe, causing their profits to climb.

Yet these benefits did not bring about a political reconciliation. Although Jefferson condemned the French Reign of Terror, he protested the Neutrality Proclamation by resigning his cabinet post. Tensions escalated when the French envoy to the United States, Edmond Genêt, sought to enlist Americans in the European war. Republican clubs poured out to hear him speak and donated generously to the French cause. The British also ignored U.S. neutrality. The Royal Navy stopped U.S. ships carrying French sugar and seized more than 250 vessels. At the same time, Britain supplied Indians in the Ohio River valley with guns and encouraged them to raid U.S. settlements.

President Washington sent John Jay to England to resolve concerns over trade with the British West Indies, compensation for seized American ships, the continued British occupation of frontier forts, and southerners' ongoing demands for reimbursement for slaves evacuated by the British during the Revolution. Jay returned from England in 1794 with a treaty, but it was widely criticized in Congress and the popular press. While securing limited U.S. trading rights in the West Indies, it failed to address British reimbursement for captured cargoes or enslaved workers and granted Britain eighteen months to leave frontier forts. It also demanded that U.S. planters repay British firms for debts accrued during the Revolution. While the **Jay Treaty** was eventually ratified, it remained a source of contention among Federalists.

Disease and Dissent.

Despite these foreign crises, it was the effect of Federalist policies on the American frontier that crystallized opposing factions. The ability of the government to respond to these crises was slowed by outbreak of yellow fever in Philadelphia, the nation's capital. In August 1793, yellow fever erupted in Philadelphia, ultimately killing some 5,000 of the city's 50,000 residents. Another 20,000 people fled the city, although nearby towns began refusing entry to these refugees, and cities such as Baltimore and New York established quarantines against Philadelphia residents and goods. The Federal Congress's summer adjournment was extended through November, and officials decided it was not even safe for President Washington to meet with his cabinet officers. Philadelphia's local leaders organized a separate "fever hospital" for those taken ill since the existing hospital did not take infectious cases. Richard Allen and Absalom Jones offered assistance from the Free African Society, assuming—as white doctors did—that blacks had immunity from this fever, much like many did from malaria. However, African Americans died at the same rate as whites, many infected while volunteering as nurses or to bury corpses. Doctors did not yet know that mosquitos carried the fever. So Dr. Benjamin Rush and his colleagues depended on isolating patients and disinfecting houses, streets, wharves, and shops to slow the spread. Residents were urged to wear masks soaked in vinegar and camphor when they were out in public. The custom of shaking hands was avoided. Among federal employees, only those at the post office and the Treasury Department continued to work through the epidemic.

Yellow fever declined in early November with colder weather, but returned to Philadelphia and appeared in New York City, Baltimore, and other port cities throughout the 1790s. When the president and Congress returned to Philadelphia, some must have feared that remnants of the disease were still lurking in the area. However, they had critical issues to address.

In the early 1790s, from Maine to Georgia, Republican societies founded to support the French Revolution demanded the removal of British and Spanish troops from frontier areas, while frontier farmers lashed out at enforcement of the so-called whiskey tax. Many farmers on the frontier grew corn and turned it into whiskey to make it easier to transport and more profitable to sell. The whiskey tax hurt these farmers, hundreds of whom petitioned the federal government for relief.

Western Pennsylvania farmers were particularly incensed and rallied in 1792 and 1793 to protest the tax and those who enforced it. Former North Carolina Regulator Hermon Husband was one of the most outspoken critics of the new excise tax. Adopting tactics from Stamp Act protests and Shays's Rebellion, farmers blocked roads, burned sheriffs in effigy, marched on courthouses, and assaulted tax collectors. The government's failure to respond only fueled the rebels' anger. By 1794 all-out rebellion had erupted.

Washington, Hamilton, and their supporters worried that the rebellion could spread and that it might encourage Indians to rise up as well. Since Spanish and British soldiers were eager to foment trouble along the frontier, the **Whiskey Rebellion** might spark their intervention. Federalists also suspected that pro-French immigrants from Scotland and Ireland helped fuel the growing insurgency.

"An Exciseman," c. 1791   This early political cartoon depicts an excise agent, carrying two casks of whiskey to "Squire Vultures," with whom he intends to divide his take. He is pursued by two farmers opposed to the whiskey tax, who yell, "let us tar and feather the rascal." The exciseman is eventually hung over a barrel of whiskey, which explodes when it is set on fire.
Fotosearch/Archive Photos/Getty Images

Unlike 1786, however, when the federal government had no power to intervene in Shays's Rebellion, Washington now federalized militias from four states, calling up nearly thirteen thousand soldiers to quash the uprising. The army that marched into western Pennsylvania in September 1794 vastly outnumbered the "whiskey rebels" and easily suppressed the uprising. Having gained victory, the federal government prosecuted only two of the leaders, who were convicted but later pardoned by Washington.

President Washington proved that the Constitution provided the necessary powers to put down internal threats. Yet in doing so, the administration horrified many Americans who viewed the force used against the farmers as excessive. Jefferson and Madison voiced this outrage from within the Federalist government. The Revolutionary generation had managed to compromise on many issues, from representation and slavery to the balance between federal and state authority. But now Hamilton's economic policies had led to a frontier uprising, and Washington had used a federal army to crush popular dissent. The Federalists were on the verge of open warfare among themselves.

Further Conflicts on the Frontier.

In one area, Federalists shared a common concern: the continued threats to U.S. sovereignty by native, British, and Spanish forces. In 1790 Congress had passed the Indian Trade and Intercourse Act to regulate race relations on the frontier and to ensure fair and equitable dealings. However, the act was widely ignored. Moreover, the government failed to stem the flood of settlers into the Ohio and Mississippi River valleys. That decision proved costly.

In 1790 Little Turtle, a war chief of the Miami nation, gathered a large force of Shawnee, Delaware, Ottawa, Chippewa, Sauk, Fox, and other Indians. This pan-Indian alliance successfully attacked federal troops in the Ohio valley that fall. A year later, the allied Indian warriors defeated a large force under General Arthur St. Clair (Map 7.2). The stunning defeat shocked Americans. In the meantime, Spanish authorities negotiated with Creeks and Cherokees to attack U.S. settlements on the southern frontier.

Washington decided to deal with problems in the Northwest Territory first, sending 2,000 men under the command of General Anthony Wayne into the Ohio frontier. In August 1794, Wayne's forces attacked 1,500 to 2,000 Indians gathered at a British fort. In the Battle of Fallen Timbers, the pan-Indian warriors, led by Little Turtle, suffered a bitter defeat. A year later, the warring tribes in the Northwest Territory signed the **Treaty of Greenville**, granting the United States vast tracts of land.

Amid this turmoil, in November 1794, John Jay signed his controversial treaty with Great Britain. With Britain agreeing to withdraw its forces from the U.S. frontier by 1796, the treaty may have helped persuade indigenous nations to accept U.S. peace terms at Greenville. Nonetheless, the Jay Treaty's requirement that Americans make "full and complete compensation" to British firms for Revolutionary War debts without the British compensating U.S. merchants or enslavers for their losses nearly led Congress to reject it. In June 1795, however, the Senate finally approved the treaty without a vote to spare. Before Jay's controversial treaty took effect, Spain agreed to negotiate an end to hostilities on the southern frontier of the United States. Envoy Thomas Pinckney negotiated that treaty, which recognized the thirty-first parallel as the boundary between U.S. and Spanish territory in the South and opened the Mississippi River and the port of New Orleans to U.S. shipping. Many Federalists, especially from the West and South, who opposed the Jay Treaty supported the **Pinckney Treaty**, which was ratified in 1796.

MAP 7.2 American Indians in the Ohio River Valley, c. 1785–1795

Until the mid-eighteenth century, despite conflicts, Indian tribes in the Ohio River valley forged trade and diplomatic relations with various colonial powers. But once the United States established the Northwest Territory in 1785, conflicts between Indians and U.S. settlers and soldiers escalated dramatically. As tribes created pan-Indian alliances, the United States constructed numerous forts in the region.

Review & Relate

■ How did events overseas shape domestic American politics and frontier policy in the 1790s?

■ What common concerns underlay the Whiskey Rebellion and Shays's Rebellion? How did the U.S. government deal differently with each?

The **First Party System**

In September 1796, when President Washington decided not to run again, he offered a Farewell Address in which he warned against the "spirit of party." "It agitates the community with ill-founded jealousies and false alarms," he claimed, and "kindles the animosity of one part against another." By then, however, Jefferson, Madison, and other opponents of Hamilton's economic policies, Washington's assault on the whiskey rebels, and Jay's Treaty had already formed a distinct party. They called themselves **Democratic-Republicans** and supported Jefferson for president. The Electoral College, hoping to bring the warring sides together, chose Federalist John Adams as president and Thomas Jefferson as vice president. The two disagreed fundamentally on a wide range of issues, and events soon heightened these divisions. Foreign crises once again fueled political antagonisms, and in this charged atmosphere, Federalists in Congress passed two acts in 1798 relating to aliens (immigrants) and to sedition (activities that promote civil disorder). Instead of resolving tensions, however, these laws exacerbated opposition to Federalist rule. By 1800, partisan differences had crystallized, and the Democratic-Republicans threatened to oust the Federalists from power.

The Adams Presidency. The election of 1796 was the first to be contested by candidates identified with opposing parties. Federalists supported John Adams for president and Thomas Pinckney for vice president. The Democratic-Republicans chose Thomas Jefferson and Aaron Burr of New York to represent their interests. When the Electoral College was established, political parties did not exist and, in fact, were seen as promoting conflict. Thus electors were asked to choose the best individuals to serve, regardless of their views. In 1796 they picked Adams for president and Jefferson for vice president, perhaps hoping to lessen partisan divisions by forcing men of different views to compromise. Instead, the effects of an administration divided against itself were nearly disastrous, and opposing interests became more thoroughly entrenched.

Adams and Jefferson had disagreed on almost every major policy issue during Washington's administration. Not surprisingly, the new president rarely took advice from his vice president. At the same time, Adams retained most of Washington's appointees, who often sought advice from Hamilton, undercutting Adams's authority. Worse still, the new president had poor political instincts and faced numerous challenges.

At first, foreign disputes enhanced the authority of the Adams administration. The Federalists remained pro-British, and French seizures of U.S. ships threatened to provoke war. In 1798 Adams tried to negotiate compensation for the losses suffered by merchants. When an American delegation arrived in Paris, however, three French agents demanded a bribe to initiate talks.

Adams made public secret correspondence from the French agents, whose names were listed only as X, Y, and Z. Americans, including Democratic-Republicans, expressed outrage at this French insult to U.S. integrity, which became known as the **XYZ affair**. Congress quickly approved an embargo act that prohibited trade with France and permitted privateering against French ships. For the next two years, the United States fought an undeclared war with France.

Despite praise for his handling of the XYZ affair, Adams feared dissent from opponents at home and abroad. Consequently, the Federalist majority in Congress passed a series of security acts in 1798. The Alien Act allowed the president to order the imprisonment or deportation of noncitizens and was directed primarily at Irish and Scottish dissenters who criticized the government's pro-British policies. Congress also approved the Naturalization

Matthew Lyon and Roger Griswold
This political cartoon depicts a fight on the floor of the House of Representatives in February 1798 between Representatives Matthew Lyon of Vermont, a Democratic-Republican brandishing tongs, and Roger Griswold of Connecticut, a Federalist waving a cane. A newspaper editor and a critic of the Alien and Sedition Acts, Lyon was later convicted of sedition but won reelection while in jail.
Library of Congress, Prints and Photographs Division [LC-DIG-ppmsca-31832]

Act, which raised the residency require-ment for citizenship from five to fourteen years. Finally, Federalists pushed through the Sedition Act, which outlawed "false, scandalous, or malicious statements against President or Congress." In the following months, nearly two dozen Democratic-Republican editors and legislators were arrested for sedition, and some were fined and imprisoned.

Democratic-Republicans were infuriated by the **Alien and Sedition Acts**. They considered the attack on immigrants an attempt to limit the votes of farmers, artisans, and frontiersmen, who formed the core of their supporters. The Sedition Act threatened Democratic-Republican critics of Federalist policies and the First Amendment's guarantee of free speech. Jeffer-son and Madison encouraged states to pass resolutions that would counter this violation of the Bill of Rights. Using language drafted by the two Democratic-Republican leaders, legislators passed the **Virginia and Kentucky Resolutions**, which declared the Alien and Sedition Acts "void and of no force." They protested against the "alarming infractions of the Constitution," particularly the freedom of speech that "has been justly deemed, the only effectual guardian of every other right." Virginia even claimed that states had a right to nullify any powers exercised by the federal government that were not explicitly granted to it.

Although the Alien and Sedition Acts curbed dissent in the short run, they reinforced popular concerns about the power wielded by the Federalists. Combined with the ongoing war with France, continuing disputes over taxes, and relentless partisan denunciations in the press, these acts set the stage for the presidential election of 1800.

The Election of 1800. By 1800 Adams had negotiated a peaceful settlement of U.S. conflicts with France, considering it one of the greatest achievements of his administration. However, other Federalists, including Hamilton, disagreed and continued to seek open warfare and an all-out victory. Thus the Federalists faced the election of 1800 deeply divided. Democratic-Republicans meanwhile united behind Jefferson and portrayed the Federalists as the "new British" tyrants.

For the first time, congressional caucuses selected candidates for each party. The Federalists agreed on Adams and Charles Cotesworth Pinckney of South Carolina. The Democratic-Republicans again chose Jefferson and Burr as their candidates. The campaign was marked by bitter accusations and denunciations.

Explore ▶

For two historians' views on partisan attacks in the Presidential election of 1800, see Sources 7.4 and 7.5.

Partisan Campaigning in the Election of 1800

While the election of 1796 was the first to involve candidates chosen by opposing parties, it was decidedly civil compared to that of 1800. Partisan differences intensified as divisions over domestic and foreign policies led each side to view the other as a threat to fundamental American values. Historians agree that the election of 1800 — between Federalist John Adams and Democratic-Republican Thomas Jefferson — marks a critical moment in U.S. history because it necessitated the peaceful transfer of power from one political party to another. Yet it was also marked by vitriol spewed by partisan newspapers. Eric Burns suggests that Federalists attacked Jefferson because they could not imagine a peaceful transfer of power to their opponents, while John Ferling focuses on the growing strength and reach of Democratic-Republican newspapers.

Source 7.4

Eric Burns | Federalists Attack Thomas Jefferson, 2006

[W]ould Federalists willingly and peacefully hand power over to their political enemies . . . , men whom they not only loathed but also considered dangerous to the republic, to private property, to economic growth and a strong central government, to everything they cherished and respected?

The answer, at least as far as federalist newspapers were concerned, was no. And to try to make sure that they would not have to report on the transfer of power to those whom they despised, they began devoting their pages to the most dire of predictions. "Should the infidel Jefferson be elected to the Presidency," wrote the *Hudson Bee* . . . , "the *seal of death* is that moment set on our holy religion, our churches will be prostrated, and some infamous prostitute, under

the title the Goddess of Reason, will preside in the Sanctuaries now devoted to the Most High." . . .

The [Democratic-]Republican counterattack was surprisingly feeble. Some papers praised Jefferson, in colorless language for the most part, for his perceptiveness and eloquence and experience. Other papers attacked Adams, but without much fire; one said that the incumbent wanted to start an American aristocracy by marrying one of his sons to a daughter of [King] George III. . . . Apparently at least some of the anti-federalist newspapers were confident of a Jeffersonian victory.

Source: Eric Burns, *Infamous Scribblers: The Founding Fathers and the Rowdy Beginnings of American Journalism.* New York: Public Affairs, Perseus Book Group, 2006, pp. 369 and 371.

In the first highly contested presidential election, the different methods states used to record voters' preferences gained more attention. Only five states determined members of the Electoral College by popular vote. In the rest, state legislatures appointed electors. Created at a time when political parties were considered injurious to good government, the Electoral College was not prepared for the situation it faced in January 1801. Federalist and Democratic-Republican caucuses nominated one candidate for president and one for vice president on party tickets. As a result, Jefferson and Burr received exactly the same number of Electoral College votes, and the House of Representatives then had to break the tie. There Burr sought to gain the presidency with the help of Federalist representatives ardently opposed to Jefferson. But Alexander Hamilton stepped in and warned against Burr's leadership. This helped Jefferson emerge victorious, but it also inflamed animosity between Burr and Hamilton that eventually led to the 1804 duel in which Burr killed Hamilton.

John Ferling | Democratic-Republicans Attack John Adams, 2013

While most of the candidates avoided the hustings [public platforms], party activists were busy. For the most part, both sides spread their messages through pamphlets, broadsides, and newspapers. The Federalists had a decided edge in the press, but [Democratic-]Republican newspapers had climbed up from 15 percent of the total in 1796 to nearly one-third by 1800. The [Democratic-]Republicans were better organized for disseminating information, as they established committees of correspondence to funnel publications to the hinterland. . . .

Some [Democratic-]Republican penmen limned [depicted]Adams as a monarchist . . . , but their essayists focused mostly on the Federalist program. One writer after another attacked the Alien and Sedition Acts, the taxes levied to pay for the debt . . . , and the very existence of a standing army. Much of their ink was [also] spilled on Hamilton's economic program. . . .

The abuse . . . directed against Hamilton paled in comparison to the calumny heaped on Jefferson. . . . Federalists charged that Jefferson's residence in France had transformed him into a dangerous radical. . . . A Federalist newspaper in Virginia alleged that Jefferson had a slave mistress. . . . [And] Federalists twisted Jefferson's advocacy of religious freedom in *Notes on the State of Virginia* to brand him an atheist.

Source: John Ferling, *Jefferson and Hamilton: The Rivalry That Forged a Nation* (New York: Bloomsbury Press, 2014), 320–321.

Examine the Sources

1. How do Ferling and Burns differ in their assessments of Federalist and Democratic-Republican attacks on each other's presidential candidates?
2. How effective are Ferling and Burns in using primary sources to make their argument? Do you find one argument more compelling than the other, and if so, why?

Put It in Context

Given the fierce attacks on Jefferson, what explains his victory in the 1800 election?

President Jefferson labeled his election a revolution achieved not "by the sword" but by "the suffrage of the people." The election of 1800 was hardly a popular revolution, given the restrictions on suffrage and the methods of selecting the Electoral College. Still, between 1796 and 1800, partisan factions had been transformed into opposing parties, and the United States had managed a peaceful transition from one party to another.

Review & Relate

What were the main issues dividing the Federalists and the Democratic-Republicans?

What do the Alien and Sedition Acts and the election of 1800 tell us about political partisanship in late-eighteenth-century America?

Conclusion: A **Young Nation** Comes of **Age**

In the 1780s and 1790s, the United States faced numerous obstacles to securing its place as a nation. Financial hardship, massive debts, hostile Indians, and European diplomacy had to be addressed by a federal government that, under the Articles of Confederation, was relatively weak. By 1787 concerns about national security, fueled by rebellious farmers and frontier conflicts, persuaded some political leaders to advocate a new governmental structure. While it required numerous compromises among groups with competing ideas and interests, the Constitution was drafted and, after a fierce battle in several states, ratified.

With the federal government's power strengthened, George Washington took office as the first American president. His administration sought to enhance U.S. power at home and abroad. Secretary of the treasury Alexander Hamilton proposed a series of measures to stabilize the American economy, pay off Revolutionary War debts, and promote trade and industry. However, these policies also aroused opposition, with leaders like Jefferson and Madison and ordinary farmers and frontiersmen questioning the benefits of Hamilton's economic priorities. Differences over the French Revolution also led to heated debates, while the imposition of an excise tax on whiskey fueled open rebellion on the Pennsylvania frontier. Although a majority of Federalists supported Hamilton and an alliance with Britain, they faced growing opposition from those who advocated agrarian ideals and supported the French Revolution.

Conflicts among Federalists drew many Americans into debates over government programs, but large groups remained marginalized or excluded from the political system. Indians, African Americans, and women had little voice in policies that directly affected them. Even white workingmen and farmers found it difficult to influence political priorities and turned to petitions, protests, and even armed uprisings to demonstrate their views.

By 1796, Jefferson and Madison, who led the opposition among Federalists, had formed a separate political party, the Democratic-Republicans. They considered passage of the Alien and Sedition Acts as a direct attack on their supporters, and in 1800 wrested control of Congress and the presidency from the Federalists. Still, this peaceful transition in power boded well for the young United States.

Despite political setbacks, the Federalist legacy remained powerful. Hamilton's policies continued to shape national economic growth, and Federalists retained political power in the Northeast for decades. Meanwhile the benefits that small farmers and frontiersmen like Daniel Shays hoped to gain under Democratic-Republican rule proved largely elusive. Marginalized Americans, including Indians and African Americans, also gained little from the transition to Democratic-Republican leadership. Indeed, the growth of slavery and U.S. westward expansion created greater burdens for these groups.

Yet the Democratic-Republican Party would not be seriously challenged for national power until 1824, giving it nearly a quarter century to implement its vision of the United States. Members of this heterogeneous party would now have to learn to compromise with each other if they were going to achieve their goal of limited federal power in an agrarian republic.

Timeline of Events

Year	Event
1783	Continental Army officers threaten to mutiny
1784	Treaty of Fort Stanwix
1785	Northwest Ordinance passed
	Annapolis Convention
1786–1787	Shays's Rebellion
1787	Constitutional Convention in Philadelphia
	Northwest Ordinance revised
1788	U.S. Constitution ratified
1789	Alexander Hamilton named secretary of the treasury
	Judiciary Act of 1789 passed
1789–1799	French Revolution
1790–1794	Little Turtle leads pan-Indian alliance in the Ohio valley
1791	Bill of Rights ratified
1793	Neutrality Proclamation
	Yellow fever epidemic paralyzes Philadelphia
1794	Whiskey Rebellion
	African Methodist Episcopal Church founded
1796	Jay Treaty and Pinckney Treaty ratified
	Democratic-Republican Party established
1798	Alien and Sedition Acts passed
1800	Election of Thomas Jefferson as president

Key Terms

Treaty of Fort Stanwix, *214*
Northwest Ordinance, *217*
republican motherhood, *220*
Shays's Rebellion, *222*
Virginia Plan, *225*
New Jersey Plan, *225*
three-fifths compromise, *225*
Federalists, *226*
Antifederalists, *227*
Bill of Rights, *228*
Jay Treaty, *232*
Whiskey Rebellion, *233*
Treaty of Greenville, *234*
Pinckney Treaty, *234*
Democratic-Republicans, *236*
XYZ affair, *236*
Alien and Sedition Acts, *237*
Virginia and Kentucky Resolutions, *237*

Review & Relate

1. What challenges did the new nation face in the immediate aftermath of the Revolutionary War?

2. How did farmers, financial leaders, foreign nations, and Indians react to government efforts to address challenges after the Revolution?

3. How did America's experience of the Revolutionary War change the lives of African Americans and women?

4. What do uprisings by farmers and debtors tell us about social and economic divisions in the early Republic?

5. What issues attracted the most intense debate during the drafting and ratification of the Constitution? Why?

6. How did Hamilton's policies stabilize the national economy, and why did they nonetheless arouse opposition?

7. How did events overseas shape domestic American politics and frontier policy in the 1790s?

8. What common concerns underlay the Whiskey Rebellion and Shays's Rebellion? How did the U.S. government deal differently with each?

9. What were the main issues dividing the Federalists and the Democratic-Republicans?

10. What do the Alien and Sedition Acts and the election of 1800 tell us about political partisanship in late-eighteenth-century America?

Debating the Constitution in New York State

▶ As Americans considered the proposed Constitution, which groups sought to increase and which groups sought to restrict federal power and why?

Although the Constitution was eventually approved by all thirteen states, the battle over its ratification revealed a deeply divided nation. Antifederalist delegates dominated conventions in Massachusetts, Virginia, and New York; and when Massachusetts and Virginia finally ratified the Constitution by close votes, the New York convention was still in session.

As elsewhere, New York delegates debated questions of representation, the increased powers of the federal government, and a bill of rights. Before the convention opened, James Madison, Alexander Hamilton, and John Jay offered fellow New Yorkers pro-Constitution arguments in *The Federalist Papers* (Source 7.6). At the convention, Hamilton emphasized the need for a strong central government in which checks and balances limited the power of any single branch and insisted on accommodating the views of diverse groups, including southern slaveowners (Source 7.8).

A secretary recorded the speeches of Hamilton and other delegates. Melancton Smith was a large landowner and a New York City merchant, but he led the state's Antifederalists and questioned the expansion of federal power and the limits on representation (Source 7.7). John Williams, a farmer from rural Washington County and thus a more typical Antifederalist, criticized the Constitution more adamantly. He distrusted federal power, disliked the system of representation, and worried about America's moral decline (Source 7.9). However, the Federalists eventually prevailed, with Hamilton, Smith, and twenty-eight other delegates voting yes and Williams one of the twenty-seven no votes. The slim victory elated the Federalist newspaper, the *Massachusetts Centinel*, which tracked each state that ratified the Constitution (Source 7.10).

The intensity of these debates highlights the competing ideas and interests among Americans. It also shows the willingness of Federalists to compromise on issues like a bill of rights while insisting on creating a new political structure.

Source 7.6

James Madison | *Federalist* 10, The Union as a Safeguard Against Domestic Faction and Insurrection, November 1787

James Madison wrote the most significant of the pro-Constitution essays known collectively as *The Federalist Papers*. In this essay, Madison challenged the widely held belief that republican governments were most likely to succeed when they were small and compact. He argued instead that a large and diverse population in which various factions competed for support would keep any one faction from subverting the freedom of other groups.

To the People of the State of New York:

AMONG the numerous advantages promised by a well-constructed Union, none deserves to be more accurately developed than its tendency to break and control the violence of faction. The friend of popular governments never finds himself so much alarmed for their character and fate, as when he contemplates their propensity to this dangerous vice. He will not fail, therefore, to set a due value on any plan which, without violating the principles to which he is attached, provides a proper cure for it. . . .

By a faction, I understand a number of citizens, whether amounting to a majority or a minority of the whole, who are united and actuated by some common impulse of passion, or of interest, adversed to the rights of other citizens, or to the permanent and aggregate interests of the community. . . .

The latent causes of faction are . . . sown in the nature of man; and we see them everywhere brought into different degrees of activity, according to the different circumstances of civil society. . . . But the most common and durable source of factions has been the various and unequal distribution of property. Those who hold and those who are without property have ever formed distinct interests in society. Those who are creditors, and those who are debtors, fall under a like discrimination. A landed interest, a manufacturing interest, a mercantile interest, a moneyed interest, with many lesser interests, grow up of necessity in civilized nations, and divide them into different classes, actuated by different sentiments and views. . . .

[I]t may be concluded that a pure democracy, by which I mean a society consisting of a small number of citizens, who assemble and administer the government in person, can admit of no cure for the mischiefs of faction. A common passion or interest will, in almost every case, be felt by a majority of the whole; a communication and concert result from the form of government itself; and there is nothing to check the inducements to sacrifice the weaker party or an obnoxious individual. . . .

A republic, by which I mean a government in which the scheme of representation takes place, opens a different prospect, and promises the cure for which we are seeking. . . .

[T]he greater number of citizens and extent of territory which may be brought within the compass of republican than of democratic government . . . is th[e] circumstance principally which renders factious combinations less to be dreaded in the former than in the latter. The smaller the society, the fewer probably will be the distinct parties and interests composing it; the fewer the distinct parties and interests, the more frequently will a majority be found of the same party; and the smaller the number of individuals composing a majority, and the smaller the compass within which they are placed, the more easily will they concert and execute their plans of oppression. Extend the sphere, and you take in a greater variety of parties and interests; you make it less probable that a majority of the whole will have a common motive to invade the rights of other citizens; or if such a common motive exists, it will be more difficult for all who feel it to discover their own strength, and to act in unison with each other. . . .

The influence of factious leaders may kindle a flame within their particular States, but will be unable to spread a general conflagration through the other States. A religious sect may degenerate into a political faction in a part of the Confederacy; but the variety of sects dispersed over the entire face of it must secure the national councils against any danger from that source.

Source: *New York Packet*, November 23, 1787, Library of Congress.

Source 7.7

Melancton Smith | Antifederalist Argument at the New York State Convention, June 1788

Melancton Smith was unusually wealthy for an Antifederalist delegate. Smith worked alongside Alexander Hamilton in the New York Manumission Society, which encouraged the gradual abolition of slavery. But while Hamilton accepted the three-fifths compromise as necessary, Smith found it odious. He also embraced the traditional view that republics were best governed by smaller governmental bodies.

In the discussion of this question, he [Smith] was disposed to make every reasonable concession, and, indeed, to sacrifice every thing for a union, except the liberties of his country. . . .

The defects of the Old Confederation needed as little proof as the necessity of an Union. But there was no proof in all this that the proposed Constitution was a good one. Defective as the Old Confederation is, . . . no one could deny but it was possible we might have a worse government. . . .

He would agree with the honorable gentlemen [Hamilton] that perfection in any system of government was not to be looked for. . . . But he would observe, that this observation applied with equal force against changing any systems, especially against material and radical changes. Fickleness and inconstancy, he said, were characteristic of a free people; and in framing a Constitution for them, it was, perhaps the most difficult thing to correct this spirit, and guard against the evil effects of it. . . .

He would now proceed to state his objections to the clause just read, (section 2, of article 1, clause 3). . . . In the first place, the rule of apportionment of the representatives is to be according to the whole number of the white inhabitants, with three fifths of all others, that is in plain English, each state is to send Representatives in proportion to the number of freemen, and three fifths of the slaves it contains. He could not see any rule by which slaves were to be included in the ratio of representation. The principle of a representation, being that every free agent should be concerned in governing himself, it was absurd to give that power to a man who could not exercise it. . . . The very operation of it was to give certain privileges to those people who were so wicked as to keep slaves. He knew it would be admitted that this rule of apportionment was founded on unjust principles, but that it was the result of accommodation; which, he supposed, we should be under the necessity of admitting, . . . though utterly repugnant to his feelings. . . .

[And] how was the will of the community to be expressed? . . . [W]e may approach a great way towards perfection by increasing the representation and limiting the powers of Congress. He considered that the great interests and liberties of the people could only be secured by the State Governments. He admitted, that if the new government was only confined to great national objects, it would be less exceptionable; but it extended to every thing dear to human nature. . . . [F]or that power which had both the purse and the sword had the government of the whole country, and might extend its powers to any and to every object.

Source: New York State Ratification Convention, Minutes, June 20, 1788.

Alexander Hamilton | Federalist Argument at the New York State Convention, June 1788

Alexander Hamilton directly countered Melancton Smith's claims about the three-fifths compromise and the benefits of relying on state governments. Noting that many states failed to provide their share of troops or funds when requisitioned by the confederation government, Hamilton feared that without a stronger central government, the United States would be weakened economically and militarily.

I will not agree with gentlemen who trifle with the weaknesses of our country; and suppose, that they are enumerated to answer a party purpose, and to terrify with ideal dangers. No; I believe these weaknesses to be real, and pregnant with destruction. Yet, however weak our country may be, I hope we never shall sacrifice our liberties. . . .

Sir, it appears to me extraordinary, that, while gentlemen in one breath acknowledge that the old confederation requires many material amendments, they should in the next deny, that its defects have been the cause of our political weakness, and the consequent calamities of our country. . . . [T]he states have almost uniformly weighed the requisitions by their own local interests; and have only executed them so far as answered their particular conveniency or advantage. Hence there have ever been thirteen different bodies to judge of the measures of Congress, and the operations of government have been distracted by their taking different courses. . . .

Shall we take the old Confederation, as the basis of a new system? . . . certainly not. Will any man who entertains a wish for the safety of his country, trust the sword and the purse with a single Assembly organized on principles so defective—so rotten? Though we might give to such a government certain powers with safety, yet to give them the full and unlimited powers of taxation and the national forces would be to establish a despotism; the definition of which is, a government in which all power is concentrated in a single body. . . . These considerations show clearly, that a government totally different must be instituted. . . . [T]he convention . . . therefore formed two branches, and divided the powers, that each might be a check upon the other. . . .

Sir, the natural situation of this country seems to divide its interests into different classes. . . . It became necessary, therefore, to compromise; or the Convention must have dissolved without effecting any thing. . . .

The first thing objected to is that clause which allows a representation for three fifths of the negroes. . . . It is the unfortunate situation of the Southern States to have a great part of their population, as well as property, in blacks. The regulation complained of was one result of the spirit of accommodation, which governed the Convention; and without this indulgence, no union could possibly have been formed. But, Sir, considering some peculiar advantages which we derive from them, it is entirely just that they should be gratified. The Southern States possess certain staples, tobacco, rice, indigo, &c. which must be capital objects in treaties of commerce with foreign nations; and the advantages which they necessarily procure in these treaties, will be felt throughout all the States. . . . [Moreover] representation and taxation go together, and one uniform rule ought to apply to both. Would it be just to compute these slaves in the assessment of taxes; and discard them from the estimate in the apportionment of representatives?

Source: New York State Ratification Convention, Minutes, June 20, 1788.

Source 7.9

John Williams | Antifederalist Argument at the New York State Convention, June 1788

One of four delegates from the northern counties of Washington and Clinton, John Williams represented the interests of rural farmers. An ardent Antifederalist, he preferred that political power be focused at local and state levels. But he also expressed deep concern about the loss of traditional values like thrift and hard work, making the nation vulnerable to mercantile and foreign interests.

I believe that this country has never before seen such a critical period in political affairs. We have felt the feebleness of those ties, by which the States are held together, and the want of that energy which is necessary to manage our general concerns. . . . Indeed, Sir, it appears to me, that many of our present distresses flow from a source very different from the defects in the Confederation. Unhappily for us, immediately after our extrication from a cruel and unnatural war, luxury and dissipation overran the country, banishing all that economy, frugality, and industry, which had been exhibited during the war. . . .

Let us, then, abandon all those foreign commodities which have hitherto deluged our country; which have loaded us with debt, and which, if continued, will forever involve us in difficulties. How many thousands are daily wearing the manufactures of Europe, when by a little industry and frugality, they might wear those of their own country! . . . What dissipation is there from the immoderate use of spirits! Is it not notorious that men cannot be hired, in time of harvest, without giving them, on an average, a pint of rum per day? . . . And, what is worse, the disposition of eight tenths of the commonalty is such, that, if they can get credit, they will purchase unnecessary articles, even to the amount of their crop, before it becomes merchantable. . . . [T]he best government ever devised, without economy and frugality will leave us in a situation no better than the present. . . .

[L]et us examine whether it [the Constitution] be calculated to preserve the invaluable blessings of liberty, and secure the inestimable rights of mankind. . . . [I]f it be found to contain principles that will lead to the subversion of liberty, . . . let us insist upon the necessary alterations and amendments. . . .

In forming a constitution for a free country like this, the greatest care should be taken to define its powers, and guard against an abuse of authority. The Constitution should be so formed as not to swallow up the State governments: the general government ought to be confined to certain national objects; and the States should retain such powers, as concern their own internal police. . . . The number of representatives is, in my opinion, too small to resist corruption. Sir, how guarded is our State Constitution on this head! The number of senate and house of representatives proposed in the Constitution does not surpass those of our State. How great the disparity, when compared with the aggregate number of the United States! . . . Can it be supposed that six men can be a complete representation of the various orders of people of this State?

Source: New York State Ratification Convention, Minutes, June 21, 1788.

Library of Congress, Serial and Government Publications Division [LC-US262-45591]

Source 7.10

The Eleventh Pillar of the Great National Dome, 1788

Throughout 1788, newspapers like the *Massachusetts Centinel* traced the results of ratifying conventions state by state. A graphic represented each state that ratified the Constitution as a pillar of the new federal superstructure. The addition of New York State is accompanied by flowery verse above and below "the beauteous DOME."

Interpret the Evidence

1. How do Melancton Smith, Alexander Hamilton, and John Williams each view the problems that exist under the confederation government (Sources 7.7, 7.8, and 7.9)?

2. What does James Madison see as the major source of factions in the United States, and how does he think they can most effectively be contained (Source 7.6)?

3. What are the main arguments for and against the three-fifths compromise over slavery in the Constitution (Sources 7.7, 7.8, and 7.9)? What other issues of representation inspired debate?

4. Are there any shared beliefs between the Federalists and Antifederalists in New York (Sources 7.6, 7.7, 7.8, and 7.9)? How might these contribute to Smith's decision to vote yes on ratification?

5. What does the Massachusetts Centinel's representation of ratification in New York State (Source 7.10) suggest about that newspaper's point of view?

Put It in Context

In what ways does the ratification process in New York State reflect larger debates and divisions in the United States in the 1780s?

The Early Republic

1790–1820

William Clark, Journal, January 28, 1805

William Clark kept a detailed journal of the 1804–1806 expedition he and Meriwether Lewis led to explore the American West. They were aided by many different native tribes, especially the Mandan community along the Missouri River. They camped near the Mandan in the winter of 1804, before heading into the Rocky Mountains. Here Clark draws a Mandan war hatchet, which was crucial to the tribe's defense. ▶ **To learn more about this primary source, see Source 8.9 on page 281.**

American Philosophical Society

After reading this chapter you will be able to:

- Analyze the ways that social and cultural leaders worked to craft an American identity and how that was complicated by racial, ethnic, and class differences.

- Interpret how the Democratic-Republican ideal of limiting federal power was transformed by international events, westward expansion, and Supreme Court rulings between 1800 and 1808.

- Explain the ways that technology reshaped the American economy and the lives of distinct groups of Americans.

Comparing American Histories

When **Parker Cleaveland** graduated from Harvard University in 1799, his parents expected him to pursue a career in medicine, law, or the ministry. Instead, he turned to teaching. In 1805 Cleaveland secured a position in Brunswick, Maine, as professor of mathematics and natural philosophy at Bowdoin College. A year later, he married Martha Bush. Over the next twenty years, the Cleavelands raised eight children on the Maine frontier, entertained visiting scholars, corresponded with families at other colleges, and boarded dozens of students. While Parker taught the students math and science, Martha trained them in manners and morals. The Cleavelands also served

as a model of new ideals of companionate marriage, in which husbands and wives shared interests and affection.

Professor Cleaveland believed in using scientific research to benefit society. When Brunswick workers asked him to identify local rocks, Parker began studying geology and chemistry. In 1816 he published his *Elementary Treatise on Mineralogy and Geology*, providing a basic text for students and interested adults. He also lectured throughout New England, displaying mineral samples and performing chemical experiments.

The Cleavelands viewed the Bowdoin College community as a laboratory in which distinctly American values and ideas could be developed and sustained. So, too, did the residents of other college towns. Although less than 1 percent of men in the United States attended universities at the time, frontier colleges were considered important vehicles for bringing virtue—especially service for the public good—to the far reaches of the early republic. Yet several of these colleges were constructed with the aid of enslaved labor, and all were built on land bought or confiscated from Indians.

The purchase of the Louisiana Territory by President Thomas Jefferson in 1803 marked a new American frontier and ensured further encroachments on native lands. The territory covered 828,000 square miles and stretched from the Mississippi River to the Rocky Mountains and from New Orleans to present-day Montana. The area was home to tens of thousands of indigenous inhabitants.

Three years before the Louisiana Purchase, a Hidatsa raiding party swept into a Shoshone village in the Rocky Mountains and seized captives, including a girl about twelve years old. The girl, **Sacagawea**, and her fellow captives were marched hundreds of miles to a Hidatsa-Mandan village on the Missouri River. Eventually Sacagawea was sold to a French trader, Toussaint Charbonneau, along with another young Shoshone woman, and both became his wives.

In November 1804, an expedition led by Meriwether Lewis and William Clark set up winter camp near this Hidatsa village. The U.S. government had sent Lewis and Clark to document flora and fauna in the Louisiana Territory, enhance trade, and explore

(*left*) **Parker Cleaveland** Courtesy the Bowdoin College Library, Brunswick, Maine, USA
(*right*) **Shoshone woman** (No image of Sacagawea exists.) Alecto Historical Editions/Bridgeman Images

routes to the Northwest. Charbonneau, who spoke French and Hidatsa, and Sacagawea, who spoke several Indian languages, joined the expedition as interpreters in April 1805.

The only woman in the party, Sacagawea gave birth during the journey and then traveled with her infant son strapped to her back. Although no portraits of her exist, her presence was crucial, as Clark noted in his journal: "The Wife of Chabono our interpreter we find reconsiles all the Indians, as to our friendly intentions." Sacagawea helped persuade native leaders to assist the expedition, but her extensive knowledge of the terrain and fluency in Indian languages were equally important. ∎

Comparing the American histories of Parker Cleaveland and Sacagawea highlights the distinct ways that individuals contributed to the development of the United States and of national identities. Cleaveland was part of a generation of intellectuals who symbolized Americans' ingenuity. Although Sacagawea was not considered learned, her understanding of Indian languages and western geography was crucial to Lewis and Clark's success. Like many other Americans, Sacagawea and Cleaveland forged new identities as the young nation developed. Still, racial, class, and gender differences made it impossible to create a single American identity. At the same time, Democratic-Republican leaders sought to shape a new national identity by promising to limit federal power and enhance state authority and individual rights. Instead, western expansion, international crises, and Supreme Court decisions all contributed to the growth of federal power.

The Dilemmas of National Identity

In his inaugural address in March 1801, President Thomas Jefferson argued that the vast distance between Europe and the United States was a blessing, allowing Americans to develop their own unique culture and institutions. For many Americans, education offered one means of ensuring a distinctive national identity. Public schools could train American children in republican values, while the wealthiest among them could attend private academies and colleges. Newspapers, sermons, books, magazines, and other printed works could also help forge a common identity among the nation's far-flung citizens. Even the presence of Indians and Africans contributed to art and literature that were uniquely American. In addition, the construction of a new capital city to house the federal government offered a potent symbol of nationhood.

Yet these developments also illuminated political and racial dilemmas in the young nation. The decision to move the U.S. capital south from Philadelphia was prompted by concerns among southern politicians about the power of northern economic and political elites. The very construction of the capital, in which enslaved and free workers labored side by side, highlighted racial and class differences. Educational opportunities differed by race and class as well as by sex. How could a singular notion of American identity be forged in a country where differences of race, class, and sex loomed so large?

Education for a New Nation.   The desire to create a specifically American culture emerged as soon as the Revolution ended. In 1783 Noah Webster, a schoolmaster, declared that "America must be as independent in *literature as in Politics*, as famous for *arts* as for *arms*." To promote his vision, Webster published the *American Spelling Book* (1810) and the

American Dictionary of the English Language (1828). His books were widely used in the nation's expanding network of schools and academies and led to more standardized spelling and pronunciation of commonly used words.

Before the Revolution, public education for children was widely available in New England and the Middle Atlantic region. In the South, only those who could afford private schooling—perhaps 25 percent of the boys and 10 percent of the girls—received any formal instruction. Few young people enrolled in high school in any part of the colonies. Following the Revolution, state and national leaders proposed ambitious plans for public education, and in 1789 Massachusetts became the first state to insist that each town provide free schools for local children, though towns set attendance policies.

The American colonies boasted nine colleges that provided higher education for young men, including Harvard, Yale, King's College (Columbia), Queen's College (Rutgers), and the College of William and Mary. After independence, many Americans worried that these institutions were tainted by British and aristocratic influences. New colleges based on republican ideals were essential.

Frontier towns offered opportunities for colleges to enrich the community and benefit the nation. The relative isolation of these villages ensured that students would focus on education. And frontier colleges provided opportunities for ethnic and religious groups outside the

Marmaduke Multiply's Merry Method of Making Minor Mathematics, c. 1815   After Noah Webster introduced his *American Spelling Book* in 1810, math instructors introduced books for young people like the one shown here. The book uses rhymes and colorful illustrations to teach students multiplication tables. More and more educational books for children were published as public schools multiplied in the decades following the Revolution. Granger

Anglo-American mainstream—like Scots-Irish Presbyterians—to cement their place in American society. The young nation benefited but, once again, at the expense of Indians and their lands. For example, the founding of Franklin College in Athens, Georgia encouraged white settlement in the state's interior, an area largely populated by the Creek and Cherokee.

Frontier colleges were organized as community institutions composed of extended families, where administrators, faculty, and their wives guided students, hosted social events, and hired local workers, including servants and slaves. Women were viewed as exemplars of virtue in the new nation, and professors' wives served as maternal figures for young adults away from home. Families of modest means could send their sons to these less expensive colleges, depending on faculty couples to expand their intellect and provide moral guidance. In some towns, students at local female academies joined college men at chaperoned events to cultivate proper relations between the sexes. Female academies multiplied as well, with institutions such as the Young Ladies Academy of Philadelphia and the Albany (New York) Female Academy opening in the decades after the Revolution. Others, like the Moravian Female Seminary in Bethlehem, Pennsylvania, expanded their curriculum in the 1780s to provide young women with a wider range of intellectual and practical knowledge.

Literary and Cultural Developments.

Older universities also contributed to the development of a national identity. A group known as the Hartford Wits, most of them Yale graduates, gave birth to a new literary tradition. Its members identified mainly as Federalists and published paeans to democracy, satires about Shays's Rebellion, and plays about the proper role of the central government in a republican nation. Developments in Europe, particularly liberal social ideas and Romantic beliefs in human perfectibility, also shaped American art, literature, philosophy, and architecture in the early nineteenth century. European Romantics, like the English poet William Wordsworth, the German philosopher Immanuel Kant, and the French painter Eugêne Delacroix, challenged Enlightenment ideas of rationality by insisting on the importance of human passion, the mysteries of nature, and the virtues of common folk.

American novelists in the early republic drew on these ideas as they sought to educate readers about virtue. Advances in printing and the manufacture of paper increased the circulation of novels, a literary genre developed in Britain and continental Europe at the turn of the eighteenth century. Improvements in girls' and young women's education then produced a growing audience for novels among women. American authors like Susanna Rowson and Charles Brockden Brown placed ordinary women and men in moments of high drama that tested their moral character. Novelists also emphasized new marital ideals, by which husbands and wives became affectionate partners and companions in creating a home and family.

Washington Irving was one of the most well-known literary figures in the early republic. He wrote a series of popular folktales, including "The Legend of Sleepy Hollow" and "Rip Van Winkle," that were published in his *Sketchbook* in 1820. They drew on Dutch culture in the Hudson valley region and often poked fun at more celebratory tales of early American history. In one serious essay, Irving challenged popular accounts of colonial wars that ignored courageous actions by Indians while applauding white atrocities.

Still, books glorifying the nation's past were also enormously popular. Just as European Romantics emphasized individual, especially heroic, action, so too did America's earliest historical writers. Among the most influential were Mason Weems, author of the *Life of Washington* (1806), a celebratory if fanciful biography, and Mercy Otis Warren, who wrote a three-volume *History of the Revolution* (1805). The influence of American authors increased as residents in both urban and rural areas purchased growing numbers of books.

Artists, too, devoted considerable attention to historical themes, though in the late eighteenth century, they tended more to Enlightenment perspectives. Charles Willson Peale painted Revolutionary generals while serving in the Continental Army and became best known for his portraits of George Washington. Samuel Jennings offered a more radical perspective on the nation's character by incorporating women and African Americans into works like *Liberty Displaying the Arts and Sciences* (1792), but highlighted the importance of learning and rationality. So, too, did William Bartram, the son of a botanist. He journeyed through the southeastern United States and Florida, and published beautiful, and scientifically accurate, engravings of plants and animals in his *Travels* (1791). Engravings were less expensive than paintings so circulated more widely, and many highlighted national symbols like flags, eagles, and Lady Liberty.

Explore ▶

See Source 8.1 for one artist's image of republican education.

In 1780, the Massachusetts legislature established the American Academy of Arts and Sciences to promote American literature and science. Six years later, Philadelphia's American Philosophical Society created the first national prize for scientific endeavor. Philadelphia was home as well to the nation's first medical college, founded at the University of Pennsylvania. Frontier colleges like Bowdoin also promoted new scientific discoveries. As in the arts, American scientists built on developments in continental Europe and Britain but prided themselves on contributing their own expertise.

Religious Renewal. Amid the wave of scientific discoveries, religious leaders sought to reinvigorate American spirituality. However, this spiritual renewal was rooted less in established churches and educated ministers than in new religious organizations and popular preachers. Methodist and Baptist churches were especially vital to this development. In 1780, only fifty Methodist churches existed in the United States. By 1820, it was the largest denomination in the nation, followed closely by Baptists. Believing that everyone could gain salvation, the two denominations appealed to small farmers, workers, and the poor as well to women and African Americans. Women already formed a majority of worshippers in many congregations, and some women — black and white — joined the popular ministries at the turn of the nineteenth century. A few women attracted followings independent of any church. In the late 1770s, Jemima Wilkinson, a white Quaker, began calling herself "the Publick Universal Friend." She developed a gender-neutral persona and proclaimed herself the "Spirit of Light." Wilkinson adopted men's clothing and gained devoted followers across New England who referred to the preacher as "he" or "him." Around the same time, Mother Ann Lee migrated from England to the United States and founded the first community of American Shakers, named after the ecstatic dances woven into their worship. Lee insisted on celibacy for herself and her followers, and women and men lived in separate dorm-like buildings. Shakers established rural communities, supporting themselves through farming and furniture making. They adopted children and welcomed converts to ensure their growth. In the early nineteenth century, a few women in the African Methodist Episcopal (AME) Church also requested the right to preach. Initially Richard Allen turned down such requests. However, in 1817, after hearing Jarena Lee offer an impromptu sermon from her seat at Mother Bethel, Allen changed his mind. In 1819, Lee was officially ordained

Guided Primary Source Analysis

Samuel Jennings | Liberty Displaying the Arts and Sciences, 1792

Samuel Jennings was born in Philadelphia and attended the College of Philadelphia before the Revolution. He taught drawing and painted portraits before moving to London to study with Benjamin West in 1787. There his allegorical paintings were exhibited at the Royal Academy. Jennings painted this image for the newly established Library Company of Philadelphia, many of whose directors were Quakers who opposed slavery. The directors requested that he include Lady Liberty with her cap on the end of a pole.

Source 8.1

The Library Company of Philadelphia

Which arts and sciences are displayed in this painting?

What does the broken chain at the feet of Lady Liberty indicate?

What distinguishes the black people inside and outside the building?

▶ Put It in Context

What does this painting suggest about how Jennings and the Library Company directors envisioned American identities in the early republic?

Jemima Wilkerson (the Publick Universal Friend) c. 1850s   Born in 1752, Jemima was one of eight children. Raised by Quaker parents, she and five siblings eventually left the Society of Friends. After a debilitating fever in 1776, Wilkerson claimed she had died and been reborn as the Publick Universal Friend. She rejected her birth name, adopted genderless pronouns, and dressed mainly in men's clothing. She attracted large numbers of young women and men and advocated universal salvation, gender equality, sexual abstinence, and the abolition of slavery. Yates County History Center

a minister, preaching to interracial audiences of Baptists and Methodists as well as the AME Church.

In the rural South and in frontier areas, Baptists, Methodists, and Presbyterians organized camp meetings, where a dozen or more preachers, mostly men and many without formal training, tapped into deep wells of spirituality. The first camp meeting, held in Cane Ridge, Kentucky in 1801, attracted some 10,000 men and women. Whites and blacks, enslaved and free, attended these meetings and were encouraged to dance, shout, sing, and pray. For the next two decades, camp meetings continued to attract large crowds across the South and West.

The Racial Limits of "American" Culture.
As white Americans sought to create a distinct national identity, they often wielded native names and symbols. Some Americans, including whiskey rebels, followed in the tradition of the Boston Tea Party, dressing as Indians to protest economic and political tyranny. More affluent whites also embraced this practice. The Tammany society, first founded in Philadelphia in 1772, expanded to other cities in the late eighteenth century. The society, named after a seventeenth-century Delaware chief called Tammend, promoted patriotism and republicanism. Its thirteen branches, named after Indian tribes, attracted large numbers of lawyers, merchants, and skilled artisans, who called their meetings "wigwams" and their leaders "sachems."

Poets, too, focused on American Indians. In his 1787 poem "Indian Burying Ground," Philip Freneau offered a sentimental portrait that highlighted the supposedly lost heritage of a nearly extinct native culture in New England. The theme of lost cultures and heroic (if still savage) Indians became even more pronounced in American poetry in the following decades. Such sentimental portraits were decidedly less popular along the nation's frontier, where indigenous communities continued to fight for their lands and rights.

White authors and artists offered far less sympathetic depictions of Africans and African Americans. Some positive images were produced in the North, intended for the rare patrons who opposed slavery. Typical images of blacks were far more demeaning, exaggerating their perceived physical and intellectual differences from whites to suggest their innate inferiority. Similarly, whites in frontier regions generally focused on natives' supposed savagery and duplicity.

Whether the depictions were realistic, sentimental, or derogatory, Africans, African Americans, and American Indians were almost always presented to the American public through the eyes of whites. Educated blacks like the Reverend Richard Allen of Philadelphia or the Reverend Thomas Paul of Boston wrote mainly for African American audiences or corresponded privately with sympathetic whites. Similarly, cultural leaders among American Indians worked mainly within their own nations either to maintain traditional languages and customs or to introduce what they considered more positive Anglo-American ideas and beliefs.

The improved educational opportunities available to white Americans generally excluded blacks and Indians. Most southern planters had little desire to teach their slaves to read and write. Even in the North, states did not generally incorporate black children into their plans for public education. African Americans in cities with large free black populations established the most long-lived schools for their race. The Reverend Allen opened a Sunday school for children in 1795 at Mother Bethel AME Church, and other free blacks formed literary and debating societies. Still, only a small percentage of African Americans received an education equivalent to that available to whites in the early republic.

U.S. political leaders were more interested in the education of American Indians, but government officials left their schooling to religious groups. Several denominations sent missionaries to the Seneca, Cherokee, and other tribes, and a few successful students were then sent to American colleges to be trained as ministers or teachers for their own people. Eleazar Wheelock established an Indian Charity School in Connecticut in the 1760s. In 1765, he sent the Reverend Samson Occam, a Mohegan Presbyterian minister, to England, where he raised 12,000 pounds for a new school. That school, Dartmouth College, opened in 1769 in Hanover, New Hampshire. However, it educated mainly white men. Angered by Wheelock's betrayal, Occam founded the Christian Indian community of Brothertown in eastern New York in the late eighteenth century. The Oneida then established New Stockbridge in central New York, welcoming Mohicans from western Massachusetts and Lenape from Delaware. Occom arranged

Benjamin Banneker's *Pennsylvania, Delaware, Maryland, and Virginia Almanac*, 1795 Benjamin Banneker (here spelled Bannaker) was a free black from Baltimore County, Maryland. Largely self-educated, he was a talented astronomer who compiled almanacs that included annual calendars, tide charts, lunar and solar observations, and statistical charts. Almanacs were widely used by farmers, sailors, and the general public. Banneker's almanac included his portrait to highlight his achievements as a black man. Granger for these villages to receive official charters in 1787. In April 1792, shortly before his death, he evicted white settlers from Brothertown.

While largely unsuccessful, the divergent approaches whites took to educating Indians and African Americans demonstrated their broader assumptions about these groups. Most white Americans believed that Indians were untamed and uncivilized, but not innately different from Europeans. Africans and African Americans, on the other hand, were assumed to be inferior, and most whites believed that no amount of education could change that. As U.S. frontiers expanded, white Americans considered ways to "civilize" Indians and incorporate them into the nation. The requirements of slavery made it much more difficult for whites to imagine African Americans as anything more than lowly laborers, despite free blacks who clearly demonstrated otherwise.

Aware of the limited opportunities available in the United States, some African Americans considered moving elsewhere. In the late 1780s, the Newport African Union Society in Rhode Island developed a plan to establish a community for American blacks in Africa. Many whites, too, viewed the settlement of blacks in Africa as a way to solve what they considered the nation's racial dilemma.

Over the next three decades, the idea of emigration (as blacks viewed it) or colonization (as whites saw it) received widespread attention. Those who opposed slavery hoped to persuade slave owners to free or sell their human property on the condition that the former slaves be shipped to Africa. Some assumed that free blacks could find opportunities in Africa not available to them in the United States. Other whites simply wanted to rid the nation of its race problem by ridding it of blacks. In 1817 a group of southern enslavers and northern merchants formed the **American Colonization Society (ACS)** to establish colonies of freed slaves and free-born American blacks in Africa. Although some African Americans supported this scheme, northern free blacks generally opposed it, viewing colonization as an effort originating "more immediately from prejudice than philanthropy." Ultimately the plans of the ACS proved impractical. Particularly as cotton production expanded from the 1790s on, few plantation owners were willing to emancipate their workers.

A New Capital for a New Nation.

A New Capital for a New Nation. While the construction of Washington City, the new national capital, provided an opportunity to highlight America's distinctive culture and identity, it also revealed enslavement as a crucial part of that identity. The capital was situated along the Potomac River between Virginia and Maryland, an area where more than 300,000 enslaved workers lived. Between 1792 and 1809, hundreds of enslaved men and a few women were hired out by their owners to build the capital. Owners were paid $5 per month for each laborer. Enslaved men cleared trees and stumps, built roads, dug trenches, baked bricks, and cut and laid sandstone while enslaved women cooked, did laundry, and nursed the sick and injured. A small number performed skilled labor as carpenters or assistants to stonemasons and surveyors. Four hundred slaves, more than half the labor force, worked on the Capitol building.

Free blacks also participated in the development of Washington. Many worked alongside enslaved laborers, but a few gained professional positions. Benjamin Banneker, for example, a self-taught clock maker, astronomer, and surveyor, was hired as an assistant to the surveyor Major Andrew Ellicott. In 1791 Banneker helped to plot the 100-square-mile site on which the capital was to be built.

African Americans often worked alongside Irish immigrants, whose wages were kept in check by the availability of enslaved labor. Most workers, regardless of race, faced poor housing, sparse meals, malarial fevers, and limited medical care. Despite these obstacles, in less than a decade, a system of roads was laid out and cleared, the Executive Mansion was built, and the north wing of the Capitol was completed.

More prosperous immigrants and foreign professionals were also involved in creating the U.S. capital. Irish-born James Hoban designed the Executive Mansion. A French engineer, Pierre Charles L'Enfant, planned the city's streets. William Thornton, a Scottish-trained physician born in the West Indies, drew the blueprints for the Capitol building, and in 1802 became head of the U.S. Patent Office. Englishman Benjamin Latrobe, who migrated to the United States in 1795, directed the building's construction and was later appointed Surveyor of Public Buildings by Thomas Jefferson. Perhaps what was most "American" about the new capital was the diverse nationalities and races of those who designed and built it.

Washington's founders envisioned the city as a beacon to the world, proclaiming the advantages of the nation's republican principles. But its location on a slow-moving river and its clay soil left the area hot, humid, and dusty in the summer and muddy and damp in the

Plan for the City of Washington, 1795   The French-born Pierre L'Enfant joined the Continental Army at age 23 in 1777 and served as a military engineer. Invited to design plans for Washington, he laid out a grand plan for broad boulevards, parks, and fountains, similar to those in major European cities. He also included a long mall stretching from the Potomac River east to the U.S. Capitol building. From The New York Public Library, https://digitalcollections.nypl.org /items/510d47da-ef95-a3d9-e040-e00a18064a99 winter and spring. When John Adams and his administration moved to Washington in June 1800, they considered themselves on the frontiers of civilization. The tree stumps that remained on the mile-long road from the Capitol to the Executive Mansion made it nearly impossible to navigate in a carriage. On rainy days, when roads proved impassable, officials walked or rode horses to work. Many early residents painted Washington in harsh tones. New Hampshire congressional representative Ebenezer Matroon wrote a friend, "If I wished to punish a culprit, I would send him to do penance in this place . . . this swamp—this lonesome dreary swamp, secluded from every delightful or pleasing thing."

Despite its critics, Washington was the seat of federal power and thus played an important role in the social and political worlds of American elites. From January through March, the height of the social season, the wives of congressmen, judges, and other officials created a lively schedule of teas, parties, and balls in the capital city. When Thomas Jefferson became president, he opened the White House to visitors on a regular basis. Yet for all his republican principles, Jefferson moved into the Executive Mansion with a retinue of slaves.

In decades to come, Washington City would become Washington, D.C., a city with broad boulevards decorated with beautiful monuments to the American political experiment. And the Executive Mansion would become the White House, a proud symbol of republican government. Yet Washington was always characterized by wide disparities in wealth, status, and power, which were especially visible when enslaved laborers worked in the Executive Mansion's kitchen, laundry, and yard. President Jefferson's efforts to incorporate new territories into the United States only exacerbated these divisions by providing more economic opportunities for white planters, investors, and farmers while ensuring the expansion of slavery and the decimation of American Indians.

Review & Relate

■ How did developments in education, literature, and the arts contribute to the emergence of a distinctly American identity?

■ How did African Americans and American Indians contribute to and challenge predominantly white views of American identity?

Extending Federal Power

Thomas Jefferson, like other Democratic-Republicans, envisioned the United States as a republic composed of small, independent farmers who had little need and less desire for expansive federal power. Despite Jefferson's early efforts to impose this vision on the government, developments in international affairs soon converged with Supreme Court rulings to expand federal power. But Jefferson, too, contributed to this expansion by purchasing the Louisiana Territory from France in 1803. The development of this vast territory increased federal authority and raised new questions about the place of Indians and African Americans in a republican society.

A New Administration Faces Challenges. In 1801 Democratic-Republicans worked quickly to implement their vision of limited federal power. Holding the majority in Congress, they repealed the whiskey tax and let the Alien and Sedition Acts expire. Jefferson significantly reduced government expenditures and immediately set about slashing the national debt, cutting it nearly in half by the end of his second term. Democratic-Republicans also worked to curb the powers granted to the Bank of the United States and the federal court system.

Soon, however, international upheavals forced Jefferson to make fuller use of his presidential powers. The U.S. government had paid tribute to the Barbary States of North Africa during the 1790s to gain protection for American merchant ships. The new president opposed this practice and in 1801 refused to continue the payments. The Barbary pirates quickly resumed their attacks, and Jefferson was forced to send the U.S. Navy and Marine Corps to retaliate. Although a combined American and Arab force did not achieve their objective of capturing Tripoli, the Ottoman viceroy agreed to negotiate a new agreement with the United States. Seeking to avoid all-out war, Congress accepted a treaty with the Barbary States that reduced the tribute payment.

Jefferson also followed the developing crisis in the West Indies during the 1790s. In 1791 slaves on the sugar-rich island of Saint Domingue launched a revolt against French rule. Inspired in part by the American Declaration of Independence, the **Haitian Revolution** escalated into a long and complicated conflict in which free people of color, white enslavers, and enslaved laborers formed competing alliances with British and Spanish forces as well as with leaders of the French Revolution. Finally, in December 1799, Toussaint L'Ouverture, a military leader and former slave, claimed the presidency of the new Republic of Haiti. But Napoleon Bonaparte seized power in France that same year and sent thousands of troops to reclaim the island. Toussaint was shipped off to France, where he died in prison. Many Haitians fled to the United States, but other Haitian rebels continued the fight.

> **Explore ▶**
>
> See Sources 8.2 and 8.3 for two views on the revolution in Haiti.

The Haitian Revolution emboldened black people throughout the Americas as it frightened whites. In the United States, whites feared it might incite uprisings among the enslaved. In 1800 Gabriel, an enslaved blacksmith in Richmond, Virginia, plotted a rebellion. Inspired by the American and Haitian revolutions, supporters rallied around the demand for "Death or Liberty." Gabriel's plan failed when informants betrayed him to authorities. Nonetheless, news of the plot traveled across the South and terrified white residents. Their anxieties were heightened when in November 1803, prolonged fighting, yellow fever, and the loss of sixty thousand soldiers forced Napoleon to admit defeat in Haiti, and it became the first independent black-led nation in the Americas.

The Louisiana Purchase and Indian Societies.
In France's defeat Jefferson saw an opportunity to gain navigation rights on the Mississippi River, which the French controlled. This was a matter of crucial concern to Americans living west of the Appalachian Mountains. Jefferson sent James Monroe to France to offer Napoleon $2 million to ensure Americans the right of navigation and deposit (i.e., offloading cargo from ships) on the Mississippi. To Jefferson's surprise, Napoleon offered instead to sell the entire Louisiana Territory for $15 million.

The president agonized over the constitutionality of this **Louisiana Purchase**. Since the Constitution contained no provisions for buying land from foreign nations, a strict interpretation would prohibit the purchase. In the end, though, the opportunity proved too tempting, and the president finally agreed to the purchase. Jefferson justified his decision by arguing that the territory would allow for the removal of more Indians from east of the Mississippi River, end European influence in the region, and expand U.S. trade networks.

Comparative Primary Source Analysis

White Responses to Black Rebellion

White southerners who feared the effect of the Haitian Revolution were nonetheless shocked when Gabriel, an enslaved blacksmith, plotted a rebellion in Virginia. Upon the plot's discovery, thirty blacks were tried and convicted, and twenty-seven executed for conspiring to rebel. In the first document, President Jefferson expresses concern about slave rebellions but also about the punishment of insurgents. The second document, by Leonore Sansay, the wife of a Saint-Domingue planter, captures the situation in Haiti in 1802 as France fought to reclaim its colony. Sansay, who had earlier met Vice President Aaron Burr, writes to him about conditions on the island.

Source 8.2

Thomas Jefferson | Letter to U.S. Minister to Great Britain Rufus King, July 1802

The course of things in the neighboring islands of the West Indies appears to have given a considerable impulse to the minds of the slaves in different parts of the U.S. A great disposition to insurgency has manifested itself among them, which, in one instance, in the state of Virginia, broke out into actual insurrection. This was easily suppressed; but many of those concerned, (between 20 and 30, I believe) fell victims to the law. So extensive an execution could not but excite sensibility in the public mind, and beget a regret that the laws had not provided, for such cases, some alternative, combining more mildness with equal efficacy. The legislature of the state, at a subsequent meeting, took the subject into consideration, and have communicated to me . . . their wish that some place could be provided, out of the limits of the U.S., to which slaves guilty of insurgency might be transported; and they have particularly looked to Africa as offering the most desirable receptacle. We might for this purpose, enter into negotiations with the natives, on some part of the coast, to obtain a settlement and, by establishing an African company, combine with it commercial operations, which might not only reimburse expenses but procure profit also.

Source: Paul Leicester Ford, ed., *The Writings of Thomas Jefferson* (New York, 1896), 8:161–64.

Opponents viewed the purchase as benefiting mainly agrarian interests and suspected Jefferson of trying to offset Federalist power in the Northeast. Still, the acquisition proved popular among ordinary Americans, most of whom focused on the opportunities it offered rather than the expansion of federal power it ensured.

Neither political party was concerned about the French, Spanish, or native peoples living in the region. When the Senate approved the purchase in October 1803, life had already changed dramatically for Indians in particular. In the late 1770s, Lakota Indians (called Sioux by Americans) expanded into the Black Hills of present-day South Dakota, forcing out the Cheyenne who had lived there. This mountainous region became a sacred site as well as the center of their bison- and horse-based society. Between 1779 and 1784, a smallpox epidemic ravaged Plains Indians, spreading along western trade routes and hitting children and pregnant women particularly hard. Some native bands lost 80 percent of their population, which led to further migration and a reconfiguration of communities. In the late eighteenth century, Russian traders — all male — discovered the value of sea otter pelts

Source 8.3

Leonora Sansay | Letter to Aaron Burr, November 1802

The so much desired general Rochambeau is at length here. His arrival was announced . . . by the firing of cannon. . . . Nothing is heard of but the public joy. He is considered as the guardian, as the saviour of the people. Every proprietor feels himself already in his habitation [plantation] and I have even heard some of them disputing about the quality of the coffee they expect soon to gather. . . .

The arrival of General Rochambeau seems to have spread terror among the negroes[.] I wish they were reduced to order so that I might see the so much vaunted habitations where I should repose beneath the shade of orange groves, walk on carpets of rose leaves and Frenchipone; be fanned to sleep by silent slaves. . . .

What a delightful existence! . . .

But the moment of enjoying these pleasures is, I fear, far distant. The negroes have felt during ten years the blessing of liberty, for a blessing it certainly is, however acquired, and then will not easily be deprived of it. They have fought and vanquished French troops, and their strength has increased from a knowledge of the weakness of their opposer, and the climate itself combats for them. . . .

Every evening several old Creoles . . . assemble at our house, and talk of their affairs. One of them . . . now lives in a miserable hut. . . . Yet he still hopes for better days, in which hope they all join him.

Source: Mary Hassal [Leonora Sansay], *Secret History of the Horrors of St. Domingo, in a Series of Letters Written by a Lady at Cape François to Colonel Burr* (Philadelphia: Bradford & Inskelp, 1808), 430–32.

Interpret the Evidence

1. How does Thomas Jefferson view the influence of West Indies rebellions on U.S. slaves, and why is he reluctant to respond to conspiracies by executing large numbers of insurgents?
2. How would you compare Leonora Sansay's response to black rebellion in Saint-Domingue/Haiti with Jefferson's response to conspiracies in Virginia? What accounts for the similarities and differences?

Put It in Context

How might reports of the Haitian Revolution and the Virginia rebellion have contributed to debates over the future of slavery in the early years of the United States?

along North America's Northwest coast. Their rush to capture the trade before Spanish and American adventurers could do so introduced new diseases as well as cloth and metal goods to native societies, led to sexual assaults on women in the region, and produced drastic changes in native economies. In these difficult circumstances, some native Alutiiq women developed long-term relationships with Siberian peasants drawn into the dangerous work of capturing sea otters. These relationships, like those in French Canada, provided Russian men with assistance in gathering pelts and Alutiiq women with greater physical security and access to food, clothing, and other Russian trade goods.

At Jefferson's request, Congress had already appropriated funds for an expedition known as the **Corps of Discovery** to explore territory along the Missouri River. That expedition would now explore much of the Louisiana Territory. The president's personal secretary, Meriwether Lewis, headed the venture and invited fellow Virginian William Clark to serve as co-captain. The two set off with about forty-five men on May 14, 1804. For two years, they traveled thousands of miles up the Missouri River, through the northern plains, over the Rocky Mountains, and beyond the Louisiana Territory to the Pacific coast. Sacagawea and her husband joined them in April 1805, serving as guides and translators as they headed into the Rocky Mountains. Throughout the expedition, members meticulously recorded observations about local plants and animals as well as Indian residents, providing valuable evidence for young scientists like Parker Cleaveland and fascinating information for ordinary Americans. **See Primary Source Project 8: The Corps of Discovery: Paeans to Peace and Instruments of War, page 279.**

Sacagawea was the only Indian to travel as a permanent member of the expedition, but many other native women and men assisted the Corps when it journeyed near their villages. They provided food and lodging for the Corps, hauled baggage up steep mountain trails, and traded food, horses, and other items. The one African American on the expedition, named York, also helped negotiate trade with local Indians. Although enslaved, York realized his value as a trader, hunter, and scout, and asked Clark for his freedom when the expedition ended in 1806. York did eventually become a free man, but it is not clear whether it was by Clark's choice or York's escape.

Other expeditions followed Lewis and Clark's venture. In 1806 Lieutenant Zebulon Pike led a group to explore the southern portion of the Louisiana Territory (Map 8.1). After traveling from St. Louis to the Rocky Mountains, the expedition entered Mexican territory. In early 1807, Pike and his men were captured by Mexican forces. They were returned to the United States at the Louisiana border that July. Pike had learned a great deal about lands that would eventually become part of the United States and about Mexican desires to overthrow Spanish rule, information that proved valuable over the next two decades.

Early in this series of expeditions, in November 1804, Jefferson easily won reelection as president. His popularity among farmers, already high, increased when Congress reduced the minimum allotment for federal land sales from 320 to 160 acres. This act allowed more farmers to purchase land on their own rather than via speculators. Yet by the time of Jefferson's second inauguration in March 1805, the president's vision of limiting federal power had been shattered by his own actions and those of the Supreme Court.

> **Explore ▸**
>
> Sources 8.4 and 8.5 offer distinct views of the interplay of religion and politics in the early republic.

The Supreme Court Extends Its Reach. In 1801, just before the Federalist-dominated Congress turned over power to the Democratic-Republicans, it passed a new **Judiciary Act**. The act created six additional circuit courts and sixteen new judgeships, which President Adams filled with Federalist "midnight appointments" before he left office. Jefferson accused the Federalists of having "retired into the judiciary" and worried that "from that battery all the works of Republicanism are to be beaten down and destroyed." Meanwhile John Marshall, chief justice of the United States (1801–1835), insisted that the powers of the Supreme Court must be equal to and balance those of the executive and legislative branches.

One of the first cases to test the Court's authority involved a dispute over President Adams's midnight appointments. Jefferson's secretary of state, James Madison, refused to deliver the appointment papers to several of the appointees, including William Marbury. Marbury and three others sued Madison to receive their commissions. In *Marbury v. Madison* (1803), the Supreme Court ruled that it was not empowered to force the executive branch to give Marbury his commission. But in his decision, Chief Justice Marshall declared that the Supreme Court did have the duty "to say what the law is." He thus asserted a

MAP 8.1   Lewis and Clark and Zebulon Pike Expeditions, 1804–1807

The expeditions led by Meriwether Lewis, William Clark, and Zebulon Pike illustrate the vast regions explored in just four years after the U.S. purchase of the Louisiana Territory. Journeying through and beyond the borders of that territory, the explorers gathered information about Indian nations, plants, animals, and the natural terrain even as Comanche and Shoshone nations, with access to horses, transformed the region.

fundamental constitutional power: that the Supreme Court had the authority to decide which federal laws were constitutional. The following year, the Court also claimed the right to rule on the constitutionality of state laws. In doing so, the justices rejected Democratic-Republicans' claim that state legislatures had the power to repudiate federal law. Instead, the Supreme Court declared that federal laws took precedence over state laws.

Over the next dozen years, the Supreme Court continued to assert Federalist principles. In 1810 it insisted that it was the proper and sole arena for determining matters of constitutional interpretation. Then in 1819, the highest court reinforced its loose interpretation of the Constitution's implied powers clause in *McCulloch v. Maryland*. This clause gave the federal government the right to "make all laws which shall be necessary and proper" for carrying out the explicit powers granted to it by the Constitution. Despite Democratic-Republicans' earlier opposition to a national bank, Congress chartered the Second Bank of the United States in 1816, and its branch banks issued notes that circulated

Comparative Secondary Source Analysis

Religion and Politics in the Early Republic

By the 1790s, the disestablishment of state churches and the guarantee of religious freedom led to a proliferation of denominations that attracted people from diverse backgrounds. Some denominations began recognizing lay preachers, those without formal training. Extended camp meetings gained popularity across the South and the frontier, with women and African Americans participating alongside white men. Historians have studied the relationships of these developments with the changing political landscape of the Early Republic. Nathan Hatch highlights the democratic spirit of popular religious movements of the period, which, he argues, echoed Anti-Federalist and Jeffersonian sentiments in politics. Amanda Porterfield, writing almost a quarter of a century later, argues that partisans on both sides of the political divide embraced evangelicalism and increasingly viewed society and politics with suspicion and distrust.

Source 8.4

Nathan O. Hatch | Religion as a Democratizing Force, 1989

These religious leaders [of the 1780s and 1790s] were fierce independents and localists. . . . Their gospel of the backcountry resonated with the powerful Anti-Federalist and Jeffersonian persuasions. . . .

[T]he most powerful popular movements in the early republic were expressly religious. . . . It was lay preachers . . . who most effectively constructed new frames of reference for people living in a period of profound transition. Religious leaders from the rank and file were phenomenally successful in reaching out to marginal people, in promoting self-education and sheltering participants from the indoctrination of elite orthodoxies, in binding people together in supportive communities, and in identifying the aspirations of common people with the will of God. . . .

This groundswell shook churches to the foundation. . . . Traditional elites, keenly aware of the fragile authority of "college learnt merchants of the gospel," scrambled to consolidate the position of orthodox churches. . . . [Yet] nurtured by sources as contradictory as George Whitfield and Tom Paine, many deeply religious people were set adrift from ecclesiastical establishments at the same time they demanded that the church begin living up to its spiritual promise. . . .

This awakening developed inversely to that commonly depicted, however. Instead of fostering a unified, cohesive movement, it splintered American Christianity and magnified the diversity of institutions claiming to be the church. It sprang from a populist upsurge rather from changing mores of established parishes. . . .

Their success may have been the most profoundly democratic upheaval in the early republic. . . .

Source: Nathan O. Hatch, *The Democratization of American Christianity* (Yale University Press, 1989), pp. 34 and 224–226.

Source 8.5

Amanda Porterfield | Religion Sows Doubt and Nurtures Partisanship, 2012

The 1790s saw rising panic about how to get along in the new world of American liberty, where old traditions of decorum had broken down. . . . As old traditions fell away, uncertainty about how to conduct oneself, cynicism with respect to other people, and ambivalence about the effects of American independence all contributed to the uneasy atmosphere of mistrustful doubt. . . .

Promoting the supreme authority of God's law, churches not only exerted moral authority as interpreters of divine governance but also fostered distrust of secular reason and government. . . .

The spike in religion's popularity around 1800 [thus] coincided with political upheavals and new forms of political organization. . . .

As public life in every region of the new republic became increasingly politicized . . . political activists channeled mistrust along partisan lines. . . . Taverns became headquarters for a new breed of political organizers who planned public events and worked to recruit voters. Alcohol flowed freely, and deals were made.

Religious organizations grew on both sides of the partisan political divide, and revivals flourished even more exuberantly outside New England, in regions where Jefferson and his party were more popular. New Light Presbyterianism from North Carolina ignited the Great Revival of 1801 in the Kentucky Cumberland, and that amazing event shaped religious expectations throughout the West and in many parts of the South. . . .

Evangelical religion surged in the context of bitter partisan conflict, the growth of libertarian policies [those opposed to federal government intervention] with respect to slavery and Indian rights, and profound ambivalence toward authority. . . .

Religion came to designate a diffuse realm, protected by the state, where people built communities, conceived relationships with God, and lamented the corruption of the state and of profane, mistrustful society. . . .

Source: Amanda Porterfield, *Conceived in Doubt: Religion and Politics in the New American Nation* (University of Chicago Press, 2012), pp. 2–4 and 11–12.

Examine the Sources

1. How do Hatch and Porterfield differ in their interpretations of the relationships between religion and politics?
2. Drawing upon evidence in Chapters 7 and 8, evaluate the strengths and weaknesses of Hatch's and Porterfield's presentations.

Put It in Context

How would you analyze religion's relationship to political transformations in the early republic?

widely in local communities. Legislators in Maryland, believing that branch banks had gained excessive power, approved a tax on their operations. Marshall's Court ruled that the establishment of the bank was "necessary and proper" for the functioning of the national government and rejected Maryland's right to tax the branch bank, claiming that "the power to tax involves the power to destroy."

By 1820 the Supreme Court, under the forceful direction of John Marshall, had established the power of judicial review—the authority of the nation's highest court to rule on cases involving states as well as the nation. From the Court's perspective, the judiciary was as important an institution in framing and preserving a national agenda as Congress or the president.

Democratic-Republicans Expand Federal Powers.

Although Democratic-Republicans generally opposed Marshall's rulings, they, too, continued to expand federal power. Once again, international developments drove the administration's political agenda. By 1805 the security of the United States was threatened by continued conflicts between France and Great Britain. Both sought alliances with the young nation, and both ignored U.S. claims of neutrality. Indeed, each nation sought to punish Americans for trading with the other. Britain's Royal Navy began stopping American ships carrying sugar and molasses from the French West Indies and, between 1802 and 1811, impressed more than eight thousand sailors from such ships, including many American citizens. France claimed a similar right to stop U.S. ships that continued to trade with Great Britain.

Unable to convince foreign powers to recognize U.S. neutrality, Jefferson and Madison pushed for congressional passage of an embargo that they hoped would, like colonial boycotts, force Great Britain's hand. In 1807 Congress passed the **Embargo Act**, which prohibited U.S. ships from leaving their home ports until Britain and France repealed their restrictions on American trade. Although the act kept the United States out of war, it had a devastating impact on national commerce.

New England merchants immediately voiced their outrage, and some began sending goods to Europe via Canada. In response, Congress passed the Force Act, granting extraordinary powers to customs officials to end such smuggling. The economic pain caused by the rapid decline in trade spread well beyond the merchant class. Parker Cleaveland was forced to sell his home to the Bowdoin trustees and become their tenant. Farmers and urban workers as well as southern planters suffered the embargo's effects more directly. Exports nearly stopped, and sailors and dockworkers faced escalating unemployment. With the recession deepening, American concerns about the expansion of federal power reemerged. Congress and the president had not simply regulated international trade; they had brought it to a halt.

Still, despite the failure of the Embargo Act, many Americans viewed Jefferson favorably. He had devoted his adult life to the creation of the United States. He had purchased the Louisiana Territory, opening up vast lands to exploration, settlement, and development. This geographical boon encouraged inventors and artisans to pursue ideas that would help the early republic take full advantage of its resources and recover from its current economic plight. Some must have wondered, however, how a Democratic-Republican president had so significantly expanded the power of the federal government.

OGRABME, or, The American Snapping-turtle.

Opposition to the Embargo Act   Although Congress repealed the Embargo Act in 1809, lawmakers still barred the United States from trading with Great Britain and France, both of which attacked American shipping in violation of U.S. neutrality. This political cartoon by Alexander Anderson criticizes the embargo, which proved costly to merchants, sailors, and dockworkers. Here a merchant carrying a barrel of goods curses the snapping turtle "Ograbme," which is *embargo* spelled backward. Bridgeman Images

Review & Relate

▪ How did the Federalist-dominated courts and the Democratic-Republican president and Congress each contribute to the expansion of the federal government?

▪ How did the purchase of the Louisiana Territory from France and international conflicts with France and Britain shape domestic issues in the late eighteenth and early nineteenth centuries?

Remaking America's Economic Character

As the United States expanded geographically, technological ingenuity became a highly valued commodity. The spread of U.S. settlements into new territories necessitated improved forms of transportation and communication and increased demands for muskets and other weapons to protect the nation's frontier. The growing population also fueled improvements in agriculture and manufacturing to meet demands for clothing, food, and farm equipment. And continued conflicts with Great Britain and France highlighted the nation's need to develop its natural resources and technological capabilities. Yet even though American ingenuity was widely praised, the daily lives of most Americans changed slowly. And for some, especially enslaved women and men, technological advances only added to their burdens.

Native Lands and American Migrations.
Although Democratic-Republicans initially hoped to limit the powers of the national government, the rapid growth of the United States pulled in the opposite direction. An increased population, combined with the exhaustion of farmland along the eastern seaboard, fueled migration to the West as well as the growth of cities. These developments heightened conflicts with native tribes and over slavery, but they also encouraged innovations in transportation and communication and improvements in agriculture and manufacturing.

As white Americans encroached more deeply on lands settled by native peoples, Indian tribes were forced ever westward. As early as 1800, groups like the Shoshone, who originally inhabited the Great Plains, had been forced into the Rocky Mountains by Indians moving into the plains from the Mississippi and Ohio valleys (Map 8.2). Sacagawea must have realized that the expedition she accompanied would only increase pressure on the Shoshone and other tribes as white migration escalated.

Indeed, President Jefferson ordered William Hull, Governor of Michigan Territory, to obtain Indian lands around military posts, such as Fort Detroit, to ensure American control should war erupt with Britain. Hull wrote Jefferson in December 1807, describing his meeting with native leaders, whom he addressed as "My Children." To Jefferson, Hull highlighted the economic benefits accruing to Indians; in discussions with Ottawa, Potawatomi, and other chiefs, he emphasized the military dangers created by ongoing tensions between the U.S. and Britain. Tribes would be "unmolested" if they agreed to cede lands and remain neutral in any future conflict. If they sided with the British, however, the United States would "lift the hatchet" and exterminate them. The 1807 Treaty of Detroit granted millions of acres of native land to the United States, encouraging more Americans to migrate west.

Thousands more moved to cities. Although the vast majority of Americans lived in rural areas, many young people sought job opportunities in manufacturing, skilled trades, and service work. Cities were defined at the time as places with 8,000 or more inhabitants, but New York City and Philadelphia both counted more than 100,000 residents by 1810. In New York a decade later, immigrants, most of them Irish, made up about 10 percent of the population and twice that percentage by 1825. At the same time, the number of African Americans in New York City increased to more than 10,000. Cities began to emerge along the nation's frontier as well. After the Louisiana Purchase, New Orleans became a key commercial center while western migration fueled cities like Cincinnati. Meanwhile Detroit, poised on the Canadian-U.S. border, maintained its multicultural population of French, British, American, Indian, and African American residents, the latter two groups including free and enslaved members. As the area gradually came under the authority of the nascent U.S. government, Detroit residents found themselves entangled in a complex web of laws and customs. Thus despite the supposed abolition of slavery via the Northwest Ordinance, many local enslavers managed to hold on to their human chattel even as the enslaved ran away, sued in court, and resisted in other ways. Smaller outposts further west, like Farnhamsburg (later Rock Island, Illinois), were founded by U.S. pioneers seeking trade with native communities. This post's location on the Mississippi River made it an important stop for migrants as trading posts multiplied throughout the Mississippi valley in the 1820s and

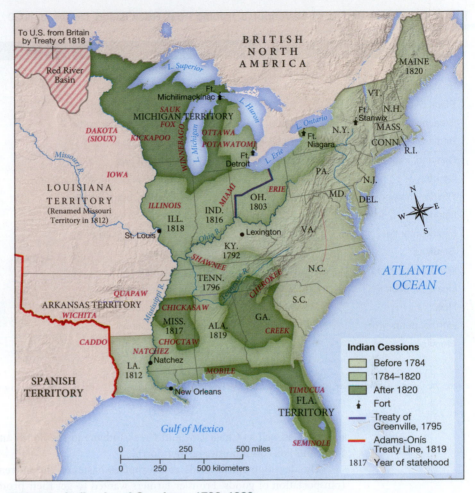

MAP 8.2   Indian Land Cessions, 1790–1820

With the ratification of the Constitution, the federal government gained greater control over Indian relations, including land cessions. At the same time, large numbers of white settlers poured into regions west of the Appalachian Mountains. The U.S. government gained most of this Indian land by purchase or treaty, but these agreements were often the consequence of military victories by the U.S. Army.

1830s. Continuing to serve as sites of exchange between Indians, French and American traders, and migrants, many created the foundation for later cities (Table 8.1).

Most Americans who headed west hoped to benefit from the increasingly liberal terms for land offered by the federal government. Yeomen farmers sought sufficient acreage to feed their families and grow some crops for sale. They were eager to settle in western sections of the original thirteen states, in the Ohio River valley, or in newly opened territories along the Missouri and Kansas Rivers. In the South, small farmers had to compete with slave-owning planters who headed west in the early nineteenth century. Migrants to the Mississippi valley also had to contend with a sizable population of Spanish and French

TABLE 8.1   Prices at George Davenport's Trading Post, Rock Island, Illinois, c. 1820

Item	Price	Item	Price
Ax	$6.00	Large copper kettle	$30.00
Beaver trap	$8.00	Lead	$0.20 per pound
Black silk handkerchief	$2.00	Lead shot for guns	$1.00 per 5 pounds
Breechcloth	$3.00	Medium copper kettle	$10.00
Bridles	$2.00–$10.00	Muskrat spear	$2.00
Chain for staking down traps	$0.75 per 6 feet	Muskrat trap	$5.00
Combs	$1.00 per pair	Muslin or calico shirt	$3.00
File (for sharpening axes)	$2.00	Ordinary butcher knife	$0.50
Flannel	$1.00 per yard	Sheet iron kettle	$10.00
Flannel mantle	$3.00	Small copper kettle	$3.00
Gunflints	$1.00 per 15	Spurs	$6.00 per pair
Hand-size mirrors	$0.25	Tin kettle	$14.00
Heavy wool cloth	$10.00 per yard	Tomahawk	$1.50
Hoe	$2.00	Trade gun	$20.00–$25.00
Horn of gunpowder	$1.50	Wool blanket	$4.00
Horses	$35.00–$50.00	Wool mantle (short cloak or shawl)	$4.00

Source: Will Leinicke, Marion Lardner, and Ferrel Anderson, *Two Nations, One Land* (Rock Island, IL: Citizens to Preserve Black Hawk Park, 1981).

residents, as well as Chickasaw and Creek Indians in the South and Shawnee, Chippewa, Sauk, and Fox communities farther north.

The development of roads and turnpikes hastened the movement of people and the transportation of goods. Frontier farmers wanted to get their produce to eastern markets quickly and cheaply. Before completion of the Lancaster Turnpike in Pennsylvania, it cost as much to carry wheat overland the sixty-two miles to Philadelphia as it did to ship it by sea from Philadelphia to London. Those who lived farther west faced even greater challenges. With the admission of Kentucky (1792), Tennessee (1796), and Ohio (1803) to the Union, demands for congressional support for building transportation routes grew louder. By 1819 five more states had been admitted along the Mississippi River, from Louisiana to Illinois.

During Jefferson's administration, secretary of the treasury Albert Gallatin urged Congress to fund roads and canals to enhance the economic development of the nation. He advocated a "great turnpike road" along the Atlantic seaboard from Maine to Georgia as well as roads to connect the four main rivers that flowed from the Appalachians to the Atlantic Ocean. Although traditionally such projects were funded by the states, in 1815 Congress approved funds for a **National Road** from western Maryland through southwestern Pennsylvania to Wheeling, West Virginia. This so-called Cumberland Road was completed in 1818 and later extended into Ohio and Illinois.

Carrying people and goods by water remained faster and cheaper than transporting them over land, but rivers ran mainly north and south. In addition, although loads could be delivered quickly downstream, the return voyage was long and slow. While politicians advocated the construction of canals along east-west routes to link river systems, inventors and mechanics focused on building boats powered by steam to overcome the problem of sending goods upriver.

In 1804 Oliver Evans, a machinist in Philadelphia, invented a high-pressure steam engine attached to a dredge that cleaned the silt around the docks in Philadelphia harbor. He had insufficient funds, however, to pursue work on a steam-powered boat. Robert Fulton, a New Yorker, improved on Evans's efforts, using the low-pressure steam engine developed in England. In 1807 Fulton launched the first successful steamboat, the *Clermont*, which traveled some 150 miles up the Hudson River from New York City to Albany in only thirty-two hours. The powerful Mississippi River proved a greater challenge, but by combining Evans's high-pressure steam engine with a flat-bottom hull that avoided the river's sandbars, mechanics who worked along the frontier improved Fulton's design and launched the steamboat era in the West.

Technology Reshapes Agriculture and Industry.

Advances in agricultural and industrial technology paralleled the development of roads and steamboats. And new inventions spurred others, inducing a **multiplier effect** that inspired additional dramatic changes. Two inventions in particular — the spinning machine and the cotton gin — transformed the deeply intertwined realms of southern agriculture and northern industry.

American developments were closely tied to the earlier rise of industry in Great Britain. Before the eighteenth century, India was the chief supplier to Europe of raw cotton and cotton cloth. As Britain gained control of crucial areas of the Indian subcontinent, notably Bengal, in the 1750s, they transformed international trade and manufacturing. The wealth gained from Bengal was used to develop British manufacturing, and by the 1770s, the English had built spinning mills in which steam-powered machines spun raw cotton into yarn. Raw cotton was imported from British-occupied India without tariffs. Cotton cloth was then exported to India, where cheaper British goods undercut homemade cloth. Eager to maintain their monopoly on industrial technology and the market in cloth, the British made it illegal for engineers to emigrate. However, officials could not stop everyone who worked in a cotton mill from leaving. At age fourteen, Samuel Slater was hired as an apprentice in an English mill that used a yarn-spinning machine designed by Richard Arkwright. Slater was promoted to supervisor of the factory but in 1789, at age twenty-one, he emigrated to America, seeking greater opportunities. While working in New York City, he learned that Moses Brown, a wealthy Rhode Island merchant, was eager to develop a machine like Arkwright's. Funded by Rhode Island investors and assisted by local craftsmen, Slater designed and built a spinning mill in Pawtucket.

The mill opened in December 1790 and began producing yarn, which was then woven into cloth in private shops and homes. By 1815 a series of cotton mills dotted the Pawtucket River. These factories offered workers, most of whom were the wives and children of farmers, a steady income, and they ensured employment for weavers in the countryside. They also increased the demand for cotton in New England just as British manufacturers sought additional sources of the crop as well.

Ensuring a steady supply of cotton required another technological innovation, this one created by Eli Whitney. After graduating from Yale, Whitney agreed to serve as a private tutor for a planter family in South Carolina. On the ship carrying him south, Whitney met the widow Catherine Greene, who invited him to stay at her Mulberry Plantation near Savannah, Georgia. There local planters complained to him about the difficulty of making a profit on cotton. Long-staple cotton, grown in the Sea Islands, yielded enormous profits, but the soil in most of the South could sustain only the short-staple variety, which required hours of intensive labor to separate its sticky green seeds from the cotton fiber.

In 1793, in as little as ten days, Eli Whitney built a machine that could speed the process of deseeding short-staple cotton. Using mesh screens, rollers, and wire brushes, Whitney's **cotton gin** could clean as much cotton fiber in one hour as several workers could clean in a day. Recognizing the gin's value, Whitney received a U.S. patent, but because the machine was easy to duplicate, he never profited from his invention. He did, however, transform southern agriculture and northern industry.

Whitney had other ideas that proved more profitable. In June 1798, amid U.S. fears of a war with France, the U.S. government granted him an extraordinary contract to produce 4,000 rifles in eighteen months. Adapting the plan of Honoré Blanc, a French mechanic who devised a musket with interchangeable parts, Whitney demonstrated the potential for using machines to produce various parts of a musket, which could then be assembled in mass quantities. With Jefferson's enthusiastic support, the federal government extended Whitney's contract, and by 1809 his New Haven factory was turning out 7,500 guns annually. Whitney's factory became a model for the **American system of manufacturing**, in which water-powered machinery and the division of production into several small tasks allowed less skilled workers to produce mass quantities of a particular item. Moreover, the factories developed by Whitney and Slater became training grounds for younger mechanics and inventors who devised improvements in machinery or set out to solve new technological puzzles. Their efforts also transformed the lives of generations of workers — enslaved and free — who planted and picked the cotton, spun the yarn, wove the cloth, and sewed the clothes that cotton gins and spinning mills made possible.

Transforming Domestic Production.

Slater and Whitney were among the most influential American inventors, but both required the assistance and collaboration of other inventors, machinists, and artisans to implement their ideas. The achievement of these enterprising individuals was seen by many Americans as part of a larger spirit of inventiveness and technological ingenuity that characterized U.S. identity. Although many Americans built on foreign ideas and models, a cascade of inventions appeared in the United States between 1790 and 1820.

Cotton gins and steam engines, steamboats and interchangeable parts, gristmills and spinning mills, clocks and woodworking lathes — each of these items and processes was improved over time and led to myriad other inventions. For instance, in 1811 Francis Cabot invented a power loom for weaving, a necessary step once spinning mills began producing more yarn than hand weavers could handle. Eventually clocks would be used to routinize the labor of workers in those mills so that they all arrived, ate lunch, and left at the same time.

Despite these rapid technological advances, the changes that occurred in the early nineteenth century were more evolutionary than revolutionary. Most political leaders and social commentators viewed gradual improvement as a blessing. For many Americans, the ideal situation consisted of either small mills scattered through the countryside or household enterprises that could supply neighbors with finer cloth, sturdier chairs, or other items that improved household comfort and productivity.

The importance of domestic manufacturing increased after passage of the Embargo Act as imports of cloth and other items fell dramatically. Small factories, like those along the Pawtucket River, increased their output, and so did ordinary housewives. Blacksmiths, carpenters, and wheelwrights busily repaired and improved the spindles, looms, and other equipment that allowed family members to produce more and better cloth from wool, flax, and cotton. These developments allowed some Americans, especially in towns and cities, to achieve a middling status between poorer laborers and wealthier elites. In this middling sector of society, new ideas about companionate marriage, which emphasized mutual obligations, may have encouraged husbands and wives to work more closely in domestic enterprises. While husbands generally carried out the heavier or more skilled parts of home manufacturing, like weaving, wives spun yarn and sewed together sections of cloth into finished goods.

At the same time, daughters, neighbors, and servants remained critical to the production of household items. In early nineteenth-century Hallowell, Maine, Martha Ballard labored alongside her daughters and a niece, producing cloth and food for domestic consumption, while she supplemented her husband's income as a surveyor by working as a midwife. Yet older forms of mutuality also continued, with neighbors sharing tools and equipment and those with specialized skills assisting neighbors in exchange for items they needed. Perhaps young couples imagined themselves embarking on more egalitarian marriages than those of their parents, but most still needed wider networks of support.

In wealthy households north and south, white servants and enslaved blacks took on a greater share of domestic labor in the late eighteenth and early nineteenth centuries. Most female servants in the North were white, young, and unmarried. Some arrived with children in tow or became pregnant on the job. Whether impregnated by consent or by force, these young women contributed to the rising rate of out-of-wedlock births following the Revolution. Meanwhile in the South, if enslaved household workers became pregnant their children added to the owner's labor supply. On larger plantations, owners increasingly assigned a few enslaved women to spin, cook, wash clothes, make candles, and wait on table. Plantation mistresses might also hire the wives of small farmers and landless laborers to spin cotton into yarn, weave yarn into cloth, and sew clothing for slaves and white children. While mistresses in both regions still engaged in household production, they expanded their roles as domestic managers.

However, most Americans at the turn of the nineteenth century continued to live on family farms, to produce or trade locally to meet their needs, and to use techniques handed down for generations. Yet by 1820 their lives, like those of wealthier Americans, were transformed by the expanding market economy, which over the next twenty years would inspire a market revolution. Gradually, more and more families would sew clothes with machine-spun thread made from cotton ginned in the American South, work their fields with newly invented cast-iron plows, and vary their diet by adding items shipped from other regions by steamboat.

Technology, Cotton, and Slaves. Some of the most dramatic technological changes occurred in agriculture, and none was more significant than the cotton gin, which led to the vast expansion of agricultural production and slavery in the South. This in turn fueled regional specialization, ensuring that residents in one area of the nation — the North, South, or West — depended on those in other areas. For instance, southern planters relied

The Cotton Gin, 1793   This colored lithograph by an anonymous American artist shows Eli Whitney's cotton gin at the center of complex transactions. Enslaved women and men haul and gin cotton. Meanwhile the planter appears to be bargaining with a cotton factor, or agent, who likely wants to purchase his crop for a northern manufacturer. Peter Newark American Pictures/Bridgeman Images

on the growing demand for cotton from northern manufacturers. At the same time, planters, merchants, manufacturers, and factory workers became more dependent on western farmers to produce grain and livestock to feed the nation. Despite their different relationships to agriculture and industry and to enslaved and free labor, Americans were increasingly bound to a **capitalist system** in which investment in and ownership of the means of production, distribution, and exchange was made and sustained primarily by private individuals and corporations rather than the government.

As cotton gins spread across the South, the system of slavery expanded into the interior of many states as well as into the lower Mississippi valley. While rice and sugar were also produced in the South, cotton quickly became the most important crop. In 1790 southern farms and plantations produced about 3,000 bales of cotton, each weighing about 300 pounds. By 1820, with the aid of the cotton gin, the South produced more than 330,000 bales annually (Table 8.2). For cotton growers, expansion meant increasing investments in cotton gins, wooden barrels, and most importantly, enslaved workers. For southern blacks, increased production meant increased burdens. Because seeds could be separated from raw

TABLE 8.2   Growth of Cotton Production in the United States, 1790–1830

Year	Production in Bales
1790	3,135
1795	16,719
1800	73,145
1805	146,290
1810	177,638
1815	208,986
1820	334,378
1825	532,915
1830	731,452

Source: Lewis Cecil Gray, *History of Agriculture in the Southern United States to 1860*, vol. 2 (Gloucester, MA: Peter Smith, 1958).

cotton with much greater efficiency, farmers could plant vastly larger quantities of the crop. Although family members, neighbors, and hired hands performed this work on small farms with no or only a few slaves, wealthy planters, with perhaps a dozen enslaved workers, took advantage of rising cotton prices in the early eighteenth century to purchase and enslave more laborers.

The dramatic increase in the amount of cotton planted and harvested each year was paralleled by a jump in the size of the enslaved population. Thus, even as northern states began to abolish the institution, albeit slowly, southern enslavers dramatically increased the number of bondsmen and women they held. In 1790 there were fewer than 700,000 enslaved persons in the United States. By 1820 there were nearly 1.5 million. Still the demand increased even faster. Despite this population increase, growing competition for field hands drove up the price of the enslaved, which roughly doubled between 1795 and 1805.

Although the international slave trade was banned in the United States in 1808, some planters smuggled in women and men from Africa and the Caribbean. Most planters, however, depended on enslaved women to bear more children, increasing the size of their labor force through natural reproduction. In addition, enslavers in the Deep South — from Georgia and the Carolinas west to Louisiana — began buying bound labor from farmers in Maryland and Virginia, where cotton and slavery were less profitable. Expanding slave markets in New Orleans and Charleston marked the continued importance of this domestic or internal slave trade as cotton moved west.

In the early nineteenth century, most white southerners believed that there was enough land to go around. And the rising price of cotton allowed small farmers to imagine they would someday be planters. Some southern Indians also placed their hopes in cotton. Cherokee and Creek Indians cultivated the crop, even purchasing enslaved blacks to increase production. Some Indian villages now welcomed ministers to their communities, hoping that embracing white culture might allow them to retain their current lands. Yet other native residents foresaw the increased pressure for land that cotton cultivation produced and organized to defend themselves from whites' invasion. Regardless of the policies adopted by

Indians, cotton and slavery expanded rapidly into Cherokee- and Creek-controlled lands in the interior of Georgia and South Carolina. And the admission of the states of Louisiana, Mississippi, and Alabama between 1812 and 1819 marked the rapid spread of southern agriculture farther west.

Enslaved men and women played critical roles in the South's geographical expansion. Without their labor, neither cotton nor sugar could have become mainstays of the South's economy. The heavy work of carving out new plantations led most planters to select young enslaved men and women to move west, breaking apart families in the process. Some enslaved people resisted their removal and, if forced to go, used their role in the labor process to limit owners' control. They resisted by working slowly, breaking tools, and feigning illness or injury. Other enslaved women and men hid out temporarily as a respite from brutal work regimes or harsh punishments. Still others ran to areas controlled by Indians, hoping for better treatment, or to regions where slavery was no longer legal.

Yet given the power and resources wielded by whites, most enslaved people had to find ways to improve their lives within the system of bondage. The end of the international slave trade helped blacks in this regard since enslavers had to depend more on natural reproduction to increase their labor supply. To ensure that the enslaved lived longer and healthier lives, planters were forced to provide better food, shelter, and clothing. Some enslaved workers gained leverage to fish, hunt, or maintain small gardens to improve their diet. With the birth of more children, southern blacks also developed more extensive kinship networks, which often allowed other family members to care for children if their parents were compelled to move west. Enslavement was still brutal, but the enslaved made small gains that improved their chances of survival.

To find release from the oppressive burdens of daily life, enslaved southerners not only joined the camp meetings and religious revivals that burned across the southern frontier in the late eighteenth and early nineteenth century but also established their own religious ceremonies. These were often held in the woods or swamps at night, away from the prying eyes of planters and overseers.

Evangelical religion, combined with revolutionary ideals promoted in the United States and Haiti, proved a potent mix, and enslavers rarely lost sight of the potential dangers this posed to the system of bondage. Outright rebellions occurred only rarely, yet victory in Haiti and Gabriel's conspiracy in Virginia reminded the enslaved and owners alike that uprisings were possible. Clearly, the power of new American identities could not be separated from the dangers embedded in the nation's oppressive racial history.

Review & Relate

▪ How did new inventions and infrastructure improvements contribute to the development of the American economy?

▪ Why did slavery expand and become more deeply entrenched in southern society in the early nineteenth century? What fears did this reinforce?

Conclusion: New Identities and New Challenges

The geographical and economic expansion that marked the period from 1790 to 1820 inspired scientific and technological advances as well as literary and artistic tributes to a distinctly American identity. For young ambitious men like Parker Cleaveland, Eli Whitney, Washington Irving, and Meriwether Lewis, the opportunities that opened in education, science, literature, and exploration offered possibilities for fame and financial success. While Whitney, Irving, and Lewis traveled widely, Cleaveland remained a professor of mathematics, mineralogy, and chemistry at Bowdoin, dying in Brunswick, Maine in 1858.

Lewis and Clark's efforts to open up the Louisiana Territory transformed the lives of many Americans. Along with the construction of roads, the invention of steamboats, and the introduction of iron plows, their Corps of Discovery opened up new lands for farming and also fueled the rise of western cities. Many white families sought fertile land, abundant wildlife, or opportunities for trade on the frontier. Yet these families often had to purchase land from speculators or compete with wealthy planters. And those who carved out farms might face Indians angered by the constant encroachment of white Americans on their lands.

New opportunities also appeared in eastern towns and cities as investors, inventors, and skilled artisans established factories and improved transportation. White women of middling or elite status could attend female academies, enter marriages based on ideals of companionship and mutual responsibilities, purchase rather than make cotton thread and cloth, and retain servants to perform the heaviest work. Yet these changes occurred gradually and unevenly. And while poorer white women might more easily find jobs in cotton mills or as servants, the pay was low and the hours long.

Transformations in white society introduced even more difficult challenges for African Americans. Despite the beginning of gradual emancipation in the North and the end of the international slave trade, slavery continued to grow. The invention of the cotton gin ensured the expansion of cotton cultivation into new areas, and many of the enslaved were forced to move west and leave family and friends behind. Enslaved women and men honed means of survival and resistance, but few could imagine a revolution like the one that took place in Haiti.

At the same time, all along the expanding U.S. frontier, American Indians faced continued pressure to leave their lands, embrace white culture, or both. In 1810 Sacagawea, Charbonneau, and their son Baptiste apparently traveled to St. Louis at the invitation of William Clark, who offered to pay for Baptiste's schooling. Sacagawea left Baptiste in Clark's care, and it is not clear whether she ever saw her son again. William Clark wrote "Se car ja we au Dead" on the cover of his cash book for 1825–1828, suggesting that she died during those years. By then, the Shoshone and Hidatsa were facing the onslaught of white settlement. They, along with Indians living in areas like Georgia, the Carolinas, and Tennessee, continued to resist U.S. expansion as they struggled to control the embattled frontier.

Indeed, the United States remained embattled throughout the early years of the republic. From 1790 to 1820, Great Britain, France, and the Barbary States of North Africa constantly challenged U.S. sovereignty from abroad while debates over slavery and conflicts over Indian lands multiplied at home. Moreover, as federal power expanded under Democratic-Republican rule, some Americans continued to worry about protecting the rights of states and of individuals. The American identities forged in the early republic would be continually tested as new challenges emerged and older conflicts intensified in the following decades.

Timeline of Events

1789	Massachusetts institutes free public elementary education
1790	Samuel Slater's spinning mill opens
1790–1820	Cotton production in the South increases from 3,000 to 330,000 bales annually
	U.S. slave population rises from 700,000 to 1.5 million
1791–1803	Haitian Revolution
1792–1809	New capital of Washington City constructed
1793	Eli Whitney invents cotton gin
1801	Judiciary Act
	U.S. forces challenge Barbary pirates
	Thousands attend camp meeting in Cane Ridge, Kentucky
1803	Louisiana Purchase
	Marbury v. Madison
1804–1806	Corps of Discovery explores Louisiana Territory and Pacific Northwest
1807	Robert Fulton launches first successful steamboat
	Embargo Act
1810	Population of New York and Philadelphia each exceeds 100,000
1817	American Colonization Society founded
1819	*McCulloch v. Maryland*
1820	Washington Irving publishes *Sketchbook*
1828	Noah Webster publishes *American Dictionary of the English Language*

Key Terms

American Colonization Society (ACS), *256*

Haitian Revolution, *259*

Louisiana Purchase, *259*

Corps of Discovery, *261*

Judiciary Act, *262*

Marbury v. Madison, 262

McCulloch v. Maryland, 263

Embargo Act, *266*

National Road, *270*

multiplier effect, *271*

cotton gin, *272*

American system of manufacturing, *272*

capitalist system, *274*

Review & Relate

1. How did developments in education, literature, and the arts contribute to the emergence of a distinctly American identity?

2. How did African Americans and American Indians contribute to and challenge the predominantly white views of American identity?

3. How did the Federalist-dominated courts and the Democratic-Republican president and Congress each contribute to the expansion of the federal government?

4. How did the purchase of the Louisiana Territory from France and international conflicts with France and Britain shape domestic issues in the late eighteenth and early nineteenth centuries?

5. How did new inventions and infrastructure improvements contribute to the development of the American economy?

6. Why did slavery expand and become more deeply entrenched in southern society in the early nineteenth century? What fears did this reinforce?

The Corps of Discovery: Paeans to Peace and Instruments of War

▶ **How did the Corps of Discovery influence relations between Indian nations and non-Indian explorers, between traders and settlers, and among Indian nations?**

From 1804 to 1806, the Corps of Discovery mapped vast regions of the West, documented plants and animals, and initiated trade relations with Indian nations. When the Corps built its winter camp at Fort Mandan in October 1804, its members hoped to develop commercial relations with local Mandan, Hidatsa, and Arikara villages. Most of these tribes had been ravaged by smallpox in the early 1780s and were now subject to raids by more powerful nations in the region. Meriwether Lewis and William Clark hoped to persuade all native tribes that peaceful relations would benefit them politically and economically. To aid negotiations, the Corps offered gifts to the indigenous leaders they encountered (Source 8.6). The Mandan, however, expected more gifts than the expedition could offer. Although Lewis and Clark assured native leaders they would benefit from future trade with and protection from the United States, the Mandan had heard such promises before and were wary of giving away vital food as winter descended (Source 8.7).

Worried about surviving the winter, Lewis and Clark finally found an unexpected item to trade with the Mandan. When their men finished building a smithy in December 1804, they discovered that natives would exchange almost any item for metal hatchets, especially those designed for battle (Sources 8.8 and 8.9).

In April the Corps moved west into present-day Idaho and traded with Shoshone leaders for horses. The Shoshone were engaged in a long and lucrative trade in horses with the Comanche, who had moved south and developed ties with the Spanish. But the Shoshone had a harder time getting guns, a concern they expressed to Lewis (Source 8.10). While Lewis and Clark advocated peace among Indian nations, one of their most desired trade items was weaponry.

Source 8.6

William Clark, Journal | October 12, 1804

As the Corps of Discovery traveled up the Missouri River from St. Louis, they stopped at Indian villages along the way to advocate peace; offer presents from President Jefferson; and learn about local plants, animals, and potential trade items. In his journal entry for October 12, Clark describes a visit to a Ricara (Arikara) village near where the Corps planned to stay for the winter.

After breakfast, we went on shore to the house of the chief of the second village named Lassel, where we found his chiefs and warriors. They made us a present of about seven bushels of corn, a pair of leggings, a twist of their tobacco, and the seeds of two different species of tobacco. The chief then delivered a speech expressive of his gratitude for the presents and the good counsels which we had given him; his intention of visiting his great father [the president of the United States] but for fear of the Sioux; and requested us to take one of the Ricara chiefs up to the Mandans and negociate a peace between the two nations. . . . After we had answered and explained the magnitude and power of the United States, the three chiefs came with

279

us to the boat. We gave them some sugar, a little salt, and a sun-glass. Two of them left us, and the chief of the third [village] . . . accompanied us to the Mandans.

[T]he Ricaras . . . were originally colonies of Pawnees, who established themselves on the Missouri. . . . From that situation, a part of the Ricaras emigrated to the neighbourhood of the Mandans, with whom they were then in alliance. The rest of the nation continued near the Chayenne [Cheyenne] till the year 1797, in the course of which, distressed by their wars with the Sioux, they joined their countrymen near the Mandans. Soon after a new war arose between the Ricaras and the Mandans, in consequence of which the former came down the river to their present position. . . .

They [the Ricara] express a disposition to keep at peace with all nations, but they are well armed with fusils [muskets], and being much under the influence of the Sioux, who exchanged the goods which they got from the British for Ricara corn, their minds are sometimes poisoned and they cannot always be depended on.

Source: William Clark Journal, October 12, 1804, *History of the Expeditions of Captains Lewis and Clark, 1804-5-6, Reprinted from the Edition of 1814, with Introduction and Index by James K. Hosmer* (Chicago: A. C. McClurg, 1902), 1:110–11, 114.

Source 8.7

Charles McKenzie | Narrative of a Fur Trader, November 1804

Charles McKenzie was a Scotsman working as a clerk for the Hudson Bay Company. He arrived with six traders at a Hidatsa village in November 1804. Over time, McKenzie adopted native dress, married a native woman, and became an advocate for native concerns. Here he recounts Lewis's frustration in his efforts to gain favor with local Indians as well as Mandan concerns about the Corps' lack of generosity.

Here we also found a party of forty Americans under the command of Captains Lewis and Clark exploring a passage by the Mississouri [Missouri] to the Pacific Ocean—they came up the River in a Boat of twenty oars accompanied by two *Peroques* [open boats or canoes]. Their fortifications for winter Quarters were already complete—they

had held a council with the Mandanes, and distributed many presents; but most of the Chiefs did not accept any thing from them. Some time after Captain Lewis with three Interpreters paid a visit to the *Gros Ventres* [Hidatsa] Village. . . . [N]ext morning he came to the village where I was—and observed to me that he was not very graciously received at the upper Village. . . .

After haranguing the Indians and explaining to them the purport of his [Lewis's] expedition to the Westward, several of them accepted clothing—but notwithstanding they could not be reconciled to like these strangers as they called them:—"Had these Whites come amongst us, Said the Chiefs, with charitable views they would have loaded their Great Boat with necessaries [trade items]. It is true they have ammunition but they prefer throwing it away idly [shooting in the air] than sparing a shot of it to a poor Mandane." . . . "Had I these White warriors in the upper plains, said the *Gros Ventres* Chief, my young men on horseback would soon do for them, as they would do for so many wolves—for, continued he, there are only two sensible men among them—the worker of Iron, and the mender of Guns."

The American Gentlemen gave flags and medals to the Chiefs on condition that they should not go to war unless the enemy attacked them in their Villages. Yet the Chief of the wolves, whose brother had been killed in the fall previous to our arrival, went soon after with a party of fifty men to revenge his death.

Source: W. Raymond Wood and Thomas D. Thiessen, eds., *Early Fur Trade on the Northern Plains: Canadian Traders among the Mandan and Hidatsa Indians, 1738–1818* (Norman: University of Oklahoma Press, 1985), 232–33.

Source 8.8

William Clark | Journal, November 18, 1804

By November 1804, the Corps had built and settled into Fort Mandan, at the convergence of the Missouri and Knife Rivers, for the winter. Lewis and Clark became increasingly aware that their trade with particular groups, like the Mandan, might shift the balance of power in the region. However given the extended journey ahead, they were limited in what goods they could give or trade with local Indians even as they sought to reassure them of U.S. support.

To-day we had a cold windy morning; the Black Cat [a Mandan chief] came to see us, and occupied us for a long time with questions on the usages [customs] of our country. He mentioned that a council had been held yesterday to deliberate on the state of their affairs. It seems that not long ago a party of Sioux fell in with some horses belonging to the Minnetarees and carried them off, but in their flight they were met by some Assiniboins, who killed the Sioux and kept the horses. A Frenchman, too, who had lived many years among the Mandans, was lately killed on his route to the British factory [trading post] on the Assiniboin . . . , all of which being discussed, the council decided that they would not resent the recent insults from the Assiniboins . . . until they had seen whether we had deceived them or not in our promises of furnishing them with arms and ammunition. They had been disappointed in their hopes of receiving them from Mr. Evans, and were afraid that we, too, like him, might tell them what was not true. We advised them to continue at peace, that supplies of every kind would no doubt arrive for them, but that time was necessary to organize the trade. The fact is that the Assiniboins treat the Mandans as the Sioux do the Ricaras; by their vicinity to the British they get all the supplies, which they withhold or give at pleasure to the remoter Indians; the consequence is that, however badly treated, the Mandans and Ricaras are very slow to retaliate lest they should lose their trade altogether.

Source: William Clark Journal, November 18, 1804, *History of the Expeditions of Captains Lewis and Clark, 1804-5-6, Reprinted from the Edition of 1814, with Introduction and Index by James K. Hosmer* (Chicago: A. C. McClurg, 1902), 1:136–37.

Source 8.9

William Clark | Journal, January 28, 1805, and Meriwether Lewis | Journal, February 1, 1805

By early 1805 it was clear to Lewis and Clark that metal goods, especially axes or hatchets, were the most valuable means of obtaining the corn and other items they needed from the Mandan and neighboring tribes. These two short entries, by Clark and then Lewis, describe both the value of the trade in hatchets to the Corps and their continued commitment to peace among Indian nations.

American Philosophical Society

28th January

Attempt to cut through the ice to get our Boat and Canoes out without success. Several Indians here wishing to get war hatchets made [image of one drawn here]. The man sick yesterday is getting well Mr. Jessome [Jessaume], our interpreter was taken very unwell this evening. Warm day.

1st February

A cold, windy day. . . . One of the Minnetaree chiefs . . . came to see us and procure a war hatchet; he also requested that we would suffer him to go to war against the Sioux and Ricaras, who had killed a Mandan some time ago; this we refused for reasons which we explained to him. He acknowledged that we were right, and promised to open his ears to our counsel.

Source: William Clark Journal, January 28, 1805, Codex C: 158 American Philosophical Society, Courtesy of the American

Philosophical Society Library; and Meriwether Lewis Journal, February 1, 1805, *History of the Expeditions of Captains Lewis and Clark, 1804-5-6, Reprinted from the Edition of 1814, with Introduction and Index by James K. Hosmer* (Chicago: A. C. McClurg, 1902), 1:168.

Source 8.10

Meriwether Lewis | Journal, August 20, 1805

The Corps was eager to encounter the Shoshone nation in hopes of getting horses and aid in crossing the mountains and the Columbia River. Sacagawea had been raised as a Shoshone, and her brother Câmeahwait was now a Shoshone chief. He and Sacagawea were shocked and excited to see each other again, and Lewis was moved by their reunion. Still, he was more interested in the relations between the Shoshone and tribes to the east as well as Spanish traders to the south.

can discover that these people are by no means friendly to the Spaniards. Their complaint is, that the Spaniards will not let them have fire arms and amunition, that they put them off by telling them that if they suffer them to have guns they will kill each other, thus leaving them defenceless and an easy prey to their bloodthirsty neighbours to the East of them, who being in possession of fire arms hunt them up and murder them without rispect to sex or age and plunder them of their horses on all occasions. They told me that to avoid their enemies who were eternally harrassing them that they were obliged to remain in the interior of these mountains at least two thirds of the year where the[y] suffered as we then saw great heardships for the want of food sometimes living for weeks without meat and only a little fish roots and berries. But this added Câmeahwait, with his ferce eyes and lank jaws grown meager for the want of food, would not be the case if we had guns, we could then live in the country of buffaloe and eat as our enimies do and not be compelled to hide ourselves in these mountains and live on roots and berries as the bear do. We do not fear our enimies when placed on an equal footing with them. I told them that the Minnetares Mandans & Recares of the Missouri had promised us to desist from making war on them & that we would indevour to find the means of making the Minnetares . . . or as they call them Pahkees desist from waging war against them also. That after our finally returning to our homes towards the rising sun whitemen would come to them with an abundance of guns and every other article necessary to their defence and comfort, and that they would be enabled to supply themselves with these articles on reasonable terms in exchange for the skins of the beaver Otter and Ermin so abundant in their country. They expressed great pleasure at this information and said they had been long anxious to see the whitemen that traded guns; and that we might rest assured of their friendship and that they would do whatever we wished them.

Source: Reuben Gold Thwaites, ed., *Original Journals of the Lewis and Clark Expedition, 1804–1808* (New York: Dodd, Mead, 1904), 383–84.

Interpret the Evidence

1. How do European traders and American explorers view the connection between trade with and peaceful relations among Indian nations (Sources 8.6 and 8.7)?
2. Describe William Clark's perspective on relations among tribes in the region (Source 8.8). Then evaluate the effects of his and Lewis's willingness to trade war hatchets for food on their desire for peace among these tribes (Sources 8.9 and 8.10)?
3. Analyze Lewis's goal in promising guns to the Shoshone when the Corps encountered Indian nations living in Spain's commercial sphere (Source 8.10)?
4. What can we learn about Indian attitudes toward European traders, American explorers, and other Indian nations from sources written by white men (Source 8.6 to 8.10)?

Put It in Context

What were the most significant problems faced by indigenous nations as more European and American explorers and traders entered the region explored by the Corps of Discovery?

Defending and Redefining the Nation

1809–1832

Window to the Past

Sequoyah's Syllabary for the Cherokee, 1821

As Cherokee contact with white Americans increased in the nineteenth century, it became clear that adopting a written language would enhance their ability to interact with U.S. traders, missionaries, and others. Sequoyah created the syllabary over two decades. Christian missionary Samuel Worcester then created this chart, which lists the syllables and their English equivalents. Both Sequoyah and Worcester then contributed significantly to translating and printing religious and other materials into Cherokee. ▶ **To learn more about this primary source, see Source 9.7 on page 314.**

North Wind Picture Library/Alamy Stock Photo

After reading this chapter you will be able to:

- Analyze the intertwined effects of conflicts on the frontier and with Britain on U.S. federal policies and the lives of white, black, and native Americans.

- Describe the role of state and federal governments in the nation's expansion and how expansion affected relations among increasingly distinct regions.

- Evaluate how the panic of 1819 and the Missouri Compromise affected and were affected by the nation's economic expansion and political divisions.

- Discuss how expanded voting rights for white working men, new racial restrictions, and continued debates over federal power led to political realignment.

- Explain the challenges that President Jackson faced in implementing federal policies on the tariff, the national bank, and the removal of the Cherokee.

Comparing American Histories

Dolley Payne was raised on a Virginia plantation. But her Quaker parents, moved by the Society of Friends' growing antislavery sentiment, decided to free their slaves. In 1783, when Dolley was fifteen, the Paynes moved to Philadelphia. There, Dolley's father suffered heavy economic losses, and Dolley lost her first husband and her younger son to yellow fever. In 1794 the young widow met and married Virginia congressman James Madison. When the newly elected president Thomas Jefferson appointed Madison secretary of state in 1801, the couple moved to the new capital city of Washington.

(*left*) **Dolley Madison** Library of Congress, Prints and Photographs Division [LC-USZ62-68175]

(*right*) **John Ross** Library of Congress, Prints and Photographs Division [LC-USZC4-3156]

Since Jefferson and his vice president, Aaron Burr, were widowers, **Dolley Madison** served as hostess for White House affairs. When James Madison succeeded Jefferson as president in 1809, he, too, depended on his wife's social skills and networks. Dolley held lively informal receptions to which she invited politicians, diplomats, cabinet officers, and their wives. These social events helped bridge the ideological differences that continued to divide Congress and proved crucial in creating a unified front when Congress declared war on Great Britain in 1812.

During the War of 1812, British forces attacked Washington City and burned the Executive Mansion, now called the White House. With the president away, his wife was left to secure important state papers, emerging as a symbol of national courage at a critical moment in the conflict. When peace came the following year, Dolley Madison quickly reestablished a busy social calendar to help mend divisions caused by the war.

In 1817, at the end of the president's second term, the Madisons left Washington just as a young trader named **John Ross** entered the political arena. Born in 1790 in the Cherokee nation, John (also known as Guwisguwi) was the son of a Scottish trader and his wife, who was both Cherokee and Scottish. John Ross was raised in an Anglo-Indian world in eastern Tennessee, where he played with Cherokee children and attended tribal events but was educated by private tutors and in Protestant missionary schools. At age twenty, Ross was appointed as a U.S. Indian agent among the Cherokee and during the War of 1812 served as an adjutant (or administrative assistant) in a Cherokee regiment.

After the war, Ross focused on business ventures in Tennessee, including the establishment of a plantation. He also became increasingly involved in Cherokee political affairs, using his bilingual skills and Protestant training to represent Indian interests to government officials. In 1819 Ross was elected president of the Cherokee legislature; and later, having moved to Georgia, he served as president of the Cherokee constitutional convention in 1827. The next year, after overseeing the first written constitution produced by an Indian nation, Ross was elected principal chief. Over the next decade, he battled to retain the Cherokee homeland against the pressures of white planters and politicians. ■

Comparing the American histories of Dolley Madison and John Ross demonstrates that, while American politics was a white man's game, it was possible for those on the political margins to influence national developments. Both Madison and Ross sought to defend and expand the democratic ideals that defined the young nation. The First Lady helped to nurture a bipartisan political culture in Washington, which was particularly important following the War of 1812. Despite the antislavery sentiments of her parents, however, she did not seem to struggle with the issue of slavery. However, that issue fueled tensions among Democratic-Republicans when the Missouri Territory sought statehood in 1819. Missouri's quest resulted from the nation's rapid geographical expansion. Its economic development proved more volatile, however, with the nation suffering its first major recession in 1819. Working men then demanded the right to vote to protect their economic interests. The Cherokee also asserted their rights. Ross encouraged Cherokees to embrace Anglo-American culture as a path to inclusion. But he could not overcome the power of planters and politicians to wrest valuable territory from his nation. President Andrew Jackson, elected in 1828, ensured Cherokee removal and supported slavery. Yet he was lauded as a democratic hero for his frontier background and promotion of working-men's rights. While the United States successfully defended itself against British intervention, Americans still could not agree on who truly belonged in the nation.

Conflicts at Home and Abroad

When Thomas Jefferson completed his second term as president in March 1809, he was succeeded by his friend and ally James Madison. Like Jefferson, Madison sought to end foreign interference in American affairs and to resolve conflicts between native and white residents on the frontier. By 1815 the United States had weathered a series of domestic and foreign crises, including another war with Britain, but American sovereignty remained fragile. At the same time, even though Madison believed in a national government with limited powers, he, like Jefferson, ultimately expanded federal authority.

Tensions at Sea and on the Frontier.
When President Madison took office, Great Britain and France remained embroiled in the Napoleonic Wars in Europe and refused to modify their policies toward American shipping or to recognize U.S. neutrality. American ships were subject to seizure by both nations, and British authorities continued to impress "deserters" into the Royal Navy. Just before Madison's inauguration in March 1809, Congress replaced the Embargo Act with the **Non-Intercourse Act**, which restricted trade with France and Britain and their colonies. Although the continued embargo against Britain encouraged U.S. manufacturing and the act allowed trade with other European nations, many Americans still opposed Congress using its power to constrain the right to trade.

In the midst of these crises, Madison also faced difficulties in the Northwest Territory. In 1794 General Anthony Wayne had won a decisive victory against a multi-tribe coalition at the **Battle of Fallen Timbers**. But this victory inspired two forceful native leaders to create a pan-Indian alliance in the Ohio River valley. The Shawnee prophet Tenskwatawa and his half-brother Tecumseh, a warrior, encouraged native peoples to resist white encroachments on their territory and to give up all aspects of white society and culture, including copper kettles, calico cloth, liquor, and other trade goods. These efforts, they believed, could create an Indian nation that stretched from the Canadian border to the Gulf of Mexico.

Indians in the upper Midwest rallied around the brothers. In 1808 Tenskwatawa and Tecumseh established the native community of Prophetstown along the Tippecanoe River in Indiana Territory. The very next year, however, territorial governor William Henry Harrison lied to several Indian leaders about U.S. intentions in the region to persuade them to sign a treaty ceding three million acres of land to the United States for only $7,600. An enraged Tecumseh dismissed the treaty, claiming the land belonged to all the Indians together. Leaving Tenskwatawa in charge, he traveled south to urge the Cherokee and Choctaw to join his alliance.

Explore ▶

Read part of Tecumseh's response to Harrison in Source 9.1.

In November 1811, in Tecumseh's absence and fearing the growing power of the Shawnee leaders, Governor Harrison attacked Prophetstown with 1,000 soldiers. With more troops and superior weapons, the U.S. army defeated the allied Indian forces, killed forty warriors, and burned Prophetstown to the ground. The rout damaged Tenskwatawa's stature as a prophet, and he and his supporters fled to Canada, where skirmishes continued along the U.S.-Canadian border. These conflicts with native tribes soon merged into a wider war with Britain.

War with Britain and Its Indian Allies.   Convinced that British officials in Canada fueled Indian resistance, many Democratic-Republicans demanded an end to British intervention on the western frontier as well as British interference in transatlantic trade. Some called for the United States to declare war. Yet merchants in the Northeast feared the commercial disruptions that war entailed. Thus New England Federalists adamantly opposed a declaration of war.

For months, Madison avoided taking a clear stand. Then in March 1811, several dozen newly elected Democratic-Republicans, including Henry Clay of Kentucky and John C. Calhoun of South Carolina, joined Congress. Known as the War Hawks, they demanded that the United States end interference from Britain in the Old Northwest Territory and stop British ships from impressing American citizens. Finally, on June 1, 1812, with diplomatic efforts exhausted, Madison sent a secret message to Congress outlining U.S. grievances against Great Britain. Within weeks, Congress declared war by sharply divided votes in the House of Representatives and the Senate.

While supporters hoped a victory would raise America's stature in Europe, the nation was ill prepared to launch a major offensive against such an imposing foe. The cost of cuts in federal spending and military resources under President Jefferson now became apparent. Jefferson, for example, reduced the U.S. navy, established under President Adams, to only six small gunboats. Democratic-Republicans had also failed to recharter the Bank of the United States when it expired in 1811, so the nation lacked a vital source of credit. Nonetheless, many in Congress believed that Britain would be too engaged by its ongoing conflict with France to attack the United States.

Meanwhile U.S. commanders devised plans to attack Canada, but the U.S. army and navy proved no match for Great Britain and its Indian allies. Instead, Tecumseh, who was appointed a brigadier general in the British army, and British troops captured Detroit in August 1812. The victory encouraged other native tribes to ally with Britain. Joint British and Indian forces then launched successful attacks on Fort Dearborn, Fort Mackinac, and other points along the U.S.-Canadian border.

Even as U.S. forces faced numerous defeats, American voters reelected James Madison as president in November 1812. Madison won most western and southern states, where the

Guided Primary Source Analysis

Tecumseh | Speech to William Henry Harrison, 1810

In 1809 William Henry Harrison, governor of the Indiana Territory, negotiated a treaty with a coalition of native leaders to cede three million acres to the United States. Angered by the treaty, Shawnee brothers Tecumseh and Tenskwatawa forged alliances with other Indian nations to resist white settlement of the region. In August 1810 Tecumseh confronted Harrison at Vincennes in the Indiana Territory and urged him to return the land. Harrison refused, and in the fall of 1811 U.S. troops attacked and defeated the Shawnees at Prophetstown.

Source 9.1

Why does Tecumseh consider white Americans untrustworthy?

How does Tecumseh's view of Indian land differ from that negotiated in the treaty?

How does Tecumseh compare U.S. actions toward Indians with Indian actions toward whites?

Brother. Since the peace was made you have kill'd some of the Shawanese, Winebagoes, Delawares, and Miamies and you have taken our lands from us, and I do not see how we can remain at peace with you if you continue to do so. You have given goods to the Kickapoos for the sale of their lands . . . which has been the cause of many deaths among them. You have promised us assistance but I do not see that you have given us any.

You try to force the red people to do some injury. It is you that is pushing them on to do mischief. You endeavor to make distinctions, you wish to prevent the Indians to do as we wish them: to unite and let them consider their land as the common property of the whole.

You take tribes aside and advise them not to come into this measure [coalition] and untill our design is accomplished we do not wish to accept of your invitation to go and visit the President.

The reason I tell you this is you want by your distinctions of Indian tribes in allotting to each a particular track of land to make them to war with each other. You never see an Indian come and endeavour to make the white people do so. You are continually driving the red people when at last you will drive them into the great Lake where they can't eather stand or work.

Source: Logan Esarey, ed., *Messages and Letters of William Henry Harrison* (Indianapolis: Indiana Historical Commission, 1922), 1:465.

■ Put It in Context

What does Tecumseh reveal about the complex relationships between American Indian nations and the U.S. government in the 1810s?

---

war was most popular, but lost in New England and New York, where Federalist opponents held sway.

After a year of fighting, U.S. forces drove the British back into Canada in 1813 (Map 9.1). A naval victory on Lake Erie led by Commodore Oliver Perry proved crucial to U.S. success. Soon after, Tecumseh was killed in battle and U.S. forces burned York (present-day Toronto). Yet just as U.S. prospects in the war improved, New England Federalists demanded retreat.

MAP 9.1 The War of 1812

Most conflicts in this war occurred in the Great Lakes region or around Washington, D.C. Yet two crucial victories occurred in the South. At Horseshoe Bend, troops under General Andrew Jackson and aided by Cherokee warriors defeated Creek allies of the British. At New Orleans, Jackson beat British forces shortly after a peace agreement was signed in Europe.

The war devastated the New England maritime trade, causing economic distress throughout the region. In 1813, state legislatures in New England withdrew their support for any invasion of "foreign British soil," and Federalists in Congress sought to block war appropriations and the deployment of local militia units into the U.S. army.

Meanwhile news arrived in March 1814 that Andrew Jackson and his Tennessee militiamen had defeated a force of Creek Indians, important allies of Tecumseh and Britain. The Creek had been fighting U.S. troops and their Cherokee allies, including John Ross, in the Mississippi Valley for ten months. At the **Battle of Horseshoe Bend**, in present-day Alabama, the combined U.S.-Cherokee forces killed eight hundred Creek warriors during the battle and the resulting retreat. Although some Americans were appalled at the slaughter, many white southerners were pleased when the Creek nation lost two-thirds of its tribal domain in the resulting treaty.

Despite such victories, the United States was no closer to winning the war. In August 1814, British ships carrying 5,000 soldiers sailed into Chesapeake Bay. They blockaded U.S. ports, launched attacks in Maryland, and marched toward Washington. As American troops retreated, Dolley Madison and an enslaved worker, Peter Jennings, gathered up government papers and valuable belongings before fleeing the White House. The redcoats then burned and sacked the capital city. U.S. troops quickly rallied, defeating the British in Maryland and expelling them from Washington and New York.

In December, as the British fleet landed thousands of troops at New Orleans, New England Federalists met secretly in Hartford, Connecticut to "deliberate upon the alarming state of public affairs." Some participants at the **Hartford Convention** called for New England states to secede from the nation. Most supported amendments to the U.S. Constitution that would eliminate the three-fifths clause, limit presidents to a single term and ensure they were elected from diverse states (ending Virginia's domination of the office),

Battle of New Orleans   On January 8, 1815, General Andrew Jackson's troops launched grapeshot and canister bombs against British forces in New Orleans in this final battle of the War of 1812. Jackson's troops included Indian allies, backcountry immigrants, and French-speaking black soldiers. This engraving by Francisco Scacki shows the slain British commander, Major General Sir Edward Pakenham, in the center foreground. Sarin Images/ Granger

A CORRECT VIEW of the BATTLE   New the City of NEW ORLEANS, on the Eighth of January 1815, Under the Command of Gen! And Jackson, Over 10,000 British Troops, in which 3 of their most distinguished Generals were killed & several wounded and upwards of 3,000 of their choicest Soldiers were killed wounded.   and made Prisoners, &c

and require a two-thirds (rather than a simple) majority vote in Congress to declare war, impose embargoes, or admit new states.

The power of Federalists to put these policies in place was never tested. Despite the increase in troops, the British were losing steam as well. Representatives of the two countries met in Ghent, Belgium in December to negotiate a peace settlement. On Christmas Eve 1814, the **Treaty of Ghent** was signed, returning to each nation the lands it controlled before the war. When news of the Hartford Convention leaked out, Federalists appeared unpatriotic to many Americans. The party never recovered, despite retaining power in a few northern states and cities.

Another post-treaty event gained a far more positive response. In January 1815, U.S. troops under General Andrew Jackson attacked and routed the British army at New Orleans. The victory cheered most Americans, who, unaware that peace had already been achieved, proclaimed Jackson a national hero.

Although the War of 1812 achieved no formal territorial gains, it did represent an important defense of U.S. sovereignty and garnered international prestige for the young nation. At the same time, Indians on the western frontier lost a powerful ally when British representatives at Ghent failed to act as advocates for their allies. Thus, in practical terms, the U.S. government gained greater control over vast expanses of land in the Ohio and Mississippi River valleys.

Review & Relate

▪ How were conflicts with Indians in the West connected to ongoing tensions between the United States and Great Britain?

▪ What were the long-term consequences of the War of 1812?

National Expansion and Regional Economies

By further expanding federal powers, the War of 1812 reinforced political changes that had been under way for more than a decade. At the Hartford Convention, Federalists who had once advocated broad national powers called for restrictions on federal authority. By contrast, Democratic-Republicans, who initially demanded restraints on federal power, now applauded its expansion. Indeed, Democratic-Republicans in Congress sought to use federal authority to settle boundary disputes in the West, make investments in transportation, and reestablish a national bank. Some state governments also invested in roads and canals. Federal power was again asserted to settle disputes with Britain and Spain over U.S. borders in the North and the South. At the same time, more secure borders and state and federal investments in transportation fueled overseas trade and the development of increasingly distinct regional economies.

Governments Fuel Economic Growth. In 1800 Thomas Jefferson captured the presidency by advocating a reduction in federal powers and a renewed emphasis on the needs of small farmers and workingmen. Once in power, however, Jefferson and his Democratic-Republican supporters faced a series of economic and political developments that led many to embrace a loose interpretation of the U.S. Constitution and support federal efforts to aid economic growth.

Population growth and commercial expansion encouraged these federal efforts. In 1811 the first steamboat traveled down the Mississippi from the Ohio River to New Orleans; over the next decade, steamboat traffic expanded. This development helped western and southern residents but hurt trade on overland routes between northeastern seaports and the Ohio River valley. The federal government began construction of the Cumberland Road in 1811 to reestablish this regional connection by linking Maryland and Ohio. Congress passed additional bills to fund ambitious federal transportation projects, but

Erie Canal, 1831   This painting by John William Hill shows the extensive need for blasting and hauling hard flinty rock along the route of the Erie Canal. Born in London, Hill moved with his parents to the United States at age 7 in 1812. Having learned engraving and aquatint skills from his father, John created landscapes and townscapes. Between 1829 and 1831, he completed a series of watercolor views of the building of the Erie Canal. Collection of the New-York Historical Society, USA/Bridgeman Images

President Madison vetoed much of this legislation, believing that it overstepped even a loose interpretation of the Constitution.

After the War of 1812, however, Democratic-Republican representative Henry Clay of Kentucky sketched out a plan to promote U.S. economic growth and advance commercial ties throughout the nation. Called the **American System**, it combined federally funded internal improvements, such as roads and canals, to aid farmers and merchants with federal tariffs to protect U.S. manufacturing. Western expansion fueled demand for these internal improvements. The non-Indian population west of the Appalachian Mountains more than doubled between 1810 and 1820, from 1,080,000 to 2,234,000. Many veterans of the War of 1812 settled there after receiving 160-acre parcels of land in the region as payment for service. These lands were largely territory taken from Britain's Indian allies. Congress admitted four new states to the Union in just four years: Indiana (1816), Mississippi (1817), Illinois (1818), and Alabama (1819). In the South, too, westward expansion depended on the dispossession of Creek and neighboring tribes.

Congress then negotiated with Indian nations to secure trade routes farther west. In the 1810s, Americans began trading along an ancient trail from Missouri to Santa Fe, a town in northern Mexico. But the trail cut across territory claimed by the Osage Indians. In 1825 Congress approved a treaty with the Osage to guarantee right of way for U.S. merchants. The Santa Fe Trail became a critical route for commerce between the United States and Mexico.

East of the Appalachian Mountains, state governments funded most internal improvement projects. The most significant of these was New York's **Erie Canal**, a 363-mile waterway stretching from the Mohawk River to Buffalo that was completed in 1825. Self-taught men directed this extraordinary engineering feat by which thousands of workers carved a swath forty feet wide and four feet deep through limestone cliffs, mountains, forests, and swamps. The canal, which rises 566 feet along its route, required the construction of 83 locks to lift and lower boats. The arduous and dangerous work was carried out mainly by Irish, Welsh, and German immigrants, many of whom settled along its route. Tolls on the Erie Canal quickly repaid the tremendous financial cost of its construction. Freight charges and shipping times plunged. And by linking western farmers to the Hudson River, the Erie Canal ensured that New York City became the nation's premier seaport (Map 9.2).

The Erie Canal's success inspired hundreds of similar projects in other states. While some of these projects failed, costing states huge sums of money, many succeeded. Canal boats carried manufactured goods from New England and the Middle Atlantic states to rural households in the Ohio River valley. They also created links across the Great Lakes. Western farmers could, thus ship agricultural products east more quickly and cheaply. Canals also linked smaller cities within Pennsylvania and Ohio, facilitating the rise of commercial and manufacturing centers like Harrisburg, Pittsburgh, and Cincinnati. Moreover, canals allowed vast quantities of coal to be transported out of the Allegheny Mountains, fueling industrial development throughout the Northeast.

Americans Expand the Nation's Borders.

In 1816, in the midst of the nation's economic resurgence, Democratic-Republican James Monroe won an easy victory in the presidential election over Rufus King, a New York Federalist. John Quincy Adams was then serving as U.S ambassador in London, sent by President Madison to improve relations with Britain and resolve ongoing problems on the frontier. He negotiated treaties that limited U.S. and British naval forces on the Great Lakes, set the U.S.-Canadian border at the

MAP 9.2   Roads and Canals to 1837

During the 1820s and 1830s, state and local governments as well as private companies built roads and canals to foster migration and commercial development. The Erie Canal, completed in 1825, was the most significant of these projects. Many other states, particularly in the Northeast and the old Northwest, sought to duplicate that canal's success over the following decade.

forty-ninth parallel, and established joint British-U.S. occupation of the Oregon Territory. In 1817 and 1818, the Senate approved these treaties, which resolved issues with Britain but further restricted Indian rights and power. By then President Monroe had recalled Adams to the United States to serve as his secretary of state.

While the U.S.-Canadian border was largely settled, Monroe harbored grave concerns about the nation's southern boundary. He sought to limit the power of Spain, which controlled Florida and vast territories in the West, and to stop Seminole Indians in Florida and Alabama from claiming lands the defeated Creeks ceded to the United States. Shifting from diplomacy to military force, the president sent General Andrew Jackson to force the Seminoles back into central Florida in 1817. He ordered Jackson to avoid direct conflict with Spanish forces for fear of igniting another war. However, in spring 1818 Jackson attacked two Spanish forts, hanged two Seminole chiefs, and executed two British citizens.

Jackson's attacks spurred outrage among Spanish and British officials and many members of Congress. The threat of conflict with Britain, Spain, and the Seminole tribe prompted President Monroe to establish the nation's first peacetime army. In the end, the British chose to ignore the execution of citizens engaged in "unauthorized" activities, while Spain decided to sell the Florida Territory to the United States. Indeed, in the **Adams-Onís Treaty** (1819), negotiated by John Quincy Adams, Spain ceded all its lands east of the Mississippi to the United States.

Success in acquiring Florida encouraged the administration to look for other opportunities to limit European influence in the Western Hemisphere. By 1822 Argentina, Chile, Peru, Colombia, and Mexico had all overthrown Spanish rule. That March, President Monroe recognized the independence of these southern neighbors, and Congress quickly established diplomatic relations with them. In his 1823 State of the Union address, President Monroe claimed that the Western Hemisphere was within the U.S. sphere of influence Although the United States did not have sufficient power to enforce what became known (in 1850) as the **Monroe Doctrine**, it declared its intention to challenge European interference in the hemisphere.

By the late 1820s, U.S. expanded its reach west and south as residents moved onto lands once belonging to Creeks and Spaniards and traded with newly independent Mexican territories. Southern whites began settling newly acquired areas of Georgia, Alabama, and Mississippi as well as Mexican-controlled lands in east Texas. At the same time, traders regularly traveled the Santa Fe Trail, and New England merchants began sending goods via clipper ships to Alta California, another Mexican territory.

Some Americans looked even farther afield. In the early nineteenth century, U.S. ships carried sea otter pelts and other Northwest coast merchandise across the Pacific, returning with Chinese porcelains and silks. In the early 1800s, the Alta California and China trades converged, expanding the reach of U.S. merchants and the demand for U.S. manufactured goods. Some Americans imagined controlling Pacific islands, especially Hawaii and Samoa.

Expanded trade routes along with wartime disruptions of European imports fueled the expansion of U.S. manufacturing, which improved opportunities for entrepreneurs and workers. By 1813 the area around Providence, Rhode Island boasted seventy-six spinning mills. Two years later, Philadelphia claimed pride of place as the nation's top industrial city, turning out glass, chemicals, metalwork, and leather goods.

Regional Economic Development.
The roads, rivers, canals, and steamboats that connected a growing nation meant that people in one region could more easily exchange the goods they produced for those they needed. This development fostered the emergence of distinct but intertwined regional economies. In the South, for instance, vast Indian land cessions, the cotton gin, and a growing enslaved population ensured the expansion of cotton cultivation just as spinning mills in New England increased the demand for raw cotton in the North.

Important changes occurred within regions as well. Soil depletion caused by the over-production of tobacco and a fall in tobacco prices in Europe made enslaved labor less valuable in the upper South. When James and Dolley Madison returned to their Virginia plantation, Montpelier, in 1817, they experienced these problems firsthand. Plantation homes in such long-settled areas had become more fashionable as they incorporated luxury goods imported from China and Europe even as the soil in the region, depleted of nutrients, limited profits and made a shift to cotton impossible. While other Virginia enslavers sold their laborers to planters farther south and west, James Madison refused to break up enslaved families who had worked his plantation for decades. Thus the Madisons were forced to reduce their standard of living.

By the 1820s, more and more southern planters carefully calculated profits and risks, and many sought to extend slavery into areas once controlled by Creeks and Spaniards. They increased production of cash crops in the area, including sugar, rice, indigo, and especially cotton. Profits from this effort then provided funds to acquire more land and more enslaved workers. Initially, these enslavers needed young men to clear land and build houses, barns, and outbuildings so they purchased bondsmen from Virginia and Maryland. They also separated families on their eastern plantations to provide young workers for newer estates

Ohio Farm and Indian Burial Ground, c. 1835–1860   American artist Charles Sullivan painted this scene in Montgomery County after moving to Ohio in the mid-1830s. It shows the diversified agriculture in this area of rolling hills and the Miamisburg Burial Mound, one of the largest conical Indian burial sites in the eastern United States. Sullivan painted native burial grounds throughout the region, some of which were later destroyed. Courtesy of the Ohio History Connection, no. Om2892_1831762_001

further west. Before the 1820s, men who traded in various goods also sold enslaved workers. After the 1820s, slave trading became a specialized occupation, one increasingly attractive to merchants north and south.

The southern cotton boom fueled economic transformations in the West and North that benefitted (mostly white) Americans across the nation. As cotton farmers and planters increased profits in the 1810s and 1820s, they purchased more grain and other agricultural goods from the Old Northwest. Towns like Cincinnati, located across the Ohio River from Kentucky, sprang up as regional centers for this growing commerce. Americans living in the Northeast increased their commercial connections with the South as well. Northern banks and merchants became deeply engaged in the southern cotton trade. They offered credit to planters, opened warehouses in cities like Savannah and Charleston, and sent agents into the countryside to bargain for cotton to be shipped north or to Europe. European countries also purchased large quantities of wheat. These regional ties both inspired and benefitted from state and federal investments in improved roads, canals, and ports.

The southern cotton boom thus helped fuel and fund northern industrial growth, a transportation revolution, and the building of larger and faster steamships and oceangoing vessels. Factory owners and merchants in New England could ship growing quantities of yarn, thread, and cloth along with shoes, tools, and leather goods to the South. Meanwhile, merchants in Philadelphia and Pittsburgh built ties to western farmers, exchanging manufactured goods for agricultural products. As importantly, in 1803 cotton became the nation's most valuable export. After 1815, with the end of the Napoleonic wars and the surge in European demand, cotton became an even more profitable export, adding to the riches of enslavers, planters, and northern merchants. Thus over time, even as America's regional economies became more distinctive, they also became increasingly interdependent.

Review & Relate

- What role did government play in early-nineteenth-century economic development?

- How and why did economic development — especially related to cotton — contribute to regional differences and shape regional ties?

Economic and Political Crises

Even as regional economies ensured economic interdependence, they inspired political differences. For instance, the growth in trade between regions led to an increase in commercial institutions, such as banks, the largest of which were established in the North. When the nation's first severe recession hit in 1819, many southern planters and midwestern farmers blamed it on the banks. In reality, falling prices for cotton and wheat abroad contributed to the recession along with banks' overextension of credit, much of it offered to southern planters and midwestern farmers who extended their reach into lands taken from the Shawnee, the Creek, and other Indian nations in the War of 1812. Whatever the cause, the interdependence of regional economies ensured that everyone suffered. Yet these economies were built on distinct forms of labor, with the South becoming increasingly dependent on enslaved labor and the North less so. When Missouri, situated between the Old Northwest Territory and expanding southern cotton lands, applied for statehood in 1819, these regional differences set off a furious national debate over slavery.

The Panic of 1819.

The **panic of 1819** resulted from the convergence of numerous economic changes and lasted far longer than its name suggests. One important factor was irresponsible banking practices in the United States and a temporary, but substantial, decline in overseas demand for American cotton and wheat. Beginning in 1816, American banks, including the newly chartered Second Bank of the United States, loaned huge sums to settlers seeking newly opened land on the southern and northern frontiers as well as merchants and manufacturers expanding their businesses. In Alabama and other states, Indian land cessions provided the financial basis for state banks to develop credit schemes that worked so long as geographical and economic expansion continued. Moreover, many loans were not backed by sufficient collateral because banks assumed that continued economic growth would ensure repayment. In the South, planters often used enslaved workers as collateral. When agricultural production in Europe revived with the end of the Napoleonic Wars, the demand for American foodstuffs dropped sharply. Farm income plummeted by roughly one-third in the late 1810s, and in the South both individual lenders and bankers discovered that the same enslaved workers had been promised to more than one borrower. The results panicked lenders and led to dire consequences for the enslaved, who found themselves traded among angry owners or ordered to move by judges, who broke up families to untangle white men's corrupt bargains.

Thus in 1818, when the directors of the Second Bank tightened the credit they provided to branch banks, this curtailment led to economic panic. Some branch banks failed immediately. Others survived by calling in loans to companies and individuals, who in turn demanded repayment from those to whom they had extended credit. But disentangling the value of Indian land cessions and the ownership of enslaved workers proved challenging as both had become enmeshed in complex financial transactions. The chain of indebtedness pushed many people to the brink of economic ruin just as factory owners cut their orders for raw materials and their workforce. Merchants, too, decreased orders for new goods. Individuals and businesses faced bankruptcy and foreclosure, and property values fell sharply.

Bankruptcies, foreclosures, unemployment, and poverty spread across the country. Cotton farmers were especially hard hit by declining exports and falling prices. Planters who had gone into debt to purchase land in Alabama and Mississippi and more enslaved workers were unable to repay these loans. Many western residents, who had invested all

Auction in Chatham Street, New York, 1820
Widespread unemployment between 1819 and 1823 resulted in evictions for thousands of families. Public auctions of the furniture, dishes, and other household goods of evicted families were held regularly in cities across the country. This depiction of an 1820 auction in New York's Chatham Square was painted by E. Didier in 1843, during the next major economic panic. Bridgeman Images

they had in new farms, lost their land or simply stopped paying their mortgages. This further strained state banks, some of which collapsed, leaving the national bank holding mortgages on vast amounts of western territory.

Many Americans viewed banks as the cause of the panic. Some states defied the Constitution and the Supreme Court by trying to tax Second Bank branches or printing state banknotes with no specie (gold or silver) to back them. Some Americans called for government relief, but there was no system to provide the kinds of assistance needed. When Congress debated how to reignite the nation's economy, regional differences quickly appeared. Northern manufacturers called for higher tariffs to protect them from foreign competition, but southern planters argued that high tariffs raised the price of manufactured goods as agricultural profits declined. Meanwhile, workingmen and small farmers feared that their economic needs were being ignored by politicians tied to bankers, planters, manufacturers, and merchants.

Although the panic dissipated for many by 1823, the prolonged economic crisis shook national confidence. Citizens became more skeptical of federal authority and more suspicious of banks, especially citizens who continued to suffer economic hardship through the 1820s. Periodic cycles of economic expansion and contraction continued to shape the U.S. economy through the 1870s.

Slavery in Missouri.

A second national crisis highlighted regional systems of labor. In February 1819 the Missouri Territory applied for statehood. New York congressman James Tallmadge Jr. proposed that Missouri be admitted only if it banned further importation of slaves and passed a gradual emancipation law. Southern congressmen blocked Tallmadge's proposals, but the northern majority in the House of Representatives then rejected Missouri's admission.

Southern politicians were outraged, claiming that since the Missouri Territory allowed slavery, so should the state of Missouri. With cotton production moving ever westward, southern congressmen wanted to ensure the availability of new lands. They also wanted to ensure the South's power in Congress. Because the northern population had grown more rapidly than that in the South, by 1819 northern politicians controlled the House of Representatives. Significant increases in the South's enslaved population did not offset this northern growth since slaves were counted as only three-fifths of a person for purposes of representation. The Senate, however, was evenly divided. If northerners could block the admission of slave states like Missouri while allowing the admission of free states, the balance of power in the Senate would also tip in the North's favor.

For southern planters, the decision on Missouri defined the future of slavery. With foreign trade in slaves outlawed since 1808, planters relied on natural increase and trading enslaved workers from older to newer areas of production to meet the demand for labor. Free blacks packed the congressional galleries in Washington to hear congressmen debate Missouri statehood, leading supporters of slavery to worry that any signs of weakness would fuel further resistance. Recent attacks on Georgia plantations by a coalition of fugitive slaves and Seminole Indians lent power to such fears.

In 1820 Representative Henry Clay of Kentucky forged a compromise that resolved the immediate issues and promised a long-term solution. Maine was to be admitted as a free state and Missouri as a slave state, thereby maintaining the balance between North and South in the U.S. Senate (Map 9.3). At the same time, Congress agreed that the southern border of Missouri — latitude 36°30' — was to serve as the boundary between slave and free states throughout the Louisiana Territory.

Explore ▶

Compare two critiques of the Missouri Compromise in Sources 9.2 and 9.3.

The **Missouri Compromise** ended the political crisis for the moment. Still, the debates made clear how quickly a disagreement over slavery could escalate into clashes that threatened the survival of the nation.

Review & Relate

■ How did regional interdependency contribute to the panic of 1819?

■ What regional divisions did the conflict over slavery in Missouri reveal?

MAP 9.3   The Missouri Compromise and Westward Expansion, 1820s

The debate over the Missouri Compromise occurred as the United States began expanding farther westward. Within a few years of its adoption, the growth of U.S. settlements in eastern Texas and increased trade with a newly independent Mexico suggested the importance of drawing a clear boundary between slave and free states.

Comparative Primary Source Analysis

Protesting the Missouri Compromise

Missouri's statehood application sparked a crisis over the future of slavery in America, and the resulting Missouri Compromise did little to ease the fears of Americans who wanted to contain its spread. Timothy Claimright and Thomas Jefferson both opposed the Missouri Compromise, but they offered different reasons for doing so. Claimright, of Brunswick, Maine, argues in this poetic broadside that his home state should not join the Union if it means inviting the admission of Missouri as a slave state. Jefferson predicts in a letter that the temporary solution of the compromise will lead only to future tragedy.

Source 9.2

Timothy Claimright | Maine Not to Be Coupled with the Missouri Question, 1820

If the South will not yield, to the West be it known,
That Maine will declare for a *King* of her own;
And *three hundred thousand* of freemen demand
The justice bestow'd on each State in the land.
Free whites of the East are not blacks of the West,
And Republican souls on this principle rest,
That if no respect to their rights can be shown,
They know how to vindicate what are their own. . . .
They are founded on freedom, humanity's right,
Ordained by God against slavery to fight.
And Heaven born liberty sooner than yield,
The whites of Missouri shall dress their own field.
We are hardy and healthy, can till our own soil,

In labour delight; make a pleasure of toil. . . .
They too lazy to work, drive slaves, whom they fear;
We school our own children, and brew our own beer.
We do a day's work and go fearless to bed;
Tho' lock'd up, they dream of slaves, whom they dread. . . .
They may boast of their blacks; we boast of our plenty,
And swear to be free, eighteen hundred and twenty. . . .
A Sister in Union admit her, as free;
To be coupled with slaves, she will never agree.

Source: Timothy Claimright, *Maine Not to Be Coupled with the Missouri Question* (Brunswick, ME, 1820), Library of Congress Ephemera Collection.

The Expansion and Limits of American Democracy

With the panic of 1819 and the debates over Missouri shaking many Americans' faith in their economic and political leaders and the frontier moving ever westward, the nation was ripe for change. Workingmen, small farmers, and frontier settlers, who had long been locked out of the electoral system by property qualifications and eastern elites, demanded the right to vote. The resulting political movement ensured voting rights for nearly all white men during the

Source 9.3

Thomas Jefferson | Letter to John Holmes, 1820

Monticello, April 22, 1820

I thank you, dear Sir, for the copy you have been so kind as to send me of the letter to your constituents on the Missouri question. It is a perfect justification to them. I had for a long time ceased to read newspapers, or pay any attention to public affairs, confident they were in good hands, and content to be a passenger in our bark [ship] to the shore from which I am not distant. But this momentous question, like a fire-bell in the night, awakened and filled me with terror. I considered it at once as the knell of the Union. It is hushed, indeed, for the moment. But this is a reprieve only, not a final sentence. A geographical line, coinciding with a marked principle, moral and political, once conceived and held up to the angry passions of men, will never be obliterated; and

every new irritation will mark it deeper and deeper. I can say, with conscious truth, that there is not a man on earth who would sacrifice more than I would to relieve us from this heavy reproach, in any *practicable* way. The cession of that kind of property [slavery], for so it is misnamed, is a bagatelle [an insignificant thing] which would not cost me a second thought, if, in that way, a general emancipation and *expatriation* could be effected; and, gradually, and with due sacrifices, I think it might be. But as it is, we have the wolf by the ears, and we can neither hold him, nor safely let him go. Justice is in one scale, and self-preservation in the other.

Source: Thomas Jefferson Randolph, ed., *Memoirs, Correspondence, and Private Papers of Thomas Jefferson* (London: Henry Colburn and Richard Bentley, 1829), 4:332.

Interpret the Evidence

1. In opposing the Missouri Compromise, how does Claimright differentiate Maine and other northern states from the slave societies of the South?

2. How does Jefferson's opposition to the Missouri Compromise differ from Claimright's and why does Jefferson believe it would exacerbate the conflict over slavery?

Put It in Context

How might supporters of the Missouri Compromise have responded to the concerns of Claimright and Jefferson?

1820s. Yet African Americans lost political and civil rights in the same period; and Indians fared poorly under the federal administrations brought to power by this expanded electorate. While some white women gained greater political influence as a result of the voting rights gained by fathers and husbands, they did not achieve independent political rights. Finally, as a wave of new voters entered the political fray, ongoing conflicts over slavery, tariffs, and the rights of Indian nations transformed party alignments.

Expanding Voting Rights. Between 1788 and 1820, the U.S. presidency was dominated by Virginia elites and after 1800 by Democratic-Republicans. With little serious

First State Election Day in Detroit, c. 1837   This painting by Thomas Mickell Burnham depicts a lively election-day crowd. However, clouds loom overhead. Stevens Thomas Mason, the successful Democratic gubernatorial candidate, appears to buy votes while drunken men fill the streets and a small African American boy begs for coins. It is possible that the Whig Party commissioned the painting after its candidate lost. Gift of Mrs. Samuel T. Carson/Bridgeman Images

political opposition at the national level, few people bothered to vote in presidential elections. Far more people engaged in political activities at the state and local levels. Many towns attracted large audiences to public celebrations on the Fourth of July and election days. Female participants sewed symbols of their partisan loyalties on their clothes and joined in parades and feasts organized by men.

The panic of 1819 increased political activity by laboring men, who were especially vulnerable to economic downturns. They now demanded the right to vote so they could hold politicians accountable. In New York State, Martin Van Buren, a rising star in the Democratic-Republican Party, led the fight to eliminate property qualifications for voting. At the state constitutional convention of 1821, the committee on suffrage argued that the only qualification for voting should be "the virtue and morality of the people." When Van Buren and the committee used the word *people*, however, they really meant white men.

Despite opposition from powerful and wealthy men, most states along the Atlantic seaboard had lowered or eliminated property qualifications on white male voters by 1825. Meanwhile states along the frontier that had joined the Union in the 1810s established universal white male suffrage from the beginning. And by 1824 three-quarters of the states (18 of 24) allowed voters, rather than state legislatures, to elect members of the Electoral College.

Yet as white workingmen gained political rights in the 1820s, democracy did not spread to other groups. Indian nations were considered sovereign entities, so native people voted in their own nations, not in U.S. elections. Moreover, tribes such as the Cherokee and the Iroquois, which had long granted women a political voice, began shifting to a male-dominated system that looked more like that of the United States. Native-born women had long been excluded from voting because of their perceived dependence on men. Among African Americans, men, too, faced growing restrictions on their political rights. No southern

Explore ▶

Examine two historians' interpretations of the expansion of voting rights in Sources 9.4 and 9.5.

legislature had ever granted blacks the right to vote, and northern states began disfranchising them as well in the 1820s. In many cases, expanded voting rights for white men went hand in hand with new restrictions on black men. In New York State, for example, the constitution of 1821, which eliminated property qualifications for white men, raised property qualifications for African American voters.

When African American men protested their disfranchisement, some northern whites spoke out on their behalf. They claimed that denying rights to men who had in no way abused the privilege of voting set "an ominous and dangerous precedent." In response, opponents of black suffrage offered explicitly racist justifications. Some argued that black voting would lead to interracial socializing, even marriage. Others feared that black voters might hold the balance of power in close elections, forcing white civic leaders to accede to their demands. Gradually, racist arguments won the day, and by 1840, 93 percent of free blacks in the North were excluded from voting.

Racist Restrictions and Racial Violence. Restrictions on voting followed other constraints on African American men and women. As early as 1790, Congress limited naturalization (the process of becoming a citizen) to white aliens, that is, immigrants. It also excluded blacks from enrolling in federal militias. In 1820 Congress authorized city officials in Washington, D.C., to adopt a separate legal code governing free and enslaved blacks. This federal legislation encouraged states, in both the North and the South, to add their own restrictions, including the segregation of public schools, transportation, and accommodations. Some northern legislatures even denied African Americans the right to settle in their state.

In addition, blacks faced mob and state-sanctioned violence across the country. In the South such violence both brutalized African Americans and inspired some to rebel, particularly in port cities that were heavily involved in the slave trade. On January 8, 1811, free and enslaved blacks of French, West Indian, and U.S. backgrounds organized a rebellion on the outskirts of New Orleans, led by Charles Deslondes, who likely came from Haiti. White Louisianans seemed preoccupied in conflicts with Spaniards on their West Florida border. As dozens of black rebels took over sugar plantations, gathered hundreds of supporters, and marched toward New Orleans, word of the revolt finally spread to whites. White enslavers, seamen, and well-armed militias from New Orleans set upon black rebels at dawn on January 10. They killed dozens and captured many more. The captives were summarily tried and executed. Their heads were displayed on tall spikes in New Orleans and along the Mississippi River as a warning to other slaves.

In 1822 officials in another port city, Charleston, South Carolina, accused Denmark Vesey, a free black, of following Haitian revolutionary Toussaint L'Ouverture and plotting a conspiracy to emancipate the city's slaves. Vesey began life enslaved in the French Caribbean. Sold to slave trader Captain Vesey, he was resold to an enslaver in Charleston but was later returned to Captain Vesey. The young black man, known as Denmark, worked onboard ship for twenty years, taking Vesey's name and traveling to many ports and learning several languages. Denmark Vesey eventually purchased his freedom and returned to Charleston, where he worked as a carpenter, joined the mixed-race but white-dominated Second Presbyterian Church in 1817, and participated in black mutual aid societies. In challenging white assumptions about black inferiority, free blacks were often considered threatening by whites. And in 1822, Vesey helped organize a secret plot to liberate slaves in the city. However, shortly before the insurrection was to begin, white authorities seized ten black men, and Vesey realized that the plot had been discovered. Vesey and thirty-four of his co-conspirators were found guilty

Comparative Secondary Source Analysis

Expanding American Democracy for Whom?

President Andrew Jackson's victory in the 1828 presidential election has been viewed by most historians as directly tied to the expansion of white male voting rights over the preceding decade. That expansion continued through the 1840s as nearly every state eliminated property requirements for white male voters. As the electorate grew, political contests became increasingly partisan and voters turned out at higher rates across the young nation. Alexander Keyssar focuses on the factors that expanded support for granting voting rights to white men without property. The Hortons highlight the ways that this supposedly democratic expansion was tied to growing racial inequities in the electorate.

Source 9.4

Alexander Keyssar | Broadening the Franchise, 2000

The much-celebrated broadening of the suffrage during the first half of the nineteenth century . . . was spawned . . . by the convergence of different factors, present in varying combinations in individual states. . . . Most fundamentally . . . all of the states that had property requirements in 1790 witnessed an increase in the number and proportion of adult males who were unable to meet those requirements. . . .

[T]he disfranchised were unable to precipitate change by themselves. When the right to vote was enlarged, it happened because some men who were already enfranchised. . . . saw themselves as having a direct interest in enlarging the electorate. One such interest was military preparedness. . . . [A]fter the War of 1812, many middle-class citizens concluded that extending the franchise to the "lower orders" would enhance their own security and help to preserve their way of life, by assuring that such

men would continue to serve in the army and the militias. . . . .

In the South, the issue had an added twist: enfranchising all white Southerners was a means of making sure that poor whites would serve in militia patrols guarding against slave rebellions. . . . [And] it would contribute to white solidarity. . . . Economic self-interest also played a role in the expansion of the franchise. . . . As territories began to organize themselves into states, inhabitants of sparsely populated regions embraced white manhood suffrage, . . . believ[ing] that a broad franchise would encourage settlement and in so doing . . . stimulate economic development. . . . After 1840, similar concerns helped to propel the alien suffrage laws. . . . Granting full political rights to immigrants appeared to be economically advantageous as well as democratic. . . .

Source: Alexander Keyssar, *The Right to Vote: The Contested History of Democracy in the United States* (New York: Basic Books, 2000) pp. 34, 35, 37, 38.

of insurrection and hanged. Although only two insurrectionists were tied to Charleston's African Methodist Episcopal Church, that center of black life was demolished.

Northern blacks also suffered from violent attacks by whites. Whites in cities across the region periodically rampaged through African American communities. Violence was often inspired by white fear over increases in the black population or immigrant anger over job competition. Both fueled white residents' outrage in Cincinnati in 1829, when attacks on black neighborhoods caused more than half of the city's black residents to flee. Many resettled in Ontario, Canada. They were joined by Philadelphia blacks after three days of rioting in August

Source 9.5

James Oliver Horton and Lois E. Horton | The Limits of Democratic Expansion, 1997

The expansion of the franchise for white men, however, was often accompanied by the restriction or elimination of the franchise for black men. . . . In 1822, Rhode Island's legislature disenfranchised blacks in that state for the first time. In New York the constitution of 1777 had guaranteed all men who could meet the property restrictions, including free blacks, the right to vote. . . . [T]hrough the early years of the nineteenth century . . . Federalists . . . foiled several attempts to institute racial restrictions. The War of 1812 was a turning point. . . . Discredited by their opposition to the war, Federalists lost control of state politics and were unable to stop Republicans . . . from limiting the black vote . . . . [B]lack males were required to . . . have more than $250 in property before they could vote. . . . As the roster of eligible white voters expanded in every state, . . . a new political grassroots style brought General Andrew Jackson to the presidency in 1828. Political parties vied for the votes of common working people, and candidates portrayed themselves as ordinary men. . . . This "age of the common man" was the age of the common white man, as black men . . . lost the franchise in many states. Party politics became a struggle between white men for the support and loyalty of other white men. Although the Jacksonians' political ideology was populist in that it attacked a somewhat vague "privilege," [it] incorporate[ed] a growing belief in white superiority and [a] distinctly racial orientation. . . .

Source: James Oliver Horton and Lois E. Horton, *In Hope of Liberty: Culture, Community and Protest Among Northern Free Blacks 1700–1860* (New York: Oxford University Press, 1997), p. 168.

Examine the Sources

1. How do Keyssar and Horton and Horton differ in their interpretation of the role of race in the expansion of voting rights in the early nineteenth century?
2. What evidence can you find in this chapter that supports Keyssar or Horton and Horton's interpretations?

Put It in Context

How do the explanations of Keyssar and Horton and Horton for changes in voting rights compare to that provided by the author of this chapter (see "Expanding Voting Rights" on pp. 299–301)?

1834. A dispute over seats on a merry-go-round led native-born and Irish mobs to tear down one church and sack another, destroy thirty black homes and several businesses, and beat dozens of black residents. Such attacks continued in northern cities throughout the 1830s.

Political Realignments. Restrictions on black political and civil rights converged with the continued decline of the Federalists. Federalist majorities in New York State had approved the gradual abolition law of 1799. In 1821 New York Federalists advocated equal rights for black and white voters as long as property qualifications limited suffrage to respectable

CLASS No. 1.

Comprises those prisoners who were found guilty and executed.

Prisoners Names.	Owners' Names.	Time of Commit.	How Disposed of.
Peter	James Poyas	June 18	
Ned	Gov. T. Bennett,	do.	Hanged on Tuesday
Rolla	do.	do	the 2d July, 1822,
Batteau	do.	do.	on Blake's lands,
Denmark Vesey	A free black man	22	near Charleston.
Jessy	Thos. Blackwood	23	
John	Elias Horry	July 5	Do. on the Lines near
Gullah Jack	Paul Pritchard	do.	Ch.; Friday July 12.
Mingo	Wm. Harth	June 21	
Lot	Forrester	27	
Joe	P. L. Jore	July 6	
Julius	Thos. Forrest	8	
Tom	Mrs. Russell	10	
Smart	Robt. Anderson	do.	
John	John Robertson	11	
Robert	do.	do.	
Adam	do.	do.	
Polydore	Mrs. Faber	do.	Hanged on the Lines
Bacchus	Benj. Hammet	do.	near Charleston,
Dick	Wm. Sims	13	on Friday, 26th
Pharaoh	— Thompson	do.	July.
Jemmy	Mrs. Clement	18	
Mauidore	Mordecai Cohen	19	
Dean	— Mitchell	do.	
Jack	Mrs. Purcell	12	
Bellisle	Est. of Jos. Yates	18	
Naphur	do.	do.	
Adam	do.	do.	
Jacob	John S. Glen	16	
Charles	John Billings	18	
Jack	N. McNeill	22	
Cæsar	Miss Smith	do.	
Jacob Stagg	Jacob Lankester	23	Do. Tues. July 30.
Tom	Wm. M. Scott	24	
William	Mrs. Garner	Aug. 2	Do. Friday, Aug. 9.

Record of Thirty-five Men Executed for Conspiring to Revolt against Their Masters   This official record of executions related to the 1822 slave conspiracy lists the name of Denmark Vesey, the only free black man accused, fifth. The enslaved men are listed next to their owners' names, including the governor of South Carolina, twenty-one other men, and six women. There were no appeals of their convictions, and the hangings took place quickly. Granger

citizens. But Federalists were losing power, and the concerns of African Americans were low on the Democratic-Republican agenda.

Struggles within the Democratic-Republican Party now turned to a large extent on the limits of federal power. Many Democratic-Republicans had come to embrace a more expansive view of federal authority and a looser interpretation of the U.S. Constitution. Others argued forcefully for a return to limited federal power and a strict construction of the Constitution. At the same time, rising young politicians—like Martin Van Buren and Andrew Jackson—joined newly enfranchised voters to seize control of the party from its longtime leaders.

The election of 1824 brought these conflicts to a head, splitting Democratic-Republicans into rival factions. By 1828 those factions coalesced into two distinct entities: the Democrats and the National Republicans. Unable to agree on a single presidential candidate in 1824, the Democratic-Republican congressional caucus fractured, backing four separate candidates: John Quincy Adams, Andrew Jackson, Henry Clay, and Secretary of the Treasury William Crawford.

As the race developed, Adams and Jackson emerged as the two strongest candidates. John Quincy Adams's stature rested on his diplomatic achievements and the reputation of his father, former president John Adams. He favored internal improvements and protective tariffs that would bolster northern industry and commerce. Jackson, who advocated limited federal power, relied largely on his fame as a war hero and Indian fighter to inspire popular support.

As a candidate who appealed to ordinary voters, Jackson held a decided edge. His supporters emphasized Jackson's humble origins, which appealed to small farmers and northern workers. Just as important, Jackson gained the support of Martin Van Buren, who also wanted to expand the political clout of the "common [white] man" and limit the reach of a central government that he insisted was becoming too powerful.

The four presidential candidates created a truly competitive race, and turnout at the polls increased significantly. Jackson won the popular vote by carrying Pennsylvania, New Jersey, the Carolinas, and much of the West and led in the Electoral College with 99 electors. But with no candidate gaining an absolute majority in the Electoral College, the Constitution called for the House of Representatives to choose the president from the three leading contenders — Jackson, Adams, and Crawford. Clay, who came in fourth, asked his supporters to back Adams, ensuring his election. Once in office, President Adams appointed Clay secretary of state. Jackson claimed that the two had engineered a "corrupt bargain," but Adams and Clay, who shared many ideas, formed a logical alliance.

Once in office, President Adams ran into vigorous opposition in Congress led by Van Buren. John C. Calhoun, a South Carolina Senator who had been elected vice president, also opposed most of Adams's policies. Van Buren argued against federal funding for internal improvements since New York State had financed the Erie Canal with its own monies. Calhoun, meanwhile, joined other southern politicians in opposing any expansion of federal power for fear it would be used to restrict the spread of slavery.

The most serious battle in Congress, however, involved tariffs. The tariff of 1816 had excluded most cheap English cotton cloth from the United States to aid New England manufacturing. In 1824 the tariff was extended to more expensive cotton and woolen cloth and to iron goods. During the presidential campaign, Adams and Clay appealed to northern voters by advocating even higher duties on these items. When Adams introduced tariff legislation that extended duties to raw materials like wool, hemp, and molasses, he gained support from both Jackson and Van Buren, who considered these tariffs beneficial to frontier farmers. Despite the opposition of Vice President Calhoun and congressmen from southeastern states, the tariff of 1828 was approved, raising duties on imports to an average of 62 percent.

The tariff of 1828, however, was Adams's only notable legislative victory. His foreign policy was also stymied by a hostile Congress. Adams thus entered the 1828 election campaign with little to show in the way of domestic or foreign achievements, and Jackson and his supporters took full advantage of the president's political vulnerability.

The Presidential Election of 1828.

The election of 1828 tested the power of the two major factions in the Democratic-Republican Party and introduced a number of innovative techniques to create enthusiasm for the opposing candidates. President Adams followed the traditional approach of "standing" for office, telling supporters, "If my country wants my services, she must ask for them." To ensure that they would ask for his services, Henry Clay campaigned widely for Adams, earning the name the "Barbecue Orator." Jackson, too, refused to run for office, but encouraged his supporters, led by Van Buren, to take his case directly to the voters. Both benefited from the expansion of cheap newspapers and other printed materials that could reach voters in small towns and villages. Rising literacy rates ensured that more voters could read these partisan views.

Van Buren managed the first truly national political campaign in U.S. history, seeking to re-create the original Democratic-Republican coalition among farmers, northern artisans, and southern planters while adding a sizable constituency of frontier voters. Calhoun aided this effort, by again running for vice president but now supporting the Tennessee war hero despite their disagreement over tariffs. Jackson's supporters organized state nominating conventions rather than relying on the congressional caucus and established local Jackson committees in critical states like Virginia and New York. Jacksonians developed a logo, the hickory leaf, based on the candidate's nickname, "Old Hickory," which symbolized strength and resilience. Enthusiastic supporters formed local Hickory Clubs across the country.

Jackson's Tennessee background, rise to wealth, and reputation as an Indian fighter ensured his popularity among southern and western voters. He also reassured southerners that he advocated "judicious" duties on imports, suggesting that he might try to lower the

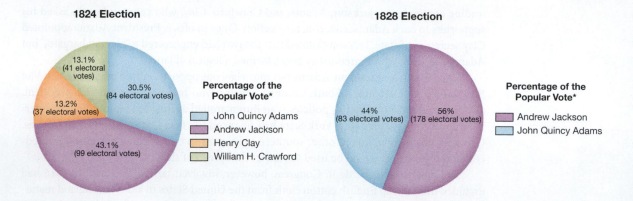

FIGURE 9.1   The Elections of 1824 and 1828

Andrew Jackson lost the 1824 election to John Quincy Adams when the decision was thrown into the House of Representatives. In 1828 Jackson launched the first popular campaign for president, mobilizing working-class white men who were newly enfranchised. Three times as many men—more than one million voters—cast ballots in 1828 than in 1824, ensuring Jackson's election as president. How did the greater number of candidates running in 1824 complicate the Electoral College system of selecting a president?

1828 rates. At the same time, his support of the tariff of 1828 and his military credentials created enthusiasm among northern workingmen and frontier farmers.

Meanwhile President Adams's advocates demeaned the "dissolute" and "rowdy" men who attended Jackson rallies. They also launched personal attacks on the candidate and his wife, Rachel. They questioned the timing of her divorce from her first husband and her remarriage to Jackson. A Cincinnati newspaper headline asked: "Ought a convicted adulteress and her paramour husband be placed in the highest offices of this free and Christian land?" Adams distanced himself from such partisan rhetoric, seeking to demonstrate his statesmanlike gentility. This strategy worked well when only men of wealth and property could vote. But with an enlarged electorate and an astonishing turnout of more than 50 percent of eligible voters, Adams's approach failed and Jackson became president (Figure 9.1).

The election of 1828 formalized a new party alignment. During the campaign Jackson and his supporters referred to themselves as "the Democracy" and forged a new national Democratic Party. In response Adams's supporters and the remaining diehard Federalists renamed themselves National Republicans. The competition between **Democrats and National Republicans** heightened interest in national politics among ordinary voters and ensured that the innovative techniques introduced in 1828 would be widely adopted in future campaigns.

Review & Relate

▪ How and why did the composition of the electorate change in the 1820s?

▪ In what ways did the 1828 presidential campaign represent a departure from earlier patterns in American politics?

Jacksonian Politics in Action

Jackson hoped to make government more responsive to the needs of white workers and frontier farmers. But the president's notion of democracy did not extend to Indians or African Americans. During his presidency, indigenous nations actively challenged his efforts to take more of their land, southern blacks continued to resist their enslavement, and growing numbers of free blacks demanded slavery's abolition. In addition, once President Jackson had to take clear positions on tariffs and other controversial issues, he could not please all of his constituents. He also confronted experienced adversaries like Henry Clay, Daniel Webster, and John Quincy Adams, who was elected to the House of Representatives from Massachusetts in 1830. The president thus faced considerable difficulty in translating popular support into public policy.

A Democratic Spirit?

On March 4, 1829, crowds of ordinary citizens came to see Jackson's inauguration. Jackson's wife, Rachel, had died of heart failure shortly after his election, leaving her husband devastated. Now Jackson, dressed in a plain black suit, walked alone to the Capitol as vast throngs of supporters waved and cheered. A somber Jackson read a brief inaugural address, took the oath of office, and then rode his horse through the crowds to the White House.

The size and enthusiasm of the crowds soon shattered the decorum of the inauguration. Author Margaret Bayard Smith reported mobs "scrambling, fighting, [and] romping" through the White House reception. Jackson was nearly crushed to death by "rabble" eager to shake his hand. Tubs of punch laced with rum, brandy, and champagne were finally placed on the lawn to draw the crowds outdoors.

While Jackson and his supporters viewed the event as a symbol of a new democratic spirit, others were less optimistic. Bayard Smith and other conservative political leaders saw echoes of the French Revolution in the unruly behavior of the masses. Supreme Court justice Joseph Story, too, feared "the reign of King 'Mob.'"

Tensions between the president and the capital's traditional leaders intensified when Jackson appointed Tennessee senator John Eaton as secretary of war. Eaton had had

President Jackson's First Inauguration, 1829   This illustration by British satirist Robert Cruikshank, entitled *President's Levee, or All Creation Going to the White House*, depicts crowds attending Jackson's inaugural reception in 1829. Washington insider Margaret Bayard Smith described the scene: "The *Majesty of the People* had disappeared, and a rabble, a mob, of boys, negros, women, children, scrambling, fighting, romping. What a pity! what a pity!" Granger an affair with a woman thought to be of questionable character and later married her. When Jackson announced his plans to appoint Eaton to his cabinet, congressional leaders urged him to reconsider. The president appointed Eaton anyway, but the wives of Washington's leading politicians snubbed Mrs. Eaton. In a sign of women's growing influence in Washington, Jackson was eventually forced to ask Eaton to resign in what became known as the **Petticoat Affair**.

In the aftermath of Eaton's resignation, Jackson asked his entire cabinet to resign so he could begin anew. Afterward, however, his legislative agenda stalled in Congress, and National Republicans regained the momentum they had lost with Adams's defeat. The Petticoat Affair reinforced concerns that the president wielded his authority to reward friends, as did his reliance on an informal group of advisers, known as the Kitchen Cabinet. While his administration opened up government posts to a wider range of individuals, ensuring more democratic access, Jackson often selected appointees based on personal ties. He believed that "to the victor goes the spoils," and the resulting **spoils system** — continued by future administrations — assigned some federal posts as gifts for partisan loyalty rather than as jobs that required experience or expertise.

Confrontations over Tariffs and the Bank.

The Democratic Party that emerged in the late 1820s was built on an unstable foundation. The coalition that formed around Jackson included northern workers who benefited from high tariffs as well as southern farmers and planters who did not. It brought together western voters who sought federal support for internal improvements and strict constructionists who believed such expenditures were unconstitutional. In nearly every legislative battle, then, decisiveness aroused conflict. In 1830 Congress passed four internal improvement bills with strong support from National Republicans. Jackson vetoed each one, which pleased his southern constituency but not his frontier supporters.

Southern congressmen, however, were more interested in his stand on tariffs. The tariff of 1828 enraged many southern planters and politicians, but most believed that once Jackson reached the White House, he would reverse course and reduce this **Tariff of Abominations**. Instead, he avoided the issue, and southern agriculture continued to suffer. Agricultural productivity in Virginia and other states of the Old South was already declining from soil exhaustion while prices for cotton and rice had not fully recovered after the panic of 1819. At the same time, southerners paid higher prices on many goods because of high tariffs.

Even as Calhoun campaigned with Jackson in 1828, the South Carolinian developed a philosophical argument to negate the effects of high tariffs on his state. In *The South Carolina Exposition and Protest*, published anonymously in 1828, Calhoun argued that states should have the ultimate power to determine the constitutionality of laws passed by Congress. When Jackson, after taking office, realized that his vice president advocated **nullification** — the right of individual states to declare individual laws void within their borders — it further damaged their relationship, which was already frayed by the Eaton affair.

When Congress debated the tariff issue in 1830, South Carolina senator Robert Hayne defended nullification. Claiming that the North intended to crush the South economically, he argued that only the right of states to nullify federal legislation could protect southern society. In response, Massachusetts senator Daniel Webster denounced nullification and the states' rights doctrine on which it was built. Jackson further antagonized southern political leaders by supporting Webster's position.

Matters worsened in 1832 when Congress confirmed the high duties set four years earlier. In response South Carolina held a special convention that approved an Ordinance of Nullification. It stated that duties on imports would not be collected in the state after February 1, 1833, and threatened secession if federal authorities tried to collect them.

The tariff crisis escalated in the fall of 1832 just as Jackson faced reelection. The tariff debates had angered many southerners, and Calhoun refused to run again as his vice president. Fortunately for Jackson, opponents in Congress had provided him with another issue that could unite his supporters and highlight his commitment to ordinary citizens: the renewal of the charter of the Bank of the United States.

Clay and Webster persuaded Nicholas Biddle, head of the bank, to request an early re-chartering of the bank. Jackson's opponents in Congress knew they had the votes to pass a new charter in the summer of 1832, and they hoped Jackson would veto the bill and thereby split the Democratic Party just before the fall elections. The Second Bank was a political quagmire. The bank had stabilized the economy during the 1820s by regularly demanding specie (gold or silver) payments from state-chartered banks. This kept those banks from issuing too much paper money and thereby prevented inflation and higher prices. This tight-money policy also kept banks from expanding too rapidly in the western states. Most financial elites applauded the bank's efforts, but its policies aroused hostility in the wider public. When state-chartered banks closed because of lack of specie, ordinary Americans were often stuck with worthless paper money. Tight-money policies also made it more difficult for individuals to get credit to purchase land, homes, or farm equipment.

As the president's opponents had hoped, Congress approved the new charter, and Jackson vetoed it. Yet rather than dividing the Democrats, Jackson's veto gained enormous support from voters across the country. In justifying his action, the president cast the Second Bank as a "monster" that was "dangerous to the liberties of the people" — particularly farmers, mechanics, and laborers — while promoting "the advancement of the few." Jackson also noted that since wealthy Britons owned substantial shares of the bank's stock, national pride demanded ending the Second Bank's reign over the U.S. economy. Jackson rode the enthusiasm for his bank veto to reelection over National Republican candidate Henry Clay. Within a year, the Second Bank was dead, deprived of government deposits by Jackson.

Soon after his reelection, however, the president faced a grave political crisis related to the tariff issue. Jackson now supported lower tariffs, but he was adamant in his opposition to nullification. In early 1833, he persuaded Congress to pass a Force Bill, which gave him authority to use the military to enforce national laws in South Carolina. At the same time, Jackson made clear that he would work with Congress to reduce tariffs, allowing South Carolina to rescind its nullification ordinance without losing face. Open conflict was averted, but the question of nullification was not resolved.

Contesting Indian Removal.

On another long-standing issue — the acquisition of Indian land — Jackson gained the support of white southerners and most frontier settlers. Yet not all Americans agreed with his effort to force southern Indians off their lands. In the 1820s nations like the Cherokee gained the support of Protestant missionaries who hoped to "civilize" Indians by converting them to Christianity and "American" ways. In 1819 Congress had granted Protestant groups federal funds to advance these goals. Jackson, however, criticized such efforts and sided with political leaders who sought to force Cherokee and other native tribes to accept homelands west of the Mississippi River. **See Primary Source Project 9: The Cherokee Engage White America, page 313.**

In 1825, three years before Jackson was elected president, Creek Indians in Georgia and Alabama were forcibly removed to the Unorganized Territory (previously part of Arkansas Territory and later called Indian Territory) based on a fraudulent treaty. Jackson supported this policy. When he became president, politicians and settlers in Georgia, Florida, the Carolinas, and Illinois demanded federal assistance to force remaining native communities out of their states.

Powerful nations, such as the Cherokee, vehemently protested their removal. The Cherokee had fought alongside Jackson at Horseshoe Bend in 1814. Thirteen years later, they adopted a republican form of government based on the U.S. Constitution. John Ross served as the president of the Cherokee constitutional convention in 1827 and a year later was elected principal chief. He and the other chiefs then declared themselves a sovereign nation within the borders of the United States. The Georgia legislature rejected Cherokee claims of independence and argued that Indians were simply guests of the state, a position that gained added significance when gold was discovered in Cherokee territory in 1829. Ross appealed to Jackson to recognize Cherokee sovereignty, but the president was affronted by what he saw as a challenge to his authority. He urged Congress to pass the **Indian Removal Act** in 1830, by which the Cherokee and other Indian nations would be forced to exchange their lands in the Southeast for a "clear title forever" on territory west of the Mississippi River. While some Cherokee leaders accepted removal and gave up their lands, the majority of Cherokees refused to accept these terms.

As the dispute between the Cherokee nation and Georgia unfolded, Jackson made clear his intention to implement the Indian Removal Act. In 1832 he sent federal troops into western Illinois to force Sauk and Fox peoples to move farther west. Instead, whole villages, led by Chief Black Hawk, fled to the Wisconsin Territory. Black Hawk and a thousand warriors confronted U.S. troops at Bad Axe, but the Sauk and Fox warriors were decimated in a brutal daylong battle. The survivors were forced to move west. Meanwhile the Seminole Indians prepared to go to war to protect their territory, while John Ross pursued legal means to resist removal through state and federal courts. The contest for Indian lands continued well past Jackson's presidency, but the president's desire to force indigenous nations westward would ultimately prevail.

Review & Relate

- What did President Jackson's response to the Eaton affair and Indian removal reveal about his vision of democracy?

- Which of Jackson's policies benefited or antagonized which groups of southerners?

Conclusion: The Nation Faces New Challenges

From the 1810s through the early 1830s, the United States was buffeted by a series of crises. Although early in the period geographical expansion and economic growth convinced the federal government to invest in internal improvements, the War of 1812 soon threatened the nation's stability and revealed significant regional divisions. The panic of 1819 then threw the nation into economic turmoil and led to demands for expanded voting rights for white men, while African American men experienced increased restrictions on their political participation. Regional differences rooted in different natural resources and economic priorities — manufacturing in the North, cotton and rice cultivation in the South, and family agriculture in the Midwest — were increasing in the 1810s. They led to greater interdependence across regions, but distinct economic needs and uncertainties intensified political debates over issues like tariffs. The admission of Missouri similarly heightened debates over slavery as white southerners saw themselves losing out to the North in population growth and political representation. At the same time, continued western expansion escalated conflicts with a diverse array of Indian nations.

In navigating these difficult issues, some Americans sought to find a middle ground. Dolley Madison worked to overcome partisan divisions through social networking. After the death of her husband, James, in 1836, she returned to Washington and transformed her home into a center of elite social life. Although her son's mismanagement of Montpelier forced her to sell the beloved estate, Dolley secured her old age when Congress purchased President James Madison's papers from her. Similarly, John Ross wielded his biracial heritage to seek rights for the Cherokee within a white-dominated world. Yet even as he served as a lobbyist for Cherokee interests in Washington, he also advocated acculturation to Anglo-American ways among the Cherokee. However, congressional passage of the Indian Removal Act challenged Ross's efforts to maintain his tribe's sovereignty and homeland. Henry Clay, too, was widely known for helping to forge compromises on issues like slavery and tariffs. In the 1820s, he brought a deeply divided Congress together, hoping that political leaders could eventually develop permanent solutions.

Despite the efforts of Madison, Ross, Clay, and others, differences often led to division in the 1820s and 1830s. Indeed, Clay's success in ensuring John Quincy Adams's selection as president in 1824 only furthered partisan divisions, leading to the emergence of two distinct political parties: the Democrats and the National Republicans. Andrew Jackson, who led the new Democratic Party, helped transform the process of political campaigning. He gave voice to white workers and frontier farmers, for example, by shutting the Second Bank of the United States. But he also introduced the spoils system to government and forced thousands of Indians off their lands. Indian removal, in turn, fostered the expansion of slavery southward and westward, which ensured future federal and sectional crises.

Dolley Madison, who lived into the late 1840s, and John Ross, who survived the Civil War, observed the continuing conflicts created by geographical expansion and partisan agendas. Ross, however, faced much more difficult circumstances as the Cherokee nation divided over whether to accept removal, facing internal dissent and pressure from the federal government for years.

Despite the dramatically different backgrounds and careers of Madison and Ross, both worked to bridge differences in the young nation, and both defended it against attack. Ultimately, however, neither had the power to overcome the partisan rivalries and economic crises that shaped the young nation or to halt the rising social, economic, and political tensions that would plague Americans in the decades to come.

chapter 9 review

Timeline of Events

1809	Non-Intercourse Act
1811	First steamboat travels down the Mississippi
	William Henry Harrison defeats Shawnees at Prophetstown
June 1812	War of 1812 begins
1814	Hartford Convention
March 1814	Battle of Horseshoe Bend
August 1814	British burn Washington City
December 1814	Treaty of Ghent
1815	Battle of New Orleans
1817–1818	Andrew Jackson fights Spanish and Seminole forces in Florida
1818	Great Britain and United States agree to joint occupation of Oregon Territory
1819	Adams-Onís Treaty
1819–1823	Panic of 1819
1820	Missouri Compromise
1821	White traders begin using Santa Fe Trail
1822	Denmark Vesey organizes a slave rebellion
1823	Monroe Doctrine proclaimed
1825	Erie Canal completed
1828	Tariff of 1828 (Tariff of Abominations)
	John Ross elected principal chief of the Cherokee nation
1829	Petticoat Affair
1830	Indian Removal Act
1832	South Carolina passes Ordinance of Nullification
1833	Force Bill

Key Terms

Non-Intercourse Act, *285*

Battle of Fallen Timbers, *285*

Battle of Horseshoe Bend, *288*

Hartford Convention, *288*

Treaty of Ghent, *289*

American System, *291*

Erie Canal, *291*

Adams-Onís Treaty, *292*

Monroe Doctrine, *293*

panic of 1819, *295*

Missouri Compromise, *297*

Democrats and National Republicans, *306*

Petticoat Affair, *308*

spoils system, *308*

Tariff of Abominations, *308*

nullification, *308*

Indian Removal Act, *310*

Review & Relate

1. How were conflicts with Indians in the West connected to ongoing tensions between the United States and Great Britain?

2. What were the long-term consequences of the War of 1812?

3. What role did government play in early-nineteenth-century economic development?

4. How and why did economic development — especially related to cotton — contribute to regional differences and shape regional ties?

5. How did regional interdependency contribute to the panic of 1819?

6. What regional divisions did the conflict over slavery in Missouri reveal?

7. How and why did the composition of the electorate change in the 1820s?

8. In what ways did the 1828 Presidential campaign represent a departure from earlier patterns in American politics?

9. What did President Jackson's response to the Eaton affair and Indian removal reveal about his vision of democracy?

10. Which of Jackson's policies benefited or antagonized which groups of southerners?

The Cherokee Engage White America

▶ **How did white Americans seek to transform Cherokee society and culture in the early 1800s, and how did Cherokee men, women and children respond to these efforts?**

By the early 1800s, decades of warfare, the collapse of the deerskin trade, and the signing of peace treaties with the United States led to dramatic transformations in Cherokee society. Still, most Cherokee sought to maintain traditional customs while benefitting from aspects of Anglo-American culture. Indeed, some Cherokee women had married British loyalists or Scottish traders in the 1780s and 1790s. Then in 1821, Sequoyah created the Cherokee Syllabary (Source 9.7). This first written form of the Cherokee language allowed writing and printing to flourish.

Other changes led to more complicated consequences. Traditionally, Cherokee were matrilineal, with goods and lineage passing through the mother's line. In general, women farmed while men hunted and made war. In the 1790s, when the U.S. government developed a "civilization" program, federal agents encouraged Cherokee men to take up farming and Cherokee women to retreat to domesticity. The U.S. government also urged Cherokee men to establish a National Council to address major issues, such as treaties. Under a matrilineal system, women retained authority in local and tribal decisions. Slowly, however, the Cherokee moved toward a patrilineal system whereby men gained economic and political power.

In 1818, women petitioned the National Council about their concerns (Source 9.6). Nine years later, the Council approved a Constitution that enshrined national over local authority and an all-male electorate. The Constitution revealed the importance of another

U.S. institution to Cherokee society — African American slavery (Source 9.8).

Christian missionaries also transformed Cherokee life. The federal government subsidized missionaries who advanced its "civilizing" policies. Wealthier Cherokee parents and women married to Anglo-American men sent children, including girls, to mission schools (Source 9.9). Eventually, some missionaries and many northern evangelical women sympathized with the Cherokee and criticized U.S. policies.

By the 1830s, with President Andrew Jackson demanding removal, a minority of Cherokee leaders negotiated the New Echota Treaty with the U.S. treaty commissioner. Most Cherokees opposed the treaty, but the U.S. Senate ratified it in 1836. John Ross, the principal chief, then published a protest explaining why the remaining Cherokee refused to move west (Source 9.10). When President Jackson left the White House in March 1837, the issue was still unresolved.

Source 9.6

Women's Petition to the Cherokee National Council, June 30, 1818

By the 1810s, Cherokee women had gradually lost traditional economic and political rights. They still met in women's councils, however, organized by elders, including Nancy Ward, who had rallied warriors after her husband's death in battle in 1755. In 1817 and 1818, the women petitioned the National Council as it considered ceding more land to the United States. In the 1830s, native women again petitioned the Council as their northern evangelical supporters petitioned the U.S. government against Cherokee removal.

Beloved Children,

We have called a meeting among ourselves to consult on the different points now before the council, relating to our national affairs. We have heard with painful feelings that the bounds of the land we now possess are to be drawn into very narrow limits. The land was given to us by the Great Spirit above as our common rights, to raise our children upon, & to make support for our rising generations. We therefore humbly petition our beloved children, the head men & warriors, to hold out to the last in support of our common rights, as the Cherokee nation have been the first settlers of this land; we therefore claim the right of the soil. . . . .

Our Father the President advised us to become farmers, to manufacture our own clothes, & to have our children instructed. To this advice we have attended in every thing as far as we were able. Now the thought of being compelled to remove to the other side of the Mississippi is dreadful to us, because it appears to us that we, by this removal, shall be brought to a savage state again, for we have . . . become too much enlightened to throw aside the privileges of a civilized life.

We therefore unanimously join in our meeting to hold our country in common as hitherto.

Some of our children have become Christians. We have missionary schools among us. . . . We have become civilized & enlightened, & are in hopes that in a few years our nation will be prepared for instruction in other branches of sciences & arts, which are both useful & necessary in civilized society.

There are some white men among us who have been raised in this country from their youth, are connected with us by marriage, & have considerable families, who are very active in encouraging the emigration of our nation. These ought to be our truest friends but prove our worst enemies. They seem only to be concerned how to increase their riches, but do not care what becomes of our Nation, nor even of their own wives and children.

Source: Theda Perdue and Michael D. Green, *The Cherokee Removal: A Brief History with Documents,* 2nd ed. (Bedford, 2005), p. 132.

Source 9.7

Sequoyah's Cherokee Syllabary, 1821

Sequoyah was born to a Cherokee mother in the 1770s. His father was likely Scottish or German. Known for his agile intellect, he worked on creating a writing system for the Cherokee language from about 1809 to 1821. He eventually created a character for each syllable. Once his syllabary was introduced to the Cherokee people, it became enormously popular. A majority of Cherokees quickly learned to use the new system. The *Cherokee Phoenix*, launched in 1828, was the first newspaper published in a native language.

North Wind Picture Library/Alamy Stock Photo

Source 9.8

Cherokee Constitution, 1827

Created in 1827 by the National Council, the Constitution mirrored the U.S. Constitution in many ways. The men who wrote the Cherokee Constitution, led by John Ross, were committed to protecting their nation's sovereignty. They were on average more literate, wealthier, and more likely to be Christian than Cherokees as a whole. Several men, including James and Joseph Vann, owned some of the almost 1,500 enslaved workers that labored in Cherokee fields and households.

We, the representatives of the people of the Cherokee Nation in Convention assembled, in order to establish justice, ensure tranquility, promote our common welfare, and secure to ourselves and our posterity, the blessing of liberty . . . do ordain and establish this Constitution for the Government of the Cherokee Nation. . . .

Article III, Sec 1. The power of this Government shall be divided into three distinct departments; the Legislative, the Executive, and Judicial. . . .

Sec. 4. No person shall be eligible for a seat in the General Council, but a free Cherokee male citizen, who shall have attained to the age of twenty-five years. The descendants of Cherokee men by all free women, except the African race, whose parents may have been living together as man and wife, according to the customs and laws of this Nation, shall be entitled to all the rights and privileges of this Nation, as well as the posterity of Cherokee women by all free men. No person who is of negro or mulatto heritage, either by the father or mother side, shall be eligible to hold any office of profit, honor or trust under this Government. . . .

Sec. 7. All free male citizens, (excepting negroes and descendants of white and Indian men by negro women who may have been set free,) who shall have attained to the age of eighteen years, shall be equally entitled to vote at all public elections.

Source: Theda Perdue and Michael D. Green, *The Cherokee Removal: A Brief History with Documents*, 2nd ed. (Bedford, 2005), pp. 60–62.

Source 9.9

Nancy Reece | Letter to Reverend Fayette Shepherd, December 25, 1828

One of the most successful schools for Cherokee children was established at the Brainerd Mission, located in present-day Chattanooga. The American Board of Commissioners for Foreign Missions ran the school and sent Presbyterian and Congregational missionaries as teachers. Those missionaries encouraged students to write letters to their benefactors, mainly ministers and northern evangelicals whose donations supported the mission. Nancy Reece was likely the daughter of William Reece, who owned a 30-acre farm, three houses, and a ferry boat.

I will tell you something of our happy school, so you may know how we shall feel if we should be separated from each other, and from our teachers and other missionaries. Miss Ames has twenty-nine scholars [and] one more is expected which will make the school full. The studies in our school are Reading, Spelling, Writing, Geography, Arithmetick, two have begun to study grammar. Eight new scholars have entered school this year. Part of them cannot talk english, and Miss Ames is obliged to have me interpret for her. I have a class of the younger children in Sabbath School. . . . [T]hose children who do not speak english . . . do not [understand the sermon] but when my father comes on sabbath days he talks in Cherokee. . . .

When school hours are over, the girls attend to domestick concerns and learn to make their own clothes and the clothes of the boys so they can do such work when they go home, to assist their parents. They can then take care of their houses and their brothers and sisters and perhaps can learn their parents something that they do not understand. . . .

The boys chop wood and in the summer help about the farm and some have left school are learning the black smiths trade. Miss Sargent goes into their school room evenings to teach them. . . .

I do not think that all the people are friends to the Cherokees. Miss Ames has been reading a part of the [newly-elected] Presid[ent's] message. Perhaps he does not like the laws of the Indian tribes for he says "This state of things requires that a remedy should be provided." Miss Ames has been talking to the scholars and she felt bad and told them that they must get a good education soon as they can, so they can teach if they should be removed where they cannot attend school and say that we try to get religion for all the instructors ought to be christians. It seems it will be a trying season to us and the missionaries if we should be separated from them. . . . I have been talking to the children about it and one says "if the white people want more land let them go back to the country they came from," another says, "they have got more land than they can use, what do they want to get ours for?"

Source: Theda Perdue and Michael D. Green, *The Cherokee Removal: A Brief History with Documents*, 2nd ed. (Bedford, 2005), 49–50.

Source: Theda Perdue and Michael D. Green, *The Cherokee Removal: A Brief History with Documents*, 2nd ed. (Bedford, 2005), 49–50.

Source 9.10

John Ross | *On the Treaty of New Echota*, 1836

In the Treaty of New Echota, the Cherokee Indians relinquished their claims to their land east of the Mississippi River, apparently clearing the way for their removal westward. But did the Treaty Party, the group of Cherokees who negotiated the treaty with the U.S. government, possess the authority to make such a deal? Cherokee Chief John Ross outlines his opposition to removal and illuminates the political fissures that had occurred among the Cherokee Indians.

It is well known that for a number of years past we have been harassed by a series of vexations, which it is deemed unnecessary to recite in detail, but the evidence of which our delegation will be prepared to furnish. With a view to bringing our troubles to a close, a delegation was appointed on the 23rd of October, 1835, by the General Council of the nation, clothed with full powers to enter into arrangements with the Government of the United States, for the final adjustment of all our existing difficulties. The delegation failing to effect an arrangement with the United States commissioner, then in the nation, proceeded, agreeably to their instructions in that case, to Washington City, for the purpose of negotiating a treaty with the authorities of the United States.

After the departure of the Delegation, a contract was made by the Rev. John F. Schermerhorn, and certain individual Cherokees, purporting to be a "treaty, concluded at New Echota, in the State of Georgia, on the 29th day of December, 1835, by General William Carroll and John F. Schermerhorn, commissioners on the part of the United States, and the chiefs, headmen, and people of the Cherokee tribes of Indians." A spurious Delegation, in violation of a special injunction of the general council of the nation, proceeded to Washington City with this pretended treaty, and by false and fraudulent representations supplanted in the favor of the Government the legal and accredited Delegation of the Cherokee people, and obtained for this instrument, after making important alterations in its provisions, the recognition of the United States Government. And now it is presented to us as a treaty, ratified by the Senate, and approved by the President [Andrew Jackson], and our acquiescence in its requirements demanded, under the sanction of the displeasure of the United States, and the threat of summary compulsion, in case of refusal. It comes to us, not through our legitimate authorities, the known and usual medium of communication between the Government of the United States and our nation, but through the agency of a complication of powers, civil and military.

By the stipulations of this instrument, we are despoiled of our private possessions, the indefeasible property of individuals. We are stripped of every attribute of freedom and eligibility for legal self-defence. Our property may be plundered before our eyes; violence may be committed on our persons; even our lives may be taken away, and there is none to regard our complaints. We are denationalized; we are disfranchised. We are deprived of membership in the human family! We have neither land nor home, nor resting place that can be called our own. And this is effected by the provisions of a compact which assumes the venerated, the sacred appellation of treaty.

We are overwhelmed! Our hearts are sickened, our utterance is paralized, when we reflect on the condition in which we are placed, by the audacious practices of unprincipled men, who have managed their stratagems with so much dexterity as to impose on the Government of the United States, in the face of our earnest, solemn, and reiterated protestations.

The instrument in question is not the act of our Nation; we are not parties to its covenants; it has not received the sanction of our people. The makers of it sustain no office nor appointment in our Nation, under the designation of Chiefs, Head men, or any other title, by which they hold, or could acquire, authority to assume the reins of Government, and to make bargain and sale of our rights, our possessions, and our common country. And we are constrained solemnly to declare, that we cannot but contemplate the enforcement of the stipulations of this instrument on us, against our consent, as an act of injustice and oppression, which, we are well persuaded, can never knowingly be countenanced by the Government and people of the United States; nor can we believe it to be the design of these honorable and highminded individuals, who stand at the head of the Govt., to bind a whole Nation, by the acts of a few unauthorized individuals. And, therefore, we, the parties to be affected by the result, appeal with confidence to the justice, the magnanimity, the compassion, of your honorable bodies, against the enforcement, on us, of the provisions of a compact, in the formation of which we have had no agency.

In truth, our cause is your own; it is the cause of liberty and of justice; it is based upon your own principles, which we have learned from yourselves; for we have gloried to count your [George] Washington and your [Thomas] Jefferson our great teachers; we have read their communications to us with veneration; we have practised their precepts with success. And the result is manifest.

The wildness of the forest has given place to comfortable dwellings and cultivated fields, stocked with the various domestic animals. Mental culture, industrious habits, and domestic enjoyments, have succeeded the rudeness of the savage state.

We have learned your religion also. We have read your Sacred books. Hundreds of our people have embraced their doctrines, practised the virtues they teach, cherished the hopes they awaken, and rejoiced in the consolations which they afford. To the spirit of your institutions, and your religion, which has been imbibed by our community, is mainly to be ascribed that patient endurance which has characterized the conduct of our people, under the laceration of their keenest woes. For assuredly, we are not ignorant of our condition; we are not insensible to our sufferings. We feel them! we groan under their pressure! And anticipation crowds our breasts with sorrows yet to come. We are, indeed, an afflicted people! Our spirits are subdued! Despair has well nigh seized upon our energies! But we speak to the representatives of a Christian country; the friends of justice; the patrons of the oppressed. And our hopes revive, and our prospects brighten, as we indulge the thought. On your sentence, our fate is suspended; prosperity or desolation depends on your word. To you, therefore, we look! Before your august assembly we present ourselves, in the attitude of deprecation, and of entreaty. On your kindness, on your humanity, on your compassion, on your benevolence, we rest our hopes. To you we address our reiterated prayers. Spare our people! Spare the wreck of our prosperity! Let not our deserted homes become the monuments of our desolation! But we forbear! We suppress the agonies which wring our hearts, when we look at our wives, our children, and our venerable sires! We restrain the forebodings of anguish and distress, of misery and devastation and death, which must be the attendants on the execution of this ruinous compact.

Source: John Ross, *The Papers of Chief John Ross, vol. 1, 1807–1839*, ed. Gary E. Moulton (Norman: University of Oklahoma Press, 1985), 458–61, http://www.pbs.org/wgbh/aia/part4/4h3083t.html.

Interpret the Evidence

1. What does the 1818 petition (Source 9.6) suggest about women's role in Cherokee society and politics? How might the elder Nancy Ward have felt about the changes that occurred in her lifetime?

2. What do Sequoyah's syllabary (Source 9.7) and the Constitution of 1827 (Source 9.8) reveal about the benefits and limits of Cherokees' acculturation to Anglo-American ideas and institutions? How does the Constitution's treatment of African Americans fit with earlier Indian and Anglo-American patterns of enslavement?

3. How does Nancy Reece's letter (Source 9.9) illustrate the changes in Cherokee society in the early 1800s, and how might the 1818 women petitioners (Source 9.6) respond to her understanding of the state of Cherokee society?

4. On what basis does John Ross challenge the 1836 Treaty of New Echota, and how does he seek to appeal to white Americans to support the Cherokee cause?

5. Taken together, what do these sources reveal about the changing character of Cherokee society, the divisions within it, and the responses of white Americans to both?

Put It in Context

In what ways was the status of Cherokees similar to and different from African Americans in the early nineteenth century? To white Americans?

In what ways were the Cherokee distinctive from or similar to other Indian nations east of the Mississippi in the early nineteenth century?

Social and Cultural Ferment in the North

1820–1850

Window to the Past

1850 Census of the Isaac Post Family in Rochester, New York

The Constitution requires the federal government to take a census of the U.S. population every ten years. The 1850 census was the first to list the names of household members, to record place of birth, and to include "color," that is race. This information along with age, sex, and occupation allows historians to calculate household and family size, occupational patterns, the class character of neighborhoods, and other demographic patterns. Despite cultural ideals emphasizing the nuclear family, many middle-class households, like that of the Posts, included other relatives, boarders, and servants. ▶ **To learn more about this primary source, see Source 10.1 on page 326.**

Dwelling-houses numbered in the order of visitation.	Families numbered in the order of visitation.	The Name of every Person whose usual place of abode on the first day of June, 1850, was in this family.	DESCRIPTION.		
			Age.	Sex.	White, black, or mulatto.
1	2	3	4	5	6
		Margaret Hennesy	20	f	
		Elizabeth Vanness	23	f	
285	338	Isaac Post	50	m	
		Amy "	45	f	
		Jacob K. "	20	m	
		Joseph "	16	m	
		Willett "	3	m	
		Sarah L. Hallowell	30	f	
		Ansel Bowen	28	m	
		Elizabeth "	28	f	
		Bridget Head	23	f	

United States Census Bureau

After reading this chapter you will be able to:

- Explain the growth of and changes in northern cities, including issues of immigration, class stratification, and gender roles.

- Analyze how industrialization transformed workers' lives, was affected by the boom and bust economic cycle, and contributed to class, ethnic, and racial tensions.

- Describe the range and appeal of religious movements that emerged in the 1830s and 1840s.

- Evaluate the emergence of reform movements and the strategies they embraced.

- Explain the importance of the transportation and communication revolution to the rise of antislavery movements and their impact on other social and political changes.

Comparing American Histories

The great revival preacher **Charles Grandison Finney** was born in 1792 and raised in rural New York State. As a young man, Finney studied the law. But in 1821, like many others of his generation, he experienced a powerful religious conversion. No longer interested in a legal career, he turned to the ministry instead.

After being ordained in the Presbyterian Church, Finney joined "New School" ministers who rejected the more conservative traditions of the Presbyterian Church and embraced a vigorous evangelicalism. In the early 1830s the Reverend Finney traveled throughout New York State preaching about Christ's place in a changing America. He held massive revivals in cities along the Erie Canal, most notably in Rochester, New York. He achieved his greatest success in places experiencing rapid economic development and an influx of migrants and immigrants, where the clash of cultures and classes fueled fears of moral decay.

Finney urged Christians to actively seek salvation. Once individuals reformed themselves, he said, they should work to abolish poverty, intemperance, prostitution, and slavery. He expected women to participate in revivals and good works but advised them to balance these efforts with their domestic responsibilities.

In many ways, **Amy Kirby Post** fit Finney's ideal. Born into a farm family in Jericho, New York, she found solace in spirituality and social reform. Like many other people in this period, Amy experienced the loss of loved ones. In 1825, at age twenty-three, Amy's fiancé died, and two years later she lost the sister to whom she was closest. The next year, Amy married a widower, Isaac Post. She mothered his two young children and bore five children of her own, two of whom died young. Yet Amy Post did not embrace evangelical revivals, but focused instead on the quiet piety preferred by her Quaker community.

Still, the personal upheavals Amy experienced in her twenties occurred amid heated controversies within the Society of Friends (Quakers). Elias Hicks claimed that the Society had abandoned its spiritual roots and become too much like a traditional church. His followers, called Hicksites, insisted that Quakers should reduce their dependence on disciplinary rules, elders, and preachers and rely instead on the "Inner Light" — the spirit of God dwelling within each individual. When the Society of Friends divided into Hicksite and Orthodox branches in 1827, Amy Kirby and Isaac Post joined the Hicksites.

In 1836 Amy Post moved with her husband and children to Rochester, New York. In a city marked by the spirit of Finney's revivals, Quakers emphasized quiet contemplation rather than emotional conversions, but the Society of Friends allowed members, including women, to preach when moved by the spirit. Quaker women also held separate meetings to discipline female congregants, evaluate marriage proposals, and write testimonies on important religious and social issues.

(*left*) **Charles Grandison Finney** Oberlin College Archives
(*right*) **Amy Kirby Post** University of Rochester Libraries, Rare Books & Special Collections

Amy Post's spiritual journey was increasingly shaped by the rising tide of abolition. Committed to ending slavery, she joined hundreds of local evangelical women in signing an 1837 antislavery petition. Four years later, she helped found the Western New York Anti-Slavery Society, which included Quakers and evangelicals, women and men, and blacks and whites. Post's growing commitment to abolition caused tensions in the Hicksite meeting since many members opposed working in "worldly" organizations alongside non-Quakers. In 1848 Post and other radical Friends formed a new, more activist-oriented Quaker meeting and joined the movement for women's rights as well as abolition. ■

C omparing the American histories of Charles Finney and Amy Post shows how individuals responded to and helped shape the dynamic religious, social, and economic developments of the early nineteenth century. Finney changed the face of American religion, aided by masses of evangelical Protestants. The transportation and communication revolutions, the expansion of the market economy, and the rise of cities, especially in the northern United States, benefitted many Americans. However, they also made problems like poverty, unemployment, alcohol abuse, crime, and prostitution more visible, drawing people to Finney's message. Like many Americans, Amy Post migrated with her family along improved roads and canals to seek better economic opportunities. But as the moral stain of slavery continued to grow, she joined other Quakers and northern blacks in refusing to purchase slave-produced goods. Bursting traditional religious bonds, she also reconsidered what it meant to do God's work. For both Finney and Post, Rochester — the fastest-growing city in the nation between 1825 and 1835 — exemplified the possibilities and problems created by the market revolution, urban expansion, and rapid social change.

The **Market Revolution**

Commercial and industrial development, immigration from Europe, and migration from rural areas led to the rapid growth of cities in the northern United States from 1820 on. Such growth both built on and furthered the expansion of roads and canals, which were funded by federal and state governments in the 1810s and 1820s. By linking northern industries with western farms and southern plantations, these innovations in transportation fueled a **market revolution** as the manufacture of goods became better organized and innovations in industry, agriculture, and communication increased efficiency and productivity. These changes fostered urbanization, which, in turn, reinforced economic growth and innovation. However, it also created social upheaval. Cultural divisions intensified in urban areas where Catholics and Protestants, workers and the well-to-do, immigrants, African Americans, and native-born whites lived side by side. Class dynamics also changed with the development of a clear middle class of shopkeepers, professionals, and clerks.

Creating an Urban Landscape.
Across the North, urban populations boomed. As commercial centers, seaports like New York and Philadelphia were the most populous cities in the early nineteenth century. Between 1820 and 1850, the number of cities with 100,000 inhabitants increased from two to six; five were seaports. The sixth was the river port of Cincinnati, Ohio. Smaller boomtowns, like Rochester, New York, emerged along inland waterways like the Erie Canal. Completed in 1825, it spurred agriculture, industry, and small business along its 363-mile route.

Development along the Erie Canal illustrates the ways that advancements in transportation transformed the surrounding landscape and ecology. As soon as the first stretch was completed in 1819, its economic benefits became clear. As the 40-foot-wide canal was extended across central and western New York State, settlers rushed to establish farms, mills, and ports. They chopped down millions of trees to construct homes and businesses and to open land for farms and orchards. Farmers shipped grain, cattle, and hogs to eastern markets or to emerging cities like Rochester. There, millers and butchers turned them into flour, beef, and pork, products that were now easier and cheaper to ship further onward. Newspapers multiplied, offering the latest news on crop prices and manufactured goods and advertising local services along the canal. The growing population of boatmen, merchants, and travelers depended on taverns for meals, rest, and information. Americans who lived along the Erie Canal, the Great Lakes, and major rivers could learn a great deal by spending time at taverns gathering news and information from far-flung ports.

As the population in western New York, the Old Northwest, and along the Great Lakes increased, residents demanded more and more manufactured goods. This demand fueled the growth of factories. Cotton, lumber, and flour mills were constructed near waterfalls for power, transforming isolated villages into mill towns while endangering the natural habitats of fish and wildlife. As thousands of newcomers cleared land in Ohio and Michigan, they expanded trade between areas fueled by the Erie Canal and the Great Lakes and older towns from New England to New York City. Midwesterners also shipped agricultural goods south via the Ohio and Mississippi Rivers, exchanging grain and other items for southern cotton, rice, and sugar. Southern trade also grew along the Atlantic coast, with cotton bales barely keeping up with the demand from New England factories.

Business and political leaders in Philadelphia and Baltimore, seeing the economic benefits created by the Erie Canal, demanded state funding for canals linking them to the Midwest. Where state funding proved insufficient, they persuaded English bankers and merchants to invest in American canals as well as railroads, which were just beginning to compete with waterways as a method to transport people and goods.

The Lure of Urban Life.

As transportation improved and the economy expanded, cities across the North increased not only in size but also in diversity. During the 1820s, some 150,000 European immigrants entered the United States; during the 1830s, nearly 600,000; and during the 1840s, more than 1,700,000. This surge of immigrants included more Irish and German settlers than ever before as well as large numbers of Scandinavians. Many settled along the eastern seaboard. Others migrated west, including thousands of Irish immigrants who labored in difficult and dangerous conditions to build the Erie Canal. Some Irish workers quit these jobs to settle in local communities along the canal's route. Others added to the growth of frontier cities such as Cincinnati, St. Louis, and Chicago.

Late-eighteenth-century Irish immigrants, many of whom were Protestants, were joined by hundreds of thousands more in the 1830s and 1840s, when Irish Catholics poured into the United States. The Irish countryside was then plagued by bad weather, a potato blight, and harsh economic policies imposed by the English government. In 1845 to 1846 a full-blown famine forced thousands more Irish Catholic families to emigrate. Young Irish women, who could easily find work as domestics or seamstresses, emigrated in especially large numbers. Poor harvests, droughts, failed revolutions, and repressive landlords convinced large numbers of Germans, including Catholics, Lutherans, and Jews, and Scandinavians to flee

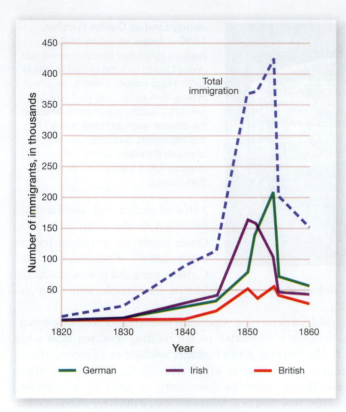

FIGURE 10.1   Immigration to the United States, 1820–1860

Famine, economic upheaval, and political persecution led masses of people from Ireland, Germany, and Britain to migrate to the United States from the 1820s through the 1850s. The vast majority settled in cities and factory towns in the North or on farms in the Midwest. An economic recession in the late 1850s finally slowed immigration, though only temporarily. What does this graph tell us about the growing diversity of the U.S. population?

their homelands as well. By 1850 the Irish made up about 40 percent of immigrants to the United States, and Germans nearly a quarter (Figure 10.1).

These immigrants provided an expanding pool of cheap labor as well as skilled artisans, adding fuel to northern commerce and industry. Banks, mercantile houses, and dry-goods stores multiplied. Urban industrial enterprises included both traditional workshops and mechanized factories. Credit and insurance agencies emerged to aid entrepreneurs in their ventures. The increase in business also drove the demand for ships, warehouses, newspapers, and other commercial necessities, which created a surge in jobs for many urban residents.

Businesses focused on leisure also flourished. In the 1830s theater became affordable to working-class families, who attended comedies, musical revues, and morality plays. They also joined middle- and upper-class audiences at productions of Shakespeare and contemporary dramas. Minstrel shows mocked self-important capitalists but also portrayed African Americans in crude caricatures. One of the most popular characters was Jim Crow, who appeared originally in an African American song. In the 1820s Thomas Rice, a white performer who blacked his face with burnt cork, incorporated Jim Crow into a song-and-dance routine.

The lures of urban life were especially attractive to the young. Single men and women and newly married couples flocked to the largest cities, ensuring their continued growth. By 1850 half the residents of New York, Philadelphia, and other seaport cities were under sixteen years old. Young men sought work in factories, construction, and the maritime trades or in banks and commercial houses, while young women competed for jobs as seamstresses and domestic servants.

The Roots of Urban Disorder.
While immigrant labor stimulated northern economic growth, immigrant families transformed the urban landscape. They crowded into houses and apartments and built ethnic institutions, including synagogues and convents — visible indicators of the growing diversity of northern cities. While most native-born Protestants applauded economic growth, cultural diversity aroused anxieties.

Jenny Lind at Castle Garden, 1850   American showman P. T. Barnum convinced Swedish opera star Jenny Lind to tour the United States in 1850. Huge crowds greeted her arrival in New York harbor and packed her concerts, leading reporters to describe the phenomenon as "Lind mania." In this lithograph, Nathaniel Currier captures the crowd at her first appearance at Castle Garden in New York. Granger

Anti-Catholicism and anti-Semitism flourished in the 1830s and 1840s. Crude stereotypes portrayed Jews as manipulative moneylenders and Catholic nuns and priests as sexually depraved. Ethnic groups also battled stereotypes. Irishmen, for example, were often pictured as habitual drunkards.

Still, rising immigration did not deter rural Americans from seeking economic opportunities in the city. Native-born white men often set out on their own, but most white women settled in cities under the supervision of a husband, landlady, or employer. African Americans, too, sought greater opportunities in urban areas. In the 1830s, more blacks joined Philadelphia's vibrant African American community, attracted by its churches, schools, and mutual aid societies. New Bedford, Massachusetts, a thriving whaling center, recruited black workers and thus attracted fugitive slaves as well.

In urban areas, many individuals lived outside the bounds of traditional families. This led some single women and widows to create or to join "housefuls." Housefuls were groups of mostly unrelated women and men, often from different ethnic and racial backgrounds, bound together by economic ties. Many served as sites of commerce, labor, and daily life. Urban housefuls existed in boardinghouses and taverns run by women and in laundries or shops with living spaces above or behind. While they allowed women, immigrants, and free and enslaved blacks to survive outside traditional families, they were still marked by hierarchies of age, skill, literacy, and other measures of economic worth.

Wherever they lived, newcomers to cities faced many dangers. Some men sought to lure young women into the sex trade, and domestic servants were often subject to sexual abuse. Thieves and scam artists regularly victimized young men new to the city, while blacks and immigrants—men and women—confronted discrimination in housing and jobs as well as on the carriages and boats that carried them to their new homes. In addition, physical battles erupted on city streets between immigrant and native-born residents, Protestant and Catholic gangs, and white and black workers. Disease also spread quickly through densely populated neighborhoods. When innovations in transportation made it possible for more affluent residents to distance themselves from crowded inner cities, they moved to less congested neighborhoods on the urban periphery. Horse-drawn streetcar lines, first built in New York City in 1832, hastened this development.

By the 1840s, economic competition intensified, fueling violence among those driven to the margins. Native-born white employers and workers pushed Irish immigrants to the bottom of the economic ladder, where they competed with African Americans. Yet Irish workers insisted that their whiteness gave them a higher status than even the most skilled blacks. When black temperance reformers organized a parade in Philadelphia in August 1842, white onlookers—mostly Irish laborers—attacked the marchers, and the conflict escalated into a riot.

Americans who lived in small towns and rural areas regularly read news of urban violence and vice. Improvements in printing created vastly more and cheaper newspapers, while the construction of the first telegraph in 1844 ensured that news could travel more quickly from town to town. Newspaper offices served as centers of activity and exchange in towns and cities across the North. Readers were asked to "enquire of the printer" if they wished further details about announcements for events, tickets, and goods for sale or advertisements for fugitive slaves and runaway spouses. Subscribers, sellers, and advertisers also came and went amid the noise and clamor that accompanied the printing process. In cities, tabloids wooed readers with sensational stories of crime, sex, and scandal. Even more respectable newspapers reported on urban mayhem, while religious periodicals warned parishioners against urban immorality. In response to both a real and a perceived increase in crime, cities replaced voluntary night watchmen with paid police forces.

The New Middle Class.

Members of the emerging middle class, which developed first in the North, included ambitious businessmen, successful shopkeepers, doctors, and lawyers as well as teachers, journalists, ministers, and other salaried employees. At the top rungs, successful entrepreneurs and professionals adopted affluent lifestyles. At the lower rungs, a growing cohort of salaried clerks and managers hoped that their hard work, honesty, and thrift would be rewarded with upward mobility.

Education, religious affiliation, and sobriety were important indicators of middle-class status. A well-read man who attended a well-established church and drank in strict moderation was marked as belonging to this new rank. He was also expected to own a comfortable home, marry a pious woman, and raise well-behaved children. The rise of the middle class inspired a flood of advice books, ladies' magazines, religious periodicals, and novels advocating new ideals of womanhood. These publications emphasized the centrality of child rearing and homemaking to women's identities. This **cult of domesticity** ideally restricted wives to home and hearth, where they provided their husbands with respite from the cares and corruptions of the world.

Explore ▶

See Source 10.1 for a statistical portrait of a middle-class family.

John Aymar and Family, New York City, c. 1838 George Twibill Jr., a student of Samuel B. Morse, painted this family portrait. John Aymar imported rum and coffee, his occupation reflected in the ship masts peeking through the window. He stands over and behind his wife Elizabeth and their daughters, the quartet surrounded by the fine carpets, rich draperies, and expensive furnishings that proclaim their elite status. The Metropolitan Museum of Art, Gift of A. Grima Johnson, 2008

Guided Primary Source Analysis

1850 U.S. Census of the Isaac and Amy Post Household

In 1850, for the first time, the federal census listed each member of the household by name as well as by age, sex, race (then labeled "Color"), and place of birth. Some census takers noted the relationship of each household member to the family head. This census taker did not, nor did he note Color. That information appears in brackets and came from other city and genealogical records. Census records provide portraits of individual households at a moment in time and also allow historians to compare families and households across place and time.

Source 10.1

1850 U.S. Census of the Isaac and Amy Post Household

Names of Residents in Household	Relation to Head of Household	Age/Sex/Color*	Occupation for Males over 15 Years	Place of Birth
Isaac Post	[Head]	50/male/[white]	Druggist	New York
Amy Post	[wife]	45**/female/[white]		New York
Jacob K. Post	[son]	20/male/[white]	Clerk	New York
Joseph Post	[son]	16/male/[white]	Clerk	New York
Willet Post	[son]	3/male/[white]		New York
Sarah Hallowell	[sister-in-law]	30/female/[white]		New York
Ansel Bowen	[boarder]	28/male/[white]	Teacher	New York
Elizabeth Bowen	[boarder]	28/female/[white]		New York
Bridget Head	[servant]	23/female/[white]		Ireland
Mary Ann Pitkin	[boarder]	10/female/[black]		New York

* The options for "Color" in the 1850 Census were "White, Black, and Mulatto."
The bracketed information is from the 1855 N.Y. State Census and Rochester city directories.

** Amy Post was 47 in summer 1850, not 45.

Source: Seventh U.S. Federal Census, 1st Ward, Rochester, N.Y., 2 August 1850.

How many different families are represented in the Isaac and Amy Post household?

What do the occupations of the men in the household tell us about these families' class status?

How would you characterize the relationships among the women in the household, and what kind of work did they likely perform?

Put It in Context

How do the families represented in the Post household conform to ideals about the middle-class family?

In reality, however, entrance to the middle class required the efforts of wives as well as husbands. While upper middle-class men were expected to provide financial security, women helped cement social and economic bonds by entertaining the wives of business associates, serving in charitable and temperance societies, and organizing Sabbath schools. Families struggling to enter the middle class might take in boarders or extended family members to help secure their financial status. The adoption of new marital ideals of affection and companionship also made the boundaries between public and domestic life more fluid. In many middle-class families, husbands and wives both participated in church, civic, and reform activities, even if they did so through single-sex organizations. At the same time, husbands joined in domestic activities in the evening, presiding over dinner or reading to children.

The ideal of separate spheres of work and home had even less relevance to the millions of women who toiled on farms and factories or as domestic servants, providing goods and services for middle-class and elite families. In turn, those middle-class families played a crucial role in the growing market economy and the jobs it created. Wives and daughters were responsible for much of the family's consumption. They purchased cloth, rugs, chairs, clocks, and housewares, and, if wealthy enough, European crystal and Chinese porcelain. Middling housewives bought goods once made at home, such as butter and candles, and arranged music lessons and other educational opportunities for their children.

Although increasingly recognized for their ability to consume wisely, middle-class women also performed significant domestic labor. While many could afford servants, they often joined domestics and daughters in household tasks. Except for those in the upper middle class, most women still cut and sewed garments, cultivated gardens, canned fruits and vegetables, cooked at least some meals, and entertained guests. As houses expanded in size and clothes became fancier, domestic servants shouldered the most laborious and time-consuming chores, while mothers and daughters performed lighter tasks. However, such work was increasingly invisible as husbands and fathers came to separate labor focused inwardly on the family from that focused outwardly in the market economy.

Middle-class men contributed significantly to the consumer economy. Of course, they created, invested in, and managed most industrial and commercial ventures. Moreover, in carrying out business and professional obligations, many enjoyed restaurants, the theater, or sporting events. Men also attended plays and lectures with their wives and visited museums and circuses with their children. And they purchased hats, suits, mustache wax, and other accoutrements of middle-class masculinity.

Review & Relate

▪ How did the market revolution, including improvements like the Erie Canal, reshape the landscape and lives of Americans in the North?

▪ As northern cities became larger and more diverse in the first half of the nineteenth century, what changes and challenges did urban residents face and what values and beliefs did the new middle class embrace?

The **Rise** of **Industry**

In the mid-nineteenth century, industrial enterprises in the Northeast transformed the nation's economy even though they employed less than 10 percent of the U.S. labor force. In the 1830s and 1840s, factories grew considerably in size, and some investors, especially in textiles, constructed factory towns. New England textile mills relied increasingly on the labor of girls and young women, while urban workshops hired children, young women and men, and older adults. Although men still dominated the skilled trades, making chairs, clocks, shoes, hats, and fine clothing, employment in these trades slowly declined as industrial jobs expanded. An economic panic in 1837 exacerbated this trend and made it even more difficult for workers to organize across differences of skill, ethnicity, race, and sex.

Factory Towns and Women Workers.   In the late 1820s investors and manufacturers joined forces to create factory towns in the New England countryside. The most famous mill town, Lowell, Massachusetts, was based on an earlier experiment in nearby Waltham. In the Waltham system, every step of the production process was mechanized; planned communities included factories, boardinghouses, government offices, and churches. Agents for the Waltham system recruited the daughters of New England farm families as workers, assuring parents that they would be watched over by managers and foremen as well as landladies. The young women were required to attend church and observe curfews while clocks and bells regulated their labor to ensure discipline and productivity.

Farm families needed more cash because of the growing market economy, and daughters in the mills could contribute to family finances and save money for the clothes and linens required for married life. Factory jobs also provided an alternative to marriage as young New England men moved west and left a surplus of women behind. Factory-owned boardinghouses provided a relatively safe, all-female environment for mill workers, and sisters and neighbors often lived together. Despite nearly constant supervision, many rural women viewed factory work as an adventure. They could set aside a bit of money for themselves, attend lectures and concerts, meet new people, and acquire a wider view of the world.

During the 1830s, however, working conditions began to deteriorate. Factory owners cut wages, lengthened hours, and sped up machines. Boardinghouses became overcrowded, and company officials regulated both rents and expenses so that higher prices for lodging did not necessarily mean better food or furnishings. Factory workers launched numerous strikes in the 1830s against longer hours, wage cuts, and speedups in factory production. The solidarity required to sustain these strikes was forged in boardinghouses and at church socials as well as on the factory floor. At age twelve, Harriet Robinson led a walkout at the Lowell Mills in 1836. In her memoir, written in 1898, she noted, "As I looked back at the long line that followed me, I was more proud than I have ever been since at any success I have achieved."

Despite mill workers' solidarity, it was difficult to overcome the economic power wielded by manufacturers. Working women's collective actions were generally short-lived, lasting only until a strike was settled. Then employees returned to their jobs until the next crisis hit. And as competition increasingly cut into profits, owners resisted mill workers' demands more vehemently. When the panic of 1837 intensified fears of job loss, women's organizing activities were doomed until the economy recovered.

"*Is Saul also among the prophets.*"

A REPOSITORY
OF ORIGINAL ARTICLES, WRITTEN BY
"FACTORY GIRLS."

LOWELL: MISSES CURTIS & FARLEY.
BOSTON: JORDAN & WILEY, 121
Washington street.
1845.

Entered according to Act of Congress, in the year 1845, in the Clerk's Office of the District Court of the District of Massachusetts.

The Lowell Offering, 1845 A local pastor launched the Lowell Offering in 1840, but it was soon taken over by millworkers, including editor Harriet Farley. In the early 1840s, women wrote articles on conditions in the mill, suicide, and labor organizing as well as poetry and lighter topics. Despite the increase in immigrant workers, the cover continued to depict a New England farm girl. Everett Collection

The Decline of Craft Work and Workingmen's Responses.

While the construction of factory towns expanded economic opportunities for young women, the gradual decline of time-honored crafts narrowed the prospects for workingmen. Craft workshops gradually increased in size and hired fewer skilled workers and more men who performed single tasks, like attaching soles to shoes. Many tasks also became mechanized during the nineteenth century. The final product was less distinctive than an entire item crafted by a skilled artisan, but it was less expensive and available in mass quantities.

The shift from craft work to factory work threatened to undermine workingmen's skills, pay, and labor conditions. Rather than skilled apprentices who worked alongside a master craftsman, masters began hiring foremen to regulate the workforce and installing bells and clocks to regulate the workday. This process of **deskilling** occurred over several decades in different trades. As it transformed shoemaking, printing, tailoring, and other trades, laboring men fought to maintain their status.

Some workers formed mutual aid societies to provide assistance in times of illness, injury, or unemployment. Others participated in religious revivals or joined fraternal orders to find the camaraderie they once enjoyed at work. The expansion of voting rights in the 1820s offered another avenue for action. The first workingmen's political party was founded in Philadelphia in 1827, and working-class men in the North joined forces to support politicians sympathetic to their needs. Most workingmen's parties focused on practical proposals: government distribution of free land in the West, abolishing compulsory militia service and imprisonment for debt, public funding for education, and regulations on banks and corporations. Although the electoral success of these parties was modest, in the 1830s Democrats and Whigs adopted many of their proposals.

Workingmen also formed unions to demand better wages and working conditions. In the 1820s and 1830s, skilled journeymen held mass meetings to protest employers' efforts to lengthen the workday, merge smaller workshops into larger factories, and cut wages. In New York City in 1834, labor activists formed a citywide federation, the General Trades Union, which provided support for striking workers. The National Trades Union was established later that year, with delegates representing more than twenty-five thousand workers across the North. These organizations aided skilled workers but refused admission to women and unskilled men.

It proved difficult to establish broader labor organizations. Most skilled men considered unskilled workers as competitors, not allies. Many workingmen also feared that women workers would undercut their wages and so refused to organize alongside them. And anti-immigrant and racist beliefs among many native-born Protestant workers interfered with organizing across racial and ethnic lines. With the onset of the panic of 1837, the common plight of workers became clearer. But the economic crisis made unified action nearly impossible as individuals sought to hold on to what little they had.

The Panic of 1837. The panic of 1837, which began in the South, hit northern cotton merchants hard (see "Van Buren and the Panic of 1837" in Chapter 11). With cotton shipments sharply curtailed, textile factories drastically cut production, unemployment rose, and merchants and investors went broke. Those still employed saw their wages cut in half. In Rochester, the Posts temporarily moved in with other family members and their oldest son left school to help save their pharmacy from foreclosure. Petty crime and prostitution also rose as men and women struggled to make ends meet.

In Lowell, hours increased and wages fell. Just as important, the process of deskilling intensified. Factory owners considered mechanization one way to improve their economic situation. A cascade of inventions, including power looms, steam boilers, and the steam press, transformed industrial occupations and led factory owners to invest more of their limited resources in machines. At the same time, the rising tide of immigrants provided a ready supply of relatively cheap labor. Artisans tried to maintain their traditional skills and status, but in many trades they were fighting a losing battle.

By the early 1840s, when the panic subsided, new technologies did spur new jobs. Factories demanded more workers to handle machines that ran at a faster pace. In printing, the steam press allowed publication of more newspapers and magazines, creating positions for editors, publishers, printers, engravers, reporters, and sales agents. Similarly, mechanical reapers sped the harvest of wheat and inspired changes in flour milling that required engineers to design machines and mechanics to build and repair them.

These changing circumstances fueled new labor organizations as well. Many of these unions comprised a particular trade or ethnic group, and almost all continued to address primarily the needs of skilled male workers. Textile operatives remained the one important group of organized female workers. In the 1840s, workingwomen even joined with workingmen in New England to fight for a ten-hour day. Slowly, however, farmers' daughters left the mills as desperate Irish immigrants flooded in and accepted lower wages, endangering the small improvements mill workers had gained.

For most women in need, charitable organizations offered more support than unions. Organizations like Philadelphia's Female Association for the Relief of Women and Children in Reduced Circumstances provided a critical safety net for many poor families since public monies for such purposes were limited. Although most northern towns and cities now provided some form of public assistance, they never had sufficient resources to meet local needs in good times, much less the extraordinary demands posed by the panic.

Review & Relate

■ How and why did American manufacturing change during the first half of the nineteenth century?

■ How did new technologies, immigration, and the panic of 1837 change the economic opportunities and organizing strategies for northern workers?

Saving the Nation from Sin

In the first half of the nineteenth century, men and women of all classes and races embraced the Protestant religious revival known as the **Second Great Awakening**, through which they expressed deeply held beliefs and reclaimed a sense of the nation's godly mission. Still, evangelical Protestantism was not the only religious tradition to thrive in this period. Catholic churches and Jewish synagogues multiplied with immigration; and in the North, Quaker meetings and Unitarian congregations flourished as well. New religious groups also attracted thousands of followers while transcendentalists sought deeper engagements with nature as another path to spiritual renewal.

The Second Great Awakening.

Although diverse religious traditions flourished in the United States, evangelical Protestantism proved the most powerful in the 1820s and 1830s. Evangelical churches hosted revivals, celebrated conversions, and organized prayer and missionary societies. This second wave of religious revivals had begun in Cane Ridge, Kentucky in 1801 and took root across the South. It then spread northward, transforming Protestant churches and the social fabric of northern life.

Ministers like Charles Grandison Finney adopted techniques first wielded by southern Methodists and Baptists: plain speaking, powerful images, and mass meetings. But Finney molded these techniques for a more affluent audience and held his "camp meetings" in established churches. By the late 1820s, boomtown growth along the Erie Canal aroused deep concerns among religious leaders about the rising tide of sin. In response, the Reverend Finney arrived in Rochester in September 1830. He began preaching in local Presbyterian churches, leading crowded prayer meetings that lasted late into the night. Individual supplicants walked to special benches designated for anxious sinners, who were prayed over in public. Female parishioners played crucial roles, encouraging their husbands, sons, friends, and neighbors to submit to God.

Thousands of Rochester residents joined in the evangelical experience as Finney's powerful message engulfed other denominations (Map 10.1). The significance of these revivals went far beyond an increase in church membership. Finney converted "the great mass of the most influential people" in the city: merchants, lawyers, doctors, master craftsmen, and shopkeepers. Equally important, he proclaimed that if Christians were "united all over the world the Millennium [Christ's Second Coming] might be brought about in three months." Preachers in Rochester and the surrounding towns took up his call, and converts committed themselves to preparing the world for Christ's arrival.

Developments in Rochester were replicated in cities across the North. Presbyterian, Congregational, and Episcopalian churches overflowed with middle-class and wealthy Americans, while Baptists and Methodists ministered to more laboring women and men. Black Baptists and Methodists evangelized in their communities, combining powerful preaching with rousing spirituals. In Philadelphia, African Americans built fifteen churches between 1799 and 1830. Black women joined men in evangelizing to their fellow African Americans as they continued to fight for the right to be ordained as ministers.

Tens of thousands of black and white converts embraced evangelicals' message of moral outreach. No reform movement gained greater impetus from the revivals than **temperance,** whose advocates sought to moderate and then ban the sale and consumption of alcohol. In the 1820s Americans fifteen years and older consumed six to seven gallons of distilled alcohol per person per year (about double the amount consumed today).

Mormons
Millerites
Fourierists
Antislavery church
1831 revival
Erie Canal

0   25   50 miles
0   25   50 kilometers

Lake Ontario

Rochester
Utica
Buffalo
Seneca Falls
Lake Erie

MAP 10.1 Religious Movements in the Burned-Over District, 1831–1848

Western and central New York State was burned over by the fires of religious revivalism in the 1830s and 1840s. But numerous other religious groups also formed or flourished in the region in these decades, including Quakers, Mormons, and Millerites. In the 1840s, Fourierist phalanxes, the Oneida community, and other utopian experiments were established here.

Source: Whitney R. Cross, *The Burned-Over District: The Social and Intellectual History of Enthusiastic Religion in Western New York, 1800–1850* (Ithaca, NY: Cornell University Press, 1950).

Middle-class evangelicals, who once accepted moderate drinking as healthful, now insisted on eliminating alcohol consumption altogether.

New Visions of Faith and Reform.

Although enthusiasm for temperance and other reforms waned during the panic of 1837 and many churches lost members, the Second Great Awakening continued in its aftermath. But evangelical ministers increasingly competed for souls with a variety of other religious groups, many of which also supported good works and social reform. The Society of Friends, the first religious group to refuse fellowship to slaveholders, expanded throughout the early nineteenth century, largely in the North and Midwest. Having divided in 1827 and again in 1848, the Society of Friends continued to grow. So, too, did its influence in reform movements as activists like Amy Post carried Quaker testimonies against alcohol, war, and slavery into the wider society. Unitarians also combined religious worship with social reform. They differed from other Christians by believing in a single unified higher spirit rather than the Trinity of the Father, the Son, and the Holy Spirit. Emerging mainly in New England in the early nineteenth century, Unitarian societies slowly spread west and south in the 1830s. Opposed to evangelical revivalism and dedicated to a rational approach to understanding the divine, Unitarians attracted prominent literary figures such as James Russell Lowell and Harvard luminaries like William Ellery Channing.

Other churches grew as a result of immigration. Dozens of Catholic churches were established to meet the needs of Irish and German immigrants. With the rapid increase in Catholic churches, Irish priests multiplied in the 1840s and 1850s, and women's religious orders became increasingly Irish as well. At the same time, synagogues, Hebrew schools, and Hebrew aid societies signaled the growing presence of Jewish immigrants, chiefly from Germany, in the United States. Between 1830 and 1860, new synagogues were built in Charleston, New Orleans, Baltimore, New York City, Cincinnati, and other cities. Most Catholics and Jews were less active in reform in the wider society and more focused on assisting their own congregants in securing a foothold in America.

Entirely new religious groups also flourished. One of the most important was the Church of Jesus Christ of Latter-Day Saints, or Mormons, founded by Joseph Smith. Smith began to receive visions from God at age fifteen and was directed to dig up gold plates inscribed with instructions for redeeming the Lost Tribes of Israel. *The Book of Mormon*

(1830), based on these inscriptions, served, along with the Bible, as the scriptural foundation for Mormons. Smith served as their Prophet.

Smith founded not only a church but a theocracy (a community governed by religious leaders). In the mid-1830s Mormons established a settlement at Nauvoo, Illinois and recruited followers—black and white—from the eastern United States and England. When Smith voiced antislavery views, some local residents expressed outrage. But it was his claim to revelations sanctioning polygamy that led local authorities to arrest him and his brother. When a mob then lynched the Smith brothers, Brigham Young, a successful missionary, took over as Prophet. In 1846 he led 12,000 followers west, 5,000 of who settled near the Great Salt Lake, in what would soon become the Utah Territory. Isolated from anti-Mormon mobs, Young established a thriving theocracy. In this settlement, leaders practiced polygamy and though accepting black members, denied them the right to become priests.

New religious groups also formed by separating from established denominations. William Miller, a prosperous farmer and Baptist preacher, claimed that the Bible proved that the Second Coming of Jesus Christ would occur in 1843. Thousands of Americans joined the Millerites. When various dates for Christ's Second Coming passed without incident, however, Millerites developed competing interpretations for the failure and divided into distinct groups. The most influential group formed the Seventh-Day Adventist Church in the 1840s.

Transcendentalism.   Another important movement for spiritual renewal was rooted in the transcendent power of nature. The founder of this transcendentalist school of thought was Ralph Waldo Emerson. Raised a Unitarian, Emerson began challenging the church's ideas. His 1836 essay entitled "Nature" expounded his newfound belief in a Universal Being. This Being existed as an ideal reality beyond the material world and was accessible through nature. Emerson's natural world was distinctly American and suggested that moral perfection could be achieved in the United States. Emerson expressed his ideas in widely read essays and books. He was also a popular speaker on the lyceum circuit, a new form of popular education and entertainment that drew tens of thousands of audience members in towns and cities across the country.

Thomas Cole, *View of the Round-Top in the Catskills Mountains*, 1827
Thomas Cole was born in England in 1801, migrated to America in 1818, and lived for many years in Catskill, New York with his wife and children until his death in 1848. Many of his paintings captured a romantic view of nature that combined a hint of wildness with the beauty of mountain mists and sunlit rivers shown here. Gift of Martha C. Karolik for the M. and M. Karolik/Bridgeman Images

Emerson's hometown of Concord, Massachusetts served as a haven for writers, poets, intellectuals, and reformers drawn to **transcendentalism**. In 1840 Margaret Fuller, a close friend of Emerson, became the first editor of *The Dial*, a journal dedicated to transcendental thought. In 1844 she moved to New York City, where Horace Greeley hired her as a critic at the *New York Tribune*. In 1845, she published *Woman in the Nineteenth Century*, which combined transcendental ideas with arguments for women's rights.

Henry David Thoreau also followed the transcendentalist path. He grew up in Concord and read "Nature" while a student at Harvard in the mid-1830s. In July 1845 Thoreau moved to a cabin near Walden Pond and launched an experiment in simple living. A year later he was imprisoned overnight for refusing to pay his taxes as a protest against slavery and the Mexican-American War. In *Civil Disobedience* (1846), Thoreau argued that individuals of conscience had the right to resist government policies they believed to be immoral. Five years later, Thoreau published *Walden*, which highlighted the intertwined virtues of simple living, natural harmony, and social justice.

Like Emerson, many American artists embraced the power of nature. Led by Thomas Cole, members of the Hudson River School painted romanticized landscapes from New York's Catskill and Adirondack Mountains. Some northern artists also traveled to the West, painting the region's grand vistas. Pennsylvanian George Catlin captured the dramatic scenery of western mountains, gorges, and waterfalls and painted moving portraits of Plains Indians.

Review & Relate

- What impact did the Second Great Awakening have in the North?

- What new religious organizations and viewpoints emerged in the first half of the nineteenth century, *outside* of Protestant evangelical denominations?

Organizing for Change

Both religious commitments and secular problems spurred social activism in the 1830s and 1840s. In cities, small towns, and rural communities, Northerners founded organizations, launched campaigns, and established institutions to better the world around them. Still, reformers often disagreed over priorities and solutions. One major divide was between activists who employed moral arguments to persuade Americans to change and those who insisted that laws were the only effective means of changing behavior.

Varieties of Reform. Middle-class Protestants formed the core of many reform movements in the mid-nineteenth-century North. They had more time and money to devote to social reform than did their working-class counterparts and were less tied to traditional ways than their wealthy neighbors. Still, workers and farmers, African Americans and immigrants, Catholics and Jews also participated in efforts to improve society.

Reformers were sometimes forced to use different techniques. Since women were excluded from direct political participation, they established charitable associations, distributed food and medicine, constructed asylums, circulated petitions, organized boycotts, arranged meetings and lectures, and published newspapers and pamphlets. Other groups with limited political rights — African Americans and immigrants, for instance — embraced similar modes of action and also formed mutual aid societies. Native-born white men wielded these forms of activism alongside political campaigning and lobbying legislators. The reform techniques chosen were also affected by the goals of a particular movement. Moral suasion worked best with families, churches, and local communities, while legislation was more likely to succeed if the goal involved transforming people's behavior across a whole state or region.

In addition, many reformers used a variety of tactics and some changed their approach over time. For instance, reformers who sought to eradicate prostitution in the 1830s prayed in front of urban brothels and attempted to rescue "fallen" women. They soon launched *The Advocate of Moral Reform*, a monthly journal filled with morality tales, advice to mothers, and lists of men who visited brothels. In small towns, moral reformers sought to alert young women and men to the dangers of city life. By the 1840s, urban reformers opened Homes for Virtuous and Friendless Females to provide safe havens for vulnerable women. And across the country, moral reformers began petitioning state legislators to make punishments for men who hired prostitutes as harsh as those for prostitutes themselves.

The Problem of Poverty.

Poverty had existed since the colonial era, but the panic of 1837 aroused greater public concern. Leaders of both government and private charitable endeavors increasingly linked relief to the moral character of those in need. Affluent Americans had long debated whether the poor would learn habits of industry and thrift if they were simply given aid without working for it. The debate was deeply gendered. Women and children were considered the worthiest recipients of aid, and middle and upper class women the appropriate dispensers of charity. Successful men, meanwhile, often linked poverty to weakness and considered giving pennies to a beggar an unmanly act that indulged the worst traits of the poor.

Explore ▶

See Sources 10.2 and 10.3 for the views of two reformers on ways to uplift the poor.

Towns and cities had long relegated the poorest residents to almshouses or workhouses. In the early nineteenth century, charitable societies sought to change the conditions that produced poverty. As the poor increased with urban growth, northern charitable ladies began visiting poor neighborhoods, offering blankets, clothing, food, and medicine to needy residents. But the problem seemed intractable, and many charitable organizations began building orphan asylums, hospitals, and homes for working women to provide deserving but vulnerable individuals with resources to improve their life chances.

Those considered the "undeserving" poor faced grimmer choices. They generally received assistance only through workhouses or jails. By the 1830s images of rowdy men who drank or gambled away what little they earned, prostitutes who tempted respectable men into vice, and immigrants who preferred idle poverty to virtuous labor became stock figures in debates over the causes of and responses to poverty.

At the same time, female reformers and novelists increasingly portrayed young poor women — if they were white and Protestant — as the victims of immoral men or unfortunate circumstance. In fictional tales, naive girls were seduced and abandoned by manipulative men. One of the first mass-produced books in the United States, Nathaniel Hawthorne's *The Scarlet Letter* (1850), was set in Puritan New England but addressed contemporary concerns about the seduction of innocents. It illustrated the social ostracism and poverty suffered by a woman who bore a child out of wedlock.

Other fictional tales placed the blame for fallen women on foreigners, especially Catholics. Such works drew vivid portraits of young nuns ravished by priests and then

Comparative Primary Source Analysis

How Can We Help the Poor?

Americans who sought to uplift the poor offered various solutions. Some supported workhouses; others provided clothes and medicine to the "deserving" poor; and still others established employment agencies for single women and widows. The sources below capture the views of two affluent northern reformers. Matthew Carey, a prominent publisher and civic leader in Philadelphia, challenged reformers to address the dire plight of working women. Emily G. Kempshall, a longtime officer of the Rochester Female Charitable Society, lost faith in the ability of female benevolence to improve the situation of impoverished families and resigned in 1838.

Source 10.2

Matthew Carey | *Appeal to the Wealthy of the Land*, 1833

Let us now turn to the appalling case of seamstresses, . . . [who are] Beset . . . by poverty and wretchedness, with scanty and poor fare, miserable lodgings, clothing inferior in quality . . . , without the most distant hope of amelioration of condition, by a course of unrelenting and unremitting industry. . . .

IT is frequently asked—what remedy can be found for the enormous and cruel oppression experienced by females employed as seamstresses . . . ? . . . [A] complete remedy for the evil is . . . impracticable. I venture, to suggest a few palliatives.

1. Public opinion, a powerful instrument, ought to be brought to bear on the subject. All honourable members of society, male and female, ought to unite in denouncing those who "grind the faces of the poor." . . .

2. Let the employments of females be multiplied as much as possible . . . especially in shop-keeping in retail stores. . . .

4. Let the Provident Societies, intended to furnish employment for women in winter, be munificently supported; and let those Societies give fair and liberal wages. . . .

6. Let schools be opened for instructing poor women in cooking. Good cooks are always scarce. . . .

8. Ladies who can afford it, ought to give out their sewing and washing, and pay fair prices. . . .

9. In the towns in the interior of the state, and in those in western states, there is generally a want of females as domestics, seamstresses, etc. . . . [The rich should] provide for sending some of the superabundant poor females of our cities to those places.

Source: Matthew Carey, *Appeal to the Wealthy of the Land, Ladies as well as Gentlemen* (Philadelphia: L. Johnson, 1833), 13, 15, 33–34.

thrown out pregnant and penniless. These stories heightened anti-Catholic sentiment, which periodically boiled over into attacks on Catholic homes, schools, churches, and convents.

That sentiment intensified as economic competition increased between immigrants and native-born Americans. By the 1840s Americans who opposed immigration took the name **nativists** and launched public political campaigns that blamed foreigners for poverty and crime. Samuel F. B. Morse, an artist and inventor of the telegraph, was among the most popular anti-immigrant spokesmen. Nativists also physically assaulted immigrants,

Source 10.3

Emily G. Kempshall | Letter to the Rochester Female Charitable Society, 1838

[T]he Board . . . have asked my reasons for withdrawing my . . . members[hip]. . . . I reply . . . that I look upon the <u>funds</u> of your society, however judiciously distributed, among the destitute sick of our city, as being wholly inadequate to meet their necessities. . . . I dare not draw a single Dollar, to relieve one poor family, lest in doing this I rob another <u>poorer</u> family, perhaps of what they must have. . . . I know [also] . . . that whole Districts are appointed to females as visitors of the S[ociety] where no decent female should go, to look after and try to assist, their vile and degraded inhabitants. . . .

And now were I addressing the . . . Common Council of this City I would say, "Give the ladies power to point, in their visits of mercy, to a work House, where idle drunken fathers and mothers <u>must</u> go and <u>work</u>." . . . [T]his being granted, the idle Drunken inhabitants . . . Being safely . . . out of the way of the sick members of their own families . . . the objection to becoming a visitor . . . will be lessened at once. . . .

[H]as not the day gone by, when your Flag of Charity may wave over its Lake, River, Canal, and Rail Road, inviting the outcasts of every city in the Union, . . . to seek . . . their subsistence from your bounty. . . . And so while your Banner, whose merciful insignia on the one side is Relief for the destitute sick, has been held up as a beacon of hope, it is painful to tell them to read the other side where want of funds has written Despair of further Relief.

Source: Emily G. Kempshall to President of the Female Charitable Society of Rochester, January 30, 1838, Rochester Female Charitable Society Papers, Rare Books and Special Collections, University of Rochester, Rochester, New York.

Interpret the Evidence

1. How are poor women and families portrayed by Matthew Carey and Emily Kempshall, both leaders in benevolent reform? Who would Kempshall send to a workhouse if one existed in Rochester?

2. How might Carey and Kempshall respond to each other's assessments of aiding the poor?

Put It in Context

What do these documents suggest about class tensions and conflicts in northern cities? How might the panic of 1837 have affected such conflicts?

---

especially Irish Catholics. In May 1844 working-class nativists clashed with Irishmen in Philadelphia after shots were fired from a firehouse. A dozen nativists and one Irishman were killed the first day. The next night, nativists looted and burned Irish businesses and Catholic churches.

Many nativists blamed poverty among immigrants on their drinking habits. Others considered alcohol abuse, whether by native-born or immigrant Americans, the root cause of many social evils.

Drunkard's Home, 1850   Temperance societies undertook a variety of activities to publicize the dangers of alcohol. This engraved illustration is from *The National Temperance Offering*, published by the Sons of Temperance, one of the oldest temperance organizations in the United States. It suggests the harm men's alcohol abuse creates for working-class women and children. From The National Temperance Offering, and Sons and Daughters of Temperance Gift, Clifton Waller Barrett Library of American Literature, Albert and Shirley Small Special Collections Library, University of Virginia

The Temperance Movement.   Temperance advocates first organized officially in 1826 with the founding of the American Temperance Society. This all-male organization was led by clergy and businessmen and focused on alcohol abuse among working-class men. Religious revivals inspired the establishment of some 5,000 local chapters, and black and white men founded other temperance organizations as well. Over time, the temperance movement changed its goal from moderation to total abstinence, targeted middle-class and elite as well as working-class men, and welcomed women's support. Wives and mothers were expected to persuade male kin to stop drinking and sign a temperance pledge. In the 1830s, women founded dozens of temperance societies and funded the circulation of didactic tales, woodcuts, and etchings about the dangers of "demon rum."

Workingmen also embraced temperance as a way to gain dignity and respect. For Protestants, in particular, abstinence distinguished them from Irish Catholic workers. Some working-class temperance advocates criticized liquor dealers, whom they claimed directed "the vilest, meanest, most earth-cursing and hell-filling business ever followed." More turned to self-improvement. In the 1840s groups of laboring men formed Washingtonian societies — named in honor of the nation's founder — to help each other stop excessive drinking. Martha Washington societies appeared shortly thereafter, composed of the wives, mothers, and sisters of male alcoholics.

Despite the rapid growth of temperance organizations, moral suasion failed to reduce alcohol consumption significantly. Many temperance advocates thus turned to legal reform. In 1851 Maine was the first state to legally prohibit the sale of alcoholic beverages. By 1855 twelve more states had restricted the manufacture or sale of alcohol. Yet these stringent measures inspired a backlash. Hostile to the imposition of middle-class Protestant standards on the population at large, Irish workers in Maine organized the Portland Rum Riot in 1855. It led Maine to repeal its law the next year. Still, the diverse strategies used by temperance advocates did gradually reduce the consumption of beer, wine, and spirits across the United States.

Utopian Communities.   While most reformers reached out to the wider society to implement change, some activists established self-contained communities to serve as models for others. The architects of these **utopian societies**, most formed in the North and Midwest, gained inspiration from European intellectuals and reformers as well as American religious and republican ideals.

"Women Drawing Water, Bishop Hill Colony," c. 1860 This painting by Olaf Kraus captures the collective labor that characterized communal life at Bishop Hill Colony, Illinois. This utopian community was founded in 1846 by Eric Jansen, a critic of the Lutheran Church in Sweden. Forced to emigrate, he recruited 1400 other dissidents to join him on the American prairie. Kraus painted several scenes while living at Bishop Hill. Granger

In the 1820s Scottish and Welsh labor radicals such as Frances Wright, Robert Owen, and his son Robert Dale Owen established several utopian communities in the United States. They perceived the young republic as open to experiments in communal labor, gender equality, and (in Wright's case) racial justice. Their efforts ultimately failed, but they did arouse impassioned debate.

Then in 1841, former Unitarian minister George Ripley established a transcendentalist community at Brook Farm in Massachusetts. Four years later, Brook Farm was reorganized according to the principles of the French socialist Charles Fourier. Fourier believed that cooperation across classes was necessary to temper conflicts inherent in capitalist society. He developed a plan for communities, called phalanxes, where residents chose jobs based on individual interest but were paid according to the contribution of each job to the community's well-being. Fourier also advocated equality for women. More than forty Fourierist phalanxes were founded in the northern United States during the 1840s.

The Oneida community was a more uniquely American experiment. John Humphrey Noyes established it in central New York in 1848. He believed that Christ's Second Coming had already occurred, and his followers embraced the communalism of the early Christian church. Noyes required members to relinquish their private property to the community and to embrace the notion of "complex marriage," in which women and men were free to have sexual intercourse with any consenting adult. He also introduced a form of birth control that sought to ensure women's freedom from constant childbearing and instituted communal child-rearing practices. Divorce and remarriage were also permitted. Despite the public outrage provoked by Oneida's economic and sexual practices, the community recruited several hundred residents and thrived for more than three decades.

Review & Relate

■ How did efforts to alleviate poverty and temper alcohol consumption reflect the range of reform tactics and participants during the 1830s and 1840s?

■ What connections can you identify between utopian communities and mainstream reform movements in the first half of the nineteenth century?

Abolitionism Expands and **Divides**

For a small percentage of Northerners, slavery was the ultimate injustice. While most Northerners considered it sufficient to rid their own region of human bondage, antislavery advocates argued that the North remained complicit in the institution. After all, enslaved workers labored under brutal conditions to provide cotton for New England factories, sugar and molasses for northern tables, and profits for urban traders. Free and enslaved blacks were the earliest advocates of abolition. As more whites joined the movement in the 1830s, the ongoing role of blacks, the unwillingness of many white churches to condemn slavery, and the propriety of women's activism stirred controversies. By the 1840s abolitionists also disagreed over whether to wield moral persuasion or organize politically and whether to focus on abolishing slavery in the South or preventing its extension into western territories. Although these debates could rupture individual organizations, they expanded the range of antislavery associations and campaigns.

The Beginnings of the Antislavery Movement.
African Americans led the movement to abolish slavery from the American Revolution through at least the 1820s. They fled slavery and sued for their freedom during the Revolution, celebrated Haitian independence and honored Toussaint L'Overture, wrote antislavery poems and essays, and fought for gradual emancipation laws throughout the North. These black abolitionists gained allies, especially among white Quakers, who joined them in forming antislavery societies and petitioning state and federal governments to end slavery and the slave trade. In the 1820s these antislavery societies also published pamphlets, lectured to (usually small) audiences, and helped runaway slaves reach freedom.

In 1829 David Walker wrote the most militant antislavery statement, ***Appeal . . . to the Colored Citizens of the World***. The free son of an enslaved father, Walker left his North Carolina home for Boston in the 1820s and became a writer for *Freedom's Journal*, the country's first African American newspaper. In his *Appeal*, Walker warned that slaves would claim their freedom by force if whites did not agree to emancipate them. Some northern blacks feared Walker's radical *Appeal* would unleash a white backlash. Quakers like Benjamin Lundy, editor of the *Genius of Universal Emancipation*, admired Walker's courage but rejected his call for violence. Nonetheless the *Appeal* circulated widely among free and enslaved blacks, with copies spreading from northern cities to Charleston, Savannah, New Orleans, and Norfolk.

William Lloyd Garrison, a white Bostonian who worked with Lundy, was inspired by Walker's radical stance. In 1831 he launched his own abolitionist newspaper, the ***Liberator***. He urged white antislavery activists to embrace the goal of immediate emancipation without compensation to slave owners, a position advocated by the English Quaker Elizabeth Heyrick in 1824.

The *Liberator* demanded that whites take an absolute stand against slavery but use moral persuasion rather than armed force to halt its spread. With like-minded black and white activists in Boston, Philadelphia, and New York City, Garrison organized the **American Anti-Slavery Society (AASS)** in 1833. Initially only men were invited to join, although Philadelphia Quaker Lucretia Mott attended the founding meeting with her husband James. By the end of the decade, the AASS boasted branches in dozens of towns and cities across the North. Members supported lecturers and petition drives, criticized churches that refused to denounce slavery, and proclaimed the U.S. Constitution a proslavery document. Some Garrisonians also participated in the work of the **underground railroad**, a secret network of black and white activists who assisted fugitives fleeing enslavement (Map 10.2).

Maria Stewart, a free black widow in Boston, spoke out against slavery in 1831–1832 in lectures to mixed-sex audiences. In addition to demanding abolition, she insisted that northern blacks take more responsibility for ending slavery and fighting discrimination. While Stewart gained large audiences, some black Bostonians criticized her for demeaning her own race or merely for being a woman. In 1833 free black and white Quaker women, led by Charlotte Forten and Lucretia Mott, formed the Philadelphia Female Anti-Slavery Society, which advocated abolition and the boycott of cotton, sugar, and other slave-produced goods. Two years later, Sarah and Angelina Grimké joined the

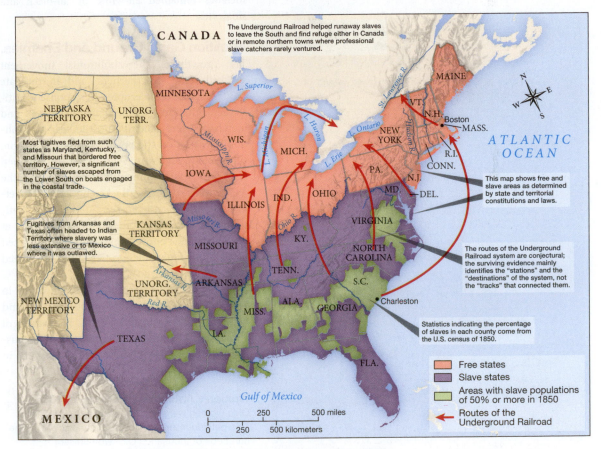

MAP 10.2   The Underground Railroad c. 1850

Free blacks and their white allies aided men and women who fled slavery from the 1790s on. By 1840, the system became more organized with individual conductors offering safe havens along well-worn routes. Former fugitives, most famously Harriet Tubman, joined the effort. In states like Arkansas and Texas, enslaved people often ran west rather than north, seeking aid from Indians or Mexicans.

Philadelphia society and the AAAS. Daughters of a prominent South Carolina planter, they moved to Philadelphia and converted to Quakerism. As white Southerners, their denunciations of slavery carried particular weight. Yet like Maria Stewart, their public stance as women aroused fierce opposition. In 1837 Congregationalist ministers in Massachusetts decried their presence in front of "promiscuous" audiences of men and women, but 1,500 female millworkers still turned out to hear them at Lowell's city hall.

The growing abolitionist movement quickly expanded to the frontier, where debates over slave and free territory were especially intense. In 1836 Ohio claimed more antislavery groups than any other state, and Ohio women initiated a petition drive to abolish slavery in the District of Columbia. The petition campaign, which spread across the North, inspired the first national meeting of women abolitionists in 1837. Other antislavery organizations, like the AASS, which had initially excluded women, now eagerly recruited them. Still, many local societies remained all-white or all-black and single-sex.

Abolition Gains Ground and Enemies.

The growth of the abolitionist movement shocked many Northerners, and in the late 1830s violence often erupted in response to antislavery agitation. Northern manufacturers and merchants were generally hostile, fearing abolitionists' effect on the profitable trade in cotton, sugar, cloth, and rum. And white workingmen feared increased competition for jobs. In the 1830s mobs routinely attacked antislavery meetings, lecturers, and presses. At the 1838 Antislavery Convention of American Women at Philadelphia's Pennsylvania Hall, mobs forced black and white women to flee and then burned the hall to the ground.

Massive antislavery petition campaigns in 1836 and 1837 generated opposition in and between the North and South. Thousands of abolitionists, including Amy Post and her husband, Isaac, signed petitions to ban slavery in

Women's Antislavery Petition, c. 1836
Ohio women were ardent antislavery petitioners. This petition from Clermont County was one of the hundreds of thousands U.S. women sent demanding the abolition of slavery or the slave trade. These women implore Congress to end slavery in the District of Columbia and focus on "the nameless wrongs of which the slaves of our own sex" are "the defenceless victims." Records of the U.S. House of Representatives and Records of the U.S. Senate, National Archives and Records Administration

the District of Columbia, end the internal slave trade, and oppose the annexation of Texas. Some evangelical women considered such efforts part of their Christian duty, but most ministers (including Finney) condemned antislavery work as outside women's sphere. In response, most female evangelicals retreated from direct involvement in the movement. Others continued their efforts but faced excommunication by their churches. **See Primary Source Project 10: Religious Faith and Women's Activism, page 350.** Meanwhile incensed Southern politicians persuaded Congress to pass the gag rule in 1836, which tabled all antislavery petitions without discussion.

But gag rules did not silence abolitionists. Indeed new groups of activists, most importantly self-emancipated slaves, offered potent personal tales of the horrors of bondage. The most famous fugitive abolitionist was Frederick Douglass. Born enslaved in Maryland around 1818, he fled to New Bedford, Massachusetts in 1838. He met Garrison in 1841, joined the AASS, and four years later published his life story, *Narrative of the Life of Frederick Douglass, as Told by Himself*. Having revealed his identity as a fugitive from slavery, Douglass sailed for England, where he launched a successful two-year lecture tour. While he was abroad, British abolitionists purchased Douglass's freedom from his owner, and Douglass returned to Massachusetts a free man.

In 1847 he decided to launch his own antislavery newspaper, the *North Star*, a decision that Garrison and other white AASS leaders opposed. Nonetheless, Douglass moved to Rochester, New York, with his wife Anna and their children. Douglass had found staunch allies in the city's black and white communities while lecturing in the region. These included Amy and Isaac Post, black barber James P. Morris, and members of the interracial and mixed-sex Western New York Anti-Slavery Society. That society and the all-black Union Anti-Slavery Sewing Society raised funds crucial for sustaining the *North Star*. Rochester men also organized single-sex abolitionist societies in the 1830s and 1840s as local anti-abolitionists became more outspoken. The latter included newspaper editor Horatio Warner, who forced a local school to reject Rosetta Douglass, Frederick and Anna's daughter, as a student. He and other anti-abolitionist editors regularly demeaned blacks and attacked abolitionists.

> **Explore ▸**
>
> Compare opposing views of the origins of the abolition movements in Sources 10.4 and 10.5.

Many white abolitionists were eager to hear fugitive slaves tell their dramatic stories, but they did not necessarily embrace racial equality. Indeed, many white abolitionists opposed slavery but believed that blacks were racially inferior; others claimed to support racial equality but assumed that black abolitionists would defer to white leaders. The independent efforts of Douglass and other black activists significantly expanded the antislavery movement but also revealed the limits of many white abolitionists' views.

Conflicts also arose over the responsibility of churches to challenge slavery. The major Protestant denominations included southern as well as northern churches. If mainstream churches—Presbyterians, Baptists, Methodists—refused communion to enslavers, their southern branches would secede. Still, from the 1830s on, abolitionists pressured churches to take Christian obligations seriously and denounce human bondage. Individual congregations responded, but aside from the Society of Friends, larger denominations failed to follow suit.

In response, abolitionists urged parishioners to break with churches that admitted slaveholders as members. Antislavery preachers pushed the issue, and some worshippers "came out" from mainstream churches to form antislavery congregations. White Wesleyan Methodists and Free Will Baptists joined African American Methodists and Baptists in

Comparative Secondary Source Analysis

Religion, Race, and the Call to End Slavery

In the 1830s, as reform movements surged across the North, some opponents of slavery began demanding an immediate end to human bondage. These *immediatists*, as they were known, included allies of white editor and activist William Lloyd Garrison and of Frederick Douglass and other outspoken fugitive slaves. They challenged not only slavery but also the economic and political structures, religious institutions, and moral values that supported it. Historians writing in the 1980s, like Lawrence Friedman, sought the roots of immediate abolitionism in evangelical movements and in the rise of a new middle class. By the 2010s, scholars represented here by Manisha Sinha highlighted the role of free blacks and fugitive slaves — women and men — in the rise and radicalism of the abolition movement. They also noted the important roles played by Quakers and by women in forging interracial alliances.

Source 10.4

Lawrence J. Friedman | The Religious Roots of Immediate Abolition, 1982

[I]mmediatist abolitionists showed a decidedly different cast of mind and personality from that of antislavery gradualists. Immediatists refused to temporize with evil. . . . They sensed that by plying slow, calculating gradualist measures such as African colonization . . . in the hope of ending slavery eventually, one compromised with sin. . . .

Like missionaries who champion temperance, Sabbath observation, [and] Bible and tract distribution, . . . immediatists constantly sought rapport with those whom they sought to proselytize; they embraced fellow immediatist abolitions, more moderate antislavery Northerners, and even a few Southerners. . . . [T]hey attempted to win these elements over to immediatist abolitionism through missionary appeals. . . .

For the most part, they were not radicals but representatives of the broad Northern middle-class benevolent reform community, subscribers to the pervasive values of market capitalism and Christian self-help. It is certainly noteworthy that members of their highly diverse local constituencies sometimes did not share their class allegiance or all of their ideological proclivities. . . . But the most revealing aspects of the immediatist experience concern the ways in which they reflected the values of the Northern middle class generally and the evangelical missionary community in particular, as well as those factors that caused them to depart in important respects from those who they most closely resembled.

Source: Lawrence J. Friedman, *Gregarious Saints: Self and Community in American Abolitionism, 1830–1870* (Cambridge: Cambridge University Press, 1982), pp. 1, 3, 4.

insisting that their members oppose slavery. Although these churches remained small, they served as a living challenge to mainstream denominations.

Abolitionism and Women's Rights. Women were increasingly active in the AASS and the "come outer" movement, but their growing participation aroused opposition even among abolitionists. In 1836–1837, female societies formed the backbone of

Source 10.5

Manisha Sinha | The Black Roots of Immediate Abolition, 2016

Slave resistance . . . lay at the heart of the abolition movement. . . . The enslaved inspired the formation of the first Quaker-dominated abolition and manumission [emancipation] societies as well as the first landmark [court] cases that inaugurated emancipation in the Western world. The actions of slave rebels and runaways, black writers and community leaders, did not lie outside of but shaped abolition and its goals. . . . Fugitive slaves united all factions of the movement and led abolitionists to justify revolutionary resistance to slavery. . . .

Black abolitionists were integral to the broader interracial milieu of the movement. . . . Black and white abolitionists also went beyond a simple appeal to the American republican tradition that sought to include African Americans in its promise. They generated a powerful critique of the slaveholding Republic and constructed a counternarrative that highlighted its origins in the slave trade and slavery. . . .

The abolition movement, in which the disenfranchised . . . played a seminal role was driven by passionate outsiders. Women were abolition's foot soldiers, and more controversially, its leaders and orators. . . . Its [the movement's] steady radicalization on women's rights, organized religion, politics and direct action made it quickly outgrow the empire of religious benevolence and moral reform. . . .

From the early Quaker and black protests against slavery to the rise of the Anglo-American movement against the slave trade . . . to the golden age of abolitionism in the years before the Civil War, abolitionists were united in their devotion to the slave's cause.

Source: Manisha Sinha, *The Slave's Cause: The History of Abolition* (New Haven: Yale University Press, 2016), pp. 1–3, 5.

Examine the Sources

1. How do Friedman and Sinha differ in their interpretations of the composition of the abolition movement? Friedman does not mention race or gender specifically, but whom do you imagine comprise his immediatists?
2. Drawing upon evidence in this chapter, how would you evaluate the strengths and weaknesses of Friedman's and Sinha's presentations?

Put It in Context

How did religion and race shape the wide range of reform movements that erupted between 1820 and 1850, and what made abolition distinct from other movements?

antislavery petition campaigns demanding an end to slavery and the slave trade in Washington, D.C. In 1837, the Anti-Slavery Convention of American Women met in New York City, and participants discussed abolition as well as the rights of women, including African American women. More women also joined the lecture circuit, notably Abby Kelley, a fiery orator who demanded that women be granted an equal role in the movement. But when Garrison and his supporters appointed Kelley to the AASS business committee in

May 1840, angry debates erupted over the propriety of women participating "in closed meetings with men." Of the 1,000 abolitionists in attendance, some 300 walked out in protest. The dissidents, including many evangelical men, soon formed a new organization, the American and Foreign Anti-Slavery Society, which excluded women from public lecturing and office holding but encouraged them to support men's efforts.

Those who remained in the AASS continued to expand women's roles. In 1840 local chapters appointed a handful of female delegates, including Lucretia Mott of Philadelphia, to the World Anti-Slavery Convention in London. The majority of men at the meeting, however, rejected the female delegates' credentials. Women were then forced to watch the proceedings from a separate section of the hall, confirming for some that women could be effective in campaigns against slavery only if they gained more rights for themselves.

As more women and blacks traveled to antislavery conventions, they confronted the difficulties of finding suitable accommodations. Most U.S. hotels and boarding houses were racially segregated and many were unwilling to house single women alongside men. Fortunately, many radical abolitionists were also active in the movement for health reform. One of its leaders, Sylvester Graham, advocated vegetarianism, sexual restraint, and temperance. Some of his followers established Graham boardinghouses in northern cities, offering food, beds, and spaces for socializing to black and white women and men. Graham Houses also provided safe haven for fugitive slaves. While rarely advertising these aspects of their work for fear of anti-abolitionist attacks, the Graham name reassured abolitionists and fugitives that they were welcome.

In spring 1844 and 1848, women in the Daughters of Zion, several of whom were abolitionists, petitioned the African Methodist Episcopal Church to grant women licenses to preach. Although some male leaders supported the claim, the conference majority twice rejected the request. In July 1848, a small circle of women, including Lucretia Mott and a young American she met in London, Elizabeth Cady Stanton, along with three progressive Quakers organized the first convention focused explicitly on women's rights. Held in Stanton's hometown of Seneca Falls, New York, the convention attracted three hundred white women and men. James Mott, husband of Lucretia, presided over the convention, and Frederick Douglass spoke, but women dominated the proceedings. One hundred participants, including Amy Post, signed the **Declaration of Sentiments**, which called for women's equality in everything from education and employment to legal rights and voting. Two weeks later, Post helped organize a second convention in Rochester. There participants elected a woman, Abigail Bush, to preside; invited working-class women to testify about their plight; and explicitly demanded equal rights for women of "every complexion," that is race. Douglass again offered his support.

Although abolitionism provided much of the impetus for women's rights advocates, other movements also contributed. Strikes by seamstresses and mill workers in the 1830s and 1840s highlighted women's economic needs. Utopian communities experimented with gender equality, and temperance reformers focused attention on domestic violence and sought changes in divorce laws. A diverse coalition also advocated for married women's property rights in the 1840s. Women's rights were debated among New York's Seneca Indians as well. Like the Cherokee, Seneca women had lost traditional rights over land and tribal policy as their nation adopted Anglo-American ways. In the summer of 1848, the creation of a written constitution threatened to enshrine these losses in writing. The Seneca constitution did strip women of their dominant role in selecting chiefs but protected their right to vote on the sale of tribal lands. Earlier in 1848, revolutions had erupted against repressive regimes in France and elsewhere in Europe. Antislavery newspapers covered developments in detail, including European women's demands for political and civil recognition. Women's rights meetings continued to draw on these ideas and influences over the next decade.

The Rise of Antislavery Parties.

As women's rights advocates demanded female suffrage, debates over the role of partisan politics in the antislavery campaign intensified. Keeping slavery out of western territories depended on the actions of Congress, as did abolishing slavery in the nation's capital and ending the internal slave trade. Moral suasion had seemingly done little to change minds in Congress or in the South. To force abolition onto the national political agenda, the **Liberty Party** was formed in 1840. Many Garrisonians were appalled at the idea of participating in national elections when the federal government supported slavery in numerous ways, from the three-fifths compromise to allowing slavery in newly acquired territories. Still, the Liberty Party gained significant support among abolitionists in New York, the Middle Atlantic states, and the Midwest.

The 1840 election was also notable for the participation of women in campaign events. Whig candidate William Henry Harrison encouraged women to support the campaign. "Mother [Elizabeth] Clarkson" of Indiana gave numerous speeches on his behalf, and local Whig committees brought wagonloads of women to Harrison's rallies. The Liberty Party, too, welcomed public support from women. Harrison's victory opened the door to women's participation across the political spectrum.

Both Whigs and Democrats had avoided the antislavery issue to keep their southern and northern wings intact, but that strategy became more difficult once the Liberty Party entered campaigns. In 1840 that party won less than 1 percent of the popular vote but organized rallies that attracted large crowds. In 1844 the party more than doubled its votes, which was sufficient to deny Henry Clay a victory in New York State and thus ensure the election of James K. Polk (see "Expanding to Oregon and Texas" in chapter 11).

When President Polk led the United States into war with Mexico, interest in the Liberty Party surged. In 1848 it gained the support of antislavery Whigs, also called Conscience Whigs; northern Democrats who opposed the extension of slavery into the territories; and African American leaders like Frederick Douglass, who began questioning Garrisonians' view that only moral suasion could end slavery. Yet more practically minded political abolitionists soon founded the **Free-Soil Party**, which quickly subsumed the Liberty Party. Free-Soilers focused less on the moral wrongs of slavery than on the benefits of keeping western territories free for northern whites seeking economic opportunity. The Free-Soil Party nominated Martin Van Buren, a former Democrat, for president in 1848 and won 10 percent of the popular vote. Once again, the result was to send a slaveholder to the White House — Zachary Taylor, a Mexican War hero. Nonetheless, the Free-Soil Party had gained far more support than the Liberty Party, raising fears in the South and in the two major parties that the battle over slavery could no longer be contained.

Review & Relate

- How did the American Anti-Slavery Society differ from earlier abolitionist organizations?

- How did conflicts over gender, race, and tactics shape the development of the abolitionist movement in the 1830s and 1840s?

Conclusion: From the North to the Nation

Charles Grandison Finney followed these political developments from Oberlin College, where he served as president in the 1840s. Skeptical that electoral politics could transform society, he continued to view individual conversions as the wellspring of change. As the nation expanded westward, he trained ministers to travel the frontier converting American Indians to Christianity and reminding pioneering families of their religious obligations. Amy Post took a more militant stand, rejecting any participation in a government that accepted slavery and fomented war. She disagreed with Douglass's decision to support the Liberty Party, but recognized that moral persuasion alone might never convince planters to end slavery.

The efforts of the tens of thousands of Northerners inspired by religious and reform movements between 1820 and 1850 had a greater impact because of the growth of cities and improvements in transportation and communication. It was far easier by the 1830s for evangelicals, Quakers, Mormons, transcendentalists, utopian communalists, and other activists to spread their ideas through sermons, lectures, newspapers, pamphlets, and conventions.

Urban development was driven by the migration of native-born Americans from rural areas and small towns as well as the increase in immigration from Ireland, Germany, and other European nations. The panic of 1837 fueled an economic crisis that lasted several years and temporarily stalled the market revolution. But the panic also inspired many Americans to organize against poverty, intemperance, prostitution, and other urban problems. At the same time, the concentration of workers, immigrants, and free blacks in cities allowed them to unite and claim rights for themselves. For workers, the need to organize was heightened by the growth of factories even as the increasing diversity of the labor force aroused tensions among distinct racial and ethnic groups. Numerous attacks occurred against free blacks, who competed for jobs with immigrants and poor whites even as the antislavery movement expanded across the North.

Of the numerous reform movements that emerged in this period, abolition carried the most powerful national implications by 1850. The growth of abolitionist sentiment was related in part to the rapid expansion of slavery. Yet the increase in the size of southern plantations and their spread westward also ensured a steady supply of raw materials, such as cotton, that drove commercial and industrial development across the North. Such developments fueled significant transformations across the South as well.

Timeline of Events

Key Terms

Review & Relate

1. How did the market revolution, including improvements like the Erie Canal, reshape the landscape and lives of Americans in the North?

2. As northern cities became larger and more diverse in the first half of the nineteenth century, what changes and challenges did urban residents face and what values and beliefs did the new middle class embrace?

3. How and why did American manufacturing change during the first half of the nineteenth century?

4. How did new technologies, immigration, and the panic of 1837 change the economic opportunities and organizing strategies for northern workers?

5. What impact did the Second Great Awakening have in the North?

6. What new religious organizations and viewpoints emerged in the first half of the nineteenth century, *outside* of Protestant evangelical denominations?

7. How did efforts to alleviate poverty and temper alcohol consumption reflect the range of reform tactics and participants during the 1830s and 1840s?

8. What connections can you identify between utopian communities and mainstream reform movements in the first half of the nineteenth century?

9. How did the American Anti-Slavery Society differ from earlier abolitionist organizations?

10. How did conflicts over gender, race, and tactics shape the development of the abolitionist movement in the 1830s and 1840s?

Religious Faith and Women's Activism

▶ **In what ways did religion limit or expand women's roles and their participation in reform movements in the 1830s?**

During the 1830s, religious revivals and growing religious diversity raised new questions about women's place in public life. In many white evangelical churches, women played prominent roles during revivals, leading prayer circles and persuading others to seek salvation. Still, male ministers retained sole authority and often emphasized women's subjection during the conversion process (Source 10.6). While accepting their subordinate role, many evangelical women nevertheless labored on behalf of temperance, moral reform, and even abolition (Source 10.7).

Male ministers also dominated black churches, but a few black women were recognized as itinerant evangelicals by the 1830s. It was Maria Stewart, however, a free black widow and evangelical convert, who spoke out most publicly about slavery, racial prejudice, and the challenges facing northern African American communities (Source 10.8).

Quaker, Unitarian, Catholic, and Jewish women also combined faith and social activism. They, too, advocated temperance, expanded charitable efforts, and promoted moral uplift. Quaker women also played prominent roles in the antislavery movement alongside white men and African Americans. These efforts generated heated debates over women's sphere. When Sarah and Angelina Grimké, daughters of a South Carolina enslaver, moved to Philadelphia and converted to Quakerism, the American Anti-Slavery Society invited them to lecture on behalf of abolition. Their 1837 lecture tour attracted large mixed-sex and interracial audiences,

leading Congregational ministers in New England to denounce the sisters' unwomanly conduct (Source 10.9). While many white evangelical women then retreated from antislavery activities, Quaker and black evangelical women continued their activities and Sarah Grimké published a spirited defense of women's antislavery activism (Source 10.10). Like Stewart, Grimké linked female efforts on behalf of racial advancement to women's need for more rights for themselves.

Source 10.6

Charles G. Finney | An Influential Woman Converts, 1830

Women were among the earliest converts in the Reverend Charles Finney's revivals in Rochester, New York. Many then persuaded friends and relatives to seek salvation. In describing the conversion of Mrs. Selah Mathews, Finney reinforces conventional ideas about female subordination while recognizing Mrs. Mathews's influence among local elites. Mrs. Mathews briefly joined a female antislavery society but by 1836 shifted her efforts to moral reform.

The wife of a prominent lawyer . . . was one of the first converts. She was a woman of high standing, a lady of culture and extensive influence. . . .

Mrs. M[athews] had been a gay, worldly woman, and very fond of society. She afterward told me that when I first came there, she greatly regretted it, and feared [that] . . . a revival would greatly interfere with the pleasures and amusements that she had promised herself that winter. On conversing with her I found that the Spirit of the Lord was indeed dealing with her. . . . She was bowed down with great conviction of sin. . . . I pressed her earnestly to renounce sin, and the world, and self, and everything for Christ. . . . [W]e knelt down to pray; and my mind being full of the subject of the pride of her heart . . . I very soon introduced the text: "Except ye be converted and become as little children, ye shall in no wise enter into the kingdom of heaven." . . . [A]lmost immediately I heard Mrs M[athews] . . . repeating that text:

"Except ye be converted and become as little children—as little children—Except ye be converted and become as little children." I observed that her mind was taken with that, and the Spirit of God was pressing it upon her heart. I therefore continued to pray, holding that subject before her mind. . . .

. . . Her heart broke down, her sensibility gushed forth, and before we rose . . . , she was indeed a little child. . . . From that moment she was out-spoken in her religious convictions, and zealous for the conversion of her friends.

Source: Charles G. Finney, *The Memoirs of Rev. Charles G. Finney, Written by Himself* (New York: F. H. Revell, 1876), 287–88.

Source 10.7

Elizabeth Emery and Mary P. Abbott | Founding a Female Anti-Slavery Society, 1836

While many women who converted during the Second Great Awakening engaged in social activism, a far smaller number remained active over time in the abolitionist movement. Elizabeth Emery and Mary Abbott, two leaders in the Andover (Massachusetts) Female Anti-Slavery Society, were in that small group. They wrote a letter to the *Liberator*, expressing their belief in Christian women's moral responsibility to end slavery.

Mr. Editor:

In these days of women's doings, it may not be amiss to report the proceedings of some ladies in Andover. . . .

The call of our female friends across the waters—the energetic appeal of those untiring sisters in the work of emancipation in Boston—above all, the sighs, the groans, the deathlike struggles of scourged sisters in the South—these have moved our hearts, our hands. We feel that woman has a place in this Godlike work, for woman's woes, and woman's wrongs, are borne to us on every breeze that flows from the South; woman has a place, for she forms a part in God's created intelligent instrumentality to reform the world. . . . When man proves recreant [remiss] to his duty and faithless to his Maker, woman, with her feeling heart, should rouse him—should start his sympathies—should cry in his ear, and raise such a storm of generous sentiment, as shall never let him sleep again. We believe God gave woman a heart to feel—an eye to weep—a hand to work—a tongue to speak. Now let her use that tongue to speak on slavery. Is it not a curse — a heaven-daring abomination? Let her employ that hand, to labor for the slave. Does not her sister in bonds, labor night and day without reward? Let her heart grieve, and her eye fill with tears, in view of a female's body dishonored — a female's mind debased — a female's soul forever ruined! Woman nothing to do with slavery! Abhorred the thought!! We will pray to abhor it more and more. Is not woman abused — woman trampled upon — woman spoiled of her virtue, her probity, her influence, her joy! And this, not in India — not in China — not in Turkey — not in Africa but in America — in the United States of America. . . .

As Christian women, we will do a Christian woman's duty. . . .

Our preamble gives our creed:

"We believe American Slavery is a sin against God — at war with the dictates of humanity, and subversive of the principles of freedom, because it regards rational beings as goods and chattel; robs them of compensation for their toil—denies to them the protection of law—disregards the relation of husband and wife, brother and sister, parent and child; shuts out from the intellect the light of knowledge; overwhelms hope in despair and ruins the soul—thus sinking to the level of brutes, more than one million of American females, who are created in God's image, a little lower than the angels', and consigns them over to degradation, physical, social, intellectual, and moral.

Source: Elizabeth Emery and Mary P. Abbott, "Letter to *The Liberator*," *Liberator*, August 27, 1836, 138.

Maria Stewart │ On Religion and the Pure Principles of Morality, 1831

Maria Stewart was orphaned in 1808 at age five. She then worked as a servant for fifteen years, gaining an education by attending Sunday school. Married at twenty-three and widowed at twenty-six, she experienced a religious conversion the next year and began speaking publicly in 1831 to mixed-sex, largely black audiences. She urged black women to claim their God-given rights and improve themselves and their community. When some black Bostonians criticized her views, Stewart moved to New York City and later Washington, D.C.

O ye daughters of Africa, awake! awake! arise! no longer sleep nor slumber, but distinguish yourselves. Show forth to the world that ye are endowed with noble and exalted faculties. . . .

I am of a strong opinion, that the day on which we unite, heart and soul, and turn our attention to knowledge and improvement, that day the hissing and reproach among the nations of the earth against us will cease. . . .

. . . Why cannot we do something to distinguish ourselves, and contribute some of our hard earnings that would reflect honor upon our memories, and cause our children to arise and call us blessed? Shall it any longer be said of the daughters of Africa, they have no ambition . . . ? By no means. Let every female heart become united; and let us raise a fund ourselves; and at the end of one year and a half, we might be able to lay the corner-stone for the building of a High School . . . and God would raise us up, and enough to aid us in our laudable designs. . . .

How long shall the fair daughters of Africa be compelled to bury their minds and talents beneath a load of iron pots and kettles? . . . How long shall a mean set of men flatter us with their smiles, and enrich themselves with our hard earnings; their wives' fingers sparkling with rings, and they

themselves laughing at our folly? Until we begin to promote and patronize each other. . . . We have never had an opportunity of displaying our talents; therefore the world thinks we know nothing. . . . Do you ask the disposition I would have you possess? Possess the spirit of independence. The Americans do, and why should not you? Possess the spirit of men, bold and enterprising, fearless and undaunted. Sue for your rights and privileges. . . . That day we, as a people, harken unto the voice of the Lord our God, . . . and we shall begin to flourish.

Source: Maria Stewart, "Religion and the Pure Principles of Morality," in *Meditations from the Pen of Mrs. Maria W. Stewart. . . . First Published by W. Lloyd Garrison & Knapp* (Washington, DC: Enterprise, 1879), 25, 31–32.

Congregational Pastoral Letter, 1837

White women's increased involvement in abolitionism generated considerable controversy. In August 1837 Congregational Church leaders circulated a letter to ministers throughout New England. They were outraged by Angelina and Sarah Grimké's lecturing on antislavery to mixed-sex audiences and condemned both them and women's public activism generally.

W e invite your attention to the dangers which at present seem to threaten the female character with wide-spread and permanent injury. The appropriate duties and influence of woman are clearly stated in the New Testament. Those duties and that influence are unobtrusive and private, but the source of mighty power. When the mild, dependent, softening influence of woman upon the sternness of man's opinions is fully exercised, society feels the effects of it in a thousand ways. The power of woman is in her dependence, flowing from the consciousness of that weakness which God has given her for her protection. . . . There are social influences which females use in promoting piety and the great objects of Christian benevolence which we cannot too highly commend. We appreciate the unostentatious prayers and efforts of woman in advancing the cause of religion at home and abroad; in Sabbath-schools; . . .

and in all such associated effort as becomes the modesty of her sex. . . .

But when she assumes the place and tone of man as a public reformer, our care and protection of her seem unnecessary; . . . and her character becomes unnatural. If the vine, whose strength and beauty is to lean upon the trellis-work and half conceal its clusters, thinks to assume the independence and the overshadowing nature of the elm, it will not only cease to bear fruit, but fall in shame and dishonor into the dust. We cannot, therefore, but regret the mistaken conduct of those who encourage females to bear an obtrusive and ostentatious part in measures of reform, and countenance any of that sex who so far forget themselves as to incinerate in the character of public lecturers and teachers. . . . We especially deplore the intimate acquaintance and promiscuous conversation of females with regard to things "which ought not to be named"; by which that modesty and delicacy . . . which constitutes the true influence of woman in society, is consumed, and the way opened . . . for degeneracy and ruin.

Source: "Pastoral Letter of the General Association of Massachusetts to the Congregational Churches under Their Care," *Liberator*, August 11, 1837.

Source 10.10

Sarah Grimké | Response to the Pastoral Letter, 1837

In response to the ministers' criticism, Sarah Grimké wrote a letter to the *Liberator* that she later published in a book of essays. Like many progressive Quakers, she and her sister felt obligated to speak out against the evils of slavery, which they had witnessed firsthand on their father's South Carolina plantation. The criticisms leveled at them inspired Sarah to develop arguments in support of women's rights as well as abolition.

Dear Friend,

. . . I am persuaded that when the minds of men and women become emancipated from the thraldom [bondage] of superstition and "traditions of men," the sentiments contained in the Pastoral Letter will be recurred to with as much astonishment as the opinions of Cotton Mather and other distinguished men of his day, on the subject of witchcraft. . . .

But to the letter. It says, "We invite your attention to the dangers which at present seem to threaten the female character with wide-spread and permanent injury." I rejoice that they have called the attention of my sex to this subject, because I believe if woman investigates it, she will soon discover that danger is impending, though from a totally different source . . . — danger from those who, having long held the reins of *usurped* authority, are unwilling to permit us to fill that sphere which God created us to move in, and who have entered into league to crush the immortal mind of woman. I rejoice, because I am persuaded that the rights of woman, like the rights of slaves, need only be examined to be understood and asserted. . . .

"The appropriate duties and influence of women are clearly stated in the New Testament. Those duties are unobtrusive and private, but the sources of *mighty power*. . . ." No one can desire more earnestly than I do, that woman may move exactly in the sphere which her Creator has assigned her; and I believe her having been displaced from that sphere has introduced confusion into the world. It is, therefore, of vast importance to herself and to all the rational creation, that she should ascertain what are her duties and her privileges as a responsible and immortal being. . . .

But . . . her light is not to shine before man like that of her brethren; but she is passively to let the lords of the creation, as they call themselves, put the bushel over it, lest peradventure [perhaps] it might appear that the world has been benefitted by the rays of *her* candle. So that her quenched light, according to their judgment, will be of more use than if it were set on the candlestick. "Her influence is the source of mighty power." This has ever been the flattering language of man since he laid aside the whip as a means to keep woman in subjection. He spares her body; but the war he has waged against her mind, her heart, and her soul, has been no less destructive to her as a moral being. . . . She has surrendered her dearest RIGHTS, and been satisfied with the privileges which man has assumed to grant her. . . . He has adorned the creature whom God gave him as a companion, with baubles and gewgaws [showy things], turned her attention to personal attractions, offered incense to her vanity, and made her the instrument of his selfish gratification. . . .

We are told, "the power of woman is in her dependence, flowing from a consciousness of that weakness which God has given her for her protection." If physical weakness is alluded to, I cheerfully concede the superiority . . . but if they mean to intimate, that mental or moral weakness belongs to woman, more than to man, I utterly disclaim the charge. . . . [N]o where does God say that he made any distinction between us, as moral and intelligent beings. . . .

As to the pretty simile . . . , "If the vine whose strength and beauty is to lean upon the trellis work, and half conceal its clusters. . . ." etc. I shall only remark that it might well suit the poet's fancy . . . ; but it seems to me utterly inconsistent with the dignity of a Christian body, to endeavor to draw such an anti-scriptural distinction between men and women. Ah! how many of my sex feel . . . , under the gentle appellation of protection, that what they have leaned upon has proved a broken reed at best, and oft a spear.

Source: Sarah Grimké, *Letters on the Equality of the Sexes and the Condition of Woman* (Boston: Isaac Knapp, 1838), 14–18, 21.

Interpret the Evidence

1. What does Charles Finney's account of Mrs. Mathews's conversion indicate about the subordination and influence of evangelical women (Source 10.6)? How does it compare in intent and attitudes with the Pastoral Letter (Source 10.9)?
2. Why do Elizabeth Emery and Mary Abbott describe enslaved women as their sisters (Source 10.7)? Would Maria Stewart agree with their view (Source 10.8)?
3. Who is Stewart's audience and why does she highlight the actions and character of free black women (Source 10.8)?
4. How do white and black women activists justify women's roles in the abolitionist movement, and whom are they trying to persuade (Sources 10.6, 10.7, and 10.9)?

Put It in Context

How do the arguments of Emery, Abbott, Stewart, and Grimké challenge dominant beliefs about men's and women's proper spheres in the mid-nineteenth century?

Why did evangelical ministers denounce the Grimkés' speeches before mixed-sex audiences but not Stewart's?

Slavery Expands South and West

1830–1850

The Slave Market

Few Americans and even fewer Europeans ever entered a slave market where black men, women, and children were auctioned off to the highest bidder. They did, however, see etchings, engravings, and paintings of the market created by artists. Some emphasized the horrors of the market; others, like German painter Friedrich Schulz, softened the reality through rich colors and respectable dress. ▶ **To learn more about this primary source, see Source 11.9 on page 390.**

Bridgeman Images

After reading this chapter you will be able to:

- Explain the development of a plantation society and the impact on planters and their families as well as enslaved workers and their families.

- Discuss the importance of enslaved labor and the development of a distinctive slave culture, including forms of resistance.

- Analyze the differences among southern whites as slavery expanded and compare the techniques used by planters to control free and enslaved blacks and non-slaveholding whites.

- Evaluate the challenges that Indians, the panic of 1837, Texas independence, and the Whig Party posed for the Democratic Party.

- Evaluate the ways that the idea of manifest destiny shaped national elections and intensified debates over slavery.

Comparing American Histories

José Antonio Menchaca was born in Spanish Texas in January 1800. His parents and nine siblings were known as Tejanos, people of Mexican descent living in Texas. His Spanish great-great-grandfather on his mother's side had been one of the founders of San Antonio de Bexar in 1718. José Antonio was raised there and learned to read, write, and speak both Spanish and English. In 1826, he married Teresa Ramón, and they had four children.

(left) **José Antonio Menchaca** Library of Congress
(right) **Solomon Northup** Documenting the American South, University Library, The University of North Carolina at Chapel Hill, http://docsouth.unc.edu/fpn/clay/ill18.html

After U.S. citizens living in Texas declared their independence from Mexico in 1835, Menchaca joined the Texian Army and served alongside other Tejanos under Captain Juan Seguin. He was stationed at the Alamo Mission in San Antonio in 1836 when word came that Mexican president Antonio Lopez de Santa Anna was leading an army to reclaim the territory. Captain Seguin and Alamo co-commander James Bowie convinced Menchaca to leave the fortress and move his family to Seguin's isolated ranch. Seguin, too, left the Alamo to recruit more Tejano volunteers. Thus Menchaca and Seguin were gone when Mexican soldiers defeated Texas forces at the Alamo.

Soon after, Menchaca rejoined Seguin's forces as an officer. Sam Houston, who had taken leadership of the Texas forces, met up with Seguin's company on March 11 and announced that delegates to the Convention of 1836 had declared Texas an independent nation. American scouts captured Mexican horsemen carrying mail for General Santa Anna, and Menchaca translated letters for Houston that revealed detailed information about Mexican strategies. Concerned that the Anglos in his own army would not differentiate between Mexican enemies and their Tejano allies, Houston ordered the latter to stay behind. Seguin convinced him to allow his men to fight. Houston agreed but insisted that they place cardboard in their hatbands as a sign that they were Texas allies. The combined forces routed the Mexican Army at the battle of San Jacinto in April 1836, ensuring Texas independence. Menchaca was among the soldiers honored by the Congress of the Republic of Texas in 1838.

Solomon Northup, a free-born African American, also ended up on the nation's southern frontier. However, his residence in Louisiana was not of his own choosing. His father Mintus had been born into slavery in New York State but was freed by his master's will in 1797. He moved to Minerva, New York, married a free woman of color, and had two sons. Solomon, born in 1807 or 1808, married Anne Hampton when he was in his early twenties. He worked transporting goods on the region's waterways and made extra cash playing the fiddle while Anne worked as a cook. In 1834, the couple moved to Saratoga Springs, New York, where they raised their three children.

In March 1841 Northup met two white circus performers who hired him to play the fiddle for them on tour. They paid his wages up front and told him to obtain documents proving his free status. After reaching Washington, D.C., however, Northup was drugged, chained, and sold to James Birch, a notorious enslaver. Northup was resold in New Orleans to William Ford, who changed his name to Platt. Ford put him to work as a raftsman while Northup tried unsuccessfully to get word to his wife.

In 1842 Ford sold "Platt" to a neighbor, John Tibeats, who, unlike Ford, whipped and abused his enslaved workers. When Tibeats attacked Northup with an ax, he fought back and fled to Ford's house. His former owner shielded him from Tibeats' wrath and arranged his sale to the planter Edwin Epps. For the next ten years, Northup worked the cotton fields on Epps's plantation.

Finally, in 1852 Samuel Bass, a Canadian carpenter who openly acknowledged his antislavery views, came to work on Epps's house. Northup persuaded Bass to send a letter to his wife in Saratoga Springs. Anne Northup, astonished to hear that her husband was still alive, took the letter to lawyer Henry Northup, the son of Mintus's former owner. After months of legal efforts, a local judge freed Solomon Northup in January 1853. ■

C omparing the American histories of José Antonio Menchaca and Solomon Northup illuminates clashes over western expansion and slavery. By siding with U.S. rebels, Menchaca and his family benefited when Texas gained its independence from Mexico. Establishing a home in San Antonio, Menchaca was elected alderman and then mayor of the city, achieving prosperity as well as political influence. His three daughters helped expand the multicultural population of the region by marrying into Anglo-American, French, and German families. In Texas and across the lower South, enslaved labor remained central to economic success and fueled market and industrial revolutions throughout the nation. Cities like New Orleans benefitted from both slavery's expansion and cotton's critical role in national and international trade. Still, from the 1830s to the 1850s, slave ownership became concentrated in the hands of a decreasing proportion of white southern families. Slave traders played a crucial role in slavery's expansion, inspiring some traders to capture free blacks like Solomon Northup and sell them into slavery. Northup labored in the harsh conditions of frontier Louisiana for masters who wielded distinct forms of brutality. He saw how the growing concentration of enslaved workers on individual plantations could both strengthen African American communities and fracture them. The enslaved laborers were also affected by the volatility of the cotton market, which created enormous economic uncertainty across the South. Planters insisted that expanding into new lands to cultivate more cotton was the only way to perpetuate economic growth, ensuring that more enslaved families would be separated from their loved ones. Democratic administrations in Washington, D.C. bolstered this expansionist effort by forcibly removing the last Indian nations from the Southeast, supporting independence and statehood for Texas, and proclaiming war on Mexico. These policies intensified clashes with Indian nations, heightened conflicts over slavery, and inspired the emergence of the Whig Party.

Planters Expand the Slave System

The cotton gin, developed in the 1790s, ensured the growth of southern agriculture into the 1850s. As the cotton kingdom spread west, those who owned the largest plantations forged a distinctive culture around the institution of slavery. While this slave-based agricultural economy limited the development of cities, technology, and educational institutions, the **planters** who wielded economic and political power calculated the benefits of the system. The South did become more dependent on the North for many of its needs, but the enormous profits from cotton, sugar, and rice allowed the planter class to live a luxurious lifestyle. Moreover, with northern businesses deeply entwined with the cotton economy, planters felt assured of northern support for policies supporting slavery. These included westward expansion, which dramatically increased the trade of enslaved people across the South. That trade shattered black families and fueled new forms of slave resistance and a growing abolition movement in the North. Still, southern planters and enslavers viewed themselves as national leaders, both the repository of traditional American values and the engine of economic progress.

A Plantation Society Develops in the South.

Plantation slavery existed throughout the Americas in the early nineteenth century. Extensive plantations worked by large numbers of enslaved people existed in the West Indies and South America. In the U.S. South, however, the volatile cotton market and a scarcity of fertile land kept most plantations relatively small before 1830. But over the next two decades, territorial expansion and profits from cotton, rice, and sugar allowed successful enslavers to build grand houses and purchase a variety of luxury goods.

As plantations grew, a wealthy aristocracy sought to ensure productivity by employing harsh methods of discipline. Even planters considered progressive in their application of modern principles of agriculture, such as James Henry Hammond of South Carolina, used the whip liberally. By these means, they hoped to ensure that their estates generated sufficient profits to support a lavish lifestyle.

Increased attention to comfort and luxury helped make the heavy workload of plantation mistresses tolerable. Mistresses were expected to manage their own families and enslaved domestic workers as well as feeding, clothing, and medical care for the entire labor force. They also organized social events, hosted relatives and friends for extended stays, and sometimes directed the plantation in their husband's absence.

Still, plantation mistresses were relieved of the most arduous labor by enslaved women, who cooked, cleaned, and washed for the family, cared for the children, and even nursed the babies. Wealthy white women benefited from the best education, the greatest access to music and literature, and the finest clothes and furnishings. The pedestal on which plantation mistresses stood was shaky, built on a patriarchal system in which husbands and fathers held enormous power. Thus, most wives tried to ignore the sexual relations that husbands initiated with enslaved women. Catherine Hammond did not. After discovering James's sexual abuse of an enslaved mother and daughter, she moved to Charleston with their two youngest children. Others, however, took out their anger and frustration on enslaved women already victimized by their husbands. Moreover, many mistresses brought enslaved women or men to their marriage. These female enslavers traded them in slave markets, often through male agents, or hired them out as wet nurses so other plantation mistresses could avoid nursing their own children. They also bestowed them as gifts or bequests to family members and friends, tearing apart families as their husbands did.

Not all enslavers were wealthy planters like the Hammonds, with fifty or more slaves and extensive landholdings. Far more planters in the 1830s and 1840s owned between twenty and fifty enslaved people, and an even larger number of farmers owned just three to six enslaved workers. As Hammond wrote a friend in 1847, "The planters here are essentially what the nobility are in other countries. They stand at the head of society & politics."

Urban Life in the Slave South.

The political and economic supremacy of enslavers had broad repercussions. The richest men in the South invested in enslaved labor, land, and household goods, with little left to develop industry, technology, or urban institutions. The largest factory in the South, the Tredegar Iron Works in Richmond, Virginia, employed several hundred free and enslaved African Americans by 1850. Most southern industrialists, however, like South Carolina textile manufacturer William Gregg, employed poor white women and children. But neither Tredegar nor scattered textile mills fundamentally reshaped the region's economy.

Even as the South fell behind in urban development, its port cities were central to economic growth throughout the nation. Northern agents, especially cotton brokers (called factors), directed much of the trade in Baltimore, Charleston, Savannah, and New Orleans. This trade formed another link in the economic bonds between North and South. Port cities were also home to the largest slave markets in the region. At the same time, nearly one-third of southern whites had no access to cash and instead bartered goods and services, which restricted the growth of smaller towns and cities across the South.

Cities were home to the largest numbers of free blacks in the South. The growing demand for cheap domestic labor in urban areas and planters' greater willingness to emancipate less valuable single enslaved women meant that free black women generally outnumbered men in southern cities. These women worked mainly as washerwomen, cooks, and general domestics, while free black men labored as skilled artisans, dockworkers, or sailors. Free blacks competed for the latter jobs with enslaved laborers and growing numbers of

New Orleans, 1841   New Orleans was one of the few major urban areas in the South and, like Baltimore and Charleston, prospered through its seaport. The port of New Orleans attracted sailing ships engaged in foreign commerce, steamships carrying goods along the Mississippi River, and enslavers from across the eastern United States. The New York Public Library/Art Resource, NY

European immigrants who flocked to port cities in the 1840s and 1850s. The presence of immigrants and free blacks and the reputation of ports as escape hatches for enslaved runaways ensured that these cities remained volatile even as they drove the South's economy.

The scarcity of cities other than ports and of industry curtailed the development of internal transportation systems in the South. State governments invested little in roads, canals, and railroads. Most small farmers traded goods locally, and most planters used the South's extensive river system to send goods to port cities, which were then carried on ships to the North, Europe, or the West Indies. Only Virginia and Maryland, with their proximity to the nation's capital, developed extensive road and rail networks.

The Consequences of Slavery's Expansion.
Outside the South, industry and agriculture increasingly benefited from technological innovation. Planters, however, continued to rely on intensive manual labor and focused on fertilizer and crop rotation rather than machines to enhance productivity. The limited use of new technologies — such as iron plows or seed drills — resulted from a lack of investment capital (which was tied up in land and labor) and planters' refusal to purchase expensive equipment that enslaved workers might break or sabotage. These enslavers also relied on continually expanding the acreage under cultivation.

One result of these practices was that a declining percentage of white Southerners came to control vast estates with large numbers of enslaved laborers. Between 1830 and 1850, the absolute number of both slaves and enslavers grew. But enslavers became a smaller proportion of all white Southerners because the white population grew faster than the number of enslavers. At the same time, distinctions among wealthy planters, small enslavers, and whites who owned no slaves also increased.

Planters' concern with productivity and profits and the concentration of more enslaved people on large plantations did have limited benefits for some black women and men. The end of the international slave trade in 1808 forced planters to rely more heavily on natural reproduction to increase their labor force. Thus many planters thought more carefully about how they treated their enslaved laborers, who were increasingly viewed as "valuable property." It was no longer good business to work enslaved people to death or cripple them by severe punishments.

Yet as slavery expanded westward, enslaved families were increasingly torn apart. By the late 1820s, enslaved workers were no longer most likely to be sold with other family members. Instead, those between fourteen and forty-five were sold in far larger numbers than younger and older workers and enslaved men far more often than women. Not until the 1850s did natural increase begin balancing out the sex ratios as enslaved men developed new families. During the 1830s and 1840s, enslavers willingly broke up families to ensure the necessary supply of young healthy men on the plantation frontier.

Moreover, owners continued to whip enslaved workers and made paltry investments in their diet and health care. Most enslaved people lived in small houses or huts with dirt floors and little furniture or clothing. They ate a diet high in calories, especially fats and carbohydrates, but with little meat, fish, fresh vegetables, or fruits. The high mortality rate among enslaved infants and children — more than twice that of white children to age five — reflected this limited care.

The spread of slavery into Mississippi, Louisiana, Alabama, Missouri, and eventually Texas affected both white and black families, though certainly not equally. The younger sons of wealthy planters were often forced to move to the frontier, and their families generally lived in rough quarters on isolated plantations. A woman traveler noted that the men "think only of making money, and their houses are hardly fit to live in." A planter's wife complained, "Mississippi and Alabama are a dreary waste." Such moves were far more difficult for enslaved laborers, however. Between 1830 and 1850, more than 440,000 enslaved people were forced to move from the Upper South to the Lower South (Map 11.1), often

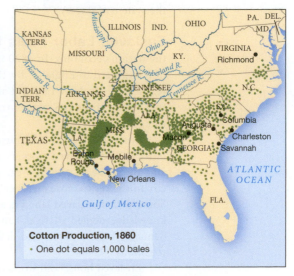

MAP 11.1   The Spread of Slavery and Cotton, 1820–1860

While tobacco, rice, and sugar remained important crops in a few states, cotton became the South's and the nation's major export. The need to find more fertile fields led planters to migrate to Alabama, Mississippi, and Louisiana. As a result of cotton's success, the number of enslaved people increased dramatically, the internal slave trade expanded, and labor demands intensified.

Explore ▶

See Source 11.1 for one
visitor's description of a slave
pen in Washington, D.C.

tearing them away from their families. On the southern frontier, they endured
incredibly harsh conditions as they cleared and cultivated new lands.

At the same time, slave markets blossomed in key cities across the South.
Solomon Northup was held in one in Washington, D.C., where a woman named
Eliza watched as her son Randall was "won" by a planter from Baton Rouge. She
promised "to be the most faithful slave that ever lived" if he would also buy her and her
daughter. The enslaver threatened the desperate mother with a hundred lashes and refused
her entreaties. As slavery spread westward, such scenes were repeated thousands of times.
Shattered family ties meant that enslaved workers on the frontier, like those initially shipped
from Africa, had to forge new kinds of bonds, including fictive kin where blood relatives
did not exist.

Review & Relate

- What role did the planter elite play in southern society and politics?
- What were the consequences of the dominance of slave-based plantation agriculture for the southern economy?

Slave Society and Culture

Because enslaved labor formed the backbone of the southern economy,
enslaved workers gained some leverage against owners and overseers. But
blacks did not simply define themselves in relation to whites. They also
developed relationships, identities, and cultural practices within the slave
quarters. Many also found small ways to resist their enslavement on an everyday basis.
Others resisted more openly, and a small number continued to organize rebellions against
the system of slavery.

Enslaved Labor Fuels the Economy. The labor of enslaved blacks drove
the nation's economy. In 1820 the South produced some 500,000 bales of cotton, much
of it exported to England. By 1850 the region produced nearly 3 million bales, feeding
textile mills in New England and abroad. A decade later, cotton accounted for nearly
two-thirds of the U.S. export trade and added nearly $200 million a year to the Ameri-
can economy.

Enslaved laborers, of course, saw little of this wealth. Carpenters, blacksmiths, and
other skilled enslaved workers were sometimes hired out and allowed to keep a small
amount of the money they earned. They traveled to nearby households, compared their
circumstances to those on other plantations, and sometimes made contact with free blacks.
Some skilled enslaved laborers also learned to read and write and had access to tools and
knowledge denied to field hands. Still, they were constantly hounded by whites who
demanded travel passes and deference, and they were often suspected of involvement in
rebellions.

Enslaved household workers sometimes received old clothes and bedding or leftover
food from their owners. Yet they were under the constant surveillance of whites, and
women especially were vulnerable to sexual abuse. Moreover, the work they performed was
physically demanding. Fugitive slave James Curry recalled that his mother, a cook in North
Carolina, rose early each morning to milk cows, bake bread, and churn butter. She was
responsible for meals for her owners and the enslaved laborers. In summer, she cooked her

Guided Primary Source Analysis

Edward Strutt Abdy | Description of Washington, D.C., Slave Pen, 1833

Slavery and the slave trade had always been legal in Washington, D.C., where enslaved laborers cleared land and constructed buildings. As the debate over slavery intensified in the nineteenth century, abolitionists often highlighted the incongruence of slavery in the capital city of American democracy. Visitors wrote with disgust about slave auctions held within sight of the Capitol steps. In the 1830s the English writer Edward Strutt Abdy toured the United States and described the scene at a slave pen.

Source 11.1

How does Abdy describe the construction of the slave pen and its relation to the U.S. Capitol?

How are whites and blacks described?

How might northern and southern audiences have reacted to this description of a slave pen? How might readers in Great Britain, where slavery had just been abolished, have responded?

One day I went to see the "slaves' pen"—a wretched hovel, "right against" the Capitol, from which it is distant about half a mile, with no house intervening. The outside alone is accessible to the eye of a visitor; what passes within being reserved for the exclusive observation of its owner (a man of the name of Robey) and his unfortunate victims. It is surrounded by a wooden paling fourteen or fifteen feet in height, with the posts outside to prevent escape, and separated from the building by a space too narrow to admit of a free circulation of air. At a small window above, which was unglazed and exposed alike to the heat of summer and the cold of winter, so trying to the constitution, two or three sable faces appeared, looking out wistfully to while away the time and catch a refreshing breeze; the weather being extremely hot. In this wretched hovel, all colors, except white—the only guilty one—both sexes, and all ages, are confined, exposed indiscriminately to all the contamination which may be expected in such society and under such seclusion. The inmates of the gaol, of this class I mean, are even worse treated; some of them, if my informants are to be believed, having been actually frozen to death, during the inclement winters which often prevail in the country. While I was in the city, Robey had got possession of a woman, whose term of slavery was limited to six years. It was expected that she would be sold before the expiration of that period, and sent away to a distance, where the assertion of her claim would subject her to ill-usage. Cases of this kind are very common.

Source: Edward Strutt Abdy, *Journal of a Residence and Tour in the United States of North America, from April, 1833, to October, 1834* (London: John Murray, 1835), 2:96–97.

Put It in Context

How did the spread of cotton to the south and west fuel the development of slave traders and slave pens?

Sale of Estates, Pictures and Slaves, 1842 J. M. Starling engraved this image of an auction in the St. Louis Hotel Rotunda in New Orleans. Three auctioneers seek bids on a painting, a family of slaves, and a manuscript. The white men, women, and children milling about considered all these items property. Only the African American family in the center fully understood the horror of the event. Interim Archives/Getty Images

last meal around eight o'clock, after which she milked the cows again. Then she returned to her quarters, put her children to bed, and often fell asleep while mending clothes.

Once enslaved children reached the age of ten to twelve, they were put to work full-time, usually in the fields. Although field labor was defined by its relentless pace and drudgery, it also brought together large numbers of enslaved people for the entire day and thus helped forge bonds among them. Songs provided a rhythm for their work and offered enslaved people the chance to communicate their frustrations or hopes.

Field labor was generally organized by task or by gang. Under the task system, typical on rice plantations, enslaved workers could return to their quarters once the day's task was completed. This left time for them to cultivate gardens, fish, or mend clothes. In the gang system, widely used on cotton plantations, men and women worked in groups under the supervision of a driver. Often working from sunup to sundown, they swept across fields hoeing, planting, or picking. **See Primary Source Project 11: Lives in Slavery, page 388.**

Many planters considered the work regimens they set as little different from northern factory owners who used bells and clocks to ensure that laborers spent maximum time at their machines. Indeed, some enslavers argued that their workers were better off because they provided them with housing, food, clothing, and health care, however minimal.

Developing an African American Culture.

Developing an African American Culture. Amid hard work and harsh treatment, enslaved people created social bonds and a rich culture of their own. For generations, African Americans continued to employ African names, like Cuffee and Binah. Even if masters gave the enslaved English names, workers might use African names in the slave quarters to sustain family memories and community networks. Elements of West African and Caribbean languages, agricultural techniques, medical practices, forms of dress, folktales, songs and musical instruments, dances, and courtship rituals demonstrated the continued importance of these cultures to African Americans. This hybrid culture was disseminated as enslaved workers hauled cotton to market, forged families across plantation boundaries, or were sold south and west. It was also passed across generations through storytelling, music, rituals, and health care. Most slave births were attended by black midwives, and African American healers sought southern equivalents to herbal cures used in West Africa.

Explore ▶

For two historians' interpretations of family life under slavery, see Sources 11.4 and 11.5.

Religious practices offer an important example of this blended culture. Africans from Muslim communities often continued to pray to Allah even if they were also required to attend Protestant churches, while black Protestant preachers developed rituals that combined African and American elements. In the early nineteenth century, many enslaved people eagerly embraced the evangelical teachings offered by Baptist and Methodist preachers, which echoed some of the expressive spiritual forms in West Africa. On Sundays, enslaved workers listened in the morning to white ministers proclaim slavery as God's will. Yet in the

"A Slave Wedding," c. 1800   This rare water color painting of an African American wedding probably dates from the turn of the nineteenth century. The distance between the slave quarters and the plantation house suggests this may be a South Carolina scene. The enslaved women and men are dressed in their finest clothing and the musicians appear to be playing African-style instruments made from gourds. MPI/Getty Images evening they might gather again to hear their own preachers declare God's love and the possibilities of liberation, at least in the hereafter. Enslaved people often incorporated drums, dancing, or other West African elements into these worship services.

Although most black preachers were men, a few enslaved women gained a spiritual following. Many female slaves embraced religion enthusiastically, hoping that Christian baptism might substitute for West African rituals that protected newborn babies. Enslaved women sometimes called on church authorities to intervene when white owners, overseers, or even enslaved men abused them. They also considered the church one means of sanctifying slave marriages that were not recognized legally.

Resistance and Rebellion.
Many enslavers worried that black preachers and West African folktales inspired blacks to resist enslavement. Fearing defiance, planters went to incredible lengths to control their enslaved population. Although they were largely successful in quelling open revolts, they were unable to eliminate more subtle forms of opposition, like slowing the pace of work, feigning illness, and damaging equipment. More overt forms of resistance — such as truancy and running away, which disrupted work and lowered profits — also proved impossible to stamp out.

The forms of everyday resistance enslaved laborers employed varied in part on their location and resources. Skilled artisans, mostly men, could do more substantial damage because they used more expensive tools, but they were less able to protect themselves through pleas of ignorance. Field laborers could often damage only hoes, but they could do so regularly without exciting suspicion. Enslaved house workers could burn dinners, scorch shirts, break china, and even poison owners. Often considered the most loyal slaves, they were also among the most feared because of their intimate contact with white families. Single male slaves were the most likely to run away, planning their escape to get as far away as possible before their absence was noticed. Women who fled plantations were more likely to hide out for short periods in the local area. Eventually, isolation, hunger, or concern for children led most of these truants to return if slave patrols did not find them first.

Despite their rarity, efforts to organize slave uprisings, such as those planned in New Orleans in 1811 and in Charleston in 1822, continued to haunt southern whites. Rebellions in the West Indies, especially the one in Saint Domingue (Haiti), also echoed through the early nineteenth century. Then in 1831 a seemingly obedient slave named Nat Turner organized a revolt in rural Virginia that stunned whites across the South. A religious visionary who believed that God had given him a mission, Turner worked through family and friendship networks, including men and women, to execute that mission. On the night of August 21, he and his followers killed his owners, the Travis family, and then headed to nearby plantations in Southampton County. The insurrection led to the deaths of 57 white men, women, and children and liberated more than 50 enslaved people. But on August 22, outraged white militiamen burst on the scene and eventually captured the black rebels. Turner hid out for two months but was eventually caught, tried, and hung. Virginia executed 55 other African Americans suspected of assisting Turner.

Nat Turner's rebellion instilled panic among white Virginians, who beat and killed some 200 blacks with no connection to the uprising. White Southerners worried they might be killed in their sleep by seemingly submissive slaves. News of the rebellion traveled through enslaved communities as well, inspiring both pride and anxiety. The execution of Turner and his followers reminded African Americans how far whites would go to protect the institution of slavery.

A mutiny on the Spanish slave ship *Amistad* in 1839 reinforced white Southerners' fears of rebellion. When Africans being transported for sale in the West Indies seized control of the ship near Cuba, the U.S. navy captured the vessel and imprisoned the enslaved rebels. But international treaties outlawing the Atlantic slave trade and pressure applied by abolitionists led to a court case in which former president John Quincy Adams defended the right of the Africans to their freedom. The widely publicized case reached the U.S. Supreme Court in 1841, and the Court freed the rebels. While abolitionists cheered the ruling, white Southerners were shocked that the justices would liberate enslaved men.

Review & Relate

- How did enslaved African Americans create ties of family, community, and culture?

- How did enslaved African Americans resist efforts to control and exploit their labor?

Planters Tighten Control

Fears of rebellion led to stricter regulations of black life, and actual uprisings temporarily reinforced white solidarity. Yet yeomen farmers, poor whites, and middle-class professionals all voiced some doubts about the ways in which slavery affected southern society. To ensure white unity, planters wielded their economic and political authority, highlighted bonds of kinship and religious fellowship, and promoted an ideology of white supremacy. Their efforts intensified as northern states and other nations began eradicating slavery.

Harsher Treatment for Southern Blacks. Slave revolts led many southern states to impose harsher controls, but Nat Turner's rebellion led some white Virginians to question slavery itself. In December 1831, the state assembly established a special committee to consider the crisis. Representatives from western counties, where slavery was never profitable, argued for gradual abolition laws and the colonization of the state's black population in Africa. Hundreds of women in the region sent petitions to the Virginia legislature supporting these positions.

While advocates of colonization gained significant support, eastern planters vehemently opposed abolition or colonization, and leading intellectuals argued for the benefits of slavery. Professor Thomas Dew, president of the College of William and Mary, insisted that enslavers performed godly work in raising Africans from the status of brute beast to civilized Christian. "Every one acquainted with southern slaves," he claimed, "knows that the slave rejoices in the elevation and prosperity of his master." In the fall of 1832 the Virginia legislature embraced Dew's proslavery argument, rejected gradual emancipation, and imposed new restrictions on enslaved and free blacks.

From the 1820s to the 1840s, more stringent codes were passed across the South. Most southern legislatures prohibited owners from manumitting their enslaved workers, made it illegal for whites to teach the enslaved to read or write, placed new limits on independent black churches, abolished slaves' limited access to courts, outlawed slave marriage, banned antislavery literature, defined rape as a crime only against white women, and outlawed assemblies of more than three blacks without a white person present.

States also regulated the lives of free blacks. Some prohibited free blacks from residing within their borders, others required large bonds to ensure good behavior, and most forbade free blacks who left the state from returning. The homes of free blacks could be raided at any time, and the children of free black women were subject to stringent apprenticeship laws that kept many in virtual slavery.

Such measures proved largely successful in controlling enslaved workers, but there was a price to pay. Restricting education and mobility for blacks hindered schooling and transportation for poor whites as well. Moreover, characterizing the region's primary labor force as savage and lazy discouraged investment in industry and other forms of economic development. And the regulations increased tensions between poorer whites, who were often responsible for enforcement, and wealthy whites, who benefited most clearly from their imposition.

White Southerners without Slaves.
Yeomen farmers, independent owners of small plots who owned few or no enslaved workers, had a complex relationship with the South's plantation economy. Many were related to enslavers, and they often depended on planters to ship their crops to market. Some made extra money by hiring themselves out to planters. Yet yeomen farmers also recognized that their economic interests and daily experiences often diverged from those of planters. This was particularly clear on slavery's frontier, where many yeoman farmers had to carve fields out of forests without the benefit of enslaved workers. They joined with friends and neighbors for barn raisings, corn shuckings, quilting bees, and other collective endeavors that combined labor with sociability. Church services and church socials also brought small farm families together.

While most yeomen farmers believed in slavery, they sometimes challenged planters' authority and assumptions. In the Virginia slavery debates, for example, small farmers from western districts advocated gradual abolition. As growing numbers gained the right to vote in the 1830s and 1840s, they voiced their concerns in county and town meetings and in local courts. They advocated more liberal policies toward debtors and demanded greater representation in state legislatures. They also protested planters' obstruction of common lands and waterways, such as building dams upriver that deprived farmers downriver of fishing rights. Yeomen farmers questioned certain ideals embraced by elites. Although plantation mistresses considered manual labor beneath them, the wives and daughters of small farmers often worked in the fields, hauled water, and chopped wood. Still, yeomen farmers' ability to diminish planter control was limited by the continued importance of cotton to the southern economy.

White Southerners who owned no property at all had fewer means of challenging planters' power. These poor whites depended on hunting and fishing in frontier areas, performing day labor on farms and plantations, or working on docks or as servants in southern cities. Poor whites competed with free and enslaved blacks for employment and often harbored resentments as a result. Yet some, including poor immigrants from Ireland, Wales, and Scotland, built alliances with blacks based on their shared economic plight.

Some poor whites remained in the same community for decades, establishing themselves on the margins of society. They attended church regularly, performed day labor for affluent families, and taught their children to defer to those higher on the social ladder. Other poor whites moved frequently and survived by combining legal and illegal ventures. They might perform day labor while also stealing food from local farmers. These men and women often had few ties to local communities and little religious training or education. Although poor whites unnerved southern elites by flouting the law and sometimes befriending poor blacks, they could not mount a significant challenge to planter control.

North Carolina Emigrants, 1845   James Henry Beard, who later gained fame for his portraits of political leaders and of dogs, captures in this painting a family of poor whites hoping to find better opportunities farther west. The family was fortunate to own a cow, but the children are barefoot and the mother cradles her infant on a horse that carries all their worldly possessions. Gift of the Proctor & Gamble Company/Bridgeman Images

The South's small but growing middle class distanced themselves from poorer whites in pursuit of stability and respectability. They worked as doctors, lawyers, teachers, and shopkeepers and often looked to the North for models to emulate. Many were educated in northern schools and developed ties with their commercial or professional counterparts in that region. They were avid readers of newspapers, religious tracts, and literary periodicals published in the North and South. And like middle-class Northerners, southern business-men often depended on their wives' social and financial skills to succeed.

Nonetheless, middle-class southern men shared many of the social attitudes and polit-ical priorities of enslavers. They participated alongside planters in benevolent, literary, and temperance societies and agricultural reform organizations. Most middle-class Southerners also adamantly supported slavery. In fact, some suggested that bound labor might be useful to industry. Despite the emergence of a small middle class, however, the gap between rich and poor continued to expand in the South.

Planters Seek to Unify Southern Whites.
Planters faced another challenge as nations in Europe and South America began to abolish slavery. In the United States, anti-slavery views were first widely expressed by free blacks and Quakers in northern and Middle Atlantic states. By the 1830s, they gained growing support among evangelical Protestants in the United States and Great Britain and among political radicals in Europe. Slave rebellions

in Saint Domingue and the British West Indies in the early nineteenth century intensified these concerns. In 1807 the British Parliament had forbidden the sale of enslaved people within its empire, and in 1834 emancipated all those who remained enslaved. France followed suit in 1848. As Spanish colonies such as Mexico and Nicaragua gained their independence in the 1820s and 1830s, they, too, eradicated the institution. Meanwhile gradual abolition laws in the northern United States slowly eliminated slavery there. Although slavery continued in Brazil and in Spanish colonies such as Cuba, and serfdom remained in Russia, international attitudes toward human bondage had shifted significantly.

In response, planters wielded their political and economic power to forge tighter bonds among white Southerners. According to the three-fifths compromise in the U.S. Constitution, areas with large enslaved populations gained more representatives in Congress than those without. The policy also applied to state elections, giving such areas disproportionate power in state politics. In addition, planters used their resources to provide credit for those in need, offer seasonal employment for poorer whites, transport crops to market for yeomen farmers, and help out in times of crisis. Few whites could afford to antagonize these affluent benefactors.

Wealthy planters also emphasized ties of family and faith. James Henry Hammond, for example, regularly assisted his siblings and other family members financially. Many enslavers worshipped alongside their less well-to-do neighbors, and both pastor and congregation benefited from maintaining good relations with the wealthiest congregants. Most church members, like many relatives and neighbors, genuinely admired and respected planter elites who looked out for them.

While planters continued to insist that the U.S. Constitution protected slavery and the right of states to enforce their own labor systems, they did not take white solidarity for granted. From the 1830s on, they relied on the ideology of **white supremacy** to cement the belief that all whites, regardless of class or education, were superior to all blacks. Following on Thomas Dew, southern elites argued with growing vehemence that the moral and intellectual failings of blacks meant that slavery was not just a necessary evil but a positive good. At the same time, they insisted that blacks harbored deep animosity toward whites, which could be controlled only by regulating every aspect of their lives. Combining racial fear and racial pride, planters forged bonds with poor and middling whites to guarantee their continued dominance. They also continued to seek support from state and national legislators.

Review & Relate

- What groups made up white southern society? How did their interests overlap or diverge?

- How and why did the planter elite seek to reinforce white solidarity?

Democrats Face Political and Economic Crises

Southern planters depended on federal power to expand and sustain the system of slavery. Despite differences on tariffs, both President Andrew Jackson and his successor, Martin Van Buren, stood with southern planters in support of Indian removal and independence for Texas from Mexico. But Van Buren faced a more well-organized opposition in the **Whig Party**, which formed in 1834. When later that decade

U.S. rebels in Texas faced powerful resistance from Mexican and Comanche forces and a prolonged and severe economic panic gripped the nation, the Whigs found their opportunity to end Democratic control of the federal government. Over the next two decades, a **Second Party System** formed that pitted Whigs against Democrats on a wide range of economic, cultural, and political issues.

The Battle for Texas. As southern agriculture expanded westward, some whites looked toward Texas for fresh land. White Southerners had begun moving into eastern Texas in the early nineteenth century, but the Adams-Onís Treaty of 1819 guaranteed Spanish control of the territory. Then in 1821 Mexicans overthrew Spanish rule and claimed Texas as part of the new Republic of Mexico. But Mexicans faced serious competition from Comanche Indians, who controlled vast areas in northern Mexico and launched frequent raids into Texas.

Eager to increase settlement in the area and to create a buffer against the Comanches, the Mexican government granted U.S. migrants some of the best land in eastern Texas. It hoped these settlers would eventually spread into the interior, where Comanche raids had devastated Mexican communities. To entice more Southerners, the Mexican government negotiated a special exemption for U.S. planters when it outlawed slavery in 1829. But rather than spreading into the interior, American migrants stayed east of the Colorado River, out of reach of Comanche raids and close to U.S. markets in Louisiana.

Moreover, U.S. settlers resisted assimilation into Mexican society. Instead, they continued to worship as Protestants, speak English, send their children to separate schools, and trade mainly with the United States. By 1835 the 27,000 white Southerners and their 3,000 enslaved workers far outnumbered the 3,000 **Tejanos** (Mexican Texans) living in eastern Texas.

Forming a majority of the east Texas population and eager to expand their plantations and trade networks, growing numbers of U.S. settlers demanded independence. Then in 1836 Mexicans elected a strong nationalist leader, General Antonio López de Santa Anna, as president. He sought to calm Tejanos angered by their vulnerability to Comanche attacks and to curb U.S. settlers seeking further concessions. However, when Santa Anna appointed a military commander to rule Texas, U.S. migrants organized a rebellion and, on March 2, declared their independence. José Antonio Menchaca and many other Tejanos, long neglected by authorities in Mexico City, sided with the rebels. But the rebellion appeared to be short-lived. On March 6, 1836, General Santa Anna crushed settlers defending the **Alamo** in San Antonio. Soon thereafter, he captured the U.S. settlement at Goliad.

At this point, Santa Anna was convinced that the uprising was over. But the U.S. government, despite its claims of neutrality, aided the rebels with funds and army officers. American newspapers picked up the story of the Alamo and published accounts of the battle, describing the Mexican fighters as brutal butchers bent on saving Texas for the Catholic Pope. These stories, though more fable than fact, increased popular support for the war at a time when many Americans were increasingly hostile to Catholic immigrants in the United States.

At this point, the ability of Menchaca and other Tejanos to translate documents captured from Mexican couriers provided the entrée American forces needed. As hundreds of armed volunteers headed to Texas, General Sam Houston led rebel forces in a critical victory at San Jacinto in April 1836. While the Mexican government refused to recognize rebel claims, it did not try to regain the lost territory. Few of the U.S. volunteers arrived in time to participate in the fighting, but some settled in the newly liberated region. The Comanche nation quickly recognized the Republic of Texas and developed trade relations with residents to gain access to the vast U.S. market. Still, Santa Anna's failure to recognize Texas independence kept the U.S. government from granting the territory statehood for fear it would lead to war with Mexico. Texans shared that fear. Thus, Menchaca commanded a frontier company that patrolled the area between the San Antonio River and the Rio Grande. In 1842, Mexican soldiers did seek to reclaim San Antonio, but Menchaca's company helped defend the city and defeat the Mexicans.

Explore ▶

See Sources 11.2 and 11.3 for opposing views on Texas independence and annexation.

Presidents Jackson and Van Buren also worried that admitting a new slave state might split the national Democratic Party. To limit debate on slavery, Congress had passed a **gag rule** in March 1836 that tabled all antislavery petitions without being read. Nevertheless, thousands of antislavery activists continued to flood the House of Representatives with petitions opposing the annexation of Texas.

Indians Resist Removal. The United States also faced continued challenges from Indian nations. After passage of the Indian Removal Act in 1830, Congress hoped to settle the most powerful eastern Indian tribes on land west of the Mississippi River. But some Indian peoples resisted. The Seminole, who had battled U.S. forces in the 1810s, continued to fight their removal. While federal authorities forcibly removed the majority of Seminoles to Indian Territory between 1832 and 1835, a minority fought back. Jackson and his military commanders expected that this **Second Seminole War** would be short-lived. However, they misjudged the Seminoles' strength; the power of their charismatic leader, Osceola; and the resistance of black fugitives living among the Seminoles.

The conflict continued long after Jackson left the presidency. During the seven-year guerrilla war, 1,600 U.S. troops died. U.S. military forces defeated the Seminole in 1842 only by luring Osceola into an army camp with false promises of a peace settlement. Instead, officers took him captive, finally breaking the back of the resistance. Still, to end the conflict, the U.S. government had to allow fugitive slaves living among the Seminoles to accompany the tribe to Indian Territory.

Unlike the Seminole, members of the Cherokee nation challenged removal by peaceful means, believing that their prolonged efforts to coexist with white society would ensure their success. Indian leaders like John Ross had urged Cherokees to embrace Christianity, white gender roles, and a republican form of government as the best means to ensure control of their communities. (See Chapter 9, "Cherokee Engage White America.") Large numbers had done so, but in 1829 and 1830, Georgia officials sought to impose new regulations on the Cherokee living within the state's borders. Tribal leaders took them to court, using evidence of their Americanization to claim their rights as an autonomous nation. In 1831 *Cherokee Nation v. Georgia* reached the U.S. Supreme Court, which denied a central part of the Cherokee claim. It ruled that all Indians were "domestic dependent nations" rather than fully sovereign governments. Yet the following year, in *Worcester v. Georgia*, the Court declared that the state of Georgia could not impose *state* laws on the Cherokee, for they had "territorial boundaries, within which their authority is exclusive," and that both their land and their rights were protected by the federal government.

President Jackson, who sought Cherokee removal, argued that only the tribe's removal west of the Mississippi River could ensure its "physical comfort," "political advancement," and "moral improvement." Most southern whites, seeking to expand cotton production or mine gold in Cherokee territory, agreed. But Protestant women and men in the North launched a massive petition campaign in 1830 supporting the Cherokees' right to their land. Cherokee women also renewed their protests against removal, and the tribe as a whole forestalled action through Jackson's second term.

In December 1835, however, U.S. officials convinced a small group of Cherokee men—without tribal sanction—to sign the **Treaty of New Echota**. It proposed the exchange of 100 million acres of Cherokee land in the Southeast for $68 million and 32 million acres in Indian Territory. Outraged Cherokee leaders like John Ross lobbied Congress to reject the treaty. But in May 1836, Congress approved the treaty by a single vote and set the date for final removal two years later (Map 11.2).

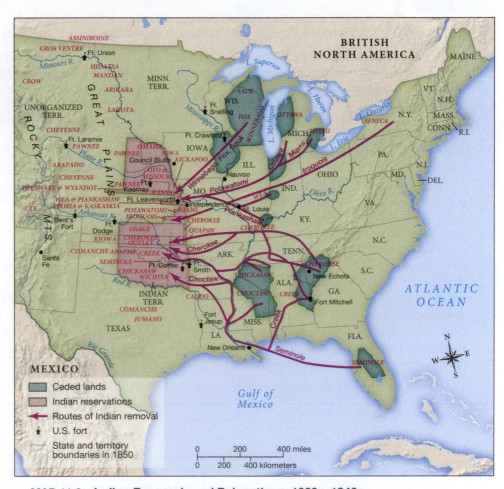

MAP 11.2   Indian Removals and Relocations, 1820s–1840s

In the 1820s and 1830s, the federal government used a variety of tactics, including military force, to expel Indian nations residing east of the Mississippi River. As these tribes resettled in the West, white migration along the Oregon and other trails began to increase. The result, by 1850, was the forced relocation of many western Indian nations as well.

Comparative Primary Source Analysis

Two Views on Texas Independence

In March 1836, U.S.-born Texans declared an independent republic. Under attack by Mexican forces at the Alamo, twenty-six–year-old Colonel William Travis and others appealed for reinforcements (Source 11.2). While all the men were killed, their appeals inspired hundreds of U.S. volunteers to join military efforts in Texas. They contributed to winning Texas independence, but that victory fueled intense debates over the question of annexation. Abolitionist and Quaker editor Benjamin Lundy was among those who argued that annexation would benefit the "Slaveholding Interest" (Source 11.3). These men offer competing perspectives on the relationship between Texas independence and national honor.

Source 11.2

Colonel William Travis | Appeal for Reinforcements, March 3, 1836

I hope your honorable body will hasten on reinforcements, ammunition, and provisions to our aid. . . . At least five hundred pounds of cannon powder, and two hundred rounds of six, nine, twelve, and eighteen pound balls—ten kegs of rifle powder, and a supply of lead, should be sent to this place without delay, under a sufficient guard.

If these things are promptly sent and large reinforcements are hastened to this frontier, this neighborhood will be the great and decisive battle ground. The power of Santa Ana is to be met here, or in the colonies; we had better meet them here, than to suffer a war of desolation to rage in our settlements. A blood-red banner waves from the church of Bejar, and in the camp above us, in token that the war is one of vengeance against rebels; they have declared us such, and demanded that we should surrender at discretion, or that this garrison should be put to the sword. Their threats have had no influence on me, or my men, but to make all fight with desperation, and that high souled courage which characterizes the patriot, who is willing to die in defence of his country's liberty and his own honor.

The citizens of this municipality are all our enemies except those who have joined us heretofore; . . . those who have not joined us in this extremity, should be declared public enemies, and their property should aid in paying the expenses of the war.

The bearer of this will give your honorable body a statement more in detail should he escape through the enemies lines.

God and Texas—Victory or Death!!
Your obedient ser't
W. Barrett Travis, Lieut. Col. Comm.

Source: *Telegraph and Texas Register*, March 12, 1836, 3.

In 1838, the U.S. army forcibly removed Cherokees who had not yet resettled in Indian Territory. That June, General Winfield Scott, assisted by 7,000 U.S. soldiers, forced some 15,000 Cherokees into forts and military camps. Indian families spent the next several months without sufficient food, water, sanitation, or medicine. In October, when the Cherokees finally began the march west, torrential rains were followed by snow. Although the U.S. army planned for a trip of less than three months, the journey actually took five

Benjamin Lundy | The War in Texas, 1836

It is generally admitted that the war in Texas has assumed a character which must seriously affect both the interests and honor of this nation. It implicates the conduct of a large number of our citizens, and even the policy and measures of the government are deeply involved in it. . . . The great fundamental principles of universal liberty—the perpetuity of our free republican institutions—the prosperity, the welfare, and the happiness of future generations—are measurably connected with the prospective issue of this fierce and bloody conflict.

But the prime cause and the real objects of this war are not distinctly understood by a large portion of the honest, disinterested, and well-meaning citizens of the United States. . . . [M]any of them have been deceived and misled by the misrepresentations of those concerned in it, and especially by hireling writers for the newspaper press. They have been induced to believe that the inhabitants of Texas were engaged in a legitimate contest for the maintenance of the sacred principles of Liberty, and the natural, inalienable Rights of Man: whereas . . . the immediate cause and the leading object of this contest originated in a settled design, among the slaveholders of this country (with land speculators and slave-traders), to wrest the large and valuable territory of Texas from the Mexican Republic, in order to re-establish the SYSTEM OF SLAVERY; to open a vast and profitable SLAVE-MARKET therein; and, ultimately, to annex it to the United States. . . . The Slaveholding Interest is now paramount in the Executive branch of our national government; and its influence operates, indirectly, yet powerfully, through that medium, in favor of this Grand Scheme of Oppression and Tyrannical Usurpation. Whether the national Legislature will join hands with the Executive, and lend its aid to this most unwarrantable, aggressive attempt, will depend on the VOICE OF THE PEOPLE, expressed in their primary assemblies, by their petitions, and through the ballot-boxes.

Source: Benjamin Lundy, *The War in Texas* (Philadelphia: Merrihew and Gunn, 1836), 3.

Interpret the Evidence

1. According to William Travis, why was it crucial for the United States to defend the Alamo and Texas independence?
2. How would you compare Travis's appeal for aid with Benjamin Lundy's claims about the rationale for the war and the interests supporting independence? How does each define U.S. national interests?

Put It in Context

What do the battle for Texas independence and debates over Texas annexation reveal about sectional divisions in the United States in the 1830s and 1840s?

months. As supplies ran short, many Indians died, including John Ross's wife. The remaining Cherokees completed this **Trail of Tears** in March 1839. But thousands remained near starvation a year later.

Following the Trail of Tears, Seneca Indians petitioned the federal government to stop their removal from western New York. Federal agents had negotiated the Treaty of Buffalo Creek with several Iroquois leaders in 1838. But some Seneca chiefs claimed the negotiation

Seminole Warriors Attack the U.S. Block House, 1837   This hand-colored lithograph offers a rare glimpse of well-armed Seminole warriors attacking a U.S. fort. The image likely shows a December 1835 attack on a fort along the Withlacoochee River. T. J. Gray and James of Charleston, South Carolina, published a series of Florida scenes in the early nineteenth century depicting Seminole villages and U.S. forts and towns. Library of Congress, LC-DIG-ppmsca-19924

was marred by bribery and fraud. With the aid of Quaker allies, the Seneca petitioned Congress and the president for redress. Perhaps reluctant to repeat the Cherokee and Seminole debacles, Congress approved a new treaty in 1842 that allowed the Seneca to retain two of their four reservations in western New York.

By the 1840s, native peoples forced into Indian Territory had rebuilt their institutions and traditions. The Cherokee established Protestant churches and the first public schools west of the Mississippi. The Choctaw, too, opened public schools and became one of the first communities in the United States to offer girls and women equal access to education. The Choctaw also reached out to help people suffering hardship elsewhere. Hearing news of the Irish famine, the tribe sent relief money to starving communities in Ireland, creating a bond between the two peoples that continues into the twenty-first century.

Van Buren and the Panic of 1837. Although President Jackson proposed the Indian Removal Act, it was President Martin Van Buren who confronted ongoing challenges from Indian nations. When Van Buren ran for president in 1836, the Whigs hoped to defeat him by bringing together diverse supporters: evangelical Protestants who objected to Jackson's Indian policy, financiers and commercial farmers who advocated internal improvements and protective tariffs, merchants and manufacturers who favored a national bank, and Southerners who were antagonized by the president's heavy-handed use of federal authority. But the Whigs could not agree on a single candidate, and this lack of unity allowed Democrats to prevail. Although Van Buren won the popular vote by only a small margin (50.9 percent), he secured an easy majority in the electoral college.

Inaugurated on March 4, 1837, President Van Buren soon faced a major financial crisis. The **panic of 1837** started in the South and was rooted in the changing fortunes of American cotton in Great Britain. Capitalist calculations undergirded economic development in all regions of the United States. In the 1820s and 1830s, southern planters borrowed huge sums from British banks to expand landholdings and purchase more enslaved laborers, sure that King Cotton would provide the profits to repay their loans. Northern cotton factors and southern entrepreneurs also borrowed funds to improve southern port facilities. At the same time, British banks lent large sums to states such as New York to fund internal improvements, which drove the market revolution but also fueled inflation.

In late 1836, the Bank of England, faced with bad harvests at home and a declining demand for textiles, tightened credit to limit the flow of money out of the country. This forced British investors to call in their loans, which drove up interest rates in the United States just as cotton prices started to fall. Some American cotton merchants were forced to declare bankruptcy. The banks where they held accounts, mainly in the South, then failed. Ninety-eight of them did so in March and April 1837 alone. Cotton prices continued to fall, cut by nearly half in less than a year. Land values declined dramatically, and port cities came to a standstill. Cotton communities on the southern frontier collapsed as overextended planters lost or abandoned newly cleared fields. Their enslaved workers faced even worse conditions than usual as enslavers lost money and credit.

Because regional economies were increasingly intertwined, the panic radiated throughout the United States. Northern brokers, shippers, and merchants were devastated by losses in the cotton trade, and northern banks were hit by unpaid debts incurred for canals and other internal improvements. In turn, entrepreneurs who borrowed money to expand their businesses defaulted in large numbers, and shopkeepers, artisans, factory workers, and farmers in the North and Midwest suffered unemployment and foreclosures.

In the North and West, many Americans blamed Jackson's war against the Bank of the United States for precipitating the panic, and Americans everywhere were outraged at Van Buren's refusal to intervene in the crisis. While it is unlikely that any federal policy could have resolved the nation's economic problems, the president's apparent disinterest in the plight of the people inspired harsh criticisms from ordinary citizens as well as political opponents. Worse, despite brief signs of recovery in 1838, the depression deepened in 1839 and continued for four more years.

The Whigs Win the White House.

Eager to exploit the weakness of Van Buren and the Democrats, the Whig Party organized its first national convention in fall 1840 and united behind military hero William Henry Harrison. Harrison was born to a wealthy planter family in Virginia, but he was portrayed as a self-made man who lived in a simple log cabin in Indiana. His running mate, John Tyler, another Virginia gentleman and a one-time Democrat, joined the Whigs because of his opposition to Jackson's stand on nullification. Whig leaders hoped he would attract southern votes. Taking their cue from Democrats, the Whigs organized rallies, barbecues, parades, and mass meetings. They turned the tables on their foe by portraying Van Buren as an aristocrat and Harrison as a war hero and friend of the common man. The Whigs supported American innovation and the entrepreneurial spirit, proclaimed prosperous farmers and skilled workers the backbone of the country, and insisted on their moral and religious superiority to Democrats. At the same time, eager to remind voters that Harrison had defeated Tenskwatawa at the Battle of Tippecanoe, the Whigs adopted the slogan "Tippecanoe and Tyler Too."

The Whigs also welcomed women into the campaign. By 1840 thousands of women had circulated petitions against Cherokee removal, organized temperance and antislavery societies, promoted religious revivals, and joined charitable associations. They embodied the kind of moral force that the Whig Party claimed to represent. In October 1840, Whig senator Daniel Webster spoke to a gathering of 1,200 women, calling on them to encourage their brothers and husbands to vote for Harrison.

The Whig strategy paid off handsomely on election day. Harrison won easily, and the Whigs gained a majority in Congress. Yet the election's promise was shattered when Harrison died of pneumonia a month after his inauguration. Whigs in Congress now had to deal with John Tyler, whose sentiments were largely southern and Democratic. Vetoing many Whig efforts at reform, Tyler allowed the Democratic Party to regroup and set the stage for close elections in 1844 and 1848.

Review & Relate

■ How did westward expansion affect white Southerners, white Northerners, enslaved blacks, and American Indians in the 1830s and 1840s?

■ What economic and political developments led to a Whig victory in the election of 1840?

The **National Government Looks** to the **West**

Despite the Whig victory in 1840, planters wielded considerable clout in Washington, D.C., because of the importance of cotton to the U.S. economy. In turn, Southerners needed federal support to expand into more fertile areas. With the economic panic of 1837–1843 finally over, the presidential election of 1844 turned on this issue. Democratic candidate James K. Polk demanded continued expansion into Mexico and Oregon. After Polk was elected, Britain and Mexico contested his claims, as did the Comanche. Still, the United States won vast Mexican territories in 1848, which intensified conflicts with Indians and debates over slavery.

Expanding to Oregon and Texas. Southerners eager to expand the plantation economy were at the forefront of the push for territorial expansion. Yet expansion was not merely a southern strategy. Northerners demanded that the United States reject British claims to the Oregon Territory, and some northern politicians and businessmen advocated acquiring Hawaii and Samoa to benefit U.S. trade. In 1844 the Democratic Party built on these expansionist dreams to recapture the White House.

The Democrats nominated a Tennessee congressman and governor, James K. Polk. The Whigs, unwilling to nominate Tyler for president, chose Kentucky senator Henry Clay. Polk declared himself in favor of the annexation of Texas. Clay, meanwhile, waffled on the issue. This proved his undoing when the Liberty Party, a small antislavery party founded in 1840, denounced annexation. Liberty Party candidate James G. Birney captured just enough votes in New York State to throw the state and the election to Polk.

In February 1845, a month before Polk took office, Congress passed a joint resolution annexing the Republic of Texas and granting it statehood. That summer, John L. O'Sullivan, editor of the *Democratic Review*, captured the American mood by declaring that nothing must interfere with "the fulfillment of our manifest destiny to overspread the continent allotted by Providence." This vision of **manifest destiny** — of the nation's God-given right to expand its borders — defined Polk's presidency.

With the Texas question seemingly resolved, President Polk turned his attention to Oregon, which stretched from the forty-second parallel to latitude 54°40′ and was jointly occupied by Great Britain and the United States. In 1842, three years before Polk took office, glowing reports of the mild climate and fertile soil around Puget Sound had inspired thousands of farmers and traders to flood into Oregon's Willamette Valley. Alarmed by this "Oregon fever," the British tried to confine Americans to areas south of the Columbia River. But U.S. settlers demanded access to the entire territory. President Polk encouraged migration into Oregon but was unwilling to risk war with Great Britain. Instead, diplomats negotiated a treaty in 1846 that extended the border with British Canada (the forty-ninth parallel) to the Pacific Ocean. Over the next two years, Congress admitted Iowa and Wisconsin to statehood, reassuring northern residents that expansion benefited all regions of the nation.

Some Americans hoped to gain even more territory by claiming northern Mexico and California for the United States. Spanish missions and forts, built in the late eighteenth century, dotted the Pacific Coast from San Diego to San Francisco. When Mexico achieved independence in 1821, it took control of this missionary and military network. Diseases carried by the Spanish and forced labor in their missions and forts had decimated some

Astoria, Oregon, 1848   In 1845 the British army sent Lieutenant Henry Warre to the Oregon Country to gather intelligence on American settlements in case of war with the United States. Warre sketched Astoria, which lies at the mouth of the Columbia River. The first permanent settlement in the Oregon Country, it was established by John Jacob Astor's Pacific Fur Company in 1811. Sarin Images/Granger

Indian tribes in the region. As Mexican soldiers took control, some married into Indian families, gaining land and social status and nurturing compound cultures. More often, however, diseases, guns, thefts of food and animals, sexual assault, and forced labor continued to debilitate native peoples.

Indians in areas newly claimed by the U.S. government faced these same dangers. In addition, as the U.S. government forced eastern tribes to move west of the Mississippi, tensions increased with Indian nations already there (see Map 11.2). Thus when the Cherokee were removed to Indian Territory, they confronted their traditional enemies, the Creek. Others, such as the Osage, whose society was forged around gender complementarity, managed to sustain much of their culture and economy despite accepting Christian missions and being forced to relocate in the Midwest. However, when white settlement pushed them onto ever less fertile land, women could no longer farm as productively and male hunters then became more critical to the community. Other native peoples were decimated by disease, including the Mandan, hosts to the Lewis and Clark expedition in 1803. When smallpox struck the Mandan in the 1830s, the Lakota and Dakota (Sioux) strengthened their domination of the region.

The flood of U.S. migrants into Texas and the southern plains also transformed relations among Indian nations and between Indians and Mexico. In the face of Spanish and then Mexican claims on their lands, for example, the Comanche forged alliances with former foes like the Wichita and the Osage. The Comanche also developed commercial ties with tribes in Indian Territory and with both Mexican and Anglo-American traders. They thereby hoped to benefit from the imperial ambitions of the United States and Mexico while strengthening bonds among Indians in the region.

For Mexicans and Tejanos, Comanche expansion was increasingly problematic. Mexico did not have sufficient resources to sustain the level of gift giving that Spanish authorities used to maintain peace. As a result, Comanche warriors launched continual raids against Mexican and Tejano settlements, failing to abide by the border between the two groups. But the Comanche also developed commercial relations with residents of New Mexico, who flaunted trade regulations promulgated in Mexico City. By 1846 Comanche trade and diplomatic relations with New Mexican settlements had seriously weakened the hold of Mexican authorities on their northern provinces. In Texas, José Antonio Menchaca was appointed an agent to native traders, including Comanche, and soon became a merchant himself.

Pursuing War with Mexico.

Pursuing War with Mexico. With Texas now part of the United States, Mexico faced growing tensions with U.S. officials over the state's western border. Mexico insisted on the Nueces River as the boundary line, while Americans claimed all the land to the Rio Grande. In January 1846, Polk secretly sent emissary John Slidell to negotiate a border treaty with Mexico. But Polk also sent U.S. troops under General Zachary Taylor across the Nueces River. Mexican officials refused to see Slidell and instead sent their own troops across the Rio Grande. Meanwhile, U.S. naval commanders prepared to seize San Francisco Bay from the Mexicans if war was declared. The Mexican government responded by sending more troops into the disputed Texas territory.

When fighting erupted near the Rio Grande in May 1846 (Map 11.3), Polk claimed that "American blood had been shed on American soil" and declared a state of war. Many Whigs in Congress opposed the declaration, arguing that the president had provoked the

MAP 11.3   The Mexican-American War, 1846–1848

Although a dispute over territory between the Nueces River and the Rio Grande initiated the Mexican-American War, most of the fighting occurred between the Rio Grande and Mexico City. In addition, U.S. forces in California launched battles to claim independence for that region even before gold was discovered there.

conflict. However, antiwar Whigs failed to convince the Democratic majority, and Congress voted to finance the war. Although northern abolitionists protested vehemently, most Americans — North and South — considered westward expansion a boon.

Once the war began, battles erupted in a variety of locations. In May 1846, U.S. troops defeated Mexican forces in Palo Alto and Resaca de la Palma. A month later, the U.S. army captured Sonoma, California with the aid of local settlers. John Frémont then

"Hanging of the San Patricios," 1847   In 1846–1847 more than two hundred immigrants, most of them Irish Catholics who defected from U.S. Army units, joined the Mexican Army. They formed the Batallón de San Patricios, which fought fiercely in many battles. When dozens were captured after the Battle of Chapultepec, the soldiers were convicted of desertion. Samuel Chamberlain painted one of two mass hangings that followed. Herbert Orth/Contributor/The LIFE Images Collection/Getty Images

led U.S. forces to Monterey, where the navy launched a successful attack and declared the California territory part of the United States. That fall, U.S. troops gained important victories at Monterrey, Mexico, just west of the Rio Grande, and Tampico, along the Gulf coast.

Despite major U.S. victories, General Santa Anna, who reclaimed the presidency of Mexico during the war, refused to give up. In February 1847, his troops attacked U.S. forces at Buena Vista and nearly secured a victory. Polk then agreed to send General Winfield Scott to Veracruz with 14,000 soldiers. Capturing the port in March, Scott's army headed to Mexico City. After a crushing defeat of Santa Anna at Cerro Gordo, the president-general was removed from power and the new Mexican government sought peace.

With victory ensured, U.S. officials faced a difficult decision: How much Mexican territory should they claim? The U.S. army in central Mexico faced continued guerrilla attacks. Meanwhile Whigs and some northern Democrats denounced the war as a southern conspiracy to expand slavery. In this context, Polk agreed to limit U.S. claims to the northern regions of Mexico. The president signed the **Treaty of Guadalupe Hidalgo** in February 1848, committing the United States to pay Mexico $15 million in return for control over Texas north and east of the Rio Grande plus California and the New Mexico territory.

Debates over Slavery Intensify. News of the U.S. victory traveled quickly across the United States. In the South, planters imagined slavery spreading into the lands acquired from Mexico. Northerners, too, applauded the expansion of U.S. territory but focused on California as a center for agriculture and commerce. Still, the acquisition of new territory heightened sectional conflicts. Debates over slavery had erupted during the war, fueled by abolitionist outrage. A few northern Democrats joined Whigs in denouncing "the power of SLAVERY" to "govern the country, its Constitutions and laws."

In August 1846, Democratic congressman David Wilmot of Pennsylvania proposed outlawing slavery in all territory acquired from Mexico so that the South could not profit from the war. While the **Wilmot Proviso** passed in the House, southern and proslavery northern Democrats defeated it in the Senate. Many Northerners shared these Democrats' views on African Americans. Legislators in Oregon Territory, too far north for slavery to be an issue, nonetheless excluded African Americans from settling within its borders. The first such law took effect in 1844, and the last of Oregon's exclusionary laws was not repealed until 1926. Ohio, Indiana, Illinois, and other Midwestern states also restricted or denied blacks the right to settle.

It was the question of slavery in the territories acquired from Mexico, however, that fueled the presidential election of 1848. With Polk declining to run for a second term, Democrats nominated Lewis Cass, a Michigan senator and ardent expansionist. Hoping to keep northern antislavery Democrats in the party, Cass argued that residents in each territory should decide whether to make the region free or slave. This strategy put the slavery question on hold but satisfied almost no one.

The Whigs, too, hoped to avoid the slavery issue for fear of losing southern votes. They nominated Mexican-American War hero General Zachary Taylor, a Louisiana enslaver who had no declared position on slavery in the western territories. But they sought to reassure their northern wing by nominating Millard Fillmore of Buffalo, New York, for vice president. As a member of Congress in the 1830s, Fillmore had opposed the annexation of Texas.

The Liberty Party, disappointed in the Whig ticket, decided to run its own candidate for president. Its leaders hoped to expand their support by reconstituting themselves as the Free-Soil Party. This party focused more on excluding enslaved labor from western territories than on the moral injustice of slavery. The party nominated former president Martin Van Buren and appealed to small farmers and urban workers hoping to benefit from western expansion.

Once again, the presence of a third party affected the outcome of the election. While Whigs and Democrats tried to avoid the slavery issue, Free-Soilers demanded attention to it. By focusing on the exclusion of slavery in western territories rather than its abolition, the party won more adherents in northern states. Indeed, Van Buren won enough northern Democrats so that Cass lost New York State and the 1848 election. Zachary Taylor and the Whigs won, but only by placing a southern enslaver in the White House.

Review & Relate

■ How did the battle over Texas affect relations among Indian nations, among white Americans, and between Indians and whites?

■ How did the Mexican-American War reshape national politics and intensify debates over slavery?

Comparative Secondary Source Analysis

Families in Slavery

Abolitionist claims about the destructive effects of slavery on enslaved families informed scholarly assessments in the twentieth century. In 1959, the historian Stanley Elkins argued that prolonged bondage limited the ability of enslaved people to forge strong emotional bonds. Six years later, scholar Daniel Patrick Moynihan claimed that slavery spawned female-dominated households, which helped explain the "pathology" of black families in the present. Robert Fogel and Stanley Engerman challenged these views in 1974 by highlighting the role of enslaved men as heads of households and leaders of the enslaved community. A decade later, Deborah Gray White argued instead that enslaved women played crucial roles and that enslaved families were surprisingly egalitarian.

Source 11.4

Robert William Fogel and Stanley L. Engerman | Planters Shape Slave Families, 1974

For better or worse, the dominant role in slave society was played by men, not women. It was men who occupied virtually all of the managerial slots available to slaves. There were very few female overseers or drivers. Men occupied nearly all the artisan crafts. . . .

While females worked along with males in the field, their role was strictly delimited. . . . Just as some jobs on the plantation were confined strictly to men, others were confined strictly to women. . . .

There was also a division of labor within the slave family, a division that began with courtship. It was the male who, at least on the surface, initiated the period of courtship. And it was the man who secured the permission of the planter to marry. After marriage, the tasks of cooking, ordinary household cleaning, laundering, and care of the children fell to the mother.

Planters recognized husbands as the head of the family. Slave families were listed in their record books with the husband at the top of the list. Houses were assigned by the names of husbands and the semiannual issues of clothing to families were made in the name of husbands. . . .

While both moral convictions and good business practice generally led planters to encourage the development of stable nuclear families, . . . there is considerable evidence that the nuclear form was not merely imposed on slaves. Slaves apparently abandoned the African family forms [such as multi-generational families living together] because they did not satisfy the needs of blacks who lived and worked under conditions and in a society much different from those which their ancestors experienced. The nuclear family took root among blacks because it did satisfy those needs.

Source: Robert William Fogelman and Stanley L. Engerman, *Time on the Cross: The Economics of American Negro Slavery* (Boston: Little, Brown and Company, 1974), pp. 139, 141, 142–143.

Source 11.5

Deborah Gray White | The Roles of Enslaved Women, 1985

[R]evisionist historians have had difficulty reconciling the slave woman's reality with Western cultural mores that dictate a subordinate familial role for women within the family. They have ignored that slave women played important provider roles and that, short of brute force, bondmen lacked the leverage by which to impose subordinate status on their wives. The extensive female network has also gone unrecognized by those who have assumed that slave woman's primary source of emotional support came from bonded men. . . . [T]he stark reality is that slave women were not sheltered from life's ugliness nor dependent on their men for subsistence goods and services. . . .

Therefore, slave families were unusually egalitarian. Equality could not have been based on sameness because . . . many jobs and responsibilities still belonged by definition to one sex or the other. This suggests that equality in the slave family was founded on complementary roles, roles that were different yet so critical to slave survival that they were of equal necessity. . . .

Nevertheless, relationships between mother and child still superseded those between husband and wife. Slaveholder practices encouraged the primacy of the mother-child relationship, and in the mores of the slave community motherhood ranked above marriage. In fact, women in their roles as mothers were the central figures in the nuclear slave family. . . .

What black women did was very much in the pattern of their female African ancestors who had for generations stood at the center of the African family. . . . Acting out a very traditional role, they made themselves a real bulwark against the destruction of the slave family's integrity.

Source: Deborah Gray White, *Ar'n't I a Woman? Female Slaves in the Plantation South* (New York: W.W. Norton & Company, 1985), pp. 158, 159, 160.

Examine the Sources

1. How do Fogel and Engerman differ from White in their interpretation of family life among the enslaved?
2. What kind of evidence do these historians draw on in making their arguments, and which interpretation do you find more compelling and why?

Put It in Context

In what ways did the enslaved and the enslavers shape black family life, and how did the expansion of slavery affect familial relationships?

Conclusion: Geographical Expansion and Political Division

By the mid-nineteenth century, the United States stood at a crossroads. Most Americans considered expansion advantageous and necessary for a strong economy. Planters certainly considered it critical to slavery's success. Yet as the number of enslaved workers and the size of plantations grew, planters also sought to impose stricter controls over blacks, enslaved and free, and to bind non-slaveowning whites more firmly to their interests. Enslaved blacks, meanwhile, developed an increasingly rich culture by combining traditions and rituals from Africa and the Caribbean with U.S. customs and beliefs. This African American culture served as one form of resistance against slavery's brutality. Many enslaved laborers resisted in other ways as well: sabotaging tools, feigning illness, running away, or committing arson or theft. Smaller numbers engaged in outright rebellions.

While most white Northerners were willing to leave slavery alone where it already existed, many hoped to keep it out of newly acquired territories. In this sense, the removal of the Cherokee did not disturb most Northerners since it was largely white yeoman farmers, they believed, who would benefit from access to their land. Still some northern whites, especially evangelical women, opposed removal on moral grounds. At the same time, many Northerners supported statehood for Texas despite abolitionist protests. When it came to the Mexican-American War, however, more Northerners—black and white—feared victory would largely benefit southern planters. Some yeomen farmers and middle-class professionals in the South also questioned whether extending slavery benefited the region economically and politically.

The vast lands gained from Mexico in 1848 intensified debates over slavery and led small but growing numbers of white Northerners to join African Americans, American Indians, and newly created Mexican Americans in protesting U.S. expansion. Tejano leaders, including José Antonio Menchaca, had supported statehood and the U.S. war against Mexico, eager to ensure the region's security. Still, after the war, Menchaca spoke out for Tejano veterans, who claimed they were denied proper compensation for their service.

These debates occurred amid a political realignment fueled by the panic of 1837. The extended depression allowed the newly formed Whig Party to gain support for its economic and reform agenda. In 1840 Whigs captured the White House and Congress just as a new antislavery force, the Liberty Party, emerged. But just four years later, James K. Polk's support of westward expansion and manifest destiny returned Democrats to power. The political volatility continued when the U.S. defeat of Mexico intensified debates over slavery, fractured the Democratic Party, and inspired the founding of the Free-Soil Party.

Political realignments continued over the next decade, as growing antislavery sentiment in the North confronted proslavery claims in the South. In 1853 Solomon Northup shocked thousands of antislavery readers with his book *Twelve Years a Slave*, which vividly described the horrors of the slave trade and life in bondage. His book and others alarmed planters, who continued to claim that slavery was a divine blessing. Yet in insisting on the benefits of enslaved labor, the planter elite reinforced conflicts with Northerners, whose lives were increasingly shaped by commercial and industrial development and the expansion of free labor.

Timeline of Events

1830	Indian Removal Act
1830–1850	440,000 enslaved people from Upper South sold to owners in Lower South
1831	*Cherokee Nation v. Georgia*
	Nat Turner leads slave uprising in Virginia
	Virginia's Assembly establishes special committee on slavery
1832	*Worcester v. Georgia*
1834	Britain abolishes slavery in its territories
1835–1842	Second Seminole War
1836	Treaty of New Echota
March 2, 1836	U.S. settlers declare eastern Texas an independent republic
March 6, 1836	General Santa Anna crushes U.S. rebels at the Alamo
March 1836	Congress passes gag rule
1837–1843	Panic of 1837 triggers extended depression
1838–1839	Cherokee driven west on Trail of Tears
1840	Whigs win the presidency and gain control of Congress
1841	Solomon Northup sold into slavery
1842	Seneca Indians win treaty to remain in New York
1845	U.S. annexes Texas
1846	U.S. settles dispute with Great Britain over Oregon
May 1846–February 1848	Mexican-American War
August 1846	David Wilmot proposes Wilmot Proviso
March 1848	Treaty of Guadalupe Hidalgo

Key Terms

planters, 358

Nat Turner's rebellion, 366

yeomen farmers, 368

white supremacy, 370

Whig Party, 370

Second Party System, 371

Tejanos, 371

Alamo, 371

gag rule, 372

Second Seminole War, 372

Treaty of New Echota, 373

Trail of Tears, 375

panic of 1837, 377

manifest destiny, 379

Treaty of Guadalupe Hidalgo, 382

Wilmot Proviso, 383

Review & Relate

1. What role did the planter elite play in southern society and politics?

2. What were the consequences of the dominant position of slave-based plantation agriculture for the southern economy?

3. How did enslaved African Americans create ties of family, community, and culture?

4. How did enslaved African Americans resist efforts to control and exploit their labor?

5. What groups made up white southern society? How did their interests overlap or diverge?

6. How and why did the planter elite seek to reinforce white solidarity?

7. How did westward expansion affect white Southerners, white Northerners, enslaved blacks, and American Indians in the 1830s and 1840s?

8. What economic and political developments led to a Whig victory in the election of 1840?

9. How did the battle over Texas affect relations among Indian nations, among white Americans, and between Indians and whites?

10. How did the Mexican-American War reshape national politics and intensify debates over slavery?

Lives in Slavery

▶ **What forms of subjugation and resistance characterized the lives of enslaved workers between 1820 and 1860?**

Enslaved workers lived under a system of severe subjugation and routinely suffered brutal working conditions, violence, and the devastating separation of families (Sources 11.6, 11.7, 11.8, and 11.9). Yet many enslaved people found ways to resist their bondage and carve out autonomous spaces. They feigned illness, ran away or hid for a few days, and developed a distinctive African American culture (Source 11.10).

A rich body of slave narratives has helped historians understand enslaved life. During the nineteenth century a few fugitive slaves published books about their lives. Often sponsored or encouraged by white abolitionists, these books highlighted the humanity of blacks and the horrors of slavery. Frederick Douglass, William Wells Brown, Solomon Northup, and Harriet Jacobs all published narratives that revealed hidden aspects of the experience of enslaved people (Sources 11.6, 11.7, and 11.8). In the twentieth century the Works Progress Administration, a federal program to provide work during the Great Depression of the 1930s, hired mostly white writers to conduct interviews with ex-slaves. Although recorded some seventy years after slavery's end, the interviews with people such as Mary Reynolds (Source 11.10) offer valuable insight into the lives of the enslaved, few of whom had recorded their own stories.

Whites also documented the lives of the enslaved in the nineteenth century. Both abolitionists and planters wrote extensively about slavery, though from opposing perspectives. Many Europeans were fascinated by American slavery, and some captured the institution in books and paintings (Source 11.9). These white-produced sources can be valuable when analyzed in the context of the stories that enslaved people tell about their own lives.

Source 11.6

William Wells Brown | Memories of Childhood

William Wells Brown was born into slavery in 1814 on a Missouri farm and later worked on Mississippi riverboats. He escaped in 1834, fleeing first to Cleveland and then to western New York and Boston. He became a popular antislavery lecturer and published his narrative in 1847. While he focuses here on his time as an enslaved household worker, he also recalls the cries of his mother being whipped in the fields.

[T]he field hands . . . were summoned to their unrequited toil every morning at four o'clock, by the ringing of a bell. . . . They were allowed half an hour to eat their breakfast, and get to the field. At half past four, a horn was blown by the overseer, which was the signal to commence work; and every one that was not on the spot at the time, had to receive ten lashes from the negro-whip, . . . The handle was about three feet long, with the butt-end filled with lead, and the lash six or seven feet in length, made of cowhide, with platted wire on the end of it. This whip was put in requisition very frequently and freely, and a small offence on the part of a slave furnished an occasion for its use. . . . I was a house servant—a situation preferable to that of a field hand, as I was better fed, better clothed, and not obliged to rise at the ringing of the bell, but about half an hour after. I have often laid and heard the crack of the whip, and the screams of the slave. My mother was a field

hand, and one morning was ten or fifteen minutes
behind the others in getting into the field. As soon as she
reached the spot where they were at work, the overseer
commenced whipping her. She cried, "Oh! pray—Oh!
pray—Oh! pray"—. . . . I heard her voice, and knew it,
and jumped out of my bunk, and went to the door.
Though the field was some distance from the house, I
could hear every crack of the whip, and every groan and
cry of my poor mother. . . . The cold chills ran over me,
and I wept aloud. After giving her ten lashes, the sound
of the whip ceased, and I returned to my bed, and found
no consolation but in my tears. It was not yet daylight.

Source: William Wells Brown, *Narrative of William W. Brown, A
Fugitive Slave, Written by Himself* (Boston: Anti-Slavery Office,
1847), 14–16.

Source 11.7

Harriet Jacobs | A Girl Threatened by Sexual Exploitation

Harriet Jacobs was born into slavery in 1813 in
Edenton, North Carolina. She made a daring escape
in 1835 but remained hidden for seven years in a
crawlspace in the house of her free black
grandmother. She finally reached the North in 1842
and became active in abolitionist circles. In her 1861
autobiography, published under the pseudonym
Linda Brent, Jacobs describes in harrowing detail her
master's attempted sexual exploitation.

But I now entered on my fifteenth year—a sad
epoch in the life of a slave girl. My master
began to whisper foul words in my ear.
Young as I was, I could not remain ignorant of their
import. I tried to treat them with indifference or
contempt. The master's age, my extreme youth, and
the fear that his conduct would be reported to my
grandmother, made him bear this treatment for
many months. He was a crafty man, and resorted to
many means to accomplish his purposes. Sometimes
he had stormy, terrific ways, that made his victims
tremble; sometimes he assumed a gentleness that he
thought must surely subdue. Of the two, I preferred
his stormy moods, although they left me trembling.
He tried his utmost to corrupt the pure principles my
grandmother had instilled. He peopled my young
mind with unclean images. . . . I turned from him
with disgust and hatred. But he was my master. I

was compelled to live under the same roof with
him—where I saw a man forty years my senior daily
violating the most sacred commandments of nature. He
told me I was his property; that I must be subject to his
will in all things. My soul revolted against the mean
tyranny. But where could I turn for protection? No
matter whether the slave girl be as black as ebony or as
fair as her mistress. In either case, there is no shadow
of law to protect her from insult, from violence, or even
from death; all these are inflicted by fiends who bear
the shape of men. The mistress, who ought to protect
the helpless victim, has no other feelings towards her
but those of jealousy and rage. . . .

Even the little child, who is accustomed to wait
on her mistress and her children, will learn, before
she is twelve years old, why it is that her mistress
hates such and such a one among the slaves. Perhaps
the child's own mother is among those hated ones. . . .
She will become prematurely knowing in evil things.
Soon she will learn to tremble when she hears her
master's footfall. She will be compelled to realize that
she is no longer a child. If God has bestowed beauty
upon her, it will prove her greatest curse. That which
commands admiration in the white woman only
hastens the degradation of the female slave.

Source: Linda Brent [Harriet Jacobs], *Incidents in the Life of a
Slave Girl* (Boston: Published for the Author, 1861), 44–46.

Source 11.8

Solomon Northup | Endless Labor and Constant Fear

Solomon Northup, who was born free in New York
State in 1808, was kidnapped and sold into slavery in
1841. After he regained his freedom in 1853, he wrote
an autobiography, *Twelve Years a Slave*, about his
experiences. In this excerpt, he describes the labor
regimen of his owner, Edwin Epps, a planter in
southern Louisiana.

The hands are required to be in the cotton field
as soon as it is light in the morning, and, with
the exception of ten or fifteen minutes, which
is given them at noon to swallow their allowance of
cold bacon, they are not permitted to be a moment
idle until it is too dark to see, and when the moon is
full, they often times labor till the middle of the night.

They do not dare to stop even at dinner time, nor return to the quarters, however late it be, until the order to halt is given by the driver.

The day's work over in the field, the baskets are . . . carried to the gin-house, where the cotton is weighed. No matter how fatigued and weary he may be—no matter how much he longs for sleep and rest—a slave never approaches the gin-house with his basket of cotton but with fear. If it falls short in weight—if he has not performed the full task appointed him, he knows that he must suffer. And if he has exceeded it by ten or twenty pounds, in all probability his master will measure the next day's task accordingly. . . . Most frequently they have too little, and therefore it is they are not anxious to leave the field. After weighing, follow the whippings; and then the baskets are carried to the cotton house, and their contents stored away like hay, all hands being sent in to tramp it down. . . .

This done, the labor of the day is not yet ended, by any means. Each one must then attend to his respective chores. One feeds the mules, another the swine—another cuts the wood, and so forth; besides, the packing is all done by candle light. Finally, at a late hour, they reach the quarters, sleepy and overcome with the long day's toil. Then a fire must be kindled in the cabin, the corn ground in the small hand-mill, and supper, and dinner for the next day in the field, prepared. All that is allowed them is corn and bacon, which is given out at the corncrib and smoke-house every Sunday morning. . . . That is all—no tea, coffee, sugar, and with the exception of a very scanty sprinkling now and then, no salt. . . .

The softest couches in the world are not to be found in the log mansion of the slave. The one whereon I reclined year after year, was a plank twelve inches wide and ten feet long. My pillow was a stick of wood. The bedding was a coarse blanket, and not a rag or shred beside. Moss might be used, were it not that it directly breeds a swarm of fleas. . . .

An hour before day light the horn is blown. . . . Then the fears and labors of another day begin.

Source: Solomon Northup, *Twelve Years a Slave* (Auburn, NY: Derby and Miller, 1853), 167–69, 171.

Source 11.9

Friedrich Shulz | *The Slave Market*

American slave markets regularly appeared in etchings, engravings, and paintings in the nineteenth century. Several images were produced by European artists traveling through the South. The German artist Friedrich Shulz (1825–1875) visited the United States in the 1840s or 1850s and painted this image of a slave auction. The beautiful colors and rich tones belie the tragic and brutal scenes taking place in this southern market.

Bridgeman Images

Mary Reynolds | Recalling Work, Punishment, and Faith c. 1850s

Ex-slaves interviewed in the 1930s offer a wealth of information. Mary Reynolds claimed to be more than a hundred years old when interviewed in 1937, but her memories were vivid. She was one of the older interviewees and thus had experienced slavery longer than many who told their stories in this period. Here she recalls life with her parents and sisters on the Kilpatrick family plantation in Black River, Louisiana. Reynolds's use of a racial epithet for black people quoted below reflects the pervasive racial language of the slave era in Louisiana and in 1930s Texas, where she was interviewed.

Massa Kilpatrick wasn't no piddlin' man. He was a man of plenty. He had a big house. . . . He was a medicine doctor and they was rooms in the second story for sick folks what come to lay in. It would take two days to go all over the land he owned. He had cattle and stock and sheep and more'n a hundred slaves and more besides. He bought the bes' of niggers near every time the spec'lators come that way. He'd make a swap of the old ones and give money for young ones what could work. . . .

He raised corn and cotton and cane and 'taters and goobers [potatoes and peanuts], 'sides the peas and other feedin' for the niggers. I 'member I helt a hoe handle mighty onsteady when they put a old women to larn me and some other chillun to scrape the fields. . . . She say, "For the love of Gawd, you better larn it right, or Solomon will beat the breath out you body." Old man Solomon was the nigger driver. . . .

The times I hated most was pickin' cotton when the frost was on the bolls. My hands git sore and crack open and bleed. We'd have a li'l fire in the fields and iffen the ones with tender hands couldn't stand it no longer, we'd run and warm our hands a li'l bit. . . .

Sometimes massa let niggers have a li'l patch. They'd raise 'taters or goobers . . . to help fill out on the victuals. . . .

Once in a while they's give us a li'l piece of Sat'day evenin' to wash out clothes. . . . When they'd git through with the clothes on Sat'day evenin's the niggers . . . brung fiddles and guitars and come out and play. The others clap they hands and stomp they feet and we young'uns cut a step round. I was plenty biggity and like to cut a step.

We was scart of Solomon and his whip, though, and he didn't like frolickin'. He didn't like for us niggers to pray, either. We never heared of no church, but us have prayin' in the cabins. . . . I know that Solomon is burnin' in hell today, and it pleasures me to know it.

Once my maw and paw taken me and Katherine after night to slip to 'nother place to a prayin' and singin'. A nigger man with white beard told us a day am comin' when niggers only be slaves of Gawd. We prays for the end of Trib'lation and the end of beatin's and for shoes that fit our feet. We prayed that us niggers could have all we wanted to eat and special for fresh meat. . . .

When we's comin' back from that prayin', I thunk I heared the nigger [tracking] dogs and somebody on horseback. . . . Maw listens and say, "Sho 'nough, them dogs am runnin' and Gawd help us!" Then she and paw . . . take us to a fence corner and stands us up 'gainst the rails and say don't move. . . . They went to the woods, so the hounds chase them and not git us. Me and Katherine stand there, holdin' hands, shakin' so we can hardly stand. We hears the hounds come nearer, but we don't move. They goes after paw and maw, but they circles round to the cabins and gits in. Maw say its the power of Gawd.

Source: Ex-Slave Stories: Mary Reynolds, in "Born in Slavery: Slave Narratives from the Federal Writers' Project, 1936–1938," American Memory, Library of Congress, Texas, vol. 16, pt. 3, pp. 238–41.

Interpret the Evidence

1. What do these documents tell us about the working lives of enslaved people? What differences and similarities do they reveal across age, sex, and region (Sources 11.6, 11.8, and 11.10)?

2. How does the likely audience for each of these sources affect the way that black writers and the black interviewee portray life in bondage? How might the German artist's portrayal be affected by his imagined audience?

3. What were the greatest threats or fears confronted by enslaved people in these sources and how did they seek to survive or resist these conditions?

4. How did enslaved women and men create a sense of community and culture, and what does this tell us about their views of enslavers and other whites?

5. In reading across these documents, how might the experience of slavery change over the course of a person's lifetime?

Put It in Context

How would proslavery Southerners respond to the experiences revealed in these documents?

What do the examples of resistance suggest about white efforts to control the behavior of enslaved labor?

Imperial Ambitions and Sectional Crises

1842–1861

Window to the Past

William C. Nell, Meeting of Colored Citizens of Boston, September 30, 1850

William C. Nell, a free black Bostonian and well-known abolitionist, fought for the racial integration of schools and government jobs and wrote a history of African Americans in the American Revolution. He also worked for abolitionist newspapers, including the *Liberator*.

In September 1850, he served as secretary for a meeting of black activists who encouraged residents to defend themselves should slave catchers appear in Boston.

▶ To learn more about this primary source, see Source 12.2 on page 406.

Resolved, That the Fugitive Slave Bill, recently adopted by the United States Congress, puts in imminent jeopardy the lives and liberties of ourselves and children; it deprives us of a trial by jury, when seized by the infernal slave-catcher, and by high penalties forbids the assistance of those who would otherwise obey their heart-promptings in our behalf; in making it obligatory upon the marshals to become bloodhounds in pursuit of human prey; leaving us no alternative (thus left without protection) but to be prepared in the emergency for self-defence; therefore, assured that God has no attribute which can take sides with the oppressors, we have counted the cost, and as we prefer *liberty* to *life*, we mutually pledge to defend ourselves and each other in resisting this God-defying and inhuman law, at any and every sacrifice, invoking Heaven's defence of the right.

Library of Congress

After reading this chapter you will be able to:

- Compare the experiences of different groups living in and migrating to the West, including Mexicans, Mexican Americans, and American Indians.

- Explain how geographical expansion heightened sectional conflicts and how those conflicts shaped and were shaped by federal policies like the Compromise of 1850 and the Fugitive Slave Act.

- Analyze the ways that the spread of antislavery sentiments, partisan politics, and federal court decisions intensified sectional divisions.

- Evaluate the importance of John Brown's raid and the election of Abraham Lincoln as president in convincing southern states to secede from the Union.

Comparing American Histories

John C. Frémont, a noted explorer and military leader, rose from humble beginnings. He was born out of wedlock to Anne Beverley Whiting Pryor of Savannah, Georgia, who abandoned her wealthy husband and ran off with a French immigrant. Frémont attended the College of Charleston, where he excelled at mathematics, but was eventually expelled for neglecting his studies. In 1833, at age twenty, he was hired to teach aboard a navy ship through the

(*left*) **John C. Frémont** Library of Congress, Prints and Photographs Division, Washington, D.C. [LC-DIG-ppmsca-03210]
(*right*) **Dred Scott** Library of Congress, Prints and Photographs Division, Washington, D.C. [LC-USZ62-79305]

help of an influential South Carolina politician. He then obtained a surveying position to map new railroad lines and Cherokee lands in Georgia and was finally appointed a second lieutenant in the Corps of Topographical Engineers.

In 1840 Lieutenant Frémont moved to Washington, D.C., where he worked on maps and reports based on his surveys. The following year, he eloped with Jessie Benton, the daughter of Missouri senator Thomas Hart Benton. Despite the scandal, Senator Benton supported his son-in-law's selection for a federally funded expedition to the West. In 1842 Frémont and his guide, Kit Carson, led twenty-three men along the emerging Oregon Trail. Two years later, John returned to Washington, where Jessie helped him turn his notes into a vivid report on the Oregon Territory and California. Congress published the report, which inspired a wave of hopeful migrants to head west.

Frémont's success was tainted, however, by a quest for personal glory. On a federal mapping expedition in 1845, he left his post and headed to Sacramento, California. In early 1846, he stirred support among U.S. settlers there for war with Mexico. His brash behavior nearly provoked a bloody battle. Frémont then fled to the Oregon Territory, where he and Kit Carson initiated conflicts with local Indians. As the United States moved closer to war with Mexico, Frémont returned to California to support Anglo-American settlers' efforts to declare the region an independent republic. After the war, Frémont worked tirelessly for California's admission to the Union and served as one of the state's first senators. With his wife's encouragement, he embraced abolition and in 1856 was nominated for president by the new Republican Party.

Dred Scott also traveled the frontier in the 1830s and 1840s, but not of his own free will. Born a slave in Southampton, Virginia around 1800, his master, Peter Blow, moved west to Alabama in 1818 and then to St. Louis, Missouri, in 1830, taking Scott with him. Three years later, Blow sold Scott to Dr. John Emerson, an assistant surgeon in the U.S. army. In 1836 Emerson took Scott to Fort Snelling in the free territory of Wisconsin Territory. There Scott met Harriet Robinson, a young enslaved African American. Her master, an Indian agent, allowed the couple to marry in 1837 and transferred ownership of Harriet to Dr.

Emerson. When Emerson moved back to St. Louis, the Scotts returned with him. After the doctor's death in 1843, the couple was hired out to local residents by Emerson's widow.

In April 1846, the Scotts initiated lawsuits to gain their freedom. The Missouri Supreme Court had ruled in earlier cases that enslaved people who resided for any time in free territory must be freed, and the Scotts had lived and married in Wisconsin.

In 1850 the Missouri Circuit Court ruled in the Scotts' favor. However, the Emerson family appealed the decision to the state supreme court, with Harriet's case to follow the outcome of her husband's. Two years later, that court ruled against all precedent and overturned the lower court's decision. Dred Scott then appealed to the U.S. Supreme Court, but it, too, ultimately ruled against the Scotts, leaving them enslaved. ∎

Comparing the American histories of John Frémont and Dred Scott demonstrates how the explosive combination of westward expansion and growing regional divisions over the issue of slavery split the nation by 1861. Whereas Frémont joined expeditions to map and conquer the West, Scott followed the migrations of enslavers and soldiers. Both Frémont and Scott were supported by strong women, and both men advocated government action to end slavery. Only Frémont, however, had the right to vote, run for office, and join the Republican Party. From their different positions, these two men reflected the dramatic changes that occurred as westward expansion pushed the issues of empire and slavery to the center of national debate.

Claiming the West

During the 1830s and 1840s, national debates over slavery intensified. The most important battles now centered on western territories gained through victory in the war with Mexico. Before 1848, government-sponsored expeditions had opened up vast new lands for American pioneers seeking opportunity, and migrants moved west in growing numbers. Following the Mexican-American War and the discovery of gold in California, tens of thousands of men rushed to the Pacific coast seeking riches. But the West was already home to a diverse population that included Indians, Mexicans, Mormons, and missionaries. Pioneers converged, and often clashed, with these groups.

Traveling the Overland Trail. In the 1830s a growing number of migrants followed overland trails to the far West. In 1836 Narcissa Whitman and Eliza Spaulding joined a group traveling to the Oregon Territory, the first white women to make the trip. They accompanied their husbands, both Presbyterian ministers, who hoped to convert the region's Indians. Their letters to friends and co-worshippers back east described the rich lands and needy souls in the Walla Walla valley. Such missives were widely shared and encouraged further migration.

The panic of 1837 also prompted families to head west. Thousands of U.S. migrants and European immigrants sought better economic prospects in Oregon, the Rocky Mountain region, and the eastern plains, while Mormons continued to settle in Salt Lake City. Some pioneers opened trading posts where Indians exchanged goods with Anglo-American settlers or with merchants back east. Small settlements developed around these posts and near the expanding system of U.S. forts that dotted the region.

For many pioneers, the journey on the **Oregon Trail** began at St. Louis. From there, they traveled by wagon train across the Great Plains and the Rocky Mountains to the Pacific coast. By 1860 some 350,000 Americans had made the journey, claimed land from the Mississippi River to the Pacific that once belonged to native peoples, and transformed the United States into an expanding empire.

Because the journey west required funds for wagons and supplies, most pioneers were of middling status. The majority of pioneers made the three- to six-month journey with family members to help share the labor. Men, mainly farmers, comprised some 60 percent of these western migrants, but women and children traveled in significant numbers, often alongside relatives or neighbors from back east. Some courageous families headed west alone, but most traveled in wagon trains — from a few wagons to a few dozen — that provided support and security.

> **Explore ▶**
>
> See Source 12.1 for one account of the journey west.

Traditional gender roles often broke down on the trail, and even conventional domestic tasks posed novel problems. Women had to cook unfamiliar food over open fires in all kinds of weather and with only a few pots and utensils. They washed laundry in rivers or streams and on the plains hauled water from great distances. Wood, too, was scarce on the plains, and women and children gathered buffalo dung (called "chips") for fuel. Men frequently had to gather food rather than hunt and fish, or they had to learn to catch strange (and sometimes dangerous) animals, such as jack rabbits and rattlesnakes. Few men were prepared for the dangerous work of floating wagons across rivers. Nor were many of them expert in shoeing horses or fixing wagon wheels, tasks that were performed by skilled artisans at home.

Emigrants Headed West, July 1859   Daniel A. Jenks and his family headed west in search of gold in spring 1859. His detailed record of the journey includes dozens of graphite, ink, and crayon images. This drawing shows the wagon train camped along the Humboldt River in Nevada. Men and women go about their "housekeeping" tasks while a couple courts in the back of a wagon. F&A Archive/Art Resource, NY

Expectations changed dramatically when men took ill or died. Then wives often drove the wagon, gathered or hunted for food, and learned to repair axles and other wagon parts. When large numbers of men were injured or ill, women might serve as scouts and guides or pick up guns to defend wagons under attack by Indians or wild animals. Yet despite their growing burdens, pioneer women gained little power over decision making. Moreover, the addition of men's jobs to women's responsibilities was rarely reciprocated. Few men cooked, did laundry, or cared for children on the trail.

Guided Primary Source Analysis

Elizabeth Smith Geer | Oregon Trail Diary, 1847

Like thousands of other families, Elizabeth and Cornelius Smith and their seven children set out for the Oregon Territory in the spring of 1847. They fared well through the summer, but in the fall heavy rains made things difficult. In November Cornelius became sick, but the Smiths arrived in Portland, Oregon by Thanksgiving. However, Cornelius died two months later, and in 1849 Elizabeth married Joseph Geer, the father of ten children whose wife also died after journeying across the Oregon Trail.

Source 12.1

November 18.

How did weather affect the ability of families to travel on the Oregon Trail?

How did children both assist and create problems for their parents?

How did the roles of husbands and wives change during the journey?

It rains and snows. We start around the falls this morning with our wagons. We have five miles to go. I carry my babe and lead, or rather carry another, through snow, mud, and water almost to my knees. It is the worst road a team could possibly travel. I went ahead with my children and I was afraid to look behind me for fear of seeing the wagons overturn into the mud and water with everything in them. My children gave out with cold and fatigue and could not travel, and the boys had to unhitch the oxen and bring them and carry the children on to camp. I was so cold and numb that I could not tell by the feeling that I had any feet. We started this morning at sunrise and did not camp until after dark, and there was not one dry thread on one of us—not even on the babe. I had carried my babe and I was so fatigued that I could scarcely speak or step. When I got here I found my husband lying in Welch's wagon very sick. He had brought Mrs. Polk down the day before and was taken sick. We had to stay up all night for our wagons were left halfway back. I have not told half we suffered. I am not adequate to the task.

Source: Theodore Thurston Geer, *Fifty Years in Oregon* (New York: Neale, 1912), 146.

Put It in Context

Despite widespread fear of Indian attacks on the trail, what were the most serious dangers that men and women pioneers faced on the journey west?

In one area, however, relative equality reigned. Men and women were equally susceptible to disease, injury, and death during the journey. Accidents, gunshot wounds, drownings, broken bones, and infections affected people on every wagon train. Some groups were struck as well by deadly epidemics of measles or cholera. In addition, about 20 percent of women on the overland trail became pregnant, which posed even greater dangers than usual given the lack of medical services and sanitation. About the same percentage of women lost children or spouses on the trip west. Overall, about one in ten to fifteen migrants died on the western journey.

The Gold Rush. Despite the hazards, more and more Americans traveled overland to the Pacific coast, although only a few thousand Americans initially settled in California. Some were agents sent there by eastern merchants to purchase fine leather made from the hides of Spanish cattle. Several agents married into families of elite Mexican ranchers, known as Californios, and adopted their culture, even converting to Catholicism.

However, the Anglo-American presence in California changed dramatically after 1848 when gold was discovered at Sutter's Mill in northeastern California. Beginning in 1849 news of the discovery brought tens of thousands of settlers from the eastern United States, South America, Europe, and Asia. In the **gold rush**, "forty-niners" raced to claim riches in California, and men vastly outnumbered women.

The rapid influx of gold seekers heightened tensions between newly arrived whites, local Indians, and Californios. Forty-niners confiscated land owned by Californios,

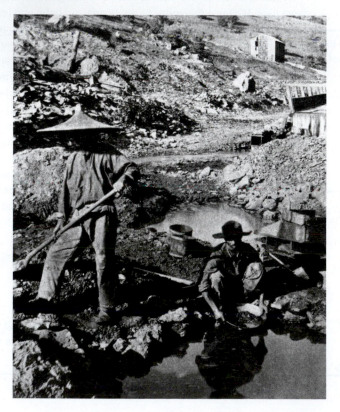

Gold Rush Miners, 1849
These prospectors were two of some 80,000 who traveled to California after gold was discovered. While many Chinese miners were run off their claims, these two men, dressed in a mix of Chinese and American attire, panned for gold with the tools of their trade — pickax, hoe, and pan. A shed in the background may have served as their home. Granger

shattered the fragile ecosystem in the California mountains, and forced Mexican and Indian men to labor for low wages or a promised share in uncertain profits. New conflicts erupted when migrants from Asia and South America joined the search for wealth. Forty-niners from the United States regularly stole from and assaulted these foreign-born competitors.

The gold rush also led to the increased exploitation of women as thousands of male migrants demanded food, shelter, laundry, and medical care. While some California women earned a good living by renting rooms, cooking meals, washing clothes, or working as prostitutes, many faced exploitation and abuse. Indian and Mexican women were especially vulnerable to sexual harassment and rape, while many Chinese women were imported specifically to provide sexual services for male miners.

Chinese men were also victims of abuse by whites, who ran them off their claims. Yet some Chinese men used the skills traditionally assigned them in their homeland — cooking and washing clothes — to earn a far steadier income than prospecting for gold could provide. Other men also took advantage of the demand for goods and services. Levi Strauss, a German Jewish immigrant, moved from New York to San Francisco to open a dry-goods store in 1853. He soon made his fortune producing canvas and then denim pants that could withstand harsh weather and long wear.

A Crowded Land.

While U.S. promoters of migration continued to depict the West as open territory, it was in fact the site of competing national ambitions in the late 1840s. Despite granting statehood to Texas in 1845 and winning the war against Mexico in 1848, the United States had to battle for control of the Great Plains with powerful Indian nations, like the Lakota and Dakota and the Cheyenne (Map 12.1).

Although attacks on wagon trains were rare, Indians did threaten frontier settlements throughout the 1840s and 1850s. Settlers often retaliated, and U.S. army troops joined them in efforts to push Indians back from areas newly claimed by whites. Yet in many parts of the West, Indians were as powerful as whites, and they did not cede territory without a fight. The Reverend Marcus Whitman and his wife, Narcissa, became victims of their success in promoting western settlement when pioneers brought a deadly measles epidemic to the region, killing thousands of Cayuse and Nez Percé Indians. In 1847, convinced that whites brought disease but no useful medicine, a group of Cayuse Indians killed the Whitmans and ten other white settlers.

Yet violence against whites could not stop the flood of migrants into the Oregon Territory. Indeed, attacks by one Indian tribe were often used to justify assaults on any Indian tribe. Thus John Frémont and Kit Carson, whose party was attacked by Modoc Indians in Oregon in 1846, retaliated by destroying a Klamath Indian village and killing its inhabitants. The defeat of Mexico and the discovery of gold in California only intensified such conflicts. Over the next quarter century, vigilante violence, kidnapping, disease, the destruction of hunting and fishing grounds and farmlands, and mass murders reduced California's native population from about 150,000 to 30,000.

Although Indians and white Americans were the main players in many battles, Indian nations also competed with each other. In the southern plains, drought and disease exacerbated those conflicts in the late 1840s and dramatically changed the balance of power there. In 1845 the southern plains were struck by a dry spell, which lasted on and off until the mid-1860s. In 1848, smallpox ravaged Comanche villages, and a virulent strain of cholera was introduced into the region the next year by forty-niners traveling to California. In the

MAP 12.1 Western Trails and Indian Nations, c. 1850

As wagon trains and traders journeyed west in rapidly growing numbers during the 1830s and 1840s, the United States established forts along the most well-traveled routes. At the same time, Indians claimed or were forced into new areas through the pressure of Indian removals, white settlement, and the demands of hunting, trade, and agriculture.

late 1840s, the Comanche nation was the largest Indian group, with about twenty thousand members; by the mid-1850s, less than half that number remained.

Yet the collapse of the Comanche empire was not simply the result of outside forces. As the Comanche expanded their trade networks and incorporated smaller Indian nations into their orbit, they overextended their reach. Most important, they allowed too many bison to be killed to meet the needs of their Indian allies and the demand of Anglo-American and European traders. The Comanche also herded growing numbers of horses, which required expansive grazing lands and winter havens in the river valleys, which forced bison onto more marginal lands. Opening the Santa Fe Trail to commerce multiplied the problems by destroying vegetation and polluting springs, thereby diminishing resources in more of the region. The prolonged drought completed the depopulation of the bison on the southern plains. Without bison, the Comanche lost a trade item critical to sustaining their commercial and political control. As the Comanche empire collapsed, former Indian allies sought to advance their own interests. These developments reignited Indian wars on the southern plains as tens of thousands of pioneers poured through the region.

African Americans also participated in these western struggles. A few southeastern tribes forced into Indian Territory brought enslaved blacks with them, but some enslaved workers were also freed and married Seminole or Cherokee spouses. The Creek proved harsh masters, prompting some of those enslaved to escape north to free states or south to Mexican or Comanche territory. As southern officers in the U.S. army moved to frontier outposts, they carried more enslaved people into the region. Many, including Dr. John Emerson, changed posts frequently, taking enslaved workers like Dred Scott into both slave and free territories. Still, it was white planters who brought the greatest numbers of African Americans into Texas, Missouri, and Kansas, pushing the frontier of slavery ever westward. At the same time, free blacks joined the migration voluntarily in hopes of finding better economic opportunities and less overt racism in the West.

Review & Relate

▪ Why did Americans go west in the 1830s and 1840s, and what was the journey like?

▪ What groups competed for land and resources in the West? How did disease, drought, and violence shape this competition?

Expansion and the Politics of Slavery

The place of slavery in the West aroused intense political debates as territories in the region began to seek statehood. Debates over the eradication of slavery and limits on its expansion had shaped the highly contested presidential election of 1848. After the Mexican-American War, the debate intensified and focused more specifically on slavery's westward expansion. Each time a territory achieved the requirements for statehood, a new crisis erupted. To resolve these crises required strong political leadership, judicial moderation, and a spirit of compromise among the American people. None of these conditions prevailed. Instead, passage of the Fugitive Slave Act in 1850 aroused deeper hostilities, and President Franklin Pierce (1853–1857) encouraged further expansion but failed to address the crises that ensued.

California and the Compromise of 1850.
In the winter of 1849, just before President Zachary Taylor's March inauguration, California applied for admission to the Union as a free state. Some California political leaders opposed slavery on principle. Others wanted to "save" the state for whites by outlawing slavery, discouraging free black migration, and restricting the rights of Mexican, Indian, and Chinese residents. Yet the internal

The United States Senate, A.D. 1850   This print captures seventy-three-year-old Henry
Clay presenting his Compromise of 1850 to colleagues in the Old Senate Chamber. An aged John
C. Calhoun, seated to the left of the Speaker's chair, denounced the compromise, as did
antislavery Whigs and Free-Soilers. Daniel Webster, sitting to the left of Clay, offered a passionate
defense but failed to gain the compromise's passage. Library of Congress, Prints and Photographs Division,
Washington, D.C. [LC-DIG-ppmsca-09398]

debates among Californians were not uppermost in the minds of politicians. Southerners
were concerned about the impact of California's free-state status on the sectional balance in
Congress, and southern Whigs in particular were shocked when President Taylor suggested
that the Senate should simply admit California as requested.

Other debates percolated in Congress at the same time. Many Northerners were horrified by the spectacle of slavery and slave trading in the nation's capital and argued that it
damaged America's international reputation. Southerners, meanwhile, complained that the
Fugitive Slave Act of 1793 was being widely ignored in the North. A boundary dispute
between Texas and New Mexico irritated western legislators, while Texas claimed that debts
it accrued while an independent republic and during the Mexican-American War should be
assumed by the federal government.

Senator Henry Clay of Kentucky, the Whig leader who had hammered out the Missouri
Compromise in 1819 and 1820, again tried to resolve the many conflicts that stalled congressional action. He offered a compromise by which California would be admitted as a free state;
the remaining land acquired from Mexico would be divided into two territories — New Mexico

and Utah—and slavery there would be decided by popular sovereignty; the border dispute between New Mexico and Texas would be decided in favor of New Mexico, but the federal government would assume Texas's war debts; the slave trade (but not slavery) would be abolished in the District of Columbia; and a new and more effective fugitive slave law would be approved. Although Clay's compromise offered something to everyone, his colleagues did not immediately embrace it.

By March 1850, after months of passionate debate, the sides remained sharply divided, as did their most esteemed leaders. John C. Calhoun, a proslavery senator from South Carolina, refused to support any compromise that allowed Congress to decide the fate of slavery in the western territories. William H. Seward, an antislavery Whig senator from New York, proclaimed he could not support a compromise that forced Northerners to help hunt down fugitives from slavery. Although Daniel Webster, a Massachusetts Whig, urged fellow senators to support the compromise to preserve the Union, Congress adjourned with the fate of California undecided.

Before the Senate reconvened in September 1850, however, the political landscape changed in unexpected ways. Henry Clay retired the previous spring, leaving the Capitol with his last great legislative effort unfinished. On March 31, 1850, Calhoun died; his absence from the Senate made compromise more likely. Then in July, President Taylor died unexpectedly, and his vice president, Millard Fillmore, became president. Fillmore then appointed Webster as secretary of state, removing him from the Senate as well.

In fall 1850, with President Fillmore's support, a younger cohort of senators and representatives steered the **Compromise of 1850** through Congress, one clause at a time. This tactic allowed legislators to support only those parts of the compromise they found palatable. In the end, all the provisions passed, and Fillmore quickly signed the bills into law.

The Compromise of 1850, like the Missouri Compromise thirty years earlier, fended off a sectional crisis but signaled future problems. Would popular sovereignty prevail when later territories sought admission to the Union, and would Northerners abide by a fugitive slave law that called on them to aid directly in the capture of enslaved runaways?

The Fugitive Slave Act Inspires Northern Protest.
The fugitive slave laws of 1793 and 1824 mandated that all states aid in apprehending and returning enslaved runaways to their enslavers. The **1850 Fugitive Slave Act** was different in two important respects. First, it eliminated jury trials for alleged fugitives. Second, the law required individual citizens, not just state officials, to help return runaways. The act angered many Northerners who believed that the federal government had gone too far in protecting the rights of enslavers and thereby aroused sympathy for the abolitionist cause.

Before 1850, free blacks led the effort to aid fugitives, including David Ruggles in New York City; William Still in Philadelphia; and, after his own successful escape, Frederick Douglass. Among their staunchest allies were white Quakers such as Amy and Isaac Post in Rochester, Lucretia Mott in Philadelphia, Thomas Garrett in Chester County, Pennsylvania, and Levi and Catherine Coffin in Newport, Indiana. Political abolitionists, like wealthy reformer Gerrit Smith, of Peterboro, New York, also aided the cause.

Following passage of the Fugitive Slave Act, the number of enslavers and hired slave catchers pursuing fugitives increased dramatically. But so, too, did the number of northern abolitionists helping blacks escape. Once escaped runaways crossed into free territory, most contacted free blacks or sought out Quaker, Baptist, or Methodist meetinghouses whose members might be sympathetic to their cause. They then began the journey along the

Anti-Fugitive Slave Law Convention, Cazenovia, New York, 1850   This rare daguerreotype captures abolitionists, outraged over the Fugitive Slave Law, at a massive protest meeting. Some 2,000 participants met in an apple orchard. Frederick Douglass sits at the left side of the table. The Edmondson sisters, in plaid shawls, stand behind him on either side of Gerrit Smith. The sisters were among fifty former enslaved people who attended the meeting. Digital image courtesy of the Getty's Open Content Program

underground railroad, from house to house or barn to barn, until they found safe haven. Harriet Tubman, herself a fugitive, returned south repeatedly and freed dozens of family members and other enslaved men and women. Abolitionists purchased the freedom of a few fugitives, including sisters Mary and Emily Edmondson who had been sold to slave traders after a failed escape attempt in 1848. Fugitives often followed disparate paths, depending on "conductors" to get them from one stop to the next. Despite its limits, the underground railroad was an important resource for fugitives seeking refuge in Canada or hoping to blend into free black communities stateside.

Free blacks were even more endangered after passage of the Fugitive Slave Act since slave catchers believed that they harbored fugitives in their midst. In Chester County, Pennsylvania, on the Maryland border, newspapers reported on at least a dozen free blacks who were kidnapped or arrested as runaways in the first three months of 1851. One provision of the Fugitive Slave Act encouraged such arrests: Commissioners were paid $10 for each slave sent back but only $5 if a runaway was not returned. Without the right to a trial, a free black could easily be sent south as a fugitive.

At the same time, a growing number of Northerners challenged the federal government's right to enforce the law. Blacks and whites organized protest meetings throughout the free states. At a meeting in Boston in 1851, William Lloyd Garrison denounced the law: "We execrate it, we spit upon it, we trample it under our feet." On July 5, 1852, Frederick Douglass asked a mixed-race audience, "What to the American slave, is your 4th of July? I answer, a day that reveals to him . . . the gross injustice and cruelty to which he is the constant victim." He then declared, "There is not a nation on the earth guilty of practices more shocking and bloody than are the people of these United States at this very hour."

Some abolitionists established vigilance committees to rescue fugitives who had been arrested. In Syracuse in October 1851, Jermaine Loguen, Samuel Ward, and the Reverend Samuel J. May led a well-organized crowd that broke into a Syracuse courthouse and rescued a fugitive known as Jerry. They successfully hid him from authorities before spiriting him to Canada.

Meanwhile Americans continued to debate the law's effects. John Frémont, one of the first two senators from California, helped defeat a federal bill that would have imposed harsher penalties on those who assisted runaways. And Congress felt growing pressure to calm the situation, including from foreign officials who were horrified by the violence required to sustain slavery in the United States. Black abolitionists denounced the Fugitive Slave Act across Canada, Ireland, and England, intensifying foreign concern over the law. Great Britain and France had abolished slavery in their West Indian colonies and could not support what they saw as extreme policies to keep the institution alive in the United States. Yet southern enslavers refused to compromise further, and increasingly northern abolitionists refused as well.

Explore ▶

See Sources 12.2 and 12.3 for two responses to the Fugitive Slave Act.

Pierce Encourages U.S. Expansion.

In the presidential election of 1852, the Whigs and the Democrats tried once again to appeal to voters across the North-South divide by running candidates who either skirted the slavery issue or voiced ambiguous views. The Democrats nominated Franklin Pierce of New Hampshire. A northern opponent of abolition, Pierce had served in his state legislature and in Congress from 1833 to 1842. He also fought in the Mexican-American War and rose to brigadier general. The Whigs rejected President Millard Fillmore, who angered many by supporting popular sovereignty and vigorous enforcement of the Fugitive Slave Act. They turned instead to General Winfield Scott of Virginia. General Scott had never expressed any proslavery views and had served with distinction in the war against Mexico. The Whigs thus hoped to gain southern support while maintaining their northern base. The Free-Soil Party, too, hoped to expand its appeal by nominating John Hale, a New Hampshire Democrat.

Franklin Pierce's eventual victory left the Whigs and the Free-Soilers in disarray. Seeking a truly proslavery party, a third of southern Whigs threw their support to the Democrats in the election. Many Democrats who had supported Free-Soilers in 1848 were driven to vote for Pierce by their enthusiasm over the admission of California as a free state. But despite the Democratic triumph, that party also remained fragile. The nation now faced some of its gravest challenges under a president with no firm base of support and a cabinet that included men of widely differing views. When confronted with difficult decisions, Pierce received contradictory advice and often pursued his own expansionist vision.

Early in his administration, Pierce focused on expanding U.S. trade and extending the "civilizing" power of the nation to other parts of the world. Trade with China had declined in the 1840s, but the United States had begun commercial negotiations with Japan in 1846. In July 1853, President Fillmore sent U.S. emissary Commodore Matthew C. Perry, a renowned naval officer and founder of the Naval Engineer Corps, to obtain a mutual trade agreement with Japan. That treaty was signed shortly after Pierce was inaugurated. Over the next four years, Pierce implemented expanded commercial ties and enhanced diplomatic relations with Japan, and the United States supported the island nation against its traditional enemies, China, Russia, and Europe.

Comparative Primary Source Analysis

The Fugitive Slave Law Contested

The Fugitive Slave Law was enacted on September 18, 1850, and soon after African Americans in Boston called a meeting to discuss their response (Source 12.2). Having heard rumors of arrests elsewhere, participants demanded the right to defend themselves. On February 15, 1851, local abolitionists, led by Lewis Hayden, rescued fugitive Shadrach Minkins from the Boston federal courthouse and spirited him to Canada. Three days later, President Millard Fillmore issued a proclamation demanding that citizens obey the law or be prosecuted (Source 12.3). Seven black men and two whites were arrested in Boston, but juries acquitted them all.

Source 12.2

William C. Nell | Meeting of Colored Citizens of Boston, September 30, 1850

The Chairman [Lewis Hayden] announced, as a prominent feature in calling the present meeting—Congress having passed the infamous Fugitive Slave Bill—the adoption of ways and means for the protection of those in Boston liable to be seized by the prowling man-thief. He said that safety was to be obtained only by an united and persevering resistance of this ungodly, anti-republican law. . . .

The following resolutions were submitted, as a platform for vigilant action in the trial hour:—

Resolved, That the Fugitive Slave Bill, recently adopted by the United States Congress, puts in imminent jeopardy the lives and liberties of ourselves and our children; it deprives us of trial by jury, when seized by the infernal slave-catcher, and by high penalties forbids the assistance of those who would otherwise obey their heart-promptings in our behalf; in making it obligatory upon marshals to become bloodhounds in pursuit of human prey; leaving us no alternative . . . but to be prepared in the emergency for self-defense; therefore, assured that God has no attribute which can take sides with oppressors, we have counted the cost, and as we prefer *liberty* to *life*, we mutually pledge to defend ourselves and each other in resisting this God-defying and inhuman law, at any and every sacrifice, invoking Heaven's defense of the right.

Resolved, That . . . eternal vigilance is the price of liberty, and that they who would be free, themselves must strike the first blow.

Source: "Meeting of the Colored Citizens of Boston," *Liberator*, October 4, 1850.

Many Americans were also eager to expand U.S. power in the Caribbean and Central America. For decades, U.S. politicians, particularly Southerners, had looked to gain control of Cuba, Mexico, and Nicaragua. A "Young America" movement within the Democratic Party imagined manifest destiny reaching southward as well as westward. Southern planters eager to expand became even more insistent about the ways that enslaved laborers benefited from the supposed care owners took in their spiritual and physical well-being.

In hopes of stirring up rebellious Cubans against Spanish rule, some Democrats joined with private adventurers to send three unauthorized expeditions, known as **filibusters**, to invade Cuba. In 1854 the capture of one of the filibustering ships led to an international

Source 12.3

President Millard Fillmore | Proclamation 56 Calling on Citizens to Assist in the Recapture of a Fugitive Slave, February 18, 1851

Whereas information has been received that sundry lawless persons, principally persons of color, combined and confederated together for the purpose of opposing by force the execution of the laws of the United States, did, at Boston, in Massachusetts, on the 15th of this month, make a violent assault on the marshal or deputy marshals of the United States for the district of Massachusetts, in the court-house, and did overcome the said officers, and did by force rescue from their custody a person arrested as a fugitive slave, and then and there a prisoner lawfully holden by the said marshal or deputy marshals of the United States, and other scandalous outrages did commit in violation of law:

Now, therefore, to the end that the authority of the laws may be maintained and those concerned in violating them brought to immediate and condign punishment, I have issued this my proclamation, calling on all well-disposed citizens to rally to the support of the laws of their country, and requiring and commanding all officers, civil and military, and all other persons, civil or military, who shall be found within the vicinity of this outrage, to be aiding and assisting by all means in their power in quelling this and other such combinations and assisting the marshal and his deputies in recapturing the above-mentioned prisoner; and I do especially direct that prosecutions be commenced against all persons who shall have made themselves aiders or abettors in or to this flagitious offense.

Source: *The Messages and Papers of the Presidents, 1789–1913* (Washington, DC: U.S. Government Printing Office, 1913), 988.

Interpret the Evidence

1. How did African Americans in Boston justify their right to defend themselves in defiance of the Fugitive Slave Law, and how would they have responded to Fillmore's Proclamation 56?
2. How does President Fillmore characterize the Boston abolitionists who sought to free fugitives like Shadrach Minkins, and what consequences does he propose for flouting the law?

Put It in Context

What do the conflicts over implementation of the Fugitive Slave Law in Boston suggest about the long-term impact of the law?

---

incident. Spanish officials confiscated the ship, and southern Democrats urged Pierce to seek an apology and redress from Spain. But many northern Democrats rejected any effort to obtain another slave state, and Pierce was forced to renounce the filibusters.

Other politicians still pressured Spain to sell Cuba to the United States. These included Pierce's secretary of state, William Marcy, and the U.S. ambassador to Great Britain, James Buchanan, as well as ministers to France and Spain. In October 1854 these ministers met in Ostend, Belgium and sent a letter to Pierce urging the conquest of Cuba. When the **Ostend Manifesto** was leaked to the press, Northerners were outraged. They viewed the episode as "a dirty plot" to gain more slave territory and forced Pierce to give up plans to obtain Cuba.

In 1855 a private adventurer named William Walker, who had organized four filibusters to Nicaragua, invaded that country and set himself up as ruler. He then invited southern enslavers to come to Nicaragua and establish plantations. Pierce and many Democrats endorsed his plan, but neighboring Hondurans forced Walker from power in 1857 and executed him three years later. Although Pierce's expansionist dreams often failed, his efforts heightened sectional tensions.

Review & Relate

- What steps did legislators take in the 1840s and early 1850s to resolve the issue of the expansion of slavery? Were they successful?

- How were slavery and American imperialist ambitions intertwined in the 1840s and 1850s?

Sectional Crises Intensify

The political crises of the early 1850s created a lively trade in antislavery literature. This cultural turmoil, combined with the weakness and fragmentation of the existing political parties, helped give rise to the Republican Party in 1854. The Republican Party soon absorbed enough Free-Soilers, Whigs, and northern Democrats to become a major political force. The events that drove these cultural and political developments included the publication of *Uncle Tom's Cabin*, continued challenges to the Fugitive Slave Act, a battle over the admission of Kansas to the Union, and a Supreme Court ruling in the *Dred Scott* case.

Popularizing Antislavery Sentiment. The Fugitive Slave Act forced Northerners to reconsider their role in sustaining the institution of slavery. In 1852, just months before Franklin Pierce was elected president, their concerns were heightened by the publication of the novel **Uncle Tom's Cabin** by Harriet Beecher Stowe. Stowe's father, Lyman Beecher, and brother Henry were among the nation's leading evangelical clergy, and her sister Catharine had opposed Cherokee removal and promoted women's education. Stowe was inspired to write *Uncle Tom's Cabin* by passage of the Fugitive Slave Act in 1850. Published in both serial and book forms, the novel created a national sensation.

Uncle Tom's Cabin built on accounts by former slaves as well as tales gathered by abolitionist lecturers and writers, which gained growing attention in the North. The autobiographies of Frederick Douglass (1845), William Wells Brown (1847), Josiah Henson (1849), and Henry Bibb (1849) set the stage for Stowe's novel. So, too, did the expansion of the antislavery press, which by the 1850s included dozens of newspapers. Antislavery poems and songs also circulated widely and were performed at abolitionist conventions and fund-raising fairs. The daguerreotype, an early form of photography, allowed abolitionists to create and circulate images of leading lecturers, fugitive slaves, and popular antislavery performers. Sojourner Truth created cartes-de-visite images to sell at her lectures, and Frederick Douglass became one of the most photographed individuals in the nineteenth century.

Still, nothing captured the public's attention as did *Uncle Tom's Cabin*. Read by millions in the United States and England and translated into French and German, the book reached a mass audience. Its sentimental portrait of saintly enslaved people and its vivid depiction of cruel masters and overseers offered white Northerners a way to identify with enslaved blacks. Although some African Americans expressed frustration that a white woman's

Hutchinson Family Singers, 1845   This daguerreotype captures the ten Hutchinson brothers, who sang with their two sisters at temperance, woman's rights, and especially abolitionist gatherings. Born in New Hampshire, they attracted large audiences across the United States in the 1840s and 1850s. In 1845, the Hutchinson singers toured England with Frederick Douglass. They became the nation's first popular social protest singers. The Metropolitan Museum of Art, Gilman Collection, Gift of The Howard Gilman Foundation, 2005

fictional account gained far more readers than their factual narratives, most recognized the book's contribution to the antislavery cause.

Still, the real-life stories of fugitives from bondage could often surpass their fictional counterparts for drama. In May 1854 abolitionists sought to free fugitive Anthony Burns from a Boston courthouse, where his enslaver was attempting to reclaim him. They failed to secure his release, and Burns was soon marched to the docks to be shipped south. Twenty-two companies of state militia held back tens of thousands of angry Bostonians who lined the streets. A year later, supporters purchased Burns's freedom from his master, but the incident raised anguished questions among local residents. In a city that was home to so many intellectual, religious, and abolitionist leaders, Bostonians wondered how they had come so far in aiding and abetting slavery.

The Kansas-Nebraska Act Stirs Dissent.   Kansas provided the first test of the effects of *Uncle Tom's Cabin* on northern sentiments toward slavery's expansion. As white Americans displaced Indian nations from their homelands, diverse groups of Indians settled in the northern half of the Louisiana Territory. This unorganized region had once been considered beyond the reach of white settlement, but Democratic senator Stephen Douglas of Illinois was eager to have a transcontinental railroad run through his home state. He needed the federal government to gain control of land along the route he proposed and thus argued for the establishment of a vast Nebraska Territory. But to support his plan, Douglas also needed to convince southern congressmen, who sought a route through their own region. According to the Missouri Compromise, states lying above the southern border of Missouri were automatically free. To gain southern support, Douglas sought to reopen the question of slavery in the territories.

When politicians began discussing further encroachment on unorganized western lands in 1851, Indian Commissioner George Manypenny reminded Congress that "the rights of person or property now pertaining to the Indians in said Territories" were inviolate, and that all lands held by Indians could "constitute no part of the [new] Territories . . . until ceded by treaty or otherwise." Numerous native peoples had been forced into this territory, including the Lakota, Dakota, Cheyenne, Navajo, and Crow. However, pressure for expansion proved unstoppable. By March 1853, Manypenny reported that "fifty-two treaties with various Indian tribes have been entered into. . . . [T]he quantity of land acquired by these treaties. . . is about one hundred and seventy-four millions of acres. . . ." Despite his previous concerns, he now proudly claimed that in "no former equal period of our history have so many treaties been made, or such vast accessions of land obtained."

In January 1854 Douglas introduced the **Kansas-Nebraska Act** to Congress. The act not only extinguished the treaty rights of any tribes remaining in the region but also repealed the Missouri Compromise. Two new territories—Kansas and Nebraska—would be carved out of the unorganized lands, and voters in each would determine whether to enter the nation as a slave or a free state (Map 12.2). The act spurred intense opposition from most Whigs and some northern Democrats who wanted to retain the Missouri Compromise line. Months of fierce debate followed, but the bill was ultimately voted into law.

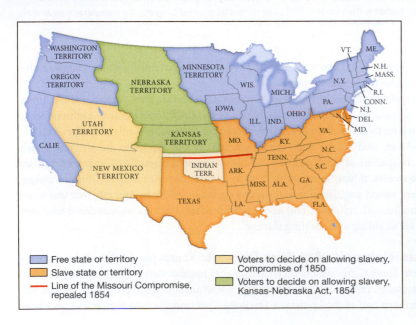

Free state or territory

Slave state or territory

Line of the Missouri Compromise, repealed 1854

Voters to decide on allowing slavery, Compromise of 1850

Voters to decide on allowing slavery, Kansas-Nebraska Act, 1854

MAP 12.2 Kansas-Nebraska Territory

From 1820 on, Congress attempted to limit sectional conflict. But the Missouri Compromise (1820) and the Compromise of 1850 failed to resolve disagreements over slavery's expansion. The creation of the Kansas and Nebraska territories in 1854 heightened sectional conflict and ensured increased hostilities with Indians in the region.

Passage of the Kansas-Nebraska Act enraged many Northerners who considered the dismantling of the Missouri Compromise a sign of the rising power of the South. They were infuriated that the South — or what some now called the "Slave Power" — had again benefited from northern politicians' willingness to compromise. Although few of these opponents considered the impact of the law on Indians, the act shattered treaty rights protecting a dozen native tribes. These Plains Indians lost half the land they had held by treaty as thousands of settlers swarmed into the newly organized territories. Nor did settlers abide by treaty provisions. The resulting upheaval aided stronger nations. The Lakota, Dakota, Arapaho, and Cheyenne forged an alliance that allowed them to dominate smaller tribes in the region. In 1854–1855, conflicts between white settlers and Indians erupted across the Great Plains. In one instance, an anxious U.S. lieutenant fired on a Brulé (Sioux) man who he accused of stealing a cow. In the resulting exchange of shots, the lieutenant and his men were killed. The U.S. army then sent six hundred troops to retaliate. They killed eighty-five Brulé residents. Incidents such as this triggered cycles of violence in the region for decades.

As tensions escalated across the nation, Americans faced the 1854 congressional elections. The Democrats, increasingly viewed as supporting the priorities of enslavers, lost badly in the North. But the Whig Party also proved weak, having failed to stop the Slave Power from extending its leverage over federal policies. A third party, the American Party, was founded in the early 1850s and attracted native-born workers and Protestant farmers who were drawn to its anti-immigrant and anti-Catholic message. They continued to seek limits on immigrants' political power and cultural influence. Responding to these political realignments, another new party, led by antislavery Whigs and Free-Soilers — the **Republican Party** — was founded in the spring of 1854. Among its early members was a Whig politician from Illinois, Abraham Lincoln.

Although established only months before the fall 1854 elections, the Republican Party gained significant support in the Midwest, particularly in state and local campaigns. Meanwhile the American Party gained control of the Massachusetts legislature and nearly captured New York. These victories marked the demise of the Whigs and the Second Party System. Unlike the Whig Party, however, with its national constituency, the Republican Party was rooted solely in the North. Like Free-Soilers, the Republicans argued that slavery should not be extended into new territories. But the Republicans also advocated a program of commercial and industrial development and internal improvements to attract a broader base than earlier antislavery parties. The Republican Party attracted both ardent abolitionists and men whose main concern was keeping western territories open to free white men. This latter group was more than willing to accept slavery where it already existed.

Bleeding Kansas and the Election of 1856.

The 1854 congressional elections exacerbated sectional tensions by bringing representatives from a strictly northern party — the Republicans — into Congress. But the conflicts over slavery reached far beyond the nation's capital. After passage of the Kansas-Nebraska Act, advocates and opponents of slavery poured into Kansas in anticipation of a vote on whether the state would enter the Union slave or free.

As Kansas prepared to hold its referendum, settlers continued to arrive daily, making it difficult to determine who was eligible to vote. In 1855 Southerners installed a proslavery government at Shawnee Mission, while abolitionists established a stronghold in Lawrence. Violence erupted when proslavery settlers invaded Lawrence, killing one resident, demolishing newspaper offices, and plundering shops and homes. Fearing that southern settlers in Kansas were better armed than antislavery Northerners in the territory, eastern abolitionists raised funds to ship rifles to Kansas.

In 1856 longtime abolitionist John Brown carried his own rifles to Kansas. Four of his sons already lived in the territory. A deeply religious man, Brown believed in the complete equality of blacks and whites. Brown held views similar to those of David Walker, whose 1829 appeal warned that enslaved people would eventually rise up and claim their freedom by force. To retaliate for proslavery attacks on Lawrence, the Browns and two friends kidnapped five proslavery advocates from their homes along Pottawatomie Creek and hacked them to death. The so-called Pottawatomie Massacre infuriated southern settlers, who then drew up the Lecompton Constitution, which declared Kansas a slave state. President Pierce made his support of the proslavery government clear, but Stephen Douglas publicly criticized his position to great acclaim from Republicans and Democrats. Pierce and Douglas then struggled over control of the Democratic Party. Congress remained divided over the issue of Kansas. While it deliberated, armed battles continued in Kansas. In the first six months of 1856, more than fifty settlers—on both sides of the conflict—were killed in what became known as **Bleeding Kansas**.

Fighting also broke out on the floor of Congress. Republican senator Charles Sumner of Massachusetts delivered an impassioned speech against the continued expansion of the Slave Power. In denouncing "The Crime against Kansas," he launched scathing attacks on planter politicians and specifically claimed that South Carolina senator Andrew Butler had "taken the harlot slavery" as his mistress. Butler's nephew, Preston Brooks, a Democratic member of the House of Representatives, rushed to defend his family's honor. He assaulted Sumner in the Senate chamber, beating him senseless with a cane. Sumner, who never fully recovered from his injuries, was considered a martyr in the North. Meanwhile Brooks was celebrated in the South, where supporters sent him canes decorated with the slogan "Hit him again!"

The presidential election of 1856 began amid an atmosphere poisoned by violence and recrimination. The Democratic Party nominated James Buchanan of Pennsylvania, a proslavery advocate. Western hero John C. Frémont headed the Republican Party ticket. The American Party, in its final presidential contest, selected former president Millard Fillmore as its candidate. The strength of nativism in politics was waning, however, and Fillmore won only the state of Maryland. Meanwhile Frémont attracted cheering throngs as he traveled across the West and North. Large numbers of women turned out to see Jessie Frémont, the first presidential candidate's wife to play a significant role in a campaign. Frémont carried most of the North and the West. Buchanan captured the South along with Pennsylvania, Indiana, and Illinois. Although Buchanan won only 45.2 percent of the popular vote, he received a comfortable majority in the electoral college, securing his victory. The nation was becoming increasingly divided along sectional lines, and President Buchanan would do little to resolve these differences.

The *Dred Scott* Decision.

Just two days after Buchanan's inauguration, the Supreme Court finally announced its decision in the *Dred Scott* case (see "Comparing American Histories"). Led by Chief Justice Roger Taney, a proslavery Southerner, the majority ruled that an enslaved person was not a citizen and therefore could not sue in court. Indeed, Taney claimed that black men had no rights that a white man was bound to respect. The ruling annulled Dred Scott's suit and meant that he and his wife remained enslaved. But the ruling went further. The **Dred Scott decision** declared that Congress had no constitutional authority to exclude slavery from any territory, thereby nullifying the Missouri Compromise and any future effort to restrict slavery's expansion. Many Northerners were outraged, now convinced that a Slave Power conspiracy had taken hold of the federal government, including the judiciary.

In 1858, when Stephen Douglas faced reelection to the U.S. Senate, the Republican Party nominated Abraham Lincoln, a successful lawyer from Springfield, Illinois, to oppose him. The candidates participated in seven debates in which they explained their positions on slavery in the wake of the *Dred Scott* decision. Pointing to the landmark ruling, Lincoln asked Douglas how he could favor popular sovereignty, which allowed residents to keep slavery out of a territory, and yet support the *Dred Scott* decision, which protected slavery in all territories. Douglas claimed that if residents did not adopt local legislation to protect enslavers' property, they could thereby exclude slavery for all practical purposes. At the same time, he accused Lincoln of advocating "negro equality," a position that went well beyond his opponent's views. Lincoln did support economic opportunity for free blacks, but not political or social equality. Nor did he politically support the abolition of slavery. Still, the Republican candidate did declare that "this government cannot endure permanently half slave and half free. . . . It will become all one thing or all the other."

The Lincoln-Douglas debates attracted national attention, but the Illinois legislature selected the state's senator. Narrowly controlled by Democrats, it returned Douglas to Washington. Although the senator retained his seat, he was concerned by how far the Democratic Party had tilted toward the South. Indeed, the Democratic Party was splitting into southern and northern wings, and the nation was on the verge of civil war.

Review & Relate

▎ What factors contributed to the spread of antislavery sentiment in the North beyond committed abolitionists?

▎ How did the violence in Kansas and the *Dred Scott* decision reflect and intensify the growing sectional divide within the nation?

From **Sectional Crisis** to **Southern Secession**

During the 1850s, a profusion of abolitionist lectures, conventions, and literature swelled antislavery sentiment in the North as did exhibits and images of instruments of torture used by enslavers. Mainstream newspapers regularly covered rescues of fugitives, the bloody crisis in Kansas, and political and judicial debates over slavery. Republican candidates in state and local elections also kept concerns about slavery's expansion and southern power alive. News of an uprising of Mexicans in Texas in summer 1859 disturbed some Americans, but nothing riveted the nation's attention as much as John Brown's raid on the federal arsenal at Harpers Ferry, Virginia that October. Less than a year later, Republican Abraham Lincoln captured the White House. In the wake of his election, seven southern states seceded from the Union. Lincoln tested their resolve by sending supplies to Fort Sumter in Charleston harbor, leading to the first battle of what would become the Civil War.

Cortina's War and John Brown's Raid.

While Americans in the eastern United States debated issues of expansion and slavery, those living on lands acquired through the Mexican-American War confronted their own racial conflicts. In 1848, Mexicans living in the northern regions of their country suddenly became citizens of the United States. In the following years, many Mexicans were deprived of their land and legal rights, assaulted, incarcerated, and murdered. Juan Nepomuceno Cortina was born in 1824 to a wealthy Mexican family living south of the Rio Grande River. In his early twenties he fought with the Mexican Army against the United States. After the U.S. victory, he watched his family and his neighbors in Brownsville (now Texas) cheated out of land and cattle, reduced to second-class citizenship, and mistreated by newly appointed sheriffs and the Texas Rangers. In July 1859, after watching one of his Mexican farmhands being brutalized by a U.S. Marshall, Cortina ordered the Marshall to stop. When he did not, Cortina shot him in the shoulder. The conflict escalated, and Cortina organized a group of Mexicans to launch a successful raid on Brownsville. In September, they proclaimed the city the Republic of the Rio Grande and raised the Mexican flag.

U.S. residents formed an armed unit, the Brownsville Tigers, to retake the city. Cortina's men retreated into Mexico but continued to raid farms and homes in Texas. As battles continued, Cortina called on Texas Governor Sam Houston to protect the rights of Mexican residents. To Mexicans, Cortina proclaimed: "The voice of revelation whispers to me that to me is entrusted the work of breaking the chains of your slavery." Eventually, the Texas Rangers and U.S. Army joined the fight. By late December, they forced Cortina's troops deeper into Mexico though sporadic battles continued through winter 1860. Despite his defeat, Cortina remained a folk hero to Mexicans in Texas, served as governor of a northern Mexican state, and continued to lead cross-border raids on Anglo-American ranchers for the next fifteen years.

John Brown was also committed to changing society through force of arms. After joining the bloody battles in Kansas, Brown became more convinced that direct action was the only answer. Following the Pottawatomie killings, he went into hiding and reappeared back east, where he hoped to initiate an uprising to overthrow slavery. Brown focused his efforts on the federal arsenal in **Harpers Ferry, Virginia**. With eighteen followers—five African Americans and thirteen whites, including three of his sons—Brown planned to capture the arsenal and distribute arms to enslaved people in the surrounding area. He hoped this action would ignite a rebellion that would destroy the plantation system throughout the South. Brown tried to convince Frederick Douglass to join the venture, but Douglass considered it a foolhardy plan. Brown did manage to persuade a small circle of white abolitionists to bankroll the effort.

On the night of October 16, 1859, Brown and his men kidnapped some leading townsmen and seized the arsenal. Local residents were stunned but managed to alert authorities, and state militia swarmed into Harpers Ferry. The next day, federal troops arrived, led by Colonel Robert E. Lee. With troops flooding into the town, Brown and his men were soon under siege, trapped in the arsenal. Fourteen rebels were killed, including two of Brown's sons. On October 18, Brown and three others were captured.

As word of the daring raid spread, Brown was hailed as a hero by many devoted abolitionists and depicted as a madman by southern planters. Southern whites were sure the raid was part of a widespread conspiracy led by power-hungry abolitionists. Federal authorities moved quickly to quell enslavers' fears and end the episode. Brown rejected his lawyer's advice to plead insanity, and a local jury found him guilty of murder, criminal conspiracy, and treason. He was hanged on December 2, 1859.

John Brown's execution unleashed a massive outpouring of grief, anger, and uncertainty across the North. Abolitionists organized parades, demonstrations, bonfires, and tributes to

John Brown, c. 1847   Black portraitist Augustus Washington took this early daguerreotype of John Brown. A decade before he joined his sons in Kansas, Brown raises his hand, pledging to dedicate his life to the destruction of slavery. He holds the flag of the "Subterranean Pass Way," a militant version of the underground rail road Brown created in New York's far northern woodlands. Smithsonian Institution Libraries/Science Source

the newest abolitionist martyr. Even many Quakers and other pacifists viewed John Brown as a hero for giving his life in the cause of emancipation. But most northern politicians and editors condemned the raid as a rash act that could only intensify sectional tensions.

Among southern whites, fear and panic greeted the raid on Harpers Ferry, and the execution of John Brown did little to quiet their outrage. By this time, southern intellectuals had developed a sophisticated proslavery argument that, to them, demonstrated the benefits of bondage for African Americans and its superiority to the northern system of wage labor. They argued that enslavers provided care and guidance for blacks from birth to death. Considering blacks too childlike to fend for themselves, proslavery advocates saw no problem with the enslaved providing labor and obedience in return for their care. Such arguments failed to convince abolitionists, who highlighted the brutality, sexual abuse, and shattered families that marked the system of bondage. In this context, Americans on both sides of the sectional divide considered the 1860 presidential election critical to the nation's future.

The Election of 1860.

Brown's hanging set the tone for the 1860 presidential campaign. The Republicans met in Chicago five months after Brown's execution and distanced themselves from the more radical wing of the abolitionist movement. The party platform condemned both John Brown and southern "Border Ruffians," who initiated the violence in Kansas. The platform accepted slavery where it already existed, but continued to advocate its exclusion from western territories. Finally, the platform insisted on the need for federally funded internal improvements and protective tariffs. The Republicans nominated Abraham Lincoln as their candidate for president. Recognizing the impossibility of gaining significant votes in the South, the party focused instead on winning large majorities in the Northeast and Midwest.

The Democrats met in Charleston, South Carolina. Stephen Douglas was the leading candidate. However when Mississippi senator Jefferson Davis introduced a resolution to protect slavery in the territories, Douglas's northern supporters rejected it, heightening southern

Republican Party Presidential Ticket, 1860 The Republican Party had no hope of gaining significant votes in the South, so this campaign banner for Abraham Lincoln and Hannibal Hamlin sought to appeal to voters in the North and West. Crowded with imagery to attract the various interests that made up the new party, the banner was displayed at campaign rallies and party offices. Library of Congress, Prints and Photographs Division, Reproduction number LC-DIG-pga-07990 (digital file from original item) LC-USZC4-7996 (color film copy transparency) LC-USZ62-5884 (b&w film copy neg.)

concerns about Douglas's commitment to the institution. President Buchanan also came out against Douglas, and the Democratic convention ended without choosing a candidate. Instead, various factions met separately. A group of largely northern Democrats met in Baltimore and nominated Douglas. Southern Democrats selected John Breckinridge, the vice president, an enslaver, and an advocate of annexing Cuba. The Constitutional Union Party, comprised mainly of former southern Whigs, advocated "no political principle other than the Constitution of the country, the union of the states, and the enforcement of the laws." Its members nominated Senator John Bell of Tennessee.

Although Lincoln won barely 40 percent of the popular vote, he carried a clear majority in the electoral college. With the admission of Minnesota and Oregon to the Union in 1858 and 1859, free states outnumbered slave states eighteen to fifteen, and Lincoln won all but one of them. Lincoln did not win a single Southern electoral vote. However, since free states were more populous than slave states, they controlled a larger number of electoral votes. Douglas ran second to Lincoln in the popular vote, but Bell and Breckinridge captured more electoral votes than Douglas because of their success in the South. Despite a deeply divided electorate, Lincoln became president (Map 12.3).

Although many abolitionists were wary of the Republicans, who were willing to leave slavery alone where it existed, most were nonetheless relieved at Lincoln's victory and hoped he would become more sympathetic to their views once in office. Meanwhile, southern whites, especially those in the deep South, were furious that a Republican had won the White House without carrying a single southern state.

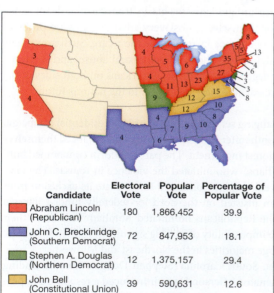

Candidate	Electoral Vote	Popular Vote	Percentage of Popular Vote
Abraham Lincoln (Republican)	180	1,866,452	39.9
John C. Breckinridge (Southern Democrat)	72	847,953	18.1
Stephen A. Douglas (Northern Democrat)	12	1,375,157	29.4
John Bell (Constitutional Union)	39	590,631	12.6

MAP 12.3 The Election of 1860

Four candidates vied for the presidency in 1860, and the voters split along clearly sectional lines. Although Stephen Douglas ran a vigorous campaign and gained votes in all regions of the country, he won a majority only in Missouri. Lincoln triumphed in the North and far West, and Breckinridge in most of the South.

From Secession to War. On December 20, 1860, six weeks after Lincoln's election, the legislature of South Carolina announced that because "a sectional party" had engineered "the election of a man to the high office of President of the United States whose opinions and purposes are hostile to slavery," the people of South Carolina dissolve their union with "the other states of North America." In early 1861, Mississippi, Florida, Alabama, Georgia, Louisiana, and Texas followed suit. Representatives from these states met on February 8 in Montgomery, Alabama, where they adopted a provisional constitution, elected Jefferson Davis as their president, and established the **Confederate States of America** (Map 12.4). **See Primary Source Project 12: Debating Secession, page 422.**

Explore ▶

See Sources 12.4 and 12.5 for two historians' interpretations of why southern states seceded from the Union.

President Buchanan did nothing to stop the secession movement. When the crisis occurred, Buchanan listened to the slave owners in his cabinet and other southern sympathizers living in Washington, D.C. Following Lincoln's election, he claimed that the federal government had no right to intervene when southern states seceded. Some Northerners were shocked as Deep South states seceded, but others supported their right to leave. Many believed those states would return to the Union when they realized they could not survive on their own. In addition, with Virginia and other Upper South slave states still part of the nation, the secession movement seemed doomed to failure. Indeed, Northerners applauded the admission of Kansas as a free state in January 1861 just as the first southern states left the Union.

In the midst of the crisis, Kentucky senator John Crittenden proposed a compromise that gained significant support. Congress approved the first part of his plan, which called for a constitutional amendment to protect slavery from federal interference in any state where it already existed. But the second part of the **Crittenden plan** would extend the Missouri Compromise line (latitude 36°30′) to the California border and bar slavery north of that line. South of that line, however, slavery would be protected, including in any territories "acquired hereafter." Fearing that passage would encourage southern planters to again seek territory in Cuba, Mexico, or Central America, Republicans rejected the proposal. Compromise seemed increasingly unlikely.

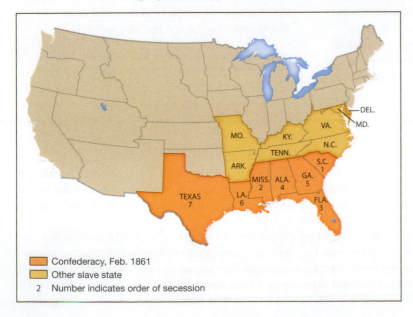

MAP 12.4 The Original Confederacy

Seven states in the Lower South seceded from the United States and formed the Confederate States of America in February 1861. While the original Confederacy was too limited in population and resources to defend itself against the U.S. government, its leaders hoped that other slave states would soon join them.

Comparative Secondary Source Analysis

White Southerners Decide to Secede

Alabama and Georgia became the fourth and fifth states to secede from the United States in winter 1861. Advocates of secession argued that they had voluntarily joined the nation and thus had the right to withdraw when their liberties were threatened. While southerners offered various reasons for seceding, since the 1960s, historians have generally agreed that the protection of slavery lay at the heart of the movement. Still, state-level studies written in the 1970s and 1980s made two important contributions to our understanding of secession. Michael Johnson and J. Mills Thorton, who focus on Georgia and Alabama respectively, show the complex issues that underlay secession debates in individual states. They also make clear that advocates of secession did not hold a significant advantage over their opponents in all southern states.

Source 12.4

Michael P. Johnson | Georgians Choose Secession, 1977

Secession was the ultimate test of the hegemony of slaveholders. Yet secession was necessary precisely because the hegemony of slaveholders was not secure. According to secessionists, . . . secession was necessary because of the internal divisions within the South [over] the degree to which the slaveholding minority could have its way in a government based ultimately on manhood suffrage. In particular, secessionists feared that many southerners would be receptive to Republican offers of patronage and would become the nucleus of a southern Republican party. . . .

In Georgia, secessionists translated that fear into a double revolution: a revolution for home rule – to eliminate the external threat; and a conservative revolution for those who ruled at home – to prevent the political realization of the internal threat. Men with conservative social and political ideas were instrumental not only in creating the small electoral margin that secessionists enjoyed in Georgia, but also in the definition and direction of the second revolution. The actions of the secession convention, including the new state constitution which they drafted, . . . represented an attempt to preserve the social status quo by reconciling the tension between the slaveholding minority and the enfranchised slaveless majority. . . .

Secession was [thus] driven by political conflict not only between the South and the North but also between the black belt and the upcountry, slaveholders and nonslaveholders, and those who feared democracy and those who valued it.

Source: Michael P. Johnson, *Toward a Patriarchal Republic: The Secession of Georgia* (Baton Rouge: Louisiana State University, 1977), pp. xx–xxi.

Confederate secessionists accused the federal government of failing to implement fully the Fugitive Slave Act and the *Dred Scott* decision. They were convinced that a Republican administration would do little to support southern interests. White Southerners also feared that Republican rule might inspire a mass uprising of slaves. Secession allowed them to maintain control over the South's black population.

Still, many legislators in the Upper South hoped a compromise could be reached, and Lincoln hoped to woo Confederates back into the Union. Most northern merchants, manufacturers, and bankers approved, wanting to maintain their economic ties to southern planters. Yet Lincoln also realized he must demonstrate Union strength to curtail further secessions. He focused on **Fort Sumter** in South Carolina's Charleston harbor, where a small Union garrison

Source 12.5

J. Mills Thornton | Alabamans Move toward Secession, 1978

Antebellum Alabama was . . . obsessed with the idea of slavery. . . . [T]he fear of an imminent loss of freedom was a part of the inheritance which Alabama's citizens had received from their Revolutionary forebears. . . . [T]his tradition was lent considerable urgency by a daily familiarity with black slavery, . . . [B]ecause servility excluded one from [citizen]ship, . . an Alabamian . . . [had] to prove his worth - his claim to possess the qualities of a free man - constantly, both to his fellows and to himself. . . . [S]lavery guaranteed, so it was believed, that very few white men would ever have to depend directly upon other white men for their sustenance. . . . [Thus,] the existence of slavery . . . came to seem an essential bulwark of freedom. . . .

[D]uring the 1850s, . . . [Alabama's] Government at all levels became much more active; its expenditures increased enormously. . . .

Control of the political mechanism began slipping from the hands of poorer citizens, as the influence of great planters . . . [increased in] significance. . . .

[A]t this time, however, leadership within the [dominant] Democratic party . . . was passing to a second generation of politicians, less sensitive to the attitudes and apprehensions of the masses. . . . Only the villains offered by the southern rights advocates among them seemed capable of striking fire with the voters. . . . If Republicans controlled the federal government, [they argued], a southerner would be able to go to the territories only if he were willing to abandon a truly egalitarian, democratic world [rooted in slavery] for a hierarchical, elitist one, on the northern model. . . .

Source: J. Mills Thornton, *Politics and Power in a Slave Society: Alabama, 1800–1860*. Baton Rouge: Louisiana State University Press, 1978, pp. xviii, xix, 402.

Examine the Sources

1. How do Johnson and Thornton differ in their understanding of the key issues behind arguments for secession?
2. How might the geographical locations of Georgia and Alabama have shaped Johnson's and Thornton's interpretations?

Put It in Context

In what ways did John Brown's raid, Lincoln's election to the presidency, and the earlier secessions of South Carolina, Mississippi, and Florida influence convention delegates in Alabama and Georgia?

was running low on food and medicine. On April 8, 1861, Lincoln dispatched ships to the fort but promised to use force only if Confederates blocked his effort to send supplies.

The Confederate government now had to choose. It could attack the Union vessels and bear responsibility for starting a war or permit a "foreign power" to maintain a fort in its territory. President Davis and his advisers chose the aggressive course, demanding Fort Sumter's immediate and unconditional surrender. The commanding officer refused, and on April 12 Confederate guns opened fire. Two days later, Fort Sumter surrendered. On April 15, Lincoln called for 75,000 volunteers to put down the southern insurrection.

Whites in the Upper South then reconsidered secession. Some small farmers and land-less whites were drawn to Republican promises of free labor and free soil and remained suspicious of the goals and power of secessionist planters. Yet the majority of southern whites, rich and poor, feared that Republicans would free the enslaved and introduce racial amalgamation, the mixing of whites and blacks, in the nation.

Lincoln used the powers of his office to keep border states that still allowed slavery—Maryland, Delaware, Missouri, and Kentucky—in the Union. He waived the right of habeas corpus (which protects citizens against arbitrary arrest and detention), jailed secessionists, arrested state legislators, and limited freedom of the press. Still, four other slave states—North Carolina, Virginia, Tennessee, and Arkansas—seceded. Virginia, with its strategic location near the nation's capital, was by far the most significant. In early April, Virginia legislators had opposed secession by a significant margin. After Fort Sumter, they reversed course, and seceded. The Confederate capital was soon moved to Richmond, which was also home to the South's largest iron manufacturer, critical for producing weapons and munitions.

At the same time, the firing on Fort Sumter prompted most Northerners to line up behind Lincoln's call to arms. Manufacturers and merchants rushed to support the president, while northern workers, including immigrants, responded to the call for volunteers. They assumed that the Union, with its greater resources and manpower, could quickly set the nation right. New York editor Horace Greeley proclaimed, "Jeff Davis and Co. will be swingin' from the battlements at Washington at least by the 4th of July."

Review & Relate

- How and why did John Brown's raid on Harpers Ferry move the country closer to civil war?

- How did Lincoln's election and the federal effort to resupply Fort Sumter affect southern politicians attitudes toward secession?

Conclusion: A Nation Divided

Dred Scott did not live to see Abraham Lincoln take the oath of office in March 1861. Following the Supreme Court's 1857 ruling, Scott was returned to Irene Emerson, who had married abolitionist Calvin Chaffee. Unwilling to be the owner of the most well-known slave in America, Chaffee quickly returned Dred Scott and his family to his original owners, the Blow family. The Blows then freed the Scotts. For the next year and a half, before dying of tuberculosis, Dred Scott lived as a free man. Although Harriet and their daughters lived to see slavery abolished, in the spring of 1861 they could not imagine how that goal would be reached.

In 1860 John C. Frémont believed the nation was headed to war; and he was willing, once again, to serve a country he had helped expand. His work as a surveyor and soldier opened new territories to white settlement, and the gold rush then ensured California's admission to the Union. Yet what Frémont and others considered the nation's manifest destiny decimated Indian nations as well as the property, civil rights, and lives of many Mexicans. Despite the efforts of the Comanche and other tribes to fend off white encroachment, the U.S. government and white settlers claimed more and more territory. It was debates over the future of these western territories that heightened conflicts over slavery.

While some Confederate enslavers hoped to expand the nation into Cuba, Nicaragua, and other southern regions, Northerners fought all such schemes. Outraged by the Fugitive Slave Act and appalled by Bleeding Kansas, militant activists applauded John Brown's raid at Harpers Ferry. As important, more moderate Northerners increasingly opposed the expansion of slavery and voted for Lincoln in 1860. His election inspired seven southern states to secede, and his efforts to resupply Fort Sumter brought the nation face-to-face with civil war.

Timeline of Events

Key Terms

Review & Relate

1. Why did Americans go west in the 1830s and 1840s, and what was the journey like?

2. What groups competed for land and resources in the West? How did disease, drought, and violence shape this competition?

3. What steps did legislators take in the 1840s and early 1850s to resolve the issue of the expansion of slavery? Were they successful?

4. How were slavery and American imperialist ambitions intertwined in the 1840s and 1850s?

5. What factors contributed to the spread of antislavery sentiment in the North beyond committed abolitionists?

6. How did the violence in Kansas and the *Dred Scott* decision reflect and intensify the growing sectional divide within the nation?

7. How and why did John Brown's raid on Harpers Ferry move the country closer to civil war?

8. How did Lincoln's election and the federal effort to resupply Fort Sumter affect southern politicians' attitudes toward secession?

Debating Secession

▶ **Which issues fueled southern politicians' drive to secede from the United States, and how did white Americans outside secession conventions respond?**

Following Abraham Lincoln's election as president in November 1860, southern states began holding conventions to consider secession. Seven states seceded before Lincoln was inaugurated in March 1861. In two of them—Alabama and Georgia—a significant minority opposed secession. While other southern states waited to see how the new president responded to the crisis, representatives from the original seven states established the Confederate States of America in February and chose Jefferson Davis as president. They did so without seeking the approval of voters. After Lincoln tried to resupply Fort Sumter, more states joined the Confederacy. In Virginia, delegates to an early April convention had voted against secession, 89-45, but after Fort Sumter, reversed their decision. Similarly in a rare statewide referendum in Tennessee in February, voters rejected secession. Yet delegates to a May convention in Nashville voted for secession. Sources 12.6 and 12.7 provide examples of secessionist and anti-secessionist arguments offered in Georgia's and Virginia's conventions, respectively. Shortly after Lincoln's inauguration, *Frank Leslie's Illustrated Weekly* offered Northerners a view of crowds celebrating the new Confederate government in its chosen capital, Montgomery (Source 12.8). On March 21, after Lincoln refused to recognize states' right to secede, Confederate vice president Alexander Stephens gave an impromptu speech celebrating secession and white supremacy (Source 12.9). Mary Boykin Chesnut, a member of South Carolina's elite enslaver class, recorded in her private diary the responses of white and black Charleston residents to Union efforts to resupply Fort Sumter (Source 12.10).

422

Source 12.6

Robert Toombs | Supporting Secession in Georgia, November 13, 1860

Immediately after Abraham Lincoln's election, several southern states began to discuss secession. The Georgia state legislature debated the issue less than two weeks after Lincoln was elected president. One of the principal speakers was Robert Toombs, a lawyer and enslaver who was elected to the Georgia legislature before serving in the U.S. House of Representatives (1844–1853) and the Senate (1853–1861). In the following selection, Senator Toombs adamantly supports secession. He later became the Confederate secretary of state.

The Executive Department of the Federal Government, for forty-eight out of the first sixty years under the present Constitution, was in the hands of Southern Presidents, and so just, fair and equitable, constitutional and advantageous to the country was the policy which they pursued, that their policy and administration were generally maintained by the people. . . .

The stern, steady march of events has brought us in conflict with our non-slaveholding confederates upon the fundamental principles of our compact of Union. We have not sought this conflict; we have sought too long to avoid it. . . . The door of conciliation and compromise is finally closed by our adversaries, and it remains only to us to meet the conflict with the dignity and firmness of men worthy of freedom. . . .

. . . The South at all times demanded nothing but equality in the common territories, equal enjoyment of them with their property, to that extended to Northern citizens and their property—nothing more. . . . In 1790 we had less than eight hundred thousand slaves. Under our mild and humane administration of the system they have increased above four millions. The country has expanded to meet this growing want, and Florida, Alabama, Mississippi, Louisiana, Texas, Arkansas, Kentucky, Tennessee, and Missouri have received this increasing tide of African labor; before the end of this century, at precisely the same rate of increase, the Africans among us in a subordinate condition will amount to eleven millions of persons. What shall be done with them? We must expand or perish. . . . The North understand it better—they have told us for twenty years that their object was to pen up slavery within its present limits—surround it with a border of free States, and like the scorpion surrounded with fire, they will make it sting itself to death. . . .

My countrymen, "if you have nature in you, bear it not." Withdraw yourselves from such a confederacy; it is your right to do so. I know not why the abolitionists should object to it, unless they want to torture and plunder you. If they resist this great sovereign right, make another war for independence. . . .

Source: Frank Moore, ed., *The Rebellion Record: A Diary of American Events* (New York: G. P. Putnam and Henry Holt, 1864), 1:362–63, 365.

Source 12.7

Waitman T. Willey | Speech at Virginia State Secession Convention, March 4, 1861

Waitman T. Willey was born on a farm in Morgantown, Virginia in 1811. He rarely attended school because his family required his labor. At age 17, he traveled to Madison College in Pennsylvania and received his B.A. degree in 1831. Returning to Morgantown, he practiced law and became active in Whig politics. He advocated temperance and universal suffrage for white men. Although he owned enslaved domestic workers, he opposed secession and supported gradual abolition. In 1863, he helped establish the state of West Virginia and served as one of its first senators.

I am here for the purpose of endeavoring to correct those grievances [raised by secessionists], and to vindicate the honor of Virginia, not by abandoning her position in this great Confederacy [meaning the United States], but by bringing her oppressors to acknowledge those errors and to redress her grievances. . . .

The first argument in favor of secession . . . were the bitterness and acrimony with which Southern institutions are constantly assailed by the Northern press, Northern schools, and by the Northern pulpit. . . . I want to know how the mere act of secession—when we have thrown off all allegiance to the common Government . . . will advance us one inch towards the silence of the Northern press, pulpit or school-house? It will aggravate the evil. . . .

Again—another argument in favor of secession . . . was to be found in the efforts made by the Northern Abolitionists to induce our slaves to abscond, in the operations of the Underground Railroad . . . and the inefficiency of the Fugitive Slave Law. . . . [S]ecession is proposed as a remedy to these evils. How will it [secession] accomplish this object? . . . I come here as a plain man from the mountains, looking to common sense as my guide. . . . How will it work, for instance, in reference to the recovery of our slaves? . . . . You dissolve the Union. What then? The common national obligation is destroyed. Will not the negro find it out? The motive to flee across the line would be increased, because the negro will know that whenever he crosses that line, he will be free. There will be no fugitive slave law for his recovery, and he will know it. . . .

But we are told that we are in a minority, and that Black Republicans may swallow us up. Who placed us in the minority? . . . What would have been the complexion of the next Congress of the United States if our sister States [the seven that seceded] had hearkened to our voice and entreaty? We implored them to wait, to pause, to deliberate and co-operate with us. . . . But they would not wait but went off, contrary to our wishes. . . . It is a fact that . . . the next House of Representatives . . . , if these States had been true to themselves and true to Virginia would have contained a majority of not less than thirty against Abraham Lincoln's policy.

Source: Furman University: http://history.furman.edu/benson/docs/willeyspeech1861.htm

Source 12.8

Frank Leslie's Illustrated Newspaper | Jefferson Davis about to become Provisional President of the Confederacy, March 16, 1861.

On February 16, 1861, an artist for *Frank Leslie's Illustrated Newspaper* in New York City produced a sketch of Jefferson Davis as he addressed a cheering throng from the balcony of the Exchange Hotel in Montgomery, Alabama. Two days later Davis would be inaugurated as the first president of the Confederate States of America. Given northern fascination and anxiety with the effects of secession, a team of engravers created this woodcut, which became the cover of the March 16 edition of Frank Leslie's newspaper.

Library of Congress, Prints and Photographs Division, Reproduction number LC-USZ62-109704 (b&w film copy neg.)

Library of Congress, Prints and Photographs Division, Reproduction number LC-USZ62-109704 (b&w film copy neg.)

Source 12.9

Alexander Stephens, Cornerstone Speech | March 21, 1861

In February 1861, Alexander Stephens, a former U.S. senator from Georgia, was chosen as vice president of the new Confederate States of America. Immediately after Lincoln's election, he had opposed secession. However, by early 1861, he embraced the cause. When President Lincoln refused to recognize the new Confederacy, Stephens gave an impromptu speech before an enthusiastic audience in Savannah. He insisted that the races were inherently unequal and that Southerners had the will and resources to create a powerful independent nation.

The new constitution has put at rest, forever, all the agitating questions relating to our peculiar institution—African slavery as it exists among us—the proper status of the negro in our form of civilization. This was the immediate cause of the late rupture and present revolution. . . . The prevailing ideas entertained by [Thomas Jefferson] and most of the leading statesmen of the time . . . were that the enslavement of the African was in violation of the laws of nature; that it was wrong in principle, socially, morally, and politically. . . . The general principle of the men of that day was that . . . the institution would be evanescent and pass away. . . . Those ideas, however, were fundamentally wrong. They rested upon the equality of the races. . . .

Our new government is founded upon exactly the opposite idea; its foundations are laid, its corner-stone rests upon the great truth, that the negro is not equal to the white man; that slavery—subordination to the superior race—is his natural and normal condition. . . . Those at the North, who still cling to these errors, with a zeal above knowledge, we justly denominate as fanatics. All fanaticism springs from an aberration of the mind—from a defect in reasoning. It is a form of insanity. . . .

May we not, therefore, look with confidence to the ultimate universal acknowledgement of the truths upon which our system rests? . . . Many governments have been founded upon the principle of the subordination and serfdom of certain classes of the same race; such were and are in violation of nature's laws. With us, however, all of the white race, however high or low, rich or poor, are equal in the eye of the law. Not so with the negro. Subordination is his place, He, by his nature or the curse against Canaan, is fitted for that condition which he occupies in our society. . . . The substratum of our society is made of the material fitted by nature for it, and by experience we know that it is best, not only for the superior, but for the inferior race, that it should be so. It is, indeed, in conformity with our Creator. . . .

Source: https://teachingamericanhistory.org/library/document/cornerstone-speech/

Source: https://teachingamericanhistory.org/library/document/cornerstone-speech/

Mary Boykin Chesnut | Diary Entries, April 4–13, 1861

Mary Boykin Chesnut and her husband James were members of Charleston, South Carolina's elite enslaver class. James was also a lawyer, U.S. senator, and Confederate officer. Mary Chesnut hosted Confederate politicians, military leaders, and other planters at the family plantation near Camden, South Carolina, and in Charleston. The Chesnuts were friends with Jefferson Davis and his wife Varina. An incisive commentator on southern society, Mary Chesnut kept detailed diaries for decades. In early April 1861, she wrote about events unfolding in Charleston and at Fort Sumter.

April 4th—. . . A ship was fired into yesterday and went back to sea. Is that the first shot? How can one settle down to anything? One's heart is in one's mouth all the time. Any minute, the cannon may open on us, the fleet come in.

April 8th—. . . [Former] Governor [John] Manning walked in, bowed gravely, seated himself by me, and said, in mock heroic style . . . "Madame, your country is invaded. . . . There are six men-of-war outside the Bar. . . .

Governor Pickens and [General] Beauregard are holding a Council of War.". . . The men went off almost immediately, and I crept silently into my room where I sat down to a good cry.

Mrs. Wigfall came in and we had it out, on the subject of civil war. We solaced ourselves with dwelling on all its known horrors, and then we added some remarks about what we had the right to expect with Yankees in front and Negroes in the rear. "The slave owners must expect a servile insurrection, of course," said Mrs. Wigfall. . . .

My husband has been made an aide-de-camp to General Beauregard. Three hours ago we were quietly packing to go home. . . . Now he tells me the attack on Fort Sumter may begin tonight. . . . [James Chesnut was sent as an emissary to Fort Sumter, April 8–12, to negotiate with Major Robert Anderson, the commander of Fort Sumter.] April 12th—Anderson will not capitulate!

Yesterday was the merriest, maddest dinner we have had yet. Men were more audaciously wise and witty. We had an unspoken foreboding that it was to be our last pleasant meeting. . . .

If Anderson does not accept terms at four o'clock [AM], the orders are he shall be fired upon. . . . At half past four, the heavy booming of the cannon! I sprang out of bed and on my knees, prostrate, I prayed as I never prayed before. . . . I put on a double-gown and shawl and went to the house top. The shells were bursting. . . .

April 13th—. . . . Not by one word or look can we detect any change in the demeanor of these Negro servants. . . . You could not tell that they even hear the awful noise that is going on in the bay, though it is dinning in their ears night and day. And people talk before them as if they were chairs and tables, and they make no sign. Are they stolidly stupid, or wiser then we are, silent and strong, biding their time. . . .

Source: Mary Boykin Chesnut, *A Diary from Dixie*, eds. Isabella D. Martin and Myrta Lockett Avary (New York: D. Appleton and Co, 1905), 31–38, https://docsouth.unc.edu/southlit/chesnut/maryches.html

Source: Mary Boykin Chesnut, *A Diary from Dixie*, eds. Isabella D. Martin and Myrta Lockett Avary (New York: D. Appleton and Co, 1905), 31–38, https://docsouth.unc.edu/southlit/chesnut/maryches.html

Interpret the Evidence

1. Compare the arguments before and against secession offered by Robert Toombs and Waitman Willey (Sources 12.6 and 12.7). What are the major areas of disagreement, and how would you explain these differences?

2. Compare Alexander Stephens's Cornerstone Speech to a public audience (Source 12.9) with those of Toombs and Willey to secession conventions. How might these distinct settings shape any differences?

3. Which groups of Southerners appear in the March 16, 1861, cover image of *Frank Leslie's Illustrated Newspaper*? What might the image suggest to northern readers?

4. What do Mary Boykin Chesnut's diary entries reveal about the crisis at Fort Sumter? How does she characterize the responses of white men and women and of enslaved blacks?

5. What kinds of historical evidence does each southern speaker or writer draw upon to support his or her claims about the secession crisis (Sources 12.6, 12.7, 12.8, 12.10)?

Put It in Context

How do these primary sources compare with the views of historians offered in Sources 12.4 and 12.5?

What two specific events or developments occurring between 1842 and 1859 were most significant in fueling the secession crisis of 1860–1861 and why?

Civil War
1861–1865

Window to the Past

Union Soldiers in Camp c. 1863

The Civil War was the first military conflict in U.S. history to be photographically documented. Many photographers took formal portraits of soldiers, individually or in groups, while others captured the bloody aftermath of battles. This picture offers a rare informal glimpse of soldiers in camp. Their range of poses and expressions suggests the various ways that soldiers responded to a lull in the conflict. ▶ **To learn more about this primary source, see Source 13.2 on page 440.**

Library of Congress Prints and Photographs Division, Washington, D.C. [LC-DIG-ppmsca-34191]

After reading this chapter you will be able to:

- Explain why southern states seceded and describe the advantages and disadvantages that marked the Confederacy and the Union at the beginning of the Civil War.

- Describe the changing roles of African Americans, free and enslaved, in the war and the growing sentiment for emancipation in the North.

- Evaluate how the war changed northern and southern political priorities and the lives of soldiers and civilians.

- Identify turning points in the Civil War, including key battles in the eastern and western theaters of war, and explain the factors that led to Union victory and the abolition of slavery.

Comparing American Histories

Born into slavery in 1818, **Frederick Douglass** became a celebrated orator, editor, and abolitionist in the 1840s. In 1845 Douglass published his autobiography, *Narrative of the Life of Frederick Douglass*, which described his enslavement in Maryland, his defiance against his masters, and his eventual escape to New York in 1838 with the help of Anna Murray, a free black servant.

After marrying in New York, Frederick and Anna moved to New Bedford, Massachusetts, and changed their last name to Douglass to avoid capture. In 1841 the American Anti-Slavery Society hired Frederick to present his vivid tale of enslaved life to public audiences. Four years later, Douglass launched a British lecture tour that attracted enthusiastic audiences. Supporters in Britain purchased his freedom, and Douglass returned to Massachusetts a free man in 1847.

Late that year, Frederick moved to Rochester, New York with Anna and their children to launch his abolitionist paper, the *North Star*. Over the next four years, Douglass gradually shifted his support from the Garrisonians to political abolitionism. When war erupted in April 1861, he lobbied President Lincoln relentlessly to make emancipation a war aim.

Initially Douglass feared that Lincoln was more committed to reconstituting the Union than abolishing slavery. But when the president issued the Emancipation Proclamation in January 1863, Douglass spoke enthusiastically on its behalf. He also argued that it was essential for black men to serve in the Union army. When African Americans were finally allowed to join in 1862–1863, Douglass helped recruit volunteers but he later protested discrimination against black troops and the denial of black civil rights.

Like Douglass, Rose O'Neal was born on a Maryland plantation, but she was white and free. Her father was John O'Neal, a planter who was killed in 1817 when Rose was about four. In her teens, she and her sister moved to Washington, D.C., where their aunt ran a fashionable boardinghouse. Her boarders included John C. Calhoun, whose states' rights views Rose eagerly embraced. Rose was welcomed into elite social circles and in 1835 married Virginian Robert Greenhow, who worked for the State Department.

Rose O'Neal Greenhow quickly became a favorite Washington hostess, entertaining congressmen, cabinet ministers, and foreign diplomats. Ardent proslavery expansionists, the Greenhows supported efforts to acquire Cuba and expand slavery into western territories. When Robert died in 1854, Rose and their four children remained in D.C. and continued to entertain powerful political leaders.

In May 1861, as the Civil War commenced, a U.S. army captain about to join the Confederate cause recruited Greenhow to head an espionage ring in Washington, D.C. With her close ties to southern sympathizers in the capital, Greenhow gathered

(*left*) **Frederick Douglass** Beinecke Rare Book and Manuscript Library, Yale University

(*right*) **Rose O'Neal Greenhow** Image courtesy of Documenting the American South, The University of North Carolina at Chapel Hill Libraries intelligence on Union plans. Although she initially avoided suspicion, by August 1861 Greenhow was investigated and placed under house arrest. After continuing to smuggle out letters, she was sent to the Old Capitol Prison in January 1862. When Greenhow again managed to transmit information, she was exiled to Richmond, where Confederate president Jefferson Davis hailed her as a hero. ■

Comparing the American histories of Frederick Douglass and Rose O'Neal Greenhow illustrates the ways that Americans, black and white, northern and southern, men and women, were shaped by and shaped the war that followed the firing on Fort Sumter. They were among hundreds of thousands of Americans who saw the war as a means to achieve their goals: a free nation, a haven for slavery, or a reunited country. Although the Confederacy launched the war, it lagged behind the Union in population, industrial and agricultural production, and railroad lines. These differences became more important as the war unfolded. Initially, however, skilled officers and knowledge of the southern terrain benefited the Confederate army as white, American Indian, and Mexican American men chose sides. On the home front, North and South, hundreds of thousands of Americans labored on farms and in factories, hospitals, and burgeoning government offices to support the war effort. After 1862, tens of thousands of African Americans joined the Union army and navy, and growing numbers of women of all races labored as cooks, laundresses, nurses, and even soldiers. The next year, the Emancipation Proclamation ensured that a Union victory would eradicate slavery. As the war dragged on, antiwar protests erupted North and South, fueled by inflation, conscription acts, and mounting casualties. Finally in 1865, the greater resources of the North, complemented by General Ulysses S. Grant's hard war strategy, led to Union victory and the final abolition of slavery.

The Nation at War, 1861–1862

When southern troops fired on northern ships seeking to resupply Fort Sumter, civil war finally erupted. The Union and the Confederacy faced very different tasks in the war. The South had to defend its territory and force the federal government to halt military action. The North had a more complicated challenge. Initially, northern political leaders believed that enslavers mainly drove secession. Lincoln and his supporters had hoped that early Union victories combined with battle deaths and property destruction would lead most southern whites to embrace reconciliation. However, this plan depended on early Union victories. Instead Confederates won early battles, and the North was forced to invade the South and isolate it from potential allies. As the conflict escalated in 1861 and 1862, both the Union and the Confederacy confronted the costs of war as well as conflicts over its meaning. Should the Union not only seek to defeat the South but also to abolish slavery? How could the Confederacy maintain the system of slavery in the midst of wartime mobilization? And how would Indians, African Americans, Mexican Americans, and immigrants envision their part in the Civil War?

Both Sides Prepare for War. At the onset of the war, the Union held a decided advantage in resources and population. The Union states held more than 60 percent of the U.S. population, and the Confederate population included several million enslaved blacks.

FIGURE 13.1 (within image: Population 61%/39%, Railroad mileage 66%/34%, Farm acreage 67%/33%, Commodity output 70%/30%, Factories 85%/15%, North / South)

FIGURE 13.1 Economies of the North and South, 1860

This figure provides graphic testimony to the enormous advantages in resources the North held on the eve of the Civil War. The North led the South in population, farm acreage, and railroad mileage as well as factories and commodity output. Over four years of war, how might the differences in each area affect the ability of the Union and the Confederacy to pursue their objectives?

Source: Data from Stanley Engerman, "The Economic Impact of the Civil War," in *The Reinterpretation of American Economic History*, ed. Robert W. Fogel and Stanley Engerman (New York: Harper and Row, 1971).

Not only would enslaved men not be armed for combat, but some men and women would also use the disruptions of war to claim their freedom. The Union also far outstripped the Confederacy in manufacturing and even led the South in agricultural production. The North's many miles of railroad track ensured greater ease in moving troops and supplies. And the Union could launch far more ships to blockade southern ports (Figure 13.1).

Yet Union forces were less prepared for war than the Confederates, who had been organizing troops and gathering munitions for months. To match their efforts, Winfield Scott, general in chief of the U.S. army, told Lincoln he would need at least 300,000 men committed to serve for two or three years. Scott believed that massing such huge numbers of soldiers would force the Confederacy to negotiate a peace. But fearing to unnerve Northerners, the president asked for only 75,000 volunteers for three months. Moreover, rather than forming a powerful national army led by seasoned officers, Lincoln left recruitment, organization, and training largely to the states. The result was disorganization and the appointment of officers based more on political connections than military expertise.

Confederate leaders also initially relied on state militia units and volunteers, but they prepared for a prolonged war from the start. Before the firing on Fort Sumter, President Davis signed up 100,000 volunteers for a year's service. Moreover, the labor provided by enslaved workers allowed a large proportion of white working-age men to volunteer for military service without harming southern agricultural production, at least initially. And Southerners were likely to be fighting mainly on home territory, where they had expert knowledge of the terrain. When the final four states joined the Confederacy, the southern army also gained important military leadership. It ultimately recruited 280 West Point graduates, including Robert E. Lee, Thomas "Stonewall" Jackson, James Longstreet, and others who had proved their mettle in the Mexican-American War.

Battle of Wilson's Creek   This colored lithograph depicts the First Iowa Regiment, led by General Nathaniel Lyon, charging Confederate forces at the Battle of Wilson's Creek, Missouri on August 10, 1861. The Confederates won the battle, and Lyon, on the ground here, became the first Union general to die in the war. The lithograph was created in 1893 based on a wartime sketch. Library of Congress, Prints and Photographs Division, Washington, D.C. [LC-DIG-pga-01861]

The South's advantages were apparent in the first major battle of the war though Confederate troops were also aided by information on Union plans sent by Rose Greenhow. When 30,000 Union troops marched on northern Virginia on July 21, 1861, Confederate forces were ready. At the **Battle of Bull Run** (or **Manassas**), later known as the First Battle of Bull Run, 22,000 Confederates repelled the Union attack. Civilians from Washington who traveled to the battle site to view the combat had to flee for their lives to escape Confederate artillery.

Despite Union defeats at Bull Run and at Wilson's Creek, Missouri that August, the Confederate army did not launch major strikes against Union forces. Meanwhile the Union navy began blockading the South's deep-water ports. By the time the armies settled into winter camps in 1861–1862, both sides had come to realize that the war was likely to be a long and costly struggle.

Wartime Roles of African Americans, Indians, and Mexican Americans.

The outbreak of war intensified debates over abolition. Some 225,000 African Americans lived in the free states, and many offered their services in an effort to end slavery. African American leaders in Cleveland proclaimed, "Today, as in the times of '76, we are ready to go forth and do battle in the common cause of our country." But Secretary of War Simon Cameron had no intention of calling up black soldiers.

Northern optimism about a quick victory contributed to the rejection of African American volunteers. Union leaders feared that whites would not enlist if they had to serve alongside blacks. In addition, Lincoln and his advisers were initially wary of letting a war to preserve the Union become a war against slavery, and they feared that any further threat to slavery might drive the four slave states that remained in the Union into the Confederacy. This political strategy, however, depended on quick and overwhelming victories. With most U.S. soldiers posted on the western frontier and a third of officers joining the Confederacy, early victories were few. Nonetheless a rush of volunteers allowed Union troops to push into Virginia while the Union navy captured crucial islands along the Confederate coast.

Regardless of official policy, wherever Union forces appeared, enslaved southerners considered freedom a possibility. Enslaved workers living near battle sites circulated information on Union troop movements. Virginia enslavers, increasingly worried about losing their workers, began sending them to more distant plantations or Confederate army units. Still, some enslaved people fled and headed to Union camps. Many enslavers tracked fugitives behind Union lines and demanded their return. Some Union commanders denied fugitives entrance to their camps or returned them to their masters. But a few Union officers recognized the fugitives' practical value. Enslaved men and women knew the local geography and could provide critical labor that freed white soldiers to fight. In addition, their loss drained the Confederate labor supply. In May 1861 at Fort Monroe, Virginia, Union General Benjamin Butler offered fugitive slaves military protection and asked his superiors in Washington to develop a general policy on the matter.

Lincoln endorsed Butler's proposal that fugitive slaves be accepted into Union camps and allowed to work there. In August 1861, Congress passed a Confiscation Act that proclaimed that any owner whose enslaved workers were used by the Confederate army would lose all claim to them. The act thus recognized fugitives as **contraband** of war, that is property forfeited by Confederates' act of rebellion. Yet the act did not free these fugitives but rather placed them under Union protection.

Explore ▶

See Source 13.1 for a Union general's reaction to fugitive slaves arriving in army camps.

This allowed the Union to strike at the institution of slavery without proclaiming a general emancipation that might prompt those border states where slavery remained legal to secede. Indeed, some Union officers in border states continued to return fugitives to their enslavers despite passage of the Confiscation Act. Although the act was far from a clear-cut declaration of freedom, it spurred the hopes of northern abolitionists and enslaved southerners.

While Northerners continued to debate African Americans' role in the war effort, the Union army recruited a wide array of other ethnic and racial groups, including American Indians. Unlike blacks, however, Indians did not all support the Union. The Comanche negotiated with both Union and Confederate agents while raiding the Texas frontier for horses and cattle. The Confederacy also gained significant support from slaveholding Indians who had earlier been removed from the Southeast. The Cherokee split over the war as they had over removal. General Stand Watie led a pan-Indian force into battle for the Confederates. Although John Ross initially joined the Confederates, he later led a group of Cherokee into Union army ranks alongside the Osage, Delaware, Seneca, and other Indian nations. Ely Parker, a Seneca sachem and engineer, became a lieutenant colonel in the Union army, serving with General Ulysses S. Grant.

Guided Primary Source Analysis

General Benjamin Butler │ Enslaved Blacks Flee to Union Army Camps, May 27, 1861

On May 24, 1861 Union General Butler, head of Fort Monroe in northern Virginia, informed the General-in-chief Winfield Scott that three slaves belonging to a Confederate colonel in Virginia had sought sanctuary from his guards. The fugitives told Butler they were about to be taken south for Confederate service. The general chose "to avail myself of their services," given the Union's great need for laborers and the desire to keep them from aiding the Confederates. Three days later, as more fugitives sought refuge at Fort Monroe, Butler asked Scott for an official policy statement on their status.

Source 13.1

How did the number and make up of fugitive slaves arriving at Fort Monroe change in the period between General Butler's first and second letters?

What policy does General Butler adopt in dealing with the fugitives?

How does Butler explain or justify his actions?

Since I wrote my last dispatch the question in regard to slave property is becoming one of very serious magnitude. The inhabitants of Virginia are using their negroes in the batteries, and are preparing to send the women and children South. The escapes from them are very numerous, and a squad has come in this morning to my pickets bringing their women and children. . . . I am in the utmost doubt what to do with this species of property. . . . I have therefore determined to employ, as I can do very profitably, the able-bodied persons in the party, issuing proper food for the support of all, and charging against their services the expense of care and sustenance of the non-laborers. . . . As a matter of property to the insurgents it will be of very great moment, the number that I now have amounting . . . to what in good times would be of the value of sixty thousand dollars. Twelve of these negroes . . . have escaped from the erection of the batteries on [nearby] Sewall's point. . . . Without them the batteries could not have been erected at least for many weeks. As a military question it would seem to be a measure of necessity to deprive their masters of their services. . . . As a political question and a question of humanity can I receive the services of a Father and a Mother and not take the children? Of the humanitarian aspect I have no doubt. Of the political one I have no right to judge. I therefore submit all this to your better judgement, and . . . have duplicate[d] the parts of my dispatch relating to this subject and forward[ed] them to the Secretary of War.

Source: Benjamin F. Butler to Lieutenant Genl. Scott, 27 May 1861, B-99 1861, Letters Received Irregular, Secretary of War, Record Group 107, National Archives

Put It in Context

What role did fugitive slaves play in the Union war effort and how did their roles compare to those of American Indians and Mexican Americans?

WeeJukeKah/James Bird, 1900   This studio portrait of Civil War veteran and scout WeeJukeKah was taken in Black River Falls, Wisconsin, home of his Ho-Chunk (Winnebago) tribe. He wears a suit and a U.S. Army hat with two crossed arrows, which indicate that he was part of Company A of the Omaha Scouts, a group of 72 Ho-Chunk soldiers led by 6 white officers. Charles Van Schaick/Wisconsin Historical Society/Getty Images

Indians played crucial roles in a number of important early battles, particularly on the Confederate side. Cherokee and Seminole warriors fought valiantly with Confederates at the Battle of Pea Ridge in Arkansas in March 1862, but were defeated by a smaller but better supplied Union force. In August 1862 Indians contributed to the Confederate victory at the Second Battle of Bull Run and the following month participated in the bloodiest single day of battle in U.S. history at Antietam (Sharpsburg). That same August, starving Dakota warriors whose treaty rights were violated and annuity payments withheld attacked white traders, settlers, and soldiers. In the largest native uprising in U.S. history, the Dakota killed hundreds of settlers. An unknown number of Dakota were killed by U.S. troops. When the army regained control in October, the Minnesota Governor sought to execute 303 Dakota prisoners, some of whom had opposed the uprising. President Lincoln intervened, sparing the lives of 265 Dakota. Thirty-eight others were hung.

Mexican Americans and Tejanos faced difficult choices when recruited by Confederate and Union officers. In May 1861, Juan Nepomuceno Cortina, whose Tejano and Mexican troops had earlier fought Anglo Texans, aided the Union at the Battle of Zapata but were defeated by the 33rd Texas Confederate Cavalry. The 33rd was led by Mexican American Captain Santos Benavides, who had also fought against Apaches and other Indians. Cortina retreated into Mexico but continued to fight against Confederate soldiers and local militias along the Texas frontier while Captain Benavides sought to recapture fugitive slaves in Mexico. Benavides also secured passage of a huge cotton shipment to a Mexican port after the U.S. Navy blockaded most southern ports. The sale of this cotton was crucial to the Confederate Treasury.

Hoping to gain control of the West's gold and silver mines, New Mexican Confederates launched an attack on Glorieta Pass, near Santa Fe, in March 1862. But a Union troop composed of Colorado miners ended that Confederate dream. New Mexico was home to many Union units, including the New Mexico Volunteer Infantry. Its 157 Mexican American officers comprised the most in any single unit fighting for the Union. It was led by Lieutenant Colonel Diego Archuleta, who was swiftly promoted to brigadier general.

While both Union and Confederate armies recruited American Indian and Mexican American regiments, African Americans were initially barred from enlisting as soldiers on either side. However, the constant call for black enlistment by Frederick Douglass and other leading abolitionists helped transform the attitudes of northern whites. So, too, did a series of Union military defeats. In spring 1862, Confederate general Stonewall Jackson won a series of stunning victories against three Union armies in Virginia's Shenandoah Valley. That June and July, General Robert E. Lee fought Union forces under General George B. McClellan to a standstill in the Seven Days Battle near Richmond. Then in August, Lee,

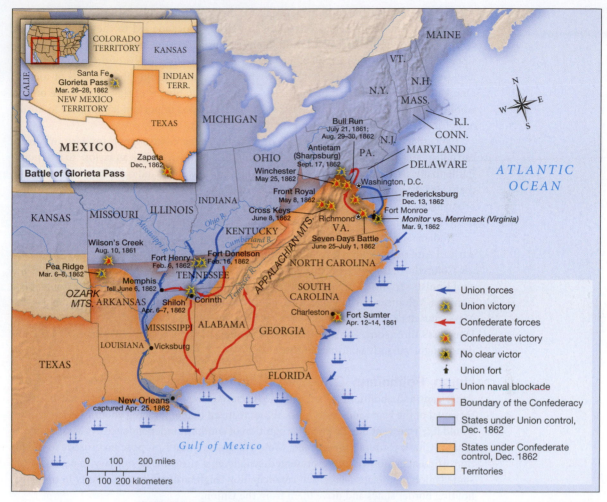

MAP 13.1 Early Civil War Battles, 1861–1862

In 1861 and 1862, the Confederate army stunned Union forces with a series of dramatic victories in Virginia, Missouri, and Texas. However, the Union army won a crucial victory at Antietam (Sharpsburg); gained control of Confederate territory in Tennessee, Arkansas, and Mississippi; fended off Confederate troops in New Mexico Territory; and established a successful blockade of Confederate ports.

Jackson, and General James Longstreet joined together to defeat Union troops at the Second Battle of Bull Run (Map 13.1).

As the war turned against the North, the North turned against slavery. In April 1862 Congress had approved a measure to abolish slavery in the District of Columbia, symbolizing this significant shift in Union sentiment. During that bloody summer, Congress passed a second confiscation act, declaring that the enslaved people of anyone who supported the Confederacy should be "forever free of their servitude, and not again held as slaves." In July Congress also approved a militia act that allowed African Americans to serve in "any military or naval service for which they may be found competent."

Support for the 1862 militia act built on the lobbying of black leaders as well as the testimony of Union soldiers. In April 1862 a Union blockade led to the capture of New Orleans, while the **Battle of Shiloh** in Tennessee provided the army entrée to the Mississippi valley. There Union troops came face-to-face with slavery. Few of these soldiers were abolitionists, but many were shocked by what they saw, including instruments of torture. One Union soldier reported he had seen "enough of the horror of slavery to make one an Abolitionist forever." In addition, enslaved blacks provided important intelligence to northern officers, making clear their value to the Union effort.

Whether in victory or defeat, rising death tolls also increased support for African American enlistment. The Battle of Shiloh was the bloodiest battle in American history to that point. Earlier battles had resulted in a few hundred or even a few thousand casualties, but with more than 23,000 casualties, Shiloh raised the carnage to a new level. As the war continued, such brutal battles became routine. The Union army would need every available man — white, black, Indian, and Mexican American — to sustain its effort against the Confederates.

Indian and Mexican American regiments had already proven themselves in battle. African Americans followed suit. In October 1862 a group of black soldiers in the First Kansas Colored Volunteers repulsed Confederates at a battle in Missouri. In the South, white abolitionists serving as Union officers organized former slaves into units like the First South Carolina Volunteers in January 1863. A few months later, another black regiment — the Massachusetts Fifty-fourth — attracted recruits from across the North, including Frederick Douglass's three sons. For the next two years, tens of thousands of African American soldiers fought valiantly in dozens of battles.

Union Politicians Consider Emancipation. By the fall of 1862, African Americans and abolitionists had gained widespread support for emancipation as a necessary goal of the war. Lincoln and his cabinet realized that embracing abolition as a war aim would likely prevent international recognition of southern independence. As Massachusetts senator Charles Sumner proclaimed, "You will observe that I propose no crusade for abolition. [Emancipation] is to be presented strictly as a measure of military necessity." Still, some Union politicians feared that emancipation might arouse deep animosity in the slave-holding border states and drive them from the Union.

From the Confederate perspective, international support was critical. Official recognition from European nations might persuade the North to accept southern independence. More immediately, recognition would ensure markets for southern agriculture and access to manufactured goods and war materiel. Confederate officials were especially focused on Britain, the leading market for cotton and a leading producer of industrial products. President Davis considered sending Rose Greenhow to England to promote the Confederate cause.

Fearing that the British might capitulate to Confederate pressure, abolitionist lecturers toured Britain, reminding residents of their early leadership in the antislavery cause. The Union's formal commitment to emancipation would certainly increase British support for its position and prevent diplomatic recognition of the Confederacy. By the summer of 1862, Lincoln was convinced, but he wanted to wait for a military victory before making a formal announcement regarding emancipation.

Instead, the Union suffered a series of defeats that summer, and Lee marched his army into Union territory in Maryland. On September 17, Longstreet joined Lee in a fierce battle along Antietam Creek as Union troops brought the Confederate advance to a standstill near the town of Sharpsburg. Union forces suffered more than 12,000 casualties and the

President Lincoln Presenting the Emancipation Proclamation to His Cabinet
In this engraving, Lincoln reads the draft of his Emancipation Proclamation to his cabinet in
September 1862. On the left are Secretary of War Edwin Stanton (seated) and Secretary of the
Treasury Salmon P. Chase, the two strongest supporters of the proclamation. Postmaster General
Montgomery Blair and Attorney General Edward Bates (seated), who opposed the plan, are on
the right. Library of Congress, Prints and Photographs Division, Washington, D.C. [LC-DIG-pga-02502]

Confederates more than 10,000, the bloodiest single day of battle in U.S. history. Yet because
Lee and his army were forced to retreat, Lincoln claimed the **Battle of Antietam** as a great
victory. Five days later, the president announced his preliminary **Emancipation Proclamation** to the assembled cabinet, promising to free the enslaved in all seceding states.

On January 1, 1863, Lincoln signed the final edict, proclaiming that enslaved people in
areas still in rebellion were "forever free" and inviting them to enlist in the Union army.
Over the next two years, tens of thousands of enslaved men fled southern plantations and
fought in the Union Army alongside equal numbers of free blacks who volunteered to
ensure the Confederacy's defeat. Still, the proclamation was a moderate document in many
ways. Its provisions exempted from emancipation the 450,000 slaves in the loyal border
states, as well as more than 300,000 enslaved people in Union-occupied areas of Tennessee,
Louisiana, and Virginia. The proclamation also justified the abolition of southern slavery
on military, not moral, grounds. Despite its limits, the Emancipation Proclamation inspired
joyous celebrations among free blacks and white abolitionists, who viewed it as the first step
toward slavery's final eradication.

Review & Relate

■ Why did American Indians, Mexicans and
Tejanos, and African Americans choose to join
Union or Confederate forces?

■ What events occurred to turn the Civil War
into a war to end slavery?

War Transforms the North and the South

For soldiers and civilians seeking to survive the upheaval of war, political pronouncements rarely alleviated the dangers they faced. The war's extraordinary death tolls shocked Americans on both sides. On the home front, the prolonged conflict created labor shortages and severe inflation in both North and South. The war initially disrupted industrial and agricultural production as men were called to service, but the North recovered quickly by building on its prewar industrial base, technological know-how, and women's labor. In the South, manufacturing increased, with enslaved laborers pressed into service as industrial workers. But this further diminished the plantation labor force as more white women were forced into managerial roles. With most of the war fought on southern soil and the Union Navy blockading Confederate ports, shortages loomed everywhere. By 1863, these dramatic transformations inspired dissent and protest as rising death tolls and rising prices made the costs of war ever clearer.

Life and Death on the Battlefield. Few soldiers entered the conflict knowing what to expect. A young private wrote that his idea of combat had been that the soldiers "would all be in line, all standing in a nice level field fighting, a number of ladies taking care of the wounded, etc., etc., but it isn't so." **See Primary Source Project 13: Firsthand Accounts of the Civil War, page 456.** Improved weaponry turned battles into scenes of bloody carnage. The shift from smoothbore muskets to rifles, which had grooves that spun the bullet, made weapons far more effective at longer distances. The use of minié balls—small bullets with a deep cavity that expanded upon firing—increased fatalities as well. By 1863 Union army sharpshooters acquired new repeating rifles with metal cartridges. With more accurate rifles and deadlier bullets, the rival armies increasingly relied on heavy fortifications, elaborate trenches, and distant mortar and artillery fire when they could. Still, casualties continued to rise, especially since the trenches served as breeding grounds for disease.

> **Explore ▸**
>
> For two images of soldiers in wartime, see Sources 13.2 and 13.3.

The hardships and discomforts of war extended beyond combat itself. As General Lee complained before Antietam, many soldiers fought in ragged uniforms and without shoes. Rations, too, ran short. Food was dispensed sporadically and was often spoiled. Many Union troops survived primarily on an unleavened biscuit called hardtack as well as small amounts of meat and beans and enormous quantities of coffee. Their diet improved over the course of the war, however, as the Union supply system grew more efficient while Confederate troops subsisted increasingly on cornmeal and fatty meat. As early as 1862, Confederate soldiers began gathering food from the haversacks of Union dead.

For every soldier who died as a result of combat, three died of disease. Measles, dysentery, typhoid, and malaria killed thousands who drank contaminated water, ate tainted food, and were exposed to the elements. And infected soldiers on both sides carried yellow fever and malaria into towns where they built fortifications. Prisoner-of-war camps were especially deadly locales. Debilitating fevers in a camp near Danville, Virginia spread to the town, killing civilians as well as soldiers.

The sufferings of African American troops were particularly severe. The death rate from disease for black Union soldiers was nearly three times greater than that for white Union soldiers, reflecting their poorer health upon enlistment, the hard labor they performed, and the minimal medical care they received in the field. Southern blacks who began their army careers in contraband camps fared even worse, with a camp near Nashville losing a quarter of its residents to death in just three months in 1864.

For all soldiers, medical assistance was primitive. Antibiotics did not exist, antiseptics were still unknown, and anesthetics were scarce. Union medical care improved with the **U.S. Sanitary Commission**, which was established by the federal government in June 1861 to promote and coordinate better medical treatment for soldiers. Nonetheless, a commentator accurately described most field hospitals as "dirty dens of butchery and horror," where amputations often occurred with whiskey as the only anesthetic.

As the horrors of war sank in, large numbers of soldiers deserted or refused to reenlist. As volunteers declined and deserters increased, both the Confederate and the Union governments were forced to institute conscription laws to draft men into service.

The Northern Economy Expands.

As the war dragged on, the North's economic advantages became more apparent. Initially, the effects of the war on northern industry had been little short of disastrous. Raw cotton for textiles disappeared, southern planters stopped ordering shoes, and trade fell off precipitously. By 1863, however, the northern economy was in high gear and could provide more arms, food, shoes, and clothing to its troops as well as for those back home. As cotton production declined, woolen manufacturing doubled, and northern iron and coal production increased 25 to 30 percent during the war. Northern factories turned out weapons and ammunition while shipyards built the fleets that blockaded southern ports.

These economic improvements were linked to a vast expansion in the federal government's activities. War Department orders fueled the industrial surge. It also created the U.S. Military Railroads unit to construct tracks in newly occupied southern territories and granted large contracts to northern railroads to carry troops and supplies. With southern Democrats out of federal office, Congress also raised tariffs on imported goods to protect northern industries. In addition, the government hired thousands of "sewing women," who were contracted to make uniforms for Union soldiers. Other women joined the federal labor force as clerical workers to sustain the expanding bureaucracy and the voluminous amounts of government-generated paperwork.

That paperwork multiplied exponentially when the federal government created a national currency and a national banking system. Before the Civil War, private banks (chartered by the states) issued their own banknotes, which were used in most economic transactions. During the war, Congress revolutionized this system, giving the federal government the power to create currency, issue federal charters to banks, and take on national debt. The government then flooded the nation with treasury bills, commonly called greenbacks. The federal budget mushroomed as well—from $63 million in 1860 to nearly $1.3 billion in 1865. By the end of the war, the federal bureaucracy had become the nation's largest single employer.

Northern manufacturers faced one daunting problem: a shortage of labor. Over half a million workers left their jobs to serve in the Union army, and others were hired by the expanding federal bureaucracy. Manufacturers dealt with the problem primarily by mechanizing more tasks and by hiring more women and children, native-born and immigrant. Combining the lower wages paid to these workers with production speedups, manufacturers improved their profits while advancing the Union cause.

Comparative Primary Source Analysis

Photographers Bring the War Home

The development of battlefield photography in the 1860s offered civilians new perspectives on warfare. Photographs were exhibited in photographers' studios and reproduced as engravings in newspapers across the country. The photographs here offer stark contrasts between soldiers on and off the battlefield. In the first, Union soldiers rest at a camp with sturdy wooden cabins. For this picture, some men stopped in the midst of work while others caroused for the camera. In the second, Union dead lie in front of the Dunker Church on the Antietam battlefield, where more than 3,600 were killed in a single day.

Source 13.2

Union Soldiers in Camp, c. 1863

Library of Congress, Prints and Photographs Division, Washington, D.C. [LC-DIG-ppmsca-34191]

Urbanization and Industrialization in the South. Although Southerners had gone to war to protect a largely rural lifestyle, the war encouraged the growth of cities and industry. The creation of a large governmental and military bureaucracy brought thousands of Southerners to the Confederate capital of Richmond. As the war expanded, refugees from the countryside also flooded into Atlanta, Savannah, Columbia, and Mobile.

Industrialization contributed to urban growth as well. With the South unable to buy industrial goods from the North and limited in its trade with Europe, military necessity spurred southern industry. Clothing and shoe factories had "sprung up almost like magic" in Natchez and Jackson, Mississippi. The Tredegar Iron Works in Richmond expanded

Source 13.3

Battlefield Dead at Antietam, 1862

Library of Congress, Prints and Photographs Division, Washington, D.C. [LC-DIG-ppmsca-32887]

Interpret the Evidence

1. How do the soldiers present themselves in the Union camp photo? How would this photograph have affected viewers on the home front?

2. How might the photograph of the Antietam battlefield affect civilians and influence soldiers like those shown in the Union camp photo?

▍Put It in Context

How might images like these affect attitudes toward the war among politicians, military leaders, and the public, North and South?

significantly as well, employing more than 2,500 men, black and white. More than 10,000 people labored in war industries in Selma, Alabama, where one factory produced cannons. With labor in short supply, widows and orphans, enslaved blacks, and white men too old or injured to fight were recruited for industrial work in many cities.

Women Aid the War Effort. Women of all classes and both races contributed to the war effort. Thousands filled jobs in agriculture, industry, and the government that were traditionally held by men while others assisted the military effort more directly. Most Union and Confederate officials initially opposed women's direct engagement in the war. Yet it was women's voluntary organization of relief efforts that inspired the federal government to establish the U.S. Sanitary Commission. By 1862 tens of thousands of women volunteered funds and assistance through hundreds of local chapters across the North. They hosted fund-raising fairs, coordinated sewing and knitting circles, rolled bandages, and sent supplies to the front lines.

With critical shortages of medical staff, some female nurses and doctors eventually gained acceptance in northern hospitals and field camps. In the North, Dorothea Dix, who had worked to improve treatment of the mentally ill, convinced Secretary of War Edwin Stanton to appoint her superintendent of nursing for the Union Army. She required nurses to be Protestant and plain looking, and Congress agreed to pay them $12 a month (one-third of what male nurses made). Some women gained positions independently of Dix's leadership. Mary Ann "Mother" Bickerdyke, a widow in her forties, showed incredible stamina and skill nursing men on the battlefield. Dr. Mary Walker, a rare female physician, also donated her services, working in field hospitals and prisoner of war camps. Since she usually dressed in men's clothing, wounded soldiers did not always recognize that a woman was caring for them.

Susie King Taylor was among the many black women who provided medical care during the war. Enslaved in South Carolina, she fled at age fifteen to a coastal island occupied by Union forces. There she laundered clothes, cleaned musketry, and served as a nurse in a segregated military hospital for black soldiers. She and other African American nurses received $10 per month, $2 less than their white counterparts. Catholic nuns also served on battlefields and in hospitals, aiding Union and Confederate soldiers. They worked in groups, their habits serving as their uniform. Despite widespread anti-Catholic prejudice, they were more widely praised by military officers due in part to their clear organization and deference to male leadership. By the end of the war, northern women almost entirely replaced men as military nurses.

In the South, too, women performed much of the medical care. But without government support, nursing was never recognized as a legitimate profession for women, and most nurses worked out of their own homes. As a result, a Confederate soldier's chance of dying from wounds or disease was greater than those of his Union counterpart. Southern women also worked tirelessly to supply soldiers with clothes, blankets, munitions, and food. But this work, too, was often performed locally and by individuals rather than as part of a coordinated Confederate effort.

Some Union and Confederate women played more unusual roles in the war. A few dozen women joined Rose Greenhow in gathering information for military and political leaders. One of the most effective spies on the Union side was the fugitive slave Harriet Tubman, who gathered intelligence in South Carolina, including from many enslaved blacks, between 1862 and 1864. Even more women served as couriers, carrying messages across battle lines to alert officers of critical changes in military orders or in the enemy's position.

In addition, at least four hundred women disguised themselves as men and fought as soldiers. There were likely hundreds more who fought for short periods of time or whose sex was never discovered. Sarah Edmonds took the name Franklin Thompson and enlisted as a private in the Second Michigan Infantry in Detroit in May 1861. She worked as a regimental nurse as well as a courier. Her regiment participated in several major battles, including First Manassas, Fredericksburg, and Antietam. After contracting malaria in April 1863,

Harry T. Buford
1 pt Lt Indpt Scouts C.S.A

Loreta Janeta Velazquez/Harry T. Buford, c. 1876 While attending school in New Orleans, Cuban-born Janeta Velazquez eloped with a Texas soldier. When the Civil War erupted, she joined her husband disguised as Lieutenant Buford. Soon widowed, she continued to serve as a Confederate soldier and spy until wounded in the Battle of Shiloh. In 1876, she published her memoir, *The Woman in Battle*, a mix of fact and fiction. The Granger Collection, New York

Edmonds deserted, fearing that doctors would discover her sex. On the Confederate side, Cuban-born Loretta Janeta Velazquez joined the army alongside her husband disguised as Harry Buford. After her husband was killed in battle, she continued to fight, serving as an officer in several regiments. Her identity was only discovered when she wrote her memoirs in 1876. Some female soldiers continued to live as men after the war; others once again donned women's clothes and embraced traditional gender roles.

Women on the home front also sought to influence wartime policies, especially in the North. Their most important effort followed the Emancipation Proclamation when Elizabeth Cady Stanton, Susan B. Anthony, and Lucy Stone founded the **Women's National Loyal League**. The League launched a massive petition drive to broaden Lincoln's policy, and female volunteers collected 260,000 signatures. Black and white signers, two-thirds of them women, demanded a congressional act "emancipating all persons of African descent" everywhere in the nation.

Dissent and Protest in the Midst of War.

The war also inspired dissent and protest North and South. Dissent roiled border states from the start of the war. From 1861 on, battles raged among residents in the border state of Missouri, with Confederate sympathizers refusing to accept living in a Union state. Pro-southern residents formed militias and staged guerrilla attacks on Union supporters. The militias, with the tacit support of Confederate officials, claimed thousands of lives during the war and forced the Union army to station troops in the area.

By 1863, frustration spread north and south as casualties increased, numbers of volunteers declined, and inflation soared. Some white Northerners had always opposed emancipation, based on racial prejudice or fear that a flood of black migrants would increase competition for jobs. Then, just two months after the Emancipation Proclamation went into effect, a new law deepened concerns among many working-class Northerners. The **Enrollment Act**, passed by Congress in March 1863, established a draft system to ensure sufficient soldiers for the Union army. While draftees were to be selected by an impartial lottery, the law allowed a person with $300 to pay the government in place of serving or to hire another man as a substitute. Many workers deeply resented the draft's profound inequality.

Dissent turned to violence in July 1863 when the new law went into effect. Riots broke out in cities across the North. In New York City, where inflation caused tremendous suffering and a large immigrant population solidly supported the Democratic Party, implementation of the draft triggered four days of the worst rioting Americans had ever seen. Women and men — including many Irish and German immigrants — attacked Republican draft officials, wealthy businessmen, and the free black community. Between July 13 and 16,

New York City Draft Riots, July 1863   On July 13 the draft riots in New York City began with an attack on the Colored Orphan Asylum on Fifth Avenue. As the matron led 233 African American children to safety, mobs of white men and women looted the building and set it ablaze. This wood engraving appeared in illustrated weeklies from New York to London. Sarin Images/Granger

rioters lynched at least a dozen African Americans and looted and burned the city's Colored Orphan Asylum. The violence ended only when Union troops put down the riots by force. By then, more than one hundred New Yorkers, most of them black, lay dead.

By 1864 inflation, which eroded the earnings of rural and urban residents, fueled further protests in the North. Women, children, and old men took over much of the field labor in the Midwest, trying to feed their families and the army while struggling to pay their bills. Factory workers, servants, and day laborers felt the pinch as well. With federal greenbacks flooding the market and military production a priority, the price of consumer goods climbed about 20 percent faster than wages. Although industrialists garnered huge profits, workers suffered. A group of Cincinnati seamstresses complained to President Lincoln in 1864 about employers "who fatten on their contracts by grinding immense profits out of the labor of their operatives." At the same time, employers persuaded some state legislatures to prohibit strikes in wartime. The federal government, too, supported business over labor. When workers at the Parrott arms factory in Cold Spring, New York struck for higher wages in 1864, the government declared martial law and arrested the strike leaders.

Northern Democrats saw the widening unrest as a political opportunity. Although some Democratic leaders supported the war effort, many others — whom opponents called **Copperheads**, after the poisonous snake — rallied behind Ohio politician Clement L. Vallandigham in opposing the war. Presenting themselves as the "peace party," these Democrats enjoyed considerable success in eastern cities where inflation was rampant and immigrant workers were caught between low wages and military service. The party was also strong in parts of the Midwest, like Missouri, where sympathy for the southern cause and antipathy to African Americans ran deep.

In the South, too, some whites expressed growing dissatisfaction with the war. Jefferson Davis signed a conscription act in April 1862, a year before Lincoln, inciting widespread opposition. Here, too, men could hire a substitute if they had enough money, and an October 1862 law exempted men owning twenty or more enslaved workers from military service. Thus, large planters, many of whom served in the Confederate legislature, had effectively exempted themselves from fighting. As one Alabama farmer fumed, "All they want is to get you pumpt up and go to fight for their infernal negroes, and after you do their fighting you may kiss their hine parts for all they care."

Small farmers were also hard hit by policies that allowed the Confederate army to take whatever supplies it needed. The army's forced acquisition of farm produce intensified food shortages that had been building since early in the war. Moreover, the lack of an extensive railroad or canal system in the South limited the distribution of what food was available.

Food shortages drove up prices on basic items like bread and corn, while the Union blockade and the focus on military needs dramatically increased prices on other consumer goods. As the Confederate government issued ever more treasury notes to finance the war, inflation soared 2,600 percent in less than three years. In spring 1863 food riots led by working-class women erupted in cities across the South, including the Confederate capital of Richmond.

Some state legislatures then tried to control food prices, but Richmond workers continued to voice their resentment. In fall 1863 a group proclaimed, "From the fact that he consumes all and produces nothing, we know that without [our] labor and production the man with money could not exist."

The devastation of the war added to all these grievances. Since most battles were fought in the Upper South or along the Confederacy's western frontier, small farmers in these regions saw their crops, animals, and fields devastated. A phrase that had seemed cynical in 1862 — "A rich man's war and a poor man's fight" — became the rallying cry of the southern peace movement in 1864. Secret peace societies flourished mainly among small farmers and in regions, like the western mountains, where plantation slavery did not develop. A secret organization centered in North Carolina provided Union forces with information on southern troop movements and encouraged desertion by Confederates. In some mountainous areas, draft evaders and deserters formed guerrilla groups that attacked draft officials and actively impeded the war effort. Women joined these efforts, hiding deserters, raiding grain depots, and burning the property of Confederate officials.

When enslavers led the South out of the Union in 1861, they had assumed the loyalty of yeomen farmers, the deference of southern ladies, and the privileges of the southern way of life. Far from preserving social harmony and social order, however, the war undermined ties between elite and poor Southerners, between planters and small farmers, and between women and men. Although most white Southerners still supported the Confederacy in 1864 and internal dissent alone did not lead to defeat, it did weaken the ties that bound soldiers to their posts in the final two years of the war.

Review & Relate

▌ In what ways did the war reshape the economy and gender roles in the North and the South?

▌ How did the death toll, inflation, and social conflicts heightened by the war fuel dissent and protest in the North and the South?

The **Tide** of **War Turns,** 1863–1865

In spring 1863, amid turmoil on the home front, General Robert E. Lee's army defeated a Union force twice its size at Chancellorsville, Virginia. The victory set the stage for a Confederate thrust into Pennsylvania, but Lee's decision to go on the offensive proved the Confederacy's undoing. In July 1863 the Union won two decisive military victories: at Gettysburg, Pennsylvania and Vicksburg, Mississippi. At the same time, the flood of African Americans, including those formerly enslaved, into Union army camps transformed the very meaning of the war. By 1864, with the momentum favoring the Union, General Ulysses S. Grant implemented policies of hard war that forced the Confederacy to consider surrender.

Key Victories for the Union.

In mid-1863 Confederate commanders believed the tide was turning in their favor. Following victories at Fredericksburg and Chancellorsville, General Lee launched an invasion of northern territory. While the Union army maneuvered to protect Washington, D.C., General Joseph Hooker resigned as head of the Union Army of the Potomac. On June 28, Lincoln appointed George A. Meade as the new Union commander, and the general immediately faced a major engagement at the **Battle of Gettysburg** in Pennsylvania. If Confederates won a victory there, European countries might finally recognize the southern nation and force the North to accept peace.

Neither Lee nor Meade set out to launch a battle in this small Pennsylvania town. But Lee was afraid of outrunning his supply lines, and Meade wanted to keep Confederates from gaining control of the roads that crossed at Gettysburg. So between July 1 and July 3, the opposing armies fought a desperate battle with Union troops occupying the high ground and Confederate forces launching deadly assaults from below (Map 13.2). Ultimately, Gettysburg proved a disaster for the South: More than 4,700 Confederates were killed, including a large number of officers; another 18,000 were wounded, captured, or missing. Although the Union suffered similar casualties, it had more men to lose, and it could claim victory.

As Lee retreated to Virginia, the South suffered another devastating defeat. Troops under General Grant had been pounding Vicksburg, Mississippi since May 1863. The **siege of Vicksburg** ended with the surrender of Confederate forces on July 4. This victory was even more important strategically than Gettysburg (Map 13.2). Combined with a victory five days later at Port Hudson, Louisiana, the Union army controlled the entire Mississippi valley, the richest plantation region in the South. This series of victories also effectively cut Louisiana, Arkansas, and Texas off from the rest of the Confederacy, ensuring Union control of the West. In November 1863 Grant's troops achieved another major victory at Chattanooga, opening up much of the South's remaining territory to invasion. Thousands of enslaved workers deserted their plantations, and many joined the Union war effort.

That same month, November 1863, President Lincoln spoke at the official dedication ceremony for the National Cemetery at Gettysburg, Pennsylvania. In his **Gettysburg Address**, Lincoln tied the war against slavery to the fulfillment of the nation's founding ideal "that all men are created equal." He insisted that the United States "shall have a new birth of freedom—and that government of the people, by the people, and for the people, shall not perish from the earth." Only in this way, he declared, could Americans ensure that the "honored dead" had not "died in vain."

MAP 13.2 Battles of Gettysburg and Vicksburg, 1863

The three-day Battle of Gettysburg and the six-week siege of Vicksburg led to critical victories for the Union. Together, these victories forced General Lee's troops back into Confederate territory and gave the Union control of the Mississippi River. Still, the war was far from over. Confederate troops controlled the southern heartland, and Northerners wearied of the ever-increasing casualties.

Explore ▶

Compare two opposing views of why soldiers fought for the Union in Sources 13.4 and 13.5.

As 1864 dawned, the Union had twice as many forces in the field as the Confederacy, whose soldiers were suffering from low morale, high mortality, and dwindling supplies. Although some difficult battles lay ahead, the war of attrition — in which the larger, better-supplied Union forces slowly wore down their Confederate opponents — had begun to pay dividends.

The changing Union fortunes increased support for Lincoln and his congressional allies. Union victories and the Emancipation Proclamation also convinced Great Britain not to recognize the Confederacy as an independent nation. And the heroics of African American soldiers, who engaged in direct and often brutal combat against southern troops, expanded support for emancipation. Republicans, who now fully embraced abolition as a war aim, were nearly assured the presidency and a congressional majority in the 1864 elections.

Northern Democrats still campaigned for peace and the readmission of Confederate states with slavery intact. They nominated George B. McClellan, the onetime Union

Comparative Secondary Source Analysis

Why Union Soldiers Fought the Civil War

The Civil War was the bloodiest war ever fought by Americans. Hoping for a quick victory, some 75,000 men volunteered to join the Union Army in spring 1861. Even as the war dragged on and the death toll rose, hundreds of thousands more rallied to the Union cause. The Confederacy recruited soldiers to protect their homeland against northern invaders. In the North, the rationale for taking up arms was less clear. Yet even those drafted into Union service generally stayed the course, throwing themselves into battle after battle in pursuit of victory. Chandra Manning suggests that soldiers' confrontation with the reality of slavery led many Union men to continue the fight and urge others to do so as well. Gary Gallagher argues instead that saving the Union was the more important reason for northern men deciding to enlist and fight.

Source 13.4

Chandra Manning | The Fight Against Slavery, 2007

Enlisted Union soldiers came to the conclusion that winning the war would require the destruction of slavery partly because soldiers' personal observations of the South led many to decide that slavery blighted everything it touched. . . .

Yet more influential than Union soldier's preexisting notions, or even their firsthand observations of the South, were their interactions with actual slaves, which led many to view slavery as a dehumanizing and evil institution that corroded the moral virtue necessary for a population to govern itself. . . .

Hostility to slavery did not necessarily mean support for racial equality. In fact, white Union soldiers strove mightily to keep the issues of slavery and black rights separate. . . .

[Still], contact with slaves and southern society convinced many Union troops that the immoral and blighting institution of slavery was antithetical to republican government, and that

any republican government that tried to accommodate slavery was doomed to eventual failure. . . . [C]lear demands for the destruction of slavery plainly emerged among enlisted Union soldiers, especially those stationed in the slave states who were witnessing slavery with their own eyes for the first time. Even some border state Union soldiers joined the clamor, either because they had witnessed for years the violence that slavery could engender or out of shock and anger that slaveholders in their home states valued the peculiar institution over the Union. Slaves themselves did the most to force emancipation onto the Union agenda, . . . [primarily] by winning over enlisted Union soldiers, who, in the first year of the war, became the first major group after black Americans and abolitionists to call for an end to slavery. . . .

Source: Chandra Manning, *What This Cruel War Was Over: Soldiers, Slavery and the Civil War* (New York: Vintage Books, 2007), pp. 47, 49, 50–51.

commander, for president. McClellan attracted working-class and immigrant voters who traditionally supported the Democrats and bore the heaviest burdens of the war. But Democratic hopes for victory in November were crushed when Union general William Tecumseh Sherman captured Atlanta, Georgia just two months before the election. Lincoln and the Republicans won easily, giving the party a clear mandate to continue the war to its conclusion.

Source 13.5

Gary Gallagher | The Fight to Save the Union, 2011

The loyal American citizenry fought a war for the Union that also killed slavery. . . . Union always remained the paramount goal, a fact clearly expressed by Abraham Lincoln in speeches and other statements designed to garner the widest popular support for the war effort. . . . That hardpan of unionism held millions of Americans to the task of suppressing the slaveholders' rebellion, even as the human and material cost mushroomed. . . .

[The Union] represented a cherished legacy of the founding generation, a democratic republic with a constitution that guaranteed political liberty and afforded individuals a chance to better themselves economically. From the perspective of loyal Americans, their republic stood as the only hope for a democracy in [the] western world . . . [following] the failed European revolutions of the 1840s. Slaveholding aristocrats who established the Confederacy . . . posed a direct threat not only to the long-term success of the American republic but also to the broader future of democracy. . . .

Issues related to the institution of slavery precipitated secession and the outbreak of fighting, but the loyal citizenry initially gave little thought to emancipation in their quest to save the Union. By the early summer of 1862, long before black men donned blue uniforms in large numbers, victorious Union armies stood poised to win the war with slavery largely intact…. Eventually, most loyal citizens, though profoundly prejudiced by twenty-first century-standards and largely indifferent toward enslaved black people, embraced emancipation as a tool to punish slaveholders, weaken the Confederacy, and protect the Union from future internal strife.

Source: Gary Gallagher, *The Union War* (Cambridge: Harvard University Press, 2011), pp. 1, 2.

Examine the Sources

1. How do Manning and Gallagher differ in their interpretations of why Union soldiers joined the war effort?
2. Based on evidence in this chapter, including the Primary Source Project, evaluate the main arguments of each author.

Put It in Context

How might the Emancipation Proclamation and the introduction of black troops in the Union Army have affected the way white Union and Confederate soldiers thought about the purpose of the war?

African Americans Contribute to Victory. Lincoln's election secured the eventual downfall of slavery, but the movement to eradicate human bondage depended on numerous actors. Most importantly, perhaps, from the fall of 1862 on, African Americans enlisted in the Union army and helped ensure that nothing short of universal emancipation would be the outcome of the war. As Private Thomas Long, a former slave serving with the First South Carolina Volunteers, explained: "If we hadn't become sojers, all might have gone back as it was before. . . . But now tings can neber go back, because we have showed our energy and our courage and our naturally manhood."

In the border states, which were exempt from the Emancipation Proclamation, enslaved men were adamant about enlisting since those who served in the Union army were granted their freedom. Because of this provision, enslavers in these states did everything in their power to prevent their enslaved workers from joining the army. Despite these efforts, between 25 and 60 percent of military-age enslaved men in the four border states stole away and joined the Union army. By the end of the war, nearly 200,000 black men had served officially in the army and navy, and some 37,000 blacks had given their lives for the Union.

Yet despite their courage and commitment, black soldiers felt the sting of racism. They were segregated in camps, given the most menial jobs, and often treated as inferiors by white soldiers and officers. Particularly galling was the Union policy of paying black soldiers less than whites. African American soldiers openly protested this discrimination even after a black sergeant who voiced his views was charged with mutiny and executed by firing squad in February 1864. The War Department finally equalized wages four months later.

One primary concern of African American soldiers was to liberate enslaved people as Union armies moved deeper into the South. At the same time, thousands of enslaved southerners headed for Union lines. Even those forced to remain on plantations learned when Union troops were nearby and talked openly of emancipation. "Now they gradually threw off the mask," an enslaved laborer remembered, "and were not afraid to let it be known that the 'freedom' in their songs meant freedom of the body in this world."

From the first year of the war, the federal government recognized enslaved men and women who reached Union lines as contraband of war. Southern blacks seeking freedom quickly turned so-called "contraband" camps into **refugee communities**. Union army camps stretched from eastern Virginia to Kansas and from northern Kentucky to southern Louisiana. Black men hoped to gain freedom and wages by fighting for the Union, but the women, children, and elderly they brought with them had to fend for themselves once their men left to fight. Women refugees sometimes worked as cooks, nurses, or laundresses for the army, but many had to survive on meager rations and aid from other refugees. Moreover, while some camps remained open for years, most moved with the battlefront. As that front shifted quickly in the final eighteen months of war, thousands of refugees were left behind, often in easy reach of their former enslavers. Nonetheless, hundreds of thousands of black refugees fled to Union lines, depriving enslavers of their labor while building free communities.

The Final Battles of a Hard War. In the spring of 1864, the war in the East entered its final stage. That March, Lincoln placed General Grant in charge of all Union forces. Grant embarked on a strategy of **hard war**, in which soldiers not only attacked military targets but also destroyed civilian crops, livestock, fields, and property to undermine morale and supply chains. Grant was also willing to accept huge casualties to achieve victory. Over the next year, he led his troops overland through western Virginia in an effort to take Richmond. Meanwhile, General Philip Sheridan devastated "The Breadbasket of the Confederacy" in Virginia's Shenandoah Valley, and General Sherman laid waste to the remnants of the plantation system in Georgia and the Carolinas.

Grant's troops headed toward Richmond, where Lee's army controlled strong defensive positions. The Confederates won a series of narrow, bloody victories, but Grant continued to push forward. Although Lee lost fewer men, they were losses he could not afford. Combining high casualties with deserters, Lee's army was melting away with each engagement.

Contraband/Refugee Camp, Fort Curtis, Helena Arkansas

Thousands of enslaved Arkansans made their way to Fort Curtis in early 1862. Initially welcomed, they hastily constructed houses there. However, a conservative general then took command and forced many refugees back to their plantations. In spring 1863, Lincoln sent General Lorenzo Thomas to such recalcitrant forts to insist that commanders assist black refugees and pay them for their service. Minnesota Historical Society

Although soldiers and civilians — North and South — called Grant "the butcher" for his seeming lack of regard for human life, the Union general was not deterred.

In the fall of 1864, implementing hard war tactics, Sheridan rendered the Shenandoah Valley a "barren waste." Called "the burning" by local residents, Sheridan's soldiers torched fields, barns, and homes and destroyed thousands of bushels of grain along with livestock, shops, and mills. His campaign demoralized civilians in the region and denied Confederate troops crucial supplies.

In the preceding months, Sherman had laid siege to Atlanta, but on September 2 his forces swept around the city and destroyed the roads and rails that connected it to the rest of the Confederacy. When General John B. Hood and his Confederate troops abandoned their posts, Sherman telegraphed Lincoln: "Atlanta is ours, and fairly won." That victory cut the South in two, but Sherman continued on. **Sherman's March to the Sea** introduced hard war tactics to Southerners along the three-hundred-mile route from the Atlantic coast north through the Carolinas. His troops cut a path of destruction fifty to sixty miles wide. They confiscated or destroyed millions of pounds of cotton, corn, wheat, and other agricultural items; tore up thousands of miles of railroad tracks; and burned Columbia, the South Carolina capital. As Eleanor Cohen Seixas, whose family had earlier fled to Columbia for safety, recorded in her journal, "The fires raged fearfully all night" and the "vile Yankees took from us clothing, food, jewels, all our cows, horses, carriages, etc." Despite later claims that Sherman's men ravaged white women, instances of such behavior were rare, although Union soldiers did ransack homes and confiscate food and clothing.

Enslaved blacks hoped that Sherman's arrival marked their emancipation. During his victorious march, nearly 18,000 enslaved men, women, and children fled ruined plantations and sought to join the victorious troops. To their dismay, soldiers refused to take them along. Union officers realized that they could not care for this vast number of people and carry out their military operations. Still, some Union soldiers abused African American men, raped black women, or stole their few possessions, treating them as enemies rather than allies. At the same time, angry Confederates captured many blacks who were turned away, killing some and re-enslaving others.

These actions caused a scandal in Washington. In January 1865, Lincoln dispatched Secretary of War Edwin Stanton to Georgia to investigate the charges. At an extraordinary meeting in Savannah, Stanton and Sherman met with black ministers to hear their complaints and hopes. The ministers spoke movingly of the war lifting "the yoke of bondage." Freed blacks, they argued, "could reap the fruit of their own labor" and, if given land, "take care of ourselves, and assist the Government in maintaining our freedom." In response, Sherman issued **Field Order Number 15**, setting aside more than 400,000 acres of captured Confederate land to be divided into small plots for the formerly enslaved. The order proved highly controversial, but it offered blacks some hope of significant change.

If many African Americans were disappointed by the actions of Union soldiers in the East, American Indians were even more devastated by developments in the West. Despite Indian nations' substantial aid to Union armies, any hope of being rewarded for their efforts vanished by 1864. Tens of thousands of whites migrated west of the Mississippi River during the Civil War, and congressional passage of the Homestead Act in 1864 increased the numbers. At the same time, the U.S. army grew exponentially during the war, using its increased power to assault western Indian nations.

Attacks on Indians were not an extension of hard war policies, but rather a government-sanctioned effort to terrorize native communities. Beginning in 1862, the Dakota went to war with the United States over broken treaties. After being defeated, four hundred warriors were arrested by military officials and thirty-eight executed. In 1863 California Volunteers slaughtered more than two hundred men, women, and children in a Shoshone-Bannock village in Idaho. Meanwhile thousands of white settlers had been flooding into Colorado after gold was discovered in 1858, forcing Cheyenne and Arapaho Indians off their land. In 1864 officers at nearby Fort Lyon promised these Indians refuge at Sand Creek. Instead, Colonel John M. Chivington led his Third Colorado Calvary in a rampage that left 125 to 160 Indian men, women, and children dead. The Sand Creek Massacre ensured that white migrants traveling in the region would be subject to Indian attacks for years to come. At the same time, in the Southwest, the Navajo were defeated by U.S. troops and their Ute allies and forced into a four-hundred-mile trek to a reservation in New Mexico.

U.S. army officers considered "winning the West" one way to restore national unity once the Civil War ended. For Indian nations, the increased migration, expanded military presence, and sheer brutality they experienced in 1863 and 1864 boded ill for their future, whichever side won the Civil War.

The War Comes to an End.
As the defeat of the Confederacy loomed, the U.S. Congress finally considered abolishing slavery throughout the nation. With intense pressure from Frederick Douglass and other abolitionists, petitioning by the Women's National Loyal League, the valiant efforts of Ohio Congressman James Ashley, and President Lincoln's lobbying of wavering senators, Congress passed the **Thirteenth Amendment** to the U.S. Constitution on January 31, 1865. It prohibited slavery and involuntary servitude anywhere in the United States. Some northern and western states had already enacted laws to ease racial inequities. Ohio, California, and Illinois repealed statutes barring blacks from testifying in court and serving on juries. Then, in May 1865, Massachusetts passed the first comprehensive public-accommodations law in U.S. history, ensuring equal treatment in stores, schools, theaters, and other social spaces. Cities from San Francisco to Cincinnati and New York also desegregated their streetcars.

Richmond in Ruins, April 1865

This photograph shows the Richmond and Petersburg Railroad Depot following the capture of the Confederate capital by General Grant and his troops in April 1865. The black man sitting amid the devastation no doubt realized that Richmond's fall marked the defeat of the South. Library of Congress, Prints and Photographs Division, Washington, D.C. [LC-DIG-cwpb-02709]

Hoping to stave off defeat, southern leaders also began rethinking their racial policies. The Confederate House passed a law to recruit enslaved men into the army in February 1865, but the Senate defeated the measure. It was too late to make a difference anyway.

In early April 1865, with Sherman heading toward Raleigh, North Carolina, Grant captured Petersburg, Virginia and then drove Lee and his forces out of Richmond. Seasoned African American troops led the final assault on the city and were among the first Union soldiers to enter the Confederate capital. On April 9, after a brief engagement at Appomattox Court House, Virginia, Lee surrendered to Grant. Within hours, Lee's troops began heading home.

Yet the war was not quite over. Sporadic fighting continued until June 23, when Cherokee General Stand Watie finally surrendered to Union forces in Oklahoma. Union General Gordon Granger also confronted Confederate intransigence. In mid-June, he arrived in Galveston to assume command of the Texas District and discovered that African Americans were still being held as enslaved laborers. On June 19, he issued General Order #3, which informed the "people of Texas" that "all slaves are free." Blacks in Texas and elsewhere continue to celebrate **Juneteenth** as their Emancipation Day. For African Americans enslaved by the Creek, Cherokee, and other southeastern tribes battles over rights lasted far longer. Post–Civil War treaties promised them tribal citizenship as well as freedom. But as Indian nations with limited resources gained federal benefits, including hospitals, housing, and scholarship funds, tribal governments excluded black members. These issues continue to be litigated.

Northerners considered Lee's surrender the end of the war. Joyous celebrations erupted, and both blacks and whites hoped that the reunited nation would be stronger and more just. Their jubilation was short-lived. On April 14, Abraham Lincoln was shot at Ford's Theatre by a Confederate fanatic named John Wilkes Booth. The president died the next day, creating great uncertainty about how peace and national unity would be achieved.

Review & Relate

■ How did African Americans claim their freedom and what roles did they play in the defeat of the Confederacy? How did the war affect white racial views in the North?

■ How did the Union win the war against the Confederacy while defeating Indians in the West?

Conclusion: An Uncertain Future

The Civil War devastated and transformed the nation. The deadliest conflict in American history—some 600,000 to 750,000 Americans died in the war—the Civil War freed nearly 4 million Americans who had been enslaved. Soldiers who survived brought new experiences and ideas back to their families and communities. But many were also marked—like the formerly enslaved—by deep physical and emotional wounds. The war transformed the home front as well. Northern and southern women entered the labor force and the public arena in numbers never before imagined. The northern economy flourished and the South became more urbanized, but the Confederacy was left economically ruined. Meanwhile the federal government significantly expanded during the war. It also initiated programs, like the Homestead Act, that fueled migration, intensifying conflicts in the West that led to further devastation among Indian nations. Altogether, the Civil War dramatically accelerated the pace of economic, political, and social change, transforming American society both during the war and for decades afterward.

Still, the legacies of the war were far from certain in 1865. Wartime protests reflected a growing sense of class inequalities while the abolition of slavery highlighted ongoing racial disparities. Moreover, even in defeat, white Southerners honored Lee and other "heroes" of the "Lost Cause" with portraits, parades, and statues. Confederate women also worked tirelessly to preserve the memory of ordinary Confederate soldiers and of heroines like Rose O'Neal Greenhow, who had drowned in 1864 while returning from a mission to gain support in Europe.

Victorious Northerners celebrated wartime heroes as well but recognized that much still needed to be done. Frederick Douglass joined other former abolitionists in seeking to enfranchise African American men to secure their rights as free people, as black and white antislavery women headed south to open schools for freedpeople. Douglass and his allies had no illusions about the lengths to which many whites would go to protect their traditional privileges. And, indeed, many northern whites, exhausted by four years of war, hoped to leave the problems of slavery and secession behind. Others sought to benefit from rebuilding the South to ensure the nation's economic future. While most black and some white Southerners worked with Republicans to create a New South, far more whites embraced the Lost Cause legacy, which highlighted the valor of Confederate soldiers and denigrated the efforts of African Americans to build new lives in freedom. These competing visions—between Northerners and Southerners and within each group—would shape the uncertainties of peace in ways few could imagine at the end of the war.

Timeline of Events

Year	Event
1861	Fort Sumter attacked
	Enslaved workers declared "contraband"
	U.S. Sanitary Commission established
	Battle of Bull Run (Manassas)
	Confiscation Act passed
1862	Battle of Shiloh
	Conscription act signed in South
	Battle of Antietam
1863	Emancipation Proclamation signed
	Enrollment Act passed in North
	Bread riots in Richmond
	New York City draft riots
	Battle of Gettysburg
	Siege of Vicksburg
	Gettysburg Address
1864	Atlanta falls
	Sand Creek Massacre
	Sherman's "March to the Sea"
1865	More than 200,000 African Americans serve in the Union army and navy
	Field Order Number 15
	Thirteenth Amendment passed
	Lee surrenders to Grant
	Lincoln assassinated

Key Terms

Battle of Bull Run (Manassas), *431*

contraband, *432*

Battle of Shiloh, *436*

Battle of Antietam, *437*

Emancipation Proclamation, *437*

U.S. Sanitary Commission, *439*

Women's National Loyal League, *443*

Enrollment Act, *443*

Copperheads, *444*

Battle of Gettysburg, *446*

siege of Vicksburg, *446*

Gettysburg Address, *446*

refugee communities, *450*

hard war, *450*

Sherman's March to the Sea, *451*

Field Order Number 15, *452*

Thirteenth Amendment, *452*

Juneteenth, *453*

Review & Relate

1. What roles did American Indians, Mexicans and Tejanos, and African Americans play in supporting the Union or the Confederacy?

2. What events occurred to turn the Civil War into a war to end slavery?

3. In what ways did the war reshape economic priorities and gender roles in the North and the South?

4. How did the death toll, inflation, and social conflicts fuel dissent and protest in the North and the South?

5. How did African Americans claim their freedom and what roles did they play in the defeat of the Confederacy? How did the war affect white racial views in the North?

6. How did the Union win the war against the Confederacy while defeating Indians in the West?

Firsthand Accounts of the Civil War

▶ **Compare the different war experiences revealed here and consider how these experiences changed over the course of the war.**

Throughout the Civil War, soldiers and their families kept in close touch by writing letters. The volume of wartime correspondence was immense, with ninety thousand letters a day processed in the Union alone. Other men and women kept journals to record their experiences, which some used as the basis for published reminiscences years later. Soldiers' letters were especially important in capturing the daily experiences of war, from the boredom of encampments to the excitement or horrors of battle to concerns about their families back home (Source 13.7). Soldiers' letters also expressed their views on the causes of the war and their changing understandings of its meaning (Source 13.6). For black soldiers this often meant coming to terms with discrimination by the very government for which they were fighting (Source 13.9). Female volunteers provide another dramatic perspective on the war. Suzy King Taylor, who escaped from a Georgia plantation to work for the Union army, is the only former slave who published her memoirs of the war (Source 13.8). Far more women experienced the war from the home front, but for some Confederate women this meant living near army outposts and even prisoner-of-war camps (Source 13.10).

The letters and journals reprinted here, from both Northerners and Southerners, represent an array of experiences, including those of soldiers and civilians, women and men, blacks and whites. Covering nearly the whole expanse of the war, they help us trace transformations among soldiers, female volunteers, and civilians.

Source 13.6

Frederick Spooner | Letter to His Brother Henry, April 30, 1861

At the start of the war, many Northerners expected a quick victory, as evidenced in this letter written by seventeen-year-old Frederick Spooner to his older brother Henry. A native of Providence, Rhode Island, Frederick believed the South was weakened by its reliance on slavery. Perhaps inspired by these same beliefs, Henry Spooner enlisted in the Union army in 1862 and later practiced law in Rhode Island and served in the U.S. House of Representatives.

Dear Henry,

Your letter was received, and I now sit down in my shirt sleeves (as it is warm) to write in return.

For the last few weeks there has been great excitement here, and nothing has been thought of scarcely except that one subject which now received the undivided attention of the whole loyal North—war.

And well may war, so hideous and disgusting in itself receive such attention when carried on for such noble and just principles as in the present case.

Traitors have begun the conflict, let us continue and end it. Let us settle it now, once and for all.

Let us settle it, even if the whole South has to be made one common graveyard, and their cotton soaked in blood. Let us do it *now* while the whole

North is aroused from the inactivity and apparent laziness in which it has been so long.

There are plenty of men, an abundance of money, and a military enthusiasm never before known in the annals of history, all of which combined will do the work nice and clean, and if need be will wipe out that palmetto, pelican, rattlesnake region entirely. The holy cause in which our volunteers are enlisted will urge them on to almost superhuman exertions. The South *may* be courageous but I doubt it, they can *gas* and *hag* [complain and bluster] first rate; they can lie and steal to perfection, but I really do believe that they cannot fight. . . .

But granting them to be brave (which I don't believe can be proven) they have no chance to overturn this government. They haven't the resources, the "almighty dollar," that powerful ally, or formidable enemy—is against them. They have no money—their property has legs and will be continually disappearing.

They have prospered dealing in human flesh—let them now take the results of it.

They have had what *they* consider the *blessings* of slavery—let them now receive the *curses* of it.

They must be put down, conquered, and thoroughly subdued if need be. . . . The fifteen weak states of the South can stand no chance against the nineteen powerful states of the North. . . .

When I began I did not intend to give a lecture or write a composition on the "crisis," . . . but unconsciously I got on the all-absorbing topic at the very commencement, and it was hard work to let go of it.

There hasn't been much studying lately, and it is very hard work to think or write concerning any other subject than that on which I've paused so long.

So therefore excuse my "crisis" beginning.

Source: Nina Silber and Mary Beth Sievens, eds., *Yankee Correspondence: Civil War Letters between New England Soldiers and the Home Front* (Charlottesville: University Press of Virginia, 1996), 55–56.

Source 13.7

John Hines | Letter to His Parents, April 22, 1862

Confederate soldier John Hines describes the Battle of Shiloh in southwestern Tennessee in this letter written to his parents in Kentucky. The bloodiest battle up to that point in the war, Shiloh was also Hines's first combat experience. As was common for soldiers on both sides of the conflict, Hines's early enthusiasm for the war and his opinion of the enemy changed with his first taste of battle.

Dear Ma and G. Pa

. . . I was in the battle of Shiloh from beginning to end. It is said to have been the hardest fought battle ever fought on this continent. Persons who were in the battles of Manassas [Bull Run] and Ft. Donelson say they were skirmishes in comparison. . . .

Our squadron was ordered close to the federal [Union] lines on Saturday evening. We stopped close enough to hear their drums beating. We were very tired and hungry. Some of the men not having et [eaten] for 36 hours. I gave a teamster 50 cents for a biscuit. Tied my horse close to me and laid down without taking off boots or pistols and slept soundly until just at dawn the loud peal of some half dozen cannons aroused us. In a few moments we were in our saddles, overcoats and extra equipment lashed to our saddles. In our shirt sleeves, we sat on our horses examining our arms, ready for the coming fray, for we knew we would give the enemy battle if they would stand.

The increased roaring of artillery and an occasional ambulance bearing off wounded soldiers told that, as we say in camp, the ball was open. Before the sun was up we were marching to the scene of action, which was perhaps a mile off. We had not marched very far before we came upon our line of infantry. For three miles in one unbroken line stood our troops, their fixed bayonets glistening in the new sunbeams, for the sun was just coming over the top of a small elevation.

Almost every hill now on both sides looked like a volcano, for the deep mouthed cannon were roaring on every side. Soon the rattle of musketry announced that our vanguard had found the foe. The dark line of men now moved quickly in. After minutes more the volleys of musketry announced that they too had entered the bloody arena. It was really a grand scene now: you could not distinguish a musket shot now, it was one continual roar like the rushing of a storm. . . . A shell or cannonball would tear some of your comrades to pieces and a person could not tell whose turn it might be next.

Being mounted and ordered to different places during the day, I had an opportunity to see everything that happened almost and I can assure you that a battlefield is far from being a pleasant place, laying aside the dangers of being hurt, because you can't get out of hearing the groans of the dying or out of sight of the dead. It seemed to me like my acquaintances were always lying in the most auspicious places. Turn what way we might I could find some ghastly looking face that perhaps an hour ago I had seen rushing to the contest with a smile on his face. . . .

We have again returned to camp which is now outside of the former federal lines and are resting quietly. I've a good slice of cheese and a can of oysters which I took out of a federal tent before setting fire to it. I have nothing to do but think over what has happened in the last few days. . . .

Your affectionate son,
J. H. Hines

Source: Rod Gragg, ed., *The Illustrated Confederate Reader* (New York: HarperCollins, 1989), 99–100.

Suzy King Taylor | Caring for the Thirty-third U.S. Colored Troops, 1863

In 1862 Suzy King Taylor escaped with other family members to a contraband camp on the Sea Islands. There she married Edward King, a black noncommissioned officer with the Thirty-third U.S. Colored Troops. Since black soldiers did not get their full pay for more than a year, many wives worked for the army as well. Suzy King was hired as a laundress but also served as a teacher, nurse, and cook. This selection is from a memoir of her experiences published in 1902.

Fort Wagner being only a mile from our camp, I went there two or three times a week, and would go up on the ramparts to watch the gunners send their shells into Charleston. . . . Outside of the fort were many skulls lying about. . . . The comrades and I would have quite a debate as to which side the men fought on. . . . They were a gruesome sight, those fleshless heads and grinning jaws, but by this time I had become accustomed to worse things. . . .

It seems strange how our aversion to seeing suffering is overcome in time of war,—how we are able to see the most sickening sights, such as men with their limbs blown off and mangled by the deadly shells without a shudder; and instead of turning away, how we hurry to assist in alleviating their pain, bind up their wounds, and press cool water to their parched lips. . . .

Finally orders were received to prepare to take Fort Gregg. . . .

About four o'clock, July 2, the charge was made. The firing could be plainly heard in camp. . . . When the wounded arrived, or rather began to arrive, the first one brought was Samuel Anderson of our company. He was badly wounded. Then others of our boys, some with their legs off, arm gone, foot off, and wounds of all kinds imaginable. . . .

My work now began. I gave my assistance to alleviate their sufferings. I asked the doctor of the hospital what I could get for them to eat. . . . I had a few cans of condensed milk and some turtle eggs, so I thought I would try to make some custard. . . . This I carried to the men, who enjoyed it very much. My services were given at all times for the comfort of these men. . . . I was enrolled as company laundress, but I did very little of it, because . . . I was employed all the time doing something for the officers and comrades.

Source: Suzy King Taylor, *Reminiscences of my Life in Camp with the 33rd United States Colored Troops, Late 1st S.C. Volunteers* (Boston: By the Author, 1902).

Thomas Freeman | Letter to His Brother-in-Law, March 26, 1864

The Massachusetts Fifty-fourth Colored Infantry, one of the Union's first black units, was recognized for its valor and heroism. The unit was also known for protesting the mistreatment of black soldiers, including a regiment-wide pay boycott to demand equal salaries for black and white soldiers. In this letter to his brother-in-law, Thomas Freeman of Worcester, Massachusetts echoes black soldiers' discontent with discrimination and poor treatment.

Jacksonville, Florida
March 26, 1864

Dear William

I will devote some spare moments I have in writing you a few lines which I hope may find you and all your family the same, also all of my many Friends in Worcester. Since the Regiment Departure from Morris Island I have enjoyed the best of health. . . . The Regiment in general are in Good Health but in Low Spirits and no reason why for they have all to a man done there duty as a soldier. It is 1 year the 1st Day of April since I enlisted and there is men here in the regiment that have been in Enlisted 13 Months and have never received one cent But there bounty and they more or less have family, and 2 thirds have never received any State Aid, and how do you think men can feel to do there duty as Soldiers, but let me say we are not Soldiers but Labourers working for Uncle Sam for nothing but our board and clothes. . . . We never can be Elevated in this country while such rascality is Performed. Slavery with all its horrorrs can not Equalise this for it is nothing but work from morning till night Building Batteries, Hauling Guns, Cleaning Bricks, clearing up land for other Regiments to settle on and if a Man Says he is sick it is the Doctors Priveledge to say yes or no. If you cannot work then you are sent to the Guard House Bucked Gagged and stay so till they see fit to relieve You and if you dont like that some white man will Give you a crack over the Head with his sword. Now do you call this Equality? If so God help such

Equality. . . . I want You to consult some counsel in Relation to the Matter and see if a man could not sue for his Discharge . . . and let me know immiedeitely for I am tired of such treatment. Please answer as soon as you can and Oblidge Yours

   T. D. Freeman

Source: Nina Silber and Mary Beth Sievens, eds., *Yankee Correspondence: Civil War Letters between New England Soldiers and the Home Front* (Charlottesville: University Press of Virginia, 1996), 47–48.

Eliza Frances Andrews | On Union Prisoners of War, 1865

Eliza Frances Andrews was the daughter of a Georgia planter and a staunch Confederate. In her early twenties when the Civil War began, she kept a journal that included reports on her visits to various army camps. In January 1865 she and a friend visited Captain Bonham at a local fort and met a Yankee prisoner, Peter Louis, who had been transferred from Andersonville Prison because of his skills as a shoemaker. Some 13,000 Union soldiers died at Andersonville.

expect the poor Yank [Peter Louis] is glad to get away from Anderson on any terms. Although matters have improved somewhat with the cool weather, the tales that are told of the condition of things there last summer are appalling. Mrs. Brisbane heard all about it from Father Hamilton, a Roman Catholic priest from Macon, who has been working like a good Samaritan in those dens of filth and misery. It is a shame to us Protestants that we have let a Roman Catholic get so far ahead of us in this work of charity and mercy. Mrs. Brisbane says Father Hamilton told her that during the summer the wretched prisoners burrowed in the ground like moles to protect themselves from the sun. It was not safe to give them material to build shanties as they might use it for clubs to overcome the guards. These underground huts, he said, were alive with vermin and stank like charnel [burial] houses. Many of the prisoners were stark naked, having not so much as a shirt to their backs. . . . Father Hamilton said that at one time the prisoners died at a rate of 150 a day. . . . Dysentery was the most fatal disease. . . . My heart aches for the poor wretches, Yankees though they are, and I am afraid God will suffer some terrible retribution to fall upon us for letting such things happen. . . . And yet, what can we do? The Yankees are really more to blame than we, for they won't exchange these prisoners, and our poor, hard-pressed Confederacy had not the means to provide for them when our own soldiers are starving in the field. Oh, what a horrible thing war is when stripped of all its pomp and circumstance!

Source: Eliza Frances Andrews, *The War-Time Journal of a Georgia Girl, 1864–1865* (New York: D. Appleton, 1908), 76–79.

Interpret the Evidence

1. According to these sources, what accounts for the early popular support for the war and when and where does that support appear to diminish?

2. Compare the letters from soldiers Fred Spooner (Source 13.6), John Hines (Source 13.7), and Thomas Freeman (Source 13.9). How did each view the enemy and the causes of the war?

3. In what ways do Suzy King Taylor (Source 13.8) and Eliza Frances Andrews (Source 13.10) defy or confirm contemporary gender roles? How does their race and their status shape these roles?

4. How do the experiences of Suzy King Taylor and Thomas Freeman (Sources 13.8 and 13.9) compare to those of the white writers (Sources 13.6, 13.7, and 13.10)?

Put It in Context

In what ways do these personal sources complement or challenge the more well-known political and military history of the Civil War?

Emancipation and Reconstruction

1863–1877

Window to the Past

Sharecropping Agreement, 1870

After the end of slavery, plantation owners needed to find new ways to work their land and formerly enslaved people needed to find employment. As a result, freedpeople sought to enter into sharecropping agreements, such as the one shown here, to farm on behalf of landowners because they lacked money and tools and wanted to farm their own land. However, despite their best efforts, they usually found themselves in debt to the white planter-merchants who controlled the accounts and sold them supplies. ▶ **To learn more about this primary source, see Source 14.8 on page 492.**

Alabama Department of Archives and History, Montgomery, Alabama

After reading this chapter you will be able to:

- Describe the challenges newly freed African Americans faced and how they responded to them.

- Analyze the influence of the president and Congress on Reconstruction policy and evaluate the successes and shortcomings of the policies they enacted.

- Evaluate the changes that took place in the society and economy of the South during Reconstruction.

- Explain how and why Reconstruction came to an end by the mid-1870s.

Comparing American Histories

Jefferson Franklin Long spent his life improving himself and the lives of others of his race. Born enslaved in Alabama in 1836, Long showed great resourcefulness in profiting from the limited opportunities available to him. His master, a tailor who moved his family to Georgia, taught him the trade, but Long taught himself to read and write. When the Civil War ended, he opened a tailor shop in Macon, Georgia. His business success allowed him to venture into Republican Party politics. Elected as Georgia's first black congressman in 1870, Long fought for the political rights of freed slaves. In his first appearance on the House floor, he opposed a bill that would allow former Confederate officials to return to Congress, noting that many belonged to secret societies, such as the Ku Klux Klan, that

intimidated black citizens. Despite his pleas, the measure passed, and Long decided not to run for reelection.

By the mid-1880s, Long had become disillusioned with the ability of black Georgians to achieve their objectives via electoral politics. Instead, he counseled African Americans to turn to institution building as the best hope for social and economic advancement. Long helped found the Union Brotherhood Lodge, a black mutual aid society with branches throughout central Georgia, which provided social and economic services for its members. He died in 1901, as political disfranchisement and racial segregation swept through Georgia and the rest of the South.

Jefferson Long and **Andrew Johnson** shared many characteristics, but their views on race could not have been more different. Whereas Long fought for the right of self-determination for African Americans, Johnson believed that whites alone should govern. Born in 1808 in Raleigh, North Carolina, Johnson grew up in poverty. At the age of thirteen or fourteen, he became a tailor's apprentice and, after moving to Tennessee in 1826, like Long, opened a tailor shop. The following year, Johnson married and began to prosper, purchasing a farm and a small number of enslaved workers.

As he made his mark in Greenville, Tennessee, Johnson became active in Democratic Party politics. A social and political outsider, Johnson gained support by championing the rights of workers and small farmers against the power of the southern aristocracy. Political success followed, and by the time the Civil War broke out, he was a U.S. senator.

When the Civil War erupted, Johnson remained loyal to the Union even after Tennessee seceded in 1861. President Abraham Lincoln rewarded Johnson by appointing him as military governor of Tennessee. In 1864 the Republican Lincoln chose the Democrat Johnson to run with him as vice president. Less than six weeks after their inauguration in March 1865, Johnson became president upon Lincoln's assassination.

Fate placed Reconstruction in the hands of Andrew Johnson. The brutal Civil War had come to a close, but the hard work of reunion remained. Toward this end, President Johnson oversaw the

(left) **Jefferson Franklin Long** Library of Congress, Prints and Photographs Division, Washington, D.C. [LC-DIG-cwpbh-00556]

(right) **Andrew Johnson** Library of Congress, Prints and Photographs Division, Washington, D.C. [LC-USZ62-13017] reestablishment of state governments in the former Confederate states. Even as southern states passed measures that restricted black civil and political rights, President Johnson declared them fit for

rejoining the Union. Most Northerners reached a different conclusion. Having won the bloody war, they feared losing the peace to Johnson and the defeated South. ■

Comparing the American histories of Andrew Johnson and Jefferson Long highlights hard-fought battles to determine the fate of the postwar South and the meaning of freedom for newly emancipated African Americans. Former enslaved people sought to reunite their families, obtain land, and gain an education. President Johnson rejected their pleas for assistance to fulfill these aims. However, Congress passed laws to ensure civil rights and extend the vote to African American men, although African American women, like white women, remained disfranchised. In the South, whites attempted to restore their economic and political power over African Americans by resorting to intimidation and violence. By 1877, they succeeded in bringing Reconstruction to an end with the consent of the federal government.

Emancipation

Even before the war came to a close, Reconstruction had begun on a small scale. During the Civil War, blacks remaining in Union-occupied areas, such as the South Carolina Sea Islands, gained some experience with freedom. When Union troops arrived, most southern whites fled, but enslaved workers chose to stay on the land. Some farmed for themselves, but most worked for northern whites who moved south to demonstrate the profitability of free black labor. After the war, however, former plantation owners returned. Rather than work for these whites, freedpeople preferred to establish their own farms. If forced to hire themselves out, they insisted on negotiating the terms of their employment. Wives and mothers often refused to labor for whites at all in favor of caring for their own families. These conflicts reflected the priorities that would shape the actions of freedpeople across the South in the immediate aftermath of the war. For freedom to be meaningful, it had to include economic independence, the power to make family decisions, and the right to control some community decisions.

African Americans Embrace Freedom.

When U.S. troops arrived in Richmond, Virginia in April 1865, the city's enslaved population knew that freedom was, finally, theirs. Four days after Union troops arrived, 1,500 African Americans, including a large number of soldiers, packed First African Baptist, the largest of the city's black churches. During the singing of the hymn "Jesus My All to Heaven Is Gone," they raised their voices at the line "This is the way I long have sought." As news of the Confederacy's defeat spread, newly freed African Americans across the South experienced similar emotions. Many years later, Houston H. Holloway, an enslaved Georgian who had been sold three times before he was twenty years old, recalled the day of emancipation: "I felt like a bird out a cage. Amen. Amen, Amen. I could hardly ask to feel any better than I did that day."

For southern whites, however, the end of the war brought fear, humiliation, and uncertainty. From their perspective, the jubilation of former slaves poured salt in their wounds. In many areas, blacks celebrated their freedom under the protection of Union soldiers.

When the army moved out, freedpeople suffered deeply for their enthusiasm. Whites beat, whipped, raped, and shot blacks who they felt had been too joyous in their celebration or too helpful to the Yankee invaders. As one North Carolina freedman testified, the Yankees "tol' us we were free," but once the army left, the planters "would get cruel to the slaves if they acted like they were free."

Newly freed blacks also faced less visible dangers. During the 1860s, disease swept through the South and through the contraband camps that housed many former slaves; widespread malnutrition and poor housing heightened the problem. A smallpox epidemic that spread south from Washington, D.C. killed more than sixty thousand freedpeople.

Despite the dangers, southern blacks eagerly pursued emancipation. They moved; they married; they attended school; they demanded wages; they refused to work for whites; they gathered together their families; they created black churches and civic associations; they held political meetings. Sometimes, black women and men acted on their own, pooling their resources to advance their freedom. At other times, they received help from private organizations — particularly northern missionary and educational associations — staffed mostly by former abolitionists, free blacks, and evangelical Christians.

Emancipated slaves also called on federal agencies for assistance and support. The most important of these agencies was the newly formed Bureau of Refugees, Freedmen, and Abandoned Lands, popularly known as the **Freedmen's Bureau**. Created by Congress in 1865 and signed into law by President Lincoln, the bureau provided ex-slaves with economic and legal resources. The Freedmen's Bureau also aided many freedpeople in achieving one of their primary goals: obtaining land. A South Carolina freedman summed up the feeling of the newly emancipated. "Give us our own land and we take care of ourselves," he remarked. "But without land, the old masters can hire or starve us, as they please." During the last years of the war, the federal government had distributed to freedpeople around 400,000 acres of abandoned land from the South Carolina Sea Islands to Florida. Immediately after hostilities ceased, the Freedmen's Bureau made available hundreds of thousands of additional acres to recently emancipated slaves.

> **Explore ▶**
>
> See Source 14.1 for freedpeople's views about ownership of land.

Reuniting Families Torn Apart by Slavery.

The first priority for many newly freed blacks was to reunite families torn apart by slavery. Men and women traveled across the South to find family members. Well into the 1870s and 1880s, parents ran advertisements in newly established black newspapers, providing what information they knew about their children's whereabouts and asking for assistance in finding them. Milly Johnson wrote to the Freedmen's Bureau in March 1867, after failing to locate the five children she had lost under slavery. She finally located three of them, but any chance of discovering the whereabouts of the other two disappeared because the records of the slave trader who purchased them burned during the war. Despite such obstacles, thousands of formerly enslaved children were reunited with their parents in the 1870s.

Husbands and wives, or those who considered themselves as such despite the absence of legal marriage under slavery, also searched for each other. Those who lived on nearby plantations could live together for the first time. Those whose spouse had been sold to distant plantations had a more difficult time. They wrote (or had letters written on their behalf) to relatives and friends who had been sold with their mate; sought assistance from

Guided Primary Source Analysis

Freedpeople Petition for Land, 1865

A committee of the formerly enslaved in Edisto Island, South Carolina wrote President Johnson requesting that they be allowed to purchase land promised them by the government during the Civil War. The president intended to restore the properties to the former rebel landholders and did not respond to the black petitioners.

Source 14.1

Edisto Island S.C. Oct 28th 1865.

. . . Here is where secession was born and Nurtured Here is were we have toiled nearly all Our lives as slaves and were treated like dumb Driven cattle, This is our home, we have made These lands what they are. we were the only true and Loyal people that were found in posession of these Lands. we have been always ready to strike for Liberty and humanity yea to fight if needs be To preserve this glorious union. Shall not we who Are freedman and have been always true to this Union have the same rights as are enjoyed by Others? Have we broken any Law of these United States? Have we forfieted our rights of property In Land?—If not then! are not our rights as A free people and good citizens of these United States To be considered before the rights of those who were Found in rebellion against this good and just Government.

We have been encouraged by government to take up these lands in small tracts, receiving Certificates of the same—we have thus far Taken Sixteen thousand (16000) acres of Land here on This Island. We are ready to pay for this land When Government calls for it and now after What has been done will the good and just government take from us all this right and make us Subject to the will of those who have cheated and Oppressed us for many years God Forbid! We the freedmen of this Island and of the State of South Carolina–Do therefore petition to you as the President of these United States, that some provisions be made by which Every colored man can purchase land. and Hold it as his own. . . .

In behalf of the Freedmen Committee
Henry Bram. Ishmael. Moultrie. yates. Sampson.

Source: Henry Bram et al. to the President of these United States, 28 Oct. 1865, filed as P-27 1865, Letters Received, series 15, Washington Headquarters, Bureau of Refugees, Freedmen, & Abandoned Lands, Record Group 105, National Archives.

Why do the freedpeople believe their request justified?

Why do they think the former landowners do not deserve the land?

How does this show the importance of landownership to them?

Put It in Context

Why was landownership so important to newly freed blacks?

Winslow Homer, *A Visit from the Old Mistress*, 1876   Civil War correspondent and artist Winslow Homer visited Virginia in the mid-1870s and visually captured the tensions existing between freedpeople and former owners. Here, a former mistress visits the home of three black women. Although the house is humble, one woman refuses to stand for the "old mistress" and the other two, one holding a freeborn child, eye her warily. Smithsonian American Art Museum, Washington, D.C./Art Resource, NY

government officials, churches, and even their former masters; and traveled to areas where they thought their spouse might reside.

These searches were complicated by long years of separation and the lack of any legal standing for slave marriages. In 1866 Philip Grey, a Virginia freedman, located his wife, Willie Ann, and their daughter Maria, who had been sold away to Kentucky years before. Willie Ann was eager to reunite with her husband, but in the years since being sold, she had remarried and borne three children. Her second husband had joined the Union army and was killed in battle. When Willie Ann wrote to Philip in April 1866, she explained her new circumstances, concluding: "If you love me you will love my children and you will have to promise me that you will provide for them all as well as if they were your own. . . . I know that I have lived with you and loved you then and love you still."

Most black spouses who found each other sought to legalize their relationship. A superintendent for marriages for the Freedmen's Bureau in northern Virginia reported that he gave out seventy-nine marriage certificates on a single day in May 1866. In another case, four couples went right from the fields to a local schoolhouse, still dressed in their work clothes, where a parson married them.

Of course, some of the formerly enslaved hoped that freedom would allow them to leave unhappy relationships. Having never been married under the law, couples could simply separate and move on. Complications arose, however, if they had children. In Lake City, Florida in 1866, a Freedmen's Bureau agent asked his superiors for advice on how to deal with Madison Day and Maria Richards. They refused to legalize the relationship forced on them under slavery, but both sought custody of their three children. As with white couples in the mid-nineteenth century, the father was granted custody on the assumption that he had the best chance of providing for the children financially.

As was the custom and law of that time, wives were subordinate to their husbands. One North Carolina freedman said of his wife, "I consider her my property." This rankled Frances Gage, an antislavery and women's rights activist, who declared, "You give us a nominal freedom, but you leave us under the heel of our husbands." Yet there was an important trade-off that black women hoped to receive from this patriarchal arrangement: protection for themselves and their children.

Freedom to Learn. Seeking land and reuniting families were only two of the many ways that southern blacks proclaimed their freedom. Learning to read and write was another. The desire to learn was all but universal. Enslaved persons had been forbidden to read and write. With emancipation they pursued what had been denied them. A newly liberated father in Mississippi proclaimed, "If I nebber does nothing more while I live, I shall give my children a chance to go to school, for I considers education [the] next best ting to liberty."

A variety of organizations opened schools for formerly enslaved persons during the 1860s and 1870s. By 1870 nearly a quarter million blacks were attending one of the 4,300 schools established by the Freedmen's Bureau. Black and white churches and missionary societies sent hundreds of teachers, black and white, into the South to establish schools in former plantation areas. Their attitudes were often paternalistic and the schools were segregated, but the institutions they founded offered important educational resources for African Americans.

Parents worked hard to keep their children in school during the day. As children gained the rudiments of education, they passed on their knowledge to parents and older siblings whose jobs prevented them from attending school. Still, many adult freedpeople insisted on getting a bit of education for themselves. In New Bern, North Carolina, where many blacks labored until eight o'clock at night, a teacher reported that they then spent at least an hour "in earnest application to study."

Freedpeople sought education for a variety of reasons. Some viewed it as a sign of liberation. Others knew the importance of reading the labor contracts they signed if they were ever to challenge exploitation by whites. Some freedpeople were eager to correspond with relatives, others to read the Bible. Growing numbers hoped to participate in politics, particularly the public meetings organized by blacks in cities across the South. When such gatherings set priorities for the future, the establishment of public schools was high on the list.

Despite the enthusiasm of blacks and the efforts of the federal government and private agencies, schooling remained severely limited throughout the South. A shortage of teachers and of funding kept enrollments low among blacks and whites alike. The isolation of black farm families and the difficulties in eking out a living limited the resources available for education. By 1880, only about a quarter of African Americans were literate.

Freedmen's Bureau School   This photograph of a one-room Freedmen's Bureau school in North Carolina in the late 1860s shows the large number and diverse ages of students who sought to obtain an education following emancipation. The teachers included white and black northern women sent by missionary and reform organizations as well as southern black women who had already received some education. *Granger*

Freedom to Worship and the Leadership Role of Black Churches.

One of the constant concerns freedpeople expressed was the desire to read the Bible and interpret it for themselves. A few black congregations had existed under slavery, but most slaves were forced to listen to white preachers who claimed that God created slavery.

From the moment of emancipation, freedpeople gathered at churches to celebrate community events. Black Methodist and Baptist congregations spread rapidly across the South following the Civil War. In these churches, African Americans were no longer forced to sit in the back benches or punished for moral infractions defined by white masters. Now blacks invested community resources in their own religious institutions where they filled the pews, hired the preachers, and selected boards of deacons and elders. Churches were the largest structures available to freedpeople in many communities and thus were used by a variety of community organizations. They often served as schools and hosted picnics, dances, weddings, funerals, festivals, and other events that brought blacks together. Church leaders also often served as arbiters of community standards of morality.

In the early years of emancipation black churches also served as important sites for political organizing. Some black ministers worried that political concerns would overwhelm spiritual devotions. Others agreed with the Reverend Charles H. Pearce of Florida, who declared, "A man in this State cannot do his whole duty as a minister except he looks out for the political interests of his people." Whatever the views of ministers, black churches were among the few places where African Americans could express their political views free from white interference.

Review & Relate

▪ What were freedpeople's highest priorities in the years immediately following the Civil War? Why?

▪ How did freedpeople define freedom? What steps did they take to make freedom real for themselves and their children?

National Reconstruction

Presidents Abraham Lincoln and Andrew Johnson viewed Reconstruction as a process of national reconciliation. They sketched out terms by which the former Confederate states could reclaim their political representation in the nation without serious penalties. Congressional Republicans, however, had a more thoroughgoing reconstruction in mind. Like many African Americans, Republican congressional leaders expected the South to extend constitutional rights to the freedmen and to provide them with the political and economic resources to sustain their freedom. Over the next decade, these competing visions of Reconstruction played out in hard-fought and tumultuous battles over the meaning of the South's defeat and the emancipation of blacks.

Abraham Lincoln Plans for Reunification.

In December 1863, even as battles continued, President Lincoln issued a **Proclamation of Amnesty and Reconstruction**, outlining his vision of the postwar world. Lincoln declared that defeated states would have to accept the abolition of slavery, but then new governments could be formed when 10 percent of those eligible to vote in 1860 (which in practice meant white southern men but not blacks) swore an oath of allegiance to the United States. Lincoln's plan granted amnesty to all but the highest-ranking Confederate officials, and the restored voters in each state would elect members to a constitutional convention and representatives to take their seats in Congress. In the next year and a half, Arkansas, Louisiana, and Tennessee — which were already under Union control — reestablished their governments under Lincoln's conciliatory "Ten Percent Plan."

Republicans in Congress had other ideas. Radical Republicans argued that the Confederate states should be treated as "conquered provinces" subject to congressional supervision. In 1864 Congress passed the Wade-Davis bill, which established much higher barriers for readmission to the Union than did Lincoln's plan. For instance, the Wade-Davis bill substituted 50 percent of voters for the president's 10 percent requirement. Lincoln put a stop to this harsher proposal by using a pocket veto — refusing to sign it within ten days of Congress's adjournment.

Although Lincoln and congressional Republicans disagreed about many aspects of postwar policy, Lincoln was flexible, and his actions mirrored his desire both to heal the Union and to help southern blacks. For example, the president supported the **Thirteenth Amendment**, abolishing slavery, which passed Congress in January 1865 and was sent to the states for ratification. In March 1865, Lincoln signed the law to create the Freedmen's Bureau. That same month, the president expressed his sincere wish for reconciliation between the North and the South. "With malice toward none, with charity for all," Lincoln declared in his second inaugural address, "let us strive on to finish the work . . . to bind up the nation's wounds." Lincoln would not, however, have the opportunity to implement his approach to Reconstruction. When he was assassinated in April 1865, it fell to Andrew Johnson, a very different sort of politician, to lead the country through the process of reintegration.

Andrew Johnson and Presidential Reconstruction.

The nation needed a president who could transmit northern desires to the South with clarity and conviction and ensure that they were carried out. Instead, the nation got a president who substituted his own aims for those of the North, refused to engage in meaningful compromise, and misled the South into believing that he could achieve restoration quickly. In the 1864 election, Lincoln chose Johnson, a southern Democrat, as his running mate in a thinly veiled effort to attract border-state voters. The vice presidency was normally an inconsequential role, so it mattered little to Lincoln that Johnson was out of step with many Republican Party positions.

As president, however, Johnson's views took on profound importance. Born into rural poverty, Johnson had no sympathy for the southern aristocracy. Yet he had been a slave owner, so his political opposition to slavery was not rooted in moral convictions. Instead, it sprang from the belief that slavery gave plantation owners inordinate power and wealth, which came at the expense of the majority of white Southerners, who owned no slaves. Johnson saw emancipation as a means to "break down an odious and dangerous [planter] aristocracy," not to empower blacks. Consequently, he was unconcerned with the fate of African Americans in the postwar South. Six months after taking office, President Johnson rescinded the wartime order to distribute confiscated land to freedpeople in the Sea Islands. He saw no reason to punish the Confederacy's leaders, because he believed that the end of slavery would doom the southern aristocracy. He hoped to bring the South back into the Union as quickly as possible and then let Southerners take care of their own affairs.

Johnson's views, combined with a lack of political savvy and skill, ensured his inability to work constructively with congressional Republicans, even the moderates who constituted the majority. Moderate Republicans shared the prevalent belief of their time that blacks were inferior to whites, but they argued that the federal government needed to protect the enslaved people who were newly emancipated. Senator Lyman Trumbull of Illinois, for example, warned that without national legislation, ex-slaves would "be tyrannized over, abused, and virtually reenslaved." The moderates expected southern states, where 90 percent of African Americans lived, to extend basic civil rights to the freedpeople, including equal protection, due process of law, and the right to work and hold property.

Nearly all Republicans shared these positions, but the Radical wing of the party wanted to go further. Led by Senator Charles Sumner of Massachusetts and Congressman Thaddeus Stevens of Pennsylvania, this small but influential group advocated suffrage, that is voting rights, for African American men as well as the redistribution of southern plantation lands to the formerly enslaved. Stevens called on the federal government to provide freedpeople "a homestead of forty acres of land," which would give them some measure of autonomy. These efforts failed, and the Republican Party proved unable to pass a comprehensive land distribution program that enabled freed blacks to gain economic independence. Nonetheless, whatever disagreements between Radicals and moderates, all Republicans believed that Congress should have a strong voice in determining the fate of the former

Mourning at Stonewall Jackson's Gravesite, 1866

Many Northerners were concerned that the defeat of the Confederacy did not lessen white Southerners' devotion to the "Lost Cause" or the heroism of soldiers who fought to maintain a society based on the domination of African Americans. Women, who led the efforts to memorialize Confederate soldiers, are shown at the gravesite of General Stonewall Jackson in Lexington, Virginia. Virginia Military Institute Archives

Confederate states. From May to December 1865, with Congress out of session, they waited to see what Johnson's restoration plan would produce, ready to assert themselves if his policies deviated too much from their own.

At first, it seemed as if Johnson would proceed as they hoped. He appointed provisional governors to convene new state constitutional conventions and urged these conventions to ratify the Thirteenth Amendment, abolishing slavery, and revoke the states' ordinances of secession. He also allowed the majority of white Southerners to obtain amnesty and a pardon by swearing their loyalty to the U.S. Constitution, but he required those who had held more than $20,000 of taxable property—the members of the southern aristocracy—to petition him for a special pardon to restore their rights. Republicans expected him to be harsh in dealing with his former political foes. Instead, Johnson relished the reversal of roles that put members of the southern elite at his mercy. As the once prominent petitioners paraded before him, the president granted almost all of their requests for pardons.

By the time Congress convened in December 1865, Johnson was satisfied that the southern states had fulfilled his requirements for restoration. Moderate and Radical Republicans disagreed, seeing few signs of change or contrition in the South. Mississippi, for example, rejected ratification of the Thirteenth Amendment. As a result of Johnson's liberal pardon policy, many former leaders of the Confederacy won election to state constitutional conventions and to Congress. Indeed, Georgians elected Confederate vice president Alexander H. Stephens to the U.S. Senate. As one white Mississippian candidly forecast, "Our negroes . . . will learn that freedom and independence are different things."

Indeed they did. Far from providing freedpeople with basic civil rights, the southern states passed a variety of **black codes** intended to reduce African Americans to a condition as close to slavery as possible. Some laws prohibited blacks from bearing arms; others outlawed intermarriage and excluded blacks from serving on juries. The codes also made it difficult for blacks to leave plantations unless they proved they could support themselves. Other provisions sought to reduce the independence of black families. They empowered southern courts to assign black children to white employers without parental consent. Echoing the slave past, laws like these were designed to ensure that white landowners had a supply of cheap black labor despite the Thirteenth Amendment abolishing slavery.

Northerners viewed this situation with alarm. In their eyes, the postwar South looked very similar to the Old South, with a few cosmetic adjustments. If the black codes prevailed, one Republican proclaimed, "then I demand to know of what practical value is the amendment abolishing slavery?" Others wondered what their wartime sacrifices meant if the South admitted no mistakes, was led by the same people, and continued to oppress its black inhabitants. **See Primary Source Project 14: Testing and Contesting Freedom, page 490.**

Johnson and Congressional Resistance.

Faced with growing opposition in the North, Johnson stubbornly held his ground. He insisted that the southern states had followed his plan and were entitled to resume their representation in Congress. Republicans objected, and in December 1865 they barred the admission of southern lawmakers. But Johnson refused to compromise. In January 1866, the president rejected a bill passed by Congress to extend the life of the Freedmen's Bureau for two years. A few months later, he vetoed the Civil Rights Act, which Congress had passed to protect freedpeople from the restrictions placed on them by the black codes. These bills represented a consensus among moderate and Radical Republicans on the federal government's responsibility toward the formerly enslaved.

Johnson justified his vetoes on both constitutional and personal grounds. He and other Democrats contended that so long as Congress refused to admit southern representatives, it could not legally pass laws affecting the South. The president also condemned the Freedmen's Bureau bill because it infringed on the right of states to handle internal affairs such as education and economic policies. Johnson's vetoes exposed his racism and his lifelong belief that the evil of slavery lay in the harm it did to poor whites, not to enslaved blacks. Johnson argued that the bills he vetoed discriminated against whites, who would receive no benefits under them, and thus put whites at a disadvantage with blacks receiving government assistance. Johnson's private secretary reported in his diary, "The president has at times exhibited a morbid distress and feeling against the Negroes."

Johnson's actions united moderates and Radicals against him. In April 1866, Congress repassed both the Freedmen's Bureau extension and Civil Rights Act over the president's vetoes. In June, lawmakers adopted the **Fourteenth Amendment**, which incorporated many of the provisions of the Civil Rights Act, and submitted it to the states for ratification (see Appendix). Reflecting its confrontational dealings with the president, Congress wanted to ensure more permanent protection for African Americans than simple legislation could provide. Lawmakers also wanted to act quickly, as the situation in the South seemed to be deteriorating rapidly. In May 1866, a race riot had broken out in Memphis, Tennessee. For a day and a half, white mobs, egged on by local police, went on a rampage, during which they terrorized blacks and burned their homes and churches. "The late riots in our city," the white editor of a Memphis newspaper asserted, "have satisfied all of one thing, that the *southern man* will not be ruled

Explore ▶

See Sources 14.2 and 14.3 for two perspectives on the Freedmen's Bureau.

Memphis Race Riot   A skirmish between white policemen and black Union veterans on May 1, 1866 resulted in three days of rioting by white mobs that attacked the black community of Memphis, Tennessee. Before federal troops restored peace, numerous women had been raped, and forty-six African Americans and two whites had been killed. This illustration from *Harper's Weekly* depicts the carnage. Sarin Images/Granger

by the *negro*." A few months later, the New Orleans police, dominated by ex-Confederates, led a mob against black and white Republicans, killing thirty-four African Americans and three whites.

The Fourteenth Amendment defined citizenship to include African Americans, thereby nullifying the ruling in the *Dred Scott* case of 1857, which declared that blacks were not citizens. It extended equal protection and due process of law to all persons, not only citizens. The amendment repudiated Confederate debts, which some state governments had refused to do, and it barred Confederate officeholders from holding elective office unless Congress removed this provision by a two-thirds vote. Although most Republicans were upset with Johnson's behavior, at this point they were not willing to embrace the Radical position entirely. Rather than granting the right to vote to black males at least twenty-one years of age, the Fourteenth Amendment gave the states the option of excluding blacks and accepting a reduction in congressional representation if they did so.

Johnson remained inflexible. Instead of counseling the southern states to accept the Fourteenth Amendment, which would have sped up their readmission to the Union, he encouraged them to reject it. In the fall of 1866, Johnson decided to take his case directly to northern voters before the midterm congressional elections. Campaigning for candidates who shared his views, he embarked on a swing through the Midwest. Out of touch with northern opinion, Johnson attacked Republican lawmakers and engaged in shouting matches with audiences. On election day, Republicans increased their majorities in

Comparative Primary Source Analysis

Debating the Freedmen's Bureau

From the start, the Freedmen's Bureau generated controversy. To its Republican supporters, it helped southern blacks make the transition from slavery to freedom. For most white Southerners and many northern Democrats, however, the bureau was little more than an expensive social welfare program that rewarded idleness in blacks. Both points of view are represented in the following documents. In a report written to the Congressional Joint Committee on Reconstruction, Colonel Eliphalet Whittlesey, the assistant head of the Freedmen's Bureau in North Carolina, outlined the bureau's initial accomplishments. The anti-bureau cartoon reprinted here was created during the height of the conflict over Reconstruction between the Republican Congress and President Andrew Johnson and depicts the pervasive racism of the era; it was intended to support the election of a Democratic candidate for governor of Pennsylvania, an ally of Johnson.

Source 14.2

Colonel Eliphalet Whittlesey │ Report on the Freedmen's Bureau, 1865

All officers of the bureau are instructed—

To aid the destitute, yet in such a way as not to encourage dependence.

To protect freedmen from injustice.

To assist freedmen in obtaining employment and fair wages for their labor.

To encourage education, intellectual and moral. . . .

. . . [W]e have in our camps at Roanoke Island and Newbern, many women and children, families of soldiers who have died in the service, and refugees from the interior during the war, for whom permanent provision must be made. . . . The reports prepared by Surgeon Hogan will show the condition of freedmen hospitals. In the early part of the summer much suffering and mortality occurred for want of medical attendance and supplies. This evil is now being remedied by the employment of surgeons by contract. . . .

Contrary to the fears and predictions of many, the great mass of colored people have remained quietly at work upon the plantations of their former masters during the entire summer. The crowds seen about the towns in the early part of the season had followed in the wake of the Union army, to escape from slavery. After hostilities ceased these refugees returned to their homes, so that but few vagrants can now be found. In truth, a much larger amount of vagrancy exists among the whites than among the blacks. It is the almost uniform report of officers of the bureau that freedmen are industrious.

The report is confirmed by the fact that out of a colored population of nearly 350,000 in the State, only about 5,000 are now receiving support from the government. Probably some others are receiving aid from kind-hearted men who have enjoyed the benefit of their services from childhood. To the general quiet and industry of this people there can be no doubt that the efforts of the bureau have contributed greatly.

Source: *The Reports of the Committees of the House of Representatives Made during the First Session, Thirty-Ninth Congress, 1865–1866* (Washington, DC: Government Printing Office, 1866), 186–87, 189.

Source 14.3

Democratic Flier Opposing the Freedmen's Bureau Bill, 1866

Library of Congress, Rare Book and Special Collections Division [LC-USZ-62-57340]

Interpret the Evidence

1. According to Colonel Whittlesey, what needs does the Freedmen's Bureau address? How does he measure the bureau's success?

2. Why might this portrayal of the Freedmen's Bureau have appealed to some whites, north and south? How would Whittlesey and other bureau supporters have responded?

Put It in Context

How did racism and prevailing racial assumptions shape both the cartoon and the report?

Congress and now controlled two-thirds of the seats, providing them with greater power to override presidential vetoes.

Congressional Reconstruction.

When the Fortieth Congress convened in 1867, Republican lawmakers charted a new course for Reconstruction. With moderates and Radicals united against the president, Congress intended to force the former Confederate states not only to protect the basic civil rights of African Americans but also to grant them the vote. Moderates now agreed with Radicals that unless blacks had access to the ballot, they would not be able to sustain their freedom. Extending the suffrage to African Americans also aided the fortunes of the Republican Party in the South by adding significant numbers of new voters. By the end of March, Congress enacted three Military Reconstruction Acts. Together they divided ten southern states into five military districts, each under the supervision of a Union general (Map 14.1). The male voters of each state, regardless of race, were to elect delegates to a constitutional convention; only former Confederate officials were disfranchised. The conventions were required to draft constitutions that guaranteed black suffrage and ratified the Fourteenth Amendment. Within a year, North Carolina, South Carolina, Florida, Alabama, Louisiana, and Arkansas had fulfilled these obligations and reentered the Union. In December 1866, only 0.5 percent of adult black males could vote in the United States; a year later the figure soared to 80.5 percent, with all of the gains made in the states subject to the military Reconstruction Acts.

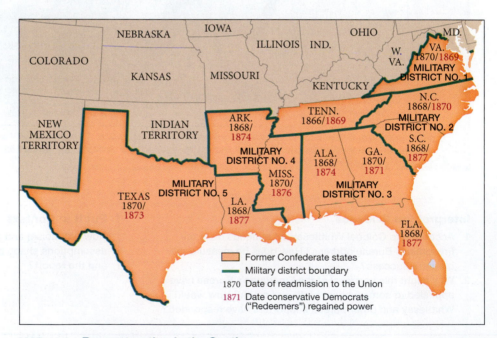

MAP 14.1   Reconstruction in the South

In 1867 Congress enacted legislation dividing the former Confederate states into five military districts. All the states were readmitted to the Union by 1870, and white conservative Democrats (Redeemers) had replaced Republicans in most states by 1875. Only in Florida, Louisiana, and South Carolina did federal troops remain until 1877.

Having ensured congressional Reconstruction in the South, Republican lawmakers turned their attention to disciplining the president. Johnson continued to resist their policies and used his power as commander in chief to order generals in the military districts to soften the intent of congressional Reconstruction. In response, Congress passed the Command of the Army Act in 1867, which required the president to issue all orders to army commanders in the field through the General of the Army in Washington, D.C., Ulysses S. Grant. The Radicals knew they could count on Grant to carry out their policies. Even more threatening to presidential power, Congress passed the **Tenure of Office Act**, which prevented Johnson from firing cabinet officers sympathetic to congressional Reconstruction. This measure barred the chief executive from removing from office any appointee that the Senate had ratified previously without returning to the Senate for approval.

Convinced that the new law was unconstitutional and outraged at this effort to limit his power, the quick-tempered Johnson chose to confront the Radical Republicans directly rather than seek a way around a congressional showdown. In February 1868, Johnson fired Secretary of War Edwin Stanton, a Lincoln appointee and a Radical sympathizer, without Senate approval. In response, congressional Radicals prepared articles of impeachment.

In late February, the House voted 126 to 47 to impeach Johnson, the first president ever to be impeached, or charged with unlawful activity. The case then went to trial in the Senate, where the chief justice of the United States presided and a two-thirds vote was necessary for conviction and removal from office. After a six-week hearing, the Senate fell one vote short of convicting Johnson. Most crucial for Johnson's fate were the votes of seven moderate Republicans who refused to find the president guilty of violating his oath to uphold the Constitution. They were convinced that Johnson's actions were insufficient to merit the enormous step of removing a president from office. Although Johnson remained in office, Congress effectively ended his power to shape Reconstruction policy.

The Republicans had restrained Johnson, and in 1868 they won back the presidency. Ulysses S. Grant, the popular Civil War general, ran against Horatio Seymour, the Democratic governor of New York. Although an ally of the Radical Republicans, Grant called for reconciliation with the South. He easily defeated Seymour, winning nearly 53 percent of the popular vote and 73 percent of the electoral vote.

The Struggle for Universal Suffrage.

In February 1869, Congress passed the **Fifteenth Amendment** to protect black male suffrage, which had initially been guaranteed by the Military Reconstruction Acts. A compromise between moderate and Radical Republicans, the amendment prohibited voting discrimination based on race, but it did not deny states the power to impose qualifications based on literacy, payment of taxes, moral character, or any other standard that did not directly relate to race. Subsequently, the wording of the amendment provided loopholes for white leaders to disfranchise large numbers of African Americans. The amendment did, however, cover the entire nation, including the North, where states like Connecticut, Kansas, Michigan, New York, Ohio, and Wisconsin still excluded blacks from voting.

The Fifteenth Amendment sparked serious conflicts not only within the South but also among old abolitionist allies. The American Anti-Slavery Society had disbanded with emancipation. Immediately following the war, the many members who believed that important work remained to be done to guarantee the rights of freedpeople formed the **American Equal Rights Association**. However, its members divided over the Fifteenth Amendment.

Frances Ellen Watkins Harper   Born a free person of color in Baltimore, Frances Ellen Watkins Harper distinguished herself as a poet, a teacher, and an abolitionist. After the Civil War, she became a staunch advocate of women's suffrage and a supporter of the Fifteenth Amendment, which set her at odds with the suffragists Susan B. Anthony and Elizabeth Cady Stanton. Documenting the American South, University Library, The University of North Carolina at Chapel Hill, http://docsouth.unc.edu/neh/brownhal/ill22.html

Some women's rights advocates, including Elizabeth Cady Stanton and Susan B. Anthony, had earlier objected to the Fourteenth Amendment because it inserted the word *male* into the Constitution for the first time when describing citizens. Although they had supported abolition before the war, Stanton and Anthony worried that postwar policies intended to enhance the rights of southern black men would further limit the rights of women. While most African American activists embraced the Fifteenth Amendment, a few voiced concern. At a meeting of the Equal Rights Association in 1867, Sojourner Truth noted, "There is quite a stir about colored men getting their rights, but not a word about colored women."

At the 1869 meeting of the Equal Rights Association, differences over the measure erupted into open conflict. Stanton and Anthony denounced suffrage for black men only, and Stanton now supported her position on racial grounds. She claimed that the "dregs of China, Germany, England, Ireland, and Africa" were degrading the U.S. polity and argued that white, educated women should certainly have the same rights as immigrant and African American men. Black and white supporters of the Fifteenth Amendment, including Frances Ellen Watkins Harper, Wendell Phillips, Abby Kelley, and Frederick Douglass, denounced Stanton's bigotry. Believing that southern black men urgently needed suffrage to protect their newly won freedom, they argued that ratification of the Fifteenth Amendment would speed progress toward the enfranchisement of women, black and white.

This conflict led to the formation of competing organizations committed to women's suffrage. The National Woman Suffrage Association, established by Stanton and Anthony, allowed only women as members and opposed ratification of the Fifteenth Amendment. The American Woman Suffrage Association, which attracted the support of women and men, white and black, supported ratification. Less than a year later, in the spring of 1870, the Fifteenth Amendment was ratified and went into effect.

Since the amendment did not grant the vote to either white or black women, women suffragists attempted to use the Fourteenth Amendment to achieve their goal. In 1875 Virginia Minor, who had been denied the ballot in Missouri, argued that the right to vote was one of the "privileges and immunities" granted to all citizens under the Fourteenth Amendment. In *Minor v. Happersett*, the Supreme Court ruled against her, and most women were denied national suffrage for decades thereafter.

Review & Relate

■ What was President Johnson's plan for reconstruction? How were his views out of step with those of most Republicans?

■ What characterized congressional Reconstruction? What priorities were reflected in congressional Reconstruction legislation?

Remaking the South

With President Johnson's power effectively curtailed, reconstruction of the South moved quickly. New state legislatures, ruled by a coalition of southern whites and blacks and white northern migrants, enacted political, economic, and social reforms that improved the overall quality of life in the South. Despite these changes, many black and white Southerners barely eked out a living under the planter-dominated sharecropping system. Moreover, the biracial Reconstruction governments lasted a relatively short time, as conservative whites used a variety of tactics, including terror and race baiting, to defeat their opponents at the polls.

Whites Reconstruct the South. During the first years of congressional Reconstruction, two groups of whites occupied the majority of elective offices in the South. A significant number of native-born Southerners joined Republicans in forging postwar constitutions and governments. Before the war, some had belonged to the Whig Party and opposed secession from the Union. Western sections of Alabama, Georgia, North Carolina, and Tennessee had demonstrated a fiercely independent strain, and many residents had remained loyal to the Union. Small merchants and farmers who detested large plantation owners also threw in their lot with the Republicans. Even a few ex-Confederates, such as General James A. Longstreet, decided that the South must change and allied with the Republicans. The majority of whites who continued to support the Democratic Party viewed these whites as traitors. They showed their distaste by calling them **scalawags**, an unflattering term meaning "scoundrels."

At the same time, Northerners came south to support Republican Reconstruction. They had varied reasons for making the journey, but most considered the South a new frontier to be conquered culturally, politically, and economically. Some—white and black—had served in the Union army during the war, liked what they saw of the region, and decided to settle there. Some of both races came to provide education and assist the freedpeople in adjusting to their new lives. As a relatively underdeveloped area, the South also beckoned fortune seekers and adventurers who saw opportunities to get rich. Southern Democrats denounced such northern interlopers, particularly whites, as **carpetbaggers**, suggesting that they invaded the region with all their possessions in a satchel, seeking to plunder it and then leave. While Northerners did seek economic opportunity, they were acting as Americans always had in settling new frontiers and pursuing dreams of success. In fact, much of the animosity directed toward them resulted primarily not from their mere presence, but from their efforts to ally with African Americans in reshaping the South.

Black Political Participation and Economic Opportunities. Still, the primary targets of southern white hostility were African Americans who attempted to exercise their hard-won freedom. Blacks constituted a majority of voters in five states — Alabama, Florida, South Carolina, Mississippi, and Louisiana — while in Georgia, North Carolina, Texas, and Virginia they fell short of a majority. They did not use their ballots to impose black rule on the South, as many white Southerners feared. Only in South Carolina did African Americans control the state legislature, and in no state did they manage to elect a governor. Nevertheless, for the first time in American history, blacks won a wide variety of elected positions. More than six hundred blacks served in state legislatures; another sixteen, including Jefferson Long, held seats in the U.S. House of Representatives; and two from Mississippi were chosen to serve in the U.S. Senate.

> **Explore ▶**
>
> Compare two opposing views of southern blacks in Reconstruction-era governments in Sources 14.4 and 14.5.

Former slaves showed enthusiasm for politics in other ways, too. African Americans considered politics a community responsibility, and in addition to casting ballots, they held rallies and mass meetings to discuss issues and choose candidates. Although they could not vote, women attended these gatherings and helped influence their outcome. Covering a Republican convention in Richmond in October 1867, held in the First African Baptist Church, the *New York Times* reported that "the entire colored population of Richmond" attended. In addition, freedpeople formed mutual aid associations to promote education, economic advancement, and social welfare programs, all of which they saw as deeply intertwined with politics.

Southern blacks also bolstered their freedom by building alliances with sympathetic whites. These interracial political coalitions produced considerable reform in the South. They created the first public school systems; provided funds for social services, such as poor relief and state hospitals; upgraded prisons; and rebuilt the South's transportation system. Moreover, the state constitutions that the Republicans wrote brought a greater measure of political democracy and equality to the South by extending suffrage to poor white men as well as black men. Some states allowed married women greater control over their property and liberalized the criminal justice system. In effect, these Reconstruction governments brought the South into the nineteenth century.

Obtaining political representation was one way in which African Americans defined freedom. Economic independence constituted a second. Without government-sponsored land redistribution, however, the options for southern blacks remained limited. Lacking capital to purchase farms, most entered into various forms of tenant contracts with large landowners. **Sharecropping** proved the most common arrangement. Blacks and poor whites became sharecroppers for much the same reasons. They received tools and supplies from landowners and farmed their own plots of land on the plantation. In exchange, sharecroppers turned over a portion of their harvest to the owner and kept the rest for themselves.

The benefits of sharecropping proved less valuable to black farmers in practice than in theory. To tide them over during the growing season, croppers had to purchase household provisions on credit from a local merchant, who was often also their landlord. At the mercy of store owners who kept the books and charged high interest rates, tenants usually found themselves in considerable debt at the end of the year. To satisfy the debt, merchants devised a crop lien system in which tenants pledged a portion of their yearly crop to satisfy what they owed. Falling prices for agricultural crops in this period ensured that most indebted tenants did not receive sufficient return on their produce to get out of debt and thus remained bound to their landlords. For many African Americans, sharecropping turned into a form of virtual slavery.

The picture for black farmers was not all bleak, however. About 20 percent of black farmers managed to buy their own land. Through careful management and extremely hard work, black families planted gardens for household consumption and raised chickens for eggs and meat. Despite its pitfalls, even sharecropping provided a limited measure of independence and allowed some blacks to accumulate small amounts of cash.

Following the war's devastation, many of the South's white small farmers, known as yeomen, also fell into sharecropping. Meanwhile, many planters' sons abandoned farming and became lawyers, bankers, and merchants. Despite these changes, one thing remained the same: White elites ruled over blacks and poor whites, and they kept these two economically exploited groups from uniting by fanning the flames of racial prejudice.

Economic hardship and racial bigotry drove many blacks to leave the South. In 1879 former slaves, known as **Exodusters**, pooled their resources to create land companies and purchase property in Kansas on which to settle. They encouraged an exodus of some 25,000 African Americans from the South. Kansas was ruled by the Republican Party and had been home to the great antislavery martyr John Brown. As one hopeful freedman from

Exodusters   This photograph of two black couples standing on their homestead was taken around 1880 in Nicodemus, Kansas. These settlers, known as Exodusters, had migrated to northwest Kansas following the end of Reconstruction. They sought economic opportunity free from the racial repression sweeping the South. Library of Congress, Prints and Photographs Division [HABS KANS, 33-NICO, 1-6]

Comparative Secondary Source Analysis

Race and Reconstruction

Although the Civil War ended slavery, it left deep and unresolved racial tensions that continued to incite conflict. In the years immediately following the war, freedmen were allowed to vote for representatives and to serve in newly formed southern state governments. These developments outraged many white Confederates who insisted that these governments were corrupt and that blacks were especially vulnerable to graft and manipulation. Many prominent historians accepted such views of postwar southern politics until the 1960s, when a younger generation of scholars argued for a reconsideration of race and Reconstruction. William A. Dunning, a white southern historian, wrote about Reconstruction in 1907, at the height of rigid racial segregation and extreme white supremacy. Fifty-three years later, the African American historian John Hope Franklin writing during the civil rights movement in 1961, reached a very different conclusion about the participation of blacks during Reconstruction. (Until the 1970s, the term *negro* or *Negro* was used by most scholars to denote African American or black.)

Source 14.4

William A. Dunning | Radical Reconstruction, 1907

. . . [T]he southerners felt that the policy of Congress had no real cause save the purpose of radical politicians to prolong and extend their party power by means of negro suffrage. . . . It was as inconceivable to the southerners that rational men of the North should seriously approve of negro suffrage *per se* as it had been in 1860 to the northerners that rational men of the South should approve of secession *per se.*

. . . . The registration of voters was so directed as to insure . . . the fullest enrollment of the blacks and the completest exclusion of disfranchised whites. . . . The result of the elections was a group of constituent assemblies whose unfitness for their task was pitiful. . . . [T]he mass of the delegates consisted of whites and blacks whose ignorance and inexperience in respect to political methods were equaled only by the crudeness and distortion of their ideas as to political and social ends.

. . . . But a solitary chance presented itself of escape from the disasters of negro political supremacy: if the freedmen could be won to look for guidance in their new duties to their old masters, all might yet be well. . . . [However], to the emancipated race all the astounding changes of the recent wonder years had come through other sources, and the vague but intoxicating delights of political privilege must, they felt, be enjoyed under the same auspices that had brought them freedom, schools, and the unlimited indulgence of those weird emotions which they called religion.

Source: William Archibald Dunning, *Reconstruction Political and Economic, 1865–1877* (New York: Harper and Brothers Publishers, 1907), pp. 110–11, 112, 114–15.

Louisiana wrote to the Kansas governor in 1879, "I am anxious to reach your state . . . because of the sacredness of her soil washed in the blood of humanitarians for the cause of black freedom." Yet poor-quality land and unpredictable weather often made farming on the Great Plains hard and unrewarding. Nevertheless, for many black migrants, the chance to own their own land and escape the oppression of the South was worth the hardships. In 1880 the census counted 40,000 blacks living in Kansas.

Source 14.5

John Hope Franklin | The South's New Leaders, 1961

The entrance of Negroes into the political arena was the most revolutionary aspect of the Reconstruction program. Out of a population of approximately four million, some 700,000 qualified as voters, but the most of them were without the qualifications to participate effectively in a democracy. In this they were not unlike the large number of Americans who were enfranchised during the Age of Jackson. . . . None of this is surprising. It had been only two years since emancipation from a system that for more than two centuries had denied slaves most rights as human beings. And it must be remembered that in these two years the former Confederates, in power all over the South, did nothing to promote the social and political education of the former slaves. What is surprising is that there were

some—and no paltry number—who in 1867 were able to assume the responsibilities of citizens and leaders.

. . . . One of the really remarkable features of the Negro leadership was the small amount of vindictiveness in their words and their actions. There was no bully, no swagger, as they took their places in the state and federal governments traditionally occupied by the white planters of the South. . . . Negroes generally wished to see political disabilities removed from the whites. . . . Negroes attempted no revolution in the social relations of the races in the South. . . . Nor did any considerable number of Negroes seek to effect an economic revolution in the South.

Source: John Hope Franklin, *Reconstruction After the Civil War* (Chicago: University of Chicago Press, 1961), pp. 86–87, 88, 89–90, 91.

Examine the Sources

1. How do Dunning and Franklin differ in their interpretations of the role played by African Americans during Reconstruction?
2. Drawing on evidence from this chapter, including the Primary Source Project, how would you evaluate the strengths and weaknesses of Dunning's and Franklin's interpretations?

Put It in Context

How might the fact that these interpretations were written fifty-four years apart (1907/1961) influence their conclusions?

White Resistance to Congressional Reconstruction.
Despite the Republican record of accomplishment during Reconstruction, white Southerners did not accept its legitimacy. They accused interracial governments of conducting a spending spree that raised taxes and encouraged corruption. Indeed, taxes did rise significantly, but mainly because legislatures funded much-needed educational and social services. Corruption on building projects and railroad construction was common during this time. Still, it is unfair

to single out Reconstruction governments and especially black legislators as inherently depraved since their Democratic opponents acted the same way when given the opportunity. Economic scandals were part of American life after the Civil War. As enormous business opportunities arose in the postwar years, many economic and political leaders made unlawful deals to enrich themselves. Furthermore, southern opponents of Reconstruction exaggerated its harshness. In contrast to revolutions and civil wars in other countries, only one rebel was executed for war crimes (the commandant of Andersonville Prison in Georgia); only one high-ranking official went to prison (Jefferson Davis); no official was forced into exile, though some fled voluntarily; and most rebels regained voting rights and the ability to hold office within seven years after the end of the rebellion.

Most important, these Reconstruction governments had only limited opportunities to transform the South. By the end of 1870, civilian rule had returned to all of the former Confederate states, and they had reentered the Union. Republican rule did not continue past 1870 in Virginia, North Carolina, and Tennessee and did not extend beyond 1871 in Georgia and 1873 in Texas. In 1874 Democrats deposed Republicans in Arkansas and Alabama; two years later, Democrats triumphed in Mississippi. In only three states — Louisiana, Florida, and South Carolina — did Reconstruction last until 1877.

The Democrats who replaced Republicans trumpeted their victories as bringing "redemption" to the South. Of course, these so-called **Redeemers** were referring to the white South. For black Republicans and their white allies, redemption meant defeat. Democratic victories came at the ballot boxes, but violence, intimidation, and fraud paved the way. In 1865 in Pulaski, Tennessee General Nathan Bedford Forrest organized Confederate veterans into a social club called the **Knights of the Ku Klux Klan (KKK)**. Spreading

throughout the South, its followers donned robes and masks to hide their identities and terrify their victims. Gun-wielding Ku Kluxers rode on horseback to the homes and churches of black and white Republicans to keep them from voting. When threats did not work, they beat and murdered their victims. In 1871, for example, 150 African Americans were killed in Jackson County in the Florida Panhandle. A black clergyman lamented, "That is where Satan has his seat." There and elsewhere, many of the individuals targeted had managed to buy property, gain political leadership, or in other ways defy white stereotypes of African American inferiority. Other white supremacist organizations joined the Klan in waging a reign of terror. During the 1875 election in Mississippi, which toppled the Republican government, armed terrorists killed hundreds of Republicans and scared many more away from the polls.

To combat the terror unleashed by the Klan and its allies, Congress passed three **Force Acts** in 1870 and 1871. These measures empowered the president to dispatch officials into the South to supervise elections and prevent voting interference. Directed specifically at the KKK, one

Ku Klux Klansmen Photographed wearing their robes and hoods, these Klansmen usually came out under cover of evening darkness to terrorize the freedpeople and keep them politically and economically subservient. The Klan also attacked northern whites (carpetbaggers) and southern white unionists (scalawags) who participated in Reconstruction. Bridgeman Images law barred secret organizations from using force to violate equal protection of the laws. In 1872 Congress established a joint committee to probe Klan tactics, and its investigations produced thirteen volumes of gripping testimony about the horrors perpetrated by the Klan. Elias Hill, a freedman from South Carolina who had become a Baptist preacher and teacher, was one of those who appeared before Congress. He and his brother lived next door to each other. The Klansmen went first to his brother's house, where, as Hill testified, they "broke open the door and attacked his wife, and I heard her screaming and mourning [moaning]. . . . At last I heard them have [rape] her in the yard." When the Klansmen discovered Elias Hill, they dragged him out of his house and beat, whipped, and threatened to kill him. On the basis of such testimony, the federal government prosecuted some 3,000 Klansmen. Only 600 were convicted, however. As the Klan disbanded in the wake of federal prosecutions, other vigilante organizations arose to take its place.

Review & Relate

■ What role did black people play in remaking southern society during Reconstruction?

■ How did southern whites fight back against Reconstruction? What role did terrorism and political violence play in this effort?

The **Unraveling** of **Reconstruction**

The violence, intimidation, and fraud perpetrated by white Redeemers does not fully explain the unraveling of Reconstruction. By the early 1870s most white Northerners had come to believe that they had done more than enough for black Southerners, and it was time to focus on other issues. Growing economic problems intensified this feeling. Still reeling from the amount of blood shed during the war, white Americans, north and south, turned their attention toward burying and memorializing the Civil War dead. White America was once again united, if only in the shared belief that it was time to move on, consigning the issues of slavery and civil rights to history.

The Republican Retreat. Most northern whites shared the racial prejudices of their counterparts in the South. Although they had supported protection of black civil rights and suffrage, they still believed that African Americans were inferior to whites and were horrified by the idea of social integration. They began to sympathize with Southern whites' racist complaints that blacks were not capable of governing honestly and effectively.

In 1872 a group calling themselves Liberal Republicans challenged the reelection of President Grant. Financial scandals had racked the Grant administration. This high-level corruption reflected other get-rich-quick schemes connected to economic speculation and development following the Civil War. Outraged by the rising level of immoral behavior in government and business, Liberal Republicans nominated Horace Greeley, editor of the *New York Tribune*, to run against Grant. They linked government corruption to the expansion of federal power that accompanied Reconstruction and called for the removal of troops from the South and amnesty for all former Confederates. They also campaigned for civil service reform, which would base government employment on a merit system and abolish the "spoils system" — in which the party in power rewarded loyal supporters with political appointments — that had been introduced by Andrew Jackson in the 1820s.

The Democratic Party believed that Liberal Republicans offered the best chance to defeat Grant, and it endorsed Greeley. Despite the scandals that surrounded him, Grant remained popular. Moreover, the main body of Republicans "waved the bloody shirt," reminding northern voters that a ballot cast for the opposition tarnished the memory of brave Union soldiers killed during the war. The president won reelection with an even greater margin than he had four years earlier. Nevertheless, the attacks against Grant foreshadowed the Republican retreat on Reconstruction. Among the Democrats sniping at Grant was Andrew Johnson. Johnson had returned to Tennessee, and in 1874 the state legislature chose the former president to serve in the U.S. Senate. He continued to speak out against the presence of federal troops in the South until his death in 1875.

Congressional and Judicial Retreat.
By the time Grant began his second term, Congress was already considering bills to restore officeholding rights to former Confederates who had not yet sworn allegiance to the Union. Black representatives, including Georgia congressman Jefferson Long, as well as some white lawmakers, remained opposed to such measures, but in 1872 Congress removed the penalties placed on former Confederates by the Fourteenth Amendment and permitted nearly all rebel leaders the right to vote and hold office. Two years later, for the first time since the start of the Civil War, the Democrats gained a majority in the House of Representatives and prepared to remove the remaining troops from the South.

Republican leaders also rethought their top priority with economic concerns increasingly replacing racial considerations. In 1873 a financial panic resulting from the collapse of the Northern Pacific Railroad triggered a severe economic depression lasting late into the decade. Tens of thousands of unemployed workers across the country worried more about finding jobs than they did about black civil rights. Businessmen, too, were plagued with widespread bankruptcies. When strikes erupted across the country in 1877, most notably the Great Railway Strike, in which more than half a million workers walked off the job, employers asked the U.S. government to remove troops from the South and dispatch them against strikers in the North and West.

While white Northerners sought ways to extricate themselves from Reconstruction, the Supreme Court weakened enforcement of the civil rights acts. In 1873 the *Slaughterhouse* cases defined the rights that African Americans were entitled to under the Fourteenth Amendment very narrowly. Reflecting the shift from moral to economic concerns, the justices interpreted the amendment as extending greater protection to corporations in conducting business than to blacks. As a result, blacks had to depend on southern state governments to protect their civil rights, the same state authorities that had deprived them of their rights in the first place. In *United States v. Cruikshank* (1876), the high court narrowed the Fourteenth Amendment further, ruling that it protected blacks against abuses only by state officials and agencies, not by private groups such as the Ku Klux Klan. Seven years later, the Court struck down the Civil Rights Act of 1875, which had extended "full and equal treatment" in public accommodations for persons of all races.

The Presidential Compromise of 1876.
The presidential election of 1876 set in motion events that officially brought Reconstruction to an end. The Republicans nominated the governor of Ohio, Rutherford B. Hayes, who was chosen partly because he was

untainted by the corruption that plagued the Grant administration. The Democrats selected their own anticorruption crusader, Governor Samuel J. Tilden of New York.

The outcome of the election depended on twenty disputed electoral votes, nineteen from the South and one from Oregon. Tilden won 51 percent of the popular vote, but Reconstruction political battles in Florida, Louisiana, and South Carolina put the election up for grabs. In each of these states, the outgoing Republican administration certified Hayes as the winner, while the incoming Democratic regime declared for Tilden.

The Constitution assigns Congress the task of counting and certifying the electoral votes submitted by the states. Normally, this is a mere formality, but 1876 was different. Democrats controlled the House, Republicans controlled the Senate, and neither branch would budge on which votes to count. Hayes needed all twenty for victory; Tilden needed only one. To break the logjam, Congress created a fifteen-member Joint Electoral Commission, composed of seven Democrats, seven Republicans, and one independent. Ultimately, a majority voted to count all twenty votes for the Republican Hayes, making him president (Map 14.2).

Still, Congress had to ratify this count, and disgruntled southern Democrats in the Senate threatened a filibuster — unlimited debate — to block certification of Hayes. With the March 4, 1877 date for the presidential inauguration creeping perilously close and no winner officially declared, behind-the-scenes negotiations finally settled the controversy. A series of meetings between Hayes supporters and southern Democrats led to a bargain. According to the agreement, Democrats would support Hayes in exchange for the president appointing a Southerner to his cabinet, withdrawing the last federal troops from the South, and endorsing construction of a transcontinental railroad through the South. This **compromise of 1877** averted a crisis over presidential succession, underscored increased southern Democratic influence within Congress, and marked the end of strong federal protections for African Americans in the South.

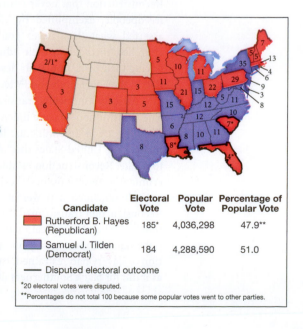

MAP 14.2   The Election of 1876

The presidential election of 1876 got swept up in Reconstruction politics. Democrats defeated Republicans in Florida, Louisiana, and South Carolina, but both parties claimed the electoral votes for their candidates. A federal electoral commission set up to investigate the twenty disputed votes, including one from Oregon, awarded the votes and the election to the Republican, Rutherford B. Hayes.

Candidate	Electoral Vote	Popular Vote	Percentage of Popular Vote
▮ Rutherford B. Hayes (Republican)	185*	4,036,298	47.9**
▮ Samuel J. Tilden (Democrat)	184	4,288,590	51.0
— Disputed electoral outcome			

*20 electoral votes were disputed.

**Percentages do not total 100 because some popular votes went to other parties.

Review & Relate

- Why did northern interest in Reconstruction wane in the 1870s?

- What common values and beliefs among white Americans were reflected in the compromise of 1877?

Conclusion: The Legacies of Reconstruction

Reconstruction was, in many ways, profoundly limited. Notwithstanding the efforts of the Freedmen's Bureau, African Americans did not receive the landownership that would have provided them with economic independence and bolstered their freedom from the racist assaults of white Southerners. The civil and political rights that the federal government conferred did not withstand the efforts of former Confederates to disfranchise and deprive the freedpeople of equal rights. The Republican Party shifted its priorities, and Democrats gained enough political power nationally to short-circuit federal intervention, even as numerous problems remained unresolved in the South. Northern support for racial equality did not run very deep, so white Northerners, who shared many of the prejudices of white Southerners, were happy to extricate themselves from further intervention in southern racial matters. Nor was there sufficient support to give women, white or black, the right to vote. Finally, federal courts, with growing concerns over economic rather than social issues, sanctioned Northerners' retreat by providing constitutional legitimacy for abandoning black Southerners and rejecting women's suffrage in court decisions that narrowed the interpretation of the Fourteenth and Fifteenth Amendments.

Despite all of this, Reconstruction did transform the country. As a result of Reconstruction, slavery was abolished and the legal basis for freedom was enshrined in the Constitution. Indeed, blacks exercised a measure of political and economic freedom during Reconstruction that never entirely disappeared over the decades to come. In many areas, freedpeople, exemplified by Congressman Jefferson Franklin Long and many others, asserted what they never could have during slavery—control over their lives, their churches, their labor, their education, and their families. What they could not practice during their own time, their descendants would one day revive through the promises codified in the Fourteenth and Fifteenth Amendments.

African Americans transformed not only themselves; they transformed the nation. The Constitution became much more democratic and egalitarian through inclusion of the Reconstruction amendments. Reconstruction lawmakers took an important step toward making the United States the "more perfect union" that the nation's Founders had pledged to create. Reconstruction established a model for expanding the power of the federal government to resolve domestic crises that lay beyond the abilities of states and ordinary citizens. It remained a powerful legacy for elected officials who dared to invoke it. And Reconstruction transformed the South to its everlasting benefit. It modernized state constitutions, expanded educational and social welfare systems, and unleashed the repressed potential for industrialization and new forms of economic development that the preservation of slavery had restrained. Ironically, Reconstruction did as much for white Southerners as it did for black Southerners in liberating them from the past.

Timeline of Events

1863	Lincoln issues Proclamation of Amnesty and Reconstruction
1865	Ku Klux Klan formed
	Freedmen's Bureau established
	Thirteenth Amendment passed
	Lincoln assassinated; Andrew Johnson becomes president
1866	Freedmen's Bureau and Civil Rights Act extended over Johnson's presidential veto
	Fourteenth Amendment passed
1867	Military Reconstruction Acts
	Command of the Army and Tenure of Office Acts passed
1868	Andrew Johnson impeached
1869	Fifteenth Amendment passed
	Women's suffrage movement splits over support of Fifteenth Amendment
1870	250,000 blacks attend schools established by the Freedmen's Bureau
	Civilian rule returns to the South
1870–1872	Congress takes steps to curb Ku Klux Klan violence in the South
1873	Financial panic sparks depression
1873–1883	Supreme Court limits rights of African Americans
1875	Civil Rights Act passed
1877	Rutherford B. Hayes becomes president
	Reconstruction ends
1879	Black Exodusters migrate from South to Kansas

Key Terms

Freedmen's Bureau, *464*

Proclamation of Amnesty and Reconstruction, *469*

Thirteenth Amendment, *469*

black codes, *471*

Fourteenth Amendment, *472*

Tenure of Office Act, *477*

Fifteenth Amendment, *477*

American Equal Rights Association, *477*

scalawags, *479*

carpetbaggers, *479*

sharecropping, *480*

Exodusters, *481*

Redeemers, *484*

Knights of the Ku Klux Klan (KKK), *484*

Force Acts, *484*

compromise of 1877, *487*

Review & Relate

1. What were freedpeople's highest priorities in the years immediately following the Civil War? Why?

2. How did freedpeople define freedom? What steps did they take to make freedom real for themselves and their children?

3. What was President Johnson's plan for reconstruction? How were his views out of step with those of most Republicans?

4. What characterized congressional Reconstruction? What priorities were reflected in congressional Reconstruction legislation?

5. What role did black people play in remaking southern society during Reconstruction?

6. How did southern whites fight back against Reconstruction? What role did terrorism and political violence play in this effort?

7. Why did northern interest in Reconstruction wane in the 1870s?

8. What common values and beliefs among white Americans were reflected in the compromise of 1877?

Testing and Contesting Freedom

▶ **How did blacks and whites view emancipation and what role did the federal government play in overseeing the transition from slavery to freedom?**

Nine months after the Civil War ended in April 1865, twenty-seven states ratified the Thirteenth Amendment, abolishing slavery throughout the United States. Freedom, however, did not guarantee equal rights or the absence of racial discrimination. Immediately following the North's victory, white southern leaders enacted black codes, which aimed to prevent freedpeople from improving their social and economic status (Source 14.6). Although Lincoln's successor, Andrew Johnson, did not support the codes, he did nothing to overturn them. A southern advocate of limited government, Johnson clashed repeatedly with Congress over Reconstruction. In 1867 the Republican majority in Congress took control and passed the Military Reconstruction Acts, placing the South under military rule and forcing whites to extend equal political and civil rights to African Americans.

Then in 1870, ratification of the Fifteenth Amendment extended suffrage to black men. In alliance with white Republicans, blacks won election to a variety of public offices, including seats in local and state governments. These interracial legislatures improved conditions for blacks and whites, providing funds for public education, hospitals, and other social services. But their opponents succeeded in tarring them with claims of fraud, corruption, wasteful spending, and "Black Rule" (Sources 14.7 and 14.10). Most newly freed blacks were eager to acquire land so they could

support themselves, but many were forced to sign sharecropping agreements with white landowners. Although sharecropping provided some benefits to freed people as well as white landowners, blacks' limited economic and political leverage ensured that these agreements gave more authority to landowners than laborers (Sources 14.7 and 14.8).

By the mid-1870s, many white Northerners sought reconciliation rather than continued conflict while southern whites created vigilante groups like the Ku Klux Klan that used violence to intimidate black and white Republicans. By the mid-1870s, northern magazines as well as southern newspapers began challenging black political rule, further isolating blacks from popular and government support (Sources 14.9 and 14.10). Ultimately, the withdrawal of federal oversight crushed southern Republicanism, leaving African Americans struggling to retain the freedoms they had supposedly gained.

Source 14.6

Mississippi Black Code, 1865

Southern legislatures created black codes primarily to limit the rights of free blacks after emancipation and return them to a condition as close as possible to slavery. Mississippi was one of the first states to enact a black code. Although its laws did legalize marriage for blacks and allowed them to own property and testify in court, its primary intent was to limit freedpeople's mobility and economic opportunities.

An Act to Confer Civil Rights on Freedmen, and for other Purposes . . .

Section 2. All freedmen, free negroes and mulattoes may intermarry with each other, in the same manner and under the same regulations that are provided by law for white persons: Provided, that the clerk of probate shall keep separate records of the same.

Section 3. All freedmen, free negroes or mulattoes who do now and have herebefore lived and cohabited together as husband and wife shall be taken and held in law as legally married, and the issue shall be taken and held as legitimate for all purposes; and it shall not be lawful for any freedman, free negro or mulatto to intermarry with any white person; nor for any person to intermarry with any freedman, free negro or mulatto; and any person who shall so intermarry shall be deemed guilty of felony, and on conviction thereof shall be confined in the State penitentiary for life; and those shall be deemed freedmen, free negroes and mulattoes who are of pure negro blood, and those descended from a negro to the third generation, inclusive, though one ancestor in each generation may have been a white person.

Section 4. In addition to cases in which freedmen, free negroes and mulattoes are now by law competent witnesses, freedmen, free negroes or mulattoes shall be competent in civil cases, when a party or parties to the suit, either plaintiff or plaintiffs, defendant or defendants; also in cases where freedmen, free negroes and mulattoes is or are either plaintiff or plaintiffs, defendant or defendants. They shall also be competent witnesses in all criminal prosecutions where the crime charged is alleged to have been committed by a white person upon or against the person or property of a freedman, free negro or mulatto. . . .

An Act to Amend the Vagrant Laws of the State . . .

Section 2. All freedmen, free negroes and mulattoes in this State, over the age of eighteen years, found on the second Monday in January, 1866, or thereafter, with no lawful employment or business, or found unlawful[ly] assembling themselves together, either in the day or night time, and all white persons assembling themselves with freedmen, free negroes or mulattoes, or usually associating with freedmen, free negroes or mulattoes, on terms of equality, or living in adultery or fornication with a freed woman, freed negro or mulatto, shall be deemed vagrants, and on conviction thereof shall be fined in a sum not exceeding, in the case of a freedman, free negro or mulatto, fifty dollars, and a white man two hundred dollars, and imprisonment at the discretion of the court, the free negro not exceeding ten days, and the white man not exceeding six months. . . .

Section 6. The same duties and liabilities existing among white persons of this State shall attach to freedmen, free negroes or mulattoes, to support their indigent families and all colored paupers; and that in order to secure a support for such indigent freedmen, free negroes, or mulattoes, it shall be lawful, and is hereby made the duty of the county police of each county in this State, to levy a poll or capitation tax on each and every freedman, free negro, or mulatto, between the ages of eighteen and sixty years, not to exceed the sum of one dollar annually to each person so taxed, which tax, when collected, shall be paid into the county treasurer's hands, and constitute a fund to be called the Freedman's Pauper Fund, . . . for the maintenance of the poor of the freedmen, free negroes and mulattoes of this State.

Source: *Laws of the State of Mississippi, Passed at a Regular Session of the Mississippi Legislature, Held in the City of Jackson, October, November, and December, 1865* (Jackson, MS, 1866), 82–86, 165–67.

Source 14.7

Richard H. Cain | Federal Aid for Land Purchase, 1868

Richard H. Cain, a free black minister raised in Ohio, went to South Carolina after the war and served as a Republican member of the U.S. House of Representatives for two terms in the 1870s. The following excerpt comes from a speech Cain made in 1868 as a representative to the South Carolina constitutional convention. Cain proposed that the convention petition Congress for a $1 million loan to purchase land that could be resold to freedmen at a reasonable price.

believe the best measure to be adopted is to bring capital to the State, and instead of causing revenge and unpleasantness, I am for even-handed justice. I am for allowing the parties who own lands to bring them into the market and sell them upon such terms as will be satisfactory to both sides. I believe a measure of this kind has a double effect: first, it brings capital, what the people want; second, it puts the people to work; it gives homesteads, what we need; it relieves the Government and takes away its responsibility of feeding the people; it inspires every man with a noble manfulness, and by the thought that he is the possessor of something in the State; it adds also to the revenue of the country. By these means men become interested in the country as they never were before. . . . I will also guarantee that after one year's time, the Freedman's Bureau will not have to give any man having one acre of land anything to eat.

Source: *Proceedings of the South Carolina Constitutional Convention of 1868* (Charleston, SC, 1868), 420–21.

Source 14.8

Willis B. Bocock and Black Laborers | Sharecropping Agreement, 1870

Because Congress did not generally provide freedpeople with land, African Americans lacked the means to start their own farms. At the same time, plantation owners needed labor now that slavery was abolished. Out of mutual necessity, white plantation owners such as Willis B. Bocock entered into sharecropping agreements with blacks to work their farms in exchange for a portion of the crop. Several of the blacks who signed this agreement had previously been enslaved to Bocock.

Contract made the 3rd day of January in the year 1870 between us the free people who have signed this paper of one part, and our employer, Willis P. Bocock, of the other part. . . . We are to furnish the necessary labor . . . and are to have all proper work done, ditching, fencing, repairing, etc., as well as cultivating and saving the crops of all kinds, so as to put and keep the land we occupy and tend in good order for cropping, and to make a good crop ourselves; and to do our fair share of job work about the place. . . . We are to be responsible for the good conduct of ourselves, our hands, and families, and agree that all shall be respectful to employer, owners, and manager, honest, industrious, and careful about every thing . . . and then our employer agrees that he and his manager shall treat us kindly, and help us to study our interest and do our duty. If any hand or family proves to be of bad character, or dishonest, or lazy, or disobedient, or any way unsuitable our employer or manager has the right, and we have the right, to have such turned off. . . .

For the labor and services of ourselves and hands rendered as above stated, we are to have one third part of all the crops, or their net-proceeds, made and secured, or prepared for market by our force. . . .

We are to be furnished by our employer through his manager with provisions if we call for them . . . to be charged to us at fair market prices.

And whatever may be due by us, or our hands to our employer for provisions or any thing else, during the year, is to be a lien on our share of the crops, and is to be retained by him out of the same before we receive our part.

Source: Waldwick Plantation Records, 1834–1971, LPR174, box 1, folder 9, Alabama Department of Archives and History.

Source 14.9

Ellen Parton | Testimony on Klan Violence, 1871

In March 1871, white mobs killed some thirty African Americans in Meridian, Mississippi. Later that month, a joint committee of the United States Congress held hearings on the violence, which included the following testimony by Ellen Parton of Mississippi, a former slave and domestic worker. The Klan suspected that Parton's husband was involved in the Union League, a southern affiliate of the Republican Party. Congress also conducted hearings on the vigilante violence against blacks throughout the South.

Ellen Parton, being sworn, states:

I reside in Meridian; have resided here nine years; occupation, washing and ironing and scouring; Wednesday night was the last night they came to my house; by "they" I mean bodies or companies of men; they came on Monday, Tuesday, and Wednesday. On Monday night they said that they came to do us no harm. On Tuesday night they said they came for the arms; I told them there was none, and they said they would take my word for it. On Wednesday night they came and broke open the wardrobe and trunks, and committed rape upon me; there were eight of them in the house; I do not know how many there were outside; they were white men; there was a light in the house; I was living in Marshal Ware's house; there were three lights burning. Mr. Ware has been one of the policemen of this town. He was concealed at the time they came; they took the claw hammer and broke open the pantry where he was lying; he was concealed in the pantry under some plunder, covered up well; I guess he covered himself up. A man said "here is Marshal's hat, where is Marshal?" I told him "I did not know"; they went then into everything in the house, and broke open the wardrobe; I called upon Mr. Mike Slamon, who was one of the crowd, for protection; I said to him "please protect me tonight, you have known me for a long time." This man covered up his head then; he had a hold of me at this time; Mr. Slamon had an oil-cloth and put it before his face, trying to conceal himself, and the man that had hold of me told me not to call Mr. Slamon's name any more. He then took me in the dining room, and told me that I had to do just what he said: I told him I could do nothing of that sort; that was not my way, and he replied "by God, you have got to," and then threw me down. This man had a black eye, where some one had beaten him; he had a black velvet cap on. After he got through with me he came through the house, and said that he was after the Union Leagues; I yielded to him because he had a pistol drawn; when he took me down he hurt me of course; I yielded to him on that account.

Source: *Report of the Joint Select Committee [of Congress] to Inquire into the Condition of Affairs in the Late Insurrectionary States, Mississippi* (Washington, DC: Government Printing Office, 1872), 1:38–39.

Source 14.10

Thomas Nast | *Colored Rule in a Reconstructed (?) State,* 1874

Thomas Nast began drawing for the popular magazine *Harper's Weekly* in 1859. Nast initially used his illustrations to rouse northern public sentiment for the plight of blacks in the South after the Civil War. By 1874, however, many Northerners had become disillusioned with federal efforts to enforce Reconstruction. Like them, Nast accepted the white southern point of view that "Black Reconstruction" was a recipe for corruption and immorality. The figure of Columbia (at the top right) represents the nation, and the caption captures the view of many Northerners by 1874: "You are Aping the lowest Whites. If you disgrace your Race in this way you had better take Back Seats."

Library of Congress, Prints and Photographs Division, Washington, D.C. [LC-USZ62-102256]

Interpret the Evidence

1. How did black codes and sharecropping agreements (Sources 14.6 and 14.8) attempt to reimpose bondage on the formerly enslaved? How did they differ from pre-Civil War slave laws?

2. Why did freedpeople consider property holding a fundamental right and to what extent did sharecropping agreements allow them to gain some economic benefits from their labor (Sources 14.7 and 14.8)?

3. Contrast the image of South Carolina's black politicians presented in Richard Cain's speech (Source 14.7) and Thomas Nast's cartoon (Source 14.10). What does Nast's cartoon suggest about white northern attitudes toward freedpeople in the South by 1874?

4. Despite the fear and physical danger caused by the Ku Klux Klan, what does the testimony of Ellen Parton (Source 14.9) reveal about black attempts to resist it?

Put It in Context

How much did Reconstruction transform the South and the nation?

What were the greatest limitations of federal Reconstruction policies and the greatest challenges to implementing them?

The Declaration of Independence

In Congress, July 4, 1776.

The unanimous Declaration of the thirteen United States of America

When in the course of human events, it becomes necessary for one people to dissolve the political bands which have connected them with another, and to assume, among the powers of the earth, the separate and equal station to which the laws of nature and of nature's God entitle them, a decent respect to the opinions of mankind requires that they should declare the causes which impel them to the separation.

We hold these truths to be self-evident, that all men are created equal; that they are endowed by their Creator with certain unalienable rights; that among these, are life, liberty, and the pursuit of happiness. That, to secure these rights, governments are instituted among men, deriving their just powers from the consent of the governed; that, whenever any form of government becomes destructive of these ends, it is the right of the people to alter or to abolish it, and to institute a new government, laying its foundation on such principles, and organizing its powers in such form, as to them shall seem most likely to effect their safety and happiness. Prudence, indeed, will dictate that governments long established, should not be changed for light and transient causes; and, accordingly, all experience hath shown, that mankind are more disposed to suffer, while evils are sufferable, than to right themselves by abolishing the forms to which they are accustomed. But, when a long train of abuses and usurpations, pursuing invariably the same object, evinces a design to reduce them under absolute despotism, it is their right, it is their duty, to throw off such government and to provide new guards for their future security. Such has been the patient sufferance of these colonies, and such is now the necessity which constrains them to alter their former systems of government. The history of the present King of Great Britain is a history of repeated injuries and usurpations, all having, in direct object, the establishment of an absolute tyranny over these States. To prove this, let facts be submitted to a candid world: He has refused his assent to laws the most wholesome and necessary for the public good.

He has forbidden his governors to pass laws of immediate and pressing importance, unless suspended in their operation till his assent should be obtained; and, when so suspended, he has utterly neglected to attend to them.

He has refused to pass other laws for the accommodation of large districts of people, unless those people would relinquish the right of representation in the legislature; a right inestimable to them, and formidable to tyrants only.

He has called together legislative bodies at places unusual, uncomfortable, and distant from the depository of their public records, for the sole purpose of fatiguing them into compliance with his measures.

He has dissolved representative houses repeatedly for opposing, with manly firmness, his invasions on the rights of the people.

He has refused, for a long time after such dissolutions, to cause others to be elected; whereby the legislative powers, incapable of annihilation, have returned to the people at large for their exercise; the state remaining in the mean-time exposed to all the danger of invasion from without, and convulsions within.

He has endeavoured to prevent the population of these States; for that purpose, obstructing the laws for naturalization of foreigners, refusing to pass others to encourage their migration hither, and raising the conditions of new appropriations of lands.

He has obstructed the administration of justice, by refusing his assent to laws for establishing judiciary powers.

He has made judges dependent on his will alone, for the tenure of their offices, and the amount and payment of their salaries.

He has erected a multitude of new offices, and sent hither swarms of officers to harass our people, and eat out their substance.

He has kept among us, in times of peace, standing armies, without the consent of our legislature.

He has affected to render the military independent of, and superior to, the civil power.

He has combined, with others, to subject us to a jurisdiction foreign to our Constitution, and unacknowledged by our laws; giving his assent to their acts of pretended legislation:

For quartering large bodies of armed troops among us:

For protecting them by a mock trial, from punishment, for any murders which they should commit on the inhabitants of these States:

For cutting off our trade with all parts of the world:

For imposing taxes on us without our consent:

For depriving us, in many cases, of the benefit of trial by jury:

For transporting us beyond seas to be tried for pretended offences:

For abolishing the free system of English laws in a neighboring province, establishing therein an arbitrary government, and enlarging its boundaries, so as to render it at once an example and fit instrument for introducing the same absolute rule into these colonies:

For taking away our charters, abolishing our most valuable laws, and altering, fundamentally, the powers of our governments:

For suspending our own legislatures, and declaring themselves invested with power to legislate for us in all cases whatsoever.

He has abdicated government here, by declaring us out of his protection, and waging war against us.

He has plundered our seas, ravaged our coasts, burnt our towns, and destroyed the lives of our people.

He is, at this time, transporting large armies of foreign mercenaries to complete the works of death, desolation, and tyranny, already begun, with circumstances of cruelty and perfidy scarcely paralleled in the most barbarous ages, and totally unworthy the head of a civilized nation.

He has constrained our fellow citizens, taken captive on the high seas, to bear arms against their country, to become the executioners of their friends, and brethren, or to fall themselves by their hands.

He has excited domestic insurrections amongst us, and has endeavored to bring on the inhabitants of our frontiers, the merciless Indian savages, whose known rule of warfare is an undistinguished destruction of all ages, sexes, and conditions.

In every stage of these oppressions, we have petitioned for redress; in the most humble terms; our repeated petitions have been answered only by repeated injury. A prince, whose character is thus marked by every act which may define a tyrant, is unfit to be the ruler of a free people.

Nor have we been wanting in attention to our British brethren. We have warned them, from time to time, of attempts made by their legislature to extend an unwarrantable jurisdiction over us. We have reminded them of the circumstances of our emigration and settlement here. We have appealed to their native justice and magnanimity, and we have conjured them, by the ties of our common kindred, to disavow these usurpations, which would inevitably interrupt our connections and correspondence. They, too, have been deaf to the voice of justice and consanguinity. We must, therefore, acquiesce in the necessity which denounces our separation, and hold them as we hold the rest of mankind, enemies in war, in peace, friends.

We, therefore, the representatives of the United States of America, in general Congress assembled, appealing to the Supreme Judge of the world for the rectitude of our intentions, do, in the name, and by authority of the good people of these colonies, solemnly publish and declare, that these united colonies are, and of right ought to be, free and independent states: that they are absolved from all allegiance to the British Crown, and that all political connection between them and the state of Great Britain is, and ought to be, totally dissolved; and that, as free and independent states, they have full power to levy war, conclude peace, contract alliances, establish commerce, and to do all other acts and things which independent states may of right do. And, for the support of this declaration, with a firm reliance on the protection of Divine Providence, we mutually pledge to each other our lives, our fortunes, and our sacred honor.

The foregoing Declaration was, by order of Congress, engrossed, and signed by the following members:

JOHN HANCOCK

New Hampshire
Josiah Bartlett
William Whipple
Matthew Thornton

Massachusetts Bay
Samuel Adams
John Adams
Robert Treat Paine
Elbridge Gerry

Rhode Island
Stephen Hopkins
William Ellery

Connecticut
Roger Sherman
Samuel Huntington
William Williams
Oliver Wolcott

New York
William Floyd
Phillip Livingston
Francis Lewis
Lewis Morris

New Jersey
Richard Stockton
John Witherspoon
Francis Hopkinson
John Hart
Abraham Clark

Pennsylvania
Robert Morris
Benjamin Rush
Benjamin Franklin
John Morton
George Clymer
James Smith
George Taylor

James Wilson
George Ross
Caesar Rodney
George Read
Thomas M'Kean

Maryland
Samuel Chase
William Paca
Thomas Stone
Charles Carroll, of Carrollton

North Carolina
William Hooper
Joseph Hewes
John Penn

South Carolina
Edward Rutledge
Thomas Heyward, Jr.

Thomas Lynch, Jr.
Arthur Middleton

Virginia
George Wythe
Richard Henry Lee
Thomas Jefferson
Benjamin Harrison
Thomas Nelson, Jr.
Francis Lightfoot Lee
Carter Braxton

Georgia
Button Gwinnett
Lyman Hall
George Walton

Resolved, That copies of the Declaration be sent to the several assemblies, conventions, and committees, or councils of safety, and to the several commanding officers of the continental troops; that it be proclaimed in each of the United States, at the head of the army.

The Articles of Confederation and Perpetual Union

Agreed to in Congress, November 15, 1777.
Ratified March 1781.

Between the states of New Hampshire, Massachusetts Bay, Rhode Island and Providence Plantations, Connecticut, New York, New Jersey, Pennsylvania, Delaware, Maryland, Virginia, North Carolina, South Carolina, Georgia.*

Article 1

The stile of this confederacy shall be "The United States of America."

Article 2

Each State retains its sovereignty, freedom and independence, and every power, jurisdiction, and right, which is not by this confederation expressly delegated to the United States, in Congress assembled.

Article 3

The said states hereby severally enter into a firm league of friendship with each other for their common defence, the security of their liberties and their mutual and general welfare; binding themselves to assist each other against all force offered to, or attacks made upon them, or any of them, on account of religion, sovereignty, trade, or any other pretence whatever.

Article 4

The better to secure and perpetuate mutual friendship and intercourse among the people of the different states in this union, the free inhabitants of each of these states, paupers, vagabonds, and fugitives from justice excepted, shall be entitled to all privileges and immunities of free citizens in the several states; and the people of each State shall have free ingress and regress to and from any other State, and shall enjoy therein all the privileges of trade and commerce, subject to the same duties, impositions, and restrictions, as the inhabitants thereof respectively; provided, that such restrictions shall not extend so far as to prevent the removal of property, imported into any State, to any other State of which the owner is an inhabitant; provided also, that no imposition, duties, or restriction, shall be laid by any State on the property of the United States, or either of them. If any person guilty of, or charged with treason, felony, or other high misdemeanor in any State, shall flee from justice and be found in any of the United States, he shall, upon demand of the governor or executive power of the State from which he fled, be delivered up and removed to the State having jurisdiction of his offence. Full faith and credit shall be given in each of these states to the records, acts, and judicial proceedings of the courts and magistrates of every other State.

Article 5

For the more convenient management of the general interests of the United States, delegates shall be annually appointed, in such manner as the legislature of each State shall direct, to meet in Congress, on the 1st Monday in November in every year, with a power reserved to each State to recall its delegates, or any of them, at any time within the year, and to send others in their stead for the remainder of the year.

*This copy of the final draft of the Articles of Confederation is from the *Journals of the Continental Congress*, 9:907–925, November 15, 1777.

No State shall be represented in Congress by less than two, nor by more than seven members; and no person shall be capable of being a delegate for more than three years in any term of six years; nor shall any person, being a delegate, be capable of holding any office under the United States, for which he, or any other for his benefit, receives any salary, fees, or emolument of any kind.

Each State shall maintain its own delegates in a meeting of the states, and while they act as members of the committee of the states.

In determining questions in the United States, in Congress assembled, each State shall have one vote.

Freedom of speech and debate in Congress shall not be impeached or questioned in any court or place out of Congress: and the members of Congress shall be protected in their persons from arrests and imprisonments, during the time of their going to and from, and attendance on Congress, except for treason, felony, or breach of the peace.

Article 6

No State, without the consent of the United States, in Congress assembled, shall send any embassy to, or receive any embassy from, or enter into any conference, agreement, alliance, or treaty with any king, prince, or state; nor shall any person, holding any office of profit or trust under the United States, or any of them, accept of any present, emolument, office or title, of any kind whatever, from any king, prince, or foreign state; nor shall the United States, in Congress assembled, or any of them, grant any title of nobility.

No two or more states shall enter into any treaty, confederation, or alliance, whatever, between them, without the consent of the United States, in Congress assembled, specifying accurately the purposes for which the same is to be entered into, and how long it shall continue.

No state shall lay any imposts or duties which may interfere with any stipulations in treaties entered into by the United States, in Congress assembled, with any king, prince, or state, in pursuance of any treaties already proposed by Congress to the courts of France and Spain.

No vessels of war shall be kept up in time of peace by any State, except such number only as shall be deemed necessary by the United States, in Congress assembled, for the defence of such State or its trade; nor shall any body of forces be kept up by any State, in time of peace, except such number only as, in the judgment of the United States, in Congress assembled, shall be deemed requisite to garrison the forts necessary for the defence of such State; but every State shall always keep up a well regulated and disciplined militia, sufficiently armed and accoutred, and shall provide, and constantly have ready for use, in public stores, a due number of field pieces and tents, and a proper quantity of arms, ammunition and camp equipage.

No State shall engage in any war without the consent of the United States, in Congress assembled, unless such State be actually invaded by enemies, or shall have received certain advice of a resolution being formed by some nation of Indians to invade such State, and the danger is so imminent as not to admit of a delay till the United States, in Congress assembled, can be consulted; nor shall any State grant commissions to any ships or vessels of war, nor letters of marque or reprisal, except it be after a declaration of war by the United States, in Congress assembled, and then only against the kingdom or state, and the subjects thereof, against which war has been so declared, and under such regulations as shall be established by the United States, in Congress assembled, unless such State be infested by pirates, in which case vessels of war may be fitted out for that occasion, and kept so long as the danger shall continue, or until the United States, in Congress assembled, shall determine otherwise.

Article 7

When land forces are raised by any State for the common defence, all officers of or under the rank of colonel, shall be appointed by the legislature of each State respectively, by whom such forces shall be raised, or in such manner as such State shall direct; and all vacancies shall be filled up by the State which first made the appointment.

Article 8

All charges of war and all other expences, that shall be incurred for the common defence or general welfare, and allowed by the United States, in Congress assembled, shall be defrayed out of a common treasury, which shall be supplied by the several states, in proportion to the value of all land within each State, granted to or surveyed for any person, as such land and the buildings and improvements thereon shall be estimated according to such mode as the United States, in Congress assembled, shall, from time to time, direct and appoint.

The taxes for paying that proportion shall be laid and levied by the authority and direction of the legislatures of the several states, within the time agreed upon by the United States, in Congress assembled.

Article 9

The United States, in Congress assembled, shall have the sole and exclusive right and power of determining on peace and war, except in the cases mentioned in the 6th article; of sending and receiving ambassadors; entering into treaties and alliances, provided that no treaty of commerce shall be made, whereby the legislative power of the respective states shall be restrained from imposing such imposts and duties on foreigners as their own people are subjected to, or from prohibiting the exportation or importation of any species of goods or commodities whatsoever; of establishing rules for deciding, in all cases, what captures on land or water shall be legal, and in what manner prizes, taken by land or naval forces in the service of the United States, shall be divided or appropriated; of granting letters of marque and reprisal in times of peace; appointing courts for the trial of piracies and felonies committed on the high seas, and establishing courts for receiving and determining, finally, appeals in all cases of captures; provided, that no member of Congress shall be appointed a judge of any of the said courts.

The United States, in Congress assembled, shall also be the last resort on appeal in all disputes and differences now subsisting, or that hereafter may arise between two or more states concerning boundary, jurisdiction or any other cause whatever; which authority shall always be exercised in the manner following: whenever the legislative or executive authority, or lawful agent of any State, in controversy with another, shall present a petition to Congress, stating the matter in question, and praying for a hearing, notice thereof shall be given, by order of Congress, to the legislative or executive authority of the other State in controversy, and a day assigned for the appearance of the parties by their lawful agents, who shall then be directed to appoint, by joint consent, commissioners or judges to constitute a court for hearing and determining the matter in question; but, if they cannot agree, Congress shall name three persons out of each of the United States, and from the list of such persons each party shall alternately strike out one, the petitioners beginning, until the number shall be reduced to thirteen; and from that number not less than seven, nor more than nine names, as Congress shall direct, shall, in the presence of Congress, be drawn out by lot; and the persons whose names shall be so drawn, or any five of them, shall be commissioners or judges to hear and finally determine the controversy, so always as a major part of the judges who shall hear the cause shall agree in the determination; and if either party shall neglect to attend at the day appointed, without shewing reasons which Congress shall judge sufficient, or, being present, shall refuse to strike, the Congress shall proceed to nominate three persons out of each State, and the secretary of Congress shall strike in behalf of such party absent or refusing; and the judgment and sentence of the court to be appointed, in the manner before prescribed, shall be final and conclusive; and if any of the parties shall refuse to submit to the authority of such court, or to appear or defend their claim or cause, the court shall nevertheless proceed to pronounce sentence or judgment, which shall, in like manner, be final and decisive, the judgment or sentence and other proceedings begin, in either case, transmitted to Congress, and lodged among the acts of Congress for the security of the parties concerned: provided, that every commissioner, before he sits in judgment, shall take an oath, to be administered by one of the judges of the supreme or superior court of the State where the cause shall be tried, "well and truly to hear and determine the matter in question, according to the best of his judgment, without favour, affection, or hope of reward:" provided, also, that no State shall be deprived of territory for the benefit of the United States.

All controversies concerning the private right of soil, claimed under different grants of two or more states, whose jurisdictions, as they may respect such lands and the states which passed such grants, are adjusted, the said grants, or either of them, being at the same time claimed to have originated antecedent to such settlement of jurisdiction, shall, on the petition of either party to the Congress of the United States, be finally determined, as near as may be, in the same manner as is before prescribed for deciding disputes respecting territorial jurisdiction between different states.

The United States, in Congress assembled, shall also have the sole and exclusive right and power of regulating the alloy and value of coin struck by their own authority, or by that of the respective states; fixing the standard of weights and measures throughout the United States; regulating the trade and managing all affairs with the Indians not members of any of the states; provided that the legislative right of any State within its own limits be not infringed or violated; establishing and regulating post offices from one State to another throughout all the United States, and exacting such postage on the papers passing through the same as may be requisite to defray the expences of the said office; appointing all officers of the land forces in the service of the United States, excepting regimental officers; appointing all the officers of the naval forces, and commissioning all officers whatever in the service of the United States; making rules for the government and regulation of the said land and naval forces, and directing their operations.

The United States, in Congress assembled, shall have authority to appoint a committee to sit in the recess of Congress, to be denominated "a Committee of the States," and to consist of one delegate from each State, and to appoint such other committees and civil officers as may be necessary for managing the general affairs of the United States, under their direction; to appoint one of their number to preside; provided that no person be allowed to serve in the office of president more than one year in any term of three years; to ascertain the necessary sums of money to be raised for the service of the United States, and to appropriate and apply the same for defraying the public expences; to borrow money or emit bills on the credit of the United States, transmitting, every half year, to the respective states, an account of the sums of money so borrowed or emitted; to build and equip a navy; to agree upon the number of land forces, and to make requisitions from each State for its quota, in proportion to the number of white inhabitants in such State; which requisitions shall be binding; and thereupon, the legislature of each State shall appoint the regimental officers, raise the men, and cloathe, arm, and equip them in a soldier-like manner, at the expence of the United States; and the officers and men so cloathed, armed, and equipped, shall march to the place appointed and within the time agreed on by the United States, in Congress assembled; but if the United States, in Congress assembled, shall, on consideration of circumstances, judge proper that any State should not raise men, or should raise a smaller number than its quota, and that any other State should raise a greater number of men than the quota thereof, such extra number shall be raised, officered, cloathed, armed, and equipped in the same manner as the quota of such State, unless the legislature of such State shall judge that such extra number cannot be safely spared out of the same, in which case they shall raise, officer, cloathe, arm, and equip as many of such extra number as they judge can be safely spared. And the officers and men so cloathed, armed, and equipped, shall march to the place appointed and within the time agreed on by the United States, in Congress assembled.

The United States, in Congress assembled, shall never engage in a war, nor grant letters of marque and reprisal in time of peace, nor enter into any treaties or alliances, nor coin money, nor regulate the value thereof, nor ascertain the sums and expences necessary for the defence and welfare of the United States, or any of them: nor emit bills, nor borrow money on the credit of the United States, nor appropriate money, nor agree upon the number of vessels of war to be built or purchased, or the number of land or sea forces to be raised, nor appoint a commander in chief of the army or navy, unless nine states assent to the same; nor shall a question on any other point, except for adjourning from day to day, be determined, unless by the votes of a majority of the United States, in Congress assembled.

The Congress of the United States shall have power to adjourn to any time within the year, and to any place within the United States, so that no period of adjournment be for a longer duration than the space of six months, and shall publish the journal of their proceedings monthly, except such parts thereof, relating to treaties, alliances or military operations, as, in their judgment, require secrecy; and the yeas and nays of the delegates of each State on any question shall be entered on the journal, when it is desired by any delegate; and the delegates of a State, or any of them, at his, or their request, shall be furnished with a transcript of the said journal, except such parts as are above excepted, to lay before the legislatures of the several states.

Article 10

The committee of the states, or any nine of them, shall be authorized to execute, in the recess of Congress, such of the powers of Congress as the United States, in Congress assembled, by the consent of nine states, shall, from time to time, think expedient to vest them with; provided, that no power be delegated to the said committee, for the exercise of which, by the articles of confederation, the voice of nine states, in the Congress of the United States assembled, is requisite.

Article 11

Canada acceding to this confederation, and joining in the measures of the United States, shall be admitted into and entitled to all the advantages of this union; but no other colony shall be admitted into the same, unless such admission be agreed to by nine states.

Article 12

All bills of credit emitted, monies borrowed and debts contracted by, or under the authority of Congress before the assembling of the United States, in pursuance of the present confederation, shall be deemed and considered as a charge against the United States, for payment and satisfaction whereof the said United States and the public faith are hereby solemnly pledged.

Article 13

Every State shall abide by the determinations of the United States, in Congress assembled, on all questions which, by this confederation, are submitted to them. And the articles of this confederation shall be inviolably observed by every State, and the union shall be perpetual; nor shall any alteration at any time hereafter be made in any of them, unless such alteration be agreed to in a Congress of the United States, and be afterwards confirmed by the legislatures of every State.

These articles shall be proposed to the legislatures of all the United States, to be considered, and if approved of by them, they are advised to authorize their delegates to ratify the same in the Congress of the United States; which being done, the same shall become conclusive.

The Constitution of the United States*

Agreed to by Philadelphia Convention, September 17, 1787. Implemented March 4, 1789.

Preamble

We the people of the United States, in order to form a more perfect union, establish justice, insure domestic tranquility, provide for the common defense, promote the general welfare, and secure the blessings of liberty to ourselves and our posterity, do ordain and establish this Constitution for the United States of America.

Article I

Section 1.   All legislative powers herein granted shall be vested in a Congress of the United States, which shall consist of a Senate and a House of Representatives.

Section 2.   The House of Representatives shall be composed of members chosen every second year by the people of the several States, and the electors in each State shall have the qualifications requisite for electors of the most numerous branch of the State Legislature.

No person shall be a Representative who shall not have attained to the age of twenty-five years, and been seven years a citizen of the United States, and who shall not, when elected, be an inhabitant of that State in which he shall be chosen.

Representatives and direct taxes shall be apportioned among the several States which may be included within this Union, according to their respective numbers, *which shall be determined by adding to the whole number of free persons, including those bound to service for a term of years and excluding Indians not taxed, three-fifths of all other persons.* The actual enumeration shall be made within three years after the first meeting of the Congress of the United States, and within every subsequent term of ten years, in such manner as they shall by law direct. The number of Representatives shall not exceed one for every thirty thousand, but each State shall have at least one Representative; and until such enumeration shall be made, *the State of New Hampshire shall be entitled to choose three, Massachusetts eight, Rhode Island and Providence Plantations one, Connecticut five, New York six, New Jersey four, Pennsylvania eight, Delaware one, Maryland six, Virginia ten, North Carolina five, South Carolina five, and Georgia three.*

---

*Passages no longer in effect are in italic type.

When vacancies happen in the representation from any State, the Executive authority thereof shall issue writs of election to fill such vacancies.

The House of Representatives shall choose their Speaker and other officers; and shall have the sole power of impeachment.

Section 3.   The Senate of the United States shall be composed of two Senators from each State, *chosen by the legislature thereof,* for six years; and each Senator shall have one vote.

Immediately after they shall be assembled in consequence of the first election, they shall be divided as equally as may be into three classes. The seats of the Senators of the first class shall be vacated at the expiration of the second year, of the second class at the expiration of the fourth year, and of the third class at the expiration of the sixth year, so that one-third may be chosen every second year; and if vacancies happen by resignation or otherwise, during the recess of the legislature of any State, the Executive thereof may make temporary appointments until the next meeting of the legislature, which shall then fill such vacancies.

No person shall be a Senator who shall not have attained to the age of thirty years, and been nine years a citizen of the United States, and who shall not, when elected, be an inhabitant of that State for which he shall be chosen.

The Vice-President of the United States shall be President of the Senate, but shall have no vote, unless they be equally divided.

The Senate shall choose their other officers, and also a President pro tempore, in the absence of the Vice-President, or when he shall exercise the office of President of the United States.

The Senate shall have the sole power to try all impeachments. When sitting for that purpose, they shall be on oath or affirmation. When the President of the United States is tried, the Chief Justice shall preside: and no person shall be convicted without the concurrence of two-thirds of the members present.

Judgment in cases of impeachment shall not extend further than to removal from the office, and disqualification to hold and enjoy any office of honor, trust or profit under the United States: but the party convicted shall nevertheless be liable and subject to indictment, trial, judgment and punishment, according to law.

Section 4.   The times, places and manner of holding elections for Senators and Representatives shall be prescribed in each State by the legislature thereof; but the Congress may at any time by law make or alter such regulations, except as to the places of choosing Senators.

The Congress shall assemble at least once in every year, and such meeting *shall be on the first Monday in December, unless they shall by law appoint a different day.*

Section 5.   Each house shall be the judge of the elections, returns and qualifications of its own members, and a majority of each shall constitute a quorum to do business; but a smaller number may adjourn from day to day, and may be authorized to compel the attendance of absent members, in such manner, and under such penalties, as each house may provide.

Each house may determine the rules of its proceedings, punish its members for disorderly behavior, and with the concurrence of two-thirds, expel a member.

Each house shall keep a journal of its proceedings, and from time to time publish the same, excepting such parts as may in their judgment require secrecy; and the yeas and nays of the members of either house on any question shall, at the desire of one fifth of those present, be entered on the journal.

Neither house, during the session of Congress, shall, without the consent of the other, adjourn for more than three days, nor to any other place than that in which the two houses shall be sitting.

Section 6.   The Senators and Representatives shall receive a compensation for their services, to be ascertained by law and paid out of the treasury of the United States. They shall in all cases except treason, felony and breach of the peace, be privileged from arrest during their attendance at the session of their respective houses, and in going to and returning from the same; and for any speech or debate in either house, they shall not be questioned in any other place.

No Senator or Representative shall, during the time for which he was elected, be appointed to any civil office under the authority of the United States, which shall have been created, or the emoluments whereof shall have been increased, during such time; and no person holding any office under the United States shall be a member of either house during his continuance in office.

Section 7.   All bills for raising revenue shall originate in the House of Representatives; but the Senate may propose or concur with amendments as on other bills.

Every bill which shall have passed the House of Representatives and the Senate, shall, before it become a law, be presented to the President of the United States; if he approve he shall sign it, but if not he shall return it with objections to that house in which it shall have originated, who shall enter the objections at large on their journal, and proceed to reconsider it. If after such reconsideration two-thirds of that house shall agree to pass the bill, it shall be sent, together with the objections, to the other house, by which it shall likewise be reconsidered, and, if approved by two-thirds of that house, it shall become a law. But in all such cases the votes of both houses shall be determined by yeas and nays, and the names of the persons voting for and against the bill shall be entered on the journal of each house respectively. If any bill shall not be returned by the President within ten days (Sundays excepted) after it shall have been presented to him, the same shall be a law, in like manner as if he had signed it, unless the Congress by their adjournment prevent its return, in which case it shall not be a law.

Every order, resolution, or vote to which the concurrence of the Senate and House of Representatives may be necessary (except on a question of adjournment) shall be presented to the President of the United States; and before the same shall take effect, shall be approved by him, or being disapproved by him, shall be repassed by two-thirds of the Senate and House of Representatives, according to the rules and limitations prescribed in the case of a bill.

Section 8.   The Congress shall have power

To lay and collect taxes, duties, imposts, and excises, to pay the debts and provide for the common defense and general welfare of the United States; but all duties, imposts and excises shall be uniform throughout the United States;

To borrow money on the credit of the United States;

To regulate commerce with foreign nations, and among the several States, and with the Indian tribes;

To establish an uniform rule of naturalization, and uniform laws on the subject of bankruptcies throughout the United States;

To coin money, regulate the value thereof, and of foreign coin, and fix the standard of weights and measures;

To provide for the punishment of counterfeiting the securities and current coin of the United States;

establish post offices and post roads;

To promote the progress of science and useful arts by securing for limited times to authors and inventors the exclusive right to their respective writings and discoveries;

To constitute tribunals inferior to the Supreme Court;

To define and punish piracies and felonies committed on the high seas and offences against the law of nations;

To declare war, grant letters of marque and reprisal, and make rules concerning captures on land and water;

To raise and support armies, but no appropriation of money to that use shall be for a longer term than two years;

To provide and maintain a navy;

To make rules for the government and regulation of the land and naval forces;

To provide for calling forth the militia to execute the laws of the Union, suppress insurrections and repel invasions;

To provide for organizing, arming, and disciplining the militia, and for governing such part of them as may be employed in the service of the United States, reserving to the States respectively the appointment of the officers, and the authority of training the militia according to the discipline prescribed by Congress;

To exercise exclusive legislation in all cases whatsoever, over such district (not exceeding ten miles square) as may, by cession of particular States, and the acceptance of Congress, become the seat of the government of the United States, and to exercise like authority over all places purchased by the consent of the legislature of the State, in which the same shall be, for erection of forts, magazines, arsenals, dock-yards, and other needful buildings;—and

To make all laws which shall be necessary and proper for carrying into execution the foregoing powers, and all other powers vested by this Constitution in the government of the United States, or in any department or officer thereof.

Section 9.   *The migration or importation of such persons as any of the States now existing shall think proper to admit shall not be prohibited by the Congress prior to the year one thousand eight hundred and eight; but a tax or duty may be imposed on such importation, not exceeding ten dollars for each person.*

The privilege of the writ of habeas corpus shall not be suspended, unless when in cases of rebellion or invasion the public safety may require it.

No bill of attainder or ex post facto law shall be passed.

No capitation, or other direct, tax shall be laid, unless in proportion to the census or enumeration herein before directed to be taken.

No tax or duty shall be laid on articles exported from any State.

No preference shall be given by any regulation of commerce or revenue to the ports of one State over those of another; nor shall vessels bound to, or from, one State be obliged to enter, clear, or pay duties in another.

No money shall be drawn from the treasury, but in consequence of appropriations made by law; and a regular statement and account of the receipts and expenditures of all public money shall be published from time to time.

No title of nobility shall be granted by the United States: and no person holding any office of profit or trust under them, shall, without the consent of the Congress, accept of any present, emolument, office, or title, of any kind whatever, from any king, prince, or foreign state.

Section 10.   No State shall enter into any treaty, alliance, or confederation; grant letters of marque and reprisal; coin money; emit bills of credit; make anything but gold and silver coin a tender in payment of debts; pass any bill of attainder, ex post facto law, or law impairing the obligation of contracts, or grant any title of nobility.

No State shall, without the consent of Congress, lay any imposts or duties on imports or exports, except what may be absolutely necessary for executing its inspection laws: and the net produce of all duties and imposts, laid by any State on imports or exports, shall be for the use of the treasury of the United States; and all such laws shall be subject to the revision and control of the Congress.

No State shall, without the consent of Congress, lay any duty of tonnage, keep troops, or ships of war in time of peace, enter into any agreement or compact with another State, or with a foreign power, or engage in war, unless actually invaded, or in such imminent danger as will not admit of delay.

Article II

Section 1.   The executive power shall be vested in a President of the United States of America. He shall hold his office during the term of four years, and, together with the Vice-President, chosen for the same term, be elected as follows:

Each State shall appoint, in such manner as the legislature thereof may direct, a number of electors, equal to the whole number of Senators and Representatives to which the State may be entitled in the Congress; but no Senator or Representative, or person holding an office of trust or profit under the United States, shall be appointed an elector.

The electors shall meet in their respective States, and vote by ballot for two persons, of whom one at least shall not be an inhabitant of the same State with themselves. And they shall make a list of all the persons voted for, and of the number of votes for each; which list they shall sign and certify, and transmit sealed to the seat of government of the United States, directed to the President of the Senate. The President of the Senate shall, in the presence of the Senate and House of Representatives, open all the certificates, and the votes shall then be counted. The person having the greatest number of votes shall be the President, if such number be a majority of the whole number of electors appointed; and if there be more than one who have such majority, and have an equal number of votes, then the House of Representatives shall immediately choose by ballot one of them for President; and if no person have a majority, then from the five highest on the list said house shall in like manner choose the President. But in choosing the President the votes shall be taken by States, the representation from each State having one vote; a quorum for this purpose shall consist of a member or members from two-thirds of the States, and a majority of all the States shall be necessary to a choice. In every case, after the choice of the President, the person having the greatest number of votes of the electors shall be the Vice-President. But if there should remain two or more who have equal votes, the Senate shall choose from them by ballot the Vice-President.

The Congress may determine the time of choosing the electors, and the day on which they shall give their votes; which day shall be the same throughout the United States.

No person except a natural-born citizen, *or a citizen of the United States at the time of the adoption of this Constitution,* shall be eligible to the office of President; neither shall any person be eligible to that office who shall not have attained to the age of thirty-five years, and been fourteen years a resident within the United States.

In cases of the removal of the President from office or of his death, resignation, or inability to discharge the powers and duties of the said office, the same shall devolve on the Vice-President, and the Congress may by law provide for the case of removal, death, resignation, or inability, both of the President and Vice-President, declaring what officer shall then act as President, and such officer shall act accordingly, until the disability be removed, or a President shall be elected.

The President shall, at stated times, receive for his services a compensation, which shall neither be increased nor diminished during the period for which he shall have been elected, and he shall not receive within that period any other emolument from the United States, or any of them.

Before he enter on the execution of his office, he shall take the following oath or affirmation:—"I do solemnly swear (or affirm) that I will faithfully execute the office of the President of the United States, and will to the best of my ability preserve, protect and defend the Constitution of the United States."

Section 2. The President shall be commander in chief of the army and navy of the United States, and of the militia of the several States, when called into the actual service of the United States; he may require the opinion, in writing, of the principal officer in each of the executive departments, upon any subject relating to the duties of their respective offices, and he shall have power to grant reprieves and pardons for offenses against the United States, except in cases of impeachment.

He shall have power, by and with the advice and consent of the Senate, to make treaties, provided two-thirds of the Senators present concur; and he shall nominate, and by and with the advice and consent of the Senate, shall appoint ambassadors, other public ministers and consuls, judges of the Supreme Court, and all other officers of the United States, whose appointments are not herein otherwise provided for, and which shall be established by law: but Congress may by law vest the appointment of such inferior officers, as they think proper, in the President alone, in the courts of law, or in the heads of departments.

The President shall have power to fill up all vacancies that may happen during the recess of the Senate, by granting commissions which shall expire at the end of their next session.

Section 3. He shall from time to time give to the Congress information of the state of the Union, and recommend to their consideration such measures as he shall judge necessary and expedient; he may, on extraordinary occasions, convene both houses, or either of them, and in case of disagreement between them, with respect to the time of adjournment, he may adjourn them to such time as he shall think proper; he shall receive ambassadors and other public ministers; he shall take care that the laws be faithfully executed, and shall commission all the officers of the United States.

Section 4. The President, Vice-President and all civil officers of the United States shall be removed from office on impeachment for, and on conviction of, treason, bribery, or other high crimes and misdemeanors.

Article III

Section 1.   The judicial power of the United States shall be vested in one Supreme Court, and in such inferior courts as the Congress may from time to time ordain and establish. The judges, both of the Supreme and inferior courts, shall hold their offices during good behavior, and shall, at stated times, receive for their services a compensation which shall not be diminished during their continuance in office.

Section 2.   The judicial power shall extend to all cases, in law and equity, arising under this Constitution, the laws of the United States, and treaties made, or which shall be made, under their authority;—to all cases affecting ambassadors, other public ministers and consuls;—to all cases of admiralty and maritime jurisdiction;—to controversies to which the United States shall be a party;—to controversies between two or more States;—between a State and citizens of another State;—between citizens of different States;—between citizens of the same State claiming lands under grants of different States, and between a State, or the citizens thereof, and foreign states, citizens or subjects.

In all cases affecting ambassadors, other public ministers and consuls, and those in which a State shall be party, the Supreme Court shall have original jurisdiction. In all the other cases before mentioned, the Supreme Court shall have appellate jurisdiction, both as to law and fact, with such exceptions, and under such regulations, as the Congress shall make.

The trial of all crimes, except in cases of impeachment, shall be by jury; and such trial shall be held in the State where said crimes shall have been committed; but when not committed within any State, the trial shall be at such place or places as the Congress may by Law have directed.

Section 3.   Treason against the United States shall consist only in levying war against them, or in adhering to their enemies, giving them aid and comfort. No person shall be convicted of treason unless on the testimony of two witnesses to the same overt act, or on confession in open court.

The Congress shall have power to declare the punishment of treason, but no attainder of treason shall work corruption of blood, or forfeiture except during the life of the person attainted.

Article IV

Section 1.   Full faith and credit shall be given in each State to the public acts, records, and judicial proceedings of every other State. And the Congress may by general laws prescribe the manner in which such acts, records, and proceedings shall be proved, and the effect thereof.

Section 2.   The citizens of each State shall be entitled to all privileges and immunities of citizens in the several States.

A person charged in any State with treason, felony, or other crime, who shall flee from justice, and be found in another State, shall on demand of the executive authority of the State from which he fled, be delivered up, to be removed to the State having jurisdiction of the crime.

No Person held to service or labor in one State, under the laws thereof, escaping into another, shall, in consequence of any law or regulation therein, be discharged from such service or labor, but shall be delivered up on claim of the party to whom such service or labor may be due.

Section 3.   New States may be admitted by the Congress into this Union; but no new State shall be formed or erected within the jurisdiction of any other State; nor any State be formed by the junction of two or more States, or parts of States, without the consent of the legislatures of the States concerned as well as of the Congress.

The Congress shall have power to dispose of and make all needful rules and regulations respecting the territory or other property belonging to the United States; and nothing in this Constitution shall be so construed as to prejudice any claims of the United States, or of any particular State.

Section 4.   The United States shall guarantee to every State in this Union a republican form of government, and shall protect each of them against invasion; and on application of the legislature, or of the executive (when the legislature cannot be convened), against domestic violence.

Article V

The Congress, whenever two-thirds of both houses shall deem it necessary, shall propose amendments to this Constitution, or, on the application of the legislatures of two-thirds of the several States, shall call a convention for proposing amendments, which, in either case, shall be valid to all intents and purposes, as part of this Constitution, when ratified by the legislatures of three-fourths of the several States, or by conventions in three-fourths thereof, as the one or the other mode of ratification may be proposed by the Congress; *provided that no amendments which may be made prior to the year one thousand eight hundred and eight shall in any manner affect the first and fourth clauses in the ninth section of the first article;* and that no State, without its consent, shall be deprived of its equal suffrage in the Senate.

Article VI

All debts contracted and engagements entered into, before the adoption of this Constitution, shall be as valid against the United States under this Constitution, as under the Confederation.

This Constitution, and the laws of the United States which shall be made in pursuance thereof; and all treaties made, or which shall be made, under the authority of the United States, shall be the supreme law of the land; and the judges in every State shall be bound thereby, anything in the Constitution or laws of any State to the contrary notwithstanding.

The Senators and Representatives before mentioned, and the members of the several State legislatures, and all executive and judicial officers, both of the United States and of the several States, shall be bound by oath or affirmation to support this Constitution; but no religious test shall ever be required as a qualification to any office or public trust under the United States.

Article VII

The ratification of the conventions of nine States shall be sufficient for the establishment of this Constitution between the States so ratifying the same.

Done in convention by the unanimous consent of the States present, the seventeenth day of September in the year of our Lord one thousand seven hundred and eighty-seven and of the Independence of the United States of America the twelfth. In witness whereof we have hereunto subscribed our names.

GEORGE WASHINGTON, President and Deputy from Virginia

New Hampshire
John Langdon
Nicholas Gilman

Massachusetts
Nathaniel Gorham
Rufus King

Connecticut
William Samuel
Johnson
Roger Sherman

New York
Alexander Hamilton

New Jersey
William Livingston
David Brearley
William Paterson
Jonathan Dayton

Pennsylvania
Benjamin Franklin
Thomas Mifflin
Robert Morris
George Clymer
Thomas FitzSimons
Jared Ingersoll
James Wilson
Gouverneur Morris

Delaware
George Read
Gunning Bedford, Jr.
John Dickinson
Richard Bassett
Jacob Broom

Maryland
James McHenry
Daniel of St. Thomas Jenifer
Daniel Carroll

Virginia
John Blair
James Madison, Jr.

North Carolina
William Blount
Richard Dobbs Spaight
Hugh Williamson

South Carolina
John Rutledge
Charles Cotesworth
Pinckney
Charles Pinckney
Pierce Butler

Georgia
William Few
Abraham Baldwin

Amendments to the Constitution

(including six unratified amendments)

Amendment I   [Ratified 1791]

Congress shall make no law respecting an establishment of religion, or prohibiting the free exercise thereof; or abridging the freedom of speech, or of the press; or the right of the people peaceably to assemble, and to petition the government for a redress of grievances.

Amendment II   [Ratified 1791]

A well-regulated militia being necessary to the security of a free State, the right of the people to keep and bear arms shall not be infringed.

Amendment III   [Ratified 1791]

No soldier shall, in time of peace, be quartered in any house without the consent of the owner, nor in time of war, but in a manner to be prescribed by law.

Amendment IV   [Ratified 1791]

The right of the people to be secure in their persons, houses, papers, and effects, against unreasonable searches and seizures, shall not be violated, and no warrants shall issue but upon probable cause, supported by oath or affirmation, and particularly describing the place to be searched, and the persons or things to be seized.

Amendment V   [Ratified 1791]

No person shall be held to answer for a capital, or otherwise infamous crime, unless on a presentment or indictment of a grand jury, except in cases arising in the land or naval forces, or in the militia, when in actual service in time of war or public danger; nor shall any person be subject for the same offence to be twice put in jeopardy of life or limb; nor shall be compelled in any criminal case to be a witness against himself, nor be deprived of life, liberty, or property, without due process of law; nor shall private property be taken for public use without just compensation.

Amendment VI   [Ratified 1791]

In all criminal prosecutions, the accused shall enjoy the right to a speedy and public trial, by an impartial jury of the State and district wherein the crime shall have been committed, which district shall have been previously ascertained by law, and to be informed of the nature and cause of the accusation; to be confronted with the witnesses against him; to have compulsory process for obtaining witnesses in his favor, and to have the assistance of counsel for his defence.

Amendment VII   [Ratified 1791]

In suits at common law, where the value in controversy shall exceed twenty dollars, the right of trial by jury shall be preserved, and no fact tried by a jury shall be otherwise reexamined in any court of the United States, than according to the rules of the common law.

Amendment VIII   [Ratified 1791]

Excessive bail shall not be required, nor excessive fines imposed, nor cruel and unusual punishments inflicted.

Amendment IX   [Ratified 1791]

The enumeration in the Constitution, of certain rights, shall not be construed to deny or disparage others retained by the people.

Amendment X   [Ratified 1791]

The powers not delegated to the United States by the Constitution, nor prohibited by it to the States, are reserved to the States respectively, or to the people.

Unratified Amendment

[Reapportionment Amendment (proposed by Congress September 25, 1789, along with the Bill of Rights)]

After the first enumeration required by the first article of the Constitution, there shall be one Representative for every thirty thousand, until the number shall amount to one hundred, after which the proportion shall be so regulated by Congress, that there shall be not less than one hundred Representatives, nor less than one Representative for every forty thousand persons, until the number of Representatives shall amount to two hundred; after which the proportion shall be so regulated by Congress, that there shall not be less than two hundred Representatives, nor more than one Representative for every fifty thousand persons.

Amendment XI   [Ratified 1798]

The judicial power of the United States shall not be construed to extend to any suit in law or equity, commenced or prosecuted against one of the United States by citizens of another State, or by citizens or subjects of any foreign state.

Amendment XII   [Ratified 1804]

The electors shall meet in their respective States, and vote by ballot for President and Vice-President, one of whom, at least, shall not be an inhabitant of the same State with themselves; they shall name in their ballots the person voted for as President, and in distinct ballots the person voted for as Vice-President, and they shall make distinct lists of all persons voted for as President, and of all persons voted for as Vice-President, and of the number of votes for each, which lists they shall sign and certify, and transmit sealed to the seat of government of the United States, directed to the President of the Senate;—the President of the Senate shall, in the presence of the Senate and House of Representatives, open all the certificates and the votes shall then be counted;—the person having the greatest number of votes for President shall be the President, if such number be a majority of the whole number of electors appointed; and if no person have such majority, then from the persons having the highest numbers not exceeding three on the list of those voted for as President, the House of Representatives shall choose immediately, by ballot, the President. But in choosing the President, the votes shall be taken by States, the representation from each State having one vote; a quorum for this purpose shall consist of a member or members from two-thirds of the States, and a majority of all the States shall be necessary to a choice. And if the House of Representatives shall not choose a President whenever the right of choice shall devolve upon them, before *the fourth day of March* next following, then the Vice-President shall act as President, as in the case of the death or other constitutional disability of the President.

The person having the greatest number of votes as Vice-President shall be the Vice-President, if such number be a majority of the whole number of electors appointed; and if no person have a majority, then from the two highest numbers on the list the Senate shall choose the Vice-President; a quorum for the purpose shall consist of two-thirds of the whole number of Senators, and a majority of the whole number shall be necessary to a choice. But no person constitutionally ineligible to the office of President shall be eligible to that of Vice-President of the United States.

Unratified Amendment

[Titles of Nobility Amendment (proposed by Congress May 1, 1810)]

If any citizen of the United States shall accept, claim, receive or retain any title of nobility or honor or shall, without the consent of Congress, accept and retain any present, pension, office or emolument of any kind whatever, from any emperor, king, prince or foreign power, such person shall cease to be a citizen of the United States, and shall be incapable of holding any office of trust or profit under them or either of them.

Unratified Amendment

[Corwin Amendment (proposed by Congress March 2, 1861)]

No amendment shall be made to the Constitution which will authorize or give to Congress the power to abolish or interfere, within any State, with the domestic institutions thereof, including that of persons held to labor or service by the laws of said State.

Amendment XIII   [Ratified 1865]

Section 1.   Neither slavery nor involuntary servitude, except as a punishment for crime whereof the party shall have been duly convicted, shall exist within the United States, or any place subject to their jurisdiction.

Section 2.   Congress shall have power to enforce this article by appropriate legislation.

Amendment XIV   [Ratified 1868]

Section 1.   All persons born or naturalized in the United States, and subject to the jurisdiction thereof, are citizens of the United States and of the State wherein they reside. No State shall make or enforce any law which shall abridge the privileges or immunities of citizens of the United States; nor shall any State deprive any person of life, liberty, or property, without due process of law; nor deny to any person within its jurisdiction the equal protection of the laws.

Section 2.   Representatives shall be appointed among the several States according to their respective numbers, counting the whole number of persons in each State, excluding Indians not taxed. But when the right to vote at any election for the choice of Electors for President and Vice-President of the United States, Representatives in Congress, the executive and judicial officers of a State, or the members of the legislature thereof, is denied to any of the *male* inhabitants of such State, being *twenty-one* years of age and citizens of the United States, or in any way abridged, except for participation in rebellion, or other crime, the basis of representation therein shall be reduced in the proportion which the number of such male citizens shall bear to the whole number of *male* citizens *twenty-one* years of age in such State.

Section 3.   No person shall be a Senator or Representative in Congress, or Elector of President and Vice-President, or hold any office, civil or military, under the United States, or under any State, who, having previously taken an oath, as a member of Congress, or as an officer of the United States, or as a member of any State legislature, or as an executive or judicial officer of any State, to support the Constitution of the United States, shall have engaged in insurrection or rebellion against the same, or given aid or comfort to the enemies thereof. Congress may, by a vote of two-thirds of each house, remove such disability.

Section 4.   The validity of the public debt of the United States, authorized by law, including debts incurred for payment of pensions and bounties for services in suppressing insurrection or rebellion, shall not be questioned. But neither the United States nor any State shall assume or pay any debt or obligation incurred in aid of insurrection or rebellion against the United States, or any claim for the loss or emancipation of any slave; but all such debts, obligations, and claims shall be held illegal and void.

Section 5.   The Congress shall have power to enforce, by appropriate legislation, the provisions of this article.

Amendment XV   [Ratified 1870]

Section 1.   The right of citizens of the United States to vote shall not be denied or abridged by the United States or by any State on account of race, color, or previous condition of servitude.

Section 2.   The Congress shall have power to enforce this article by appropriate legislation.

Amendment XVI   [Ratified 1913]

The Congress shall have power to lay and collect taxes on incomes, from whatever source derived, without apportionment among the several States, and without regard to any census or enumeration.

Amendment XVII   [Ratified 1913]

Section 1.   The Senate of the United States shall be composed of two Senators from each State, elected by the people thereof, for six years; and each Senator shall have one vote. The electors in each State shall have the qualifications requisite for electors of [voters for] the most numerous branch of the State legislatures.

Section 2.   When vacancies happen in the representation of any State in the Senate, the executive authority of such State shall issue writs of election to fill such vacancies: Provided, that the Legislature of any State may empower the executive thereof to make temporary appointments until the people fill the vacancies by election as the Legislature may direct.

Section 3.   *This amendment shall not be so construed as to affect the election or term of any Senator chosen before it becomes valid as part of the Constitution.*

Amendment XVIII

[Ratified 1919; repealed 1933 by Amendment XXI]

Section 1.   *After one year from the ratification of this article the manufacture, sale, or transportation of intoxicating liquors within, the importation thereof into, or the exportation thereof from the United States and all territory subject to the jurisdiction thereof, for beverage purposes, is hereby prohibited.*

Section 2.   *The Congress and the several States shall have concurrent power to enforce this article by appropriate legislation.*

Section 3.   *This article shall be inoperative unless it shall have been ratified as an amendment to the Constitution by the legislatures of the several States, as provided by the Constitution, within seven years from the date of the submission thereof to the States by the Congress.*

Amendment XIX   [Ratified 1920]

Section 1.   The right of citizens of the United States to vote shall not be denied or abridged by the United States or by any State on account of sex.

Section 2.   Congress shall have the power to enforce this article by appropriate legislation.

Unratified Amendment

[Child Labor Amendment (proposed by Congress June 2, 1924)]

Section 1.   *The Congress shall have power to limit, regulate, and prohibit the labor of persons under eighteen years of age.*

Section 2.   *The power of the several States is unimpaired by this article except that the operation of State laws shall be suspended to the extent necessary to give effect to legislation enacted by Congress.*

Amendment XX   [Ratified 1933]

Section 1.   The terms of the President and Vice-President shall end at noon on the 20th day of January, and the terms of Senators and Representatives at noon on the 3rd day of January, of the years in which such terms would have ended if this article had not been ratified; and the terms of their successors shall then begin.

Section 2. The Congress shall assemble at least once in every year, and such meeting shall begin at noon on the 3rd day of January, unless they shall by law appoint a different day.

Section 3. If, at the time fixed for the beginning of the term of the President, the President-elect shall have died, the Vice-President-elect shall become President. If a President shall not have been chosen before the time fixed for the beginning of his term, or if the President-elect shall have failed to qualify, then the Vice-President-elect shall act as President until a President shall have qualified; and the Congress may by law provide for the case wherein neither a President-elect nor a Vice-President-elect shall have qualified, declaring who shall then act as President, or the manner in which one who is to act shall be selected, and such person shall act accordingly until a President or Vice-President shall have qualified.

Section 4. The Congress may by law provide for the case of the death of any of the persons from whom the House of Representatives may choose a President whenever the right of choice shall have devolved upon them, and for the case of the death of any of the persons from whom the Senate may choose a Vice-President whenever the right of choice shall have devolved upon them.

Section 5. Sections 1 and 2 shall take effect on the 15th day of October following the ratification of this article.

Section 6. This article shall be inoperative unless it shall have been ratified as an amendment to the Constitution by the Legislatures of three-fourths of the several States within seven years from the date of its submission.

Amendment XXI [Ratified 1933]

Section 1. The eighteenth article of amendment to the Constitution of the United States is hereby repealed.

Section 2. The transportation or importation into any State, Territory, or Possession of the United States for delivery or use therein of intoxicating liquors, in violation of the laws thereof, is hereby prohibited.

Section 3. This article shall be inoperative unless it shall have been ratified as an amendment to the Constitution by conventions in the several States, as provided in the Constitution, within seven years from the date of the submission thereof to the States by the Congress.

Amendment XXII [Ratified 1951]

Section 1. No person shall be elected to the office of the President more than twice, and no person who has held the office of President, or acted as President, for more than two years of a term to which some other person was elected President shall be elected to the office of President more than once. But this article shall not apply to any person holding the office of President when this Article was proposed by the Congress, and shall not prevent any person who may be holding the office of President, or acting as President, during the term within which this Article becomes operative from holding the office of President or acting as President during the remainder of such term.

Section 2. This article shall be inoperative unless it shall have been ratified as an amendment to the Constitution by the legislatures of three-fourths of the several States within seven years from the date of its submission to the States by the Congress.

Amendment XXIII   [Ratified 1961]

Section 1.   The District constituting the seat of Government of the United States shall appoint in such manner as the Congress may direct: A number of electors of President and Vice-President equal to the whole number of Senators and Representatives in Congress to which the District would be entitled if it were a State, but in no event more than the least populous State; they shall be in addition to those appointed by the States, but they shall be considered for the purposes of the election of President and Vice-President, to be electors appointed by a State; and they shall meet in the District and perform such duties as provided by the twelfth article of amendment.

Section 2.   The Congress shall have the power to enforce this article by appropriate legislation.

Amendment XXIV   [Ratified 1964]

Section 1.   The right of citizens of the United States to vote in any primary or other election for President or Vice-President, for electors for President or Vice-President, or for Senator or Representative in Congress, shall not be denied or abridged by the United States or any State by reason of failure to pay any poll tax or other tax.

Section 2.   The Congress shall have the power to enforce this article by appropriate legislation.

Amendment XXV   [Ratified 1967]

Section 1.   In case of the removal of the President from office or of his death or resignation, the Vice-President shall become President.

Section 2.   Whenever there is a vacancy in the office of the Vice-President, the President shall nominate a Vice-President who shall take office upon confirmation by a majority vote of both Houses of Congress.

Section 3.   Whenever the President transmits to the President pro tempore of the Senate and the Speaker of the House of Representatives his written declaration that he is unable to discharge the powers and duties of his office, and until he transmits to them a written declaration to the contrary, such powers and duties shall be discharged by the Vice-President as Acting President.

Section 4.   Whenever the Vice-President and a majority of either the principal officers of the executive departments or of such other body as Congress may by law provide, transmit to the President pro tempore of the Senate and the Speaker of the House of Representatives their written declaration that the President is unable to discharge the powers and duties of his office, the Vice-President shall immediately assume the powers and duties of the office as Acting President.

Thereafter, when the President transmits to the President pro tempore of the Senate and the Speaker of the House of Representatives his written declaration that no inability exists, he shall resume the powers and duties of his office unless the Vice-President and a majority of either the principal officers of the executive department[s] or of such other body as Congress may by law provide, transmit within four days to the President pro tempore of the Senate and the Speaker of the House of Representatives their written declaration that the President is unable to discharge the powers and duties of his office. Thereupon Congress shall decide the issue, assembling within forty-eight hours for that purpose if not in session. If the Congress, within twenty-one days after receipt of the latter written declaration, or, if Congress is not in session, within twenty-one days after Congress is required to assemble, determines by two-thirds vote of both Houses that the President is unable to discharge the powers and duties of his office, the Vice-President shall continue to discharge the same as Acting President; otherwise, the President shall resume the powers and duties of his office.

Amendment XXVI   [Ratified 1971]

Section 1.   The right of citizens of the United States, who are eighteen years of age or older, to vote shall not be denied or abridged by the United States or by any State on account of age.

Section 2.   The Congress shall have power to enforce this article by appropriate legislation.

Unratified Amendment

[Equal Rights Amendment (proposed by Congress March 22, 1972; seven-year deadline for ratification extended to June 30, 1982)]

Section 1.   *Equality of rights under the law shall not be denied or abridged by the United States or by any State on account of sex.*

Section 2.   *The Congress shall have the power to enforce, by appropriate legislation, the provisions of this article.*

Section 3.   *This amendment shall take effect two years after the date of ratification.*

Unratified Amendment

[D.C. Statehood Amendment (proposed by Congress August 22, 1978)]

Section 1.   *For purposes of representation in the Congress, election of the President and Vice-President, and article V of this Constitution, the District constituting the seat of government of the United States shall be treated as though it were a State.*

Section 2.   *The exercise of the rights and powers conferred under this article shall be by the people of the District constituting the seat of government, and as shall be provided by Congress.*

Section 3.   *The twenty-third article of amendment to the Constitution of the United States is hereby repealed.*

Section 4.   *This article shall be inoperative, unless it shall have been ratified as an amendment to the Constitution by the legislatures of three-fourths of the several states within seven years from the date of its submission.*

Amendment XXVII   [Ratified 1992]

No law, varying the compensation for the services of the Senators and Representatives, shall take effect, until an election of Representatives shall have intervened.

Admission of States to the Union

State	Year of Admission
Delaware	1787
Pennsylvania	1787
New Jersey	1787
Georgia	1788
Connecticut	1788
Massachusetts	1788
Maryland	1788
South Carolina	1788
New Hampshire	1788
Virginia	1788
New York	1788
North Carolina	1789
Rhode Island	1790
Vermont	1791
Kentucky	1792
Tennessee	1796
Ohio	1803
Louisiana	1812
Indiana	1816
Mississippi	1817
Illinois	1818
Alabama	1819
Maine	1820
Missouri	1821
Arkansas	1836

State	Year of Admission
Michigan	1837
Florida	1845
Texas	1845
Iowa	1846
Wisconsin	1848
California	1850
Minnesota	1858
Oregon	1859
Kansas	1861
West Virginia	1863
Nevada	1864
Nebraska	1867
Colorado	1876
North Dakota	1889
South Dakota	1889
Montana	1889
Washington	1889
Idaho	1890
Wyoming	1890
Utah	1896
Oklahoma	1907
New Mexico	1912
Arizona	1912
Alaska	1959
Hawaii	1959

Presidents of the United States

President	Term
George Washington	1789–1797
John Adams	1797–1801
Thomas Jefferson	1801–1809
James Madison	1809–1817
James Monroe	1817–1825
John Quincy Adams	1825–1829
Andrew Jackson	1829–1837
Martin Van Buren	1837–1841
William H. Harrison	1841
John Tyler	1841–1845
James K. Polk	1845–1849
Zachary Taylor	1849–1850
Millard Fillmore	1850–1853
Franklin Pierce	1853–1857
James Buchanan	1857–1861
Abraham Lincoln	1861–1865
Andrew Johnson	1865–1869
Ulysses S. Grant	1869–1877
Rutherford B. Hayes	1877–1881
James A. Garfield	1881
Chester A. Arthur	1881–1885
Grover Cleveland	1885–1889
Benjamin Harrison	1889–1893

President	Term
Grover Cleveland	1893–1897
William McKinley	1897–1901
Theodore Roosevelt	1901–1909
William H. Taft	1909–1913
Woodrow Wilson	1913–1921
Warren G. Harding	1921–1923
Calvin Coolidge	1923–1929
Herbert Hoover	1929–1933
Franklin D. Roosevelt	1933–1945
Harry S. Truman	1945–1953
Dwight D. Eisenhower	1953–1961
John F. Kennedy	1961–1963
Lyndon B. Johnson	1963–1969
Richard M. Nixon	1969–1974
Gerald R. Ford	1974–1977
Jimmy Carter	1977–1981
Ronald Reagan	1981–1989
George H. W. Bush	1989–1993
Bill Clinton	1993–2001
George W. Bush	2001–2009
Barack Obama	2009–2017
Donald J. Trump	2017–2021
Joseph R. Biden	2021–Present

Glossary of Key Terms

Adams-Onís Treaty Treaty negotiated by John Quincy Adams and signed in 1819 by which Spain ceded all of its lands east of the Mississippi River to the United States. (p. 292)

Alamo Texas fort captured by General Santa Anna on March 6, 1836, from rebel defenders. Sensationalist accounts of the siege of the Alamo increased popular support in the United States for Texas independence. (p. 371)

Albany Congress June 1754 meeting in Albany, New York, of Iroquois and colonial representatives meant to facilitate better relations between Britain and the Iroquois Confederacy. Benjamin Franklin also put forward a plan for colonial union that was never implemented. (p. 145)

Alien and Sedition Acts 1798 security acts passed by the Federalist-controlled Congress. The Alien Act allowed the president to imprison or deport noncitizens; the Sedition Act placed significant restrictions on political speech. (p. 237)

American Anti-Slavery Society (AASS) Abolitionist society founded by William Lloyd Garrison in 1833 that became the most important northern abolitionist organization of the period. (p. 340)

American Colonization Society (ACS) Organization formed in 1817 to establish colonies of freed slaves and freeborn blacks in Africa. The ACS was led by a group of white elites whose primary goal was to rid the nation of African Americans. (p. 256)

American Equal Rights Association Group of black and white women and men formed in 1866 to promote gender and racial equality. The organization split in 1869 over support for the Fifteenth Amendment. (p. 477)

American System Plan proposed by Henry Clay to promote the U.S. economy by combining federally funded internal improvements to aid farmers with federal tariffs to protect U.S. manufacturing and a national bank to oversee economic development. (p. 291)

American system of manufacturing Production system focused on water-powered machinery, division of labor, and the use of interchangeable parts.

The introduction of the American system in the early nineteenth century greatly increased the productivity of American manufacturing. (p. 272)

Antifederalists Opponents of ratification of the Constitution. Antifederalists were generally more rural and less wealthy than the Federalists. (p. 227)

Appeal . . . to the Colored Citizens of the World Radical abolitionist pamphlet published by David Walker in 1829. Walker's work inspired some white abolitionists to take a more radical stance on slavery. (p. 340)

Articles of Confederation Plan for national government proposed by the Continental Congress in 1777 and ratified in March 1781. The Articles of Confederation gave the national government limited powers, reflecting widespread fear of centralized authority. (p. 195)

Atlantic economy The systematic exchange of goods and people between Europe and the Americas that emerged in the seventeenth century. (p. 42)

Aztecs Spanish term for the Mexica, an indigenous people who built an empire in present-day Mexico in the centuries before the arrival of the Spaniards. The Aztecs built their empire through conquest. (p. 4)

Bacon's Rebellion 1676 uprising in Virginia led by Nathaniel Bacon. Bacon and his followers, many of whom were former servants, were upset by the Virginia governor's unwillingness to send troops to intervene in conflicts between settlers and Indians and by the lack of representation of western settlers in the House of Burgesses. (p. 52)

Battle of Antietam Fought in September 1862, this Civil War battle was the bloodiest single day in U.S. military history, but it gave Abraham Lincoln the victory he sought before announcing the Emancipation Proclamation. (p. 437)

Battle of Bull Run (Manassas) First major battle of the Civil War at which Confederate troops routed Union forces in July 1861. (p. 431)

Battle of Bunker Hill Early Revolutionary War battle in which British troops narrowly defeated patriot militias, emboldening patriot forces. (p. 181)

Battle of Fallen Timbers Battle at which U.S. General Anthony Wayne won a major victory over a multi-tribe coalition of American Indians in the Northwest Territory in 1794. (p. 285)

Battle of Gettysburg Key July 1863 battle that helped turn the tide for the Union. The Union victory at Gettysburg, combined with a victory at Vicksburg that same month, positioned the Union to push farther into the South. (p. 446)

Battle of Horseshoe Bend In 1814, Tennessee militia led by Andrew Jackson fought alongside Cherokee warriors to defeat Creek forces allied with Britain during the War of 1812. (p. 288)

Battle of Oriskany In one of the bloodiest Revolutionary War battles, a force of German-American farmers and Oneida Indians deterred British troops and their Indian allies in central New York State, leaving British forces further east vulnerable to attack by the Continental Army. (p. 192)

Battle of Saratoga Key Revolutionary War battle fought at Saratoga, New York. The patriot victory there in October 1777 provided hope that the colonists could prevail and increased the chances that the French would formally join the patriot side. (p. 192)

Battle of Shiloh April 1862 battle in Tennessee that provided the Union entrance to the Mississippi valley. Shiloh was the bloodiest battle in American history to that point. (p. 436)

Battle of Yorktown Decisive battle in which the surrender of British forces on October 19, 1781, at Yorktown, Virginia, effectively sealed the patriot victory in the Revolutionary War. (p. 203)

benign neglect British colonial policy from about 1700 to 1760 that relaxed supervision of internal colonial affairs as long as the North American colonies produced sufficient raw materials and revenue; also known as *salutary neglect*. (p. 156)

Beringia Land bridge that linked Siberia and Alaska during the Wisconsin period. Migrants from northeast Asia used this bridge to travel to North America. (p. 3)

Bill of Rights The first ten amendments to the Constitution. These ten amendments helped reassure Americans who feared that the federal government established under the Constitution would infringe on the rights of individuals and states. (p. 228)

black codes Racial laws passed in the immediate aftermath of the Civil War by southern legislatures. The black codes were intended to reduce free African Americans to a condition as close to slavery as possible. (p. 471)

Black Death The epidemic of bubonic plague that swept through Europe beginning in the mid-fourteenth century and wiped out roughly half of Europe's population. (p. 10)

Bleeding Kansas The Kansas Territory during a period of violent conflicts over the fate of slavery in the mid-1850s. The violence in Kansas intensified the sectional division over slavery. (p. 412)

Boston Massacre 1770 clash between colonial protesters and British soldiers in Boston that led to the death of five colonists. The bloody conflict was used to promote the patriot cause. (p. 164)

capitalist system Economy in which private individuals and corporations rather than the government primarily own and sustain the means of production, distribution, and exchange. (p. 274)

carpetbaggers Derogatory term for white Northerners who moved to the South in the years following the Civil War. Many white Southerners believed that such migrants were intent on exploiting their suffering. (p. 479)

Church of England National church established by Henry VIII after he split with the Catholic Church. (p. 40)

Coercive Acts (Intolerable Acts) 1774 act of Parliament passed in response to the Boston Tea Party. The Coercive Acts were meant to force the colonists into submission, but they only resulted in increased resistance. Colonial patriots called them the Intolerable Acts. (p. 165)

Columbian exchange The biological exchange between the Americas and the rest of the world. Although the initial impact of the Columbian exchange was strongest in the Americas and Europe, it was soon felt all over the world. (p. 20)

committee of correspondence Type of committee first established in Massachusetts to circulate concerns and reports of protests and other events to leaders in other colonies in the aftermath of the Sugar Act. (p. 157)

Common Sense Pamphlet arguing in favor of independence written by Thomas Paine and published in 1776. *Common Sense* was widely read and had an important impact on the debate over declaring independence from Britain. (p. 182)

Compromise of 1850 Series of acts following California's application for admission as a free state. Meant to quell sectional tensions over slavery, the act was intended to provide something for all sides but ended up fueling more conflicts. (p. 403)

Compromise of 1877 Compromise between Republicans and southern Democrats that resulted in the election of Rutherford B. Hayes. Southern Democrats agreed to support Hayes in the disputed presidential election in exchange for his promise to end Reconstruction. (p. 487)

Confederate States of America Nation established in 1861 by the eleven slave states that seceded between December 1860 and April 1861. (p. 417)

conquistadors Spanish soldiers who were central to the conquest of the civilizations of the Americas. Once conquest was complete, conquistadors often extracted wealth from the people and lands they now ruled. (p. 22)

Continental Congress Congress convened in Philadelphia in 1774 in response to the Coercive Acts. The delegates hoped to reestablish the freedoms colonists had enjoyed in earlier times. (p. 166)

contraband Designation assigned to escaped slaves by Union general Benjamin Butler in May 1861. By designating slaves as property forfeited by the act of rebellion, the Union was able to strike at slavery without proclaiming a general emancipation. (p. 432)

Copperheads Northern Democrats who did not support the Union war effort. Such Democrats enjoyed considerable support in eastern cities and parts of the Midwest. (p. 444)

Corps of Discovery Expedition organized by the U.S. government to explore the Louisiana Territory. Led by Meriwether Lewis and William Clark, the expedition set out in May 1804 and journeyed to the Pacific coast and back by 1806 with the aid of interpreters like Sacagawea. (p. 261)

cotton gin Machine invented by Eli Whitney in 1793 to deseed short-staple cotton. The cotton gin dramatically reduced the time and labor involved in deseeding, facilitating the expansion of cotton production in the South and West. (p. 272)

Crittenden plan A political compromise over slavery which failed after seven southern states seceded from the Union in early 1861. It would have protected slavery from federal interference where it already existed and extended the Missouri Compromise line to California. (p. 417)

Crusades Eleventh- and twelfth-century campaigns to reclaim the Holy Land for the Roman Catholic Church. The Crusades were, on the whole, a military failure, but they did stimulate trade and inspire Europeans to seek better connections with the larger world. (p. 9)

cult of domesticity New ideals of womanhood that emerged alongside the middle class in the 1830s and 1840s that advocated women's relegation to the domestic sphere where they could devote themselves to the care of children, the home, and hard-working husbands. (p. 325)

Declaration of Independence Document declaring the independence of the colonies from Great Britain. Drafted by Thomas Jefferson and then debated and revised by the Continental Congress, the Declaration was made public on July 4, 1776. (p. 184)

Declaration of Sentiments Call for women's rights in marriage, family, religion, politics, and law issued at the 1848 Seneca Falls convention. It was signed by 100 of the 300 participants. (p. 346)

Democratic-Republicans Political party that emerged out of opposition to Federalist policies in the 1790s. The Democratic-Republicans chose Thomas Jefferson as their presidential candidate in 1796, 1800, and 1804. (p. 236)

Democrats and National Republicans Two parties that resulted from the split of the Democratic-Republicans in the early 1820s. Andrew Jackson emerged as the leader of the Democrats. (p. 306)

deskilling The replacement of skilled labor with unskilled labor and machines. (p. 329)

Dred Scott decision 1857 Supreme Court case centered on the status of Dred Scott and his family. In its ruling, the Court denied the claim that black men had any rights and blocked Congress from excluding slavery from any territory. (p. 413)

Dunmore's Proclamation 1775 proclamation issued by the British commander Lord Dunmore that offered freedom to all enslaved African Americans who joined the British army. The proclamation heightened concerns among some patriots about the consequences of independence. (p. 182)

Emancipation Proclamation January 1, 1863, proclamation that declared all slaves in areas still in rebellion "forever free." While stopping short of abolishing slavery, the Emancipation Proclamation was, nonetheless, seen by blacks and abolitionists as a great victory. (p. 437)

Embargo Act 1807 act that prohibited American ships from leaving their home ports until Britain and France repealed restrictions on U.S. trade. The act had a devastating impact on American commerce. (p. 266)

encomienda System first established by Christopher Columbus by which Spanish leaders in the Americas received land and the labor of all Indians residing on it. From the Indian point of view, the encomienda system amounted to little more than enslavement. (p. 15)

Enlightenment European cultural movement that emphasized rational and scientific thinking over traditional religion and superstition. Enlightenment thought appealed to many colonial elites. (p. 128)

Enrollment Act March 1863 Union draft law that provided for draftees to be selected by an impartial lottery. A loophole in the law that allowed wealthy Americans to escape service by paying $300 or hiring a substitute created widespread resentment. (p. 443)

enslavers Those who traded or owned enslaved people; see also planters. (p. 93)

Enterprise of the Indies Christopher Columbus's proposal to sail west across the Atlantic to Japan and China. In 1492 Columbus gained support for the venture from Ferdinand and Isabella of Spain. (p. 15)

Erie Canal Canal built in the early 1820s that made water transport from the Great Lakes to New York City possible. The success of the Erie Canal inspired many similar projects and ensured New York City's place as the premier international port in the United States. (p. 291)

Exodusters Blacks who migrated from the South to Kansas in 1879 seeking land and a better way of life. (p. 481)

Federalists Supporters of ratification of the Constitution, many of whom came from urban and commercial backgrounds. (p. 226)

Field Order Number 15 Order issued by General William Sherman in January 1865, setting aside more than 400,000 acres of Confederate land to be divided into plots for former slaves. Sherman's order came in response to pressure from African American leaders. (p. 452)

Fifteenth Amendment Amendment to the Constitution prohibiting the abridgment of a citizen's right to vote on the basis of "race, color, or previous condition of servitude." From the 1870s on, southern states devised numerous strategies for circumventing the Fifteenth Amendment. (p. 477)

filibusters Unauthorized military expeditions launched by U.S. adventurers to gain control of Cuba, Nicaragua, and other Spanish territories in the 1850s. (p. 406)

Force Acts Three acts passed by the U.S. Congress in 1870 and 1871 in response to vigilante attacks on southern blacks. The acts were designed to protect black political rights and end violence by the Ku Klux Klan and similar organizations. (p. 484)

Fort Sumter Union fort that guarded the harbor in Charleston, South Carolina. The Confederacy's decision to fire on the fort and block resupply in April 1861 marked the beginning of the Civil War. (p. 418)

Fourteenth Amendment Amendment to the Constitution defining citizenship and protecting individual civil and political rights from abridgment by the states. Adopted during Reconstruction, the Fourteenth Amendment overturned the *Dred Scott* decision. (p. 472)

Freedmen's Bureau Federal agency created in 1865 to provide ex-slaves with economic and legal resources. The Freedmen's Bureau played an active role in shaping black life in the postwar South. (p. 464)

Free-Soil Party Party founded by political abolitionists in 1848 to expand the appeal of the Liberty Party by focusing less on the moral wrongs of slavery and more on the benefits of providing economic opportunities for northern whites in western territories. (p. 347)

Fugitive Slave Act of 1850 Act strengthening earlier fugitive slave laws, passed as part of the Compromise of 1850. The Fugitive Slave Act provoked widespread anger in the North and intensified sectional tensions. (p. 403)

gag rule Rule passed by the House of Representatives in 1836 to table, or postpone action on, all antislavery petitions without hearing them read to stifle debate over slavery. It was renewed annually until it was rescinded in 1844. (p. 372)

Gettysburg Address Speech given by Abraham Lincoln in November 1863, at a dedication of the National Cemetery created at Gettysburg, Pennsylvania. (p. 446)

Glorious Revolution 1688 rebellion that forced James II from the English throne and replaced him with William and Mary. The Glorious Revolution led to greater political and commercial autonomy for the British colonies. (p. 74)

gold rush The rapid influx of migrants into California after the discovery of gold in 1848. Migrants came from all over the world seeking riches. (p. 398)

Great Awakening Series of religious revivals in colonial America that began in 1720 and lasted to about 1750. (p. 130)

Haitian Revolution Revolt against French rule by free and enslaved blacks in the 1790s on the island of Saint Domingue. The revolution led in 1803 to the establishment of Haiti, the first independent black-led nation in the Americas. (p. 259)

hard war The strategy promoted by General Ulysses S. Grant in which Union forces destroyed civilian crops, livestock, fields, and property to undermine Confederate morale and supply chains. (p. 450)

Harpers Ferry, Virginia Site of an 1859 raid on a federal arsenal led by John Brown, who hoped to inspire an uprising by enslaved Americans. (p. 414)

Hartford Convention 1814 convention of Federalists opposed to the War of 1812. Delegates to the convention considered a number of constitutional amendments, as well as the possibility of secession. (p. 288)

Hopewell people Indian people who established a thriving culture near the Mississippi River in the early centuries C.E. (p. 7)

horticulture A form of agriculture in which people work small plots of land with simple tools. (p. 4)

House of Burgesses Local governing body in Virginia established by the English crown in 1619. (p. 49)

import duty Tax imposed on goods imported into the colonies, paid by the importer rather than directly by the consumer; also known as a *tariff*. (p. 157)

impressment The forced enlistment of civilians into the army or navy. The impressment of residents of colonial seaports into the British navy was a major source of complaint in the eighteenth century. (p. 134)

Incas Andean people who built an empire in the centuries before the arrival of the Spaniards. At the height of their power in the fifteenth century, the Incas controlled some sixteen million people. (p. 6)

indentured servants Servants contracted to work for a set period of time without pay. Many early migrants to the English colonies indentured themselves in exchange for the price of passage to North America. (p. 49)

Indian Removal Act 1830 act by which Indian peoples in the East were forced to exchange their lands for territory west of the Mississippi River. Andrew Jackson was an ardent supporter of Indian removal. (p. 310)

Intolerable Acts *See* Coercive Acts.

Jamestown The first successful English colony in North America. Settled in 1607, Jamestown was founded by soldiers and adventurers under the leadership of Captain John Smith. (p. 47)

Jay Treaty 1796 treaty that required British forces to withdraw from U.S. soil, required American repayment of debts to British firms, and limited U.S. trade with the British West Indies. (p. 232)

Judiciary Act Act passed in 1801 by the Federalist-controlled Congress to expand the federal court system by creating sixteen circuit (regional) courts, with new judges appointed for each, just before Democratic-Republicans took control of the presidency and Congress. (p. 262)

Juneteenth June 19, 1865, the day when General Gordon Granger informed all enslaved people in Texas that they were free. The day is still celebrated by many African Americans as Emancipation Day. (p. 453)

Kansas-Nebraska Act 1854 act creating the territories of Kansas and Nebraska out of what was then Indian land. The act stipulated that the issue of slavery would be settled by a popular referendum in each territory. (p. 410)

King Philip's War 1675–1676 conflict between New England settlers and the region's Indians. The settlers were the eventual victors, but fighting was fierce and casualties on both sides were high. (p. 63)

King William's War 1689–1697 war that began as a conflict over competing French and English interests on the European continent but soon spread to the American frontier. Both sides pulled Indian allies into the war. (p. 78)

Knights of the Ku Klux Klan (KKK) Organization formed in 1865 by General Nathan Bedford Forrest to enforce prewar racial norms. Members of the KKK used threats and violence to intimidate blacks and white Republicans. (p. 484)

Liberator Radical abolitionist newspaper launched by William Lloyd Garrison in 1831. Through the *Liberator*, Garrison called for immediate, uncompensated emancipation of slaves. (p. 340)

Liberty Party Antislavery political party formed in 1840. The Liberty Party, along with the Free-Soil Party, helped place slavery at the center of national political debates. (p. 347)

Louisiana Purchase U.S. government's 1803 purchase from France of the vast territory stretching from the Mississippi River to the Rocky Mountains and from New Orleans to present-day Montana, doubling the size of the nation. (p. 259)

loyalist A colonial supporter of the British during the Revolutionary War. Loyalists came from all economic backgrounds and had a variety of motives for siding with the British. (p. 185)

manifest destiny Term coined by John L. O'Sullivan in 1845 to describe what he saw as the nation's God-given right to expand its borders. Throughout the nineteenth century, the concept of manifest destiny was used to justify U.S. expansion. (p. 379)

Marbury v. Madison 1803 Supreme Court decision that established the authority of the Supreme Court to rule on the constitutionality of federal laws. (p. 262)

market revolution Innovations in agriculture, industry, communication, and transportation in the early 1800s fueled increased efficiency and productivity and linked northern industry with western farms and southern plantations. (p. 321)

Maya People who established large cities in the Yucatán peninsula. Mayan civilization was strongest between 300 and 800 C.E. (p. 6)

Mayflower Compact Written constitution created by the Pilgrims upon their arrival in Plymouth. The Mayflower Compact was the first written constitution adopted in North America. (p. 56)

McCulloch v. Maryland 1819 Supreme Court decision that reinforced the federal government's ability to employ an expansive understanding of the implied powers clause of the Constitution. (p. 263)

mercantilism Economic system centered on the maintenance of a favorable balance of trade for the home country, with more gold and silver flowing into that country than flowed out. Seventeenth- and eighteenth-century British colonial policy was heavily shaped by mercantilism. (p. 85)

metis Term for mixed-race children of French men and Indian women in colonial North America. (p. 43)

Middle Passage The brutal voyage of slave ships laden with human cargo from Africa to the Americas. The voyage was the middle segment in a triangular journey that began in Europe, went first to Africa, then to the Americas, and finally back to Europe. (p. 86)

Missouri Compromise 1820 act that allowed Missouri to enter the Union as a slave state and Maine to enter as a free state and established the southern border of Missouri as the boundary between slave and free states throughout the Louisiana Territory. (p. 297)

Monroe Doctrine Assertion by President James Monroe in 1823 that the Western Hemisphere was part of the U.S. sphere of influence. Although the United States lacked the power to back up this claim, it signaled an intention to challenge Europeans for authority in the Atlantic world. (p. 293)

multiplier effect The diverse changes spurred by a single invention, including other inventions it spawns and the broader economic, social, and political transformations it fuels. (p. 271)

Nat Turner's rebellion 1831 slave uprising in Virginia led by Nat Turner. Turner's rebellion instilled panic among white Southerners, leading to tighter control of African Americans and reconsideration of the institution of slavery. (p. 366)

National Republicans *See* Democrats and National Republicans.

National Road Road constructed using federal funds that ran from western Maryland through southwestern Pennsylvania to Wheeling, West Virginia; also called the Cumberland Road. Completed in 1818, the road was part of a larger push to improve the nation's infrastructure. (p. 270)

nativists Anti-immigrant Americans who launched public campaigns against foreigners in the 1840s. Nativism emerged as a response to increased immigration to the United States in the 1830s and 1840s, particularly the large influx of Catholic immigrants. (p. 336)

Navigation Acts Acts passed by Parliament in the 1650s and 1660s that prohibited smuggling, established guidelines for legal commerce, and set duties on trade items. In the 1760s, British authorities sought to enforce these laws fully, leading to resistance by colonists. (pp. 85, 157)

New Jersey Plan A proposal to the 1787 Constitutional Convention that highlighted the needs of small states by creating one legislative house in the federal government and granting each state equal representation in it. (p. 225)

New Light clergy Colonial clergy who called for religious revivals and emphasized the emotional aspects of spiritual commitment. The New Lights were leaders in the Great Awakening. (p. 128)

Non-Intercourse Act Act passed by Congress in 1809 allowing Americans to trade with every nation except France and Britain. The act failed to stop the seizure of American ships or improve the economy. (p. 285)

Northwest Ordinance Act of the confederation congress that provided for the survey, sale, and eventual division into states of the Northwest Territory. The 1787

act clarified the process by which territories could become states. (p. 217)

nullification The doctrine that individual states have the right to declare federal laws unconstitutional and, therefore, void within their borders. South Carolina attempted to invoke the doctrine of nullification in response to the tariff of 1832. (p. 308)

Old Light clergy Colonial clergy from established churches who supported the religious status quo in the early eighteenth century. (p. 128)

Oregon Trail The route west from the Missouri River to the Oregon Territory. By 1860, some 350,000 Americans had made the three- to six-month journey along the trail. (p. 396)

Ostend Manifesto This 1854 letter from U.S. ambassadors and the Secretary of State to President Franklin Pierce urged him to conquer Cuba. When it was leaked to the press, Northerners voiced outrage at what they saw as a plot to expand slave territories. (p. 407)

pandemic A disease prevalent in a country, continent, or the world. Examples include the Black Death, the 1918 influenza pandemic, and the 2020 coronavirus pandemic. (pp. 10, 697, 1035)

panic of 1819 The nation's first severe recession. This panic, which lasted for a decade in some areas, resulted from irresponsible banking practices, the declining European demand for American goods, and the expansion of settlement and slavery into Indian lands. (p. 295)

panic of 1837 Severe economic recession that began shortly after Martin Van Buren's presidential inauguration. The panic of 1837 started in the South and was rooted in the changing fortunes of American cotton in Great Britain. (p. 377)

patriarchal family Model of the family in which fathers have absolute authority over wives, children, and servants. Most colonial Americans accepted the patriarchal model of the family, at least as an ideal. (p. 113)

Peace of Paris 1763 peace treaty that brought the Seven Years' War to a close. Under the terms of the treaty, Britain gained control of North America east of the Mississippi River and of present-day Canada. (p. 149)

Pequot War 1636–1637 conflict between New England settlers, their Narragansett allies, and the Pequots. The

English saw the Pequots as both a threat and an obstacle to further English expansion. (p. 62)

Petticoat Affair 1829 political conflict over Andrew Jackson's appointment of John Eaton as secretary of war. Eaton was married to a woman of allegedly questionable character, and the wives of many prominent Washington politicians organized a campaign to snub her. (p. 308)

Pietists German protestants who decried the power of established churches and urged individuals to follow their hearts rather than their heads in spiritual matters. Pietism had a profound influence on the leaders of the Great Awakening. (p. 128)

Pilgrims Group of English religious dissenters who established a settlement at Plymouth, Massachusetts, in 1620. Unlike more mainstream Protestants, the Pilgrims were separatists who aimed to sever all connections with the Church of England. (p. 56)

Pinckney Treaty 1796 treaty that defined the boundary between U.S. and Spanish territory in the South and opened the Mississippi River and New Orleans to U.S. shipping. (p. 234)

planters Southern whites who owned the largest plantations and forged a distinct culture and economy around the institution of slavery. (p. 358)

Powhatan Confederacy Large and powerful Indian confederation in Virginia. The Jamestown settlers had a complicated and contentious relationship with the leaders of the Powhatan Confederacy. (p. 47)

Proclamation Line of 1763 Act of Parliament that restricted colonial settlement west of the Appalachian Mountains. The Proclamation Line sparked protests from rich and poor colonists alike. (p. 150)

Proclamation of Amnesty and Reconstruction 1863 proclamation that established the basic parameters of President Abraham Lincoln's approach to Reconstruction. Lincoln's plan would have readmitted the South to the Union on relatively lenient terms. (p. 469)

proprietary colonies Colonies granted to individuals, rather than held directly by the crown or given to chartered companies. Proprietors of such colonies, such as William Penn of Pennsylvania, had considerable leeway to distribute land and govern as they pleased. (p. 74)

Protestantism Religious movement initiated in the early sixteenth century that resulted in a permanent division

within European Christianity. Protestants differed with Catholics over the nature of salvation, the role of priests, and the organization of the church. (p. 39)

Pueblo revolt 1680 uprising of Pueblo Indians against Spanish forces in New Mexico that led to the Spaniards' temporary retreat from the area. The uprising was sparked by mistreatment and the suppression of Indian culture and religion. (p. 76)

Puritans Radical English Protestants who hoped to reform the Church of England. The first Puritan settlers in the Americas arrived in Massachusetts in 1630. (p. 57)

Redeemers White, conservative Democrats who challenged and overthrew Republican rule in the South during Reconstruction. (p. 484)

redemptioners Immigrants who borrowed money from shipping agents to cover the costs of transport to America, loans that were repaid, or "redeemed," by colonial employers. Redemptioners worked for their "redeemers" for a set number of years. (p. 92)

refugee communities Settlements of formerly enslaved peoples during the Civil War. The Union recognized enslaved people who reached Union Army camps as contraband of war, but southern blacks turned these settlements into refugee communities to sustain themselves under desperate circumstances. (p. 450)

Regulators Local organizations formed in North and South Carolina to protest and resist unpopular policies from 1766–1771. After first seeking redress through official institutions, Regulators went on to establish militias and other institutions of self-governance. (p. 164)

Renaissance The cultural and intellectual flowering that began in Italy in the fifteenth century and then spread north. The Renaissance occurred at the same time that European rulers were pushing for greater political unification of their states. (p. 10)

republican motherhood In the 1790s, some leaders supported women's education so that they could instruct their sons in principles of republican government. (p. 220)

Republican Party Party formed in 1854 that was committed to stopping the expansion of slavery and advocated economic development and internal improvements. Although their appeal was limited to the North, the Republicans quickly became a major political force. (p. 411)

scalawags Derisive term for white Southerners who supported Reconstruction. (p. 479)

Second Continental Congress Assembly of colonial representatives that served as a national government during the Revolutionary War. Despite limited formal powers, the Continental Congress coordinated the war effort and conducted negotiations with outside powers. (p. 181)

Second Great Awakening Evangelical revival movement that began in the South in the early nineteenth century and then spread to the North. The social and economic changes of the first half of the nineteenth century were a major spur to religious revivals, which in turn spurred social reform movements. (p. 331)

Second Party System When the Whig Party formed in 1834, they posed the first significant challenge to Democratic Party control in two decades. (p. 371)

Second Seminole War 1835–1842 war between the Seminoles, including fugitive slaves who had joined the tribe, and the U.S. government over whether the Seminoles would be forced to leave Florida and settle west of the Mississippi River. Despite substantial investments of men, money, and resources, it took seven years for the United States to achieve victory. (p. 372)

sharecropping A system that emerged as the dominant mode of agricultural production in the South in the years after the Civil War. Under the sharecropping system, sharecroppers received tools and supplies from landowners in exchange for a share of the eventual harvest. (p. 480)

Shays's Rebellion 1786 rebellion by western Massachusetts farmers caused primarily by economic turmoil in the aftermath of the Revolutionary War. (p. 222)

Sherman's March to the Sea Hard war tactics employed by General William Tecumseh Sherman to capture Atlanta and huge swaths of Georgia and the Carolinas, devastating this crucial region of the Confederacy in 1864. (p. 451)

siege of Vicksburg After a prolonged siege, Union troops forced Confederate forces to surrender at Vicksburg, Mississippi, leading to Union control of the rich Mississippi River valley. (p. 446)

slave laws A series of laws that defined slavery as a distinct status based on racial identity and which passed that status on through future generations. (p. 95)

Sons of Liberty Boston organization first formed to protest the Stamp Act. The Sons of Liberty spread to other colonies and played an important role in the unrest leading to the American Revolution. (p. 159)

spoils system Patronage system introduced by Andrew Jackson in which federal offices were awarded on the basis of political loyalty. The system remained in place until the late nineteenth century. (p. 308)

Stamp Act 1765 act of Parliament that imposed a duty on all transactions involving paper items. The Stamp Act prompted widespread, coordinated protests and was eventually repealed. (p. 158)

Stono rebellion 1739 uprising by enslaved Africans and African Americans in South Carolina. In the aftermath of the uprising, white fear of slave revolts intensified. (p. 99)

Sugar Act 1764 act of Parliament that imposed an import tax on sugar, coffee, wines, and other luxury items. The Sugar Act sparked colonial protests that would escalate over time as new revenue measures were enacted. (p. 157)

Tariff of Abominations White Southerners' name for the 1828 Congressional tariff act that benefited northern manufacturers and merchants at the expense of agriculture, especially southern plantations. (p. 308)

Tejanos Mexican residents of Texas. Although some Tejano elites allied themselves with American settlers, most American settlers resisted the adoption of Tejano culture. (p. 371)

temperance The movement to moderate and then ban the sale and consumption of alcohol. The American temperance movement emerged in the early nineteenth century as part of the larger push for improving society from the 1820s to the 1850s. (p. 331)

Tenure of Office Act Law passed by Congress in 1867 to prevent President Andrew Johnson from removing cabinet members sympathetic to the Republican Party's approach to congressional Reconstruction without Senate approval. Johnson was impeached, but not convicted, for violating the act. (p. 477)

Thirteenth Amendment Amendment to the Constitution abolishing slavery. The Thirteenth Amendment was passed in January 1865 and sent to the states for ratification. (pp. 452, 469)

three-fifths compromise Compromise between northern and southern delegates to the 1787

Constitutional Convention to count enslaved persons as three-fifths of a free person in apportioning representation in the House of Representatives and taxation by the federal government. (p. 225)

Townshend Act 1767 act of Parliament that instituted an import tax on a range of items including glass, lead, paint, paper, and tea. The Townshend Act prompted a boycott of British goods and contributed to violence between British soldiers and colonists. (p. 160)

Trail of Tears The forced march of some 15,000 Cherokees from Georgia to Indian Territory. Inadequate planning, food, water, sanitation, and medicine led to the deaths of thousands of Cherokees. (p. 375)

transcendentalism A movement founded by Ralph Waldo Emerson in the 1830s that proposed that individuals look inside themselves and to nature for spiritual and moral guidance rather than to the dogmas of formal religion. Transcendentalism attracted a number of important American writers and artists to its vision. (p. 334)

Treaty of Fort Stanwix 1784 treaty in which U.S. commissioners coerced Iroquois delegates into ceding vast tracts of land in western New York and the Ohio River Valley to the United States. (p. 214)

Treaty of Ghent Accord signed in December 1814 ending the War of 1812 and returning to U.S. and Britain the lands each controlled before the war. (p. 289)

Treaty of Greenville 1795 treaty signed following the Battle of Fallen Timbers through which Indians in the Northwest Territory were forced to ceded vast tracts of land to the United States. (p. 234)

Treaty of Guadalupe Hidalgo 1848 treaty ending the Mexican-American War. By the terms of the treaty, the United States acquired control over Texas north and east of the Rio Grande plus the New Mexico territory, which included present-day Arizona and New Mexico and parts of Utah, Nevada, and Colorado. The treaty also ceded Alta California, which had declared itself an independent republic during the war, to the United States. (p. 382)

Treaty of New Echota 1836 treaty in which a group of Cherokee men agreed to exchange their land in the Southeast for money and land in Indian Territory. Despite the fact that the treaty was obtained without tribal sanction, it was approved by the U.S. Congress. (p. 373)

Treaty (Peace) of Paris 1783 treaty that formally ended the conflict between Britain and its North American colonies. The newly established United States gained benefits from the treaty. (p. 203)

Tuscarora War War launched by Tuscarora Indians from 1711 to 1715 against European settlers in North Carolina and their allies from the Yamasee, Catawba, and Cherokee nations. The Tuscaroras forfeited their lands when they signed the peace treaty and many then joined the Iroquois Confederacy to the north. (p. 80)

U.S. Sanitary Commission Federal organization established in June 1861 to improve and coordinate the medical care of Union soldiers. Northern women played a key role in the work of the commission. (p. 439)

Uncle Tom's Cabin Novel published in 1852 by Harriet Beecher Stowe. Meant to publicize the evils of slavery, the novel struck an emotional chord in the North and was an international best seller. (p. 408)

underground railroad A series of routes from southern plantation areas to northern free states and Canada along which abolitionist supporters, known as conductors, provided hiding places and transportation for runaway slaves seeking freedom. (p. 341)

utopian societies Communities formed in the first half of the nineteenth century to embody alternative social and economic visions and to create models for society at large to follow. (p. 338)

Valley Forge Site of Continental Army winter encampment in 1777–1778. Despite the harsh conditions, the Continental Army emerged from its encampment at Valley Forge as a more effective fighting force. (p. 194)

Virginia and Kentucky Resolutions Resolutions passed by legislatures in Virginia and Kentucky that declared the Alien and Sedition Acts (1798) "void and of no force" in their states. (p. 237)

Virginia Plan Plan put forth at the beginning of the 1787 Constitutional Convention that introduced the ideas of a strong central government, a bicameral legislature, and a system of representation based on population. (p. 225)

Walking Purchase 1737 treaty that allowed Pennsylvania to expand its boundaries at the expense of the Delaware Indians. The treaty, quite possibly a forgery, allowed the British to add territory that could be walked off in a day and a half. (p. 123)

War of the Spanish Succession 1702–1713 war over control of Spain and its colonies; also called Queen Anne's War. Although the Treaty of Utrecht that ended the war in 1713 was intended to bring peace through the establishment of a balance of power, imperial conflict continued to escalate. (p. 78)

Whig Party Political party formed in the 1830s to challenge the power of the Democratic Party. The Whigs attempted to forge a diverse coalition from around the country by promoting commercial interests and moral reforms. (p. 370)

Whiskey Rebellion Uprising by western Pennsylvania farmers who led protests against the excise tax on whiskey in the early 1790s. (p. 233)

white supremacy An ideology promoted by southern planters and intellectuals that maintained that all whites, regardless of class or education, were superior to all blacks. (p. 370)

Wilmot Proviso 1846 proposal by Democratic congressman David Wilmot of Pennsylvania to outlaw slavery in all territory acquired from Mexico. The proposal was defeated, but the fight over its adoption foreshadowed the sectional conflicts of the 1850s. (p. 383)

Women's National Loyal League Organization founded by abolitionist women during the Civil War to press Lincoln and Congress to enact universal emancipation. (p. 443)

XYZ affair 1798 incident in which French agents demanded bribes before meeting with American diplomatic representatives. (p. 236)

Yamasee War A pan-Indian war from 1715 to 1717 led by the Yamasee who intended, but failed, to oust the British from South Carolina. (p. 81)

yeomen farmers Southern independent landowners who did not own slaves. Although yeomen farmers had connections to the South's plantation economy, many realized that their interests were not always identical to those of the planter elite. (p. 368)

Chapter 1

The Voyage of Magellan, the Journal of Antonio Pigafetta, trans. Paula Spurlin Paige (Englewood Cliffs, NJ: Prentice Hall, 1969), 76–78. Used with permission from the author.

Camilla Townsend, ed. and trans., *American Indian History: A Documentary Reader* (Malden, MA: Wiley-Blackwell, 2009), 29–30. Used with permission from the author.

Chapter 2

Marie de L'Incarnation, Correspondence, ed. Dom Guy Oury (Abbaye de Saint-Pierre, 1971), trans. Natalie Zemon Davis, *Women on the Margins: Three Seventeenth-Century Lives* (Cambridge, MA: Harvard University Press, 1995), 111–12. Used with permission.

Chapter 3

James A. Henretta, "Families and Farms: Mentalité in Pre-Industrial America," *William and Mary Quarterly* 35, no. 1 (1978): 4–5. Copyright © 1978 by Omohundro Institute of Early American History and Culture. Used with permission.

Chapter 8

Republished with permission of University of Oklahoma Press from W. Raymond Wood and Thomas D. Thiessen, eds., *Early Fur Trade on the Northern Plains: Canadian Traders among the Mandan and Hidatsa Indians, 1738–1818* (Norman: University of Oklahoma Press, 1985), 232–33. Copyright © 1985. Permission conveyed through Copyright Clearance Center, Inc.

Chapter 9

Republished with permission of University of Oklahoma Press from John Ross, ed. Gary E. Moulton, *The Papers of Chief John Ross, vol. 1, 1807–1839* (Norman: University of Oklahoma Press, 1985), 458–61. Copyright © 1985. Permission conveyed through Copyright Clearance Center, Inc.

Chapter 13

John Hines, letter to his parents, April 22, 1862. Hines Family Collection, MSS 91, Department of Library Special Collections, Western Kentucky University. Courtesy of Department of Library Special Collections, Western Kentucky University.

Nina Silber and Mary Beth Sievens, eds., *Yankee Correspondence: Civil War Letters between New England Soldiers and the Home Front* (Charlottesville: University Press of Virginia, 1996), 55–56. Copyright © 1996 by the Rhode Island Historical Society. Used with permission.

Index

Letters in parentheses following page numbers refer to figures *(f)*, illustrations *(i)*, maps *(m)*, sources *(s)*, and tables *(t)*.

About the Authors

Authors Nancy A. Hewitt and Steven F. Lawson

Nancy A. Hewitt (PhD, University of Pennsylvania) is Professor Emerita of History and of Women's and Gender Studies at Rutgers University. Her publications include *Radical Friend: Amy Kirby Post and Her Activist Worlds*, for which she won the SHEAR prize in biography; *Women's Activism and Social Change: Rochester, New York, 1822–1872*; *Southern Discomfort: Women's Activism in Tampa, Florida, 1880s–1920s*, and the second edition of *A Companion to American Women's History*, edited with Anne M. Valk.

Steven F. Lawson (PhD, Columbia University) is Professor Emeritus of History at Rutgers University. His research interests include U.S. politics since 1945 and the history of the civil rights movement, with a particular focus on black politics and the interplay between civil rights and political culture in the mid-twentieth century. He is the author of many works including *Running for Freedom: Civil Rights and Black Politics in America since 1941*; *Debating the Civil Rights Movement*; *Black Ballots: Voting Rights in the South, 1944–1969*; and *In Pursuit of Power: Southern Blacks and Electoral Politics, 1965–1982*.